NIV

WOMEN'S

DEVOTIONAL

NEW TESTAMENT

WITH PSALMS & PROVERBS

NEW INTERNATIONAL VERSION

ZondervanPublishingHouse

GRAND RAPIDS, MICHIGAN 49530, U.S.A.

Women's Devotional 2 New Testament with Psalms and Proverbs
New International Version®
Copyright © 1995 by Zondervan Corporation
All rights reserved

Copyright information on devotional material begins on page 548 and is regarded as an extension of the copyright page.

The Holy Bible, New International Version
Copyright © 1973, 1978, 1984 by International Bible Society

Library of Congress Catalog Card Number 95-61484

Published by Zondervan Publishing House
Grand Rapids, Michigan 49530, U.S.A.
Printed in the United States of America
All rights reserved

Supplementary Materials:
Project Management and Editorial: Ruth DeJager and Catherine DeVries
Editorial Assistance: Sarah Hupp
Graphics Design: Sharon Wright

98 99 0 10 9 8 7 6 5 4

CONTENTS

INTRODUCTION

WOMEN'S DEVOTIONAL 2 NEW TESTAMENT
WITH PSALMS AND PROVERBS

WELCOME to the Women's Devotional 2 New Testament with Psalms and Proverbs! If you are like most women today, your life is full—maybe even too full. There are so many things to do, so many demands on your time. The Women's Devotional 2 New Testament provides you with a convenient Bible reading/devotional plan. Following the same format as the original Women's Devotional New Testament, the Women's Devotional 2 New Testament offers a brand new selection of devotions that will take you into the thoughts of well-known Christian women writers. We hope these meditations will give you new perspective, encouragement and inspiration.

Even though the Bible was written approximately two thousand years ago, it contains themes not unlike today—struggling between good and evil, dealing with suffering and loss, celebrating in laughter and joy, seeing God's promises fulfilled. As you read this Bible, you will discover how relevant God's Word is to your life today. Several features make the Women's Devotional 2 New Testament an exceptional guide:

Devotions

The devotions in the Women's Devotional 2 New Testament follow the days of the week: Monday, Tuesday, Wednesday, Thursday, Friday. For something a bit different on the weekend, we have developed "Weekending"—combining one thought-provoking devotion with two short Scripture readings, one for Saturday, one for Sunday. At the top of each devotion is "Verse" and "Passage." The subject of each devotion is tied to the designated Scripture verse. And the passage provides the context, or Scripture that surrounds the verse.

No matter on what day of the week you begin, simply turn to a devotion for that day. For the next day, look to the bottom of the devotion for the page number of the next day's devotion. For example, if you start on a Monday, you could turn to the first devotion in the book of Genesis. Glance at the bottom of Monday's devotion and you will see the page number where Tuesday's devotion is—and so on as you keep reading on through Friday.

Friday's devotion will direct you to a "Weekending." The bottom of the "Weekending" will send you to the next Monday devotion. And you are well on your way—through a year of spending precious time in God's Word and growing closer to him.

Book Introductions

Each of the books in this New Testament begins with an introduction. The introductions succinctly highlight themes, provide helpful background information and offer practical applications to your life.

Reading Plans

On page 554 you will find a plan that can help you read through the New Testament, Psalms and Proverbs in one year. God's Word has wonderful continuity. You will discover many of its treasures as you read through chapter after chapter, book after book.

Author Biographies

On page 558 you will find the author index. You might recognize many names of the women who contributed to this New Testament. In this index, discover interesting information about each person and find where her devotions appear in this New Testament.

Subject Index

The subject index on page 563 will help you locate material on specific topics, items of interest or virtually any problem confronting you. The subjects of the devotions are many and varied, including joy, depression, parenting, nature, career, death, grandparenting and more.

The Word of God

Far more important than any of the tools we've provided, however, is the text itself, the Word of God. The Bible is a supernaturally powerful book, one that can be explained simply to preschoolers and at the same time studied inexhaustively by scholars. Whatever your situation, whatever your need, we offer this New Testament edition with the hope and the prayer that the power of God's Word may penetrate and transform your heart.

So, come on along. You are invited to open the pages of the Women's Devotional 2 New Testament and start along a pathway to growing in God. The treasures of God's Word await you at every step of the way, and the meditations of the women who have shared a bit of themselves will encourage you to keep moving ahead. And as you go, we pray you will become all that God intends you to be.

PREFACE

THE NEW INTERNATIONAL VERSION is a completely new translation of the Holy Bible made by over a hundred scholars working directly from the best available Hebrew, Aramaic and Greek texts. It had its beginning in 1965 when, after several years of exploratory study by committees from the Christian Reformed Church and the National Association of Evangelicals, a group of scholars met at Palos Heights, Illinois, and concurred in the need for a new translation of the Bible in contemporary English. This group, though not made up of official church representatives, was transdenominational. Its conclusion was endorsed by a large number of leaders from many denominations who met in Chicago in 1966.

Responsibility for the new version was delegated by the Palos Heights group to a self-governing body of fifteen, the Committee on Bible Translation, composed for the most part of biblical scholars from colleges, universities and seminaries. In 1967 the New York Bible Society (now the International Bible Society) generously undertook the financial sponsorship of the project—a sponsorship that made it possible to enlist the help of many distinguished scholars. The fact that participants from the United States, Great Britain, Canada, Australia and New Zealand worked together gave the project its international scope. That they were from many denominations—including Anglican, Assemblies of God, Baptist, Brethren, Christian Reformed, Church of Christ, Evangelical Free, Lutheran, Mennonite, Methodist, Nazarene, Presbyterian, Wesleyan and other churches—helped to safeguard the translation from sectarian bias.

How it was made helps to give the New International Version its distinctiveness. The translation of each book was assigned to a team of scholars. Next, one of the Intermediate Editorial Committees revised the initial translation, with constant reference to the Hebrew, Aramaic or Greek. Their work then went to one of the General Editorial Committees, which checked it in detail and made another thorough revision. This revision in turn was carefully reviewed by the Committee on Bible Translation, which made further changes and then released the final version for publication. In this way the entire Bible underwent three revisions, during each of which the translation was examined for its faithfulness to the original languages and for its English style.

All this involved many thousands of hours of research and discussion regarding the meaning of the texts and the precise way of putting them into English. It may well be that no other translation has been made by a more thorough process of review and revision from committee to committee than this one.

From the beginning of the project, the Committee on Bible Translation held to certain goals for the New International Version: that it would be an accurate translation and one that would have clarity and literary quality and so prove suitable for public and private reading, teaching, preaching, memorizing and liturgical use. The Committee also sought to preserve some measure of continuity with the long tradition of translating the Scriptures into English.

In working toward these goals, the translators were united in their commitment to the authority and infallibility of the Bible as God's Word in written form. They believe that it contains the divine answer to the deepest needs of humanity, that it sheds unique light on our path in a dark world, and that it sets forth the way to our eternal well-being.

The first concern of the translators has been the accuracy of the translation and its fidelity to the thought of the biblical writers. They have weighed the significance of the lexical and grammatical details of the Hebrew, Aramaic and Greek texts. At the same time, they have striven for more than a word-for-word translation. Because thought patterns and syntax differ from language to language, faithful communication of the meaning of the writers of the Bible demands frequent modifications in sentence structure and constant regard for the contextual meanings of words.

A sensitive feeling for style does not always accompany scholarship. Accordingly the Committee on Bible Translation submitted the developing version to a number of stylistic consultants. Two of them read every book of both Old and New Testaments twice—once before and once after the last major revision—and made invaluable suggestions. Samples of the translation were tested for clarity and ease of reading by various kinds of people—young and old, highly educated and less well educated, ministers and laymen.

Concern for clear and natural English—that the New International Version should be idiomatic but not idiosyncratic, contemporary but not dated—motivated the translators and consultants. At the same time, they tried to reflect the differing styles of the biblical writers. In view of the international use of English, the translators sought to avoid obvious Americanisms on the one hand and obvious Anglicisms on the other. A British edition reflects the comparatively few differences of significant idiom and of spelling.

As for the traditional pronouns "thou," "thee" and "thine" in reference to the Deity, the translators judged that to use these archaisms (along with the old verb forms such as "doest," "wouldest" and "hadst") would violate accuracy in translation. Neither Hebrew, Aramaic nor Greek uses special pronouns for the persons of the Godhead. A present-day translation is not enhanced by forms that in the time of the King James Version were used in everyday speech, whether referring to God or man.

For the Old Testament the standard Hebrew text, the Masoretic Text as published in the latest editions of *Biblia Hebraica*, was used throughout. The Dead Sea Scrolls contain material bearing on an earlier stage of the Hebrew text. They were consulted, as were the Samaritan Pentateuch and the ancient scribal traditions relating to textual changes. Sometimes a variant Hebrew reading in the margin of the Masoretic Text was followed instead of the text itself. Such instances, being variants within the Masoretic tradition, are not specified by footnotes. In rare cases, words in the consonantal text were divided differently from the way they appear in the Masoretic Text. Footnotes indicate this. The translators also consulted the more important early versions—the Septuagint; Aquila, Symmachus and Theodotion; the Vulgate; the Syriac Peshitta; the Targums; and for the Psalms the *Juxta Hebraica* of Jerome. Readings from these versions were occasionally followed where the Masoretic Text seemed doubtful and where accepted principles of textual criticism showed that one or more of these textual witnesses appeared to provide the correct reading. Such instances are footnoted. Sometimes vowel letters and vowel signs did not, in the judgment of the translators, represent the correct vowels for the original consonantal text. Accordingly some words were read with a different set of vowels. These instances are usually not indicated by footnotes.

The Greek text used in translating the New Testament was an eclectic one. No other piece of ancient literature has such an abundance of manuscript witnesses as does the New Testament. Where existing manuscripts differ, the translators made their choice of readings according to accepted principles of New Testament textual criticism. Footnotes call attention to places where there was uncertainty about what the original text was. The best current printed texts of the Greek New Testament were used.

There is a sense in which the work of translation is never wholly finished. This applies to all great literature and uniquely so to the Bible. In 1973 the New Testament in the New International Version was published. Since then, suggestions for corrections and revisions have been received from various sources. The Committee on Bible Translation carefully considered the suggestions and adopted a number of them. These were incorporated in the first printing of the entire Bible in 1978. Additional revisions were made by the Committee on Bible Translation in 1983 and appear in printings after that date.

As in other ancient documents, the precise meaning of the biblical texts is sometimes uncertain. This is more often the case with the Hebrew and Aramaic texts than with the Greek text. Although archaeological and linguistic discoveries in this century aid in understanding difficult passages, some uncertainties remain. The more significant of these have been called to the reader's attention in the footnotes.

In regard to the divine name *YHWH*, commonly referred to as the *Tetragrammaton*, the translators adopted the device used in most English versions of rendering that name as "LORD" in capital letters to distinguish it from *Adonai*, another Hebrew word rendered "Lord," for which small letters are used. Wherever the two names stand together in the Old Testament as a compound name of God, they are rendered "Sovereign LORD."

Because for most readers today the phrases "the LORD of hosts" and "God of hosts" have little meaning, this version renders them "the LORD Almighty" and "God Almighty." These renderings convey the sense of the Hebrew, namely, "he who is sovereign over all the 'hosts' (powers) in heaven and on earth, especially over the "hosts" (armies) of Israel." For readers unacquainted with Hebrew this does not make clear the distinction between *Sabaoth* ("hosts" or "Almighty") and *Shaddai* (which can also be translated "Almighty"), but the latter occurs infrequently and is always footnoted. When *Adonai* and *YHWH Sabaoth* occur together, they are rendered "the Lord, the LORD Almighty."

As for other proper nouns, the familiar spellings of the King James Version are generally retained. Names traditionally spelled with "ch," except where it is final, are usually spelled in this translation with "k" or "c," since the biblical languages do not have the sound that "ch" frequently indicates in English—for example, in *chant*. For well-known names such as Zechariah, however, the traditional spelling has been retained. Variation in the spelling of names in the original languages has usually not been indicated. Where a person or place has two or more different names in the Hebrew, Aramaic or Greek texts, the more familiar one has generally been used, with footnotes where needed.

To achieve clarity the translators sometimes supplied words not in the original texts but required by the context. If there was uncertainty about such material, it is enclosed in brackets. Also for the sake of clarity or style, nouns, including some proper nouns, are sometimes substituted for pronouns, and vice versa. And though the Hebrew writers often shifted back and forth between first, second and third personal pronouns without change of antecedent, this translation often makes them uniform, in accordance with English style and without the use of footnotes.

Poetical passages are printed as poetry, that is, with indentation of lines with separate stanzas. These are generally designed to reflect the structure of Hebrew poetry. This poetry is normally characterized by parallelism in balanced lines. Most of the poetry in the Bible is in the Old Testament, and scholars differ regarding the scansion of Hebrew lines. The translators determined the stanza divisions for the most part by analysis of the subject matter. The stanzas therefore serve as poetic paragraphs.

As an aid to the reader, italicized sectional headings are inserted in most of the books. They are not to be regarded as part of the NIV text, are not for oral reading, and are not intended to dictate the interpretation of the sections they head.

The footnotes in this version are of several kinds, most of which need no explanation. Those giving alternative translations begin with "Or" and generally introduce the alternative with the last word preceding it in the text, except when it is a single-word alternative; in poetry quoted in a footnote a slant mark indicates a line division. Footnotes introduced by "Or" do not have uniform significance. In some cases two possible translations were considered to have about equal validity. In other cases, though the translators were convinced that the translation in the text was correct, they judged that another interpretation was possible and of sufficient importance to be represented in a footnote.

In the New Testament, footnotes that refer to uncertainty regarding the original text are introduced by "Some manuscripts" or similar expressions. In the Old Testament, evidence for the reading chosen is given first and evidence for the alternative is added after a semicolon (for example: Septuagint; Hebrew *father*). In such notes the term "Hebrew" refers to the Masoretic Text.

It should be noted that minerals, flora and fauna, architectural details, articles of clothing and jewelry, musical instruments and other articles cannot always be identified with precision. Also measures of capacity in the biblical period are particularly uncertain (see the table of weights and measures following the text).

Like all translations of the Bible, made as they are by imperfect man, this one undoubtedly falls short of its goals. Yet we are grateful to God for the extent to which he has enabled us to realize these goals and for the strength he has given us and our colleagues to complete our task. We offer this version of the Bible to him in whose name and for whose glory it has been made. We pray that it will lead many into a better understanding of the Holy Scriptures and a fuller knowledge of Jesus Christ the incarnate Word, of whom the Scriptures so faithfully testify.

The Committee on Bible Translation

June 1978
(Revised August 1983)

Names of the translators and editors may be secured from the International Bible Society, translation sponsors of the New International Version, 1820 Jet Stream Drive, Colorado Springs, Colorado 80921-3696 U.S.A.

NEW
TESTAMENT

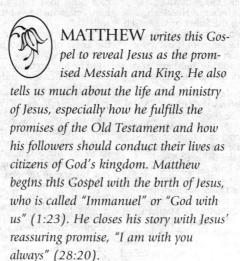

MATTHEW *writes this Gospel to reveal Jesus as the promised Messiah and King. He also tells us much about the life and ministry of Jesus, especially how he fulfills the promises of the Old Testament and how his followers should conduct their lives as citizens of God's kingdom. Matthew begins this Gospel with the birth of Jesus, who is called "Immanuel" or "God with us" (1:23). He closes his story with Jesus' reassuring promise, "I am with you always" (28:20).*

MATTHEW

The Genealogy of Jesus

1 A record of the genealogy of Jesus Christ the son of David, the son of Abraham:

² Abraham was the father of Isaac,
Isaac the father of Jacob,
Jacob the father of Judah and his brothers,
³ Judah the father of Perez and Zerah, whose mother was Tamar,
Perez the father of Hezron,
Hezron the father of Ram,
⁴ Ram the father of Amminadab,
Amminadab the father of Nahshon,
Nahshon the father of Salmon,
⁵ Salmon the father of Boaz, whose mother was Rahab,
Boaz the father of Obed, whose mother was Ruth,
Obed the father of Jesse,
⁶ and Jesse the father of King David.

David was the father of Solomon, whose mother had been Uriah's wife,
⁷ Solomon the father of Rehoboam,
Rehoboam the father of Abijah,
Abijah the father of Asa,
⁸ Asa the father of Jehoshaphat,
Jehoshaphat the father of Jehoram,

Jehoram the father of Uzziah,
⁹Uzziah the father of Jotham,
Jotham the father of Ahaz,
Ahaz the father of Hezekiah,
¹⁰Hezekiah the father of Manasseh,
Manasseh the father of Amon,
Amon the father of Josiah,
¹¹and Josiah the father of Jeconiah*ᵃ* and his brothers at the time of the exile to Babylon.

¹²After the exile to Babylon:
Jeconiah was the father of Shealtiel,
Shealtiel the father of Zerubbabel,
¹³Zerubbabel the father of Abiud,
Abiud the father of Eliakim,
Eliakim the father of Azor,
¹⁴Azor the father of Zadok,
Zadok the father of Akim,
Akim the father of Eliud,
¹⁵Eliud the father of Eleazar,
Eleazar the father of Matthan,
Matthan the father of Jacob,
¹⁶and Jacob the father of Joseph, the husband of Mary, of whom was born Jesus, who is called Christ.

¹⁷Thus there were fourteen generations in all from Abraham to David, fourteen from David to the exile to Babylon, and fourteen from the exile to the Christ.ᵇ

The Birth of Jesus Christ

¹⁸This is how the birth of Jesus Christ came about: His mother Mary was pledged to be married to Joseph, but before they came together, she was found to be with child through the Holy Spirit. ¹⁹Because Joseph her husband was a righteous man and did not want to expose her to public disgrace, he had in mind to divorce her quietly.

²⁰But after he had considered this, an angel of the Lord appeared to him in a dream and said, "Joseph son of David, do not be afraid to take Mary home as your wife, because what is conceived in her is from the Holy Spirit. ²¹She will give birth to a son, and you are to give him the name Jesus,ᶜ because he will save his people from their sins."

²²All this took place to fulfill what the Lord had said through the prophet: ²³"The virgin will be with child and will give birth to a son, and they will call him Immanuel"ᵈ—which means, "God with us."

²⁴When Joseph woke up, he did what the angel of the Lord had commanded him and took Mary home as his wife. ²⁵But he had no union with her until she gave birth to a son. And he gave him the name Jesus.

The Visit of the Magi

2 After Jesus was born in Bethlehem in Judea, during the time of King Herod, Magiᵉ from the east came to Jerusalem ²and asked, "Where is the one who has been born king of the Jews? We saw his star in the eastᶠ and have come to worship him."

³When King Herod heard this he was disturbed, and all Jerusalem with him. ⁴When he had called together all the people's chief priests and teachers of the law, he asked them where the Christᵍ was to be born. ⁵"In Bethlehem in Judea," they replied, "for this is what the prophet has written:

⁶" 'But you, Bethlehem, in the land of Judah,
are by no means least among the rulers of Judah;
for out of you will come a ruler
who will be the shepherd of my people Israel.'ʰ"

⁷Then Herod called the Magi secretly and found out from them the exact time the star had appeared. ⁸He sent them to Bethlehem and said, "Go and make a careful search for the child. As soon as you find him, report to me, so that I too may go and worship him."

⁹After they had heard the king, they went on their way, and the star they had seen in the eastⁱ went ahead of them until it stopped over the place where the child was. ¹⁰When they saw the star, they were overjoyed. ¹¹On coming to the house, they saw the child with his mother Mary, and they bowed down and worshiped him. Then they opened their treasures and presented him with gifts of gold and of incense and of myrrh. ¹²And

ᵃ11 That is, Jehoiachin; also in verse 12   ᵇ17 Or Messiah. "The Christ" (Greek) and "the Messiah" (Hebrew) both mean "the Anointed One."   ᶜ21 Jesus is the Greek form of Joshua, which means the LORD saves.   ᵈ23 Isaiah 7:14   ᵉ1 Traditionally Wise Men   ᶠ2 Or star when it rose   ᵍ4 Or Messiah   ʰ6 Micah 5:2   ⁱ9 Or seen when it rose

having been warned in a dream not to go back to Herod, they returned to their country by another route.

The Escape to Egypt

[13]When they had gone, an angel of the Lord appeared to Joseph in a dream. "Get up," he said, "take the child and his mother and escape to Egypt. Stay there until I tell you, for Herod is going to search for the child to kill him."

[14]So he got up, took the child and his mother during the night and left for Egypt, [15]where he stayed until the death of Herod. And so was fulfilled what the Lord had said through the prophet: "Out of Egypt I called my son."[a]

[16]When Herod realized that he had been outwitted by the Magi, he was furious, and he gave orders to kill all the boys in Bethlehem and its vicinity who were two years old and under, in accordance with the time he had learned from the Magi. [17]Then what was said through the prophet Jeremiah was fulfilled:

[18]"A voice is heard in Ramah,
  weeping and great mourning,
Rachel weeping for her children
  and refusing to be comforted,
because they are no more."[b]

The Return to Nazareth

[19]After Herod died, an angel of the Lord appeared in a dream to Joseph in Egypt [20]and said, "Get up, take the child and his mother and go to the land of Israel, for those who were trying to take the child's life are dead."

[21]So he got up, took the child and his mother and went to the land of Israel. [22]But when he heard that Archelaus was reigning in Judea in place of his father Herod, he was afraid to go there. Having been warned in a dream, he withdrew to the district of Galilee, [23]and he went and lived in a town called Nazareth. So was fulfilled what was said through the prophets: "He will be called a Nazarene."

John the Baptist Prepares the Way

3 In those days John the Baptist came, preaching in the Desert of Judea [2]and saying, "Repent, for the kingdom of heaven is near." [3]This is he who was spoken of through the prophet Isaiah:

"A voice of one calling in the desert,
'Prepare the way for the Lord,
  make straight paths for him.' "[c]

[4]John's clothes were made of camel's hair, and he had a leather belt around his waist. His food was locusts and wild honey. [5]People went out to him from Jerusalem and all Judea and the whole region of the Jordan. [6]Confessing their sins, they were baptized by him in the Jordan River.

[7]But when he saw many of the Pharisees and Sadducees coming to where he was baptizing, he said to them: "You brood of vipers! Who warned you to flee from the coming wrath? [8]Produce fruit in keeping with repentance. [9]And do not think you can say to yourselves, 'We have Abraham as our father.' I tell you that out of these stones God can raise up children for Abraham. [10]The ax is already at the root of the trees, and every tree that does not produce good fruit will be cut down and thrown into the fire.

[11]"I baptize you with[d] water for repentance. But after me will come one who is more powerful than I, whose sandals I am not fit to carry. He will baptize you with the Holy Spirit and with fire. [12]His winnowing fork is in his hand, and he will clear his threshing floor, gathering his wheat into the barn and burning up the chaff with unquenchable fire."

The Baptism of Jesus

[13]Then Jesus came from Galilee to the Jordan to be baptized by John. [14]But John tried to deter him, saying, "I need to be baptized by you, and do you come to me?"

[15]Jesus replied, "Let it be so now; it is proper for us to do this to fulfill all righteousness." Then John consented.

[16]As soon as Jesus was baptized, he went up out of the water. At that moment heaven was opened, and he saw the Spirit of God descending like a dove and lighting on him. [17]And a voice from heaven said, "This is my Son, whom I love; with him I am well pleased."

---

[a]15 Hosea 11:1   [b]18 Jer. 31:15   [c]3 Isaiah 40:3   [d]11 Or in

The Temptation of Jesus

4 Then Jesus was led by the Spirit into the desert to be tempted by the devil. ²After fasting forty days and forty nights, he was hungry. ³The tempter came to him and said, "If you are the Son of God, tell these stones to become bread."

⁴Jesus answered, "It is written: 'Man does not live on bread alone, but on every word that comes from the mouth of God.'ᵃ"

⁵Then the devil took him to the holy city and had him stand on the highest point of the temple. ⁶"If you are the Son of God," he said, "throw yourself down. For it is written:

" 'He will command his angels
        concerning you,
    and they will lift you up in their
        hands,
so that you will not strike your foot
        against a stone.'ᵇ"

⁷Jesus answered him, "It is also written: 'Do not put the Lord your God to the test.'ᶜ"

⁸Again, the devil took him to a very high mountain and showed him all the kingdoms of the world and their splendor. ⁹"All this I will give you," he said, "if you will bow down and worship me."

¹⁰Jesus said to him, "Away from me, Satan! For it is written: 'Worship the Lord your God, and serve him only.'ᵈ"

¹¹Then the devil left him, and angels came and attended him.

Jesus Begins to Preach

¹²When Jesus heard that John had been put in prison, he returned to Galilee. ¹³Leaving Nazareth, he went and lived in Capernaum, which was by the lake in the area of Zebulun and Naphtali— ¹⁴to fulfill what was said through the prophet Isaiah:

¹⁵"Land of Zebulun and land of
        Naphtali,
    the way to the sea, along the
        Jordan,
    Galilee of the Gentiles—
¹⁶the people living in darkness
    have seen a great light;

on those living in the land of the
        shadow of death
    a light has dawned."ᵉ

¹⁷From that time on Jesus began to preach, "Repent, for the kingdom of heaven is near."

The Calling of the First Disciples

¹⁸As Jesus was walking beside the Sea of Galilee, he saw two brothers, Simon called Peter and his brother Andrew. They were casting a net into the lake, for they were fishermen. ¹⁹"Come, follow me," Jesus said, "and I will make you fishers of men." ²⁰At once they left their nets and followed him.

²¹Going on from there, he saw two other brothers, James son of Zebedee and his brother John. They were in a boat with their father Zebedee, preparing their nets. Jesus called them, ²²and immediately they left the boat and their father and followed him.

Jesus Heals the Sick

²³Jesus went throughout Galilee, teaching in their synagogues, preaching the good news of the kingdom, and healing every disease and sickness among the people. ²⁴News about him spread all over Syria, and people brought to him all who were ill with various diseases, those suffering severe pain, the demon-possessed, those having seizures, and the paralyzed, and he healed them. ²⁵Large crowds from Galilee, the Decapolis,ᶠ Jerusalem, Judea and the region across the Jordan followed him.

The Beatitudes

5 Now when he saw the crowds, he went up on a mountainside and sat down. His disciples came to him, ²and he began to teach them, saying:

³"Blessed are the poor in spirit,
    for theirs is the kingdom of
        heaven.
⁴Blessed are those who mourn,
    for they will be comforted.
⁵Blessed are the meek,
    for they will inherit the earth.
⁶Blessed are those who hunger and
        thirst for righteousness,
    for they will be filled.

ᵃ4 Deut. 8:3   ᵇ6 Psalm 91:11,12   ᶜ7 Deut. 6:16   ᵈ10 Deut. 6:13   ᵉ16 Isaiah 9:1,2
ᶠ25 That is, the Ten Cities

7Blessed are the merciful,
  for they will be shown mercy.
8Blessed are the pure in heart,
  for they will see God.
9Blessed are the peacemakers,
  for they will be called sons of
    God.
10Blessed are those who are persecuted
    because of righteousness,
  for theirs is the kingdom of
    heaven.

11"Blessed are you when people insult you, persecute you and falsely say all kinds of evil against you because of me. **12**Rejoice and be glad, because great is your reward in heaven, for in the same way they persecuted the prophets who were before you.

Salt and Light

13"You are the salt of the earth. But if the salt loses its saltiness, how can it be made salty again? It is no longer good for anything, except to be thrown out and trampled by men.

14"You are the light of the world. A city on a hill cannot be hidden. **15**Neither do people light a lamp and put it under a bowl. Instead they put it on its stand, and it gives light to everyone in the house. **16**In the same way, let your light shine before men, that they may see your good deeds and praise your Father in heaven.

The Fulfillment of the Law

17"Do not think that I have come to abolish the Law or the Prophets; I have not come to abolish them but to fulfill them. **18**I tell you the truth, until heaven and earth disappear, not the smallest letter, not the least stroke of a pen, will by any means disappear from the Law until everything is accomplished. **19**Anyone who breaks one of the least of these commandments and teaches others to do the same will be called least in the kingdom of heaven, but whoever practices and teaches these commands will be called great in the kingdom of heaven. **20**For I tell you that unless your righteousness surpasses that of the Pharisees and the teachers of the law, you will certainly not enter the kingdom of heaven.

Murder

21"You have heard that it was said to the people long ago, 'Do not murder,[a] and anyone who murders will be subject to judgment.' **22**But I tell you that anyone who is angry with his brother[b] will be subject to judgment. Again, anyone who says to his brother, 'Raca,[c]' is answerable to the Sanhedrin. But anyone who says, 'You fool!' will be in danger of the fire of hell.

23"Therefore, if you are offering your gift at the altar and there remember that your brother has something against you, **24**leave your gift there in front of the altar. First go and be reconciled to your brother; then come and offer your gift.

25"Settle matters quickly with your adversary who is taking you to court. Do it while you are still with him on the way, or he may hand you over to the judge, and the judge may hand you over to the officer, and you may be thrown into prison. **26**I tell you the truth, you will not get out until you have paid the last penny.[d]

Adultery

27"You have heard that it was said, 'Do not commit adultery.'[e] **28**But I tell you that anyone who looks at a woman lustfully has already committed adultery with her in his heart. **29**If your right eye causes you to sin, gouge it out and throw it away. It is better for you to lose one part of your body than for your whole body to be thrown into hell. **30**And if your right hand causes you to sin, cut it off and throw it away. It is better for you to lose one part of your body than for your whole body to go into hell.

Divorce

31"It has been said, 'Anyone who divorces his wife must give her a certificate of divorce.'[f] **32**But I tell you that anyone who divorces his wife, except for marital unfaithfulness, causes her to become an adulteress, and anyone who marries the divorced woman commits adultery.

Oaths

33"Again, you have heard that it was said to the people long ago, 'Do not

---

[a]21 Exodus 20:13   [b]22 Some manuscripts *brother without cause*   [c]22 An Aramaic term of contempt   [d]26 Greek *kodrantes*   [e]27 Exodus 20:14   [f]31 Deut. 24:1

break your oath, but keep the oaths you have made to the Lord.' **34**But I tell you, Do not swear at all: either by heaven, for it is God's throne; **35**or by the earth, for it is his footstool; or by Jerusalem, for it is the city of the Great King. **36**And do not swear by your head, for you cannot make even one hair white or black. **37**Simply let your 'Yes' be 'Yes,' and your 'No,' 'No'; anything beyond this comes from the evil one.

An Eye for an Eye

38"You have heard that it was said, 'Eye for eye, and tooth for tooth.'*a* **39**But I tell you, Do not resist an evil person. If someone strikes you on the right cheek, turn to him the other also. **40**And if someone wants to sue you and take your tunic, let him have your cloak as well. **41**If someone forces you to go one mile, go with him two miles. **42**Give to the one who asks you, and do not turn away from the one who wants to borrow from you.

Love for Enemies

43"You have heard that it was said, 'Love your neighbor*b* and hate your enemy.' **44**But I tell you: Love your enemies*c* and pray for those who persecute you, **45**that you may be sons of your Father in heaven. He causes his sun to rise on the evil and the good, and sends rain on the righteous and the unrighteous. **46**If you love those who love you, what reward will you get? Are not even the tax collectors doing that? **47**And if you greet only your brothers, what are you doing more than others? Do not even pagans do that? **48**Be perfect, therefore, as your heavenly Father is perfect.

Giving to the Needy

6 "Be careful not to do your 'acts of righteousness' before men, to be seen by them. If you do, you will have no reward from your Father in heaven.

2"So when you give to the needy, do not announce it with trumpets, as the hypocrites do in the synagogues and on the streets, to be honored by men. I tell you the truth, they have received their reward in full. **3**But when you give to the needy, do not let your left hand know

what your right hand is doing, **4**so that your giving may be in secret. Then your Father, who sees what is done in secret, will reward you.

Prayer

5"And when you pray, do not be like the hypocrites, for they love to pray standing in the synagogues and on the street corners to be seen by men. I tell you the truth, they have received their reward in full. **6**But when you pray, go into your room, close the door and pray to your Father, who is unseen. Then your Father, who sees what is done in secret, will reward you. **7**And when you pray, do not keep on babbling like pagans, for they think they will be heard because of their many words. **8**Do not be like them, for your Father knows what you need before you ask him.

9"This, then, is how you should pray:

" 'Our Father in heaven,
     hallowed be your name,
10your kingdom come,
     your will be done
         on earth as it is in heaven.
11Give us today our daily bread.
12Forgive us our debts,
     as we also have forgiven our
         debtors.
13And lead us not into temptation,
     but deliver us from the evil one.*d* '

14For if you forgive men when they sin against you, your heavenly Father will also forgive you. **15**But if you do not forgive men their sins, your Father will not forgive your sins.

Fasting

16"When you fast, do not look somber as the hypocrites do, for they disfigure their faces to show men they are fasting. I tell you the truth, they have received their reward in full. **17**But when you fast, put oil on your head and wash your face, **18**so that it will not be obvious to men that you are fasting, but only to your Father, who is unseen; and your Father, who sees what is done in secret, will reward you.

Treasures in Heaven

19"Do not store up for yourselves

---

a38 Exodus 21:24; Lev. 24:20; Deut. 19:21   *b43* Lev. 19:18   *c44* Some late manuscripts *enemies,*
bless those who curse you, do good to those who hate you   *d13* Or *from evil*; some late manuscripts *one, /*
for yours is the kingdom and the power and the glory forever. Amen.

treasures on earth, where moth and rust destroy, and where thieves break in and steal. 20But store up for yourselves treasures in heaven, where moth and rust do not destroy, and where thieves do not break in and steal. 21For where your treasure is, there your heart will be also.

22"The eye is the lamp of the body. If your eyes are good, your whole body will be full of light. 23But if your eyes are bad, your whole body will be full of darkness. If then the light within you is darkness, how great is that darkness!

24"No one can serve two masters. Either he will hate the one and love the other, or he will be devoted to the one and despise the other. You cannot serve both God and Money.

Do Not Worry

25"Therefore I tell you, do not worry about your life, what you will eat or drink; or about your body, what you will wear. Is not life more important than food, and the body more important than clothes? 26Look at the birds of the air; they do not sow or reap or store away in barns, and yet your heavenly Father feeds them. Are you not much more valuable than they? 27Who of you by worrying can add a single hour to his life*a*?

28"And why do you worry about clothes? See how the lilies of the field grow. They do not labor or spin. 29Yet I tell you that not even Solomon in all his splendor was dressed like one of these. 30If that is how God clothes the grass of the field, which is here today and tomorrow is thrown into the fire, will he not much more clothe you, O you of little faith? 31So do not worry, saying, 'What shall we eat?' or 'What shall we drink?' or 'What shall we wear?' 32For the pagans run after all these things, and your heavenly Father knows that you need them. 33But seek first his kingdom and his righteousness, and all these things will be given to you as well. 34Therefore do not worry about tomorrow, for tomorrow will worry about itself. Each day has enough trouble of its own.

Judging Others

7 "Do not judge, or you too will be judged. 2For in the same way you judge others, you will be judged, and with the measure you use, it will be measured to you.

3"Why do you look at the speck of sawdust in your brother's eye and pay no attention to the plank in your own eye? 4How can you say to your brother, 'Let me take the speck out of your eye,' when all the time there is a plank in your own eye? 5You hypocrite, first take the plank out of your own eye, and then you will see clearly to remove the speck from your brother's eye.

6"Do not give dogs what is sacred; do not throw your pearls to pigs. If you do, they may trample them under their feet, and then turn and tear you to pieces.

Ask, Seek, Knock

7"Ask and it will be given to you; seek and you will find; knock and the door will be opened to you. 8For everyone who asks receives; he who seeks finds; and to him who knocks, the door will be opened.

9"Which of you, if his son asks for bread, will give him a stone? 10Or if he asks for a fish, will give him a snake? 11If you, then, though you are evil, know how to give good gifts to your children, how much more will your Father in heaven give good gifts to those who ask him! 12So in everything, do to others what you would have them do to you, for this sums up the Law and the Prophets.

The Narrow and Wide Gates

13"Enter through the narrow gate. For wide is the gate and broad is the road that leads to destruction, and many enter through it. 14But small is the gate and narrow the road that leads to life, and only a few find it.

A Tree and Its Fruit

15"Watch out for false prophets. They come to you in sheep's clothing, but inwardly they are ferocious wolves. 16By their fruit you will recognize them. Do people pick grapes from thornbushes, or figs from thistles? 17Likewise every good tree bears good fruit, but a bad tree bears bad fruit. 18A good tree cannot bear bad fruit, and a bad tree cannot bear good fruit. 19Every tree that does not bear good fruit is cut down and

a27 Or single cubit to his height

thrown into the fire. **20**Thus, by their fruit you will recognize them.

21"Not everyone who says to me, 'Lord, Lord,' will enter the kingdom of heaven, but only he who does the will of my Father who is in heaven. **22**Many will say to me on that day, 'Lord, Lord, did we not prophesy in your name, and in your name drive out demons and perform many miracles?' **23**Then I will tell them plainly, 'I never knew you. Away from me, you evildoers!'

The Wise and Foolish Builders

24"Therefore everyone who hears these words of mine and puts them into practice is like a wise man who built his house on the rock. **25**The rain came down, the streams rose, and the winds blew and beat against that house; yet it did not fall, because it had its foundation on the rock. **26**But everyone who hears these words of mine and does not put them into practice is like a foolish man who built his house on sand. **27**The rain came down, the streams rose, and the winds blew and beat against that house, and it fell with a great crash."

28When Jesus had finished saying these things, the crowds were amazed at his teaching, **29**because he taught as one who had authority, and not as their teachers of the law.

The Man With Leprosy

8 When he came down from the mountainside, large crowds followed him. **2**A man with leprosy[a] came and knelt before him and said, "Lord, if you are willing, you can make me clean."

3Jesus reached out his hand and touched the man. "I am willing," he said. "Be clean!" Immediately he was cured[b] of his leprosy. **4**Then Jesus said to him, "See that you don't tell anyone. But go, show yourself to the priest and offer the gift Moses commanded, as a testimony to them."

The Faith of the Centurion

5When Jesus had entered Capernaum, a centurion came to him, asking for help. **6**"Lord," he said, "my servant lies at home paralyzed and in terrible suffering."

7Jesus said to him, "I will go and heal him."

8The centurion replied, "Lord, I do not deserve to have you come under my roof. But just say the word, and my servant will be healed. **9**For I myself am a man under authority, with soldiers under me. I tell this one, 'Go,' and he goes; and that one, 'Come,' and he comes. I say to my servant, 'Do this,' and he does it."

10When Jesus heard this, he was astonished and said to those following him, "I tell you the truth, I have not found anyone in Israel with such great faith. **11**I say to you that many will come from the east and the west, and will take their places at the feast with Abraham, Isaac and Jacob in the kingdom of heaven. **12**But the subjects of the kingdom will be thrown outside, into the darkness, where there will be weeping and gnashing of teeth."

13Then Jesus said to the centurion, "Go! It will be done just as you believed it would." And his servant was healed at that very hour.

Jesus Heals Many

14When Jesus came into Peter's house, he saw Peter's mother-in-law lying in bed with a fever. **15**He touched her hand and the fever left her, and she got up and began to wait on him.

16When evening came, many who were demon-possessed were brought to him, and he drove out the spirits with a word and healed all the sick. **17**This was to fulfill what was spoken through the prophet Isaiah:

"He took up our infirmities
    and carried our diseases."[c]

The Cost of Following Jesus

18When Jesus saw the crowd around him, he gave orders to cross to the other side of the lake. **19**Then a teacher of the law came to him and said, "Teacher, I will follow you wherever you go."

20Jesus replied, "Foxes have holes and birds of the air have nests, but the Son of Man has no place to lay his head."

21Another disciple said to him, "Lord, first let me go and bury my father."

---

*a*2 The Greek word was used for various diseases affecting the skin—not necessarily leprosy.
*b*3 Greek *made clean*   *c*17 Isaiah 53:4

WEEKENDING

REFLECT

Prayer is the expression of a human heart in conversation with God. The more natural the prayer, the more real he becomes. It has all been simplified for me to this extent: Prayer is a dialogue between two persons who love each other.

Rosalind Rinker

REVIVE

Saturday: Matthew 6:8–13
Sunday: Romans 8:25–27

Go to page 12 for your next devotional reading.

22But Jesus told him, "Follow me, and let the dead bury their own dead."

Jesus Calms the Storm

23Then he got into the boat and his disciples followed him. **24**Without warning, a furious storm came up on the lake, so that the waves swept over the boat. But Jesus was sleeping. **25**The disciples went and woke him, saying, "Lord, save us! We're going to drown!"

26He replied, "You of little faith, why are you so afraid?" Then he got up and rebuked the winds and the waves, and it was completely calm.

27The men were amazed and asked, "What kind of man is this? Even the winds and the waves obey him!"

The Healing of Two Demon-possessed Men

28When he arrived at the other side in the region of the Gadarenes,[a] two demon-possessed men coming from the tombs met him. They were so violent that no one could pass that way. **29**"What do you want with us, Son of God?" they shouted. "Have you come here to torture us before the appointed time?"

30Some distance from them a large herd of pigs was feeding. **31**The demons begged Jesus, "If you drive us out, send us into the herd of pigs."

32He said to them, "Go!" So they came out and went into the pigs, and the whole herd rushed down the steep bank into the lake and died in the water. **33**Those tending the pigs ran off, went into the town and reported all this, including what had happened to the demon-possessed men. **34**Then the whole town went out to meet Jesus. And when they saw him, they pleaded with him to leave their region.

Jesus Heals a Paralytic

9 Jesus stepped into a boat, crossed over and came to his own town. **2**Some men brought to him a paralytic, lying on a mat. When Jesus saw their faith, he said to the paralytic, "Take heart, son; your sins are forgiven."

3At this, some of the teachers of the law said to themselves, "This fellow is blaspheming!"

4Knowing their thoughts, Jesus said, "Why do you entertain evil thoughts in your hearts? **5**Which is easier: to say, 'Your sins are forgiven,' or to say, 'Get up and walk'? **6**But so that you may know that the Son of Man has authority on earth to forgive sins. . . ." Then he said to the paralytic, "Get up, take your mat and go home." **7**And the man got up and went home. **8**When the crowd saw this, they were filled with awe; and they praised God, who had given such authority to men.

The Calling of Matthew

9As Jesus went on from there, he saw a man named Matthew sitting at the tax collector's booth. "Follow me," he told him, and Matthew got up and followed him.

10While Jesus was having dinner at Matthew's house, many tax collectors and "sinners" came and ate with him and his disciples. **11**When the Pharisees saw this, they asked his disciples, "Why does your teacher eat with tax collectors and 'sinners'?"

12On hearing this, Jesus said, "It is not the healthy who need a doctor, but the sick. **13**But go and learn what this means: 'I desire mercy, not sacrifice.'[b] For I have not come to call the righteous, but sinners."

Jesus Questioned About Fasting

14Then John's disciples came and asked him, "How is it that we and the Pharisees fast, but your disciples do not fast?"

15Jesus answered, "How can the guests of the bridegroom mourn while he is with them? The time will come when the bridegroom will be taken from them; then they will fast.

16"No one sews a patch of unshrunk cloth on an old garment, for the patch will pull away from the garment, making the tear worse. **17**Neither do men pour new wine into old wineskins. If they do, the skins will burst, the wine will run out and the wineskins will be ruined. No, they pour new wine into new wineskins, and both are preserved."

A Dead Girl and a Sick Woman

18While he was saying this, a ruler came and knelt before him and said,

---

a28 Some manuscripts *Gergesenes*; others *Gerasenes*   *b13* Hosea 6:6

"My daughter has just died. But come and put your hand on her, and she will live." [19]Jesus got up and went with him, and so did his disciples.

[20]Just then a woman who had been subject to bleeding for twelve years came up behind him and touched the edge of his cloak. [21]She said to herself, "If I only touch his cloak, I will be healed."

[22]Jesus turned and saw her. "Take heart, daughter," he said, "your faith has healed you." And the woman was healed from that moment.

[23]When Jesus entered the ruler's house and saw the flute players and the noisy crowd, [24]he said, "Go away. The girl is not dead but asleep." But they laughed at him. [25]After the crowd had been put outside, he went in and took the girl by the hand, and she got up. [26]News of this spread through all that region.

Jesus Heals the Blind and Mute

[27]As Jesus went on from there, two blind men followed him, calling out, "Have mercy on us, Son of David!"

[28]When he had gone indoors, the blind men came to him, and he asked them, "Do you believe that I am able to do this?"

"Yes, Lord," they replied.

[29]Then he touched their eyes and said, "According to your faith will it be done to you"; [30]and their sight was restored. Jesus warned them sternly, "See that no one knows about this." [31]But they went out and spread the news about him all over that region.

[32]While they were going out, a man who was demon-possessed and could not talk was brought to Jesus. [33]And when the demon was driven out, the man who had been mute spoke. The crowd was amazed and said, "Nothing like this has ever been seen in Israel."

[34]But the Pharisees said, "It is by the prince of demons that he drives out demons."

The Workers Are Few

[35]Jesus went through all the towns and villages, teaching in their synagogues, preaching the good news of the kingdom and healing every disease and sickness. [36]When he saw the crowds, he had compassion on them, because they were harassed and helpless, like sheep without a shepherd. [37]Then he said to his disciples, "The harvest is plentiful but the workers are few. [38]Ask the Lord of the harvest, therefore, to send out workers into his harvest field."

Jesus Sends Out the Twelve

10 He called his twelve disciples to him and gave them authority to drive out evil[a] spirits and to heal every disease and sickness.

[2]These are the names of the twelve apostles: first, Simon (who is called Peter) and his brother Andrew; James son of Zebedee, and his brother John; [3]Philip and Bartholomew; Thomas and Matthew the tax collector; James son of Alphaeus, and Thaddaeus; [4]Simon the Zealot and Judas Iscariot, who betrayed him.

[5]These twelve Jesus sent out with the following instructions: "Do not go among the Gentiles or enter any town of the Samaritans. [6]Go rather to the lost sheep of Israel. [7]As you go, preach this message: 'The kingdom of heaven is near.' [8]Heal the sick, raise the dead, cleanse those who have leprosy,[b] drive out demons. Freely you have received, freely give. [9]Do not take along any gold or silver or copper in your belts; [10]take no bag for the journey, or extra tunic, or sandals or a staff; for the worker is worth his keep.

[11]"Whatever town or village you enter, search for some worthy person there and stay at his house until you leave. [12]As you enter the home, give it your greeting. [13]If the home is deserving, let your peace rest on it; if it is not, let your peace return to you. [14]If anyone will not welcome you or listen to your words, shake the dust off your feet when you leave that home or town. [15]I tell you the truth, it will be more bearable for Sodom and Gomorrah on the day of judgment than for that town. [16]I am sending you out like sheep among wolves. Therefore be as shrewd as snakes and as innocent as doves.

[17]"Be on your guard against men; they will hand you over to the local councils and flog you in their synagogues. [18]On

---

[a]1 Greek *unclean*   [b]8 The Greek word was used for various diseases affecting the skin—not necessarily leprosy.

my account you will be brought before governors and kings as witnesses to them and to the Gentiles. **19**But when they arrest you, do not worry about what to say or how to say it. At that time you will be given what to say, **20**for it will not be you speaking, but the Spirit of your Father speaking through you.

21"Brother will betray brother to death, and a father his child; children will rebel against their parents and have them put to death. **22**All men will hate you because of me, but he who stands firm to the end will be saved. **23**When you are persecuted in one place, flee to another. I tell you the truth, you will not finish going through the cities of Israel before the Son of Man comes.

24"A student is not above his teacher, nor a servant above his master. **25**It is

---

MONDAY

VERSE:	AUTHOR:	PASSAGE:
Matthew 10:8	Babbie Mason	Matthew 10:5–10

Right Here at Home

You don't have to go overseas to be a missionary.

I used to think you had to be white, older, single, wear your hair in a bun and never use makeup to qualify as a missionary—and here I am, a black married woman with a family! But I've learned you don't need a degree in missions to be qualified to love people. You just go into your world and do your best to make a difference. A century ago, there were no social agencies like the welfare system—the church met the needs of the poor, the widow, the hungry, the orphan. If Christians took a more active role in reaching people—no matter what their color—that would take care of a lot of our social problems.

However, we have to ask ourselves: *Do we really want to get our hands dirty?* For example, a few years ago, my integrated church bussed people in from the inner city to see our large singing Christmas tree. It was a great idea—but we had problems we didn't expect. These people were homeless, so the kids had lice. Some had wet their pants. Men and women hadn't bathed. So here they were in this affluent suburban church, watching the Christmas pageant with the rest of us. There were a lot of complaints from our congregation.

But what is church for? We are the hands and feet of Christ. We need to do what Christ would do. If people are hungry, feed them. If they're naked, clothe them. If they're lonely, talk to them. If they're discouraged, encourage them. Do it by whatever means you can—if you can bake, take them some banana bread. If you can read, then go to the youth detention center and read to the people there. Do what you can to make a difference in somebody's life—one life at a time, right here at home.

ADDITIONAL SCRIPTURE READINGS:
Matthew 25:31–46; 1 Corinthians 13; James 2:1–14

Go to page 18 for your next devotional reading.

enough for the student to be like his teacher, and the servant like his master. If the head of the house has been called Beelzebub,[a] how much more the members of his household!

26 "So do not be afraid of them. There is nothing concealed that will not be disclosed, or hidden that will not be made known. 27What I tell you in the dark, speak in the daylight; what is whispered in your ear, proclaim from the roofs. 28Do not be afraid of those who kill the body but cannot kill the soul. Rather, be afraid of the One who can destroy both soul and body in hell. 29Are not two sparrows sold for a penny[b]? Yet not one of them will fall to the ground apart from the will of your Father. 30And even the very hairs of your head are all numbered. 31So don't be afraid; you are worth more than many sparrows.

32 "Whoever acknowledges me before men, I will also acknowledge him before my Father in heaven. 33But whoever disowns me before men, I will disown him before my Father in heaven.

34 "Do not suppose that I have come to bring peace to the earth. I did not come to bring peace, but a sword. 35For I have come to turn

" 'a man against his father,
    a daughter against her mother,
a daughter-in-law against her
        mother-in-law—
36   a man's enemies will be the
        members of his own
        household.'[c]

37 "Anyone who loves his father or mother more than me is not worthy of me; anyone who loves his son or daughter more than me is not worthy of me; 38and anyone who does not take his cross and follow me is not worthy of me. 39Whoever finds his life will lose it, and whoever loses his life for my sake will find it.

40 "He who receives you receives me, and he who receives me receives the one who sent me. 41Anyone who receives a prophet because he is a prophet will receive a prophet's reward, and anyone who receives a righteous man because he is a righteous man will receive a righteous man's reward. 42And if anyone

gives even a cup of cold water to one of these little ones because he is my disciple, I tell you the truth, he will certainly not lose his reward."

Jesus and John the Baptist

11 After Jesus had finished instructing his twelve disciples, he went on from there to teach and preach in the towns of Galilee.[d]

2When John heard in prison what Christ was doing, he sent his disciples 3to ask him, "Are you the one who was to come, or should we expect someone else?"

4Jesus replied, "Go back and report to John what you hear and see: 5The blind receive sight, the lame walk, those who have leprosy[e] are cured, the deaf hear, the dead are raised, and the good news is preached to the poor. 6Blessed is the man who does not fall away on account of me."

7As John's disciples were leaving, Jesus began to speak to the crowd about John: "What did you go out into the desert to see? A reed swayed by the wind? 8If not, what did you go out to see? A man dressed in fine clothes? No, those who wear fine clothes are in kings' palaces. 9Then what did you go out to see? A prophet? Yes, I tell you, and more than a prophet. 10This is the one about whom it is written:

" 'I will send my messenger ahead
        of you,
    who will prepare your way before
        you.'[f]

11I tell you the truth: Among those born of women there has not risen anyone greater than John the Baptist; yet he who is least in the kingdom of heaven is greater than he. 12From the days of John the Baptist until now, the kingdom of heaven has been forcefully advancing, and forceful men lay hold of it. 13For all the Prophets and the Law prophesied until John. 14And if you are willing to accept it, he is the Elijah who was to come. 15He who has ears, let him hear.

16 "To what can I compare this generation? They are like children sitting in the marketplaces and calling out to others:

a25 Greek *Beezeboul* or *Beelzeboul*   b29 Greek *an assarion*   c36 Micah 7:6   d1 Greek *in their towns*   e5 The Greek word was used for various diseases affecting the skin—not necessarily leprosy.   f10 Mal. 3:1

17 " 'We played the flute for you,
      and you did not dance;
we sang a dirge,
      and you did not mourn.'

18 For John came neither eating nor drinking, and they say, 'He has a demon.' 19 The Son of Man came eating and drinking, and they say, 'Here is a glutton and a drunkard, a friend of tax collectors and "sinners." ' But wisdom is proved right by her actions."

Woe on Unrepentant Cities

20 Then Jesus began to denounce the cities in which most of his miracles had been performed, because they did not repent. 21 "Woe to you, Korazin! Woe to you, Bethsaida! If the miracles that were performed in you had been performed in Tyre and Sidon, they would have repented long ago in sackcloth and ashes. 22 But I tell you, it will be more bearable for Tyre and Sidon on the day of judgment than for you. 23 And you, Capernaum, will you be lifted up to the skies? No, you will go down to the depths.^a If the miracles that were performed in you had been performed in Sodom, it would have remained to this day. 24 But I tell you that it will be more bearable for Sodom on the day of judgment than for you."

Rest for the Weary

25 At that time Jesus said, "I praise you, Father, Lord of heaven and earth, because you have hidden these things from the wise and learned, and revealed them to little children. 26 Yes, Father, for this was your good pleasure.

27 "All things have been committed to me by my Father. No one knows the Son except the Father, and no one knows the Father except the Son and those to whom the Son chooses to reveal him.

28 "Come to me, all you who are weary and burdened, and I will give you rest. 29 Take my yoke upon you and learn from me, for I am gentle and humble in heart, and you will find rest for your souls. 30 For my yoke is easy and my burden is light."

Lord of the Sabbath

12 At that time Jesus went through the grainfields on the Sabbath.

His disciples were hungry and began to pick some heads of grain and eat them. 2 When the Pharisees saw this, they said to him, "Look! Your disciples are doing what is unlawful on the Sabbath."

3 He answered, "Haven't you read what David did when he and his companions were hungry? 4 He entered the house of God, and he and his companions ate the consecrated bread—which was not lawful for them to do, but only for the priests. 5 Or haven't you read in the Law that on the Sabbath the priests in the temple desecrate the day and yet are innocent? 6 I tell you that one^b greater than the temple is here. 7 If you had known what these words mean, 'I desire mercy, not sacrifice,'^c you would not have condemned the innocent. 8 For the Son of Man is Lord of the Sabbath."

9 Going on from that place, he went into their synagogue, 10 and a man with a shriveled hand was there. Looking for a reason to accuse Jesus, they asked him, "Is it lawful to heal on the Sabbath?"

11 He said to them, "If any of you has a sheep and it falls into a pit on the Sabbath, will you not take hold of it and lift it out? 12 How much more valuable is a man than a sheep! Therefore it is lawful to do good on the Sabbath."

13 Then he said to the man, "Stretch out your hand." So he stretched it out and it was completely restored, just as sound as the other. 14 But the Pharisees went out and plotted how they might kill Jesus.

God's Chosen Servant

15 Aware of this, Jesus withdrew from that place. Many followed him, and he healed all their sick, 16 warning them not to tell who he was. 17 This was to fulfill what was spoken through the prophet Isaiah:

18 "Here is my servant whom I have
            chosen,
      the one I love, in whom I delight;
   I will put my Spirit on him,
      and he will proclaim justice to the
            nations.
19 He will not quarrel or cry out;
      no one will hear his voice in the
            streets.
20 A bruised reed he will not break,

---

^a23 Greek *Hades*   ^b6 Or *something*; also in verses 41 and 42   ^c7 Hosea 6:6

and a smoldering wick he will not
   snuff out,
till he leads justice to victory.
21 In his name the nations will put
   their hope." [a]

Jesus and Beelzebub

22Then they brought him a demon-possessed man who was blind and mute, and Jesus healed him, so that he could both talk and see. 23All the people were astonished and said, "Could this be the Son of David?"

24But when the Pharisees heard this, they said, "It is only by Beelzebub, [b] the prince of demons, that this fellow drives out demons."

25Jesus knew their thoughts and said to them, "Every kingdom divided against itself will be ruined, and every city or household divided against itself will not stand. 26If Satan drives out Satan, he is divided against himself. How then can his kingdom stand? 27And if I drive out demons by Beelzebub, by whom do your people drive them out? So then, they will be your judges. 28But if I drive out demons by the Spirit of God, then the kingdom of God has come upon you.

29"Or again, how can anyone enter a strong man's house and carry off his possessions unless he first ties up the strong man? Then he can rob his house. 30"He who is not with me is against me, and he who does not gather with me scatters. 31And so I tell you, every sin and blasphemy will be forgiven men, but the blasphemy against the Spirit will not be forgiven. 32Anyone who speaks a word against the Son of Man will be forgiven, but anyone who speaks against the Holy Spirit will not be forgiven, either in this age or in the age to come.

33"Make a tree good and its fruit will be good, or make a tree bad and its fruit will be bad, for a tree is recognized by its fruit. 34You brood of vipers, how can you who are evil say anything good? For out of the overflow of the heart the mouth speaks. 35The good man brings good things out of the good stored up in him, and the evil man brings evil things out of the evil stored up in him. 36But I tell you that men will have to give account on the day of judgment for every careless word they have spoken. 37For by your words you will be acquitted, and by your words you will be condemned."

The Sign of Jonah

38Then some of the Pharisees and teachers of the law said to him, "Teacher, we want to see a miraculous sign from you."

39He answered, "A wicked and adulterous generation asks for a miraculous sign! But none will be given it except the sign of the prophet Jonah. 40For as Jonah was three days and three nights in the belly of a huge fish, so the Son of Man will be three days and three nights in the heart of the earth. 41The men of Nineveh will stand up at the judgment with this generation and condemn it; for they repented at the preaching of Jonah, and now one[c] greater than Jonah is here. 42The Queen of the South will rise at the judgment with this generation and condemn it; for she came from the ends of the earth to listen to Solomon's wisdom, and now one greater than Solomon is here.

43"When an evil[d] spirit comes out of a man, it goes through arid places seeking rest and does not find it. 44Then it says, 'I will return to the house I left.' When it arrives, it finds the house unoccupied, swept clean and put in order. 45Then it goes and takes with it seven other spirits more wicked than itself, and they go in and live there. And the final condition of that man is worse than the first. That is how it will be with this wicked generation."

Jesus' Mother and Brothers

46While Jesus was still talking to the crowd, his mother and brothers stood outside, wanting to speak to him. 47Someone told him, "Your mother and brothers are standing outside, wanting to speak to you."[e]

48He replied to him, "Who is my mother, and who are my brothers?" 49Pointing to his disciples, he said, "Here are my mother and my brothers. 50For whoever does the will of my Father in heaven is my brother and sister and mother."

[a]21 Isaiah 42:1-4   [b]24 Greek *Beezeboul* or *Beelzeboul*; also in verse 27   [c]41 Or *something*; also in verse 42   [d]43 Greek *unclean*   [e]47 Some manuscripts do not have verse 47.

The Parable of the Sower

13 That same day Jesus went out of the house and sat by the lake. ²Such large crowds gathered around him that he got into a boat and sat in it, while all the people stood on the shore. ³Then he told them many things in parables, saying: "A farmer went out to sow his seed. ⁴As he was scattering the seed, some fell along the path, and the birds came and ate it up. ⁵Some fell on rocky places, where it did not have much soil. It sprang up quickly, because the soil was shallow. ⁶But when the sun came up, the plants were scorched, and they withered because they had no root. ⁷Other seed fell among thorns, which grew up and choked the plants. ⁸Still other seed fell on good soil, where it produced a crop—a hundred, sixty or thirty times what was sown. ⁹He who has ears, let him hear."

¹⁰The disciples came to him and asked, "Why do you speak to the people in parables?"

¹¹He replied, "The knowledge of the secrets of the kingdom of heaven has been given to you, but not to them. ¹²Whoever has will be given more, and he will have an abundance. Whoever does not have, even what he has will be taken from him. ¹³This is why I speak to them in parables:

"Though seeing, they do not see;
    though hearing, they do not hear
    or understand.

¹⁴In them is fulfilled the prophecy of Isaiah:

" 'You will be ever hearing but never
    understanding;
you will be ever seeing but never
    perceiving.
¹⁵For this people's heart has become
    calloused;
    they hardly hear with their ears,
    and they have closed their eyes.
Otherwise they might see with their
    eyes,
    hear with their ears,
    understand with their hearts
and turn, and I would heal them.' ᵃ

¹⁶But blessed are your eyes because they see, and your ears because they hear. ¹⁷For I tell you the truth, many prophets and righteous men longed to see what you see but did not see it, and to hear what you hear but did not hear it.

¹⁸"Listen then to what the parable of the sower means: ¹⁹When anyone hears the message about the kingdom and does not understand it, the evil one comes and snatches away what was sown in his heart. This is the seed sown along the path. ²⁰The one who received the seed that fell on rocky places is the man who hears the word and at once receives it with joy. ²¹But since he has no root, he lasts only a short time. When trouble or persecution comes because of the word, he quickly falls away. ²²The one who received the seed that fell among the thorns is the man who hears the word, but the worries of this life and the deceitfulness of wealth choke it, making it unfruitful. ²³But the one who received the seed that fell on good soil is the man who hears the word and understands it. He produces a crop, yielding a hundred, sixty or thirty times what was sown."

The Parable of the Weeds

²⁴Jesus told them another parable: "The kingdom of heaven is like a man who sowed good seed in his field. ²⁵But while everyone was sleeping, his enemy came and sowed weeds among the wheat, and went away. ²⁶When the wheat sprouted and formed heads, then the weeds also appeared.

²⁷"The owner's servants came to him and said, 'Sir, didn't you sow good seed in your field? Where then did the weeds come from?'

²⁸" 'An enemy did this,' he replied.

"The servants asked him, 'Do you want us to go and pull them up?'

²⁹" 'No,' he answered, 'because while you are pulling the weeds, you may root up the wheat with them. ³⁰Let both grow together until the harvest. At that time I will tell the harvesters: First collect the weeds and tie them in bundles to be burned; then gather the wheat and bring it into my barn.' "

The Parables of the Mustard Seed and the Yeast

³¹He told them another parable: "The kingdom of heaven is like a mustard

ᵃ15 Isaiah 6:9,10

seed, which a man took and planted in his field. [32]Though it is the smallest of all your seeds, yet when it grows, it is the largest of garden plants and becomes a tree, so that the birds of the air come and perch in its branches."

[33]He told them still another parable: "The kingdom of heaven is like yeast that a woman took and mixed into a large amount[a] of flour until it worked all through the dough."

[34]Jesus spoke all these things to the crowd in parables; he did not say anything to them without using a parable. [35]So was fulfilled what was spoken through the prophet:

"I will open my mouth in parables,
I will utter things hidden since the creation of the world."[b]

The Parable of the Weeds Explained

[36]Then he left the crowd and went into the house. His disciples came to him and said, "Explain to us the parable of the weeds in the field."

[37]He answered, "The one who sowed the good seed is the Son of Man. [38]The field is the world, and the good seed stands for the sons of the kingdom. The weeds are the sons of the evil one, [39]and the enemy who sows them is the devil. The harvest is the end of the age, and the harvesters are angels.

[40]"As the weeds are pulled up and burned in the fire, so it will be at the end of the age. [41]The Son of Man will send out his angels, and they will weed out of his kingdom everything that causes sin and all who do evil. [42]They will throw them into the fiery furnace, where there will be weeping and gnashing of teeth. [43]Then the righteous will shine like the sun in the kingdom of their Father. He who has ears, let him hear.

The Parables of the Hidden Treasure and the Pearl

[44]"The kingdom of heaven is like treasure hidden in a field. When a man found it, he hid it again, and then in his joy went and sold all he had and bought that field.

[45]"Again, the kingdom of heaven is like a merchant looking for fine pearls. [46]When he found one of great value, he went away and sold everything he had and bought it.

The Parable of the Net

[47]"Once again, the kingdom of heaven is like a net that was let down into the lake and caught all kinds of fish. [48]When it was full, the fishermen pulled it up on the shore. Then they sat down and collected the good fish in baskets, but threw the bad away. [49]This is how it will be at the end of the age. The angels will come and separate the wicked from the righteous [50]and throw them into the fiery furnace, where there will be weeping and gnashing of teeth.

[51]"Have you understood all these things?" Jesus asked.

"Yes," they replied.

[52]He said to them, "Therefore every teacher of the law who has been instructed about the kingdom of heaven is like the owner of a house who brings out of his storeroom new treasures as well as old."

A Prophet Without Honor

[53]When Jesus had finished these parables, he moved on from there. [54]Coming to his hometown, he began teaching the people in their synagogue, and they were amazed. "Where did this man get this wisdom and these miraculous powers?" they asked. [55]"Isn't this the carpenter's son? Isn't his mother's name Mary, and aren't his brothers James, Joseph, Simon and Judas? [56]Aren't all his sisters with us? Where then did this man get all these things?" [57]And they took offense at him.

But Jesus said to them, "Only in his hometown and in his own house is a prophet without honor."

[58]And he did not do many miracles there because of their lack of faith.

John the Baptist Beheaded

14 At that time Herod the tetrarch heard the reports about Jesus, [2]and he said to his attendants, "This is John the Baptist; he has risen from the dead! That is why miraculous powers are at work in him."

[3]Now Herod had arrested John and bound him and put him in prison because of Herodias, his brother Philip's wife, [4]for John had been saying to him:

---

[a]33 Greek *three satas* (probably about 1/2 bushel or 22 liters)   [b]35 Psalm 78:2

"It is not lawful for you to have her." [5]Herod wanted to kill John, but he was afraid of the people, because they considered him a prophet.

[6]On Herod's birthday the daughter of Herodias danced for them and pleased Herod so much [7]that he promised with an oath to give her whatever she asked. [8]Prompted by her mother, she said, "Give me here on a platter the head of John the Baptist." [9]The king was distressed, but because of his oaths and

TUESDAY

VERSE:
Matthew 13:46

AUTHOR:
Sarah Jepson Coleman

PASSAGE:
Matthew 13:24–52

The Pearl

Here we have our glorious gospel likened to a hidden treasure. People who live in lands that fear invasion are often forced to take their riches and conceal them. From Japan comes a story of a family that did just that.

For generations their ancestors had been pearl divers. There was always a thrill in opening the oyster and examining its contents. To an untrained eye, many of the pearls they found would appear to be "of great value." But experts would point out the imperfections: a speck here, a dent there, too oblong; and so it was as day after day the pearls were brought to the surface and examined. Then one day the eldest son of the family had found an unusually rich oyster bed. He stayed down too long and soon afterward died. But he had brought up with him an oyster containing the most perfect pearl the family had ever seen. At last they had obtained their pearl of great value, but it had cost them a son. The family came to the United States and World War II broke out. During their internment the pearl was hidden. When they were released, they knew the time had come to sell the treasure. It was appraised, but on the day the buyer came to pick up the pearl, the father of the house explained that they had made a new decision. The pearl was beyond price; no amount of money could console them for the costly death of their son!

The gospel too is a treasure, much of which was hidden in the Old Testament, and then revealed when God gave his Son. The Son he sacrificed was beyond price, so salvation cannot be purchased. Nothing will buy it and no one can earn it. It is only granted as a free gift.

This short, stirring parable likens Christ to the precious pearl, and we through faith may possess him. It is time to reflect on the treasure that becomes ours when we receive the gift of God, the treasure of life and truth, and know for a certainty it is beyond price.

ADDITIONAL SCRIPTURE READINGS:
Romans 8:32; 2 Corinthians 4:7; Ephesians 1:16–18

Go to page 22 for your next devotional reading.

his dinner guests, he ordered that her request be granted ¹⁰and had John beheaded in the prison. ¹¹His head was brought in on a platter and given to the girl, who carried it to her mother. ¹²John's disciples came and took his body and buried it. Then they went and told Jesus.

Jesus Feeds the Five Thousand

¹³When Jesus heard what had happened, he withdrew by boat privately to a solitary place. Hearing of this, the crowds followed him on foot from the towns. ¹⁴When Jesus landed and saw a large crowd, he had compassion on them and healed their sick.

¹⁵As evening approached, the disciples came to him and said, "This is a remote place, and it's already getting late. Send the crowds away, so they can go to the villages and buy themselves some food."

¹⁶Jesus replied, "They do not need to go away. You give them something to eat."

¹⁷"We have here only five loaves of bread and two fish," they answered.

¹⁸"Bring them here to me," he said. ¹⁹And he directed the people to sit down on the grass. Taking the five loaves and the two fish and looking up to heaven, he gave thanks and broke the loaves. Then he gave them to the disciples, and the disciples gave them to the people. ²⁰They all ate and were satisfied, and the disciples picked up twelve basketfuls of broken pieces that were left over. ²¹The number of those who ate was about five thousand men, besides women and children.

Jesus Walks on the Water

²²Immediately Jesus made the disciples get into the boat and go on ahead of him to the other side, while he dismissed the crowd. ²³After he had dismissed them, he went up on a mountainside by himself to pray. When evening came, he was there alone, ²⁴but the boat was already a considerable distance[a] from land, buffeted by the waves because the wind was against it.

²⁵During the fourth watch of the night Jesus went out to them, walking on the lake. ²⁶When the disciples saw him

walking on the lake, they were terrified. "It's a ghost," they said, and cried out in fear.

²⁷But Jesus immediately said to them: "Take courage! It is I. Don't be afraid."

²⁸"Lord, if it's you," Peter replied, "tell me to come to you on the water."

²⁹"Come," he said.

Then Peter got down out of the boat, walked on the water and came toward Jesus. ³⁰But when he saw the wind, he was afraid and, beginning to sink, cried out, "Lord, save me!"

³¹Immediately Jesus reached out his hand and caught him. "You of little faith," he said, "why did you doubt?"

³²And when they climbed into the boat, the wind died down. ³³Then those who were in the boat worshiped him, saying, "Truly you are the Son of God."

³⁴When they had crossed over, they landed at Gennesaret. ³⁵And when the men of that place recognized Jesus, they sent word to all the surrounding country. People brought all their sick to him ³⁶and begged him to let the sick just touch the edge of his cloak, and all who touched him were healed.

Clean and Unclean

15 Then some Pharisees and teachers of the law came to Jesus from Jerusalem and asked, ²"Why do your disciples break the tradition of the elders? They don't wash their hands before they eat!"

³Jesus replied, "And why do you break the command of God for the sake of your tradition? ⁴For God said, 'Honor your father and mother'[b] and 'Anyone who curses his father or mother must be put to death.'[c] ⁵But you say that if a man says to his father or mother, 'Whatever help you might otherwise have received from me is a gift devoted to God,' ⁶he is not to 'honor his father'[d] with it. Thus you nullify the word of God for the sake of your tradition. ⁷You hypocrites! Isaiah was right when he prophesied about you:

⁸" 'These people honor me with their
      lips,
  but their hearts are far from me.
⁹They worship me in vain;

---

a 24 Greek *many stadia*   *b* 4 Exodus 20:12; Deut. 5:16   *c* 4 Exodus 21:17; Lev. 20:9   *d* 6 Some manuscripts *father or his mother*

their teachings are but rules taught by men.'*"

¹⁰Jesus called the crowd to him and said, "Listen and understand. ¹¹What goes into a man's mouth does not make him 'unclean,' but what comes out of his mouth, that is what makes him 'unclean.'"

¹²Then the disciples came to him and asked, "Do you know that the Pharisees were offended when they heard this?"

¹³He replied, "Every plant that my heavenly Father has not planted will be pulled up by the roots. ¹⁴Leave them; they are blind guides.*b* If a blind man leads a blind man, both will fall into a pit."

¹⁵Peter said, "Explain the parable to us."

¹⁶"Are you still so dull?" Jesus asked them. ¹⁷"Don't you see that whatever enters the mouth goes into the stomach and then out of the body? ¹⁸But the things that come out of the mouth come from the heart, and these make a man 'unclean.' ¹⁹For out of the heart come evil thoughts, murder, adultery, sexual immorality, theft, false testimony, slander. ²⁰These are what make a man 'unclean'; but eating with unwashed hands does not make him 'unclean.'"

The Faith of the Canaanite Woman

²¹Leaving that place, Jesus withdrew to the region of Tyre and Sidon. ²²A Canaanite woman from that vicinity came to him, crying out, "Lord, Son of David, have mercy on me! My daughter is suffering terribly from demon-possession."

²³Jesus did not answer a word. So his disciples came to him and urged him, "Send her away, for she keeps crying out after us."

²⁴He answered, "I was sent only to the lost sheep of Israel."

²⁵The woman came and knelt before him. "Lord, help me!" she said.

²⁶He replied, "It is not right to take the children's bread and toss it to their dogs."

²⁷"Yes, Lord," she said, "but even the dogs eat the crumbs that fall from their masters' table."

²⁸Then Jesus answered, "Woman, you have great faith! Your request is granted." And her daughter was healed from that very hour.

Jesus Feeds the Four Thousand

²⁹Jesus left there and went along the Sea of Galilee. Then he went up on a mountainside and sat down. ³⁰Great crowds came to him, bringing the lame, the blind, the crippled, the mute and many others, and laid them at his feet; and he healed them. ³¹The people were amazed when they saw the mute speaking, the crippled made well, the lame walking and the blind seeing. And they praised the God of Israel.

³²Jesus called his disciples to him and said, "I have compassion for these people; they have already been with me three days and have nothing to eat. I do not want to send them away hungry, or they may collapse on the way."

³³His disciples answered, "Where could we get enough bread in this remote place to feed such a crowd?"

³⁴"How many loaves do you have?" Jesus asked.

"Seven," they replied, "and a few small fish."

³⁵He told the crowd to sit down on the ground. ³⁶Then he took the seven loaves and the fish, and when he had given thanks, he broke them and gave them to the disciples, and they in turn to the people. ³⁷They all ate and were satisfied. Afterward the disciples picked up seven basketfuls of broken pieces that were left over. ³⁸The number of those who ate was four thousand, besides women and children. ³⁹After Jesus had sent the crowd away, he got into the boat and went to the vicinity of Magadan.

The Demand for a Sign

16 The Pharisees and Sadducees came to Jesus and tested him by asking him to show them a sign from heaven.

²He replied,*c* "When evening comes, you say, 'It will be fair weather, for the sky is red,' ³and in the morning, 'Today it will be stormy, for the sky is red and overcast.' You know how to interpret the appearance of the sky, but you cannot

---

*a*9 Isaiah 29:13   *b*14 Some manuscripts *guides of the blind*   *c*2 Some early manuscripts do not have the rest of verse 2 and all of verse 3.

interpret the signs of the times. [4]A wicked and adulterous generation looks for a miraculous sign, but none will be given it except the sign of Jonah." Jesus then left them and went away.

The Yeast of the Pharisees and Sadducees

[5]When they went across the lake, the disciples forgot to take bread. [6]"Be careful," Jesus said to them. "Be on your guard against the yeast of the Pharisees and Sadducees."

[7]They discussed this among themselves and said, "It is because we didn't bring any bread."

[8]Aware of their discussion, Jesus asked, "You of little faith, why are you talking among yourselves about having no bread? [9]Do you still not understand? Don't you remember the five loaves for the five thousand, and how many basketfuls you gathered? [10]Or the seven loaves for the four thousand, and how many basketfuls you gathered? [11]How is it you don't understand that I was not talking to you about bread? But be on your guard against the yeast of the Pharisees and Sadducees." [12]Then they understood that he was not telling them to guard against the yeast used in bread, but against the teaching of the Pharisees and Sadducees.

Peter's Confession of Christ

[13]When Jesus came to the region of Caesarea Philippi, he asked his disciples, "Who do people say the Son of Man is?"

[14]They replied, "Some say John the Baptist; others say Elijah; and still others, Jeremiah or one of the prophets."

[15]"But what about you?" he asked. "Who do you say I am?"

[16]Simon Peter answered, "You are the Christ,[a] the Son of the living God."

[17]Jesus replied, "Blessed are you, Simon son of Jonah, for this was not revealed to you by man, but by my Father in heaven. [18]And I tell you that you are Peter,[b] and on this rock I will build my church, and the gates of Hades[c] will not overcome it.[d] [19]I will give you the keys of the kingdom of heaven; whatever you bind on earth will be[e] bound

in heaven, and whatever you loose on earth will be[e] loosed in heaven." [20]Then he warned his disciples not to tell anyone that he was the Christ.

Jesus Predicts His Death

[21]From that time on Jesus began to explain to his disciples that he must go to Jerusalem and suffer many things at the hands of the elders, chief priests and teachers of the law, and that he must be killed and on the third day be raised to life.

[22]Peter took him aside and began to rebuke him. "Never, Lord!" he said. "This shall never happen to you!"

[23]Jesus turned and said to Peter, "Get behind me, Satan! You are a stumbling block to me; you do not have in mind the things of God, but the things of men."

[24]Then Jesus said to his disciples, "If anyone would come after me, he must deny himself and take up his cross and follow me. [25]For whoever wants to save his life[f] will lose it, but whoever loses his life for me will find it. [26]What good will it be for a man if he gains the whole world, yet forfeits his soul? Or what can a man give in exchange for his soul? [27]For the Son of Man is going to come in his Father's glory with his angels, and then he will reward each person according to what he has done. [28]I tell you the truth, some who are standing here will not taste death before they see the Son of Man coming in his kingdom."

The Transfiguration

17 After six days Jesus took with him Peter, James and John the brother of James, and led them up a high mountain by themselves. [2]There he was transfigured before them. His face shone like the sun, and his clothes became as white as the light. [3]Just then there appeared before them Moses and Elijah, talking with Jesus.

[4]Peter said to Jesus, "Lord, it is good for us to be here. If you wish, I will put up three shelters—one for you, one for Moses and one for Elijah."

[5]While he was still speaking, a bright cloud enveloped them, and a voice from

the cloud said, "This is my Son, whom I love; with him I am well pleased. Listen to him!"

⁶When the disciples heard this, they fell facedown to the ground, terrified. ⁷But Jesus came and touched them. "Get up," he said. "Don't be afraid." ⁸When they looked up, they saw no one except Jesus.

⁹As they were coming down the mountain, Jesus instructed them, "Don't tell anyone what you have seen, until the Son of Man has been raised from the dead."

¹⁰The disciples asked him, "Why then do the teachers of the law say that Elijah must come first?"

¹¹Jesus replied, "To be sure, Elijah comes and will restore all things. ¹²But I tell you, Elijah has already come, and they did not recognize him, but have done to him everything they wished. In the same way the Son of Man is going to suffer at their hands." ¹³Then the disci-

---

WEDNESDAY

VERSE:
Matthew 17:4

AUTHOR:
Ruth Senter

PASSAGE:
Matthew 17:1–13

The Road Down the Mountain

Paths to the top of this mountain should be one way. No one ever wants to go down. This path leads to the sun—a place of peace and tranquility.

The glory of the Lord breathes in every lodgepole pine and giant fir up here. We have climbed so far I feel almost celestial.

Viewed from this pinnacle of majesty, life below takes on different meaning. Why do humans rush to and fro, frantically chasing their tails?

Life in the clouds gives perspective. Authenticity. Simplicity. A log cabin provides our shelter, and a helicopter delivers our daily bread. We fill our cups from glacier runoff and breathe deeply of nature's pure air. No one wears a watch; there's no reason to look at one. We feed the ground creatures—the chipmunks and the marmots—and talk to the white-breasted grosbeak that sits on our table.

Surely this is hallowed ground. I can worship in this place.

"Peter said to Jesus, 'Lord, it is good for us to be here. If you wish, I will put up . . . shelters' " (v. 4). But Jesus pointed Peter to the path down the mountain. As they went, Jesus instructed them about his suffering which was soon to come.

Once home I find a friend in the hospital, a neighbor who is dying, and a man who is drunk, depressed and reaching out for help. "God is a presence, not a place," I say to myself. And so I look at the photographs of my moments on the mountain, remember what God did for me there, but reluctantly agree to live life on the plains.

ADDITIONAL SCRIPTURE READINGS:
Psalm 8:1; John 17:6–15

Go to page 25 for your next devotional reading.

ples understood that he was talking to them about John the Baptist.

The Healing of a Boy With a Demon

14When they came to the crowd, a man approached Jesus and knelt before him. **15**"Lord, have mercy on my son," he said. "He has seizures and is suffering greatly. He often falls into the fire or into the water. **16**I brought him to your disciples, but they could not heal him."

17"O unbelieving and perverse generation," Jesus replied, "how long shall I stay with you? How long shall I put up with you? Bring the boy here to me." **18**Jesus rebuked the demon, and it came out of the boy, and he was healed from that moment.

19Then the disciples came to Jesus in private and asked, "Why couldn't we drive it out?"

20He replied, "Because you have so little faith. I tell you the truth, if you have faith as small as a mustard seed, you can say to this mountain, 'Move from here to there' and it will move. Nothing will be impossible for you.*a*"

22When they came together in Galilee, he said to them, "The Son of Man is going to be betrayed into the hands of men. **23**They will kill him, and on the third day he will be raised to life." And the disciples were filled with grief.

The Temple Tax

24After Jesus and his disciples arrived in Capernaum, the collectors of the two-drachma tax came to Peter and asked, "Doesn't your teacher pay the temple tax*b*?"

25"Yes, he does," he replied.

When Peter came into the house, Jesus was the first to speak. "What do you think, Simon?" he asked. "From whom do the kings of the earth collect duty and taxes—from their own sons or from others?"

26"From others," Peter answered.

"Then the sons are exempt," Jesus said to him. **27**"But so that we may not offend them, go to the lake and throw out your line. Take the first fish you catch; open its mouth and you will find a four-drachma coin. Take it and give it to them for my tax and yours."

The Greatest in the Kingdom of Heaven

18 At that time the disciples came to Jesus and asked, "Who is the greatest in the kingdom of heaven?"

2He called a little child and had him stand among them. **3**And he said: "I tell you the truth, unless you change and become like little children, you will never enter the kingdom of heaven. **4**Therefore, whoever humbles himself like this child is the greatest in the kingdom of heaven.

5"And whoever welcomes a little child like this in my name welcomes me. **6**But if anyone causes one of these little ones who believe in me to sin, it would be better for him to have a large millstone hung around his neck and to be drowned in the depths of the sea.

7"Woe to the world because of the things that cause people to sin! Such things must come, but woe to the man through whom they come! **8**If your hand or your foot causes you to sin, cut it off and throw it away. It is better for you to enter life maimed or crippled than to have two hands or two feet and be thrown into eternal fire. **9**And if your eye causes you to sin, gouge it out and throw it away. It is better for you to enter life with one eye than to have two eyes and be thrown into the fire of hell.

The Parable of the Lost Sheep

10"See that you do not look down on one of these little ones. For I tell you that their angels in heaven always see the face of my Father in heaven.*c*

12"What do you think? If a man owns a hundred sheep, and one of them wanders away, will he not leave the ninety-nine on the hills and go to look for the one that wandered off? **13**And if he finds it, I tell you the truth, he is happier about that one sheep than about the ninety-nine that did not wander off. **14**In the same way your Father in heaven is not willing that any of these little ones should be lost.

A Brother Who Sins Against You

15"If your brother sins against you,*d* go and show him his fault, just between

---

a20 Some manuscripts *you.* *21But this kind does not go out except by prayer and fasting.*   *b24* Greek *the two drachmas*   *c10* Some manuscripts *heaven.* *11The Son of Man came to save what was lost.*
d15 Some manuscripts do not have *against you.*

the two of you. If he listens to you, you have won your brother over. **16**But if he will not listen, take one or two others along, so that 'every matter may be established by the testimony of two or three witnesses.'*a* **17**If he refuses to listen to them, tell it to the church; and if he refuses to listen even to the church, treat him as you would a pagan or a tax collector.

18"I tell you the truth, whatever you bind on earth will be*b* bound in heaven, and whatever you loose on earth will be*b* loosed in heaven.

19"Again, I tell you that if two of you on earth agree about anything you ask for, it will be done for you by my Father in heaven. **20**For where two or three come together in my name, there am I with them."

The Parable of the Unmerciful Servant

21Then Peter came to Jesus and asked, "Lord, how many times shall I forgive my brother when he sins against me? Up to seven times?"

22Jesus answered, "I tell you, not seven times, but seventy-seven times.*c*

23"Therefore, the kingdom of heaven is like a king who wanted to settle accounts with his servants. **24**As he began the settlement, a man who owed him ten thousand talents*d* was brought to him. **25**Since he was not able to pay, the master ordered that he and his wife and his children and all that he had be sold to repay the debt.

26"The servant fell on his knees before him. 'Be patient with me,' he begged, 'and I will pay back everything.' **27**The servant's master took pity on him, canceled the debt and let him go.

28"But when that servant went out, he found one of his fellow servants who owed him a hundred denarii.*e* He grabbed him and began to choke him. 'Pay back what you owe me!' he demanded.

29"His fellow servant fell to his knees and begged him, 'Be patient with me, and I will pay you back.'

30"But he refused. Instead, he went off and had the man thrown into prison until he could pay the debt. **31**When the other servants saw what had happened,

they were greatly distressed and went and told their master everything that had happened.

32"Then the master called the servant in. 'You wicked servant,' he said, 'I canceled all that debt of yours because you begged me to. **33**Shouldn't you have had mercy on your fellow servant just as I had on you?' **34**In anger his master turned him over to the jailers to be tortured, until he should pay back all he owed.

35"This is how my heavenly Father will treat each of you unless you forgive your brother from your heart."

Divorce

19 When Jesus had finished saying these things, he left Galilee and went into the region of Judea to the other side of the Jordan. **2**Large crowds followed him, and he healed them there.

3Some Pharisees came to him to test him. They asked, "Is it lawful for a man to divorce his wife for any and every reason?"

4"Haven't you read," he replied, "that at the beginning the Creator 'made them male and female,'*f* **5**and said, 'For this reason a man will leave his father and mother and be united to his wife, and the two will become one flesh'*g*? **6**So they are no longer two, but one. Therefore what God has joined together, let man not separate."

7"Why then," they asked, "did Moses command that a man give his wife a certificate of divorce and send her away?"

8Jesus replied, "Moses permitted you to divorce your wives because your hearts were hard. But it was not this way from the beginning. **9**I tell you that anyone who divorces his wife, except for marital unfaithfulness, and marries another woman commits adultery."

10The disciples said to him, "If this is the situation between a husband and wife, it is better not to marry."

11Jesus replied, "Not everyone can accept this word, but only those to whom it has been given. **12**For some are eunuchs because they were born that way; others were made that way by men; and others have renounced marriage*h*

---

*a*16 Deut. 19:15   *b*18 Or *have been*
dollars   *e*28 That is, a few dollars   *f*4 Gen. 1:27   *c*22 Or *seventy times seven*   *d*24 That is, millions of
*g*5 Gen. 2:24   *h*12 Or *have made*
themselves eunuchs

because of the kingdom of heaven. The one who can accept this should accept it."

The Little Children and Jesus

¹³Then little children were brought to Jesus for him to place his hands on them and pray for them. But the disciples rebuked those who brought them.

¹⁴Jesus said, "Let the little children come to me, and do not hinder them,

---

⟨ THURSDAY ⟩

VERSE:	AUTHOR:	PASSAGE:
Matthew 19:14	Karen Burton Mains	Matthew 19:13–15

Welcome, Child, to My Home

Recently the Lord has convicted me that my largest lack in hospitality is toward my own children's friends. It was hard to open my cleaned rooms to toy-oriented hands and feet. My own children knew they were expected to pick up after themselves, but this standard was a little harder to impose on the neighbors' kids.

Coming downstairs one day, arms loaded with soiled sheets and blankets, I nudged my way around two little forms huddled in conference on the treads. *Why do children love stairs so much?* Excusing myself, we shifted positions a bit, and I balanced my load on its way to the washer in the basement. I had not gone too far when I heard a little voice pipe, "I love to come to your house. Your mother doesn't yell all the time the way my mother does."

It gave me pause, and I suddenly realized this little girl had been around frequently. I didn't know her mother so I hadn't any way to judge the comment about yelling, but I did sense she had found shelter, a quiet space in a noisy world. *You are welcome, child, to my stairway any time.*

This is such a Christlike quality, this hospitality toward children. It is not simply a matter of being open toward our own, difficult as that often is, but it requires that we accept, encourage and want those born of someone else, whether we are married or not, whether we have children of our own or not. The story of Christ blessing the children is not only for the nursery but for adult Sunday school as well. If he could welcome the interruption of his ministry by wiggling, wonderstruck, bouncing, impertinent humanity, can we dare do less? . . . We really have no choice—we who know the one who is the living water, this same one who creates new songs in our hearts—we have no choice but to open our homes and our lives to those who may leave their telltale marks.

ADDITIONAL SCRIPTURE READINGS:
1 Timothy 5:10; Hebrews 13:2; 1 Peter 4:9

Go to page 28 for your next devotional reading.

for the kingdom of heaven belongs to such as these." ¹⁵When he had placed his hands on them, he went on from there.

The Rich Young Man

¹⁶Now a man came up to Jesus and asked, "Teacher, what good thing must I do to get eternal life?"

¹⁷"Why do you ask me about what is good?" Jesus replied. "There is only One who is good. If you want to enter life, obey the commandments."

¹⁸"Which ones?" the man inquired.

Jesus replied, " 'Do not murder, do not commit adultery, do not steal, do not give false testimony, ¹⁹honor your father and mother,'ᵃ and 'love your neighbor as yourself.'ᵇ "

²⁰"All these I have kept," the young man said. "What do I still lack?"

²¹Jesus answered, "If you want to be perfect, go, sell your possessions and give to the poor, and you will have treasure in heaven. Then come, follow me."

²²When the young man heard this, he went away sad, because he had great wealth.

²³Then Jesus said to his disciples, "I tell you the truth, it is hard for a rich man to enter the kingdom of heaven. ²⁴Again I tell you, it is easier for a camel to go through the eye of a needle than for a rich man to enter the kingdom of God."

²⁵When the disciples heard this, they were greatly astonished and asked, "Who then can be saved?"

²⁶Jesus looked at them and said, "With man this is impossible, but with God all things are possible."

²⁷Peter answered him, "We have left everything to follow you! What then will there be for us?"

²⁸Jesus said to them, "I tell you the truth, at the renewal of all things, when the Son of Man sits on his glorious throne, you who have followed me will also sit on twelve thrones, judging the twelve tribes of Israel. ²⁹And everyone who has left houses or brothers or sisters or father or motherᶜ or children or fields for my sake will receive a hundred times as much and will inherit eternal life. ³⁰But many who are first will be last, and many who are last will be first.

The Parable of the Workers in the Vineyard

20 "For the kingdom of heaven is like a landowner who went out early in the morning to hire men to work in his vineyard. ²He agreed to pay them a denarius for the day and sent them into his vineyard.

³About the third hour he went out and saw others standing in the marketplace doing nothing. ⁴He told them, 'You also go and work in my vineyard, and I will pay you whatever is right.' ⁵So they went.

"He went out again about the sixth hour and the ninth hour and did the same thing. ⁶About the eleventh hour he went out and found still others standing around. He asked them, 'Why have you been standing here all day long doing nothing?'

⁷" 'Because no one has hired us,' they answered.

"He said to them, 'You also go and work in my vineyard.'

⁸"When evening came, the owner of the vineyard said to his foreman, 'Call the workers and pay them their wages, beginning with the last ones hired and going on to the first.'

⁹"The workers who were hired about the eleventh hour came and each received a denarius. ¹⁰So when those came who were hired first, they expected to receive more. But each one of them also received a denarius. ¹¹When they received it, they began to grumble against the landowner. ¹²'These men who were hired last worked only one hour,' they said, 'and you have made them equal to us who have borne the burden of the work and the heat of the day.'

¹³"But he answered one of them, 'Friend, I am not being unfair to you. Didn't you agree to work for a denarius? ¹⁴Take your pay and go. I want to give the man who was hired last the same as I gave you. ¹⁵Don't I have the right to do what I want with my own money? Or are you envious because I am generous?'

¹⁶"So the last will be first, and the first will be last."

Jesus Again Predicts His Death

¹⁷Now as Jesus was going up to Jeru-

ᵃ19 Exodus 20:12-16; Deut. 5:16-20   ᵇ19 Lev. 19:18   ᶜ29 Some manuscripts mother or wife

salem, he took the twelve disciples aside and said to them, **18** "We are going up to Jerusalem, and the Son of Man will be betrayed to the chief priests and the teachers of the law. They will condemn him to death **19** and will turn him over to the Gentiles to be mocked and flogged and crucified. On the third day he will be raised to life!"

A Mother's Request

20 Then the mother of Zebedee's sons came to Jesus with her sons and, kneeling down, asked a favor of him.

21 "What is it you want?" he asked.

She said, "Grant that one of these two sons of mine may sit at your right and the other at your left in your kingdom."

22 "You don't know what you are asking," Jesus said to them. "Can you drink the cup I am going to drink?"

"We can," they answered.

23 Jesus said to them, "You will indeed drink from my cup, but to sit at my right or left is not for me to grant. These places belong to those for whom they have been prepared by my Father."

24 When the ten heard about this, they were indignant with the two brothers. **25** Jesus called them together and said, "You know that the rulers of the Gentiles lord it over them, and their high officials exercise authority over them. **26** Not so with you. Instead, whoever wants to become great among you must be your servant, **27** and whoever wants to be first must be your slave— **28** just as the Son of Man did not come to be served, but to serve, and to give his life as a ransom for many."

Two Blind Men Receive Sight

29 As Jesus and his disciples were leaving Jericho, a large crowd followed him. **30** Two blind men were sitting by the roadside, and when they heard that Jesus was going by, they shouted, "Lord, Son of David, have mercy on us!"

31 The crowd rebuked them and told them to be quiet, but they shouted all the louder, "Lord, Son of David, have mercy on us!"

32 Jesus stopped and called them. "What do you want me to do for you?" he asked.

33 "Lord," they answered, "we want our sight."

34 Jesus had compassion on them and touched their eyes. Immediately they received their sight and followed him.

The Triumphal Entry

21 As they approached Jerusalem and came to Bethphage on the Mount of Olives, Jesus sent two disciples, **2** saying to them, "Go to the village ahead of you, and at once you will find a donkey tied there, with her colt by her. Untie them and bring them to me. **3** If anyone says anything to you, tell him that the Lord needs them, and he will send them right away."

4 This took place to fulfill what was spoken through the prophet:

5 "Say to the Daughter of Zion,
　'See, your king comes to you,
gentle and riding on a donkey,
　on a colt, the foal of a donkey.' " *a*

6 The disciples went and did as Jesus had instructed them. **7** They brought the donkey and the colt, placed their cloaks on them, and Jesus sat on them. **8** A very large crowd spread their cloaks on the road, while others cut branches from the trees and spread them on the road. **9** The crowds that went ahead of him and those that followed shouted,

"Hosanna *b* to the Son of David!"

"Blessed is he who comes in the
　name of the Lord!" *c*

"Hosanna *b* in the highest!"

10 When Jesus entered Jerusalem, the whole city was stirred and asked, "Who is this?"

11 The crowds answered, "This is Jesus, the prophet from Nazareth in Galilee."

Jesus at the Temple

12 Jesus entered the temple area and drove out all who were buying and selling there. He overturned the tables of the money changers and the benches of those selling doves. **13** "It is written," he said to them, " 'My house will be called a house of prayer,' *d* but you are making it a 'den of robbers.' *e* "

---

a5 Zech. 9:9   *b9* A Hebrew expression meaning "Save!" which became an exclamation of praise; also in verse 15   *c9* Psalm 118:26   *d13* Isaiah 56:7   *e13* Jer. 7:11

¹⁴The blind and the lame came to him at the temple, and he healed them. ¹⁵But when the chief priests and the teachers of the law saw the wonderful things he did and the children shouting in the temple area, "Hosanna to the Son of David," they were indignant.

¹⁶"Do you hear what these children are saying?" they asked him.

"Yes," replied Jesus, "have you never read,

FRIDAY

VERSE:
Matthew 20:28

AUTHOR:
Cynthia Culp Allen

PASSAGE:
Matthew 20:20–28

"Hooray! I'm a Servant!"

When Charity was small, I was the janitor of our church. She would accompany me on the day I cleaned "God's house" and help with the small tasks like dusting and taking out the trash.

I wish I could say she loved it, but some days Charity would rather have been anywhere else. One day she was especially disgruntled over having to clean with me. She came over to where I was mopping and, with wide eyes, asked, "Mommy, is God really for real?"

I leaned on my mop and assured her that God is the most real person she will ever know.

Immediately she snapped, "Well, if he's real, why can't he clean his own house?"

Clever thinking! Why not? Of course, he could if he wanted to. The Almighty had cleaned up the chaos of the world at creation. Why not clean his own house? Child's play!

Then I remembered another time that Jesus had done some cleaning. I told Charity about it:

"In Jesus' day, because of the dusty roads and sandaled feet, a servant would meet visitors at the front door and wash the dirt from their feet. One night Jesus and his disciples attended a banquet. They needed their dirty feet washed and there was no servant to do it. Do you know who washed the disciples' feet?"

Charity's eyes were wide again as she shook her head.

"Jesus washed those dirty feet. Jesus became their servant. Even that lowly job was not below him, and he was a King. But he loved his disciples and he could show them his love by serving them."

"Charity," I said, "that's why God allows me to clean his house. He wants me to know the joy of being a servant. And I'm glad to do it because this is one way I can show Jesus that I love him."

I continued my cleaning that day, and for several more years, but Charity did not continue her complaining.

ADDITIONAL SCRIPTURE READINGS:
Matthew 26:26–28; John 13:1–18; Philippians 2:3

Go to page 31 for your next devotional reading.

" 'From the lips of children and
    infants
  you have ordained praise'ᵃ?"

17And he left them and went out of
the city to Bethany, where he spent the
night.

The Fig Tree Withers

18Early in the morning, as he was on
his way back to the city, he was hungry.
19Seeing a fig tree by the road, he went
up to it but found nothing on it except
leaves. Then he said to it, "May you never bear fruit again!" Immediately the tree
withered.

20When the disciples saw this, they
were amazed. "How did the fig tree wither so quickly?" they asked.

21Jesus replied, "I tell you the truth, if
you have faith and do not doubt, not
only can you do what was done to the
fig tree, but also you can say to this
mountain, 'Go, throw yourself into the
sea,' and it will be done. **22**If you believe,
you will receive whatever you ask for in
prayer."

The Authority of Jesus Questioned

23Jesus entered the temple courts,
and, while he was teaching, the chief
priests and the elders of the people
came to him. "By what authority are you
doing these things?" they asked. "And
who gave you this authority?"

24Jesus replied, "I will also ask you
one question. If you answer me, I will
tell you by what authority I am doing
these things. **25**John's baptism—where
did it come from? Was it from heaven,
or from men?"

They discussed it among themselves
and said, "If we say, 'From heaven,' he
will ask, 'Then why didn't you believe
him?' **26**But if we say, 'From men'—we
are afraid of the people, for they all hold
that John was a prophet."

27So they answered Jesus, "We don't
know."

Then he said, "Neither will I tell you
by what authority I am doing these
things.

The Parable of the Two Sons

28"What do you think? There was a
man who had two sons. He went to the

first and said, 'Son, go and work today
in the vineyard.'

29" 'I will not,' he answered, but later
he changed his mind and went.

30"Then the father went to the other
son and said the same thing. He answered, 'I will, sir,' but he did not go.

31"Which of the two did what his father wanted?"

"The first," they answered.

Jesus said to them, "I tell you the
truth, the tax collectors and the prostitutes are entering the kingdom of God
ahead of you. **32**For John came to you to
show you the way of righteousness, and
you did not believe him, but the tax collectors and the prostitutes did. And even
after you saw this, you did not repent
and believe him.

The Parable of the Tenants

33"Listen to another parable: There
was a landowner who planted a vineyard. He put a wall around it, dug a
winepress in it and built a watchtower.
Then he rented the vineyard to some
farmers and went away on a journey.
34When the harvest time approached, he
sent his servants to the tenants to collect his fruit.

35"The tenants seized his servants;
they beat one, killed another, and
stoned a third. **36**Then he sent other
servants to them, more than the first
time, and the tenants treated them the
same way. **37**Last of all, he sent his son
to them. 'They will respect my son,' he
said.

38"But when the tenants saw the son,
they said to each other, 'This is the heir.
Come, let's kill him and take his inheritance.' **39**So they took him and threw
him out of the vineyard and killed him.

40"Therefore, when the owner of the
vineyard comes, what will he do to
those tenants?"

41"He will bring those wretches to a
wretched end," they replied, "and he will
rent the vineyard to other tenants, who
will give him his share of the crop at
harvest time."

42Jesus said to them, "Have you never
read in the Scriptures:

" 'The stone the builders rejected
  has become the capstoneᵇ;

ᵃ16 Psalm 8:2   ᵇ42 Or cornerstone

the Lord has done this,
   and it is marvelous in our eyes'[a]?

43"Therefore I tell you that the kingdom of God will be taken away from you and given to a people who will produce its fruit. **44**He who falls on this stone will be broken to pieces, but he on whom it falls will be crushed."[b]

45When the chief priests and the Pharisees heard Jesus' parables, they knew he was talking about them. **46**They looked for a way to arrest him, but they were afraid of the crowd because the people held that he was a prophet.

The Parable of the Wedding Banquet

22 Jesus spoke to them again in parables, saying: **2**"The kingdom of heaven is like a king who prepared a wedding banquet for his son. **3**He sent his servants to those who had been invited to the banquet to tell them to come, but they refused to come.

4"Then he sent some more servants and said, 'Tell those who have been invited that I have prepared my dinner: My oxen and fattened cattle have been butchered, and everything is ready. Come to the wedding banquet.'

5"But they paid no attention and went off—one to his field, another to his business. **6**The rest seized his servants, mistreated them and killed them. **7**The king was enraged. He sent his army and destroyed those murderers and burned their city.

8"Then he said to his servants, 'The wedding banquet is ready, but those I invited did not deserve to come. **9**Go to the street corners and invite to the banquet anyone you find.' **10**So the servants went out into the streets and gathered all the people they could find, both good and bad, and the wedding hall was filled with guests.

11"But when the king came in to see the guests, he noticed a man there who was not wearing wedding clothes. **12**'Friend,' he asked, 'how did you get in here without wedding clothes?' The man was speechless.

13"Then the king told the attendants, 'Tie him hand and foot, and throw him outside, into the darkness, where there will be weeping and gnashing of teeth.'

14"For many are invited, but few are chosen."

Paying Taxes to Caesar

15Then the Pharisees went out and laid plans to trap him in his words. **16**They sent their disciples to him along with the Herodians. "Teacher," they said, "we know you are a man of integrity and that you teach the way of God in accordance with the truth. You aren't swayed by men, because you pay no attention to who they are. **17**Tell us then, what is your opinion? Is it right to pay taxes to Caesar or not?"

18But Jesus, knowing their evil intent, said, "You hypocrites, why are you trying to trap me? **19**Show me the coin used for paying the tax." They brought him a denarius, **20**and he asked them, "Whose portrait is this? And whose inscription?"

21"Caesar's," they replied.

Then he said to them, "Give to Caesar what is Caesar's, and to God what is God's."

22When they heard this, they were amazed. So they left him and went away.

Marriage at the Resurrection

23That same day the Sadducees, who say there is no resurrection, came to him with a question. **24**"Teacher," they said, "Moses told us that if a man dies without having children, his brother must marry the widow and have children for him. **25**Now there were seven brothers among us. The first one married and died, and since he had no children, he left his wife to his brother. **26**The same thing happened to the second and third brother, right on down to the seventh. **27**Finally, the woman died. **28**Now then, at the resurrection, whose wife will she be of the seven, since all of them were married to her?"

29Jesus replied, "You are in error because you do not know the Scriptures or the power of God. **30**At the resurrection people will neither marry nor be given in marriage; they will be like the angels in heaven. **31**But about the resurrection of the dead—have you not read what God said to you, **32**'I am the God of Abraham, the God of Isaac, and the God of Jacob'[c]? He is not the God of the dead but of the living."

---

[a]42 Psalm 118:22,23   [b]44 Some manuscripts do not have verse 44.   [c]32 Exodus 3:6

WEEKENDING

REJOICE

God has given us a vision, a delightful
picture of his purpose—a bridegroom
coming for his bride, a love song, a love
feast . . . God courts us patiently and
lovingly; he woos us diligently and
imaginatively. No lover has ever given
his loved one so much beauty. What is
a basket of flowers compared to a grove
of birches, a stand of pines, a meadow
of daisies? God is extravagant in his
love . . . he says just come to the wedding feast; let me look at your loveliness
. . . He has added all the ceremony, all
the sights, smells, tastes, textures to help
his courting of us, his bride.

Cheryl Forbes

RECALL

Saturday: Song of Songs 2; Revelation 19:1–10
Sunday: Matthew 22:2–14

*Go to page 36 for your next
devotional reading.*

[33]When the crowds heard this, they were astonished at his teaching.

The Greatest Commandment

[34]Hearing that Jesus had silenced the Sadducees, the Pharisees got together. [35]One of them, an expert in the law, tested him with this question: [36]"Teacher, which is the greatest commandment in the Law?"

[37]Jesus replied: "'Love the Lord your God with all your heart and with all your soul and with all your mind.'[a] [38]This is the first and greatest commandment. [39]And the second is like it: 'Love your neighbor as yourself.'[b] [40]All the Law and the Prophets hang on these two commandments."

Whose Son Is the Christ?

[41]While the Pharisees were gathered together, Jesus asked them, [42]"What do you think about the Christ[c]? Whose son is he?"

"The son of David," they replied.

[43]He said to them, "How is it then that David, speaking by the Spirit, calls him 'Lord'? For he says,

[44]"'The Lord said to my Lord:
"Sit at my right hand
until I put your enemies
under your feet."'[d]

[45]If then David calls him 'Lord,' how can he be his son?" [46]No one could say a word in reply, and from that day on no one dared to ask him any more questions.

Seven Woes

23 Then Jesus said to the crowds and to his disciples: [2]"The teachers of the law and the Pharisees sit in Moses' seat. [3]So you must obey them and do everything they tell you. But do not do what they do, for they do not practice what they preach. [4]They tie up heavy loads and put them on men's shoulders, but they themselves are not willing to lift a finger to move them.

[5]"Everything they do is done for men to see: They make their phylacteries[e]

wide and the tassels on their garments long; [6]they love the place of honor at banquets and the most important seats in the synagogues; [7]they love to be greeted in the marketplaces and to have men call them 'Rabbi.'

[8]"But you are not to be called 'Rabbi,' for you have only one Master and you are all brothers. [9]And do not call anyone on earth 'father,' for you have one Father, and he is in heaven. [10]Nor are you to be called 'teacher,' for you have one Teacher, the Christ.[c] [11]The greatest among you will be your servant. [12]For whoever exalts himself will be humbled, and whoever humbles himself will be exalted.

[13]"Woe to you, teachers of the law and Pharisees, you hypocrites! You shut the kingdom of heaven in men's faces. You yourselves do not enter, nor will you let those enter who are trying to.[f]

[15]"Woe to you, teachers of the law and Pharisees, you hypocrites! You travel over land and sea to win a single convert, and when he becomes one, you make him twice as much a son of hell as you are.

[16]"Woe to you, blind guides! You say, 'If anyone swears by the temple, it means nothing; but if anyone swears by the gold of the temple, he is bound by his oath.' [17]You blind fools! Which is greater: the gold, or the temple that makes the gold sacred? [18]You also say, 'If anyone swears by the altar, it means nothing; but if anyone swears by the gift on it, he is bound by his oath.' [19]You blind men! Which is greater: the gift, or the altar that makes the gift sacred? [20]Therefore, he who swears by the altar swears by it and by everything on it. [21]And he who swears by the temple swears by it and by the one who dwells in it. [22]And he who swears by heaven swears by God's throne and by the one who sits on it.

[23]"Woe to you, teachers of the law and Pharisees, you hypocrites! You give a tenth of your spices—mint, dill and cummin. But you have neglected the more important matters of the law—jus-

---

[a]37 Deut. 6:5   [b]39 Lev. 19:18   [c]42,10 Or *Messiah*   [d]44 Psalm 110:1   [e]5 That is, boxes containing Scripture verses, worn on forehead and arm   [f]13 Some manuscripts to. [14]*Woe to you, teachers of the law and Pharisees, you hypocrites! You devour widows' houses and for a show make lengthy prayers. Therefore you will be punished more severely.*

tice, mercy and faithfulness. You should have practiced the latter, without neglecting the former. [24]You blind guides! You strain out a gnat but swallow a camel.

[25]"Woe to you, teachers of the law and Pharisees, you hypocrites! You clean the outside of the cup and dish, but inside they are full of greed and self-indulgence. [26]Blind Pharisee! First clean the inside of the cup and dish, and then the outside also will be clean.

[27]"Woe to you, teachers of the law and Pharisees, you hypocrites! You are like whitewashed tombs, which look beautiful on the outside but on the inside are full of dead men's bones and everything unclean. [28]In the same way, on the outside you appear to people as righteous but on the inside you are full of hypocrisy and wickedness.

[29]"Woe to you, teachers of the law and Pharisees, you hypocrites! You build tombs for the prophets and decorate the graves of the righteous. [30]And you say, 'If we had lived in the days of our forefathers, we would not have taken part with them in shedding the blood of the prophets.' [31]So you testify against yourselves that you are the descendants of those who murdered the prophets. [32]Fill up, then, the measure of the sin of your forefathers!

[33]"You snakes! You brood of vipers! How will you escape being condemned to hell? [34]Therefore I am sending you prophets and wise men and teachers. Some of them you will kill and crucify; others you will flog in your synagogues and pursue from town to town. [35]And so upon you will come all the righteous blood that has been shed on earth, from the blood of righteous Abel to the blood of Zechariah son of Berekiah, whom you murdered between the temple and the altar. [36]I tell you the truth, all this will come upon this generation.

[37]"O Jerusalem, Jerusalem, you who kill the prophets and stone those sent to you, how often I have longed to gather your children together, as a hen gathers her chicks under her wings, but you were not willing. [38]Look, your house is left to you desolate. [39]For I tell you, you will not see me again until you say, 'Blessed is he who comes in the name of the Lord.'[a]"

Signs of the End of the Age

24 Jesus left the temple and was walking away when his disciples came up to him to call his attention to its buildings. [2]"Do you see all these things?" he asked. "I tell you the truth, not one stone here will be left on another; every one will be thrown down."

[3]As Jesus was sitting on the Mount of Olives, the disciples came to him privately. "Tell us," they said, "when will this happen, and what will be the sign of your coming and of the end of the age?"

[4]Jesus answered: "Watch out that no one deceives you. [5]For many will come in my name, claiming, 'I am the Christ,[b]' and will deceive many. [6]You will hear of wars and rumors of wars, but see to it that you are not alarmed. Such things must happen, but the end is still to come. [7]Nation will rise against nation, and kingdom against kingdom. There will be famines and earthquakes in various places. [8]All these are the beginning of birth pains.

[9]"Then you will be handed over to be persecuted and put to death, and you will be hated by all nations because of me. [10]At that time many will turn away from the faith and will betray and hate each other, [11]and many false prophets will appear and deceive many people. [12]Because of the increase of wickedness, the love of most will grow cold, [13]but he who stands firm to the end will be saved. [14]And this gospel of the kingdom will be preached in the whole world as a testimony to all nations, and then the end will come.

[15]"So when you see standing in the holy place 'the abomination that causes desolation,'[c] spoken of through the prophet Daniel—let the reader understand— [16]then let those who are in Judea flee to the mountains. [17]Let no one on the roof of his house go down to take anything out of the house. [18]Let no one in the field go back to get his cloak. [19]How dreadful it will be in those days for pregnant women and nursing mothers! [20]Pray that your flight will not take place in winter or on the Sabbath. [21]For then there will be great distress, unequaled from the beginning of the world until now—and never to be equaled again. [22]If those days had not been cut

---

[a]39 Psalm 118:26   [b]5 Or *Messiah*; also in verse 23   [c]15 Daniel 9:27; 11:31; 12:11

short, no one would survive, but for the sake of the elect those days will be shortened. ²³At that time if anyone says to you, 'Look, here is the Christ!' or, 'There he is!' do not believe it. ²⁴For false Christs and false prophets will appear and perform great signs and miracles to deceive even the elect—if that were possible. ²⁵See, I have told you ahead of time.

²⁶"So if anyone tells you, 'There he is, out in the desert,' do not go out; or, 'Here he is, in the inner rooms,' do not believe it. ²⁷For as lightning that comes from the east is visible even in the west, so will be the coming of the Son of Man. ²⁸Wherever there is a carcass, there the vultures will gather.

²⁹"Immediately after the distress of those days

" 'the sun will be darkened,
    and the moon will not give its
        light;
the stars will fall from the sky,
    and the heavenly bodies will be
        shaken.'ᵃ

³⁰"At that time the sign of the Son of Man will appear in the sky, and all the nations of the earth will mourn. They will see the Son of Man coming on the clouds of the sky, with power and great glory. ³¹And he will send his angels with a loud trumpet call, and they will gather his elect from the four winds, from one end of the heavens to the other.

³²"Now learn this lesson from the fig tree: As soon as its twigs get tender and its leaves come out, you know that summer is near. ³³Even so, when you see all these things, you know that itᵇ is near, right at the door. ³⁴I tell you the truth, this generationᶜ will certainly not pass away until all these things have happened. ³⁵Heaven and earth will pass away, but my words will never pass away.

The Day and Hour Unknown

³⁶"No one knows about that day or hour, not even the angels in heaven, nor the Son,ᵈ but only the Father. ³⁷As it was in the days of Noah, so it will be at the coming of the Son of Man. ³⁸For in the days before the flood, people were eating and drinking, marrying and giving

in marriage, up to the day Noah entered the ark; ³⁹and they knew nothing about what would happen until the flood came and took them all away. That is how it will be at the coming of the Son of Man. ⁴⁰Two men will be in the field; one will be taken and the other left. ⁴¹Two women will be grinding with a hand mill; one will be taken and the other left.

⁴²"Therefore keep watch, because you do not know on what day your Lord will come. ⁴³But understand this: If the owner of the house had known at what time of night the thief was coming, he would have kept watch and would not have let his house be broken into. ⁴⁴So you also must be ready, because the Son of Man will come at an hour when you do not expect him.

⁴⁵"Who then is the faithful and wise servant, whom the master has put in charge of the servants in his household to give them their food at the proper time? ⁴⁶It will be good for that servant whose master finds him doing so when he returns. ⁴⁷I tell you the truth, he will put him in charge of all his possessions. ⁴⁸But suppose that servant is wicked and says to himself, 'My master is staying away a long time,' ⁴⁹and he then begins to beat his fellow servants and to eat and drink with drunkards. ⁵⁰The master of that servant will come on a day when he does not expect him and at an hour he is not aware of. ⁵¹He will cut him to pieces and assign him a place with the hypocrites, where there will be weeping and gnashing of teeth.

The Parable of the Ten Virgins

25 "At that time the kingdom of heaven will be like ten virgins who took their lamps and went out to meet the bridegroom. ²Five of them were foolish and five were wise. ³The foolish ones took their lamps but did not take any oil with them. ⁴The wise, however, took oil in jars along with their lamps. ⁵The bridegroom was a long time in coming, and they all became drowsy and fell asleep.

⁶"At midnight the cry rang out: 'Here's the bridegroom! Come out to meet him!'

⁷"Then all the virgins woke up and trimmed their lamps. ⁸The foolish ones

---

ᵃ29 Isaiah 13:10; 34:4   ᵇ33 Or he   ᶜ34 Or race   ᵈ36 Some manuscripts do not have nor the Son.

said to the wise, 'Give us some of your oil; our lamps are going out.'

⁹ " 'No,' they replied, 'there may not be enough for both us and you. Instead, go to those who sell oil and buy some for yourselves.'

¹⁰ "But while they were on their way to buy the oil, the bridegroom arrived. The virgins who were ready went in with him to the wedding banquet. And the door was shut.

¹¹ "Later the others also came. 'Sir! Sir!' they said. 'Open the door for us!'

¹² "But he replied, 'I tell you the truth, I don't know you.'

¹³ "Therefore keep watch, because you do not know the day or the hour.

The Parable of the Talents

¹⁴ "Again, it will be like a man going on a journey, who called his servants and entrusted his property to them. ¹⁵To one he gave five talents*ᵃ* of money, to another two talents, and to another one talent, each according to his ability. Then he went on his journey. ¹⁶The man who had received the five talents went at once and put his money to work and gained five more. ¹⁷So also, the one with the two talents gained two more. ¹⁸But the man who had received the one talent went off, dug a hole in the ground and hid his master's money.

¹⁹ "After a long time the master of those servants returned and settled accounts with them. ²⁰The man who had received the five talents brought the other five. 'Master,' he said, 'you entrusted me with five talents. See, I have gained five more.'

²¹ "His master replied, 'Well done, good and faithful servant! You have been faithful with a few things; I will put you in charge of many things. Come and share your master's happiness!'

²² "The man with the two talents also came. 'Master,' he said, 'you entrusted me with two talents; see, I have gained two more.'

²³ "His master replied, 'Well done, good and faithful servant! You have been faithful with a few things; I will put you in charge of many things. Come and share your master's happiness!'

²⁴ "Then the man who had received the one talent came. 'Master,' he said, 'I knew that you are a hard man, harvest-

ing where you have not sown and gathering where you have not scattered seed. ²⁵So I was afraid and went out and hid your talent in the ground. See, here is what belongs to you.'

²⁶ "His master replied, 'You wicked, lazy servant! So you knew that I harvest where I have not sown and gather where I have not scattered seed? ²⁷Well then, you should have put my money on deposit with the bankers, so that when I returned I would have received it back with interest.

²⁸ " 'Take the talent from him and give it to the one who has the ten talents. ²⁹For everyone who has will be given more, and he will have an abundance. Whoever does not have, even what he has will be taken from him. ³⁰And throw that worthless servant outside, into the darkness, where there will be weeping and gnashing of teeth.'

The Sheep and the Goats

³¹ "When the Son of Man comes in his glory, and all the angels with him, he will sit on his throne in heavenly glory. ³²All the nations will be gathered before him, and he will separate the people one from another as a shepherd separates the sheep from the goats. ³³He will put the sheep on his right and the goats on his left.

³⁴ "Then the King will say to those on his right, 'Come, you who are blessed by my Father; take your inheritance, the kingdom prepared for you since the creation of the world. ³⁵For I was hungry and you gave me something to eat, I was thirsty and you gave me something to drink, I was a stranger and you invited me in, ³⁶I needed clothes and you clothed me, I was sick and you looked after me, I was in prison and you came to visit me.'

³⁷ "Then the righteous will answer him, 'Lord, when did we see you hungry and feed you, or thirsty and give you something to drink? ³⁸When did we see you a stranger and invite you in, or needing clothes and clothe you? ³⁹When did we see you sick or in prison and go to visit you?'

⁴⁰ "The King will reply, 'I tell you the truth, whatever you did for one of the least of these brothers of mine, you did for me.'

ᵃ15 A talent was worth more than a thousand dollars.

⁴¹"Then he will say to those on his left, 'Depart from me, you who are cursed, into the eternal fire prepared for the devil and his angels. ⁴²For I was hungry and you gave me nothing to eat, I was thirsty and you gave me nothing to drink, ⁴³I was a stranger and you did not invite me in, I needed clothes and you did not clothe me, I was sick and in prison and you did not look after me.'

⁴⁴"They also will answer, 'Lord, when did we see you hungry or thirsty or a

MONDAY

VERSE:
Matthew 25:15

AUTHOR:
Jeanette Lockerbie

PASSAGE:
Matthew 25:14–18

The Fulfillment of the Right Job

Many working women drag themselves, day after day, to a job in which they have little interest. Consequently, they find a minimum of fulfillment and probably do not achieve much success at what they are doing.

In the parable of the talents, it's evident that resources are given according to our ability to use them. As the distributor of the talents, God knows what abilities he has given each individual.

It makes sense that we will do best the work that coincides with our God-given talents. So it's important that we try to find out what these are. But how to do it?

Along this line, Dr. Clyde Narramore has a saying which is simple and yet profound: "Your natural abilities are God's suggestions for your life's work." If this were heeded, many square pegs would be spared the frustration of being squeezed into round holes!

God has given every one of us some unique ability to do a certain thing or things about which we feel comfortable and competent. It's wise to ask, while we can do something about it, What *is* my particular "thing"? It may be a bent for the technical: business machines and such, a much-in-demand skill; or, it may be skill in the arts: music, painting, writing or something else, which also has its place.

It can be disastrous for the company, and frustrating to the individual, when the job and the person's natural abilities are poles apart. But it happens. I recall a summer when I had a job in a very large bank. At first I was placed at a machine, but after a few days, lest I wreck too much, I was hastily transferred to a public relations desk. Later—much later, in fact—the Lord made it possible for me to pursue another area of ability he has given me.

God will always make it possible for us to do what he has gifted us to do if we really want his will in our lives. We need, then, to discover or uncover our talent(s) and put them to work. And one day we will know the ultimate fulfillment: Christ's "Well done."

ADDITIONAL SCRIPTURE READINGS:
Ezra 2:69; Luke 19:17; 1 Corinthians 12:22–25

Go to page 40 for your next devotional reading.

stranger or needing clothes or sick or in prison, and did not help you?'

45 "He will reply, 'I tell you the truth, whatever you did not do for one of the least of these, you did not do for me.'

46 "Then they will go away to eternal punishment, but the righteous to eternal life."

The Plot Against Jesus

26 When Jesus had finished saying all these things, he said to his disciples, **2** "As you know, the Passover is two days away—and the Son of Man will be handed over to be crucified."

3 Then the chief priests and the elders of the people assembled in the palace of the high priest, whose name was Caiaphas, **4** and they plotted to arrest Jesus in some sly way and kill him. **5** "But not during the Feast," they said, "or there may be a riot among the people."

Jesus Anointed at Bethany

6 While Jesus was in Bethany in the home of a man known as Simon the Leper, **7** a woman came to him with an alabaster jar of very expensive perfume, which she poured on his head as he was reclining at the table.

8 When the disciples saw this, they were indignant. "Why this waste?" they asked. **9** "This perfume could have been sold at a high price and the money given to the poor."

10 Aware of this, Jesus said to them, "Why are you bothering this woman? She has done a beautiful thing to me. **11** The poor you will always have with you, but you will not always have me. **12** When she poured this perfume on my body, she did it to prepare me for burial. **13** I tell you the truth, wherever this gospel is preached throughout the world, what she has done will also be told, in memory of her."

Judas Agrees to Betray Jesus

14 Then one of the Twelve—the one called Judas Iscariot—went to the chief priests **15** and asked, "What are you willing to give me if I hand him over to you?" So they counted out for him thirty silver coins. **16** From then on Judas watched for an opportunity to hand him over.

The Lord's Supper

17 On the first day of the Feast of Unleavened Bread, the disciples came to Jesus and asked, "Where do you want us to make preparations for you to eat the Passover?"

18 He replied, "Go into the city to a certain man and tell him, 'The Teacher says: My appointed time is near. I am going to celebrate the Passover with my disciples at your house.' " **19** So the disciples did as Jesus had directed them and prepared the Passover.

20 When evening came, Jesus was reclining at the table with the Twelve. **21** And while they were eating, he said, "I tell you the truth, one of you will betray me."

22 They were very sad and began to say to him one after the other, "Surely not I, Lord?"

23 Jesus replied, "The one who has dipped his hand into the bowl with me will betray me. **24** The Son of Man will go just as it is written about him. But woe to that man who betrays the Son of Man! It would be better for him if he had not been born."

25 Then Judas, the one who would betray him, said, "Surely not I, Rabbi?"

Jesus answered, "Yes, it is you."[a]

26 While they were eating, Jesus took bread, gave thanks and broke it, and gave it to his disciples, saying, "Take and eat; this is my body."

27 Then he took the cup, gave thanks and offered it to them, saying, "Drink from it, all of you. **28** This is my blood of the[b] covenant, which is poured out for many for the forgiveness of sins. **29** I tell you, I will not drink of this fruit of the vine from now on until that day when I drink it anew with you in my Father's kingdom."

30 When they had sung a hymn, they went out to the Mount of Olives.

Jesus Predicts Peter's Denial

31 Then Jesus told them, "This very night you will all fall away on account of me, for it is written:

" 'I will strike the shepherd,
    and the sheep of the flock will be
        scattered.'[c]

a25 Or *"You yourself have said it"*   *b28* Some manuscripts *the new*   *c31* Zech. 13:7

³²But after I have risen, I will go ahead of you into Galilee."

³³Peter replied, "Even if all fall away on account of you, I never will."

³⁴"I tell you the truth," Jesus answered, "this very night, before the rooster crows, you will disown me three times."

³⁵But Peter declared, "Even if I have to die with you, I will never disown you." And all the other disciples said the same.

Gethsemane

³⁶Then Jesus went with his disciples to a place called Gethsemane, and he said to them, "Sit here while I go over there and pray." ³⁷He took Peter and the two sons of Zebedee along with him, and he began to be sorrowful and troubled. ³⁸Then he said to them, "My soul is overwhelmed with sorrow to the point of death. Stay here and keep watch with me."

³⁹Going a little farther, he fell with his face to the ground and prayed, "My Father, if it is possible, may this cup be taken from me. Yet not as I will, but as you will."

⁴⁰Then he returned to his disciples and found them sleeping. "Could you men not keep watch with me for one hour?" he asked Peter. ⁴¹"Watch and pray so that you will not fall into temptation. The spirit is willing, but the body is weak."

⁴²He went away a second time and prayed, "My Father, if it is not possible for this cup to be taken away unless I drink it, may your will be done."

⁴³When he came back, he again found them sleeping, because their eyes were heavy. ⁴⁴So he left them and went away once more and prayed the third time, saying the same thing.

⁴⁵Then he returned to the disciples and said to them, "Are you still sleeping and resting? Look, the hour is near, and the Son of Man is betrayed into the hands of sinners. ⁴⁶Rise, let us go! Here comes my betrayer!"

Jesus Arrested

⁴⁷While he was still speaking, Judas, one of the Twelve, arrived. With him was a large crowd armed with swords and clubs, sent from the chief priests and the elders of the people. ⁴⁸Now the betrayer had arranged a signal with them: "The one I kiss is the man; arrest him." ⁴⁹Going at once to Jesus, Judas said, "Greetings, Rabbi!" and kissed him.

⁵⁰Jesus replied, "Friend, do what you came for." ᵃ

Then the men stepped forward, seized Jesus and arrested him. ⁵¹With that, one of Jesus' companions reached for his sword, drew it out and struck the servant of the high priest, cutting off his ear.

⁵²"Put your sword back in its place," Jesus said to him, "for all who draw the sword will die by the sword. ⁵³Do you think I cannot call on my Father, and he will at once put at my disposal more than twelve legions of angels? ⁵⁴But how then would the Scriptures be fulfilled that say it must happen in this way?"

⁵⁵At that time Jesus said to the crowd, "Am I leading a rebellion, that you have come out with swords and clubs to capture me? Every day I sat in the temple courts teaching, and you did not arrest me. ⁵⁶But this has all taken place that the writings of the prophets might be fulfilled." Then all the disciples deserted him and fled.

Before the Sanhedrin

⁵⁷Those who had arrested Jesus took him to Caiaphas, the high priest, where the teachers of the law and the elders had assembled. ⁵⁸But Peter followed him at a distance, right up to the courtyard of the high priest. He entered and sat down with the guards to see the outcome.

⁵⁹The chief priests and the whole Sanhedrin were looking for false evidence against Jesus so that they could put him to death. ⁶⁰But they did not find any, though many false witnesses came forward.

Finally two came forward ⁶¹and declared, "This fellow said, 'I am able to destroy the temple of God and rebuild it in three days.'"

⁶²Then the high priest stood up and said to Jesus, "Are you not going to answer? What is this testimony that these men are bringing against you?" ⁶³But Jesus remained silent.

ᵃ50 Or "Friend, why have you come?"

The high priest said to him, "I charge you under oath by the living God: Tell us if you are the Christ,[a] the Son of God."

64 "Yes, it is as you say," Jesus replied. "But I say to all of you: In the future you will see the Son of Man sitting at the right hand of the Mighty One and coming on the clouds of heaven."

65 Then the high priest tore his clothes and said, "He has spoken blasphemy! Why do we need any more witnesses? Look, now you have heard the blasphemy. **66** What do you think?"

"He is worthy of death," they answered.

67 Then they spit in his face and struck him with their fists. Others slapped him **68** and said, "Prophesy to us, Christ. Who hit you?"

Peter Disowns Jesus

69 Now Peter was sitting out in the courtyard, and a servant girl came to him. "You also were with Jesus of Galilee," she said.

70 But he denied it before them all. "I don't know what you're talking about," he said.

71 Then he went out to the gateway, where another girl saw him and said to the people there, "This fellow was with Jesus of Nazareth."

72 He denied it again, with an oath: "I don't know the man!"

73 After a little while, those standing there went up to Peter and said, "Surely you are one of them, for your accent gives you away."

74 Then he began to call down curses on himself and he swore to them, "I don't know the man!"

Immediately a rooster crowed. **75** Then Peter remembered the word Jesus had spoken: "Before the rooster crows, you will disown me three times." And he went outside and wept bitterly.

Judas Hangs Himself

27 Early in the morning, all the chief priests and the elders of the people came to the decision to put Jesus to death. **2** They bound him, led him away and handed him over to Pilate, the governor.

3 When Judas, who had betrayed him, saw that Jesus was condemned, he was seized with remorse and returned the thirty silver coins to the chief priests and the elders. **4** "I have sinned," he said, "for I have betrayed innocent blood."

"What is that to us?" they replied. "That's your responsibility."

5 So Judas threw the money into the temple and left. Then he went away and hanged himself.

6 The chief priests picked up the coins and said, "It is against the law to put this into the treasury, since it is blood money." **7** So they decided to use the money to buy the potter's field as a burial place for foreigners. **8** That is why it has been called the Field of Blood to this day. **9** Then what was spoken by Jeremiah the prophet was fulfilled: "They took the thirty silver coins, the price set on him by the people of Israel, **10** and they used them to buy the potter's field, as the Lord commanded me."[b]

Jesus Before Pilate

11 Meanwhile Jesus stood before the governor, and the governor asked him, "Are you the king of the Jews?"

"Yes, it is as you say," Jesus replied. **12** When he was accused by the chief priests and the elders, he gave no answer. **13** Then Pilate asked him, "Don't you hear the testimony they are bringing against you?" **14** But Jesus made no reply, not even to a single charge—to the great amazement of the governor.

15 Now it was the governor's custom at the Feast to release a prisoner chosen by the crowd. **16** At that time they had a notorious prisoner, called Barabbas. **17** So when the crowd had gathered, Pilate asked them, "Which one do you want me to release to you: Barabbas, or Jesus who is called Christ?" **18** For he knew it was out of envy that they had handed Jesus over to him.

19 While Pilate was sitting on the judge's seat, his wife sent him this message: "Don't have anything to do with that innocent man, for I have suffered a great deal today in a dream because of him."

20 But the chief priests and the elders persuaded the crowd to ask for Barabbas and to have Jesus executed.

21 "Which of the two do you want me

---

[a]63 Or *Messiah*; also in verse 68   [b]10 See Zech. 11:12,13; Jer. 19:1-13; 32:6-9.

to release to you?" asked the governor.

"Barabbas," they answered.

²²"What shall I do, then, with Jesus who is called Christ?" Pilate asked.

They all answered, "Crucify him!"

²³"Why? What crime has he committed?" asked Pilate.

But they shouted all the louder, "Crucify him!"

²⁴When Pilate saw that he was getting nowhere, but that instead an uproar was starting, he took water and washed his hands in front of the crowd. "I am innocent of this man's blood," he said. "It is your responsibility!"

²⁵All the people answered, "Let his blood be on us and on our children!"

²⁶Then he released Barabbas to them. But he had Jesus flogged, and handed him over to be crucified.

TUESDAY

VERSE:	AUTHOR:	PASSAGE:
Matthew 27:19	Eugenia Price	Matthew 27:11–44

Claudia: Too Little, Too Late

There are those who believe Claudia may have been a secret believer in Jesus. Perhaps she was. Certainly she had been convinced in her heart that [Jesus] was a good man, not worthy of execution, harming no one, only blessing all those who came in contact with him.

Claudia did a courageous and daring thing, sending her plea for his life to Pilate in that tense moment. But her good act was weakened because, if she was a believer, she had kept it such a secret her plea lacked influence with her husband.

Evidently Pilate had never heard anything definite about Jesus until that night. The whole incident was new and troublesome and difficult for him. Had Claudia begun sharing her feelings about this man before that night, she might have prevailed upon her husband. But she had not, and her note came only as an annoying surprise, for which he was not prepared.

Our defense of Christianity today can be weakened in exactly the same way, if we keep our faith a secret. When, in some sudden emergency, we reveal it to those who have heard little of him, how can we expect them to listen to us? How can we expect them not to be annoyed, not to turn away, ignoring our urgency? For that matter, if we have not openly pursued our walk with Christ, how can we expect our own inner strength to be great enough for the times of sudden tension and tragedy? Claudia made a last desperate effort to defend him, but her influence was not great enough. Her interest in this man was all new to her husband, and being Pilate, he could not have been expected to pay much attention to this last minute effort on the part of his well-meaning but ineffectual wife.

ADDITIONAL SCRIPTURE READINGS:
Luke 8:16–17; Acts 1:8; Colossians 2:6

Go to page 47 for your next devotional reading.

The Soldiers Mock Jesus

27Then the governor's soldiers took Jesus into the Praetorium and gathered the whole company of soldiers around him. **28**They stripped him and put a scarlet robe on him, **29**and then twisted together a crown of thorns and set it on his head. They put a staff in his right hand and knelt in front of him and mocked him. "Hail, king of the Jews!" they said. **30**They spit on him, and took the staff and struck him on the head again and again. **31**After they had mocked him, they took off the robe and put his own clothes on him. Then they led him away to crucify him.

The Crucifixion

32As they were going out, they met a man from Cyrene, named Simon, and they forced him to carry the cross. **33**They came to a place called Golgotha (which means The Place of the Skull). **34**There they offered Jesus wine to drink, mixed with gall; but after tasting it, he refused to drink it. **35**When they had crucified him, they divided up his clothes by casting lots.*a* **36**And sitting down, they kept watch over him there. **37**Above his head they placed the written charge against him: THIS IS JESUS, THE KING OF THE JEWS. **38**Two robbers were crucified with him, one on his right and one on his left. **39**Those who passed by hurled insults at him, shaking their heads **40**and saying, "You who are going to destroy the temple and build it in three days, save yourself! Come down from the cross, if you are the Son of God!" **41**In the same way the chief priests, the teachers of the law and the elders mocked him. **42**"He saved others," they said, "but he can't save himself! He's the King of Israel! Let him come down now from the cross, and we will believe in him. **43**He trusts in God. Let God rescue him now if he wants him, for he said, 'I am the Son of God.'" **44**In the same way the robbers who were crucified with him also heaped insults on him.

The Death of Jesus

45From the sixth hour until the ninth hour darkness came over all the land. **46**About the ninth hour Jesus cried out in a loud voice, *"Eloi, Eloi,b lama sabachthani?"*—which means, "My God, my God, why have you forsaken me?"*c*

47When some of those standing there heard this, they said, "He's calling Elijah."

48Immediately one of them ran and got a sponge. He filled it with wine vinegar, put it on a stick, and offered it to Jesus to drink. **49**The rest said, "Now leave him alone. Let's see if Elijah comes to save him."

50And when Jesus had cried out again in a loud voice, he gave up his spirit.

51At that moment the curtain of the temple was torn in two from top to bottom. The earth shook and the rocks split. **52**The tombs broke open and the bodies of many holy people who had died were raised to life. **53**They came out of the tombs, and after Jesus' resurrection they went into the holy city and appeared to many people.

54When the centurion and those with him who were guarding Jesus saw the earthquake and all that had happened, they were terrified, and exclaimed, "Surely he was the Son*d* of God!"

55Many women were there, watching from a distance. They had followed Jesus from Galilee to care for his needs. **56**Among them were Mary Magdalene, Mary the mother of James and Joses, and the mother of Zebedee's sons.

The Burial of Jesus

57As evening approached, there came a rich man from Arimathea, named Joseph, who had himself become a disciple of Jesus. **58**Going to Pilate, he asked for Jesus' body, and Pilate ordered that it be given to him. **59**Joseph took the body, wrapped it in a clean linen cloth, **60**and placed it in his own new tomb that he had cut out of the rock. He rolled a big stone in front of the entrance to the tomb and went away. **61**Mary Magdalene and the other Mary were sitting there opposite the tomb.

The Guard at the Tomb

62The next day, the one after Prepara-

---

a35 A few late manuscripts *lots that the word spoken by the prophet might be fulfilled: "They divided my garments among themselves and cast lots for my clothing"* (Psalm 22:18)   *b46* Some manuscripts *Eli, Eli*   *c46* Psalm 22:1   *d54* Or *a son*

tion Day, the chief priests and the Pharisees went to Pilate. [63]"Sir," they said, "we remember that while he was still alive that deceiver said, 'After three days I will rise again.' [64]So give the order for the tomb to be made secure until the third day. Otherwise, his disciples may come and steal the body and tell the people that he has been raised from the dead. This last deception will be worse than the first."

[65]"Take a guard," Pilate answered. "Go, make the tomb as secure as you know how." [66]So they went and made the tomb secure by putting a seal on the stone and posting the guard.

The Resurrection

28 After the Sabbath, at dawn on the first day of the week, Mary Magdalene and the other Mary went to look at the tomb.

[2]There was a violent earthquake, for an angel of the Lord came down from heaven and, going to the tomb, rolled back the stone and sat on it. [3]His appearance was like lightning, and his clothes were white as snow. [4]The guards were so afraid of him that they shook and became like dead men.

[5]The angel said to the women, "Do not be afraid, for I know that you are looking for Jesus, who was crucified. [6]He is not here; he has risen, just as he said. Come and see the place where he lay. [7]Then go quickly and tell his disciples: 'He has risen from the dead and is going ahead of you into Galilee. There you will see him.' Now I have told you."

[8]So the women hurried away from the tomb, afraid yet filled with joy, and ran to tell his disciples. [9]Suddenly Jesus met them. "Greetings," he said. They came to him, clasped his feet and worshiped him. [10]Then Jesus said to them, "Do not be afraid. Go and tell my brothers to go to Galilee; there they will see me."

The Guards' Report

[11]While the women were on their way, some of the guards went into the city and reported to the chief priests everything that had happened. [12]When the chief priests had met with the elders and devised a plan, they gave the soldiers a large sum of money, [13]telling them, "You are to say, 'His disciples came during the night and stole him away while we were asleep.' [14]If this report gets to the governor, we will satisfy him and keep you out of trouble." [15]So the soldiers took the money and did as they were instructed. And this story has been widely circulated among the Jews to this very day.

The Great Commission

[16]Then the eleven disciples went to Galilee, to the mountain where Jesus had told them to go. [17]When they saw him, they worshiped him; but some doubted. [18]Then Jesus came to them and said, "All authority in heaven and on earth has been given to me. [19]Therefore go and make disciples of all nations, baptizing them in[a] the name of the Father and of the Son and of the Holy Spirit, [20]and teaching them to obey everything I have commanded you. And surely I am with you always, to the very end of the age."

---

[a]19 Or into; see Acts 8:16; 19:5; Romans 6:3; 1 Cor. 1:13; 10:2 and Gal. 3:27.

THE *Gospel of Mark takes a fast-paced approach to introducing Jesus Christ, the Son of God. Mark shows Jesus moving quickly from teaching his disciples to healing sick people to confronting religious leaders on his way to death on the cross. Note Mark's sensitive portrayal of the compassionate suffering servant, Jesus, full of life and emotion and purpose. Note also his call to us to be disciples of Jesus. Keep in mind the love Jesus showed his disciples and ask yourself, "If Jesus was willing to suffer for me, what am I willing to do as his disciple?"*

MARK

John the Baptist Prepares the Way

1 The beginning of the gospel about Jesus Christ, the Son of God.[a]

[2] It is written in Isaiah the prophet:

"I will send my messenger ahead of
    you,
  who will prepare your way"[b] —
[3] "a voice of one calling in the desert,
'Prepare the way for the Lord,
  make straight paths for him.' "[c]

[4] And so John came, baptizing in the desert region and preaching a baptism of repentance for the forgiveness of sins. [5] The whole Judean countryside and all the people of Jerusalem went out to him. Confessing their sins, they were baptized by him in the Jordan River. [6] John wore clothing made of camel's hair, with a leather belt around his waist, and he ate locusts and wild honey. [7] And this was his message: "After me will come one more powerful than I, the thongs of whose sandals I am not worthy to stoop down and untie. [8] I baptize you with[d] water, but he will baptize you with the Holy Spirit."

a1 Some manuscripts do not have *the Son of God.*   *b2* Mal. 3:1   *c3* Isaiah 40:3   *d8* Or *in*

The Baptism and Temptation of Jesus

⁹At that time Jesus came from Nazareth in Galilee and was baptized by John in the Jordan. ¹⁰As Jesus was coming up out of the water, he saw heaven being torn open and the Spirit descending on him like a dove. ¹¹And a voice came from heaven: "You are my Son, whom I love; with you I am well pleased."

¹²At once the Spirit sent him out into the desert, ¹³and he was in the desert forty days, being tempted by Satan. He was with the wild animals, and angels attended him.

The Calling of the First Disciples

¹⁴After John was put in prison, Jesus went into Galilee, proclaiming the good news of God. ¹⁵"The time has come," he said. "The kingdom of God is near. Repent and believe the good news!"

¹⁶As Jesus walked beside the Sea of Galilee, he saw Simon and his brother Andrew casting a net into the lake, for they were fishermen. ¹⁷"Come, follow me," Jesus said, "and I will make you fishers of men." ¹⁸At once they left their nets and followed him.

¹⁹When he had gone a little farther, he saw James son of Zebedee and his brother John in a boat, preparing their nets. ²⁰Without delay he called them, and they left their father Zebedee in the boat with the hired men and followed him.

Jesus Drives Out an Evil Spirit

²¹They went to Capernaum, and when the Sabbath came, Jesus went into the synagogue and began to teach. ²²The people were amazed at his teaching, because he taught them as one who had authority, not as the teachers of the law. ²³Just then a man in their synagogue who was possessed by an evil[a] spirit cried out, ²⁴"What do you want with us, Jesus of Nazareth? Have you come to destroy us? I know who you are—the Holy One of God!"

²⁵"Be quiet!" said Jesus sternly. "Come out of him!" ²⁶The evil spirit shook the man violently and came out of him with a shriek.

²⁷The people were all so amazed that they asked each other, "What is this? A new teaching—and with authority! He even gives orders to evil spirits and they obey him." ²⁸News about him spread quickly over the whole region of Galilee.

Jesus Heals Many

²⁹As soon as they left the synagogue, they went with James and John to the home of Simon and Andrew. ³⁰Simon's mother-in-law was in bed with a fever, and they told Jesus about her. ³¹So he went to her, took her hand and helped her up. The fever left her and she began to wait on them.

³²That evening after sunset the people brought to Jesus all the sick and demon-possessed. ³³The whole town gathered at the door, ³⁴and Jesus healed many who had various diseases. He also drove out many demons, but he would not let the demons speak because they knew who he was.

Jesus Prays in a Solitary Place

³⁵Very early in the morning, while it was still dark, Jesus got up, left the house and went off to a solitary place, where he prayed. ³⁶Simon and his companions went to look for him, ³⁷and when they found him, they exclaimed: "Everyone is looking for you!"

³⁸Jesus replied, "Let us go somewhere else—to the nearby villages—so I can preach there also. That is why I have come." ³⁹So he traveled throughout Galilee, preaching in their synagogues and driving out demons.

A Man With Leprosy

⁴⁰A man with leprosy[b] came to him and begged him on his knees, "If you are willing, you can make me clean."

⁴¹Filled with compassion, Jesus reached out his hand and touched the man. "I am willing," he said. "Be clean!" ⁴²Immediately the leprosy left him and he was cured.

⁴³Jesus sent him away at once with a strong warning: ⁴⁴"See that you don't tell this to anyone. But go, show yourself to the priest and offer the sacrifices that Moses commanded for your cleansing, as a testimony to them." ⁴⁵Instead he went out and began to talk freely, spreading the news. As a result, Jesus could no longer enter a town openly but

---

[a]23 Greek *unclean*; also in verses 26 and 27 affecting the skin—not necessarily leprosy.   [b]40 The Greek word was used for various diseases

stayed outside in lonely places. Yet the people still came to him from everywhere.

Jesus Heals a Paralytic

2 A few days later, when Jesus again entered Capernaum, the people heard that he had come home. ²So many gathered that there was no room left, not even outside the door, and he preached the word to them. ³Some men came, bringing to him a paralytic, carried by four of them. ⁴Since they could not get him to Jesus because of the crowd, they made an opening in the roof above Jesus and, after digging through it, lowered the mat the paralyzed man was lying on. ⁵When Jesus saw their faith, he said to the paralytic, "Son, your sins are forgiven."

⁶Now some teachers of the law were sitting there, thinking to themselves, ⁷"Why does this fellow talk like that? He's blaspheming! Who can forgive sins but God alone?"

⁸Immediately Jesus knew in his spirit that this was what they were thinking in their hearts, and he said to them, "Why are you thinking these things? ⁹Which is easier: to say to the paralytic, 'Your sins are forgiven,' or to say, 'Get up, take your mat and walk'? ¹⁰But that you may know that the Son of Man has authority on earth to forgive sins . . . ." He said to the paralytic, ¹¹"I tell you, get up, take your mat and go home." ¹²He got up, took his mat and walked out in full view of them all. This amazed everyone and they praised God, saying, "We have never seen anything like this!"

The Calling of Levi

¹³Once again Jesus went out beside the lake. A large crowd came to him, and he began to teach them. ¹⁴As he walked along, he saw Levi son of Alphaeus sitting at the tax collector's booth. "Follow me," Jesus told him, and Levi got up and followed him.

¹⁵While Jesus was having dinner at Levi's house, many tax collectors and "sinners" were eating with him and his disciples, for there were many who followed him. ¹⁶When the teachers of the law who were Pharisees saw him eating with the "sinners" and tax collectors, they asked his disciples: "Why does he eat with tax collectors and 'sinners'?"

¹⁷On hearing this, Jesus said to them, "It is not the healthy who need a doctor, but the sick. I have not come to call the righteous, but sinners."

Jesus Questioned About Fasting

¹⁸Now John's disciples and the Pharisees were fasting. Some people came and asked Jesus, "How is it that John's disciples and the disciples of the Pharisees are fasting, but yours are not?"

¹⁹Jesus answered, "How can the guests of the bridegroom fast while he is with them? They cannot, so long as they have him with them. ²⁰But the time will come when the bridegroom will be taken from them, and on that day they will fast.

²¹"No one sews a patch of unshrunk cloth on an old garment. If he does, the new piece will pull away from the old, making the tear worse. ²²And no one pours new wine into old wineskins. If he does, the wine will burst the skins, and both the wine and the wineskins will be ruined. No, he pours new wine into new wineskins."

Lord of the Sabbath

²³One Sabbath Jesus was going through the grainfields, and as his disciples walked along, they began to pick some heads of grain. ²⁴The Pharisees said to him, "Look, why are they doing what is unlawful on the Sabbath?"

²⁵He answered, "Have you never read what David did when he and his companions were hungry and in need? ²⁶In the days of Abiathar the high priest, he entered the house of God and ate the consecrated bread, which is lawful only for priests to eat. And he also gave some to his companions."

²⁷Then he said to them, "The Sabbath was made for man, not man for the Sabbath. ²⁸So the Son of Man is Lord even of the Sabbath."

3 Another time he went into the synagogue, and a man with a shriveled hand was there. ²Some of them were looking for a reason to accuse Jesus, so they watched him closely to see if he would heal him on the Sabbath. ³Jesus said to the man with the shriveled hand, "Stand up in front of everyone."

⁴Then Jesus asked them, "Which is lawful on the Sabbath: to do good or to

do evil, to save life or to kill?" But they remained silent.

⁵He looked around at them in anger and, deeply distressed at their stubborn hearts, said to the man, "Stretch out your hand." He stretched it out, and his hand was completely restored. ⁶Then the Pharisees went out and began to plot with the Herodians how they might kill Jesus.

Crowds Follow Jesus

⁷Jesus withdrew with his disciples to the lake, and a large crowd from Galilee followed. ⁸When they heard all he was doing, many people came to him from Judea, Jerusalem, Idumea, and the regions across the Jordan and around Tyre and Sidon. ⁹Because of the crowd he told his disciples to have a small boat ready for him, to keep the people from crowding him. ¹⁰For he had healed many, so that those with diseases were pushing forward to touch him. ¹¹Whenever the evil*a* spirits saw him, they fell down before him and cried out, "You are the Son of God." ¹²But he gave them strict orders not to tell who he was.

The Appointing of the Twelve Apostles

¹³Jesus went up on a mountainside and called to him those he wanted, and they came to him. ¹⁴He appointed twelve—designating them apostles*b*— that they might be with him and that he might send them out to preach ¹⁵and to have authority to drive out demons. ¹⁶These are the twelve he appointed: Simon (to whom he gave the name Peter); ¹⁷James son of Zebedee and his brother John (to them he gave the name Boanerges, which means Sons of Thunder); ¹⁸Andrew, Philip, Bartholomew, Matthew, Thomas, James son of Alphaeus, Thaddaeus, Simon the Zealot ¹⁹and Judas Iscariot, who betrayed him.

Jesus and Beelzebub

²⁰Then Jesus entered a house, and again a crowd gathered, so that he and his disciples were not even able to eat. ²¹When his family heard about this, they went to take charge of him, for they said, "He is out of his mind."

²²And the teachers of the law who came down from Jerusalem said, "He is possessed by Beelzebub*c*! By the prince of demons he is driving out demons."

²³So Jesus called them and spoke to them in parables: "How can Satan drive out Satan? ²⁴If a kingdom is divided against itself, that kingdom cannot stand. ²⁵If a house is divided against itself, that house cannot stand. ²⁶And if Satan opposes himself and is divided, he cannot stand; his end has come. ²⁷In fact, no one can enter a strong man's house and carry off his possessions unless he first ties up the strong man. Then he can rob his house. ²⁸I tell you the truth, all the sins and blasphemies of men will be forgiven them. ²⁹But whoever blasphemes against the Holy Spirit will never be forgiven; he is guilty of an eternal sin."

³⁰He said this because they were saying, "He has an evil spirit."

Jesus' Mother and Brothers

³¹Then Jesus' mother and brothers arrived. Standing outside, they sent someone in to call him. ³²A crowd was sitting around him, and they told him, "Your mother and brothers are outside looking for you."

³³"Who are my mother and my brothers?" he asked.

³⁴Then he looked at those seated in a circle around him and said, "Here are my mother and my brothers! ³⁵Whoever does God's will is my brother and sister and mother."

The Parable of the Sower

4 Again Jesus began to teach by the lake. The crowd that gathered around him was so large that he got into a boat and sat in it out on the lake, while all the people were along the shore at the water's edge. ²He taught them many things by parables, and in his teaching said: ³"Listen! A farmer went out to sow his seed. ⁴As he was scattering the seed, some fell along the path, and the birds came and ate it up. ⁵Some fell on rocky places, where it did not have much soil. It sprang up quickly, because the soil was shallow. ⁶But when the sun came up, the plants were scorched, and

---

*a*11 Greek *unclean*; also in verse 30   *b*14 Some manuscripts do not have *designating them apostles.*
*c*22 Greek *Beezeboul* or *Beelzeboul*

they withered because they had no root. ⁷Other seed fell among thorns, which grew up and choked the plants, so that they did not bear grain. ⁸Still other seed fell on good soil. It came up, grew and produced a crop, multiplying thirty, sixty, or even a hundred times."

⁹Then Jesus said, "He who has ears to hear, let him hear."

¹⁰When he was alone, the Twelve and the others around him asked him about the parables. ¹¹He told them, "The secret of the kingdom of God has been given to you. But to those on the outside everything is said in parables ¹²so that,

" 'they may be ever seeing but never
    perceiving,
and ever hearing but never
    understanding;

⟨ WEDNESDAY ⟩

VERSE:	AUTHOR:	PASSAGE:
Mark 3:27	Alice C. Peter	Mark 3:20–30

He Never Sleeps

My computer drones most of the day and my busy life bubbles with fresh escapades as long as there is daylight. But night comes swiftly in Seattle and I feel a little shiver as I check my apartment door latch, then run my finger along the metal frame to make sure each window is locked.

I love living in downtown Seattle, where lectures at the main library, the symphony, the ballet and art museums are all within walking distance. But I spend countless hours shaking under the covers at night, wondering what I can do to keep myself safe.

The evening news carries so many stories about robberies, stabbings and the like that I panic when a strange noise shatters the darkness or an unfamiliar shadow presses against the wall. I am often anxious, allowing myself to climb into bed with fear and dread as my companions.

Evil lurks all around me. And I allow Satan to break down my defenses until I'm left with dread. My "house"—me, myself—is divided, bombarded with nightly bouts of negativism.

I wonder, *Are my nightly fears symptoms of a too-busy life? Am I going about my nightly ritual all wrong?*

I check to make sure that I do not overlook the proper precautions out of carelessness. But I will not forget the one thing that casts fear from my mind—God's promise to me in Mark 3:27: "No one can enter a strong man's house and carry off his possessions unless he first ties up the strong man."

So, instead of wasting time wondering what I can do to keep myself safe, I . . . crawl into bed praising the Lord for his Word. My "house" is placed into the loving arms of Jesus; I . . . rest in him and sleep without fear.

ADDITIONAL SCRIPTURE READINGS:
Psalm 3:5–6; Psalm 121; Romans 8:31

Go to page 49 for your next devotional reading.

otherwise they might turn and be
forgiven!'[a]"

[13]Then Jesus said to them, "Don't you
understand this parable? How then will
you understand any parable? [14]The
farmer sows the word. [15]Some people
are like seed along the path, where the
word is sown. As soon as they hear it,
Satan comes and takes away the word
that was sown in them. [16]Others, like
seed sown on rocky places, hear the
word and at once receive it with joy.
[17]But since they have no root, they last
only a short time. When trouble or persecution comes because of the word,
they quickly fall away. [18]Still others, like
seed sown among thorns, hear the
word; [19]but the worries of this life, the
deceitfulness of wealth and the desires
for other things come in and choke the
word, making it unfruitful. [20]Others, like
seed sown on good soil, hear the word,
accept it, and produce a crop—thirty, sixty or even a hundred times what was
sown."

A Lamp on a Stand

[21]He said to them, "Do you bring in a
lamp to put it under a bowl or a bed?
Instead, don't you put it on its stand?
[22]For whatever is hidden is meant to be
disclosed, and whatever is concealed is
meant to be brought out into the open.
[23]If anyone has ears to hear, let him
hear."

[24]"Consider carefully what you hear,"
he continued. "With the measure you
use, it will be measured to you—and
even more. [25]Whoever has will be given
more; whoever does not have, even what
he has will be taken from him."

The Parable of the Growing Seed

[26]He also said, "This is what the kingdom of God is like. A man scatters seed
on the ground. [27]Night and day, whether
he sleeps or gets up, the seed sprouts
and grows, though he does not know
how. [28]All by itself the soil produces
grain—first the stalk, then the head, then
the full kernel in the head. [29]As soon as
the grain is ripe, he puts the sickle to it,
because the harvest has come."

The Parable of the Mustard Seed

[30]Again he said, "What shall we say
the kingdom of God is like, or what parable shall we use to describe it? [31]It is
like a mustard seed, which is the smallest seed you plant in the ground. [32]Yet
when planted, it grows and becomes the
largest of all garden plants, with such
big branches that the birds of the air can
perch in its shade."

[33]With many similar parables Jesus
spoke the word to them, as much as
they could understand. [34]He did not say
anything to them without using a parable. But when he was alone with his
own disciples, he explained everything.

Jesus Calms the Storm

[35]That day when evening came, he
said to his disciples, "Let us go over to
the other side." [36]Leaving the crowd behind, they took him along, just as he
was, in the boat. There were also other
boats with him. [37]A furious squall came
up, and the waves broke over the boat,
so that it was nearly swamped. [38]Jesus
was in the stern, sleeping on a cushion.
The disciples woke him and said to him,
"Teacher, don't you care if we drown?"

[39]He got up, rebuked the wind and
said to the waves, "Quiet! Be still!" Then
the wind died down and it was completely calm.

[40]He said to his disciples, "Why are
you so afraid? Do you still have no
faith?"

[41]They were terrified and asked each
other, "Who is this? Even the wind and
the waves obey him!"

The Healing of a Demon-possessed
Man

5 They went across the lake to the region of the Gerasenes.[b] [2]When
Jesus got out of the boat, a man with an
evil[c] spirit came from the tombs to
meet him. [3]This man lived in the tombs,
and no one could bind him any more,
not even with a chain. [4]For he had often
been chained hand and foot, but he tore
the chains apart and broke the irons on
his feet. No one was strong enough to
subdue him. [5]Night and day among the
tombs and in the hills he would cry out
and cut himself with stones.

⁶When he saw Jesus from a distance, he ran and fell on his knees in front of him. ⁷He shouted at the top of his voice, "What do you want with me, Jesus, Son of the Most High God? Swear to God that you won't torture me!" ⁸For Jesus had said to him, "Come out of this man, you evil spirit!"

⁹Then Jesus asked him, "What is your name?"

"My name is Legion," he replied, "for we are many." ¹⁰And he begged Jesus again and again not to send them out of the area.

¹¹A large herd of pigs was feeding on the nearby hillside. ¹²The demons begged Jesus, "Send us among the pigs; allow us to go into them." ¹³He gave them permission, and the evil spirits came out and went into the pigs. The herd, about two thousand in number, rushed down the steep bank into the lake and were drowned.

¹⁴Those tending the pigs ran off and reported this in the town and countryside, and the people went out to see what had happened. ¹⁵When they came to Jesus, they saw the man who had been possessed by the legion of demons, sitting there, dressed and in his right mind; and they were afraid. ¹⁶Those who had seen it told the people what had happened to the demon-possessed man—and told about the pigs as well. ¹⁷Then the people began to plead with Jesus to leave their region.

¹⁸As Jesus was getting into the boat, the man who had been demon-possessed begged to go with him. ¹⁹Jesus did not let him, but said, "Go home to your family and tell them how much the Lord has done for you, and how he has had mercy on you." ²⁰So the man went away and began to tell in the Decapolisᵃ how much Jesus had done for him. And all the people were amazed.

ᵃ20 That is, the Ten Cities

⟨ THURSDAY ⟩

VERSE:	AUTHOR:	PASSAGE:
Mark 4:41	Betsy Lee	Mark 4:35–41

Quiet, Be Still!

We all go through storms in life. Whether we are caught up in the agitation of little daily traumas that tear away at our peace of mind, or face real fears that rage within our hearts, Jesus can calm any storm with a word: "Quiet, be still!" (v. 39) When the disciples first witnessed Jesus' power to bring peace, they were amazed: "Who is this? Even the wind and the waves obey him!" (v. 41). We will be amazed too.

The gift of peace can come quietly, unexpectedly—as you gaze at the soft glow of a candle during a hushed quiet time, as you walk in the woods and feel God close. It can come even in a glimpse out the window, as your eye beholds the beauty outside. It can come through the loving gesture of a friend. It can come through laughter or tears . . . or simply silence. It can come through prayer.

"Peace be to you," Jesus says. To *you*.

ADDITIONAL SCRIPTURE READINGS:
Psalm 34:14; Isaiah 26:3; John 14:27; 2 Thessalonians 3:16

Go to page 51 for your next devotional reading.

A Dead Girl and a Sick Woman

21When Jesus had again crossed over by boat to the other side of the lake, a large crowd gathered around him while he was by the lake. **22**Then one of the synagogue rulers, named Jairus, came there. Seeing Jesus, he fell at his feet **23**and pleaded earnestly with him, "My little daughter is dying. Please come and put your hands on her so that she will be healed and live." **24**So Jesus went with him.

A large crowd followed and pressed around him. **25**And a woman was there who had been subject to bleeding for twelve years. **26**She had suffered a great deal under the care of many doctors and had spent all she had, yet instead of getting better she grew worse. **27**When she heard about Jesus, she came up behind him in the crowd and touched his cloak, **28**because she thought, "If I just touch his clothes, I will be healed." **29**Immediately her bleeding stopped and she felt in her body that she was freed from her suffering.

30At once Jesus realized that power had gone out from him. He turned around in the crowd and asked, "Who touched my clothes?"

31"You see the people crowding against you," his disciples answered, "and yet you can ask, 'Who touched me?' "

32But Jesus kept looking around to see who had done it. **33**Then the woman, knowing what had happened to her, came and fell at his feet and, trembling with fear, told him the whole truth. **34**He said to her, "Daughter, your faith has healed you. Go in peace and be freed from your suffering."

35While Jesus was still speaking, some men came from the house of Jairus, the synagogue ruler. "Your daughter is dead," they said. "Why bother the teacher any more?"

36Ignoring what they said, Jesus told the synagogue ruler, "Don't be afraid; just believe."

37He did not let anyone follow him except Peter, James and John the brother of James. **38**When they came to the home of the synagogue ruler, Jesus saw a commotion, with people crying and wailing loudly. **39**He went in and said to them, "Why all this commotion and wailing? The child is not dead but asleep." **40**But they laughed at him.

After he put them all out, he took the child's father and mother and the disciples who were with him, and went in where the child was. **41**He took her by the hand and said to her, *"Talitha koum!"* (which means, "Little girl, I say to you, get up!"). **42**Immediately the girl stood up and walked around (she was twelve years old). At this they were completely astonished. **43**He gave strict orders not to let anyone know about this, and told them to give her something to eat.

A Prophet Without Honor

6 Jesus left there and went to his hometown, accompanied by his disciples. **2**When the Sabbath came, he began to teach in the synagogue, and many who heard him were amazed.

"Where did this man get these things?" they asked. "What's this wisdom that has been given him, that he even does miracles! **3**Isn't this the carpenter? Isn't this Mary's son and the brother of James, Joseph,*a* Judas and Simon? Aren't his sisters here with us?" And they took offense at him.

4Jesus said to them, "Only in his hometown, among his relatives and in his own house is a prophet without honor." **5**He could not do any miracles there, except lay his hands on a few sick people and heal them. **6**And he was amazed at their lack of faith.

Jesus Sends Out the Twelve

Then Jesus went around teaching from village to village. **7**Calling the Twelve to him, he sent them out two by two and gave them authority over evil*b* spirits.

8These were his instructions: "Take nothing for the journey except a staff—no bread, no bag, no money in your belts. **9**Wear sandals but not an extra tunic. **10**Whenever you enter a house, stay there until you leave that town. **11**And if any place will not welcome you or listen to you, shake the dust off your feet when you leave, as a testimony against them."

12They went out and preached that people should repent. **13**They drove out many demons and anointed many sick people with oil and healed them.

---

a3 Greek *Joses,* a variant of *Joseph*   *b7* Greek *unclean*

John the Baptist Beheaded

[14] King Herod heard about this, for Jesus' name had become well known. Some were saying,[a] "John the Baptist has been raised from the dead, and that is why miraculous powers are at work in him."

[15] Others said, "He is Elijah."

[a] 14 Some early manuscripts *He was saying*

FRIDAY

| VERSE:
Mark 5:29 | AUTHOR:
Ruth DeJager | PASSAGE:
Mark 5:25–34 |

Personal Healing

Poor woman. She had been "subject to bleeding for twelve years" (v. 25)! It's easy to read over those words quickly but what suffering they represent! By Jewish law she was considered unclean. No mixing socially. No sexual relations. She must have been exhausted from anemia. At the end of her rope. She had spent all her money on doctor bills and not one of those doctors had given her health or hope.

Many of us can relate to this sick woman. We might suffer from health problems that are unique to us women. They may be too personal to share or to talk about much, so we feel isolated and alone. Our condition may not be life threatening, but it saps our strength and provides one more irritation in our already busy and complicated lives. The medical community may be unable to help, or the help forthcoming may be patronizing and discount our emotions and ignore our instincts about our own bodies.

The story in Mark 5 offers us encouragement. This woman was desperate, but she had heard about Jesus and her hope was renewed. She didn't want to call attention to herself—she had lived long with embarrassment—but she quietly worked her way through the crowd just to touch the hem of his cloak. I don't think Jesus had to turn around to know who had touched him. I think he did so to show her (and all those around him) how much he cared for her. I can picture him lifting her from her knees where she huddled in fear and, to her joy, calling her "Daughter." He looked her full in the eyes and ended her ordeal with his loving words, "Go in peace and be freed from your suffering" (v. 34).

Whatever problems we have, none are too personal to take to Jesus. He might offer us instant healing or inspiration to try a different approach or treatment to our health problems. We may indeed have to live with them for a long time. But in any case, we are his "daughters," and he offers hope of healing in every aspect of our lives, personal or not.

ADDITIONAL SCRIPTURE READINGS:
Psalm 103:1–5; Malachi 4:1–2; Matthew 9:35–36

Go to page 53 for your next devotional reading.

And still others claimed, "He is a prophet, like one of the prophets of long ago."

¹⁶But when Herod heard this, he said, "John, the man I beheaded, has been raised from the dead!"

¹⁷For Herod himself had given orders to have John arrested, and he had him bound and put in prison. He did this because of Herodias, his brother Philip's wife, whom he had married. ¹⁸For John had been saying to Herod, "It is not lawful for you to have your brother's wife." ¹⁹So Herodias nursed a grudge against John and wanted to kill him. But she was not able to, ²⁰because Herod feared John and protected him, knowing him to be a righteous and holy man. When Herod heard John, he was greatly puzzled[a]; yet he liked to listen to him.

²¹Finally the opportune time came. On his birthday Herod gave a banquet for his high officials and military commanders and the leading men of Galilee. ²²When the daughter of Herodias came in and danced, she pleased Herod and his dinner guests.

The king said to the girl, "Ask me for anything you want, and I'll give it to you." ²³And he promised her with an oath, "Whatever you ask I will give you, up to half my kingdom."

²⁴She went out and said to her mother, "What shall I ask for?"

"The head of John the Baptist," she answered.

²⁵At once the girl hurried in to the king with the request: "I want you to give me right now the head of John the Baptist on a platter."

²⁶The king was greatly distressed, but because of his oaths and his dinner guests, he did not want to refuse her. ²⁷So he immediately sent an executioner with orders to bring John's head. The man went, beheaded John in the prison, ²⁸and brought back his head on a platter. He presented it to the girl, and she gave it to her mother. ²⁹On hearing of this, John's disciples came and took his body and laid it in a tomb.

Jesus Feeds the Five Thousand

³⁰The apostles gathered around Jesus and reported to him all they had done and taught. ³¹Then, because so many people were coming and going that they did not even have a chance to eat, he said to them, "Come with me by yourselves to a quiet place and get some rest."

³²So they went away by themselves in a boat to a solitary place. ³³But many who saw them leaving recognized them and ran on foot from all the towns and got there ahead of them. ³⁴When Jesus landed and saw a large crowd, he had compassion on them, because they were like sheep without a shepherd. So he began teaching them many things.

³⁵By this time it was late in the day, so his disciples came to him. "This is a remote place," they said, "and it's already very late. ³⁶Send the people away so they can go to the surrounding countryside and villages and buy themselves something to eat."

³⁷But he answered, "You give them something to eat."

They said to him, "That would take eight months of a man's wages[b]! Are we to go and spend that much on bread and give it to them to eat?"

³⁸"How many loaves do you have?" he asked. "Go and see."

When they found out, they said, "Five—and two fish."

³⁹Then Jesus directed them to have all the people sit down in groups on the green grass. ⁴⁰So they sat down in groups of hundreds and fifties. ⁴¹Taking the five loaves and the two fish and looking up to heaven, he gave thanks and broke the loaves. Then he gave them to his disciples to set before the people. He also divided the two fish among them all. ⁴²They all ate and were satisfied, ⁴³and the disciples picked up twelve basketfuls of broken pieces of bread and fish. ⁴⁴The number of the men who had eaten was five thousand.

Jesus Walks on the Water

⁴⁵Immediately Jesus made his disciples get into the boat and go on ahead of him to Bethsaida, while he dismissed the crowd. ⁴⁶After leaving them, he went up on a mountainside to pray.

⁴⁷When evening came, the boat was in the middle of the lake, and he was alone on land. ⁴⁸He saw the disciples straining at the oars, because the wind was against them. About the fourth watch of

---

[a]20 Some early manuscripts *he did many things*   [b]37 Greek *take two hundred denarii*

WEEKENDING

REJOICE

Hooray for Christmas trees
And candlelight
And the good old church pageant.
Hooray for shepherd boys
   who forget their lines
And wise men whose beards fall off
And a Mary who giggles.
O Lord, you were born!
And I will celebrate!
I rejoice for the carnival of Christmas!
I clap for the pajama-clad cherubs
And the Christmas cards jammed
   in the mail slot.
I o-o-o-oh for the turkey
And ah-h-h-h for the Christmas pudding
And thank God for the alleluias
   I see in the faces of people.
O Lord, there aren't enough choir
   boys to sing what I feel.
There aren't enough trumpets to blow.
O Lord, I want bells to peal!
I want to dance in the streets of
   Bethlehem!
I want to sing with the heavenly host!
For unto us a Son was given
And he was called *God With Us*.
For those of us who believe,
The whole world is decorated
   in love!

Ann Weems

REFLECT

Saturday: Luke 2:12–14
Sunday: Isaiah 9:6–7

*Go to page 54 for your next
devotional reading.*

the night he went out to them, walking on the lake. He was about to pass by them, ⁴⁹but when they saw him walking on the lake, they thought he was a ghost. They cried out, ⁵⁰because they all saw him and were terrified.

Immediately he spoke to them and said, "Take courage! It is I. Don't be afraid." ⁵¹Then he climbed into the boat with them, and the wind died down. They were completely amazed, ⁵²for they had not understood about the loaves; their hearts were hardened.

⁵³When they had crossed over, they landed at Gennesaret and anchored there. ⁵⁴As soon as they got out of the boat, people recognized Jesus. ⁵⁵They ran throughout that whole region and carried the sick on mats to wherever they heard he was. ⁵⁶And wherever he went—into villages, towns or country-side—they placed the sick in the market-places. They begged him to let them touch even the edge of his cloak, and all who touched him were healed.

Clean and Unclean

7 The Pharisees and some of the teachers of the law who had come from Jerusalem gathered around Jesus and ²saw some of his disciples eating food with hands that were "unclean," that is, unwashed. ³(The Pharisees and all the Jews do not eat unless they give their hands a ceremonial washing, holding to the tradition of the elders. ⁴When they come from the marketplace they do not eat unless they wash. And they observe many other traditions, such as the

---

MONDAY

VERSE: AUTHOR: PASSAGE:
Mark 6:31   Millie Stamm   Mark 6:30–44

Rest and Relaxation

Are you exhausted today? Are you taking pills for energy to get through the day? Or are you on a nervous high and need something to slow you down? Perhaps what your body is really crying for is rest. Is there rest for anyone in this tension-filled world?

As the disciples returned from a missionary journey, they were elated with their success. They gave glowing reports of how God had worked. Jesus was glad to hear their accounts, but he knew that they needed physical rest after their arduous journey. He invited them to come rest with him in a quiet place.

We, too, need to refresh ourselves to maintain physical and spiritual strength. Our schedules are demanding. They drain our physical, mental, emotional and spiritual life.

God's Holy Spirit gives us strength for his schedule for us. I believe God plans for us to include times of rest and relaxation in our schedule. If the disciples needed rest, so do we.

Our rest times may consist of a vacation where we can rest and relax, a change of environment, or simply a respite right where we are. Time spent with the Lord brings renewal and refreshment.

ADDITIONAL SCRIPTURE READINGS:
Exodus 33:14; Isaiah 40:27–31; Matthew 11:28–30

Go to page 60 for your next devotional reading.

washing of cups, pitchers and kettles.[a])

[5]So the Pharisees and teachers of the law asked Jesus, "Why don't your disciples live according to the tradition of the elders instead of eating their food with 'unclean' hands?"

[6]He replied, "Isaiah was right when he prophesied about you hypocrites; as it is written:

" 'These people honor me with their lips,
  but their hearts are far from me.
[7]They worship me in vain;
  their teachings are but rules taught by men.'[b]

[8]You have let go of the commands of God and are holding on to the traditions of men."

[9]And he said to them: "You have a fine way of setting aside the commands of God in order to observe[c] your own traditions! [10]For Moses said, 'Honor your father and your mother,'[d] and, 'Anyone who curses his father or mother must be put to death.'[e] [11]But you say that if a man says to his father or mother: 'Whatever help you might otherwise have received from me is Corban' (that is, a gift devoted to God), [12]then you no longer let him do anything for his father or mother. [13]Thus you nullify the word of God by your tradition that you have handed down. And you do many things like that."

[14]Again Jesus called the crowd to him and said, "Listen to me, everyone, and understand this. [15]Nothing outside a man can make him 'unclean' by going into him. Rather, it is what comes out of a man that makes him 'unclean.'[f]"

[17]After he had left the crowd and entered the house, his disciples asked him about this parable. [18]"Are you so dull?" he asked. "Don't you see that nothing that enters a man from the outside can make him 'unclean'? [19]For it doesn't go into his heart but into his stomach, and then out of his body." (In saying this, Jesus declared all foods "clean.")

[20]He went on: "What comes out of a man is what makes him 'unclean.' [21]For from within, out of men's hearts, come evil thoughts, sexual immorality, theft, murder, adultery, [22]greed, malice, deceit, lewdness, envy, slander, arrogance and folly. [23]All these evils come from inside and make a man 'unclean.' "

The Faith of a Syrophoenician Woman

[24]Jesus left that place and went to the vicinity of Tyre.[g] He entered a house and did not want anyone to know it; yet he could not keep his presence secret. [25]In fact, as soon as she heard about him, a woman whose little daughter was possessed by an evil[h] spirit came and fell at his feet. [26]The woman was a Greek, born in Syrian Phoenicia. She begged Jesus to drive the demon out of her daughter.

[27]"First let the children eat all they want," he told her, "for it is not right to take the children's bread and toss it to their dogs."

[28]"Yes, Lord," she replied, "but even the dogs under the table eat the children's crumbs."

[29]Then he told her, "For such a reply, you may go; the demon has left your daughter."

[30]She went home and found her child lying on the bed, and the demon gone.

The Healing of a Deaf and Mute Man

[31]Then Jesus left the vicinity of Tyre and went through Sidon, down to the Sea of Galilee and into the region of the Decapolis.[i] [32]There some people brought to him a man who was deaf and could hardly talk, and they begged him to place his hand on the man.

[33]After he took him aside, away from the crowd, Jesus put his fingers into the man's ears. Then he spit and touched the man's tongue. [34]He looked up to heaven and with a deep sigh said to him, "Ephphatha!" (which means, "Be opened!"). [35]At this, the man's ears were opened, his tongue was loosened and he began to speak plainly.

[36]Jesus commanded them not to tell anyone. But the more he did so, the more they kept talking about it. [37]People were overwhelmed with amazement. "He has done everything well," they

---

[a]4 Some early manuscripts *pitchers, kettles and dining couches*   [b]6,7 Isaiah 29:13   [c]9 Some manuscripts *set up*   [d]10 Exodus 20:12; Deut. 5:16   [e]10 Exodus 21:17; Lev. 20:9   [f]15 Some early manuscripts *'unclean.'* [16]*If anyone has ears to hear, let him hear.*   [g]24 Many early manuscripts *Tyre and Sidon*   [h]25 Greek *unclean*   [i]31 That is, the Ten Cities

said. "He even makes the deaf hear and the mute speak."

Jesus Feeds the Four Thousand

8 During those days another large crowd gathered. Since they had nothing to eat, Jesus called his disciples to him and said, [2]"I have compassion for these people; they have already been with me three days and have nothing to eat. [3]If I send them home hungry, they will collapse on the way, because some of them have come a long distance."

[4]His disciples answered, "But where in this remote place can anyone get enough bread to feed them?"

[5]"How many loaves do you have?" Jesus asked.

"Seven," they replied.

[6]He told the crowd to sit down on the ground. When he had taken the seven loaves and given thanks, he broke them and gave them to his disciples to set before the people, and they did so. [7]They had a few small fish as well; he gave thanks for them also and told the disciples to distribute them. [8]The people ate and were satisfied. Afterward the disciples picked up seven basketfuls of broken pieces that were left over. [9]About four thousand men were present. And having sent them away, [10]he got into the boat with his disciples and went to the region of Dalmanutha.

[11]The Pharisees came and began to question Jesus. To test him, they asked him for a sign from heaven. [12]He sighed deeply and said, "Why does this generation ask for a miraculous sign? I tell you the truth, no sign will be given to it." [13]Then he left them, got back into the boat and crossed to the other side.

The Yeast of the Pharisees and Herod

[14]The disciples had forgotten to bring bread, except for one loaf they had with them in the boat. [15]"Be careful," Jesus warned them. "Watch out for the yeast of the Pharisees and that of Herod."

[16]They discussed this with one another and said, "It is because we have no bread."

[17]Aware of their discussion, Jesus asked them: "Why are you talking about having no bread? Do you still not see or understand? Are your hearts hardened?

[18]Do you have eyes but fail to see, and ears but fail to hear? And don't you remember? [19]When I broke the five loaves for the five thousand, how many basketfuls of pieces did you pick up?"

"Twelve," they replied.

[20]"And when I broke the seven loaves for the four thousand, how many basketfuls of pieces did you pick up?"

They answered, "Seven."

[21]He said to them, "Do you still not understand?"

The Healing of a Blind Man at Bethsaida

[22]They came to Bethsaida, and some people brought a blind man and begged Jesus to touch him. [23]He took the blind man by the hand and led him outside the village. When he had spit on the man's eyes and put his hands on him, Jesus asked, "Do you see anything?"

[24]He looked up and said, "I see people; they look like trees walking around."

[25]Once more Jesus put his hands on the man's eyes. Then his eyes were opened, his sight was restored, and he saw everything clearly. [26]Jesus sent him home, saying, "Don't go into the village.[a]"

Peter's Confession of Christ

[27]Jesus and his disciples went on to the villages around Caesarea Philippi. On the way he asked them, "Who do people say I am?"

[28]They replied, "Some say John the Baptist; others say Elijah; and still others, one of the prophets."

[29]"But what about you?" he asked. "Who do you say I am?"

Peter answered, "You are the Christ.[b]"

[30]Jesus warned them not to tell anyone about him.

Jesus Predicts His Death

[31]He then began to teach them that the Son of Man must suffer many things and be rejected by the elders, chief priests and teachers of the law, and that he must be killed and after three days rise again. [32]He spoke plainly about this, and Peter took him aside and began to rebuke him.

---

[a]26 Some manuscripts *Don't go and tell anyone in the village* and "the Messiah" (Hebrew) both mean "the Anointed One."

[b]29 Or *Messiah.* "The Christ" (Greek)

33But when Jesus turned and looked at his disciples, he rebuked Peter. "Get behind me, Satan!" he said. "You do not have in mind the things of God, but the things of men."

34Then he called the crowd to him along with his disciples and said: "If anyone would come after me, he must deny himself and take up his cross and follow me. **35**For whoever wants to save his life[a] will lose it, but whoever loses his life for me and for the gospel will save it. **36**What good is it for a man to gain the whole world, yet forfeit his soul? **37**Or what can a man give in exchange for his soul? **38**If anyone is ashamed of me and my words in this adulterous and sinful generation, the Son of Man will be ashamed of him when he comes in his Father's glory with the holy angels."

9 And he said to them, "I tell you the truth, some who are standing here will not taste death before they see the kingdom of God come with power."

The Transfiguration

2After six days Jesus took Peter, James and John with him and led them up a high mountain, where they were all alone. There he was transfigured before them. **3**His clothes became dazzling white, whiter than anyone in the world could bleach them. **4**And there appeared before them Elijah and Moses, who were talking with Jesus.

5Peter said to Jesus, "Rabbi, it is good for us to be here. Let us put up three shelters—one for you, one for Moses and one for Elijah." **6**(He did not know what to say, they were so frightened.)

7Then a cloud appeared and enveloped them, and a voice came from the cloud: "This is my Son, whom I love. Listen to him!"

8Suddenly, when they looked around, they no longer saw anyone with them except Jesus.

9As they were coming down the mountain, Jesus gave them orders not to tell anyone what they had seen until the Son of Man had risen from the dead. **10**They kept the matter to themselves, discussing what "rising from the dead" meant.

11And they asked him, "Why do the teachers of the law say that Elijah must come first?"

12Jesus replied, "To be sure, Elijah does come first, and restores all things. Why then is it written that the Son of Man must suffer much and be rejected? **13**But I tell you, Elijah has come, and they have done to him everything they wished, just as it is written about him."

The Healing of a Boy With an Evil Spirit

14When they came to the other disciples, they saw a large crowd around them and the teachers of the law arguing with them. **15**As soon as all the people saw Jesus, they were overwhelmed with wonder and ran to greet him.

16"What are you arguing with them about?" he asked.

17A man in the crowd answered, "Teacher, I brought you my son, who is possessed by a spirit that has robbed him of speech. **18**Whenever it seizes him, it throws him to the ground. He foams at the mouth, gnashes his teeth and becomes rigid. I asked your disciples to drive out the spirit, but they could not."

19"O unbelieving generation," Jesus replied, "how long shall I stay with you? How long shall I put up with you? Bring the boy to me."

20So they brought him. When the spirit saw Jesus, it immediately threw the boy into a convulsion. He fell to the ground and rolled around, foaming at the mouth.

21Jesus asked the boy's father, "How long has he been like this?"

"From childhood," he answered. **22**"It has often thrown him into fire or water to kill him. But if you can do anything, take pity on us and help us."

23"'If you can'?" said Jesus. "Everything is possible for him who believes."

24Immediately the boy's father exclaimed, "I do believe; help me overcome my unbelief!"

25When Jesus saw that a crowd was running to the scene, he rebuked the evil[b] spirit. "You deaf and mute spirit," he said, "I command you, come out of him and never enter him again."

26The spirit shrieked, convulsed him violently and came out. The boy looked

---

[a]35 The Greek word means either *life* or *soul*; also in verse 36.   [b]25 Greek *unclean*

so much like a corpse that many said, "He's dead." **27**But Jesus took him by the hand and lifted him to his feet, and he stood up.

28After Jesus had gone indoors, his disciples asked him privately, "Why couldn't we drive it out?"

29He replied, "This kind can come out only by prayer.*a*"

30They left that place and passed through Galilee. Jesus did not want anyone to know where they were, **31**because he was teaching his disciples. He said to them, "The Son of Man is going to be betrayed into the hands of men. They will kill him, and after three days he will rise." **32**But they did not understand what he meant and were afraid to ask him about it.

Who Is the Greatest?

33They came to Capernaum. When he was in the house, he asked them, "What were you arguing about on the road?" **34**But they kept quiet because on the way they had argued about who was the greatest.

35Sitting down, Jesus called the Twelve and said, "If anyone wants to be first, he must be the very last, and the servant of all."

36He took a little child and had him stand among them. Taking him in his arms, he said to them, **37**"Whoever welcomes one of these little children in my name welcomes me; and whoever welcomes me does not welcome me but the one who sent me."

Whoever Is Not Against Us Is for Us

38"Teacher," said John, "we saw a man driving out demons in your name and we told him to stop, because he was not one of us."

39"Do not stop him," Jesus said. "No one who does a miracle in my name can in the next moment say anything bad about me, **40**for whoever is not against us is for us. **41**I tell you the truth, anyone who gives you a cup of water in my name because you belong to Christ will certainly not lose his reward.

Causing to Sin

42"And if anyone causes one of these little ones who believe in me to sin, it would be better for him to be thrown into the sea with a large millstone tied around his neck. **43**If your hand causes you to sin, cut it off. It is better for you to enter life maimed than with two hands to go into hell, where the fire never goes out.*b* **45**And if your foot causes you to sin, cut it off. It is better for you to enter life crippled than to have two feet and be thrown into hell.*c* **47**And if your eye causes you to sin, pluck it out. It is better for you to enter the kingdom of God with one eye than to have two eyes and be thrown into hell, **48**where

> " 'their worm does not die,
>   and the fire is not quenched.'*d*

49Everyone will be salted with fire. **50**"Salt is good, but if it loses its saltiness, how can you make it salty again? Have salt in yourselves, and be at peace with each other."

Divorce

10 Jesus then left that place and went into the region of Judea and across the Jordan. Again crowds of people came to him, and as was his custom, he taught them.

2Some Pharisees came and tested him by asking, "Is it lawful for a man to divorce his wife?"

3"What did Moses command you?" he replied.

4They said, "Moses permitted a man to write a certificate of divorce and send her away."

5"It was because your hearts were hard that Moses wrote you this law," Jesus replied. **6**"But at the beginning of creation God 'made them male and female.'*e* **7**'For this reason a man will leave his father and mother and be united to his wife,*f* **8**and the two will become one flesh.'*g* So they are no longer two, but one. **9**Therefore what God has joined together, let man not separate."

10When they were in the house again, the disciples asked Jesus about this. **11**He answered, "Anyone who divorces his wife and marries another woman

---

*a*29 Some manuscripts *prayer and fasting*   *b*43 Some manuscripts *out, 44where / " 'their worm does not die, / and the fire is not quenched.'*   *c*45 Some manuscripts *hell, 46where / " 'their worm does not die, / and the fire is not quenched.'*   *d*48 Isaiah 66:24   *e*6 Gen. 1:27   *f*7 Some early manuscripts do not have *and be united to his wife.*   *g*8 Gen. 2:24

commits adultery against her. ¹²And if she divorces her husband and marries another man, she commits adultery."

The Little Children and Jesus

¹³People were bringing little children to Jesus to have him touch them, but the disciples rebuked them. ¹⁴When Jesus saw this, he was indignant. He said to them, "Let the little children come to me, and do not hinder them, for the kingdom of God belongs to such as these. ¹⁵I tell you the truth, anyone who will not receive the kingdom of God like a little child will never enter it." ¹⁶And he took the children in his arms, put his hands on them and blessed them.

The Rich Young Man

¹⁷As Jesus started on his way, a man ran up to him and fell on his knees before him. "Good teacher," he asked, "what must I do to inherit eternal life?"

¹⁸"Why do you call me good?" Jesus answered. "No one is good—except God alone. ¹⁹You know the commandments: 'Do not murder, do not commit adultery, do not steal, do not give false testimony, do not defraud, honor your father and mother.'ᵃ"

²⁰"Teacher," he declared, "all these I have kept since I was a boy."

²¹Jesus looked at him and loved him. "One thing you lack," he said. "Go, sell everything you have and give to the poor, and you will have treasure in heaven. Then come, follow me."

²²At this the man's face fell. He went away sad, because he had great wealth.

²³Jesus looked around and said to his disciples, "How hard it is for the rich to enter the kingdom of God!"

²⁴The disciples were amazed at his words. But Jesus said again, "Children, how hard it isᵇ to enter the kingdom of God! ²⁵It is easier for a camel to go through the eye of a needle than for a rich man to enter the kingdom of God."

²⁶The disciples were even more amazed, and said to each other, "Who then can be saved?"

²⁷Jesus looked at them and said, "With man this is impossible, but not with God; all things are possible with God."

²⁸Peter said to him, "We have left everything to follow you!"

²⁹"I tell you the truth," Jesus replied, "no one who has left home or brothers or sisters or mother or father or children or fields for me and the gospel ³⁰will fail to receive a hundred times as much in this present age (homes, brothers, sisters, mothers, children and fields—and with them, persecutions) and in the age to come, eternal life. ³¹But many who are first will be last, and the last first."

Jesus Again Predicts His Death

³²They were on their way up to Jerusalem, with Jesus leading the way, and the disciples were astonished, while those who followed were afraid. Again he took the Twelve aside and told them what was going to happen to him. ³³"We are going up to Jerusalem," he said, "and the Son of Man will be betrayed to the chief priests and teachers of the law. They will condemn him to death and will hand him over to the Gentiles, ³⁴who will mock him and spit on him, flog him and kill him. Three days later he will rise."

The Request of James and John

³⁵Then James and John, the sons of Zebedee, came to him. "Teacher," they said, "we want you to do for us whatever we ask."

³⁶"What do you want me to do for you?" he asked.

³⁷They replied, "Let one of us sit at your right and the other at your left in your glory."

³⁸"You don't know what you are asking," Jesus said. "Can you drink the cup I drink or be baptized with the baptism I am baptized with?"

³⁹"We can," they answered.

Jesus said to them, "You will drink the cup I drink and be baptized with the baptism I am baptized with, ⁴⁰but to sit at my right or left is not for me to grant. These places belong to those for whom they have been prepared."

⁴¹When the ten heard about this, they became indignant with James and John. ⁴²Jesus called them together and said, "You know that those who are regarded as rulers of the Gentiles lord it over them, and their high officials exercise authority over them. ⁴³Not so with you.

ᵃ19 Exodus 20:12-16; Deut. 5:16-20   ᵇ24 Some manuscripts *is for those who trust in riches*

Instead, whoever wants to become great among you must be your servant, 44and whoever wants to be first must be slave of all. 45For even the Son of Man did not come to be served, but to serve, and to give his life as a ransom for many."

Blind Bartimaeus Receives His Sight

46Then they came to Jericho. As Jesus and his disciples, together with a large crowd, were leaving the city, a blind man, Bartimaeus (that is, the Son of Timaeus), was sitting by the roadside begging. 47When he heard that it was Jesus of Nazareth, he began to shout, "Jesus, Son of David, have mercy on me!"

48Many rebuked him and told him to be quiet, but he shouted all the more, "Son of David, have mercy on me!"

49Jesus stopped and said, "Call him."

So they called to the blind man, "Cheer up! On your feet! He's calling you." 50Throwing his cloak aside, he jumped to his feet and came to Jesus.

51"What do you want me to do for you?" Jesus asked him.

The blind man said, "Rabbi, I want to see."

52"Go," said Jesus, "your faith has healed you." Immediately he received his sight and followed Jesus along the road.

⟨ TUESDAY ⟩

VERSE:
Mark 10:21

AUTHOR:
Catherine Doherty

PASSAGE:
Mark 10:17–31

The Gospel Is Risky Business

The security to which most people cling is mere illusion. We are not secure walking big-city streets. In planes we never know if we'll stay up or not. Wars flare up in almost every part of the world. So where is that security everybody is supposed to value so dearly? God doesn't give us this material security. Instead he offers faith . . . which begins, in a sense, where reason ends.

God's security begins when we start loving him with our whole heart, our whole mind, our whole soul—and our neighbor as ourselves. I speak of this so often, but it is the only message that can never be overstressed. We must clothe the skeletons of our lives with the flesh of his love, or we shall perish.

For this kind of loving we have the Holy Spirit in us. With his help, we will have the courage to risk loving our neighbor. It's a tremendous risk, because we must also love our enemies. We have the power to change them into friends and beloved neighbors. To love one's neighbor is the ultimate risk, for it may even mean death for my brother or sister's sake if need be.

All this sounds idealistic and unobtainable, but Christ assures us it *is* attainable. Through little steps day after day, one slowly accepts the other as he or she is, and begins to love totally, tenderly, compassionately. Once begun, the involvement becomes deeper and deeper and deeper.

ADDITIONAL SCRIPTURE READINGS:
Matthew 22:36–38; 2 Timothy 1:6–7; 1 John 3:18

Go to page 65 for your next devotional reading.

The Triumphal Entry

11 As they approached Jerusalem and came to Bethphage and Bethany at the Mount of Olives, Jesus sent two of his disciples, **2**saying to them, "Go to the village ahead of you, and just as you enter it, you will find a colt tied there, which no one has ever ridden. Untie it and bring it here. **3**If anyone asks you, 'Why are you doing this?' tell him, 'The Lord needs it and will send it back here shortly.' "

4They went and found a colt outside in the street, tied at a doorway. As they untied it, **5**some people standing there asked, "What are you doing, untying that colt?" **6**They answered as Jesus had told them to, and the people let them go. **7**When they brought the colt to Jesus and threw their cloaks over it, he sat on it. **8**Many people spread their cloaks on the road, while others spread branches they had cut in the fields. **9**Those who went ahead and those who followed shouted,

"Hosanna!*a*

"Blessed is he who comes in the name of the Lord!"*b*

10"Blessed is the coming kingdom of our father David!"

"Hosanna in the highest!"

11Jesus entered Jerusalem and went to the temple. He looked around at everything, but since it was already late, he went out to Bethany with the Twelve.

Jesus Clears the Temple

12The next day as they were leaving Bethany, Jesus was hungry. **13**Seeing in the distance a fig tree in leaf, he went to find out if it had any fruit. When he reached it, he found nothing but leaves, because it was not the season for figs. **14**Then he said to the tree, "May no one ever eat fruit from you again." And his disciples heard him say it.

15On reaching Jerusalem, Jesus entered the temple area and began driving out those who were buying and selling there. He overturned the tables of the money changers and the benches of those selling doves, **16**and would not allow anyone to carry merchandise through the temple courts. **17**And as he taught them, he said, "Is it not written:

" 'My house will be called
a house of prayer for all
nations'*c*?

But you have made it 'a den of robbers.'*d*"

18The chief priests and the teachers of the law heard this and began looking for a way to kill him, for they feared him, because the whole crowd was amazed at his teaching.

19When evening came, they*e* went out of the city.

The Withered Fig Tree

20In the morning, as they went along, they saw the fig tree withered from the roots. **21**Peter remembered and said to Jesus, "Rabbi, look! The fig tree you cursed has withered!"

22"Have*f* faith in God," Jesus answered. **23**"I tell you the truth, if anyone says to this mountain, 'Go, throw yourself into the sea,' and does not doubt in his heart but believes that what he says will happen, it will be done for him. **24**Therefore I tell you, whatever you ask for in prayer, believe that you have received it, and it will be yours. **25**And when you stand praying, if you hold anything against anyone, forgive him, so that your Father in heaven may forgive you your sins.*g*"

The Authority of Jesus Questioned

27They arrived again in Jerusalem, and while Jesus was walking in the temple courts, the chief priests, the teachers of the law and the elders came to him. **28**"By what authority are you doing these things?" they asked. "And who gave you authority to do this?"

29Jesus replied, "I will ask you one question. Answer me, and I will tell you by what authority I am doing these things. **30**John's baptism—was it from heaven, or from men? Tell me!"

31They discussed it among themselves and said, "If we say, 'From heaven,' he will ask, 'Then why didn't you

---

a9 A Hebrew expression meaning "Save!" which became an exclamation of praise; also in verse 10
b9 Psalm 118:25,26   *c17* Isaiah 56:7   *d17* Jer. 7:11   *e19* Some early manuscripts *he*
f22 Some early manuscripts *If you have*   *g25* Some manuscripts *sins.* 26*But if you do not forgive, neither will your Father who is in heaven forgive your sins.*

believe him?' ³²But if we say, 'From men' . . . ." (They feared the people, for everyone held that John really was a prophet.)

³³So they answered Jesus, "We don't know."

Jesus said, "Neither will I tell you by what authority I am doing these things."

The Parable of the Tenants

12 He then began to speak to them in parables: "A man planted a vineyard. He put a wall around it, dug a pit for the winepress and built a watchtower. Then he rented the vineyard to some farmers and went away on a journey. ²At harvest time he sent a servant to the tenants to collect from them some of the fruit of the vineyard. ³But they seized him, beat him and sent him away empty-handed. ⁴Then he sent another servant to them; they struck this man on the head and treated him shamefully. ⁵He sent still another, and that one they killed. He sent many others; some of them they beat, others they killed.

⁶"He had one left to send, a son, whom he loved. He sent him last of all, saying, 'They will respect my son.'

⁷"But the tenants said to one another, 'This is the heir. Come, let's kill him, and the inheritance will be ours.' ⁸So they took him and killed him, and threw him out of the vineyard.

⁹"What then will the owner of the vineyard do? He will come and kill those tenants and give the vineyard to others. ¹⁰Haven't you read this scripture:

" 'The stone the builders rejected
    has become the capstone[a];
¹¹the Lord has done this,
    and it is marvelous in our
        eyes'[b]?"

¹²Then they looked for a way to arrest him because they knew he had spoken the parable against them. But they were afraid of the crowd; so they left him and went away.

Paying Taxes to Caesar

¹³Later they sent some of the Pharisees and Herodians to Jesus to catch him in his words. ¹⁴They came to him and said, "Teacher, we know you are a man of integrity. You aren't swayed by men, because you pay no attention to who they are; but you teach the way of God in accordance with the truth. Is it right to pay taxes to Caesar or not? ¹⁵Should we pay or shouldn't we?"

But Jesus knew their hypocrisy. "Why are you trying to trap me?" he asked. "Bring me a denarius and let me look at it." ¹⁶They brought the coin, and he asked them, "Whose portrait is this? And whose inscription?"

"Caesar's," they replied.

¹⁷Then Jesus said to them, "Give to Caesar what is Caesar's and to God what is God's."

And they were amazed at him.

Marriage at the Resurrection

¹⁸Then the Sadducees, who say there is no resurrection, came to him with a question. ¹⁹"Teacher," they said, "Moses wrote for us that if a man's brother dies and leaves a wife but no children, the man must marry the widow and have children for his brother. ²⁰Now there were seven brothers. The first one married and died without leaving any children. ²¹The second one married the widow, but he also died, leaving no child. It was the same with the third. ²²In fact, none of the seven left any children. Last of all, the woman died too. ²³At the resurrection[c] whose wife will she be, since the seven were married to her?"

²⁴Jesus replied, "Are you not in error because you do not know the Scriptures or the power of God? ²⁵When the dead rise, they will neither marry nor be given in marriage; they will be like the angels in heaven. ²⁶Now about the dead rising—have you not read in the book of Moses, in the account of the bush, how God said to him, 'I am the God of Abraham, the God of Isaac, and the God of Jacob'[d]? ²⁷He is not the God of the dead, but of the living. You are badly mistaken!"

The Greatest Commandment

²⁸One of the teachers of the law came and heard them debating. Noticing that Jesus had given them a good answer, he asked him, "Of all the commandments, which is the most important?"

²⁹"The most important one," an-

---

[a]10 Or cornerstone   [b]11 Psalm 118:22,23   [c]23 Some manuscripts resurrection, when men rise from the dead,   [d]26 Exodus 3:6

swered Jesus, "is this: 'Hear, O Israel, the Lord our God, the Lord is one.[a] ³⁰Love the Lord your God with all your heart and with all your soul and with all your mind and with all your strength.'[b] ³¹The second is this: 'Love your neighbor as yourself.'[c] There is no commandment greater than these."

³²"Well said, teacher," the man replied. "You are right in saying that God is one and there is no other but him. ³³To love him with all your heart, with all your understanding and with all your strength, and to love your neighbor as yourself is more important than all burnt offerings and sacrifices."

³⁴When Jesus saw that he had answered wisely, he said to him, "You are not far from the kingdom of God." And from then on no one dared ask him any more questions.

Whose Son Is the Christ?

³⁵While Jesus was teaching in the temple courts, he asked, "How is it that the teachers of the law say that the Christ[d] is the son of David? ³⁶David himself, speaking by the Holy Spirit, declared:

" 'The Lord said to my Lord:
  "Sit at my right hand
until I put your enemies
  under your feet." '[e]

³⁷David himself calls him 'Lord.' How then can he be his son?"

The large crowd listened to him with delight.

³⁸As he taught, Jesus said, "Watch out for the teachers of the law. They like to walk around in flowing robes and be greeted in the marketplaces, ³⁹and have the most important seats in the synagogues and the places of honor at banquets. ⁴⁰They devour widows' houses and for a show make lengthy prayers. Such men will be punished most severely."

The Widow's Offering

⁴¹Jesus sat down opposite the place where the offerings were put and watched the crowd putting their money into the temple treasury. Many rich people threw in large amounts. ⁴²But a poor widow came and put in two very small copper coins,[f] worth only a fraction of a penny.[g]

⁴³Calling his disciples to him, Jesus said, "I tell you the truth, this poor widow has put more into the treasury than all the others. ⁴⁴They all gave out of their wealth; but she, out of her poverty, put in everything—all she had to live on."

Signs of the End of the Age

13 As he was leaving the temple, one of his disciples said to him, "Look, Teacher! What massive stones! What magnificent buildings!"

²"Do you see all these great buildings?" replied Jesus. "Not one stone here will be left on another; every one will be thrown down."

³As Jesus was sitting on the Mount of Olives opposite the temple, Peter, James, John and Andrew asked him privately, ⁴"Tell us, when will these things happen? And what will be the sign that they are all about to be fulfilled?"

⁵Jesus said to them: "Watch out that no one deceives you. ⁶Many will come in my name, claiming, 'I am he,' and will deceive many. ⁷When you hear of wars and rumors of wars, do not be alarmed. Such things must happen, but the end is still to come. ⁸Nation will rise against nation, and kingdom against kingdom. There will be earthquakes in various places, and famines. These are the beginning of birth pains.

⁹"You must be on your guard. You will be handed over to the local councils and flogged in the synagogues. On account of me you will stand before governors and kings as witnesses to them. ¹⁰And the gospel must first be preached to all nations. ¹¹Whenever you are arrested and brought to trial, do not worry beforehand about what to say. Just say whatever is given you at the time, for it is not you speaking, but the Holy Spirit.

¹²"Brother will betray brother to death, and a father his child. Children will rebel against their parents and have them put to death. ¹³All men will hate you because of me, but he who stands firm to the end will be saved.

¹⁴"When you see 'the abomination that causes desolation'[h] standing where

a29 Or the Lord our God is one Lord   b30 Deut. 6:4,5   c31 Lev. 19:18   d35 Or Messiah   e36 Psalm 110:1   f42 Greek two lepta   g42 Greek kodrantes   h14 Daniel 9:27; 11:31; 12:11

it[a] does not belong—let the reader understand—then let those who are in Judea flee to the mountains. [15]Let no one on the roof of his house go down or enter the house to take anything out. [16]Let no one in the field go back to get his cloak. [17]How dreadful it will be in those days for pregnant women and nursing mothers! [18]Pray that this will not take place in winter, [19]because those will be days of distress unequaled from the beginning, when God created the world, until now—and never to be equaled again. [20]If the Lord had not cut short those days, no one would survive. But for the sake of the elect, whom he has chosen, he has shortened them. [21]At that time if anyone says to you, 'Look, here is the Christ[b]!' or, 'Look, there he is!' do not believe it. [22]For false Christs and false prophets will appear and perform signs and miracles to deceive the elect—if that were possible. [23]So be on your guard; I have told you everything ahead of time.

[24]"But in those days, following that distress,

" 'the sun will be darkened,
   and the moon will not give its
      light;
[25]the stars will fall from the sky,
   and the heavenly bodies will be
      shaken.'[c]

[26]"At that time men will see the Son of Man coming in clouds with great power and glory. [27]And he will send his angels and gather his elect from the four winds, from the ends of the earth to the ends of the heavens.

[28]"Now learn this lesson from the fig tree: As soon as its twigs get tender and its leaves come out, you know that summer is near. [29]Even so, when you see these things happening, you know that it is near, right at the door. [30]I tell you the truth, this generation[d] will certainly not pass away until all these things have happened. [31]Heaven and earth will pass away, but my words will never pass away.

The Day and Hour Unknown

[32]"No one knows about that day or hour, not even the angels in heaven, nor the Son, but only the Father. [33]Be on

guard! Be alert[e]! You do not know when that time will come. [34]It's like a man going away: He leaves his house and puts his servants in charge, each with his assigned task, and tells the one at the door to keep watch.

[35]"Therefore keep watch because you do not know when the owner of the house will come back—whether in the evening, or at midnight, or when the rooster crows, or at dawn. [36]If he comes suddenly, do not let him find you sleeping. [37]What I say to you, I say to everyone: 'Watch!' "

Jesus Anointed at Bethany

14 Now the Passover and the Feast of Unleavened Bread were only two days away, and the chief priests and the teachers of the law were looking for some sly way to arrest Jesus and kill him. [2]"But not during the Feast," they said, "or the people may riot."

[3]While he was in Bethany, reclining at the table in the home of a man known as Simon the Leper, a woman came with an alabaster jar of very expensive perfume, made of pure nard. She broke the jar and poured the perfume on his head.

[4]Some of those present were saying indignantly to one another, "Why this waste of perfume? [5]It could have been sold for more than a year's wages[f] and the money given to the poor." And they rebuked her harshly.

[6]"Leave her alone," said Jesus. "Why are you bothering her? She has done a beautiful thing to me. [7]The poor you will always have with you, and you can help them any time you want. But you will not always have me. [8]She did what she could. She poured perfume on my body beforehand to prepare for my burial. [9]I tell you the truth, wherever the gospel is preached throughout the world, what she has done will also be told, in memory of her."

[10]Then Judas Iscariot, one of the Twelve, went to the chief priests to betray Jesus to them. [11]They were delighted to hear this and promised to give him money. So he watched for an opportunity to hand him over.

The Lord's Supper

[12]On the first day of the Feast of Un-

---

a[14] Or he; also in verse 29   b[21] Or Messiah   c[25] Isaiah 13:10; 34:4   d[30] Or race
e[33] Some manuscripts alert and pray   f[5] Greek than three hundred denarii

leavened Bread, when it was customary to sacrifice the Passover lamb, Jesus' disciples asked him, "Where do you want us to go and make preparations for you to eat the Passover?"

¹³So he sent two of his disciples, telling them, "Go into the city, and a man carrying a jar of water will meet you. Follow him. ¹⁴Say to the owner of the house he enters, 'The Teacher asks: Where is my guest room, where I may eat the Passover with my disciples?' ¹⁵He will show you a large upper room, furnished and ready. Make preparations for us there."

¹⁶The disciples left, went into the city and found things just as Jesus had told them. So they prepared the Passover.

¹⁷When evening came, Jesus arrived with the Twelve. ¹⁸While they were reclining at the table eating, he said, "I tell

you the truth, one of you will betray me—one who is eating with me."

¹⁹They were saddened, and one by one they said to him, "Surely not I?"

²⁰"It is one of the Twelve," he replied, "one who dips bread into the bowl with me. ²¹The Son of Man will go just as it is written about him. But woe to that man who betrays the Son of Man! It would be better for him if he had not been born."

²²While they were eating, Jesus took bread, gave thanks and broke it, and gave it to his disciples, saying, "Take it; this is my body."

²³Then he took the cup, gave thanks and offered it to them, and they all drank from it.

²⁴"This is my blood of the*a* covenant, which is poured out for many," he said to them. ²⁵"I tell you the truth, I will not drink again of the fruit of the vine until

a24 Some manuscripts *the new*

WEDNESDAY

VERSE:
Mark 14:6

AUTHOR:
Millie Stamm

PASSAGE:
Mark 14:1–11

A Gift for Jesus

Jesus was being entertained in the home of Simon the Leper. As he sat there a woman came to him, bringing an alabaster box of ointment of spikenard, very precious. This she broke and poured on his head. Judas was critical. It seemed such a waste, such an extravagance, accomplishing no useful purpose. He felt it should have been sold and the money given to the poor.

But Jesus could see into her heart. It was filled with love for him and he was encouraged by her display of love. She had used her money to purchase the ointment. She used her time to pour it out on his head. He knew that her desire was to give him that which was precious to her, so he said, "She did what she could" (v. 8).

It was not the value of her gift that was important, but her motive in giving. For this she received the praise of the Savior. "Wherever the gospel is preached throughout the world, what she has done will also be told, in memory of her" (v. 9). Nothing ever given to Jesus is wasted.

ADDITIONAL SCRIPTURE READINGS:
Luke 14:25–26; Romans 12:1

Go to page 69 for your next devotional reading.

that day when I drink it anew in the kingdom of God."

26When they had sung a hymn, they went out to the Mount of Olives.

Jesus Predicts Peter's Denial

27"You will all fall away," Jesus told them, "for it is written:

" 'I will strike the shepherd,
and the sheep will be scattered.'*a*

28But after I have risen, I will go ahead of you into Galilee."

29Peter declared, "Even if all fall away, I will not."

30"I tell you the truth," Jesus answered, "today—yes, tonight—before the rooster crows twice*b* you yourself will disown me three times."

31But Peter insisted emphatically, "Even if I have to die with you, I will never disown you." And all the others said the same.

Gethsemane

32They went to a place called Gethsemane, and Jesus said to his disciples, "Sit here while I pray." 33He took Peter, James and John along with him, and he began to be deeply distressed and troubled. 34"My soul is overwhelmed with sorrow to the point of death," he said to them. "Stay here and keep watch."

35Going a little farther, he fell to the ground and prayed that if possible the hour might pass from him. 36"Abba,*c* Father," he said, "everything is possible for you. Take this cup from me. Yet not what I will, but what you will."

37Then he returned to his disciples and found them sleeping. "Simon," he said to Peter, "are you asleep? Could you not keep watch for one hour? 38Watch and pray so that you will not fall into temptation. The spirit is willing, but the body is weak."

39Once more he went away and prayed the same thing. 40When he came back, he again found them sleeping, because their eyes were heavy. They did not know what to say to him.

41Returning the third time, he said to them, "Are you still sleeping and resting? Enough! The hour has come. Look, the Son of Man is betrayed into the hands of sinners. 42Rise! Let us go! Here comes my betrayer!"

Jesus Arrested

43Just as he was speaking, Judas, one of the Twelve, appeared. With him was a crowd armed with swords and clubs, sent from the chief priests, the teachers of the law, and the elders.

44Now the betrayer had arranged a signal with them: "The one I kiss is the man; arrest him and lead him away under guard." 45Going at once to Jesus, Judas said, "Rabbi!" and kissed him. 46The men seized Jesus and arrested him. 47Then one of those standing near drew his sword and struck the servant of the high priest, cutting off his ear.

48"Am I leading a rebellion," said Jesus, "that you have come out with swords and clubs to capture me? 49Every day I was with you, teaching in the temple courts, and you did not arrest me. But the Scriptures must be fulfilled." 50Then everyone deserted him and fled.

51A young man, wearing nothing but a linen garment, was following Jesus. When they seized him, 52he fled naked, leaving his garment behind.

Before the Sanhedrin

53They took Jesus to the high priest, and all the chief priests, elders and teachers of the law came together. 54Peter followed him at a distance, right into the courtyard of the high priest. There he sat with the guards and warmed himself at the fire.

55The chief priests and the whole Sanhedrin were looking for evidence against Jesus so that they could put him to death, but they did not find any. 56Many testified falsely against him, but their statements did not agree.

57Then some stood up and gave this false testimony against him: 58"We heard him say, 'I will destroy this man-made temple and in three days will build another, not made by man.'" 59Yet even then their testimony did not agree.

60Then the high priest stood up before them and asked Jesus, "Are you not going to answer? What is this testimony that these men are bringing against you?" 61But Jesus remained silent and gave no answer.

Again the high priest asked him, "Are

---

a27 Zech. 13:7   *b30* Some early manuscripts do not have *twice.*   *c36* Aramaic for *Father* you the Christ,[a] the Son of the Blessed One?"

62"I am," said Jesus. "And you will see the Son of Man sitting at the right hand of the Mighty One and coming on the clouds of heaven."

63The high priest tore his clothes. "Why do we need any more witnesses?" he asked. **64**"You have heard the blasphemy. What do you think?"

They all condemned him as worthy of death. **65**Then some began to spit at him; they blindfolded him, struck him with their fists, and said, "Prophesy!" And the guards took him and beat him.

Peter Disowns Jesus

66While Peter was below in the courtyard, one of the servant girls of the high priest came by. **67**When she saw Peter warming himself, she looked closely at him.

"You also were with that Nazarene, Jesus," she said.

68But he denied it. "I don't know or understand what you're talking about," he said, and went out into the entryway.[b]

69When the servant girl saw him there, she said again to those standing around, "This fellow is one of them." **70**Again he denied it.

After a little while, those standing near said to Peter, "Surely you are one of them, for you are a Galilean."

71He began to call down curses on himself, and he swore to them, "I don't know this man you're talking about."

72Immediately the rooster crowed the second time.[c] Then Peter remembered the word Jesus had spoken to him: "Before the rooster crows twice[d] you will disown me three times." And he broke down and wept.

Jesus Before Pilate

15 Very early in the morning, the chief priests, with the elders, the teachers of the law and the whole Sanhedrin, reached a decision. They bound Jesus, led him away and handed him over to Pilate.

2"Are you the king of the Jews?" asked Pilate.

"Yes, it is as you say," Jesus replied.

3The chief priests accused him of many things. **4**So again Pilate asked him, "Aren't you going to answer? See how many things they are accusing you of."

5But Jesus still made no reply, and Pilate was amazed.

6Now it was the custom at the Feast to release a prisoner whom the people requested. **7**A man called Barabbas was in prison with the insurrectionists who had committed murder in the uprising. **8**The crowd came up and asked Pilate to do for them what he usually did.

9"Do you want me to release to you the king of the Jews?" asked Pilate, **10**knowing it was out of envy that the chief priests had handed Jesus over to him. **11**But the chief priests stirred up the crowd to have Pilate release Barabbas instead.

12"What shall I do, then, with the one you call the king of the Jews?" Pilate asked them.

13"Crucify him!" they shouted.

14"Why? What crime has he committed?" asked Pilate.

But they shouted all the louder, "Crucify him!"

15Wanting to satisfy the crowd, Pilate released Barabbas to them. He had Jesus flogged, and handed him over to be crucified.

The Soldiers Mock Jesus

16The soldiers led Jesus away into the palace (that is, the Praetorium) and called together the whole company of soldiers. **17**They put a purple robe on him, then twisted together a crown of thorns and set it on him. **18**And they began to call out to him, "Hail, king of the Jews!" **19**Again and again they struck him on the head with a staff and spit on him. Falling on their knees, they paid homage to him. **20**And when they had mocked him, they took off the purple robe and put his own clothes on him. Then they led him out to crucify him.

The Crucifixion

21A certain man from Cyrene, Simon, the father of Alexander and Rufus, was passing by on his way in from the country, and they forced him to carry the cross. **22**They brought Jesus to the place called Golgotha (which means The Place of the Skull). **23**Then they offered him

---

a61 Or *Messiah*   *b68* Some early manuscripts *entryway and the rooster crowed*   *c72* Some early manuscripts do not have *the second time*.   *d72* Some early manuscripts do not have *twice*.

wine mixed with myrrh, but he did not take it. 24And they crucified him. Dividing up his clothes, they cast lots to see what each would get.

25It was the third hour when they crucified him. 26The written notice of the charge against him read: THE KING OF THE JEWS. 27They crucified two robbers with him, one on his right and one on his left.*a* 29Those who passed by hurled insults at him, shaking their heads and saying, "So! You who are going to destroy the temple and build it in three days, 30come down from the cross and save yourself!"

31In the same way the chief priests and the teachers of the law mocked him among themselves. "He saved others," they said, "but he can't save himself! 32Let this Christ,*b* this King of Israel, come down now from the cross, that we may see and believe." Those crucified with him also heaped insults on him.

The Death of Jesus

33At the sixth hour darkness came over the whole land until the ninth hour. 34And at the ninth hour Jesus cried out in a loud voice, *"Eloi, Eloi, lama sabachthani?"*—which means, "My God, my God, why have you forsaken me?"*c*

35When some of those standing near heard this, they said, "Listen, he's calling Elijah."

36One man ran, filled a sponge with wine vinegar, put it on a stick, and offered it to Jesus to drink. "Now leave him alone. Let's see if Elijah comes to take him down," he said.

37With a loud cry, Jesus breathed his last.

38The curtain of the temple was torn in two from top to bottom. 39And when the centurion, who stood there in front of Jesus, heard his cry and*d* saw how he died, he said, "Surely this man was the Son*e* of God!"

40Some women were watching from a distance. Among them were Mary Magdalene, Mary the mother of James the younger and of Joses, and Salome. 41In Galilee these women had followed him and cared for his needs. Many other women who had come up with him to Jerusalem were also there.

The Burial of Jesus

42It was Preparation Day (that is, the day before the Sabbath). So as evening approached, 43Joseph of Arimathea, a prominent member of the Council, who was himself waiting for the kingdom of God, went boldly to Pilate and asked for Jesus' body. 44Pilate was surprised to hear that he was already dead. Summoning the centurion, he asked him if Jesus had already died. 45When he learned from the centurion that it was so, he gave the body to Joseph. 46So Joseph bought some linen cloth, took down the body, wrapped it in the linen, and placed it in a tomb cut out of rock. Then he rolled a stone against the entrance of the tomb. 47Mary Magdalene and Mary the mother of Joses saw where he was laid.

The Resurrection

16 When the Sabbath was over, Mary Magdalene, Mary the mother of James, and Salome bought spices so that they might go to anoint Jesus' body. 2Very early on the first day of the week, just after sunrise, they were on their way to the tomb 3and they asked each other, "Who will roll the stone away from the entrance of the tomb?"

4But when they looked up, they saw that the stone, which was very large, had been rolled away. 5As they entered the tomb, they saw a young man dressed in a white robe sitting on the right side, and they were alarmed.

6"Don't be alarmed," he said. "You are looking for Jesus the Nazarene, who was crucified. He has risen! He is not here. See the place where they laid him. 7But go, tell his disciples and Peter, 'He is going ahead of you into Galilee. There you will see him, just as he told you.'"

8Trembling and bewildered, the women went out and fled from the tomb. They said nothing to anyone, because they were afraid.

[The earliest manuscripts and some other ancient witnesses do not have Mark 16:9–20.]

---

a27 Some manuscripts *left, 28and the scripture was fulfilled which says, "He was counted with the lawless ones"* (Isaiah 53:12)   *b32* Or *Messiah*   *c34* Psalm 22:1   *d39* Some manuscripts do not have *heard his cry and*   *e39* Or *a son*

⁹When Jesus rose early on the first day of the week, he appeared first to Mary Magdalene, out of whom he had driven seven demons. ¹⁰She went and told those who had been with him and who were mourning and weeping. ¹¹When they heard that Jesus was alive and that she had seen him, they did not believe it.

¹²Afterward Jesus appeared in a different form to two of them while they were walking in the country. ¹³These returned

THURSDAY

VERSE:
Mark 15:21

AUTHOR:
Elisabeth Elliot

PASSAGE:
Mark 15:21–32

Pick Up Your Cross

Jesus invites us to be his disciples. If we choose to accept his loving invitation, we must understand that there are certain conditions to be fulfilled. One of them is a willingness to accept the cross. Is this a once-for-all taking up of one particular burden? I don't think so. It seems to me that my "cross" is each particular occasion when I am given the chance to "die"— that is, to offer up my own will whenever it crosses Christ's. This happens very often. A disagreement with my husband can cause an argument and harsh words, even if the matter is ridiculously small—"When are you going to get that dashboard light fixed in the car?" I have already mentioned the light three times. It may be time to keep my mouth shut, but I don't want to keep my mouth shut. Here, then, is a chance to die. A decision which affects both of us may be a fairly big one, but we find ourselves on two sides of the fence. One of us, then, must "die." It is never easy for me. Shall I make excuses for myself (that's the way I am; it's my personality; it's the way I was raised; I'm tired; I can't hack it; you don't understand)—or shall I pick up this cross?

Perhaps my illustration seems to trivialize the cross of Christ. His was so unimaginably greater. What cross could I possibly take up which would be analogous? When Jesus took up his cross, he was saying yes with all his being to the will of the Father. If I am unwilling to say yes in even a very little thing, how shall I accept a more painful thing? What sort of practice does it take for a disciple to learn to follow the Crucified? A friend hurts us, a plan goes awry, an effort fails—small things indeed. But then cancer strikes, a daughter marries unwisely, a business folds, a wife abandons her home and family. The call still comes to us: *Take up your cross and come with me.* With you, Lord? *Yes, with me.* Will you give me strength and show me the way? *That was my promise—is it my custom to break promises?*

ADDITIONAL SCRIPTURE READINGS:
Psalm 40:8; Romans 6:11; Galatians 2:20; Hebrews 12:2–6

Go to page 73 for your next devotional reading.

and reported it to the rest; but they did not believe them either.

[14]Later Jesus appeared to the Eleven as they were eating; he rebuked them for their lack of faith and their stubborn refusal to believe those who had seen him after he had risen.

[15]He said to them, "Go into all the world and preach the good news to all creation. [16]Whoever believes and is baptized will be saved, but whoever does not believe will be condemned. [17]And these signs will accompany those who believe: In my name they will drive out demons; they will speak in new tongues; [18]they will pick up snakes with their hands; and when they drink deadly poison, it will not hurt them at all; they will place their hands on sick people, and they will get well."

[19]After the Lord Jesus had spoken to them, he was taken up into heaven and he sat at the right hand of God. [20]Then the disciples went out and preached everywhere, and the Lord worked with them and confirmed his word by the signs that accompanied it.

LUKE *writes this Gospel to share the good news of salvation—a message intended for everyone. A physician by profession, Luke shows compassion for people considered outcasts, including tax collectors, women, children and the poor. Not only does Luke show great regard for people but he also shows a deep concern for prayer, discipleship, joy and the ministry of the Spirit. As you read Luke's account of the life of Jesus, may you be like him who was "full of joy through the Holy Spirit" (10:21).*

LUKE

Introduction

1 Many have undertaken to draw up an account of the things that have been fulfilled[a] among us, ²just as they were handed down to us by those who from the first were eyewitnesses and servants of the word. ³Therefore, since I myself have carefully investigated everything from the beginning, it seemed good also to me to write an orderly account for you, most excellent Theophilus, ⁴so that you may know the certainty of the things you have been taught.

The Birth of John the Baptist Foretold

⁵In the time of Herod king of Judea there was a priest named Zechariah, who belonged to the priestly division of Abijah; his wife Elizabeth was also a descendant of Aaron. ⁶Both of them were upright in the sight of God, observing all the Lord's commandments and regulations blamelessly. ⁷But they had no children, because Elizabeth was barren; and they were both well along in years.

⁸Once when Zechariah's division was on duty and he was serving as priest

before God, **9**he was chosen by lot, according to the custom of the priesthood, to go into the temple of the Lord and burn incense. **10**And when the time for the burning of incense came, all the assembled worshipers were praying outside.

11Then an angel of the Lord appeared to him, standing at the right side of the altar of incense. **12**When Zechariah saw him, he was startled and was gripped with fear. **13**But the angel said to him: "Do not be afraid, Zechariah; your prayer has been heard. Your wife Elizabeth will bear you a son, and you are to give him the name John. **14**He will be a joy and delight to you, and many will rejoice because of his birth, **15**for he will be great in the sight of the Lord. He is never to take wine or other fermented drink, and he will be filled with the Holy Spirit even from birth.*a* **16**Many of the people of Israel will he bring back to the Lord their God. **17**And he will go on before the Lord, in the spirit and power of Elijah, to turn the hearts of the fathers to their children and the disobedient to the wisdom of the righteous—to make ready a people prepared for the Lord."

18Zechariah asked the angel, "How can I be sure of this? I am an old man and my wife is well along in years."

19The angel answered, "I am Gabriel. I stand in the presence of God, and I have been sent to speak to you and to tell you this good news. **20**And now you will be silent and not able to speak until the day this happens, because you did not believe my words, which will come true at their proper time."

21Meanwhile, the people were waiting for Zechariah and wondering why he stayed so long in the temple. **22**When he came out, he could not speak to them. They realized he had seen a vision in the temple, for he kept making signs to them but remained unable to speak.

23When his time of service was completed, he returned home. **24**After this his wife Elizabeth became pregnant and for five months remained in seclusion. **25**"The Lord has done this for me," she said. "In these days he has shown his favor and taken away my disgrace among the people."

The Birth of Jesus Foretold

26In the sixth month, God sent the angel Gabriel to Nazareth, a town in Galilee, **27**to a virgin pledged to be married to a man named Joseph, a descendant of David. The virgin's name was Mary. **28**The angel went to her and said, "Greetings, you who are highly favored! The Lord is with you."

29Mary was greatly troubled at his words and wondered what kind of greeting this might be. **30**But the angel said to her, "Do not be afraid, Mary, you have found favor with God. **31**You will be with child and give birth to a son, and you are to give him the name Jesus. **32**He will be great and will be called the Son of the Most High. The Lord God will give him the throne of his father David, **33**and he will reign over the house of Jacob forever; his kingdom will never end."

34"How will this be," Mary asked the angel, "since I am a virgin?"

35The angel answered, "The Holy Spirit will come upon you, and the power of the Most High will overshadow you. So the holy one to be born will be called*b* the Son of God. **36**Even Elizabeth your relative is going to have a child in her old age, and she who was said to be barren is in her sixth month. **37**For nothing is impossible with God."

38"I am the Lord's servant," Mary answered. "May it be to me as you have said." Then the angel left her.

Mary Visits Elizabeth

39At that time Mary got ready and hurried to a town in the hill country of Judea, **40**where she entered Zechariah's home and greeted Elizabeth. **41**When Elizabeth heard Mary's greeting, the baby leaped in her womb, and Elizabeth was filled with the Holy Spirit. **42**In a loud voice she exclaimed: "Blessed are you among women, and blessed is the child you will bear! **43**But why am I so favored, that the mother of my Lord should come to me? **44**As soon as the sound of your greeting reached my ears, the baby in my womb leaped for joy. **45**Blessed is she who has believed that what the Lord has said to her will be accomplished!"

---

a15 Or *from his mother's womb*   *b35* Or *So the child to be born will be called holy,*

Mary's Song

⁴⁶And Mary said:

"My soul glorifies the Lord
⁴⁷ and my spirit rejoices in God my
Savior,
⁴⁸for he has been mindful
of the humble state of his servant.
From now on all generations will call
me blessed,
⁴⁹ for the Mighty One has done great
things for me—
holy is his name.
⁵⁰His mercy extends to those who fear
him,
from generation to generation.
⁵¹He has performed mighty deeds with
his arm;
he has scattered those who are
proud in their inmost
thoughts.
⁵²He has brought down rulers from
their thrones
but has lifted up the humble.

⁵³He has filled the hungry with good
things
but has sent the rich away empty.
⁵⁴He has helped his servant Israel,
remembering to be merciful
⁵⁵to Abraham and his descendants
forever,
even as he said to our fathers."

⁵⁶Mary stayed with Elizabeth for
about three months and then returned
home.

The Birth of John the Baptist

⁵⁷When it was time for Elizabeth to
have her baby, she gave birth to a son.
⁵⁸Her neighbors and relatives heard that
the Lord had shown her great mercy,
and they shared her joy.
⁵⁹On the eighth day they came to circumcise the child, and they were going
to name him after his father Zechariah,
⁶⁰but his mother spoke up and said,
"No! He is to be called John."
⁶¹They said to her, "There is no one

=====< **FRIDAY** >=====

VERSE:	AUTHOR:	PASSAGE:
Luke 1:35	Luci Shaw	Luke 1:26–38

Virgin

As if until that moment
nothing real
had happened since creation

As if outside the world were empty
so that she and he were all
there was—he mover, she moved upon

As if her submission were the most
dynamic of all works; as if
no one had ever said Yes like that

As if one day the sun had no place
in all the universe to pour its gold
but her small room.

ADDITIONAL SCRIPTURE READINGS:
Isaiah 7:14; Philippians 2:6–7

Go to page 75 for your next devotional reading.

among your relatives who has that name."

⁶²Then they made signs to his father, to find out what he would like to name the child. ⁶³He asked for a writing tablet, and to everyone's astonishment he wrote, "His name is John." ⁶⁴Immediately his mouth was opened and his tongue was loosed, and he began to speak, praising God. ⁶⁵The neighbors were all filled with awe, and throughout the hill country of Judea people were talking about all these things. ⁶⁶Everyone who heard this wondered about it, asking, "What then is this child going to be?" For the Lord's hand was with him.

Zechariah's Song

⁶⁷His father Zechariah was filled with the Holy Spirit and prophesied:

⁶⁸"Praise be to the Lord, the God of
    Israel,
    because he has come and has
       redeemed his people.
⁶⁹He has raised up a horn[a] of
       salvation for us
    in the house of his servant David
⁷⁰(as he said through his holy
       prophets of long ago),
⁷¹salvation from our enemies
    and from the hand of all who hate
       us—
⁷²to show mercy to our fathers
    and to remember his holy
       covenant,
⁷³   the oath he swore to our father
       Abraham:
⁷⁴to rescue us from the hand of our
       enemies,
    and to enable us to serve him
       without fear
⁷⁵   in holiness and righteousness
       before him all our days.

⁷⁶And you, my child, will be called a
    prophet of the Most High;
    for you will go on before the Lord
       to prepare the way for him,
⁷⁷to give his people the knowledge of
    salvation
    through the forgiveness of their
       sins,
⁷⁸because of the tender mercy of our
    God,

    by which the rising sun will come
       to us from heaven
⁷⁹to shine on those living in darkness
    and in the shadow of death,
    to guide our feet into the path of
       peace."

⁸⁰And the child grew and became strong in spirit; and he lived in the desert until he appeared publicly to Israel.

The Birth of Jesus

2 In those days Caesar Augustus issued a decree that a census should be taken of the entire Roman world. ²(This was the first census that took place while Quirinius was governor of Syria.) ³And everyone went to his own town to register.

⁴So Joseph also went up from the town of Nazareth in Galilee to Judea, to Bethlehem the town of David, because he belonged to the house and line of David. ⁵He went there to register with Mary, who was pledged to be married to him and was expecting a child. ⁶While they were there, the time came for the baby to be born, ⁷and she gave birth to her firstborn, a son. She wrapped him in cloths and placed him in a manger, because there was no room for them in the inn.

The Shepherds and the Angels

⁸And there were shepherds living out in the fields nearby, keeping watch over their flocks at night. ⁹An angel of the Lord appeared to them, and the glory of the Lord shone around them, and they were terrified. ¹⁰But the angel said to them, "Do not be afraid. I bring you good news of great joy that will be for all the people. ¹¹Today in the town of David a Savior has been born to you; he is Christ[b] the Lord. ¹²This will be a sign to you: You will find a baby wrapped in cloths and lying in a manger."

¹³Suddenly a great company of the heavenly host appeared with the angel, praising God and saying,

¹⁴"Glory to God in the highest,
    and on earth peace to men on
       whom his favor rests."

¹⁵When the angels had left them and

ᵃ69 Horn here symbolizes strength.   ᵇ11 Or Messiah. "The Christ" (Greek) and "the Messiah" (Hebrew) both mean "the Anointed One"; also in verse 26.

WEEKENDING

RECALL

We are the beneficiaries of God's two
ways of revealing himself. His special
revelation, through Scripture and Jesus
Christ, shows us how God looks and
acts; his general revelation is the whole
universe, the manuscript in which the
Creator has written his character and
signed his name.

So I take comfort not just from the
words on a page but also from a different message—the images I see written
on the sky, the configurations of a flock
of birds, the gift of a glossy chestnut. In
dew, rocks, rain, flowers, finches I see
divine "syllables of light and color" that
say, "I care for you." The deer and the
great blue heron, daily visitors to my
woodland home, remind me of how
wild things find their way through the
wilderness, as I do, guided by God.

Luci Shaw

RECHARGE

Saturday: Luke 12:22–34
Sunday: Psalm 19

*Go to page 76 for your next
devotional reading.*

gone into heaven, the shepherds said to one another, "Let's go to Bethlehem and see this thing that has happened, which the Lord has told us about."

¹⁶So they hurried off and found Mary and Joseph, and the baby, who was lying in the manger. ¹⁷When they had seen him, they spread the word concerning what had been told them about this child, ¹⁸and all who heard it were amazed at what the shepherds said to them. ¹⁹But Mary treasured up all these things and pondered them in her heart. ²⁰The shepherds returned, glorifying and praising God for all the things they had heard and seen, which were just as they had been told.

Jesus Presented in the Temple

²¹On the eighth day, when it was time to circumcise him, he was named Jesus, the name the angel had given him before he had been conceived.

²²When the time of their purification according to the Law of Moses had been completed, Joseph and Mary took him to Jerusalem to present him to the Lord ²³(as it is written in the Law of the Lord, "Every firstborn male is to be consecrat-

---

MONDAY

VERSE:	AUTHOR:	PASSAGE:
Luke 2:19	Mary C. & Robert G. Wells, Judy & Ken Gire	Luke 2:1–20

This Little Boy

Dear Lord,

I want this little boy to know how much I love him. I want him to know how much joy he has brought to my life. I realize, Lord, that he won't understand these things, at least not fully, until someday when he has children of his own. But Lord, help him even now to understand this: Help him to know how much he is wanted.

Help me to show him how much. By the sparkle of delight in my eyes when I smile at him. By how quick I am to drop a mother's chores and play with him. By the unhurried way I read him stories, even stories I've read to him a hundred times before. Especially those stories, Lord, because they will create such a vivid memory for him.

Help me to give this boy a happy childhood, filled with late nights and pillow fights and stories read by flashlight under his covers. May his mornings be filled with building forts, his noons with peanut butter sandwiches eaten in a tree house and his afternoons with baseball with the neighbor kids.

May his childhood be filled with such happy times, Lord, that when he looks back on them, twenty, thirty, forty years hence, the memories will bring a smile to his face and a reassurance to his heart that he was wanted, and that he was loved.

ADDITIONAL SCRIPTURE READINGS:
Psalm 127; Matthew 19:14; Luke 2:51–52

Go to page 78 for your next devotional reading.

ed to the Lord"[a]), 24and to offer a sacrifice in keeping with what is said in the Law of the Lord: "a pair of doves or two young pigeons."[b]

25Now there was a man in Jerusalem called Simeon, who was righteous and devout. He was waiting for the consolation of Israel, and the Holy Spirit was upon him. 26It had been revealed to him by the Holy Spirit that he would not die before he had seen the Lord's Christ. 27Moved by the Spirit, he went into the temple courts. When the parents brought in the child Jesus to do for him what the custom of the Law required, 28Simeon took him in his arms and praised God, saying:

29"Sovereign Lord, as you have
          promised,
     you now dismiss[c] your servant in
          peace.
30For my eyes have seen your
          salvation,
31   which you have prepared in the
          sight of all people,
32a light for revelation to the Gentiles
     and for glory to your people
          Israel."

33The child's father and mother marveled at what was said about him. 34Then Simeon blessed them and said to Mary, his mother: "This child is destined to cause the falling and rising of many in Israel, and to be a sign that will be spoken against, 35so that the thoughts of many hearts will be revealed. And a sword will pierce your own soul too."

36There was also a prophetess, Anna, the daughter of Phanuel, of the tribe of Asher. She was very old; she had lived with her husband seven years after her marriage, 37and then was a widow until she was eighty-four.[d] She never left the temple but worshiped night and day, fasting and praying. 38Coming up to them at that very moment, she gave thanks to God and spoke about the child to all who were looking forward to the redemption of Jerusalem.

39When Joseph and Mary had done everything required by the Law of the Lord, they returned to Galilee to their own town of Nazareth. 40And the child grew and became strong; he was filled with wisdom, and the grace of God was upon him.

The Boy Jesus at the Temple

41Every year his parents went to Jerusalem for the Feast of the Passover. 42When he was twelve years old, they went up to the Feast, according to the custom. 43After the Feast was over, while his parents were returning home, the boy Jesus stayed behind in Jerusalem, but they were unaware of it. 44Thinking he was in their company, they traveled on for a day. Then they began looking for him among their relatives and friends. 45When they did not find him, they went back to Jerusalem to look for him. 46After three days they found him in the temple courts, sitting among the teachers, listening to them and asking them questions. 47Everyone who heard him was amazed at his understanding and his answers. 48When his parents saw him, they were astonished. His mother said to him, "Son, why have you treated us like this? Your father and I have been anxiously searching for you."

49"Why were you searching for me?" he asked. "Didn't you know I had to be in my Father's house?" 50But they did not understand what he was saying to them.

51Then he went down to Nazareth with them and was obedient to them. But his mother treasured all these things in her heart. 52And Jesus grew in wisdom and stature, and in favor with God and men.

John the Baptist Prepares the Way

3 In the fifteenth year of the reign of Tiberius Caesar—when Pontius Pilate was governor of Judea, Herod tetrarch of Galilee, his brother Philip tetrarch of Iturea and Traconitis, and Lysanias tetrarch of Abilene— 2during the high priesthood of Annas and Caiaphas, the word of God came to John son of Zechariah in the desert. 3He went into all the country around the Jordan, preaching a baptism of repentance for the forgiveness of sins. 4As is written in the book of the words of Isaiah the prophet:

     "A voice of one calling in the desert,

---

[a]23 Exodus 13:2,12   [b]24 Lev. 12:8   [c]29 Or promised, / now dismiss   [d]37 Or widow for eighty-four years

'Prepare the way for the Lord,
    make straight paths for him.
[5]Every valley shall be filled in,
    every mountain and hill made low.
The crooked roads shall become
    straight,
    the rough ways smooth.
[6]And all mankind will see God's
    salvation.'"[a]

[7]John said to the crowds coming out
to be baptized by him, "You brood of
vipers! Who warned you to flee from the
coming wrath? [8]Produce fruit in keeping
with repentance. And do not begin to
say to yourselves, 'We have Abraham
as our father.' For I tell you that out of
these stones God can raise up children
for Abraham. [9]The ax is already at the
root of the trees, and every tree that does
not produce good fruit will be cut down
and thrown into the fire."

[10]"What should we do then?" the
crowd asked.

[11]John answered, "The man with two
tunics should share with him who has

[a]6 Isaiah 40:3-5

TUESDAY

VERSE:	AUTHOR:	PASSAGE:
Luke 2:46	Marcia Hollis	Luke 2:41–52

Waiting on Grace

The story of Jesus in the temple can teach us something about
our own relationship with God. Mary and Joseph had made
their plans to return to Nazareth. They set off early in the
morning with their family and traveled for a whole day without Jesus, assuming he was with them. Sometimes, I think we
tend to do the same thing. We make our plans, tell God what we
intend to do, and then travel for quite a while before we realize that
he simply isn't with us! It isn't that he leaves us on purpose
because he wants to embarrass us or show us who's really the
boss. It's just that in the rush and hurry to get something done, we
may ride roughshod over love, humility or what we know to be
God's will for us, and we leave him far behind, lost in the crowd.

Brother Lawrence provides beautiful insight about this very
thing in his book, *The Practice of the Presence of God*. When writing
to a friend about a young woman in spiritual difficulties, the ven-
erable monk assessed her situation this way: "She seems to me full
of good will, but she would go faster than grace."

We cannot go faster than grace. If we try to go ahead of God's
enabling power, then we, like Joseph and Mary, will have to retrace
our steps. Certainly the goal may lie clearly ahead. It may be purely
spiritual, or it may be a more immediate piece of practical work. In
either case, we can't go at it any faster than God wants us to. We
have to wait and learn the lessons on the road. If God will not go
ahead with us, we must wait and go with God.

ADDITIONAL SCRIPTURE READINGS:
Psalm 27:14; Psalm 37:5

Go to page 82 for your next devotional reading.

none, and the one who has food should do the same."

[12] Tax collectors also came to be baptized. "Teacher," they asked, "what should we do?"

[13] "Don't collect any more than you are required to," he told them.

[14] Then some soldiers asked him, "And what should we do?"

He replied, "Don't extort money and don't accuse people falsely—be content with your pay."

[15] The people were waiting expectantly and were all wondering in their hearts if John might possibly be the Christ.[a] [16] John answered them all, "I baptize you with[b] water. But one more powerful than I will come, the thongs of whose sandals I am not worthy to untie. He will baptize you with the Holy Spirit and with fire. [17] His winnowing fork is in his hand to clear his threshing floor and to gather the wheat into his barn, but he will burn up the chaff with unquenchable fire." [18] And with many other words John exhorted the people and preached the good news to them.

[19] But when John rebuked Herod the tetrarch because of Herodias, his brother's wife, and all the other evil things he had done, [20] Herod added this to them all: He locked John up in prison.

The Baptism and Genealogy of Jesus

[21] When all the people were being baptized, Jesus was baptized too. And as he was praying, heaven was opened [22] and the Holy Spirit descended on him in bodily form like a dove. And a voice came from heaven: "You are my Son, whom I love; with you I am well pleased."

[23] Now Jesus himself was about thirty years old when he began his ministry. He was the son, so it was thought, of Joseph,

the son of Heli, [24] the son of Matthat,
the son of Levi, the son of Melki, the son of Jannai, the son of Joseph,
[25] the son of Mattathias, the son of Amos,
the son of Nahum, the son of Esli,

the son of Naggai, [26] the son of Maath,
the son of Mattathias, the son of Semein,
the son of Josech, the son of Joda,
[27] the son of Joanan, the son of Rhesa,
the son of Zerubbabel, the son of Shealtiel,
the son of Neri, [28] the son of Melki,
the son of Addi, the son of Cosam,
the son of Elmadam, the son of Er,
[29] the son of Joshua, the son of Eliezer,
the son of Jorim, the son of Matthat,
the son of Levi, [30] the son of Simeon,
the son of Judah, the son of Joseph,
the son of Jonam, the son of Eliakim,
[31] the son of Melea, the son of Menna,
the son of Mattatha, the son of Nathan,
the son of David, [32] the son of Jesse,
the son of Obed, the son of Boaz,
the son of Salmon,[c] the son of Nahshon,
[33] the son of Amminadab, the son of Ram,[d]
the son of Hezron, the son of Perez,
the son of Judah, [34] the son of Jacob,
the son of Isaac, the son of Abraham,
the son of Terah, the son of Nahor,
[35] the son of Serug, the son of Reu,
the son of Peleg, the son of Eber,
the son of Shelah, [36] the son of Cainan,
the son of Arphaxad, the son of Shem,
the son of Noah, the son of Lamech,
[37] the son of Methuselah, the son of Enoch,
the son of Jared, the son of Mahalalel,
the son of Kenan, [38] the son of Enosh,
the son of Seth, the son of Adam,
the son of God.

[a]15 Or *Messiah*   [b]16 Or *in*   [c]32 Some early manuscripts *Sala*   [d]33 Some manuscripts *Amminadab, the son of Admin, the son of Arni*; other manuscripts vary widely.

The Temptation of Jesus

4 Jesus, full of the Holy Spirit, returned from the Jordan and was led by the Spirit in the desert, ²where for forty days he was tempted by the devil. He ate nothing during those days, and at the end of them he was hungry.

³The devil said to him, "If you are the Son of God, tell this stone to become bread."

⁴Jesus answered, "It is written: 'Man does not live on bread alone.'ᵃ"

⁵The devil led him up to a high place and showed him in an instant all the kingdoms of the world. ⁶And he said to him, "I will give you all their authority and splendor, for it has been given to me, and I can give it to anyone I want to. ⁷So if you worship me, it will all be yours."

⁸Jesus answered, "It is written: 'Worship the Lord your God and serve him only.'ᵇ"

⁹The devil led him to Jerusalem and had him stand on the highest point of the temple. "If you are the Son of God," he said, "throw yourself down from here. ¹⁰For it is written:

" 'He will command his angels
        concerning you
    to guard you carefully;
¹¹they will lift you up in their hands,
    so that you will not strike your
        foot against a stone.'ᶜ"

¹²Jesus answered, "It says: 'Do not put the Lord your God to the test.'ᵈ"

¹³When the devil had finished all this tempting, he left him until an opportune time.

Jesus Rejected at Nazareth

¹⁴Jesus returned to Galilee in the power of the Spirit, and news about him spread through the whole countryside. ¹⁵He taught in their synagogues, and everyone praised him.

¹⁶He went to Nazareth, where he had been brought up, and on the Sabbath day he went into the synagogue, as was his custom. And he stood up to read. ¹⁷The scroll of the prophet Isaiah was handed to him. Unrolling it, he found the place where it is written:

¹⁸"The Spirit of the Lord is on me,
    because he has anointed me
    to preach good news to the poor.
He has sent me to proclaim freedom
        for the prisoners
    and recovery of sight for the blind,
    to release the oppressed,
¹⁹   to proclaim the year of the Lord's
        favor."ᵉ

²⁰Then he rolled up the scroll, gave it back to the attendant and sat down. The eyes of everyone in the synagogue were fastened on him, ²¹and he began by saying to them, "Today this scripture is fulfilled in your hearing."

²²All spoke well of him and were amazed at the gracious words that came from his lips. "Isn't this Joseph's son?" they asked.

²³Jesus said to them, "Surely you will quote this proverb to me: 'Physician, heal yourself! Do here in your hometown what we have heard that you did in Capernaum.' "

²⁴"I tell you the truth," he continued, "no prophet is accepted in his hometown. ²⁵I assure you that there were many widows in Israel in Elijah's time, when the sky was shut for three and a half years and there was a severe famine throughout the land. ²⁶Yet Elijah was not sent to any of them, but to a widow in Zarephath in the region of Sidon. ²⁷And there were many in Israel with leprosyᶠ in the time of Elisha the prophet, yet not one of them was cleansed—only Naaman the Syrian."

²⁸All the people in the synagogue were furious when they heard this. ²⁹They got up, drove him out of the town, and took him to the brow of the hill on which the town was built, in order to throw him down the cliff. ³⁰But he walked right through the crowd and went on his way.

Jesus Drives Out an Evil Spirit

³¹Then he went down to Capernaum, a town in Galilee, and on the Sabbath began to teach the people. ³²They were amazed at his teaching, because his message had authority.

³³In the synagogue there was a man possessed by a demon, an evilᵍ spirit. He cried out at the top of his voice,

---

ᵃ4 Deut. 8:3   ᵇ8 Deut. 6:13   ᶜ11 Psalm 91:11,12   ᵈ12 Deut. 6:16   ᵉ19 Isaiah 61:1,2
ᶠ27 The Greek word was used for various diseases affecting the skin—not necessarily leprosy.
ᵍ33 Greek unclean; also in verse 36

[34]"Ha! What do you want with us, Jesus of Nazareth? Have you come to destroy us? I know who you are—the Holy One of God!"

[35]"Be quiet!" Jesus said sternly. "Come out of him!" Then the demon threw the man down before them all and came out without injuring him.

[36]All the people were amazed and said to each other, "What is this teaching? With authority and power he gives orders to evil spirits and they come out!" [37]And the news about him spread throughout the surrounding area.

Jesus Heals Many

[38]Jesus left the synagogue and went to the home of Simon. Now Simon's mother-in-law was suffering from a high fever, and they asked Jesus to help her. [39]So he bent over her and rebuked the fever, and it left her. She got up at once and began to wait on them.

[40]When the sun was setting, the people brought to Jesus all who had various kinds of sickness, and laying his hands on each one, he healed them. [41]Moreover, demons came out of many people, shouting, "You are the Son of God!" But he rebuked them and would not allow them to speak, because they knew he was the Christ.[a]

[42]At daybreak Jesus went out to a solitary place. The people were looking for him and when they came to where he was, they tried to keep him from leaving them. [43]But he said, "I must preach the good news of the kingdom of God to the other towns also, because that is why I was sent." [44]And he kept on preaching in the synagogues of Judea.[b]

The Calling of the First Disciples

5 One day as Jesus was standing by the Lake of Gennesaret,[c] with the people crowding around him and listening to the word of God, [2]he saw at the water's edge two boats, left there by the fishermen, who were washing their nets. [3]He got into one of the boats, the one belonging to Simon, and asked him to put out a little from shore. Then he sat down and taught the people from the boat.

[4]When he had finished speaking, he said to Simon, "Put out into deep water, and let down[d] the nets for a catch."

[5]Simon answered, "Master, we've worked hard all night and haven't caught anything. But because you say so, I will let down the nets."

[6]When they had done so, they caught such a large number of fish that their nets began to break. [7]So they signaled their partners in the other boat to come and help them, and they came and filled both boats so full that they began to sink.

[8]When Simon Peter saw this, he fell at Jesus' knees and said, "Go away from me, Lord; I am a sinful man!" [9]For he and all his companions were astonished at the catch of fish they had taken, [10]and so were James and John, the sons of Zebedee, Simon's partners.

Then Jesus said to Simon, "Don't be afraid; from now on you will catch men." [11]So they pulled their boats up on shore, left everything and followed him.

The Man With Leprosy

[12]While Jesus was in one of the towns, a man came along who was covered with leprosy.[e] When he saw Jesus, he fell with his face to the ground and begged him, "Lord, if you are willing, you can make me clean."

[13]Jesus reached out his hand and touched the man. "I am willing," he said. "Be clean!" And immediately the leprosy left him.

[14]Then Jesus ordered him, "Don't tell anyone, but go, show yourself to the priest and offer the sacrifices that Moses commanded for your cleansing, as a testimony to them."

[15]Yet the news about him spread all the more, so that crowds of people came to hear him and to be healed of their sicknesses. [16]But Jesus often withdrew to lonely places and prayed.

Jesus Heals a Paralytic

[17]One day as he was teaching, Pharisees and teachers of the law, who had come from every village of Galilee and from Judea and Jerusalem, were sitting there. And the power of the Lord was present for him to heal the sick. [18]Some men came carrying a paralytic on a mat

---

[a]41 Or *Messiah*   [b]44 Or *the land of the Jews*; some manuscripts *Galilee*   [c]1 That is, Sea of Galilee
[d]4 The Greek verb is plural.   [e]12 The Greek word was used for various diseases affecting the skin—not necessarily leprosy.

and tried to take him into the house to lay him before Jesus. **19**When they could not find a way to do this because of the crowd, they went up on the roof and lowered him on his mat through the tiles into the middle of the crowd, right in front of Jesus.

20When Jesus saw their faith, he said, "Friend, your sins are forgiven."

21The Pharisees and the teachers of the law began thinking to themselves, "Who is this fellow who speaks blasphemy? Who can forgive sins but God alone?"

22Jesus knew what they were thinking and asked, "Why are you thinking these things in your hearts? **23**Which is easier: to say, 'Your sins are forgiven,' or to say, 'Get up and walk'? **24**But that you may know that the Son of Man has authority on earth to forgive sins. . . ." He said to the paralyzed man, "I tell you, get up, take your mat and go home." **25**Immediately he stood up in front of them, took what he had been lying on and went home praising God. **26**Everyone

was amazed and gave praise to God. They were filled with awe and said, "We have seen remarkable things today."

The Calling of Levi

27After this, Jesus went out and saw a tax collector by the name of Levi sitting at his tax booth. "Follow me," Jesus said to him, **28**and Levi got up, left everything and followed him.

29Then Levi held a great banquet for Jesus at his house, and a large crowd of tax collectors and others were eating with them. **30**But the Pharisees and the teachers of the law who belonged to their sect complained to his disciples, "Why do you eat and drink with tax collectors and 'sinners'?"

31Jesus answered them, "It is not the healthy who need a doctor, but the sick. **32**I have not come to call the righteous, but sinners to repentance."

Jesus Questioned About Fasting

33They said to him, "John's disciples often fast and pray, and so do the disci-

---

WEDNESDAY

VERSE:	AUTHOR:	PASSAGE:
Luke 5:16	Joan C. Webb	Luke 5:12–16

Taking Time to Replenish

Jesus' days were filled with counseling the confused, encouraging the disappointed, hugging children, protecting the abused, feeding the hungry, questioning false teaching, challenging the weather, crusading for justice and fair play, withstanding ridicule, teaching his staff of apostles and loving his opponents. Increasing crowds clamored around Jesus daily.

Jesus was extremely busy. Yet he knew the limitations of his human body and soul. He realized he needed to separate himself from the day-to-day demands. Although Jesus acknowledged the people's tremendous need, he did not call himself selfish when he *often* withdrew to replenish his mind and spirit.

Learning to take care of ourselves is worthwhile and nurturing. Jesus did it; so can we.

ADDITIONAL SCRIPTURE READINGS:
Matthew 14:23; Mark 6:30; Hebrews 4:8–10

Go to page 84 for your next devotional reading.

ples of the Pharisees, but yours go on eating and drinking."

34Jesus answered, "Can you make the guests of the bridegroom fast while he is with them? **35**But the time will come when the bridegroom will be taken from them; in those days they will fast."

36He told them this parable: "No one tears a patch from a new garment and sews it on an old one. If he does, he will have torn the new garment, and the patch from the new will not match the old. **37**And no one pours new wine into old wineskins. If he does, the new wine will burst the skins, the wine will run out and the wineskins will be ruined. **38**No, new wine must be poured into new wineskins. **39**And no one after drinking old wine wants the new, for he says, 'The old is better.'"

Lord of the Sabbath

6 One Sabbath Jesus was going through the grainfields, and his disciples began to pick some heads of grain, rub them in their hands and eat the kernels. **2**Some of the Pharisees asked, "Why are you doing what is unlawful on the Sabbath?"

3Jesus answered them, "Have you never read what David did when he and his companions were hungry? **4**He entered the house of God, and taking the consecrated bread, he ate what is lawful only for priests to eat. And he also gave some to his companions." **5**Then Jesus said to them, "The Son of Man is Lord of the Sabbath."

6On another Sabbath he went into the synagogue and was teaching, and a man was there whose right hand was shriveled. **7**The Pharisees and the teachers of the law were looking for a reason to accuse Jesus, so they watched him closely to see if he would heal on the Sabbath. **8**But Jesus knew what they were thinking and said to the man with the shriveled hand, "Get up and stand in front of everyone." So he got up and stood there.

9Then Jesus said to them, "I ask you, which is lawful on the Sabbath: to do good or to do evil, to save life or to destroy it?"

10He looked around at them all, and then said to the man, "Stretch out your hand." He did so, and his hand was completely restored. **11**But they were fu-

rious and began to discuss with one another what they might do to Jesus.

The Twelve Apostles

12One of those days Jesus went out to a mountainside to pray, and spent the night praying to God. **13**When morning came, he called his disciples to him and chose twelve of them, whom he also designated apostles: **14**Simon (whom he named Peter), his brother Andrew, James, John, Philip, Bartholomew, **15**Matthew, Thomas, James son of Alphaeus, Simon who was called the Zealot, **16**Judas son of James, and Judas Iscariot, who became a traitor.

Blessings and Woes

17He went down with them and stood on a level place. A large crowd of his disciples was there and a great number of people from all over Judea, from Jerusalem, and from the coast of Tyre and Sidon, **18**who had come to hear him and to be healed of their diseases. Those troubled by evil[a] spirits were cured, **19**and the people all tried to touch him, because power was coming from him and healing them all.

20Looking at his disciples, he said:

"Blessed are you who are poor,
   for yours is the kingdom of God.
21Blessed are you who hunger now,
   for you will be satisfied.
Blessed are you who weep now,
   for you will laugh.
22Blessed are you when men hate you,
   when they exclude you and insult
     you
   and reject your name as evil,
     because of the Son of Man.

23"Rejoice in that day and leap for joy, because great is your reward in heaven. For that is how their fathers treated the prophets.

24"But woe to you who are rich,
   for you have already received your
     comfort.
25Woe to you who are well fed now,
   for you will go hungry.
Woe to you who laugh now,
   for you will mourn and weep.
26Woe to you when all men speak well
     of you,

---

a18 Greek *unclean*

for that is how their fathers treated the false prophets.

Love for Enemies

27 "But I tell you who hear me: Love your enemies, do good to those who hate you, 28 bless those who curse you, pray for those who mistreat you. 29 If someone strikes you on one cheek, turn to him the other also. If someone takes your cloak, do not stop him from taking your tunic. 30 Give to everyone who asks you, and if anyone takes what belongs to you, do not demand it back. 31 Do to others as you would have them do to you.

THURSDAY

VERSE:	AUTHOR:	PASSAGE:
Luke 6:31	Marcia Hollis	Luke 6:27-31

Shock Absorbers

Considering the increasing violence around us, what our society needs is some good, heavy-duty shock absorbers. If only we could wrap everybody in felt pads before they went out for the day! Unfortunately . . . we are enormously complicated creatures. We feel injuries not only in our bodies but also in our emotions. And sometimes deep wounds in our inner selves fester for years, causing us to reach out and hurt anyone who comes near us. One painful blow to our psyche can create the motive for innumerable blows outward in the years to come.

The Old Testament law was very explicit: an eye for an eye, and a tooth for a tooth (Exodus 21:24). Harsh as it seems to us now, this principle was a vast improvement. Before then, a person's life might have been demanded for that eye or tooth, or two eyes might have been put out in exchange for the loss of one. Again and again our human nature wants to "teach people a lesson" or make things worse for them than they made it for us. We see revenge as a way of getting back, of making ourselves whole again. But it never works.

The solution Jesus offers is radical. There is no question of revenge or even bare restitution. He suggests simply that we become the shock absorbers of this world.

To receive a blow and to refuse to pass it on is an act that requires extraordinary generosity. For most people, it does not come naturally. We are too hard and resistant to be able to absorb the effect of an injury before we pass it on to a neighbor. We must become softer, gentler, more loving people, receiving a blow but unable by the fabric of our lives to transmit the force of it.

Love and forgiveness are the special vocation of the Christian, and when we exercise them we are able to find healing for our own wounds and offer balm for the healing of others.

ADDITIONAL SCRIPTURE READINGS:
Isaiah 53:5; Galatians 6:2; Ephesians 4:29–32

Go to page 90 for your next devotional reading.

³²"If you love those who love you, what credit is that to you? Even 'sinners' love those who love them. ³³And if you do good to those who are good to you, what credit is that to you? Even 'sinners' do that. ³⁴And if you lend to those from whom you expect repayment, what credit is that to you? Even 'sinners' lend to 'sinners,' expecting to be repaid in full. ³⁵But love your enemies, do good to them, and lend to them without expecting to get anything back. Then your reward will be great, and you will be sons of the Most High, because he is kind to the ungrateful and wicked. ³⁶Be merciful, just as your Father is merciful.

Judging Others

³⁷"Do not judge, and you will not be judged. Do not condemn, and you will not be condemned. Forgive, and you will be forgiven. ³⁸Give, and it will be given to you. A good measure, pressed down, shaken together and running over, will be poured into your lap. For with the measure you use, it will be measured to you."

³⁹He also told them this parable: "Can a blind man lead a blind man? Will they not both fall into a pit? ⁴⁰A student is not above his teacher, but everyone who is fully trained will be like his teacher.

⁴¹"Why do you look at the speck of sawdust in your brother's eye and pay no attention to the plank in your own eye? ⁴²How can you say to your brother, 'Brother, let me take the speck out of your eye,' when you yourself fail to see the plank in your own eye? You hypocrite, first take the plank out of your eye, and then you will see clearly to remove the speck from your brother's eye.

A Tree and Its Fruit

⁴³"No good tree bears bad fruit, nor does a bad tree bear good fruit. ⁴⁴Each tree is recognized by its own fruit. People do not pick figs from thornbushes, or grapes from briers. ⁴⁵The good man brings good things out of the good stored up in his heart, and the evil man brings evil things out of the evil stored up in his heart. For out of the overflow of his heart his mouth speaks.

The Wise and Foolish Builders

⁴⁶"Why do you call me, 'Lord, Lord,' and do not do what I say? ⁴⁷I will show you what he is like who comes to me and hears my words and puts them into practice. ⁴⁸He is like a man building a house, who dug down deep and laid the foundation on rock. When a flood came, the torrent struck that house but could not shake it, because it was well built. ⁴⁹But the one who hears my words and does not put them into practice is like a man who built a house on the ground without a foundation. The moment the torrent struck that house, it collapsed and its destruction was complete."

The Faith of the Centurion

7 When Jesus had finished saying all this in the hearing of the people, he entered Capernaum ²There a centurion's servant, whom his master valued highly, was sick and about to die. ³The centurion heard of Jesus and sent some elders of the Jews to him, asking him to come and heal his servant. ⁴When they came to Jesus, they pleaded earnestly with him, "This man deserves to have you do this, ⁵because he loves our nation and has built our synagogue." ⁶So Jesus went with them.

He was not far from the house when the centurion sent friends to say to him: "Lord, don't trouble yourself, for I do not deserve to have you come under my roof. ⁷That is why I did not even consider myself worthy to come to you. But say the word, and my servant will be healed. ⁸For I myself am a man under authority, with soldiers under me. I tell this one, 'Go,' and he goes; and that one, 'Come,' and he comes. I say to my servant, 'Do this,' and he does it."

⁹When Jesus heard this, he was amazed at him, and turning to the crowd following him, he said, "I tell you, I have not found such great faith even in Israel." ¹⁰Then the men who had been sent returned to the house and found the servant well.

Jesus Raises a Widow's Son

¹¹Soon afterward, Jesus went to a town called Nain, and his disciples and a large crowd went along with him. ¹²As he approached the town gate, a dead person was being carried out—the only son of his mother, and she was a widow. And a large crowd from the town was with her. ¹³When the Lord saw her,

his heart went out to her and he said, "Don't cry."

14Then he went up and touched the coffin, and those carrying it stood still. He said, "Young man, I say to you, get up!" **15**The dead man sat up and began to talk, and Jesus gave him back to his mother.

16They were all filled with awe and praised God. "A great prophet has appeared among us," they said. "God has come to help his people." **17**This news about Jesus spread throughout Judea*a* and the surrounding country.

Jesus and John the Baptist

18John's disciples told him about all these things. Calling two of them, **19**he sent them to the Lord to ask, "Are you the one who was to come, or should we expect someone else?"

20When the men came to Jesus, they said, "John the Baptist sent us to you to ask, 'Are you the one who was to come, or should we expect someone else?'"

21At that very time Jesus cured many who had diseases, sicknesses and evil spirits, and gave sight to many who were blind. **22**So he replied to the messengers, "Go back and report to John what you have seen and heard: The blind receive sight, the lame walk, those who have leprosy*b* are cured, the deaf hear, the dead are raised, and the good news is preached to the poor. **23**Blessed is the man who does not fall away on account of me."

24After John's messengers left, Jesus began to speak to the crowd about John: "What did you go out into the desert to see? A reed swayed by the wind? **25**If not, what did you go out to see? A man dressed in fine clothes? No, those who wear expensive clothes and indulge in luxury are in palaces. **26**But what did you go out to see? A prophet? Yes, I tell you, and more than a prophet. **27**This is the one about whom it is written:

" 'I will send my messenger ahead
      of you,
    who will prepare your way before
      you.'*c*

28I tell you, among those born of women there is no one greater than John; yet

the one who is least in the kingdom of God is greater than he."

29(All the people, even the tax collectors, when they heard Jesus' words, acknowledged that God's way was right, because they had been baptized by John. **30**But the Pharisees and experts in the law rejected God's purpose for themselves, because they had not been baptized by John.)

31"To what, then, can I compare the people of this generation? What are they like? **32**They are like children sitting in the marketplace and calling out to each other:

" 'We played the flute for you,
      and you did not dance;
    we sang a dirge,
      and you did not cry.'

33For John the Baptist came neither eating bread nor drinking wine, and you say, 'He has a demon.' **34**The Son of Man came eating and drinking, and you say, 'Here is a glutton and a drunkard, a friend of tax collectors and "sinners."' **35**But wisdom is proved right by all her children."

Jesus Anointed by a Sinful Woman

36Now one of the Pharisees invited Jesus to have dinner with him, so he went to the Pharisee's house and reclined at the table. **37**When a woman who had lived a sinful life in that town learned that Jesus was eating at the Pharisee's house, she brought an alabaster jar of perfume, **38**and as she stood behind him at his feet weeping, she began to wet his feet with her tears. Then she wiped them with her hair, kissed them and poured perfume on them.

39When the Pharisee who had invited him saw this, he said to himself, "If this man were a prophet, he would know who is touching him and what kind of woman she is—that she is a sinner."

40Jesus answered him, "Simon, I have something to tell you."

"Tell me, teacher," he said.

41"Two men owed money to a certain moneylender. One owed him five hundred denarii,*d* and the other fifty. **42**Neither of them had the money to pay him

---

a 17 Or *the land of the Jews*   *b 22* The Greek word was used for various diseases affecting the skin—not necessarily leprosy.   *c 27* Mal. 3:1   *d 41* A denarius was a coin worth about a day's wages.

back, so he canceled the debts of both. Now which of them will love him more?"

43Simon replied, "I suppose the one who had the bigger debt canceled."

"You have judged correctly," Jesus said.

44Then he turned toward the woman and said to Simon, "Do you see this woman? I came into your house. You did not give me any water for my feet, but she wet my feet with her tears and wiped them with her hair. 45You did not give me a kiss, but this woman, from the time I entered, has not stopped kissing my feet. 46You did not put oil on my head, but she has poured perfume on my feet. 47Therefore, I tell you, her many sins have been forgiven—for she loved much. But he who has been forgiven little loves little."

48Then Jesus said to her, "Your sins are forgiven."

49The other guests began to say among themselves, "Who is this who even forgives sins?"

50Jesus said to the woman, "Your faith has saved you; go in peace."

The Parable of the Sower

8 After this, Jesus traveled about from one town and village to another, proclaiming the good news of the kingdom of God. The Twelve were with him, 2and also some women who had been cured of evil spirits and diseases: Mary (called Magdalene) from whom seven demons had come out; 3Joanna the wife of Cuza, the manager of Herod's household; Susanna; and many others. These women were helping to support them out of their own means.

4While a large crowd was gathering and people were coming to Jesus from town after town, he told this parable: 5"A farmer went out to sow his seed. As he was scattering the seed, some fell along the path; it was trampled on, and the birds of the air ate it up. 6Some fell on rock, and when it came up, the plants withered because they had no moisture. 7Other seed fell among thorns, which grew up with it and choked the plants. 8Still other seed fell on good soil. It came up and yielded a crop, a hundred times more than was sown."

When he said this, he called out, "He who has ears to hear, let him hear."

9His disciples asked him what this parable meant. 10He said, "The knowledge of the secrets of the kingdom of God has been given to you, but to others I speak in parables, so that,

" 'though seeing, they may not see;
　though hearing, they may not
　　understand.' [a]

11"This is the meaning of the parable: The seed is the word of God. 12Those along the path are the ones who hear, and then the devil comes and takes away the word from their hearts, so that they may not believe and be saved. 13Those on the rock are the ones who receive the word with joy when they hear it, but they have no root. They believe for a while, but in the time of testing they fall away. 14The seed that fell among thorns stands for those who hear, but as they go on their way they are choked by life's worries, riches and pleasures, and they do not mature. 15But the seed on good soil stands for those with a noble and good heart, who hear the word, retain it, and by persevering produce a crop.

A Lamp on a Stand

16"No one lights a lamp and hides it in a jar or puts it under a bed. Instead, he puts it on a stand, so that those who come in can see the light. 17For there is nothing hidden that will not be disclosed, and nothing concealed that will not be known or brought out into the open. 18Therefore consider carefully how you listen. Whoever has will be given more; whoever does not have, even what he thinks he has will be taken from him."

Jesus' Mother and Brothers

19Now Jesus' mother and brothers came to see him, but they were not able to get near him because of the crowd. 20Someone told him, "Your mother and brothers are standing outside, wanting to see you."

21He replied, "My mother and brothers are those who hear God's word and put it into practice."

a10 Isaiah 6:9

Jesus Calms the Storm

22One day Jesus said to his disciples, "Let's go over to the other side of the lake." So they got into a boat and set out. **23**As they sailed, he fell asleep. A squall came down on the lake, so that the boat was being swamped, and they were in great danger.

24The disciples went and woke him, saying, "Master, Master, we're going to drown!"

He got up and rebuked the wind and the raging waters; the storm subsided, and all was calm. **25**"Where is your faith?" he asked his disciples.

In fear and amazement they asked one another, "Who is this? He commands even the winds and the water, and they obey him."

The Healing of a Demon-possessed Man

26They sailed to the region of the Gerasenes,*a* which is across the lake from Galilee. **27**When Jesus stepped ashore, he was met by a demon-possessed man from the town. For a long time this man had not worn clothes or lived in a house, but had lived in the tombs. **28**When he saw Jesus, he cried out and fell at his feet, shouting at the top of his voice, "What do you want with me, Jesus, Son of the Most High God? I beg you, don't torture me!" **29**For Jesus had commanded the evil*b* spirit to come out of the man. Many times it had seized him, and though he was chained hand and foot and kept under guard, he had broken his chains and had been driven by the demon into solitary places.

30Jesus asked him, "What is your name?"

"Legion," he replied, because many demons had gone into him. **31**And they begged him repeatedly not to order them to go into the Abyss.

32A large herd of pigs was feeding there on the hillside. The demons begged Jesus to let them go into them, and he gave them permission. **33**When the demons came out of the man, they went into the pigs, and the herd rushed down the steep bank into the lake and was drowned.

34When those tending the pigs saw what had happened, they ran off and reported this in the town and countryside, **35**and the people went out to see what had happened. When they came to Jesus, they found the man from whom the demons had gone out, sitting at Jesus' feet, dressed and in his right mind; and they were afraid. **36**Those who had seen it told the people how the demon-possessed man had been cured. **37**Then all the people of the region of the Gerasenes asked Jesus to leave them, because they were overcome with fear. So he got into the boat and left.

38The man from whom the demons had gone out begged to go with him, but Jesus sent him away, saying, **39**"Return home and tell how much God has done for you." So the man went away and told all over town how much Jesus had done for him.

A Dead Girl and a Sick Woman

40Now when Jesus returned, a crowd welcomed him, for they were all expecting him. **41**Then a man named Jairus, a ruler of the synagogue, came and fell at Jesus' feet, pleading with him to come to his house **42**because his only daughter, a girl of about twelve, was dying.

As Jesus was on his way, the crowds almost crushed him. **43**And a woman was there who had been subject to bleeding for twelve years,*c* but no one could heal her. **44**She came up behind him and touched the edge of his cloak, and immediately her bleeding stopped.

45"Who touched me?" Jesus asked.

When they all denied it, Peter said, "Master, the people are crowding and pressing against you."

46But Jesus said, "Someone touched me; I know that power has gone out from me."

47Then the woman, seeing that she could not go unnoticed, came trembling and fell at his feet. In the presence of all the people, she told why she had touched him and how she had been instantly healed. **48**Then he said to her, "Daughter, your faith has healed you. Go in peace."

49While Jesus was still speaking, someone came from the house of Jairus, the synagogue ruler. "Your daughter is

---

a26 Some manuscripts *Gadarenes*; other manuscripts *Gergesenes*; also in verse 37   *b29* Greek *unclean*
c43 Many manuscripts *years, and she had spent all she had on doctors*

dead," he said. "Don't bother the teacher any more."

⁵⁰Hearing this, Jesus said to Jairus, "Don't be afraid; just believe, and she will be healed."

⁵¹When he arrived at the house of Jairus, he did not let anyone go in with him except Peter, John and James, and the child's father and mother. ⁵²Meanwhile, all the people were wailing and mourning for her. "Stop wailing," Jesus said. "She is not dead but asleep."

⁵³They laughed at him, knowing that she was dead. ⁵⁴But he took her by the hand and said, "My child, get up!" ⁵⁵Her spirit returned, and at once she stood up. Then Jesus told them to give her something to eat. ⁵⁶Her parents were astonished, but he ordered them not to tell anyone what had happened.

Jesus Sends Out the Twelve

9 When Jesus had called the Twelve together, he gave them power and authority to drive out all demons and to cure diseases, ²and he sent them out to preach the kingdom of God and to heal the sick. ³He told them: "Take nothing for the journey—no staff, no bag, no bread, no money, no extra tunic. ⁴Whatever house you enter, stay there until you leave that town. ⁵If people do not welcome you, shake the dust off your feet when you leave their town, as a testimony against them." ⁶So they set out and went from village to village, preaching the gospel and healing people everywhere.

⁷Now Herod the tetrarch heard about all that was going on. And he was perplexed, because some were saying that John had been raised from the dead, ⁸others that Elijah had appeared, and still others that one of the prophets of long ago had come back to life. ⁹But Herod said, "I beheaded John. Who, then, is this I hear such things about?" And he tried to see him.

Jesus Feeds the Five Thousand

¹⁰When the apostles returned, they reported to Jesus what they had done. Then he took them with him and they withdrew by themselves to a town called Bethsaida, ¹¹but the crowds learned about it and followed him. He welcomed them and spoke to them about the kingdom of God, and healed those who needed healing.

¹²Late in the afternoon the Twelve came to him and said, "Send the crowd away so they can go to the surrounding villages and countryside and find food and lodging, because we are in a remote place here."

¹³He replied, "You give them something to eat."

They answered, "We have only five loaves of bread and two fish—unless we go and buy food for all this crowd." ¹⁴(About five thousand men were there.)

But he said to his disciples, "Have them sit down in groups of about fifty each." ¹⁵The disciples did so, and everybody sat down. ¹⁶Taking the five loaves and the two fish and looking up to heaven, he gave thanks and broke them. Then he gave them to the disciples to set before the people. ¹⁷They all ate and were satisfied, and the disciples picked up twelve basketfuls of broken pieces that were left over.

Peter's Confession of Christ

¹⁸Once when Jesus was praying in private and his disciples were with him, he asked them, "Who do the crowds say I am?"

¹⁹They replied, "Some say John the Baptist; others say Elijah; and still others, that one of the prophets of long ago has come back to life."

²⁰"But what about you?" he asked. "Who do you say I am?"

Peter answered, "The Christ^a of God."

²¹Jesus strictly warned them not to tell this to anyone. ²²And he said, "The Son of Man must suffer many things and be rejected by the elders, chief priests and teachers of the law, and he must be killed and on the third day be raised to life."

²³Then he said to them all: "If anyone would come after me, he must deny himself and take up his cross daily and follow me. ²⁴For whoever wants to save his life will lose it, but whoever loses his life for me will save it. ²⁵What good is it for a man to gain the whole world, and yet lose or forfeit his very self? ²⁶If anyone is ashamed of me and my words, the Son of Man will be ashamed of him when he comes in his glory and

VERSE:
Luke 9:1

AUTHOR:
Jeanette Lockerbie

PASSAGE:
Luke 9:1–6

Motivated by Trust

It must have been a great day for the chosen twelve. One phase of their training over, they were being sent out on the road. Their instructions were explicit, what to do and what not to do. The master teacher combined *realism*—they would encounter rejection—and *encouragement*. They would not be alone, for the Spirit of the Father would accompany them. Add to that Christ's assurance to them of their *personal value* to God, his trust in them, and they were ready for the task!

Employers can learn a lot from Christ's confidence in his followers. They were human; they had weaknesses as well as strengths. Knowing all about them, Jesus trusted them with great responsibility—and they rose to the challenge.

How often, by contrast, does the employer (Christian as well as non-Christian) impose the responsibility but deny the authority or the trust that should accompany it.

Marie, for example, complained justifiably. "She [the boss] loads responsibility on me, then she acts as though she can't trust me to do things right. She stands over me, giving me the feeling that she thinks I'll flub."

What does it do for us when we're given a position of trust on the job? Generally, when it's a task we're competent at, responsible for and being trusted to carry out, it brings out the very best in us. We strive to prove worthy of the trust placed in us. We aim to do greater things. We become even more responsible, more dependable.

But when the responsibility does not carry the corresponding trust and the authority to fulfill it, such responsibility is a mockery.

It's a wise superior who will let an employee prove herself, even if at first she may need guidance and help in decision making. There's no better way to foster confidence in a person.

Jesus had thoroughly trained very ordinary men. He then commissioned them and expected that they would succeed. How much, we might ponder, did their phenomenal success have to do with their master's good expectations of them? "Even greater things than these" will you do (John 14:12), he had assured them. And they did!

Our Lord was too wise to delegate responsibility and withhold trust.

ADDITIONAL SCRIPTURE READINGS:
John 14:12; Acts 6:1–8; 2 Timothy 1:13–14

Go to page 92 for your next devotional reading.

in the glory of the Father and of the holy angels. **27**I tell you the truth, some who are standing here will not taste death before they see the kingdom of God."

The Transfiguration

28About eight days after Jesus said this, he took Peter, John and James with him and went up onto a mountain to pray. **29**As he was praying, the appearance of his face changed, and his clothes became as bright as a flash of lightning. **30**Two men, Moses and Elijah, **31**appeared in glorious splendor, talking with Jesus. They spoke about his departure, which he was about to bring to fulfillment at Jerusalem. **32**Peter and his companions were very sleepy, but when they became fully awake, they saw his glory and the two men standing with him. **33**As the men were leaving Jesus, Peter said to him, "Master, it is good for us to be here. Let us put up three shelters—one for you, one for Moses and one for Elijah." (He did not know what he was saying.)

34While he was speaking, a cloud appeared and enveloped them, and they were afraid as they entered the cloud. **35**A voice came from the cloud, saying, "This is my Son, whom I have chosen; listen to him." **36**When the voice had spoken, they found that Jesus was alone. The disciples kept this to themselves, and told no one at that time what they had seen.

The Healing of a Boy With an Evil Spirit

37The next day, when they came down from the mountain, a large crowd met him. **38**A man in the crowd called out, "Teacher, I beg you to look at my son, for he is my only child. **39**A spirit seizes him and he suddenly screams; it throws him into convulsions so that he foams at the mouth. It scarcely ever leaves him and is destroying him. **40**I begged your disciples to drive it out, but they could not."

41"O unbelieving and perverse generation," Jesus replied, "how long shall I stay with you and put up with you? Bring your son here."

42Even while the boy was coming, the demon threw him to the ground in a convulsion. But Jesus rebuked the evil[a] spirit, healed the boy and gave him back to his father. **43**And they were all amazed at the greatness of God.

While everyone was marveling at all that Jesus did, he said to his disciples, **44**"Listen carefully to what I am about to tell you: The Son of Man is going to be betrayed into the hands of men." **45**But they did not understand what this meant. It was hidden from them, so that they did not grasp it, and they were afraid to ask him about it.

Who Will Be the Greatest?

46An argument started among the disciples as to which of them would be the greatest. **47**Jesus, knowing their thoughts, took a little child and had him stand beside him. **48**Then he said to them, "Whoever welcomes this little child in my name welcomes me; and whoever welcomes me welcomes the one who sent me. For he who is least among you all—he is the greatest."

49"Master," said John, "we saw a man driving out demons in your name and we tried to stop him, because he is not one of us."

50"Do not stop him," Jesus said, "for whoever is not against you is for you."

Samaritan Opposition

51As the time approached for him to be taken up to heaven, Jesus resolutely set out for Jerusalem. **52**And he sent messengers on ahead, who went into a Samaritan village to get things ready for him; **53**but the people there did not welcome him, because he was heading for Jerusalem. **54**When the disciples James and John saw this, they asked, "Lord, do you want us to call fire down from heaven to destroy them[b]?" **55**But Jesus turned and rebuked them, **56**and[c] they went to another village.

The Cost of Following Jesus

57As they were walking along the road, a man said to him, "I will follow you wherever you go."

58Jesus replied, "Foxes have holes and birds of the air have nests, but the Son of Man has no place to lay his head."

---

*a*42 Greek *unclean*   *b*54 Some manuscripts *them, even as Elijah did*   *c*55,56 Some manuscripts *them. And he said, "You do not know what kind of spirit you are of, for the Son of Man did not come to destroy men's lives, but to save them." 56And*

WEEKENDING

RECALL

I think that *welcome* is one of the most Christlike words we can speak to each other.

And yet, how rarely this happens. This word is shriveling because of disuse. How rarely do people stop in their busyness to greet one another, to chat on the block, to have a cup of coffee and talk about their day. How infrequently we inquire as to strangers' names, ask questions that indicate interest in their lives and families. How wonderfully rare it is when someone whispers, "I haven't seen you for so long, I missed you." How marvelous to hear, "You always make our times together special." We must learn to give to one another the words of welcome.

Karen Burton Mains

REFLECT

Saturday: Luke 9:46–50
Sunday: Philemon 4–22

Go to page 95 for your next devotional reading.

⁵⁹He said to another man, "Follow me."

But the man replied, "Lord, first let me go and bury my father."

⁶⁰Jesus said to him, "Let the dead bury their own dead, but you go and proclaim the kingdom of God."

⁶¹Still another said, "I will follow you, Lord; but first let me go back and say good-by to my family."

⁶²Jesus replied, "No one who puts his hand to the plow and looks back is fit for service in the kingdom of God."

Jesus Sends Out the Seventy-two

10 After this the Lord appointed seventy-two[a] others and sent them two by two ahead of him to every town and place where he was about to go. ²He told them, "The harvest is plentiful, but the workers are few. Ask the Lord of the harvest, therefore, to send out workers into his harvest field. ³Go! I am sending you out like lambs among wolves. ⁴Do not take a purse or bag or sandals; and do not greet anyone on the road.

⁵"When you enter a house, first say, 'Peace to this house.' ⁶If a man of peace is there, your peace will rest on him; if not, it will return to you. ⁷Stay in that house, eating and drinking whatever they give you, for the worker deserves his wages. Do not move around from house to house.

⁸"When you enter a town and are welcomed, eat what is set before you. ⁹Heal the sick who are there and tell them, 'The kingdom of God is near you.' ¹⁰But when you enter a town and are not welcomed, go into its streets and say, ¹¹'Even the dust of your town that sticks to our feet we wipe off against you. Yet be sure of this: The kingdom of God is near.' ¹²I tell you, it will be more bearable on that day for Sodom than for that town.

¹³"Woe to you, Korazin! Woe to you, Bethsaida! For if the miracles that were performed in you had been performed in Tyre and Sidon, they would have repented long ago, sitting in sackcloth and ashes. ¹⁴But it will be more bearable for Tyre and Sidon at the judgment than for you. ¹⁵And you, Capernaum, will you be lifted up to the skies? No, you will go down to the depths.[b]

¹⁶"He who listens to you listens to me; he who rejects you rejects me; but he who rejects me rejects him who sent me."

¹⁷The seventy-two returned with joy and said, "Lord, even the demons submit to us in your name."

¹⁸He replied, "I saw Satan fall like lightning from heaven. ¹⁹I have given you authority to trample on snakes and scorpions and to overcome all the power of the enemy; nothing will harm you. ²⁰However, do not rejoice that the spirits submit to you, but rejoice that your names are written in heaven."

²¹At that time Jesus, full of joy through the Holy Spirit, said, "I praise you, Father, Lord of heaven and earth, because you have hidden these things from the wise and learned, and revealed them to little children. Yes, Father, for this was your good pleasure.

²²"All things have been committed to me by my Father. No one knows who the Son is except the Father, and no one knows who the Father is except the Son and those to whom the Son chooses to reveal him."

²³Then he turned to his disciples and said privately, "Blessed are the eyes that see what you see. ²⁴For I tell you that many prophets and kings wanted to see what you see but did not see it, and to hear what you hear but did not hear it."

The Parable of the Good Samaritan

²⁵On one occasion an expert in the law stood up to test Jesus. "Teacher," he asked, "what must I do to inherit eternal life?"

²⁶"What is written in the Law?" he replied. "How do you read it?"

²⁷He answered: "'Love the Lord your God with all your heart and with all your soul and with all your strength and with all your mind'[c]; and, 'Love your neighbor as yourself.'[d]"

²⁸"You have answered correctly," Jesus replied. "Do this and you will live."

²⁹But he wanted to justify himself, so he asked Jesus, "And who is my neighbor?"

³⁰In reply Jesus said: "A man was go-

a1 Some manuscripts *seventy*; also in verse 17   *b15* Greek *Hades*   *c27* Deut. 6:5
d27 Lev.19:18

ing down from Jerusalem to Jericho, when he fell into the hands of robbers. They stripped him of his clothes, beat him and went away, leaving him half dead. **31**A priest happened to be going down the same road, and when he saw the man, he passed by on the other side. **32**So too, a Levite, when he came to the place and saw him, passed by on the other side. **33**But a Samaritan, as he traveled, came where the man was; and when he saw him, he took pity on him. **34**He went to him and bandaged his wounds, pouring on oil and wine. Then he put the man on his own donkey, took him to an inn and took care of him. **35**The next day he took out two silver coins*a* and gave them to the innkeeper. 'Look after him,' he said, 'and when I return, I will reimburse you for any extra expense you may have.'

36"Which of these three do you think was a neighbor to the man who fell into the hands of robbers?"

37The expert in the law replied, "The one who had mercy on him."

Jesus told him, "Go and do likewise."

At the Home of Martha and Mary

38As Jesus and his disciples were on their way, he came to a village where a woman named Martha opened her home to him. **39**She had a sister called Mary, who sat at the Lord's feet listening to what he said. **40**But Martha was distracted by all the preparations that had to be made. She came to him and asked, "Lord, don't you care that my sister has left me to do the work by myself? Tell her to help me!"

41"Martha, Martha," the Lord answered, "you are worried and upset about many things, **42**but only one thing is needed.*b* Mary has chosen what is better, and it will not be taken away from her."

Jesus' Teaching on Prayer

11 One day Jesus was praying in a certain place. When he finished, one of his disciples said to him, "Lord, teach us to pray, just as John taught his disciples."

2He said to them, "When you pray, say:

" 'Father,*c*
hallowed be your name,
   your kingdom come.*d*
3Give us each day our daily bread.
4Forgive us our sins,
   for we also forgive everyone who
     sins against us.*e*
And lead us not into temptation.*f* '"

5Then he said to them, "Suppose one of you has a friend, and he goes to him at midnight and says, 'Friend, lend me three loaves of bread, **6**because a friend of mine on a journey has come to me, and I have nothing to set before him.'

7"Then the one inside answers, 'Don't bother me. The door is already locked, and my children are with me in bed. I can't get up and give you anything.' **8**I tell you, though he will not get up and give him the bread because he is his friend, yet because of the man's boldness*g* he will get up and give him as much as he needs.

9"So I say to you: Ask and it will be given to you; seek and you will find; knock and the door will be opened to you. **10**For everyone who asks receives; he who seeks finds; and to him who knocks, the door will be opened.

11"Which of you fathers, if your son asks for*h* a fish, will give him a snake instead? **12**Or if he asks for an egg, will give him a scorpion? **13**If you then, though you are evil, know how to give good gifts to your children, how much more will your Father in heaven give the Holy Spirit to those who ask him!"

Jesus and Beelzebub

14Jesus was driving out a demon that was mute. When the demon left, the man who had been mute spoke, and the crowd was amazed. **15**But some of them said, "By Beelzebub,*i* the prince of demons, he is driving out demons." **16**Others tested him by asking for a sign from heaven.

17Jesus knew their thoughts and said to them: "Any kingdom divided against itself will be ruined, and a house divided

---

a35 Greek *two denarii*   *b42* Some manuscripts *but few things are needed—or only one*   *c2* Some manuscripts *Our Father in heaven*   *d2* Some manuscripts *come. May your will be done on earth as it is in heaven.*   *e4* Greek *everyone who is indebted to us*   *f4* Some manuscripts *temptation but deliver us from the evil one*   *g8* Or *persistence*   *h11* Some manuscripts *for bread, will give him a stone; or if he asks for*   *i15* Greek *Beezeboul* or *Beelzeboul*; also in verses 18 and 19

against itself will fall. **18**If Satan is divided against himself, how can his kingdom stand? I say this because you claim that I drive out demons by Beelzebub. **19**Now if I drive out demons by Beelzebub, by whom do your followers drive them out? So then, they will be your judges. **20**But if I drive out demons by the finger of God, then the kingdom of God has come to you.

21"When a strong man, fully armed, guards his own house, his possessions

---

MONDAY

VERSE:	AUTHOR:	PASSAGE:
Luke 10:42	Sue Monk Kidd	Luke 10:38–42

Sitting at Jesus' Feet

One day, while flipping through the New Testament, I came upon the familiar story of Mary and Martha. Jesus came to Mary's house for a visit. There was a lot of fuss and flurry in the kitchen, and Mary's sister, Martha, got completely wound up in it and missed the point of everything. Mary, on the other hand defied a lot of taboos by entering the circle of men who had gathered as disciples around Jesus. The Bible says that she sat at his feet and fixed her listening heart upon him.

I thought about the daring that she had mustered to break out of expected patterns that confined the deeper contemplative part of her and to position herself as she did. I tried imagining how she looked there—sitting still, watching Christ's face, focusing not only her eyes but her heart on him.

This sitting at the feet of the divine with an attentive and loving heart is a posture we all long to assume, whether we recognize that longing or not. Our longing for it is deep and universal . . . God created us in order to share the joy of being alive with us, in order to love us and taste our love, to delight in us and enjoy our delight. God wants our hearts.

As I attempted to take on the posture of Mary at the divine feet, I didn't struggle to set a "quiet time" or do a lot of mental exercises. I simply took time out now and then to sit still and experience attention of the heart. I often sat on the patio in the early morning, listening to the owl that always sang invisibly from a distant tree. Sometimes I sat in the dusk in a near-blizzard of fireflies. Once I went away for a weekend and sat in my stillness for even longer, unbroken spaces of time. Inwardly I fixed my heart on God. I tried to watch, to be attentive, to love and be present to God, creation, my own aliveness, even to the holiness of an owl's call.

For me, that's the posture of Mary—the still prayer of waiting that transforms us in unseen ways.

ADDITIONAL SCRIPTURE READINGS:
Psalm 84; 2 Corinthians 3:17–18; Revelation 2:17

Go to page 101 for your next devotional reading.

are safe. ²²But when someone stronger attacks and overpowers him, he takes away the armor in which the man trusted and divides up the spoils.

²³"He who is not with me is against me, and he who does not gather with me, scatters.

²⁴"When an evil[a] spirit comes out of a man, it goes through arid places seeking rest and does not find it. Then it says, 'I will return to the house I left.' ²⁵When it arrives, it finds the house swept clean and put in order. ²⁶Then it goes and takes seven other spirits more wicked than itself, and they go in and live there. And the final condition of that man is worse than the first."

²⁷As Jesus was saying these things, a woman in the crowd called out, "Blessed is the mother who gave you birth and nursed you."

²⁸He replied, "Blessed rather are those who hear the word of God and obey it."

The Sign of Jonah

²⁹As the crowds increased, Jesus said, "This is a wicked generation. It asks for a miraculous sign, but none will be given it except the sign of Jonah. ³⁰For as Jonah was a sign to the Ninevites, so also will the Son of Man be to this generation. ³¹The Queen of the South will rise at the judgment with the men of this generation and condemn them; for she came from the ends of the earth to listen to Solomon's wisdom, and now one[b] greater than Solomon is here. ³²The men of Nineveh will stand up at the judgment with this generation and condemn it; for they repented at the preaching of Jonah, and now one greater than Jonah is here.

The Lamp of the Body

³³"No one lights a lamp and puts it in a place where it will be hidden, or under a bowl. Instead he puts it on its stand, so that those who come in may see the light. ³⁴Your eye is the lamp of your body. When your eyes are good, your whole body also is full of light. But when they are bad, your body also is full of darkness. ³⁵See to it, then, that the light within you is not darkness. ³⁶Therefore, if your whole body is full of light, and no part of it dark, it will be completely lighted, as when the light of a lamp shines on you."

Six Woes

³⁷When Jesus had finished speaking, a Pharisee invited him to eat with him; so he went in and reclined at the table. ³⁸But the Pharisee, noticing that Jesus did not first wash before the meal, was surprised.

³⁹Then the Lord said to him, "Now then, you Pharisees clean the outside of the cup and dish, but inside you are full of greed and wickedness. ⁴⁰You foolish people! Did not the one who made the outside make the inside also? ⁴¹But give what is inside ₍the dish₎[c] to the poor, and everything will be clean for you.

⁴²"Woe to you Pharisees, because you give God a tenth of your mint, rue and all other kinds of garden herbs, but you neglect justice and the love of God. You should have practiced the latter without leaving the former undone.

⁴³"Woe to you Pharisees, because you love the most important seats in the synagogues and greetings in the marketplaces.

⁴⁴"Woe to you, because you are like unmarked graves, which men walk over without knowing it."

⁴⁵One of the experts in the law answered him, "Teacher, when you say these things, you insult us also."

⁴⁶Jesus replied, "And you experts in the law, woe to you, because you load people down with burdens they can hardly carry, and you yourselves will not lift one finger to help them.

⁴⁷"Woe to you, because you build tombs for the prophets, and it was your forefathers who killed them. ⁴⁸So you testify that you approve of what your forefathers did; they killed the prophets, and you build their tombs. ⁴⁹Because of this, God in his wisdom said, 'I will send them prophets and apostles, some of whom they will kill and others they will persecute.' ⁵⁰Therefore this generation will be held responsible for the blood of all the prophets that has been shed since the beginning of the world, ⁵¹from the blood of Abel to the blood of Zechariah, who was killed between the altar and the sanctuary. Yes, I tell you, this generation will be held responsible for it all.

---

[a]24 Greek *unclean*   [b]31 Or *something*; also in verse 32   [c]41 Or *what you have*

52 "Woe to you experts in the law, because you have taken away the key to knowledge. You yourselves have not entered, and you have hindered those who were entering."

53 When Jesus left there, the Pharisees and the teachers of the law began to oppose him fiercely and to besiege him with questions, 54 waiting to catch him in something he might say.

Warnings and Encouragements

12 Meanwhile, when a crowd of many thousands had gathered, so that they were trampling on one another, Jesus began to speak first to his disciples, saying: "Be on your guard against the yeast of the Pharisees, which is hypocrisy. 2 There is nothing concealed that will not be disclosed, or hidden that will not be made known. 3 What you have said in the dark will be heard in the daylight, and what you have whispered in the ear in the inner rooms will be proclaimed from the roofs.

4 "I tell you, my friends, do not be afraid of those who kill the body and after that can do no more. 5 But I will show you whom you should fear: Fear him who, after the killing of the body, has power to throw you into hell. Yes, I tell you, fear him. 6 Are not five sparrows sold for two pennies[a]? Yet not one of them is forgotten by God. 7 Indeed, the very hairs of your head are all numbered. Don't be afraid; you are worth more than many sparrows.

8 "I tell you, whoever acknowledges me before men, the Son of Man will also acknowledge him before the angels of God. 9 But he who disowns me before men will be disowned before the angels of God. 10 And everyone who speaks a word against the Son of Man will be forgiven, but anyone who blasphemes against the Holy Spirit will not be forgiven.

11 "When you are brought before synagogues, rulers and authorities, do not worry about how you will defend yourselves or what you will say, 12 for the Holy Spirit will teach you at that time what you should say."

The Parable of the Rich Fool

13 Someone in the crowd said to him, "Teacher, tell my brother to divide the inheritance with me."

14 Jesus replied, "Man, who appointed me a judge or an arbiter between you?" 15 Then he said to them, "Watch out! Be on your guard against all kinds of greed; a man's life does not consist in the abundance of his possessions."

16 And he told them this parable: "The ground of a certain rich man produced a good crop. 17 He thought to himself, 'What shall I do? I have no place to store my crops.'

18 "Then he said, 'This is what I'll do. I will tear down my barns and build bigger ones, and there I will store all my grain and my goods. 19 And I'll say to myself, "You have plenty of good things laid up for many years. Take life easy, eat, drink and be merry." '

20 "But God said to him, 'You fool! This very night your life will be demanded from you. Then who will get what you have prepared for yourself?'

21 "This is how it will be with anyone who stores up things for himself but is not rich toward God."

Do Not Worry

22 Then Jesus said to his disciples: "Therefore I tell you, do not worry about your life, what you will eat; or about your body, what you will wear. 23 Life is more than food, and the body more than clothes. 24 Consider the ravens: They do not sow or reap, they have no storeroom or barn; yet God feeds them. And how much more valuable you are than birds! 25 Who of you by worrying can add a single hour to his life[b]? 26 Since you cannot do this very little thing, why do you worry about the rest?

27 "Consider how the lilies grow. They do not labor or spin. Yet I tell you, not even Solomon in all his splendor was dressed like one of these. 28 If that is how God clothes the grass of the field, which is here today, and tomorrow is thrown into the fire, how much more will he clothe you, O you of little faith! 29 And do not set your heart on what you will eat or drink; do not worry about it. 30 For the pagan world runs after all such things, and your Father knows that you need them. 31 But seek his kingdom, and these things will be given to you as well.

32 "Do not be afraid, little flock, for

---

a 6 Greek *two assaria*   b 25 Or *single cubit to his height* your Father has been pleased to give you the kingdom. ³³Sell your possessions and give to the poor. Provide purses for yourselves that will not wear out, a treasure in heaven that will not be exhausted, where no thief comes near and no moth destroys. ³⁴For where your treasure is, there your heart will be also.

Watchfulness

³⁵"Be dressed ready for service and keep your lamps burning, ³⁶like men waiting for their master to return from a wedding banquet, so that when he comes and knocks they can immediately open the door for him. ³⁷It will be good for those servants whose master finds them watching when he comes. I tell you the truth, he will dress himself to serve, will have them recline at the table and will come and wait on them. ³⁸It will be good for those servants whose master finds them ready, even if he comes in the second or third watch of the night. ³⁹But understand this: If the owner of the house had known at what hour the thief was coming, he would not have let his house be broken into. ⁴⁰You also must be ready, because the Son of Man will come at an hour when you do not expect him."

⁴¹Peter asked, "Lord, are you telling this parable to us, or to everyone?"

⁴²The Lord answered, "Who then is the faithful and wise manager, whom the master puts in charge of his servants to give them their food allowance at the proper time? ⁴³It will be good for that servant whom the master finds doing so when he returns. ⁴⁴I tell you the truth, he will put him in charge of all his possessions. ⁴⁵But suppose the servant says to himself, 'My master is taking a long time in coming,' and he then begins to beat the menservants and maidservants and to eat and drink and get drunk. ⁴⁶The master of that servant will come on a day when he does not expect him and at an hour he is not aware of. He will cut him to pieces and assign him a place with the unbelievers.

⁴⁷"That servant who knows his master's will and does not get ready or does not do what his master wants will be beaten with many blows. ⁴⁸But the one who does not know and does things deserving punishment will be beaten with few blows. From everyone who has been given much, much will be demanded; and from the one who has been entrusted with much, much more will be asked.

Not Peace but Division

⁴⁹"I have come to bring fire on the earth, and how I wish it were already kindled! ⁵⁰But I have a baptism to undergo, and how distressed I am until it is completed! ⁵¹Do you think I came to bring peace on earth? No, I tell you, but division. ⁵²From now on there will be five in one family divided against each other, three against two and two against three. ⁵³They will be divided, father against son and son against father, mother against daughter and daughter against mother, mother-in-law against daughter-in-law and daughter-in-law against mother-in-law."

Interpreting the Times

⁵⁴He said to the crowd: "When you see a cloud rising in the west, immediately you say, 'It's going to rain,' and it does. ⁵⁵And when the south wind blows, you say, 'It's going to be hot,' and it is. ⁵⁶Hypocrites! You know how to interpret the appearance of the earth and the sky. How is it that you don't know how to interpret this present time?

⁵⁷"Why don't you judge for yourselves what is right? ⁵⁸As you are going with your adversary to the magistrate, try hard to be reconciled to him on the way, or he may drag you off to the judge, and the judge turn you over to the officer, and the officer throw you into prison. ⁵⁹I tell you, you will not get out until you have paid the last penny.ᵃ"

Repent or Perish

13 Now there were some present at that time who told Jesus about the Galileans whose blood Pilate had mixed with their sacrifices. ²Jesus answered, "Do you think that these Galileans were worse sinners than all the other Galileans because they suffered this way? ³I tell you, no! But unless you repent, you too will all perish. ⁴Or those eighteen who died when the tower in Siloam fell on them—do you think they were more guilty than all the others living in Jerusalem? ⁵I tell you, no! But unless you repent, you too will all perish."

ᵃ59 Greek *lepton*

[6]Then he told this parable: "A man had a fig tree, planted in his vineyard, and he went to look for fruit on it, but did not find any. [7]So he said to the man who took care of the vineyard, 'For three years now I've been coming to look for fruit on this fig tree and haven't found any. Cut it down! Why should it use up the soil?'

[8]"'Sir,' the man replied, 'leave it alone for one more year, and I'll dig around it and fertilize it. [9]If it bears fruit next year, fine! If not, then cut it down.'"

A Crippled Woman Healed on the Sabbath

[10]On a Sabbath Jesus was teaching in one of the synagogues, [11]and a woman was there who had been crippled by a spirit for eighteen years. She was bent over and could not straighten up at all. [12]When Jesus saw her, he called her forward and said to her, "Woman, you are set free from your infirmity." [13]Then he put his hands on her, and immediately she straightened up and praised God.

[14]Indignant because Jesus had healed on the Sabbath, the synagogue ruler said to the people, "There are six days for work. So come and be healed on those days, not on the Sabbath."

[15]The Lord answered him, "You hypocrites! Doesn't each of you on the Sabbath untie his ox or donkey from the stall and lead it out to give it water? [16]Then should not this woman, a daughter of Abraham, whom Satan has kept bound for eighteen long years, be set free on the Sabbath day from what bound her?"

[17]When he said this, all his opponents were humiliated, but the people were delighted with all the wonderful things he was doing.

The Parables of the Mustard Seed and the Yeast

[18]Then Jesus asked, "What is the kingdom of God like? What shall I compare it to? [19]It is like a mustard seed, which a man took and planted in his garden. It grew and became a tree, and the birds of the air perched in its branches."

[20]Again he asked, "What shall I compare the kingdom of God to? [21]It is like yeast that a woman took and mixed into a large amount[a] of flour until it worked all through the dough."

The Narrow Door

[22]Then Jesus went through the towns and villages, teaching as he made his way to Jerusalem. [23]Someone asked him, "Lord, are only a few people going to be saved?"

He said to them, [24]"Make every effort to enter through the narrow door, because many, I tell you, will try to enter and will not be able to. [25]Once the owner of the house gets up and closes the door, you will stand outside knocking and pleading, 'Sir, open the door for us.'

"But he will answer, 'I don't know you or where you come from.'

[26]"Then you will say, 'We ate and drank with you, and you taught in our streets.'

[27]"But he will reply, 'I don't know you or where you come from. Away from me, all you evildoers!'

[28]"There will be weeping there, and gnashing of teeth, when you see Abraham, Isaac and Jacob and all the prophets in the kingdom of God, but you yourselves thrown out. [29]People will come from east and west and north and south, and will take their places at the feast in the kingdom of God. [30]Indeed there are those who are last who will be first, and first who will be last."

Jesus' Sorrow for Jerusalem

[31]At that time some Pharisees came to Jesus and said to him, "Leave this place and go somewhere else. Herod wants to kill you."

[32]He replied, "Go tell that fox, 'I will drive out demons and heal people today and tomorrow, and on the third day I will reach my goal.' [33]In any case, I must keep going today and tomorrow and the next day—for surely no prophet can die outside Jerusalem!

[34]"O Jerusalem, Jerusalem, you who kill the prophets and stone those sent to you, how often I have longed to gather your children together, as a hen gathers her chicks under her wings, but you were not willing! [35]Look, your house is left to you desolate. I tell you, you will not see me again until you say, 'Blessed

---

a21 Greek *three satas* (probably about 1/2 bushel or 22 liters)

is he who comes in the name of the Lord.'*a*"

Jesus at a Pharisee's House

14 One Sabbath, when Jesus went to eat in the house of a prominent Pharisee, he was being carefully watched. **2**There in front of him was a man suffering from dropsy. **3**Jesus asked the Pharisees and experts in the law, "Is it lawful to heal on the Sabbath or not?" **4**But they remained silent. So taking hold of the man, he healed him and sent him away.

5Then he asked them, "If one of you has a son*b* or an ox that falls into a well on the Sabbath day, will you not immediately pull him out?" **6**And they had nothing to say.

7When he noticed how the guests picked the places of honor at the table, he told them this parable: **8**"When someone invites you to a wedding feast, do not take the place of honor, for a person more distinguished than you may have been invited. **9**If so, the host who invited both of you will come and say to you, 'Give this man your seat.' Then, humiliated, you will have to take the least important place. **10**But when you are invited, take the lowest place, so that when your host comes, he will say to you, 'Friend, move up to a better place.' Then you will be honored in the presence of all your fellow guests. **11**For everyone who exalts himself will be humbled, and he who humbles himself will be exalted."

12Then Jesus said to his host, "When you give a luncheon or dinner, do not invite your friends, your brothers or relatives, or your rich neighbors; if you do, they may invite you back and so you will be repaid. **13**But when you give a banquet, invite the poor, the crippled, the lame, the blind, **14**and you will be blessed. Although they cannot repay you, you will be repaid at the resurrection of the righteous."

The Parable of the Great Banquet

15When one of those at the table with him heard this, he said to Jesus, "Blessed is the man who will eat at the feast in the kingdom of God."

16Jesus replied: "A certain man was preparing a great banquet and invited many guests. **17**At the time of the banquet he sent his servant to tell those who had been invited, 'Come, for everything is now ready.'

18"But they all alike began to make excuses. The first said, 'I have just bought a field, and I must go and see it. Please excuse me.'

19"Another said, 'I have just bought five yoke of oxen, and I'm on my way to try them out. Please excuse me.'

20"Still another said, 'I just got married, so I can't come.'

21"The servant came back and reported this to his master. Then the owner of the house became angry and ordered his servant, 'Go out quickly into the streets and alleys of the town and bring in the poor, the crippled, the blind and the lame.'

22" 'Sir,' the servant said, 'what you ordered has been done, but there is still room.'

23"Then the master told his servant, 'Go out to the roads and country lanes and make them come in, so that my house will be full. **24**I tell you, not one of those men who were invited will get a taste of my banquet.' "

The Cost of Being a Disciple

25Large crowds were traveling with Jesus, and turning to them he said: **26**"If anyone comes to me and does not hate his father and mother, his wife and children, his brothers and sisters—yes, even his own life—he cannot be my disciple. **27**And anyone who does not carry his cross and follow me cannot be my disciple.

28"Suppose one of you wants to build a tower. Will he not first sit down and estimate the cost to see if he has enough money to complete it? **29**For if he lays the foundation and is not able to finish it, everyone who sees it will ridicule him, **30**saying, 'This fellow began to build and was not able to finish.'

31"Or suppose a king is about to go to war against another king. Will he not first sit down and consider whether he is able with ten thousand men to oppose the one coming against him with twenty thousand? **32**If he is not able, he will send a delegation while the other is still a long way off and will ask for terms of peace. **33**In the same way, any of you

---

a35 Psalm 118:26   *b5* Some manuscripts *donkey*

who does not give up everything he has cannot be my disciple.

³⁴"Salt is good, but if it loses its saltiness, how can it be made salty again? ³⁵It is fit neither for the soil nor for the manure pile; it is thrown out.

"He who has ears to hear, let him hear."

The Parable of the Lost Sheep

15 Now the tax collectors and "sinners" were all gathering around to hear him. ²But the Pharisees and the teachers of the law muttered, "This man welcomes sinners and eats with them."

³Then Jesus told them this parable: ⁴"Suppose one of you has a hundred sheep and loses one of them. Does he not leave the ninety-nine in the open country and go after the lost sheep until he finds it? ⁵And when he finds it, he joyfully puts it on his shoulders ⁶and goes home. Then he calls his friends and neighbors together and says, 'Rejoice with me; I have found my lost sheep.' ⁷I tell you that in the same way there will be more rejoicing in heaven over one sinner who repents than over ninety-nine righteous persons who do not need to repent.

The Parable of the Lost Coin

⁸"Or suppose a woman has ten silver coins*a* and loses one. Does she not light a lamp, sweep the house and search carefully until she finds it? ⁹And when she finds it, she calls her friends and neighbors together and says, 'Rejoice with me; I have found my lost coin.' ¹⁰In the same way, I tell you, there is rejoicing in the presence of the angels of God over one sinner who repents."

a8 Greek ten drachmas, each worth about a day's wages

TUESDAY

VERSE:	AUTHOR:	PASSAGE:
Luke 14:27	Susanna Wesley	Luke 14:25–35

Consider the Cost

Forbid, O Lord, that I should take on myself the profession of a Christian, without first considering the end of such a profession, without weighing the difficulties I must encounter in order to obtain that end: the number and strength of my enemies, what my own powers are, what succors I may expect and rely on. The end I seek is thy glory, O God, and my happiness; not the happiness of the body, but of the mind, which is incapable of true happiness till renewed and sanctified, till restored to its native liberty, till recovered from its lapse and in all things made conformable to thy will and thy laws. So may happiness and purity hold just proportion to each other.

The difficulties are many and enemies very powerful. But our Savior has said: "If anyone would come after me, he must deny himself and take up his cross and follow me" (Matthew 16:24). I am my own worst enemy. Grant me thy grace, O Lord. *Amen.*

ADDITIONAL SCRIPTURE READINGS:
Psalm 25:19–22; Matthew 16:24–25

Go to page 103 for your next devotional reading.

The Parable of the Lost Son

11Jesus continued: "There was a man who had two sons. **12**The younger one said to his father, 'Father, give me my share of the estate.' So he divided his property between them.

13"Not long after that, the younger son got together all he had, set off for a distant country and there squandered his wealth in wild living. **14**After he had spent everything, there was a severe famine in that whole country, and he began to be in need. **15**So he went and hired himself out to a citizen of that country, who sent him to his fields to feed pigs. **16**He longed to fill his stomach with the pods that the pigs were eating, but no one gave him anything.

17"When he came to his senses, he said, 'How many of my father's hired men have food to spare, and here I am starving to death! **18**I will set out and go back to my father and say to him: Father, I have sinned against heaven and against you. **19**I am no longer worthy to be called your son; make me like one of your hired men.' **20**So he got up and went to his father.

"But while he was still a long way off, his father saw him and was filled with compassion for him; he ran to his son, threw his arms around him and kissed him.

21"The son said to him, 'Father, I have sinned against heaven and against you. I am no longer worthy to be called your son.*a*'

22"But the father said to his servants, 'Quick! Bring the best robe and put it on him. Put a ring on his finger and sandals on his feet. **23**Bring the fattened calf and kill it. Let's have a feast and celebrate. **24**For this son of mine was dead and is alive again; he was lost and is found.' So they began to celebrate.

25"Meanwhile, the older son was in the field. When he came near the house, he heard music and dancing. **26**So he called one of the servants and asked him what was going on. **27**'Your brother has come,' he replied, 'and your father has killed the fattened calf because he has him back safe and sound.'

28"The older brother became angry and refused to go in. So his father went

out and pleaded with him. **29**But he answered his father, 'Look! All these years I've been slaving for you and never disobeyed your orders. Yet you never gave me even a young goat so I could celebrate with my friends. **30**But when this son of yours who has squandered your property with prostitutes comes home, you kill the fattened calf for him!'

31" 'My son,' the father said, 'you are always with me, and everything I have is yours. **32**But we had to celebrate and be glad, because this brother of yours was dead and is alive again; he was lost and is found.' "

The Parable of the Shrewd Manager

16 Jesus told his disciples: "There was a rich man whose manager was accused of wasting his possessions. **2**So he called him in and asked him, 'What is this I hear about you? Give an account of your management, because you cannot be manager any longer.'

3"The manager said to himself, 'What shall I do now? My master is taking away my job. I'm not strong enough to dig, and I'm ashamed to beg— **4**I know what I'll do so that, when I lose my job here, people will welcome me into their houses.'

5"So he called in each one of his master's debtors. He asked the first, 'How much do you owe my master?'

6" 'Eight hundred gallons*b* of olive oil,' he replied.

"The manager told him, 'Take your bill, sit down quickly, and make it four hundred.'

7"Then he asked the second, 'And how much do you owe?'

" 'A thousand bushels*c* of wheat,' he replied.

"He told him, 'Take your bill and make it eight hundred.'

8"The master commended the dishonest manager because he had acted shrewdly. For the people of this world are more shrewd in dealing with their own kind than are the people of the light. **9**I tell you, use worldly wealth to gain friends for yourselves, so that when it is gone, you will be welcomed into eternal dwellings.

10"Whoever can be trusted with very

---

*a*21 Some early manuscripts *son. Make me like one of your hired men.*   *b*6 Greek *one hundred batous*
(probably about 3 kiloliters)   *c*7 Greek *one hundred korous* (probably about 35 kiloliters)

little can also be trusted with much, and whoever is dishonest with very little will also be dishonest with much. ¹¹So if you have not been trustworthy in handling worldly wealth, who will trust you with true riches? ¹²And if you have not been trustworthy with someone else's property, who will give you property of your own?

¹³"No servant can serve two masters. Either he will hate the one and love the other, or he will be devoted to the one

---

WEDNESDAY

VERSE:
Luke 15:11

AUTHOR:
Luci Shaw

PASSAGE:
Luke 15:11–32

The Celebration

We might well
feel sorry for the
elder brother.

All he gets for his pains is
promises—promises,
a firm reproach, a truthful telling
that virtue brings
its own reward
while in the ballroom
across the hall
the black sheep and all his
loud friends
think it a fine Homecoming,
dance, laugh, live it up.

The firstborn's lack is
he's only a brother.

He hasn't tasted
parenthood, hasn't learned
the hard way
that love, longing,
endurance, disappointment,
bitter concern
often flower in stronger love
and later,
a more merry heart.

We would hate
to wish it on him, but
he can understand
only if, someday, *he* has
a prodigal son.

ADDITIONAL SCRIPTURE READINGS:
Nehemiah 1:9; Luke 1:1–17

Go to page 108 for your next devotional reading.

and despise the other. You cannot serve both God and Money."

14The Pharisees, who loved money, heard all this and were sneering at Jesus. **15**He said to them, "You are the ones who justify yourselves in the eyes of men, but God knows your hearts. What is highly valued among men is detestable in God's sight.

Additional Teachings

16"The Law and the Prophets were proclaimed until John. Since that time, the good news of the kingdom of God is being preached, and everyone is forcing his way into it. **17**It is easier for heaven and earth to disappear than for the least stroke of a pen to drop out of the Law.

18"Anyone who divorces his wife and marries another woman commits adultery, and the man who marries a divorced woman commits adultery.

The Rich Man and Lazarus

19"There was a rich man who was dressed in purple and fine linen and lived in luxury every day. **20**At his gate was laid a beggar named Lazarus, covered with sores **21**and longing to eat what fell from the rich man's table. Even the dogs came and licked his sores.

22"The time came when the beggar died and the angels carried him to Abraham's side. The rich man also died and was buried. **23**In hell,*a* where he was in torment, he looked up and saw Abraham far away, with Lazarus by his side. **24**So he called to him, 'Father Abraham, have pity on me and send Lazarus to dip the tip of his finger in water and cool my tongue, because I am in agony in this fire.'

25"But Abraham replied, 'Son, remember that in your lifetime you received your good things, while Lazarus received bad things, but now he is comforted here and you are in agony. **26**And besides all this, between us and you a great chasm has been fixed, so that those who want to go from here to you cannot, nor can anyone cross over from there to us.'

27"He answered, 'Then I beg you, father, send Lazarus to my father's house, **28**for I have five brothers. Let him warn

them, so that they will not also come to this place of torment.'

29"Abraham replied, 'They have Moses and the Prophets; let them listen to them.'

30"'No, father Abraham,' he said, 'but if someone from the dead goes to them, they will repent.'

31"He said to him, 'If they do not listen to Moses and the Prophets, they will not be convinced even if someone rises from the dead.'"

Sin, Faith, Duty

17 Jesus said to his disciples: "Things that cause people to sin are bound to come, but woe to that person through whom they come. **2**It would be better for him to be thrown into the sea with a millstone tied around his neck than for him to cause one of these little ones to sin. **3**So watch yourselves.

"If your brother sins, rebuke him, and if he repents, forgive him. **4**If he sins against you seven times in a day, and seven times comes back to you and says, 'I repent,' forgive him."

5The apostles said to the Lord, "Increase our faith!"

6He replied, "If you have faith as small as a mustard seed, you can say to this mulberry tree, 'Be uprooted and planted in the sea,' and it will obey you.

7"Suppose one of you had a servant plowing or looking after the sheep. Would he say to the servant when he comes in from the field, 'Come along now and sit down to eat'? **8**Would he not rather say, 'Prepare my supper, get yourself ready and wait on me while I eat and drink; after that you may eat and drink'? **9**Would he thank the servant because he did what he was told to do? **10**So you also, when you have done everything you were told to do, should say, 'We are unworthy servants; we have only done our duty.'"

Ten Healed of Leprosy

11Now on his way to Jerusalem, Jesus traveled along the border between Samaria and Galilee. **12**As he was going into a village, ten men who had leprosy*b* met him. They stood at a distance **13**and called out in a loud voice, "Jesus, Master, have pity on us!"

---

a 23 Greek *Hades*   *b 12* The Greek word was used for various diseases affecting the skin—not necessarily leprosy.

¹⁴When he saw them, he said, "Go, show yourselves to the priests." And as they went, they were cleansed.

¹⁵One of them, when he saw he was healed, came back, praising God in a loud voice. ¹⁶He threw himself at Jesus' feet and thanked him—and he was a Samaritan.

¹⁷Jesus asked, "Were not all ten cleansed? Where are the other nine? ¹⁸Was no one found to return and give praise to God except this foreigner?" ¹⁹Then he said to him, "Rise and go; your faith has made you well."

The Coming of the Kingdom of God

²⁰Once, having been asked by the Pharisees when the kingdom of God would come, Jesus replied, "The kingdom of God does not come with your careful observation, ²¹nor will people say, 'Here it is,' or 'There it is,' because the kingdom of God is within*ᵃ* you."

²²Then he said to his disciples, "The time is coming when you will long to see one of the days of the Son of Man, but you will not see it. ²³Men will tell you, 'There he is!' or 'Here he is!' Do not go running off after them. ²⁴For the Son of Man in his dayᵇ will be like the lightning, which flashes and lights up the sky from one end to the other. ²⁵But first he must suffer many things and be rejected by this generation.

²⁶"Just as it was in the days of Noah, so also will it be in the days of the Son of Man. ²⁷People were eating, drinking, marrying and being given in marriage up to the day Noah entered the ark. Then the flood came and destroyed them all.

²⁸"It was the same in the days of Lot. People were eating and drinking, buying and selling, planting and building. ²⁹But the day Lot left Sodom, fire and sulfur rained down from heaven and destroyed them all.

³⁰"It will be just like this on the day the Son of Man is revealed. ³¹On that day no one who is on the roof of his house, with his goods inside, should go down to get them. Likewise, no one in the field should go back for anything. ³²Remember Lot's wife! ³³Whoever tries to keep his life will lose it, and whoever loses his life will preserve it. ³⁴I tell you, on that night two people will be in one bed; one will be taken and the other left. ³⁵Two women will be grinding grain together; one will be taken and the other left.ᶜ"

³⁷"Where, Lord?" they asked.

He replied, "Where there is a dead body, there the vultures will gather."

The Parable of the Persistent Widow

18 Then Jesus told his disciples a parable to show them that they should always pray and not give up. ²He said: "In a certain town there was a judge who neither feared God nor cared about men. ³And there was a widow in that town who kept coming to him with the plea, 'Grant me justice against my adversary.'

⁴"For some time he refused. But finally he said to himself, 'Even though I don't fear God or care about men, ⁵yet because this widow keeps bothering me, I will see that she gets justice, so that she won't eventually wear me out with her coming!' "

⁶And the Lord said, "Listen to what the unjust judge says. ⁷And will not God bring about justice for his chosen ones, who cry out to him day and night? Will he keep putting them off? ⁸I tell you, he will see that they get justice, and quickly. However, when the Son of Man comes, will he find faith on the earth?"

The Parable of the Pharisee and the Tax Collector

⁹To some who were confident of their own righteousness and looked down on everybody else, Jesus told this parable: ¹⁰"Two men went up to the temple to pray, one a Pharisee and the other a tax collector. ¹¹The Pharisee stood up and prayed aboutᵈ himself: 'God, I thank you that I am not like other men—robbers, evildoers, adulterers—or even like this tax collector. ¹²I fast twice a week and give a tenth of all I get.'

¹³"But the tax collector stood at a distance. He would not even look up to heaven, but beat his breast and said, 'God, have mercy on me, a sinner.'

¹⁴"I tell you that this man, rather than the other, went home justified before God. For everyone who exalts himself will be humbled, and he who humbles himself will be exalted."

ᵃ21 Or among   ᵇ24 Some manuscripts do not have *in his day.*   ᶜ35 Some manuscripts *left.*
³⁶*Two men will be in the field; one will be taken and the other left.*   ᵈ11 Or *to*

The Little Children and Jesus

15People were also bringing babies to Jesus to have him touch them. When the disciples saw this, they rebuked them. **16**But Jesus called the children to him and said, "Let the little children come to me, and do not hinder them, for the kingdom of God belongs to such as these. **17**I tell you the truth, anyone who will not receive the kingdom of God like a little child will never enter it."

The Rich Ruler

18A certain ruler asked him, "Good teacher, what must I do to inherit eternal life?"

19"Why do you call me good?" Jesus answered. "No one is good—except God alone. **20**You know the commandments: 'Do not commit adultery, do not murder, do not steal, do not give false testimony, honor your father and mother.'*a*"

21"All these I have kept since I was a boy," he said.

22When Jesus heard this, he said to him, "You still lack one thing. Sell everything you have and give to the poor, and you will have treasure in heaven. Then come, follow me."

23When he heard this, he became very sad, because he was a man of great wealth. **24**Jesus looked at him and said, "How hard it is for the rich to enter the kingdom of God! **25**Indeed, it is easier for a camel to go through the eye of a needle than for a rich man to enter the kingdom of God."

26Those who heard this asked, "Who then can be saved?"

27Jesus replied, "What is impossible with men is possible with God."

28Peter said to him, "We have left all we had to follow you!"

29"I tell you the truth," Jesus said to them, "no one who has left home or wife or brothers or parents or children for the sake of the kingdom of God **30**will fail to receive many times as much in this age and, in the age to come, eternal life."

Jesus Again Predicts His Death

31Jesus took the Twelve aside and told them, "We are going up to Jerusalem, and everything that is written by the prophets about the Son of Man will be fulfilled. **32**He will be handed over to the Gentiles. They will mock him, insult him, spit on him, flog him and kill him. **33**On the third day he will rise again."

34The disciples did not understand any of this. Its meaning was hidden from them, and they did not know what he was talking about.

A Blind Beggar Receives His Sight

35As Jesus approached Jericho, a blind man was sitting by the roadside begging. **36**When he heard the crowd going by, he asked what was happening. **37**They told him, "Jesus of Nazareth is passing by."

38He called out, "Jesus, Son of David, have mercy on me!"

39Those who led the way rebuked him and told him to be quiet, but he shouted all the more, "Son of David, have mercy on me!"

40Jesus stopped and ordered the man to be brought to him. When he came near, Jesus asked him, **41**"What do you want me to do for you?"

"Lord, I want to see," he replied.

42Jesus said to him, "Receive your sight; your faith has healed you." **43**Immediately he received his sight and followed Jesus, praising God. When all the people saw it, they also praised God.

Zacchaeus the Tax Collector

19 Jesus entered Jericho and was passing through. **2**A man was there by the name of Zacchaeus; he was a chief tax collector and was wealthy. **3**He wanted to see who Jesus was, but being a short man he could not, because of the crowd. **4**So he ran ahead and climbed a sycamore-fig tree to see him, since Jesus was coming that way.

5When Jesus reached the spot, he looked up and said to him, "Zacchaeus, come down immediately. I must stay at your house today." **6**So he came down at once and welcomed him gladly.

7All the people saw this and began to mutter, "He has gone to be the guest of a 'sinner.'"

8But Zacchaeus stood up and said to the Lord, "Look, Lord! Here and now I give half of my possessions to the poor, and if I have cheated anybody out of

a20 Exodus 20:12-16; Deut. 5:16-20

anything, I will pay back four times the amount."

⁹Jesus said to him, "Today salvation has come to this house, because this man, too, is a son of Abraham. ¹⁰For the Son of Man came to seek and to save what was lost."

The Parable of the Ten Minas

¹¹While they were listening to this, he went on to tell them a parable, because he was near Jerusalem and the people thought that the kingdom of God was going to appear at once. ¹²He said: "A man of noble birth went to a distant country to have himself appointed king and then to return. ¹³So he called ten of his servants and gave them ten minas.ᵃ 'Put this money to work,' he said, 'until I come back.'

¹⁴"But his subjects hated him and sent a delegation after him to say, 'We don't want this man to be our king.'

¹⁵"He was made king, however, and returned home. Then he sent for the servants to whom he had given the money, in order to find out what they had gained with it.

¹⁶"The first one came and said, 'Sir, your mina has earned ten more.'

¹⁷" 'Well done, my good servant!' his master replied. 'Because you have been trustworthy in a very small matter, take charge of ten cities.'

¹⁸"The second came and said, 'Sir, your mina has earned five more.'

¹⁹"His master answered, 'You take charge of five cities.'

²⁰"Then another servant came and said, 'Sir, here is your mina; I have kept it laid away in a piece of cloth. ²¹I was afraid of you, because you are a hard man. You take out what you did not put in and reap what you did not sow.'

²²"His master replied, 'I will judge you by your own words, you wicked servant! You knew, did you, that I am a hard man, taking out what I did not put in, and reaping what I did not sow? ²³Why then didn't you put my money on deposit, so that when I came back, I could have collected it with interest?'

²⁴"Then he said to those standing by, 'Take his mina away from him and give it to the one who has ten minas.'

²⁵" 'Sir,' they said, 'he already has ten!'

²⁶"He replied, 'I tell you that to everyone who has, more will be given, but as for the one who has nothing, even what he has will be taken away. ²⁷But those enemies of mine who did not want me to be king over them—bring them here and kill them in front of me.' "

The Triumphal Entry

²⁸After Jesus had said this, he went on ahead, going up to Jerusalem. ²⁹As he approached Bethphage and Bethany at the hill called the Mount of Olives, he sent two of his disciples, saying to them, ³⁰"Go to the village ahead of you, and as you enter it, you will find a colt tied there, which no one has ever ridden. Untie it and bring it here. ³¹If anyone asks you, 'Why are you untying it?' tell him, 'The Lord needs it.' "

³²Those who were sent ahead went and found it just as he had told them. ³³As they were untying the colt, its owners asked them, "Why are you untying the colt?"

³⁴They replied, "The Lord needs it."

³⁵They brought it to Jesus, threw their cloaks on the colt and put Jesus on it. ³⁶As he went along, people spread their cloaks on the road.

³⁷When he came near the place where the road goes down the Mount of Olives, the whole crowd of disciples began joyfully to praise God in loud voices for all the miracles they had seen:

³⁸"Blessed is the king who comes in
    the name of the Lord!"ᵇ

"Peace in heaven and glory in the
    highest!"

³⁹Some of the Pharisees in the crowd said to Jesus, "Teacher, rebuke your disciples!"

⁴⁰"I tell you," he replied, "if they keep quiet, the stones will cry out."

⁴¹As he approached Jerusalem and saw the city, he wept over it ⁴²and said, "If you, even you, had only known on this day what would bring you peace—but now it is hidden from your eyes. ⁴³The days will come upon you when your enemies will build an embankment against you and encircle you and hem you in on every side. ⁴⁴They will dash you to the ground, you and the children within your walls. They will not leave

---

ᵃ13 A mina was about three months' wages.   ᵇ38 Psalm 118:26

VERSE:
Luke 19:15

AUTHOR:
Jeanette Lockerbie

PASSAGE:
Luke 19:12–15

The Aura of Success

Anne found it necessary to join the world of working women after years of being a homemaker. Confiding her fears and uncertainties to a friend, she asked, "Do you have some advice for me?"

The friend thought for a minute and then said, "Yes. Become good at something." She went on to explain: "There's something about being successful at what you're doing—a kind of aura. People tend to be willing to listen to you, and they filter what you're saying through their concept that because you are successful, what you say is worth hearing."

Our generation abounds with successful Christians: in the arts, in business, in politics, in education—in practically every area of life. These are persons who have "gotten good at something," and other people have taken notice.

There's an often-repeated saying, "God has not called us to be successful, he has called us to be faithful." Not for an instant would I dispute the latter truth. But I would like to pose the question: How much is real success dependent on *faithfulness* to what one is doing? It's my thinking that God places no premium on mediocrity.

There are, obviously, material benefits for the person who is successful in her business or profession. But as Christians seeking first the kingdom of God, we can look beyond the material and temporal, for there are also *spiritual* rewards. The greatest of these is the opportunity of obtaining a hearing when we witness to our faith in Christ. When we speak of God's guidance in our life, and it has apparently gotten us somewhere, our witness may be all the more credible to "the man [or woman who] without the Spirit does not accept the things that come from the Spirit of God" (1 Corinthians 2:14). Some people will only heed those whom they view as "having made it."

Moreover, if the parable of the talents teaches anything, it is that God has success expectations. He is looking to us to use successfully those talents with which he has endowed us. Only then, according to the words of Jesus, will we hear his "Well done, good and faithful servant" (Matthew 25:21).

So it pays great dividends when we assess our abilities and then become good at something. Wouldn't you agree?

ADDITIONAL SCRIPTURE READINGS:
Genesis 24:12; Ecclesiastes 10:10; Daniel 6:26–28

Go to page 113 for your next devotional reading.

one stone on another, because you did not recognize the time of God's coming to you."

Jesus at the Temple

45Then he entered the temple area and began driving out those who were selling. **46**"It is written," he said to them, "'My house will be a house of prayer'*a*; but you have made it 'a den of robbers.'*b*"

47Every day he was teaching at the temple. But the chief priests, the teachers of the law and the leaders among the people were trying to kill him. **48**Yet they could not find any way to do it, because all the people hung on his words.

The Authority of Jesus Questioned

20 One day as he was teaching the people in the temple courts and preaching the gospel, the chief priests and the teachers of the law, together with the elders, came up to him. **2**"Tell us by what authority you are doing these things," they said. "Who gave you this authority?"

3He replied, "I will also ask you a question. Tell me, **4**John's baptism—was it from heaven, or from men?"

5They discussed it among themselves and said, "If we say, 'From heaven,' he will ask, 'Why didn't you believe him?' **6**But if we say, 'From men,' all the people will stone us, because they are persuaded that John was a prophet."

7So they answered, "We don't know where it was from."

8Jesus said, "Neither will I tell you by what authority I am doing these things."

The Parable of the Tenants

9He went on to tell the people this parable: "A man planted a vineyard, rented it to some farmers and went away for a long time. **10**At harvest time he sent a servant to the tenants so they would give him some of the fruit of the vineyard. But the tenants beat him and sent him away empty-handed. **11**He sent another servant, but that one also they beat and treated shamefully and sent away empty-handed. **12**He sent still a third, and they wounded him and threw him out.

13"Then the owner of the vineyard said, 'What shall I do? I will send my son, whom I love; perhaps they will respect him.'

14"But when the tenants saw him, they talked the matter over. 'This is the heir,' they said. 'Let's kill him, and the inheritance will be ours.' **15**So they threw him out of the vineyard and killed him.

"What then will the owner of the vineyard do to them? **16**He will come and kill those tenants and give the vineyard to others."

When the people heard this, they said, "May this never be!"

17Jesus looked directly at them and asked, "Then what is the meaning of that which is written:

" 'The stone the builders rejected
has become the capstone*c' d*?

18Everyone who falls on that stone will be broken to pieces, but he on whom it falls will be crushed."

19The teachers of the law and the chief priests looked for a way to arrest him immediately, because they knew he had spoken this parable against them. But they were afraid of the people.

Paying Taxes to Caesar

20Keeping a close watch on him, they sent spies, who pretended to be honest. They hoped to catch Jesus in something he said so that they might hand him over to the power and authority of the governor. **21**So the spies questioned him: "Teacher, we know that you speak and teach what is right, and that you do not show partiality but teach the way of God in accordance with the truth. **22**Is it right for us to pay taxes to Caesar or not?"

23He saw through their duplicity and said to them, **24**"Show me a denarius. Whose portrait and inscription are on it?"

25"Caesar's," they replied.

He said to them, "Then give to Caesar what is Caesar's, and to God what is God's."

26They were unable to trap him in what he had said there in public. And astonished by his answer, they became silent.

The Resurrection and Marriage

27Some of the Sadducees, who say there is no resurrection, came to Jesus

---

a46 Isaiah 56:7   *b46* Jer. 7:11   *c17* Or *cornerstone*   *d17* Psalm 118:22

with a question. 28"Teacher," they said, "Moses wrote for us that if a man's brother dies and leaves a wife but no children, the man must marry the widow and have children for his brother. 29Now there were seven brothers. The first one married a woman and died childless. 30The second 31and then the third married her, and in the same way the seven died, leaving no children. 32Finally, the woman died too. 33Now then, at the resurrection whose wife will she be, since the seven were married to her?"

34Jesus replied, "The people of this age marry and are given in marriage. 35But those who are considered worthy of taking part in that age and in the resurrection from the dead will neither marry nor be given in marriage, 36and they can no longer die; for they are like the angels. They are God's children, since they are children of the resurrection. 37But in the account of the bush, even Moses showed that the dead rise, for he calls the Lord 'the God of Abraham, and the God of Isaac, and the God of Jacob.'a 38He is not the God of the dead, but of the living, for to him all are alive."

39Some of the teachers of the law responded, "Well said, teacher!" 40And no one dared to ask him any more questions.

Whose Son Is the Christ?

41Then Jesus said to them, "How is it that they say the Christb is the Son of David? 42David himself declares in the Book of Psalms:

" 'The Lord said to my Lord:
"Sit at my right hand
43until I make your enemies
a footstool for your feet." 'c

44David calls him 'Lord.' How then can he be his son?"

45While all the people were listening, Jesus said to his disciples, 46"Beware of the teachers of the law. They like to walk around in flowing robes and love to be greeted in the marketplaces and have the most important seats in the synagogues and the places of honor at banquets. 47They devour widows' houses and for a show make lengthy prayers. Such men will be punished most severely."

The Widow's Offering

21 As he looked up, Jesus saw the rich putting their gifts into the temple treasury. 2He also saw a poor widow put in two very small copper coins.d 3"I tell you the truth," he said, "this poor widow has put in more than all the others. 4All these people gave their gifts out of their wealth; but she out of her poverty put in all she had to live on."

Signs of the End of the Age

5Some of his disciples were remarking about how the temple was adorned with beautiful stones and with gifts dedicated to God. But Jesus said, 6"As for what you see here, the time will come when not one stone will be left on another; every one of them will be thrown down."

7"Teacher," they asked, "when will these things happen? And what will be the sign that they are about to take place?"

8He replied: "Watch out that you are not deceived. For many will come in my name, claiming, 'I am he,' and, 'The time is near.' Do not follow them. 9When you hear of wars and revolutions, do not be frightened. These things must happen first, but the end will not come right away."

10Then he said to them: "Nation will rise against nation, and kingdom against kingdom. 11There will be great earthquakes, famines and pestilences in various places, and fearful events and great signs from heaven.

12"But before all this, they will lay hands on you and persecute you. They will deliver you to synagogues and prisons, and you will be brought before kings and governors, and all on account of my name. 13This will result in your being witnesses to them. 14But make up your mind not to worry beforehand how you will defend yourselves. 15For I will give you words and wisdom that none of your adversaries will be able to resist or contradict. 16You will be betrayed even by parents, brothers, relatives and friends, and they will put some of you to death. 17All men will hate you because of me. 18But not a hair of your head will perish. 19By standing firm you will gain life.

---

a37 Exodus 3:6   b41 Or Messiah   c43 Psalm 110:1   d2 Greek two lepta

²⁰"When you see Jerusalem being surrounded by armies, you will know that its desolation is near. ²¹Then let those who are in Judea flee to the mountains, let those in the city get out, and let those in the country not enter the city. ²²For this is the time of punishment in fulfillment of all that has been written. ²³How dreadful it will be in those days for pregnant women and nursing mothers! There will be great distress in the land and wrath against this people. ²⁴They will fall by the sword and will be taken as prisoners to all the nations. Jerusalem will be trampled on by the Gentiles until the times of the Gentiles are fulfilled.

²⁵"There will be signs in the sun, moon and stars. On the earth, nations will be in anguish and perplexity at the roaring and tossing of the sea. ²⁶Men will faint from terror, apprehensive of what is coming on the world, for the heavenly bodies will be shaken. ²⁷At that time they will see the Son of Man coming in a cloud with power and great glory. ²⁸When these things begin to take place, stand up and lift up your heads, because your redemption is drawing near."

²⁹He told them this parable: "Look at the fig tree and all the trees. ³⁰When they sprout leaves, you can see for yourselves and know that summer is near. ³¹Even so, when you see these things happening, you know that the kingdom of God is near.

³²"I tell you the truth, this generation[a] will certainly not pass away until all these things have happened. ³³Heaven and earth will pass away, but my words will never pass away.

³⁴"Be careful, or your hearts will be weighed down with dissipation, drunkenness and the anxieties of life, and that day will close on you unexpectedly like a trap. ³⁵For it will come upon all those who live on the face of the whole earth. ³⁶Be always on the watch, and pray that you may be able to escape all that is about to happen, and that you may be able to stand before the Son of Man."

³⁷Each day Jesus was teaching at the temple, and each evening he went out to spend the night on the hill called the Mount of Olives, ³⁸and all the people came early in the morning to hear him at the temple.

Judas Agrees to Betray Jesus

22 Now the Feast of Unleavened Bread, called the Passover, was approaching, ²and the chief priests and the teachers of the law were looking for some way to get rid of Jesus, for they were afraid of the people. ³Then Satan entered Judas, called Iscariot, one of the Twelve. ⁴And Judas went to the chief priests and the officers of the temple guard and discussed with them how he might betray Jesus. ⁵They were delighted and agreed to give him money. ⁶He consented, and watched for an opportunity to hand Jesus over to them when no crowd was present.

The Last Supper

⁷Then came the day of Unleavened Bread on which the Passover lamb had to be sacrificed. ⁸Jesus sent Peter and John, saying, "Go and make preparations for us to eat the Passover."

⁹"Where do you want us to prepare for it?" they asked.

¹⁰He replied, "As you enter the city, a man carrying a jar of water will meet you. Follow him to the house that he enters, ¹¹and say to the owner of the house, 'The Teacher asks: Where is the guest room, where I may eat the Passover with my disciples?' ¹²He will show you a large upper room, all furnished. Make preparations there."

¹³They left and found things just as Jesus had told them. So they prepared the Passover.

¹⁴When the hour came, Jesus and his apostles reclined at the table. ¹⁵And he said to them, "I have eagerly desired to eat this Passover with you before I suffer. ¹⁶For I tell you, I will not eat it again until it finds fulfillment in the kingdom of God."

¹⁷After taking the cup, he gave thanks and said, "Take this and divide it among you. ¹⁸For I tell you I will not drink again of the fruit of the vine until the kingdom of God comes."

¹⁹And he took bread, gave thanks and broke it, and gave it to them, saying, "This is my body given for you; do this in remembrance of me."

²⁰In the same way, after the supper he

[a]32 Or race

took the cup, saying, "This cup is the new covenant in my blood, which is poured out for you. ²¹But the hand of him who is going to betray me is with mine on the table. ²²The Son of Man will go as it has been decreed, but woe to that man who betrays him." ²³They began to question among themselves which of them it might be who would do this.

²⁴Also a dispute arose among them as to which of them was considered to be greatest. ²⁵Jesus said to them, "The kings of the Gentiles lord it over them; and those who exercise authority over them call themselves Benefactors. ²⁶But you are not to be like that. Instead, the greatest among you should be like the youngest, and the one who rules like the one who serves. ²⁷For who is greater, the one who is at the table or the one who serves? Is it not the one who is at the table? But I am among you as one who serves. ²⁸You are those who have stood by me in my trials. ²⁹And I confer on you a kingdom, just as my Father conferred one on me, ³⁰so that you may eat and drink at my table in my kingdom and sit on thrones, judging the twelve tribes of Israel.

³¹"Simon, Simon, Satan has asked to sift you*ᵃ* as wheat. ³²But I have prayed for you, Simon, that your faith may not fail. And when you have turned back, strengthen your brothers."

³³But he replied, "Lord, I am ready to go with you to prison and to death."

³⁴Jesus answered, "I tell you, Peter, before the rooster crows today, you will deny three times that you know me."

³⁵Then Jesus asked them, "When I sent you without purse, bag or sandals, did you lack anything?"

"Nothing," they answered.

³⁶He said to them, "But now if you have a purse, take it, and also a bag; and if you don't have a sword, sell your cloak and buy one. ³⁷It is written: 'And he was numbered with the transgressors'ᵇ; and I tell you that this must be fulfilled in me. Yes, what is written about me is reaching its fulfillment."

³⁸The disciples said, "See, Lord, here are two swords."

"That is enough," he replied.

Jesus Prays on the Mount of Olives

³⁹Jesus went out as usual to the Mount of Olives, and his disciples followed him. ⁴⁰On reaching the place, he said to them, "Pray that you will not fall into temptation." ⁴¹He withdrew about a stone's throw beyond them, knelt down and prayed, ⁴²"Father, if you are willing, take this cup from me; yet not my will, but yours be done." ⁴³An angel from heaven appeared to him and strengthened him. ⁴⁴And being in anguish, he prayed more earnestly, and his sweat was like drops of blood falling to the ground.ᶜ

⁴⁵When he rose from prayer and went back to the disciples, he found them asleep, exhausted from sorrow. ⁴⁶"Why are you sleeping?" he asked them. "Get up and pray so that you will not fall into temptation."

Jesus Arrested

⁴⁷While he was still speaking a crowd came up, and the man who was called Judas, one of the Twelve, was leading them. He approached Jesus to kiss him, ⁴⁸but Jesus asked him, "Judas, are you betraying the Son of Man with a kiss?"

⁴⁹When Jesus' followers saw what was going to happen, they said, "Lord, should we strike with our swords?" ⁵⁰And one of them struck the servant of the high priest, cutting off his right ear.

⁵¹But Jesus answered, "No more of this!" And he touched the man's ear and healed him.

⁵²Then Jesus said to the chief priests, the officers of the temple guard, and the elders, who had come for him, "Am I leading a rebellion, that you have come with swords and clubs? ⁵³Every day I was with you in the temple courts, and you did not lay a hand on me. But this is your hour—when darkness reigns."

Peter Disowns Jesus

⁵⁴Then seizing him, they led him away and took him into the house of the high priest. Peter followed at a distance. ⁵⁵But when they had kindled a fire in the middle of the courtyard and had sat down together, Peter sat down with them. ⁵⁶A servant girl saw him seated there in the

---

ᵃ31 The Greek is plural.   ᵇ37 Isaiah 53:12   ᶜ44 Some early manuscripts do not have verses 43 and 44.

firelight. She looked closely at him and said, "This man was with him."

57But he denied it. "Woman, I don't know him," he said.

58A little later someone else saw him and said, "You also are one of them."

"Man, I am not!" Peter replied.

59About an hour later another asserted, "Certainly this fellow was with him, for he is a Galilean."

60Peter replied, "Man, I don't know what you're talking about!" Just as he

---

═══ FRIDAY ═══

VERSE:	AUTHOR:	PASSAGE:
Luke 22:61–62	Brenda M. Josee, Ed.	Luke 22:54–62

The Look

Few stories in the Bible give me goose bumps like the account of Peter's denial of Jesus. All four Gospels report the event, but Luke's Gospel is the only account which includes "the look."

I know "the look." I was raised with it. It is silent, yet speaks volumes. My father was a master of "the look." This meant he seldom had to yell or spank. "The look" was enough.

Once when I was about six years old, I became angry at my friend, Betsy. I stood in my driveway calling her every name I could think of. "Big baby" and "ugly dummy" were about the extent of my verbal arsenal, and they just didn't seem effective. Then I remembered a name, one I certainly had not heard in my house, and lobbed that one. It must have been a good one, because Betsy screamed and ran inside to tell her mother.

I did an about face and marched triumphantly toward my house. Unfortunately, I had not seen my father cleaning out his car. He had heard every word. When my eyes met his, my heart broke. He was giving me "the look." I burst into tears, ran into the house and down the hall into my room, where I cried for two hours.

Imagine Peter's reaction to Jesus' look. He must have been overwhelmed by the conviction of his sin, the denial of his Lord and friend. All he could do was flee the scene of the crime and mourn his mistake. But beyond that, maybe there was a newfound awareness of Jesus' meekness; that Jesus, who had the power to instantly annihilate Peter, simply looked at him. Was it a look of disappointment? Anger? Pain? Love? Concern? Maybe a combination of all. That's what I always saw in my father's eyes. And it was enough.

As you read this account of Peter's denial, try to imagine the scene from both perspectives, Jesus' and Peter's. When have you denied your Lord by your words and actions? Can you imagine Jesus looking at you just as he looked at the apostle Peter all those centuries ago?

ADDITIONAL SCRIPTURE READINGS:
Ezra 9:6; Mark 8:38; John 21:15–19

Go to page 115 for your next devotional reading.

was speaking, the rooster crowed. **61**The Lord turned and looked straight at Peter. Then Peter remembered the word the Lord had spoken to him: "Before the rooster crows today, you will disown me three times." **62**And he went outside and wept bitterly.

The Guards Mock Jesus

63The men who were guarding Jesus began mocking and beating him. **64**They blindfolded him and demanded, "Prophesy! Who hit you?" **65**And they said many other insulting things to him.

Jesus Before Pilate and Herod

66At daybreak the council of the elders of the people, both the chief priests and teachers of the law, met together, and Jesus was led before them. **67**"If you are the Christ,*a*" they said, "tell us."

Jesus answered, "If I tell you, you will not believe me, **68**and if I asked you, you would not answer. **69**But from now on, the Son of Man will be seated at the right hand of the mighty God."

70They all asked, "Are you then the Son of God?"

He replied, "You are right in saying I am."

71Then they said, "Why do we need any more testimony? We have heard it from his own lips."

23 Then the whole assembly rose and led him off to Pilate. **2**And they began to accuse him, saying, "We have found this man subverting our nation. He opposes payment of taxes to Caesar and claims to be Christ,*b* a king."

3So Pilate asked Jesus, "Are you the king of the Jews?"

"Yes, it is as you say," Jesus replied.

4Then Pilate announced to the chief priests and the crowd, "I find no basis for a charge against this man."

5But they insisted, "He stirs up the people all over Judea*c* by his teaching. He started in Galilee and has come all the way here."

6On hearing this, Pilate asked if the man was a Galilean. **7**When he learned that Jesus was under Herod's jurisdiction, he sent him to Herod, who was also in Jerusalem at that time.

8When Herod saw Jesus, he was greatly pleased, because for a long time he had been wanting to see him. From what he had heard about him, he hoped to see him perform some miracle. **9**He plied him with many questions, but Jesus gave him no answer. **10**The chief priests and the teachers of the law were standing there, vehemently accusing him. **11**Then Herod and his soldiers ridiculed and mocked him. Dressing him in an elegant robe, they sent him back to Pilate. **12**That day Herod and Pilate became friends—before this they had been enemies.

13Pilate called together the chief priests, the rulers and the people, **14**and said to them, "You brought me this man as one who was inciting the people to rebellion. I have examined him in your presence and have found no basis for your charges against him. **15**Neither has Herod, for he sent him back to us; as you can see, he has done nothing to deserve death. **16**Therefore, I will punish him and then release him.*d*"

18With one voice they cried out, "Away with this man! Release Barabbas to us!" **19**(Barabbas had been thrown into prison for an insurrection in the city, and for murder.)

20Wanting to release Jesus, Pilate appealed to them again. **21**But they kept shouting, "Crucify him! Crucify him!"

22For the third time he spoke to them: "Why? What crime has this man committed? I have found in him no grounds for the death penalty. Therefore I will have him punished and then release him."

23But with loud shouts they insistently demanded that he be crucified, and their shouts prevailed. **24**So Pilate decided to grant their demand. **25**He released the man who had been thrown into prison for insurrection and murder, the one they asked for, and surrendered Jesus to their will.

The Crucifixion

26As they led him away, they seized Simon from Cyrene, who was on his way in from the country, and put the cross on him and made him carry it behind Jesus. **27**A large number of people followed him, including women who mourned and wailed for him. **28**Jesus

---

*a*67 Or *Messiah*   *b*2 Or *Messiah*; also in verses 35 and 39   *c*5 Or *over the land of the Jews*
*d*16 Some manuscripts *him."* *17Now he was obliged to release one man to them at the Feast.*

WEEKENDING

REALIZE

Each of us has an important decision to make here. Is Jesus really who he claimed to be—the *only begotten son* of the Father, "very God of very God"? Is he entitled to be called "the Christ"? For the name *Christ* means "the Messiah," the one prophesied through all the centuries . . . There can be only one Christus—the Crowned One.

Until we catch a glimpse of the full glory of this crowned Christ, of the honors heaped upon him, of the extent of the power the Father has placed in his hands, we can never grasp the significance of Jesus' question, "Who do you say I am?"

Catherine Marshall

RESTORE

Saturday: John 1:1–18
Sunday: Matthew 16:13–19; Colossians 1:15–23

Go to page 117 for your next devotional reading.

turned and said to them, "Daughters of Jerusalem, do not weep for me; weep for yourselves and for your children. ²⁹For the time will come when you will say, 'Blessed are the barren women, the wombs that never bore and the breasts that never nursed!' ³⁰Then

> " 'they will say to the mountains,
>   "Fall on us!"
>   and to the hills, "Cover us!" ' ᵃ

³¹For if men do these things when the tree is green, what will happen when it is dry?"

³²Two other men, both criminals, were also led out with him to be executed. ³³When they came to the place called the Skull, there they crucified him, along with the criminals—one on his right, the other on his left. ³⁴Jesus said, "Father, forgive them, for they do not know what they are doing." ᵇ And they divided up his clothes by casting lots.

³⁵The people stood watching, and the rulers even sneered at him. They said, "He saved others; let him save himself if he is the Christ of God, the Chosen One."

³⁶The soldiers also came up and mocked him. They offered him wine vinegar ³⁷and said, "If you are the king of the Jews, save yourself."

³⁸There was a written notice above him, which read: THIS IS THE KING OF THE JEWS.

³⁹One of the criminals who hung there hurled insults at him: "Aren't you the Christ? Save yourself and us!"

⁴⁰But the other criminal rebuked him. "Don't you fear God," he said, "since you are under the same sentence? ⁴¹We are punished justly, for we are getting what our deeds deserve. But this man has done nothing wrong."

⁴²Then he said, "Jesus, remember me when you come into your kingdom.ᶜ"

⁴³Jesus answered him, "I tell you the truth, today you will be with me in paradise."

Jesus' Death

⁴⁴It was now about the sixth hour, and darkness came over the whole land until the ninth hour, ⁴⁵for the sun stopped shining. And the curtain of the temple was torn in two. ⁴⁶Jesus called

out with a loud voice, "Father, into your hands I commit my spirit." When he had said this, he breathed his last.

⁴⁷The centurion, seeing what had happened, praised God and said, "Surely this was a righteous man." ⁴⁸When all the people who had gathered to witness this sight saw what took place, they beat their breasts and went away. ⁴⁹But all those who knew him, including the women who had followed him from Galilee, stood at a distance, watching these things.

Jesus' Burial

⁵⁰Now there was a man named Joseph, a member of the Council, a good and upright man, ⁵¹who had not consented to their decision and action. He came from the Judean town of Arimathea and he was waiting for the kingdom of God. ⁵²Going to Pilate, he asked for Jesus' body. ⁵³Then he took it down, wrapped it in linen cloth and placed it in a tomb cut in the rock, one in which no one had yet been laid. ⁵⁴It was Preparation Day, and the Sabbath was about to begin.

⁵⁵The women who had come with Jesus from Galilee followed Joseph and saw the tomb and how his body was laid in it. ⁵⁶Then they went home and prepared spices and perfumes. But they rested on the Sabbath in obedience to the commandment.

The Resurrection

24 On the first day of the week, very early in the morning, the women took the spices they had prepared and went to the tomb. ²They found the stone rolled away from the tomb, ³but when they entered, they did not find the body of the Lord Jesus. ⁴While they were wondering about this, suddenly two men in clothes that gleamed like lightning stood beside them. ⁵In their fright the women bowed down with their faces to the ground, but the men said to them, "Why do you look for the living among the dead? ⁶He is not here; he has risen! Remember how he told you, while he was still with you in Galilee: ⁷'The Son of Man must be delivered into the hands of sinful men, be crucified and on the third day be

---

ᵃ30 Hosea 10:8   ᵇ34 Some early manuscripts do not have this sentence.   ᶜ42 Some manuscripts *come with your kingly power*

VERSE:	AUTHOR:	PASSAGE:
Luke 23:49	Ruth Senter	Luke 23:26–49

Rainy Nights and Wooden Crosses

We've come away from the cross. In our sleek, sophisticated society we allow no time for plain wooden planks that meet in the middle. I don't pay much attention to symbols that dominated the eve of Passover 2,000 years ago. I feed my children, shop for groceries and drive to the post office, but I don't think much about the Roman style of execution and rocky hillsides shaped like skulls. Life is much too modern for archaic sentimentality.

But tonight calls to the past. My past. His past. Everyone's past. I slip into the semi-dark cathedral. One dim light from somewhere high in the vaulted ceiling makes me barely aware of muted figures passing by me as though in stocking feet. No one talks. Only the Gregorian chant from the far corner of the long, gothic nave breaks the silence.

All eyes focus on a simple crossbeam suspended high above the altar. The light from above shines directly on the cross. Otherwise, all is dark.

"The Word became flesh and made his dwelling among us . . ." (John 1:14). The chant goes on, echoing off the vaulted ceiling. What does it mean to me—these simple wooden planks that meet in the middle?

I am in the middle of a fast-paced, upwardly mobile metropolis. But tonight I stop, study the cross and kneel in shame for so quickly forgetting. This cross, like a wedding band, bonds me forever in love. I am loved. I am loved enough for Roman execution on a rocky, skull-shaped hill.

". . . now dismiss your servant in peace" (Luke 2:29). The choir voice grows soft. The light dims. The muted forms around me start to move. I cast one last glance at the hanging wood and know I must return again and again. What tragedy to wander from the cross.

I pull my coat around me and head out into a rainy Seattle night. Returning to the cross compels me also to leave it, because the cross points me outward, to the world. I am loved, yes, but so are they. I see the lights of a million people in the city below. What tragedy should they miss the cross. I must return to the cross for their sakes, as well as for mine.

ADDITIONAL SCRIPTURE READINGS:
Matthew 10:38; Matthew 28:16–20; Hebrews 13:12–21

Go to page 122 for your next devotional reading.

raised again.' " **8**Then they remembered his words.

9When they came back from the tomb, they told all these things to the Eleven and to all the others. **10**It was Mary Magdalene, Joanna, Mary the mother of James, and the others with them who told this to the apostles. **11**But they did not believe the women, because their words seemed to them like nonsense. **12**Peter, however, got up and ran to the tomb. Bending over, he saw the strips of linen lying by themselves, and he went away, wondering to himself what had happened.

On the Road to Emmaus

13Now that same day two of them were going to a village called Emmaus, about seven miles*a* from Jerusalem. **14**They were talking with each other about everything that had happened. **15**As they talked and discussed these things with each other, Jesus himself came up and walked along with them; **16**but they were kept from recognizing him.

17He asked them, "What are you discussing together as you walk along?"

They stood still, their faces downcast. **18**One of them, named Cleopas, asked him, "Are you only a visitor to Jerusalem and do not know the things that have happened there in these days?"

19"What things?" he asked.

"About Jesus of Nazareth," they replied. "He was a prophet, powerful in word and deed before God and all the people. **20**The chief priests and our rulers handed him over to be sentenced to death, and they crucified him; **21**but we had hoped that he was the one who was going to redeem Israel. And what is more, it is the third day since all this took place. **22**In addition, some of our women amazed us. They went to the tomb early this morning **23**but didn't find his body. They came and told us that they had seen a vision of angels, who said he was alive. **24**Then some of our companions went to the tomb and found it just as the women had said, but him they did not see."

25He said to them, "How foolish you are, and how slow of heart to believe all that the prophets have spoken! **26**Did not the Christ*b* have to suffer these things and then enter his glory?" **27**And beginning with Moses and all the Prophets, he explained to them what was said in all the Scriptures concerning himself.

28As they approached the village to which they were going, Jesus acted as if he were going farther. **29**But they urged him strongly, "Stay with us, for it is nearly evening; the day is almost over." So he went in to stay with them.

30When he was at the table with them, he took bread, gave thanks, broke it and began to give it to them. **31**Then their eyes were opened and they recognized him, and he disappeared from their sight. **32**They asked each other, "Were not our hearts burning within us while he talked with us on the road and opened the Scriptures to us?"

33They got up and returned at once to Jerusalem. There they found the Eleven and those with them, assembled together **34**and saying, "It is true! The Lord has risen and has appeared to Simon." **35**Then the two told what had happened on the way, and how Jesus was recognized by them when he broke the bread.

Jesus Appears to the Disciples

36While they were still talking about this, Jesus himself stood among them and said to them, "Peace be with you."

37They were startled and frightened, thinking they saw a ghost. **38**He said to them, "Why are you troubled, and why do doubts rise in your minds? **39**Look at my hands and my feet. It is I myself! Touch me and see; a ghost does not have flesh and bones, as you see I have."

40When he had said this, he showed them his hands and feet. **41**And while they still did not believe it because of joy and amazement, he asked them, "Do you have anything here to eat?" **42**They gave him a piece of broiled fish, **43**and he took it and ate it in their presence.

44He said to them, "This is what I told you while I was still with you: Everything must be fulfilled that is written about me in the Law of Moses, the Prophets and the Psalms."

45Then he opened their minds so they could understand the Scriptures. **46**He told them, "This is what is written: The

a13 Greek *sixty stadia* (about 11 kilometers)   *b26* Or *Messiah*; also in verse 46

Christ will suffer and rise from the dead on the third day, [47]and repentance and forgiveness of sins will be preached in his name to all nations, beginning at Jerusalem. [48]You are witnesses of these things. [49]I am going to send you what my Father has promised; but stay in the city until you have been clothed with power from on high."

The Ascension

[50]When he had led them out to the vicinity of Bethany, he lifted up his hands and blessed them. [51]While he was blessing them, he left them and was taken up into heaven. [52]Then they worshiped him and returned to Jerusalem with great joy. [53]And they stayed continually at the temple, praising God.

WHY *did God's Son come to earth? The Gospel of John has the answer: "For God so loved the world that he gave his one and only Son, that whoever believes in him shall not perish but have eternal life" (3:16). John's writings are designed to convince people to believe in Jesus as God in human form and, as a result, to "have life" (20:31). Reflect on the One who once lived among people like us and renew your trust that he will give you life to the full.*

JOHN

The Word Became Flesh

1 In the beginning was the Word, and the Word was with God, and the Word was God. ²He was with God in the beginning.

³Through him all things were made; without him nothing was made that has been made. ⁴In him was life, and that life was the light of men. ⁵The light shines in the darkness, but the darkness has not understood*ᵃ* it.

⁶There came a man who was sent from God; his name was John. ⁷He came as a witness to testify concerning that light, so that through him all men might believe. ⁸He himself was not the light; he came only as a witness to the light. ⁹The true light that gives light to every man was coming into the world.*ᵇ*

¹⁰He was in the world, and though the world was made through him, the world did not recognize him. ¹¹He came to that which was his own, but his own did not receive him. ¹²Yet to all who received him, to those who believed in his name, he gave the right to become children of God— ¹³children born not of natural descent,*ᶜ* nor of human decision or a husband's will, but born of God.

¹⁴The Word became flesh and made

his dwelling among us. We have seen his glory, the glory of the One and Only,[a] who came from the Father, full of grace and truth.

[15]John testifies concerning him. He cries out, saying, "This was he of whom I said, 'He who comes after me has surpassed me because he was before me.'" [16]From the fullness of his grace we have all received one blessing after another. [17]For the law was given through Moses; grace and truth came through Jesus Christ. [18]No one has ever seen God, but God the One and Only,[a,b] who is at the Father's side, has made him known.

John the Baptist Denies Being the Christ

[19]Now this was John's testimony when the Jews of Jerusalem sent priests and Levites to ask him who he was. [20]He did not fail to confess, but confessed freely, "I am not the Christ.[c]"

[21]They asked him, "Then who are you? Are you Elijah?"

He said, "I am not."

"Are you the Prophet?"

He answered, "No."

[22]Finally they said, "Who are you? Give us an answer to take back to those who sent us. What do you say about yourself?"

[23]John replied in the words of Isaiah the prophet, "I am the voice of one calling in the desert, 'Make straight the way for the Lord.'"[d]

[24]Now some Pharisees who had been sent [25]questioned him, "Why then do you baptize if you are not the Christ, nor Elijah, nor the Prophet?"

[26]"I baptize with[e] water," John replied, "but among you stands one you do not know. [27]He is the one who comes after me, the thongs of whose sandals I am not worthy to untie."

[28]This all happened at Bethany on the other side of the Jordan, where John was baptizing.

Jesus the Lamb of God

[29]The next day John saw Jesus coming toward him and said, "Look, the Lamb of God, who takes away the sin of the world! [30]This is the one I meant when I said, 'A man who comes after me has surpassed me because he was before me.' [31]I myself did not know him, but the reason I came baptizing with water was that he might be revealed to Israel."

[32]Then John gave this testimony: "I saw the Spirit come down from heaven as a dove and remain on him. [33]I would not have known him, except that the one who sent me to baptize with water told me, 'The man on whom you see the Spirit come down and remain is he who will baptize with the Holy Spirit.' [34]I have seen and I testify that this is the Son of God."

Jesus' First Disciples

[35]The next day John was there again with two of his disciples. [36]When he saw Jesus passing by, he said, "Look, the Lamb of God!"

[37]When the two disciples heard him say this, they followed Jesus. [38]Turning around, Jesus saw them following and asked, "What do you want?"

They said, "Rabbi" (which means Teacher), "where are you staying?"

[39]"Come," he replied, "and you will see."

So they went and saw where he was staying, and spent that day with him. It was about the tenth hour.

[40]Andrew, Simon Peter's brother, was one of the two who heard what John had said and who had followed Jesus. [41]The first thing Andrew did was to find his brother Simon and tell him, "We have found the Messiah" (that is, the Christ). [42]And he brought him to Jesus.

Jesus looked at him and said, "You are Simon son of John. You will be called Cephas" (which, when translated, is Peter[f]).

Jesus Calls Philip and Nathanael

[43]The next day Jesus decided to leave for Galilee. Finding Philip, he said to him, "Follow me."

[44]Philip, like Andrew and Peter, was from the town of Bethsaida. [45]Philip found Nathanael and told him, "We have found the one Moses wrote about

---

[a]14,18 Or the Only Begotten   [b]18 Some manuscripts but the only (or only begotten) Son   [c]20 Or Messiah. "The Christ" (Greek) and "the Messiah" (Hebrew) both mean "the Anointed One"; also in verse 25.   [d]23 Isaiah 40:3   [e]26 Or in; also in verses 31 and 33   [f]42 Both Cephas (Aramaic) and Peter (Greek) mean rock.

in the Law, and about whom the prophets also wrote—Jesus of Nazareth, the son of Joseph."

⁴⁶"Nazareth! Can anything good come from there?" Nathanael asked.

"Come and see," said Philip.

⁴⁷When Jesus saw Nathanael approaching, he said of him, "Here is a true Israelite, in whom there is nothing false."

⁴⁸"How do you know me?" Nathanael asked.

Jesus answered, "I saw you while you were still under the fig tree before Philip called you."

⁴⁹Then Nathanael declared, "Rabbi, you are the Son of God; you are the King of Israel."

⁵⁰Jesus said, "You believe*a* because I told you I saw you under the fig tree. You shall see greater things than that." ⁵¹He then added, "I tell you*b* the truth, you*b* shall see heaven open, and the angels of God ascending and descending on the Son of Man."

Jesus Changes Water to Wine

2 On the third day a wedding took place at Cana in Galilee. Jesus' mother was there, ²and Jesus and his

---

a50 Or *Do you believe . . . ?*   *b51* The Greek is plural.

TUESDAY

VERSE:
John 1:38

AUTHOR:
Jeanie Miley

PASSAGE:
John 1:35-42

What Do You Want?

"What do you want?" Jesus asks you.

It is such a simple question, and yet you know that how you answer that question is going to shape the rest of your days.

"I saw you following me," Jesus says. You turn to your friend as a slight blush washes across your face. Then you look back to Jesus. His compelling force is so great that you don't concern yourself with being embarrassed.

Standing there, poised between your old life and the future, you feel alive as never before. Time seems to stand still. All the colors around you are vivid; the sounds are clear and almost musical.

What do you say when Jesus asks what you want? Do you even know what you want? As you stand there, enclosed in a holy space even in the midst of a crowd, you examine your heart.

Are you coming to Jesus out of curiosity? Do you have some need you think he might meet or an intellectual question he might answer? Is there something in you that needs to be healed? Is there some brokenness, a piercing or unrelenting pain, a failure from your past that you would like him to carry? Do you need forgiveness? Are you dying for love? Is there something you have tried to fix that escapes your skill?

Exactly what is it that you want from Jesus of Nazareth? Tell him, in your prayer of the heart, exactly what you need.

ADDITIONAL SCRIPTURE READINGS:
Psalm 103:1-5; Psalm 148; Matthew 7:7-11

Go to page 124 for your next devotional reading.

disciples had also been invited to the wedding. ³When the wine was gone, Jesus' mother said to him, "They have no more wine."

⁴"Dear woman, why do you involve me?" Jesus replied. "My time has not yet come."

⁵His mother said to the servants, "Do whatever he tells you."

⁶Nearby stood six stone water jars, the kind used by the Jews for ceremonial washing, each holding from twenty to thirty gallons.ᵃ

⁷Jesus said to the servants, "Fill the jars with water"; so they filled them to the brim.

⁸Then he told them, "Now draw some out and take it to the master of the banquet."

They did so, ⁹and the master of the banquet tasted the water that had been turned into wine. He did not realize where it had come from, though the servants who had drawn the water knew. Then he called the bridegroom aside ¹⁰and said, "Everyone brings out the choice wine first and then the cheaper wine after the guests have had too much to drink; but you have saved the best till now."

¹¹This, the first of his miraculous signs, Jesus performed at Cana in Galilee. He thus revealed his glory, and his disciples put their faith in him.

Jesus Clears the Temple

¹²After this he went down to Capernaum with his mother and brothers and his disciples. There they stayed for a few days.

¹³When it was almost time for the Jewish Passover, Jesus went up to Jerusalem. ¹⁴In the temple courts he found men selling cattle, sheep and doves, and others sitting at tables exchanging money. ¹⁵So he made a whip out of cords, and drove all from the temple area, both sheep and cattle; he scattered the coins of the money changers and overturned their tables. ¹⁶To those who sold doves he said, "Get these out of here! How dare you turn my Father's house into a market!"

¹⁷His disciples remembered that it is written: "Zeal for your house will consume me."ᵇ

¹⁸Then the Jews demanded of him, "What miraculous sign can you show us to prove your authority to do all this?"

¹⁹Jesus answered them, "Destroy this temple, and I will raise it again in three days."

²⁰The Jews replied, "It has taken forty-six years to build this temple, and you are going to raise it in three days?" ²¹But the temple he had spoken of was his body. ²²After he was raised from the dead, his disciples recalled what he had said. Then they believed the Scripture and the words that Jesus had spoken.

²³Now while he was in Jerusalem at the Passover Feast, many people saw the miraculous signs he was doing and believed in his name.ᶜ ²⁴But Jesus would not entrust himself to them, for he knew all men. ²⁵He did not need man's testimony about man, for he knew what was in a man.

Jesus Teaches Nicodemus

3 Now there was a man of the Pharisees named Nicodemus, a member of the Jewish ruling council. ²He came to Jesus at night and said, "Rabbi, we know you are a teacher who has come from God. For no one could perform the miraculous signs you are doing if God were not with him."

³In reply Jesus declared, "I tell you the truth, no one can see the kingdom of God unless he is born again.ᵈ"

⁴"How can a man be born when he is old?" Nicodemus asked. "Surely he cannot enter a second time into his mother's womb to be born!"

⁵Jesus answered, "I tell you the truth, no one can enter the kingdom of God unless he is born of water and the Spirit. ⁶Flesh gives birth to flesh, but the Spiritᵉ gives birth to spirit. ⁷You should not be surprised at my saying, 'Youᶠ must be born again.' ⁸The wind blows wherever it pleases. You hear its sound, but you cannot tell where it comes from or where it is going. So it is with everyone born of the Spirit."

ᵃ6 Greek *two to three metretes* (probably about 75 to 115 liters)   ᵇ17 Psalm 69:9   ᶜ23 Or *and believed in him*   ᵈ3 Or *born from above*; also in verse 7   ᵉ6 Or *but spirit*   ᶠ7 The Greek is plural.

⁹"How can this be?" Nicodemus asked.

¹⁰"You are Israel's teacher," said Jesus, "and do you not understand these things? ¹¹I tell you the truth, we speak of what we know, and we testify to what we have seen, but still you people do not accept our testimony. ¹²I have spoken to you of earthly things and you do not believe; how then will you believe if I speak of heavenly things? ¹³No one has ever gone into heaven except the

WEDNESDAY

VERSE:	AUTHOR:	PASSAGE:
John 3:3	Sue Monk Kidd	John 3:1–21

Aching to Be Born

"There is a self within each one of us aching to be born," says theologian Alan Jones.* And when this aching breaks into our lives . . . we must somehow find the courage to say yes. Yes to this more real, more Christlike self struggling to be born.

That cold February day I tried very hard to say yes to what was struggling inside me. I burrowed into the wind, my head down. I happened to look up again as I passed beneath the branches of a dogwood tree, and my eyes fell upon a curious little appendage suspended from a twig just over my head.

I kept walking. *No, stop . . . look closer.* Not knowing what else to do but obey the inner impulse, I backed up and looked again. *I had come upon a cocoon.*

I was caught suddenly by a sweep of reverence, a sensation that made me want to sink to my knees. Somehow I knew I had stumbled upon an epiphany, a strange gracing of my darkness. I touched the bottom tip of the tiny brown cocoon and felt something like light move in me. In that moment God seemed to speak to me about transformation. About the descent and emergence of the soul. About hope.

I broke the twig from the limb and carried the cocoon home. For this was *my* cocoon. My darkness. My soul incubating within.

Back home I carefully taped the twig with the cocoon to a branch of a crab apple tree in my backyard. [Later,] I stood at the window watching the cocoon, which hung in the winter air like an upside-down question mark. *Live the question,* God whispered.

Knowledge descended into my heart and I understood. Crisis, change, all the myriad upheavals that blister the spirit and leave us groping—they aren't voices simply of pain but also of creativity. And if we would only listen, we might hear such times beckoning us to a season of waiting, to the place of fertile emptiness.

*Journey into Christ (San Francisco: Harper & Row, 1977)

ADDITIONAL SCRIPTURE READINGS:
Ephesians 4:20–23; Titus 3:5; 1 Peter 1:3

Go to page 126 for your next devotional reading.

one who came from heaven—the Son of Man.[a] [14]Just as Moses lifted up the snake in the desert, so the Son of Man must be lifted up, [15]that everyone who believes in him may have eternal life.[b]

[16]"For God so loved the world that he gave his one and only Son,[c] that whoever believes in him shall not perish but have eternal life. [17]For God did not send his Son into the world to condemn the world, but to save the world through him. [18]Whoever believes in him is not condemned, but whoever does not believe stands condemned already because he has not believed in the name of God's one and only Son.[d] [19]This is the verdict: Light has come into the world, but men loved darkness instead of light because their deeds were evil. [20]Everyone who does evil hates the light, and will not come into the light for fear that his deeds will be exposed. [21]But whoever lives by the truth comes into the light, so that it may be seen plainly that what he has done has been done through God."[e]

John the Baptist's Testimony About Jesus

[22]After this, Jesus and his disciples went out into the Judean countryside, where he spent some time with them, and baptized. [23]Now John also was baptizing at Aenon near Salim, because there was plenty of water, and people were constantly coming to be baptized. [24](This was before John was put in prison.) [25]An argument developed between some of John's disciples and a certain Jew[f] over the matter of ceremonial washing. [26]They came to John and said to him, "Rabbi, that man who was with you on the other side of the Jordan—the one you testified about—well, he is baptizing, and everyone is going to him."

[27]To this John replied, "A man can receive only what is given him from heaven. [28]You yourselves can testify that I said, 'I am not the Christ[g] but am sent ahead of him.' [29]The bride belongs to the bridegroom. The friend who attends the bridegroom waits and listens for him, and is full of joy when he hears the bridegroom's voice. That joy is mine, and it is now complete. [30]He must become greater; I must become less.

[31]"The one who comes from above is above all; the one who is from the earth belongs to the earth, and speaks as one from the earth. The one who comes from heaven is above all. [32]He testifies to what he has seen and heard, but no one accepts his testimony. [33]The man who has accepted it has certified that God is truthful. [34]For the one whom God has sent speaks the words of God, for God[h] gives the Spirit without limit. [35]The Father loves the Son and has placed everything in his hands. [36]Whoever believes in the Son has eternal life, but whoever rejects the Son will not see life, for God's wrath remains on him."[i]

Jesus Talks With a Samaritan Woman

4 The Pharisees heard that Jesus was gaining and baptizing more disciples than John, [2]although in fact it was not Jesus who baptized, but his disciples. [3]When the Lord learned of this, he left Judea and went back once more to Galilee.

[4]Now he had to go through Samaria. [5]So he came to a town in Samaria called Sychar, near the plot of ground Jacob had given to his son Joseph. [6]Jacob's well was there, and Jesus, tired as he was from the journey, sat down by the well. It was about the sixth hour.

[7]When a Samaritan woman came to draw water, Jesus said to her, "Will you give me a drink?" [8](His disciples had gone into the town to buy food.)

[9]The Samaritan woman said to him, "You are a Jew and I am a Samaritan woman. How can you ask me for a drink?" (For Jews do not associate with Samaritans.[j])

[10]Jesus answered her, "If you knew the gift of God and who it is that asks you for a drink, you would have asked him and he would have given you living water."

[11]"Sir," the woman said, "you have nothing to draw with and the well is deep. Where can you get this living water? [12]Are you greater than our father Ja-

---

[a]13 Some manuscripts Man, who is in heaven   [b]15 Or believes may have eternal life in him   [c]16 Or his only begotten Son   [d]18 Or God's only begotten Son   [e]21 Some interpreters end the quotation after verse 15.   [f]25 Some manuscripts and certain Jews   [g]28 Or Messiah   [h]34 Greek he [i]36 Some interpreters end the quotation after verse 30.   [j]9 Or do not use dishes Samaritans have used

cob, who gave us the well and drank from it himself, as did also his sons and his flocks and herds?"

¹³Jesus answered, "Everyone who drinks this water will be thirsty again, ¹⁴but whoever drinks the water I give him will never thirst. Indeed, the water I give him will become in him a spring of water welling up to eternal life."

¹⁵The woman said to him, "Sir, give me this water so that I won't get thirsty and have to keep coming here to draw water."

¹⁶He told her, "Go, call your husband and come back."

¹⁷"I have no husband," she replied.

Jesus said to her, "You are right when you say you have no husband. ¹⁸The fact is, you have had five husbands, and the man you now have is not your husband. What you have just said is quite true."

¹⁹"Sir," the woman said, "I can see that you are a prophet. ²⁰Our fathers worshiped on this mountain, but you Jews claim that the place where we must worship is in Jerusalem."

²¹Jesus declared, "Believe me, woman, a time is coming when you will worship the Father neither on this mountain nor

---

THURSDAY

VERSE:	AUTHOR:	PASSAGE:
John 4:10	Gigi Graham Tchividjian	John 4:1–26

The Green Ribbon

It was Saturday, Israel's day of worship. After church [my husband] Stephan, the children and I decided to drive out of the city and into the hills around Jerusalem. They are rugged and barren—beautiful in an almost mystical sort of way—and we never tired of exploring them.

After stopping at a small cafe for *pita* and *falafel*, we found ourselves on the old dirt road that winds through the wilderness from Jerusalem down to the plains of Jericho. We pulled the car over to look at the hills of Moab silhouetted against the eastern sky, and to watch the afternoon shadows playing eerie games of hide-and-seek with the deep ravines and steep precipices.

As I stood gazing at these ancient hills and soaking up their mysterious beauty, my eyes fell on a ribbon of lush greenery. It was so out of character, so cool and inviting in the midst of the heat and dust of the desert. All of a sudden I realized that here, in the middle of the wilderness, there must be an underground stream, providing nourishment and refreshment to the trees whose roots were firmly embedded along its banks.

Immediately Psalm 1 came to mind: "He is like a tree planted by streams of water, which yields its fruit in season and whose leaf does not wither. Whatever he does prospers" (Psalm 1:3).

How encouraging that even in times of dryness, even when I go through a desert experience, I can flourish and bear fruit if I am deeply rooted in the source of living water.

ADDITIONAL SCRIPTURE READINGS:
Psalm 63:1; Psalm 92:12–14; Isaiah 12:3

Go to page 130 for your next devotional reading.

in Jerusalem. 22You Samaritans worship what you do not know; we worship what we do know, for salvation is from the Jews. 23Yet a time is coming and has now come when the true worshipers will worship the Father in spirit and truth, for they are the kind of worshipers the Father seeks. 24God is spirit, and his worshipers must worship in spirit and in truth."

25The woman said, "I know that Messiah" (called Christ) "is coming. When he comes, he will explain everything to us."

26Then Jesus declared, "I who speak to you am he."

The Disciples Rejoin Jesus

27Just then his disciples returned and were surprised to find him talking with a woman. But no one asked, "What do you want?" or "Why are you talking with her?"

28Then, leaving her water jar, the woman went back to the town and said to the people, 29"Come, see a man who told me everything I ever did. Could this be the Christ*?" 30They came out of the town and made their way toward him.

31Meanwhile his disciples urged him, "Rabbi, eat something."

32But he said to them, "I have food to eat that you know nothing about."

33Then his disciples said to each other, "Could someone have brought him food?"

34"My food," said Jesus, "is to do the will of him who sent me and to finish his work. 35Do you not say, 'Four months more and then the harvest'? I tell you, open your eyes and look at the fields! They are ripe for harvest. 36Even now the reaper draws his wages, even now he harvests the crop for eternal life, so that the sower and the reaper may be glad together. 37Thus the saying 'One sows and another reaps' is true. 38I sent you to reap what you have not worked for. Others have done the hard work, and you have reaped the benefits of their labor."

Many Samaritans Believe

39Many of the Samaritans from that town believed in him because of the woman's testimony, "He told me everything I ever did." 40So when the Samari-

tans came to him, they urged him to stay with them, and he stayed two days. 41And because of his words many more became believers.

42They said to the woman, "We no longer believe just because of what you said; now we have heard for ourselves, and we know that this man really is the Savior of the world."

Jesus Heals the Official's Son

43After the two days he left for Galilee. 44(Now Jesus himself had pointed out that a prophet has no honor in his own country.) 45When he arrived in Galilee, the Galileans welcomed him. They had seen all that he had done in Jerusalem at the Passover Feast, for they also had been there.

46Once more he visited Cana in Galilee, where he had turned the water into wine. And there was a certain royal official whose son lay sick at Capernaum. 47When this man heard that Jesus had arrived in Galilee from Judea, he went to him and begged him to come and heal his son, who was close to death.

48"Unless you people see miraculous signs and wonders," Jesus told him, "you will never believe."

49The royal official said, "Sir, come down before my child dies."

50Jesus replied, "You may go. Your son will live."

The man took Jesus at his word and departed. 51While he was still on the way, his servants met him with the news that his boy was living. 52When he inquired as to the time when his son got better, they said to him, "The fever left him yesterday at the seventh hour."

53Then the father realized that this was the exact time at which Jesus had said to him, "Your son will live." So he and all his household believed.

54This was the second miraculous sign that Jesus performed, having come from Judea to Galilee.

The Healing at the Pool

5 Some time later, Jesus went up to Jerusalem for a feast of the Jews. 2Now there is in Jerusalem near the Sheep Gate a pool, which in Aramaic is called Bethesda* and which is surrounded by five covered colonnades. 3Here a great number of disabled people

---

a29 Or Messiah   *b2* Some manuscripts Bethzatha; other manuscripts Bethsaida

used to lie—the blind, the lame, the paralyzed.[a] 5One who was there had been an invalid for thirty-eight years. 6When Jesus saw him lying there and learned that he had been in this condition for a long time, he asked him, "Do you want to get well?"

7"Sir," the invalid replied, "I have no one to help me into the pool when the water is stirred. While I am trying to get in, someone else goes down ahead of me."

8Then Jesus said to him, "Get up! Pick up your mat and walk." 9At once the man was cured; he picked up his mat and walked.

The day on which this took place was a Sabbath, 10and so the Jews said to the man who had been healed, "It is the Sabbath; the law forbids you to carry your mat."

11But he replied, "The man who made me well said to me, 'Pick up your mat and walk.' "

12So they asked him, "Who is this fellow who told you to pick it up and walk?"

13The man who was healed had no idea who it was, for Jesus had slipped away into the crowd that was there.

14Later Jesus found him at the temple and said to him, "See, you are well again. Stop sinning or something worse may happen to you." 15The man went away and told the Jews that it was Jesus who had made him well.

Life Through the Son

16So, because Jesus was doing these things on the Sabbath, the Jews persecuted him. 17Jesus said to them, "My Father is always at his work to this very day, and I, too, am working." 18For this reason the Jews tried all the harder to kill him; not only was he breaking the Sabbath, but he was even calling God his own Father, making himself equal with God.

19Jesus gave them this answer: "I tell you the truth, the Son can do nothing by himself; he can do only what he sees his Father doing, because whatever the Father does the Son also does. 20For the Father loves the Son and shows him all he does. Yes, to your amazement he will show him even greater things than these. 21For just as the Father raises the dead and gives them life, even so the Son gives life to whom he is pleased to give it. 22Moreover, the Father judges no one, but has entrusted all judgment to the Son, 23that all may honor the Son just as they honor the Father. He who does not honor the Son does not honor the Father, who sent him.

24"I tell you the truth, whoever hears my word and believes him who sent me has eternal life and will not be condemned; he has crossed over from death to life. 25I tell you the truth, a time is coming and has now come when the dead will hear the voice of the Son of God and those who hear will live. 26For as the Father has life in himself, so he has granted the Son to have life in himself. 27And he has given him authority to judge because he is the Son of Man.

28"Do not be amazed at this, for a time is coming when all who are in their graves will hear his voice 29and come out—those who have done good will rise to live, and those who have done evil will rise to be condemned. 30By myself I can do nothing; I judge only as I hear, and my judgment is just, for I seek not to please myself but him who sent me.

Testimonies About Jesus

31"If I testify about myself, my testimony is not valid. 32There is another who testifies in my favor, and I know that his testimony about me is valid.

33"You have sent to John and he has testified to the truth. 34Not that I accept human testimony; but I mention it that you may be saved. 35John was a lamp that burned and gave light, and you chose for a time to enjoy his light.

36"I have testimony weightier than that of John. For the very work that the Father has given me to finish, and which I am doing, testifies that the Father has sent me. 37And the Father who sent me has himself testified concerning me. You have never heard his voice nor seen his form, 38nor does his word dwell in you, for you do not believe the one he sent. 39You diligently study[b] the Scriptures because you think that by them

---

[a]3 Some less important manuscripts paralyzed—and they waited for the moving of the waters. 4From time to time an angel of the Lord would come down and stir up the waters. The first one into the pool after each such disturbance would be cured of whatever disease he had.   [b]39 Or Study diligently (the imperative)

you possess eternal life. These are the Scriptures that testify about me, **40**yet you refuse to come to me to have life.

41"I do not accept praise from men, **42**but I know you. I know that you do not have the love of God in your hearts. **43**I have come in my Father's name, and you do not accept me; but if someone else comes in his own name, you will accept him. **44**How can you believe if you accept praise from one another, yet make no effort to obtain the praise that comes from the only God*a*?

45"But do not think I will accuse you before the Father. Your accuser is Moses, on whom your hopes are set. **46**If you believed Moses, you would believe me, for he wrote about me. **47**But since you do not believe what he wrote, how are you going to believe what I say?"

Jesus Feeds the Five Thousand

6 Some time after this, Jesus crossed to the far shore of the Sea of Galilee (that is, the Sea of Tiberias), **2**and a great crowd of people followed him because they saw the miraculous signs he had performed on the sick. **3**Then Jesus went up on a mountainside and sat down with his disciples. **4**The Jewish Passover Feast was near.

5When Jesus looked up and saw a great crowd coming toward him, he said to Philip, "Where shall we buy bread for these people to eat?" **6**He asked this only to test him, for he already had in mind what he was going to do.

7Philip answered him, "Eight months' wages*b* would not buy enough bread for each one to have a bite!"

8Another of his disciples, Andrew, Simon Peter's brother, spoke up, **9**"Here is a boy with five small barley loaves and two small fish, but how far will they go among so many?"

10Jesus said, "Have the people sit down." There was plenty of grass in that place, and the men sat down, about five thousand of them. **11**Jesus then took the loaves, gave thanks, and distributed to those who were seated as much as they wanted. He did the same with the fish.

12When they had all had enough to eat, he said to his disciples, "Gather the pieces that are left over. Let nothing be wasted." **13**So they gathered them and filled twelve baskets with the pieces of the five barley loaves left over by those who had eaten.

14After the people saw the miraculous sign that Jesus did, they began to say, "Surely this is the Prophet who is to come into the world." **15**Jesus, knowing that they intended to come and make him king by force, withdrew again to a mountain by himself.

Jesus Walks on the Water

16When evening came, his disciples went down to the lake, **17**where they got into a boat and set off across the lake for Capernaum. By now it was dark, and Jesus had not yet joined them. **18**A strong wind was blowing and the waters grew rough. **19**When they had rowed three or three and a half miles,*c* they saw Jesus approaching the boat, walking on the water; and they were terrified. **20**But he said to them, "It is I; don't be afraid." **21**Then they were willing to take him into the boat, and immediately the boat reached the shore where they were heading.

22The next day the crowd that had stayed on the opposite shore of the lake realized that only one boat had been there, and that Jesus had not entered it with his disciples, but that they had gone away alone. **23**Then some boats from Tiberias landed near the place where the people had eaten the bread after the Lord had given thanks. **24**Once the crowd realized that neither Jesus nor his disciples were there, they got into the boats and went to Capernaum in search of Jesus.

Jesus the Bread of Life

25When they found him on the other side of the lake, they asked him, "Rabbi, when did you get here?"

26Jesus answered, "I tell you the truth, you are looking for me, not because you saw miraculous signs but because you ate the loaves and had your fill. **27**Do not work for food that spoils, but for food that endures to eternal life, which the Son of Man will give you. On him God the Father has placed his seal of approval."

28Then they asked him, "What must we do to do the works God requires?"

a44 Some early manuscripts *the Only One*   *b7* Greek *two hundred denarii*   *c19* Greek *rowed twenty-five or thirty stadia* (about 5 or 6 kilometers)

²⁹Jesus answered, "The work of God is this: to believe in the one he has sent."

³⁰So they asked him, "What miraculous sign then will you give that we may see it and believe you? What will you do? ³¹Our forefathers ate the manna in the desert; as it is written: 'He gave them bread from heaven to eat.'ᵃ"

³²Jesus said to them, "I tell you the truth, it is not Moses who has given you the bread from heaven, but it is my Father who gives you the true bread from heaven. ³³For the bread of God is he who comes down from heaven and gives life to the world."

³⁴"Sir," they said, "from now on give us this bread."

³⁵Then Jesus declared, "I am the bread of life. He who comes to me will never go hungry, and he who believes in me will never be thirsty. ³⁶But as I told you, you have seen me and still you do not believe. ³⁷All that the Father gives me will come to me, and whoever comes to me I will never drive away. ³⁸For I have

ᵃ31 Exodus 16:4; Neh. 9:15; Psalm 78:24,25

FRIDAY

VERSE:	AUTHOR:	PASSAGE:
John 6:3	Nellie C. Savicki	John 6:1–15

Come Away With Me!

The clear, crisp mountain air—the breath of God—renewed my spirit. I had come with other women of our church for a winter retreat at the Lazy F.

The cascading mountain stream proclaimed God's glory. The stream's crescendo, like the Hallelujah Chorus, lifted my emotions. I saw the grandeur of God in the shadows and the rich earth tones and in the herd of elk and deer at the feeding station.

Falls broke through the frozen mountainside—faith bursting forth in praise.

The crystalline flakes enwrapped the earth—God's mantle of love.

There was sharing time and a time of silent meditation. Reflecting on the direction I was going and communing with God enriched me.

The crowds following Jesus left little time for teaching God's way. Jesus gained new strength when he retreated to commune with his Father. "Come apart with me," Jesus urged his disciples. It was in times of solitude that he was best able to teach them.

I need to respond to Jesus' invitation. When I hunger for God's way, I am filled with the bread of life. When I search diligently God's Word, I discover truth. When I reach out in prayer, I am given a cup of living water to quench my thirst.

God's love feast is spread before me, a spiritual feast for all my needs.

ADDITIONAL SCRIPTURE READINGS:
Jeremiah 17:12–13; Matthew 5:6; John 6:35

Go to page 132 for your next devotional reading.

come down from heaven not to do my will but to do the will of him who sent me. **39**And this is the will of him who sent me, that I shall lose none of all that he has given me, but raise them up at the last day. **40**For my Father's will is that everyone who looks to the Son and believes in him shall have eternal life, and I will raise him up at the last day."

41At this the Jews began to grumble about him because he said, "I am the bread that came down from heaven." **42**They said, "Is this not Jesus, the son of Joseph, whose father and mother we know? How can he now say, 'I came down from heaven'?"

43"Stop grumbling among yourselves," Jesus answered. **44**"No one can come to me unless the Father who sent me draws him, and I will raise him up at the last day. **45**It is written in the Prophets: 'They will all be taught by God.'[a] Everyone who listens to the Father and learns from him comes to me. **46**No one has seen the Father except the one who is from God; only he has seen the Father. **47**I tell you the truth, he who believes has everlasting life. **48**I am the bread of life. **49**Your forefathers ate the manna in the desert, yet they died. **50**But here is the bread that comes down from heaven, which a man may eat and not die. **51**I am the living bread that came down from heaven. If anyone eats of this bread, he will live forever. This bread is my flesh, which I will give for the life of the world."

52Then the Jews began to argue sharply among themselves, "How can this man give us his flesh to eat?"

53Jesus said to them, "I tell you the truth, unless you eat the flesh of the Son of Man and drink his blood, you have no life in you. **54**Whoever eats my flesh and drinks my blood has eternal life, and I will raise him up at the last day. **55**For my flesh is real food and my blood is real drink. **56**Whoever eats my flesh and drinks my blood remains in me, and I in him. **57**Just as the living Father sent me and I live because of the Father, so the one who feeds on me will live because of me. **58**This is the bread that came down from heaven. Your forefathers ate manna and died, but he who feeds on this bread will live forever."

59He said this while teaching in the synagogue in Capernaum.

Many Disciples Desert Jesus

60On hearing it, many of his disciples said, "This is a hard teaching. Who can accept it?"

61Aware that his disciples were grumbling about this, Jesus said to them, "Does this offend you? **62**What if you see the Son of Man ascend to where he was before! **63**The Spirit gives life; the flesh counts for nothing. The words I have spoken to you are spirit[b] and they are life. **64**Yet there are some of you who do not believe." For Jesus had known from the beginning which of them did not believe and who would betray him. **65**He went on to say, "This is why I told you that no one can come to me unless the Father has enabled him."

66From this time many of his disciples turned back and no longer followed him.

67"You do not want to leave too, do you?" Jesus asked the Twelve.

68Simon Peter answered him, "Lord, to whom shall we go? You have the words of eternal life. **69**We believe and know that you are the Holy One of God."

70Then Jesus replied, "Have I not chosen you, the Twelve? Yet one of you is a devil!" **71**(He meant Judas, the son of Simon Iscariot, who, though one of the Twelve, was later to betray him.)

Jesus Goes to the Feast of Tabernacles

7 After this, Jesus went around in Galilee, purposely staying away from Judea because the Jews there were waiting to take his life. **2**But when the Jewish Feast of Tabernacles was near, **3**Jesus' brothers said to him, "You ought to leave here and go to Judea, so that your disciples may see the miracles you do. **4**No one who wants to become a public figure acts in secret. Since you are doing these things, show yourself to the world." **5**For even his own brothers did not believe in him.

6Therefore Jesus told them, "The right time for me has not yet come; for you any time is right. **7**The world cannot hate you, but it hates me because I testify that what it does is evil. **8**You go to the Feast. I am not yet[c] going up to this Feast,

---

[a]45 Isaiah 54:13   [b]63 Or *Spirit*   [c]8 Some early manuscripts do not have *yet.*

WEEKENDING

RECALL

I recall the beauty of the sanctuary of a large city church I used to attend. The loveliness was enhanced by beautiful stained glass windows. As the last rays of the late afternoon sun streamed in through the windows, they took on the colors of the rainbow—reds, blues and yellows radiating a special splendor. Just as the windows reflected the beauty of the sun, we are to reflect the beauty of the light of the world, Jesus Christ, through the windows of our lives. Are you a light for Christ in today's dark world, guiding someone to him? . . . God's part is to place us where he wants us; our part is to shine.

Millie Stamm

RESTORE

Saturday: John 8:12
Sunday: Matthew 5:14

Go to page 135 for your next devotional reading.

because for me the right time has not yet come." **9**Having said this, he stayed in Galilee.

10However, after his brothers had left for the Feast, he went also, not publicly, but in secret. **11**Now at the Feast the Jews were watching for him and asking, "Where is that man?"

12Among the crowds there was widespread whispering about him. Some said, "He is a good man."

Others replied, "No, he deceives the people." **13**But no one would say anything publicly about him for fear of the Jews.

Jesus Teaches at the Feast

14Not until halfway through the Feast did Jesus go up to the temple courts and begin to teach. **15**The Jews were amazed and asked, "How did this man get such learning without having studied?"

16Jesus answered, "My teaching is not my own. It comes from him who sent me. **17**If anyone chooses to do God's will, he will find out whether my teaching comes from God or whether I speak on my own. **18**He who speaks on his own does so to gain honor for himself, but he who works for the honor of the one who sent him is a man of truth; there is nothing false about him. **19**Has not Moses given you the law? Yet not one of you keeps the law. Why are you trying to kill me?"

20"You are demon-possessed," the crowd answered. "Who is trying to kill you?"

21Jesus said to them, "I did one miracle, and you are all astonished. **22**Yet, because Moses gave you circumcision (though actually it did not come from Moses, but from the patriarchs), you circumcise a child on the Sabbath. **23**Now if a child can be circumcised on the Sabbath so that the law of Moses may not be broken, why are you angry with me for healing the whole man on the Sabbath? **24**Stop judging by mere appearances, and make a right judgment."

Is Jesus the Christ?

25At that point some of the people of Jerusalem began to ask, "Isn't this the man they are trying to kill? **26**Here he is, speaking publicly, and they are not say-

ing a word to him. Have the authorities really concluded that he is the Christ[a]? **27**But we know where this man is from; when the Christ comes, no one will know where he is from."

28Then Jesus, still teaching in the temple courts, cried out, "Yes, you know me, and you know where I am from. I am not here on my own, but he who sent me is true. You do not know him, **29**but I know him because I am from him and he sent me."

30At this they tried to seize him, but no one laid a hand on him, because his time had not yet come. **31**Still, many in the crowd put their faith in him. They said, "When the Christ comes, will he do more miraculous signs than this man?"

32The Pharisees heard the crowd whispering such things about him. Then the chief priests and the Pharisees sent temple guards to arrest him.

33Jesus said, "I am with you for only a short time, and then I go to the one who sent me. **34**You will look for me, but you will not find me; and where I am, you cannot come."

35The Jews said to one another, "Where does this man intend to go that we cannot find him? Will he go where our people live scattered among the Greeks, and teach the Greeks? **36**What did he mean when he said, 'You will look for me, but you will not find me,' and 'Where I am, you cannot come'?"

37On the last and greatest day of the Feast, Jesus stood and said in a loud voice, "If anyone is thirsty, let him come to me and drink. **38**Whoever believes in me, as[b] the Scripture has said, streams of living water will flow from within him." **39**By this he meant the Spirit, whom those who believed in him were later to receive. Up to that time the Spirit had not been given, since Jesus had not yet been glorified.

40On hearing his words, some of the people said, "Surely this man is the Prophet."

41Others said, "He is the Christ."

Still others asked, "How can the Christ come from Galilee? **42**Does not the Scripture say that the Christ will come from David's family[c] and from Bethlehem, the town where David

---

[a]26 Or *Messiah*; also in verses 27, 31, 41 and 42   [b]37,38 Or / *If anyone is thirsty, let him come to me.*
/ *And let him drink,* **38***who believes in me.* / *As*   [c]42 Greek *seed*

lived?" **43**Thus the people were divided because of Jesus. **44**Some wanted to seize him, but no one laid a hand on him.

Unbelief of the Jewish Leaders

45Finally the temple guards went back to the chief priests and Pharisees, who asked them, "Why didn't you bring him in?"

46"No one ever spoke the way this man does," the guards declared.

47"You mean he has deceived you also?" the Pharisees retorted. **48**"Has any of the rulers or of the Pharisees believed in him? **49**No! But this mob that knows nothing of the law—there is a curse on them."

50Nicodemus, who had gone to Jesus earlier and who was one of their own number, asked, **51**"Does our law condemn anyone without first hearing him to find out what he is doing?"

52They replied, "Are you from Galilee, too? Look into it, and you will find that a prophet*a* does not come out of Galilee."

[The earliest manuscripts and many other ancient witnesses do not have John 7:53–8:11.]

53Then each went to his own home.

8 But Jesus went to the Mount of Olives. **2**At dawn he appeared again in the temple courts, where all the people gathered around him, and he sat down to teach them. **3**The teachers of the law and the Pharisees brought in a woman caught in adultery. They made her stand before the group **4**and said to Jesus, "Teacher, this woman was caught in the act of adultery. **5**In the Law Moses commanded us to stone such women. Now what do you say?" **6**They were using this question as a trap, in order to have a basis for accusing him.

But Jesus bent down and started to write on the ground with his finger. **7**When they kept on questioning him, he straightened up and said to them, "If any one of you is without sin, let him be the first to throw a stone at her." **8**Again he stooped down and wrote on the ground.

9At this, those who heard began to go away one at a time, the older ones first, until only Jesus was left, with the woman still standing there. **10**Jesus straightened up and asked her, "Woman, where are they? Has no one condemned you?"

11"No one, sir," she said.

"Then neither do I condemn you," Jesus declared. "Go now and leave your life of sin."

The Validity of Jesus' Testimony

12When Jesus spoke again to the people, he said, "I am the light of the world. Whoever follows me will never walk in darkness, but will have the light of life."

13The Pharisees challenged him, "Here you are, appearing as your own witness; your testimony is not valid."

14Jesus answered, "Even if I testify on my own behalf, my testimony is valid, for I know where I came from and where I am going. But you have no idea where I come from or where I am going. **15**You judge by human standards; I pass judgment on no one. **16**But if I do judge, my decisions are right, because I am not alone. I stand with the Father, who sent me. **17**In your own Law it is written that the testimony of two men is valid. **18**I am one who testifies for myself; my other witness is the Father, who sent me."

19Then they asked him, "Where is your father?"

"You do not know me or my Father," Jesus replied. "If you knew me, you would know my Father also." **20**He spoke these words while teaching in the temple area near the place where the offerings were put. Yet no one seized him, because his time had not yet come.

21Once more Jesus said to them, "I am going away, and you will look for me, and you will die in your sin. Where I go, you cannot come."

22This made the Jews ask, "Will he kill himself? Is that why he says, 'Where I go, you cannot come'?"

23But he continued, "You are from below; I am from above. You are of this world; I am not of this world. **24**I told you that you would die in your sins; if you do not believe that I am ˌthe one I claim to beˌ,[a] you will indeed die in your sins."

[25] "Who are you?" they asked.

"Just what I have been claiming all along," Jesus replied. [26] "I have much to say in judgment of you. But he who sent

me is reliable, and what I have heard from him I tell the world."

[27] They did not understand that he was telling them about his Father. [28] So Jesus said, "When you have lifted up the Son of Man, then you will know that I am ˌthe one I claim to beˌ and that I do

[a] 24 Or I am he; also in verse 28

MONDAY

VERSE:	AUTHOR:	PASSAGE:
John 8:3	Betsy Lee	John 8:3–11

Mercy

"Guilty!" cries the crowd, and they take up stones. The woman has no defender. Caught in the act, dragged naked out of the bedroom, a cloak thrown quickly around her shoulders to keep out the cold. But it cannot hide her sin. Picture yourself as that woman—humiliated, terrified.

You are thrust in front of your neighbors, townspeople, people you know. You feel so ashamed. They look at you with disdain. You feel like a small child battered by the condemning look of an accusing parent. You want to run and hide, but where can you go?

Even your own heart condemns you. "Guilty!" It points a finger. A sharp stab of pain cuts at the core of who you are. Overwhelmed by waves of sadness and shame, you sink to the ground, huddled in a heap.

The crowd presses in. They tower over you, not only bearing down on you but also on Jesus, the one they are questioning. Instead of answering their questions, he bends down and writes in the dust. There is a stillness about him, a composure that will not be hurried. He glances up at you. His eyes are not like the others; they are soft with mercy.

Then he speaks to the crowd with a voice sure and steady, with authority. There is silence. A long silence . . . Now *their* heads are bowed. *Thud.* A hard rock hits the ground. *Thud. Thud.* Another, then another. One by one, your accusers walk away.

You are left alone with Jesus. Quietly, he comes close. He reaches out and lifts your chin up with his hand. He smiles and wipes away the tears that stain your cheeks. His touch takes your breath away. He makes you feel cherished. Lovely.

Slowly, he helps you to your feet.

"Go now," he says, "and leave your life of sin" (v.11).

ADDITIONAL SCRIPTURE READINGS:
Hosea 6:1–3; Ephesians 2:4–7; 2 Timothy 1:9–11

Go to page 137 for your next devotional reading.

nothing on my own but speak just what the Father has taught me. [29]The one who sent me is with me; he has not left me alone, for I always do what pleases him." [30]Even as he spoke, many put their faith in him.

The Children of Abraham

[31]To the Jews who had believed him, Jesus said, "If you hold to my teaching, you are really my disciples. [32]Then you will know the truth, and the truth will set you free."

[33]They answered him, "We are Abraham's descendants[a] and have never been slaves of anyone. How can you say that we shall be set free?"

[34]Jesus replied, "I tell you the truth, everyone who sins is a slave to sin. [35]Now a slave has no permanent place in the family, but a son belongs to it forever. [36]So if the Son sets you free, you will be free indeed. [37]I know you are Abraham's descendants. Yet you are ready to kill me, because you have no room for my word. [38]I am telling you what I have seen in the Father's presence, and you do what you have heard from your father.[b]"

[39]"Abraham is our father," they answered.

"If you were Abraham's children," said Jesus, "then you would[c] do the things Abraham did. [40]As it is, you are determined to kill me, a man who has told you the truth that I heard from God. Abraham did not do such things. [41]You are doing the things your own father does."

"We are not illegitimate children," they protested. "The only Father we have is God himself."

The Children of the Devil

[42]Jesus said to them, "If God were your Father, you would love me, for I came from God and now am here. I have not come on my own; but he sent me. [43]Why is my language not clear to you? Because you are unable to hear what I say. [44]You belong to your father, the devil, and you want to carry out your father's desire. He was a murderer from the beginning, not holding to the truth, for there is no truth in him. When he

lies, he speaks his native language, for he is a liar and the father of lies. [45]Yet because I tell the truth, you do not believe me! [46]Can any of you prove me guilty of sin? If I am telling the truth, why don't you believe me? [47]He who belongs to God hears what God says. The reason you do not hear is that you do not belong to God."

The Claims of Jesus About Himself

[48]The Jews answered him, "Aren't we right in saying that you are a Samaritan and demon-possessed?"

[49]"I am not possessed by a demon," said Jesus, "but I honor my Father and you dishonor me. [50]I am not seeking glory for myself; but there is one who seeks it, and he is the judge. [51]I tell you the truth, if anyone keeps my word, he will never see death."

[52]At this the Jews exclaimed, "Now we know that you are demon-possessed! Abraham died and so did the prophets, yet you say that if anyone keeps your word, he will never taste death. [53]Are you greater than our father Abraham? He died, and so did the prophets. Who do you think you are?"

[54]Jesus replied, "If I glorify myself, my glory means nothing. My Father, whom you claim as your God, is the one who glorifies me. [55]Though you do not know him, I know him. If I said I did not, I would be a liar like you, but I do know him and keep his word. [56]Your father Abraham rejoiced at the thought of seeing my day; he saw it and was glad."

[57]"You are not yet fifty years old," the Jews said to him, "and you have seen Abraham!"

[58]"I tell you the truth," Jesus answered, "before Abraham was born, I am!" [59]At this, they picked up stones to stone him, but Jesus hid himself, slipping away from the temple grounds.

Jesus Heals a Man Born Blind

9 As he went along, he saw a man blind from birth. [2]His disciples asked him, "Rabbi, who sinned, this man or his parents, that he was born blind?"

[3]"Neither this man nor his parents

---

[a]33 Greek seed; also in verse 37   [b]38 Or presence. Therefore do what you have heard from the Father.
[c]39 Some early manuscripts "If you are Abraham's children," said Jesus, "then

sinned," said Jesus, "but this happened so that the work of God might be displayed in his life. [4]As long as it is day, we must do the work of him who sent me. Night is coming, when no one can work. [5]While I am in the world, I am the light of the world."

[6]Having said this, he spit on the ground, made some mud with the saliva, and put it on the man's eyes. [7]"Go," he told him, "wash in the Pool of Siloam" (this word means Sent). So the man went and washed, and came home seeing.

[8]His neighbors and those who had formerly seen him begging asked, "Isn't this the same man who used to sit and beg?" [9]Some claimed that he was.

Others said, "No, he only looks like him."

But he himself insisted, "I am the man."

[10]"How then were your eyes opened?" they demanded.

[11]He replied, "The man they call Jesus made some mud and put it on my eyes. He told me to go to Siloam and wash. So I went and washed, and then I could see."

[12]"Where is this man?" they asked him.

"I don't know," he said.

TUESDAY

VERSE:	AUTHOR:	PASSAGE:
John 9:5	Joni Eareckson Tada	John 9:1–12

Shattered Glass

My art studio is a mess of half-chewed pastel pencils, old tubes of paint and piles of illustrations overflowing my file drawers. Recently while cleaning up, I discovered some broken glass on the counter by the window. I also discovered that when sunlight struck the shattered glass, brilliant, colorful rays scattered everywhere.

Shattered glass is full of a thousand different angles, each one picking up a ray of light and shooting it off in a thousand directions. That doesn't happen with plain glass, such as a jar. The glass must be broken into many pieces.

What's true of shattered glass is true of a broken life. Shattered dreams. A heart full of fissures. Hopes that are splintered. A life in pieces that appears to be ruined. But given time and prayer, such a person's life can shine more brightly than if the brokenness had never happened. When the light of the Lord Jesus falls upon a shattered life, that believer's hopes can be brightened.

Only our great God can reach down into what otherwise would be brokenness and produce something beautiful. With him, nothing is wasted. Every broken dream and heart that hurts can be redeemed by his loving, warm touch. Your life may be shattered by sorrow, pain or sin, but God has in mind a kaleidoscope through which his light can shine more brilliantly.

ADDITIONAL SCRIPTURE READINGS:
Psalm 34:18; Psalm 51:17; Philippians 1:29

Go to page 139 for your next devotional reading.

The Pharisees Investigate the Healing

[13]They brought to the Pharisees the man who had been blind. [14]Now the day on which Jesus had made the mud and opened the man's eyes was a Sabbath. [15]Therefore the Pharisees also asked him how he had received his sight. "He put mud on my eyes," the man replied, "and I washed, and now I see."

[16]Some of the Pharisees said, "This man is not from God, for he does not keep the Sabbath."

But others asked, "How can a sinner do such miraculous signs?" So they were divided.

[17]Finally they turned again to the blind man, "What have you to say about him? It was your eyes he opened."

The man replied, "He is a prophet."

[18]The Jews still did not believe that he had been blind and had received his sight until they sent for the man's parents. [19]"Is this your son?" they asked. "Is this the one you say was born blind? How is it that now he can see?"

[20]"We know he is our son," the parents answered, "and we know he was born blind. [21]But how he can see now, or who opened his eyes, we don't know. Ask him. He is of age; he will speak for himself." [22]His parents said this because they were afraid of the Jews, for already the Jews had decided that anyone who acknowledged that Jesus was the Christ[a] would be put out of the synagogue. [23]That was why his parents said, "He is of age; ask him."

[24]A second time they summoned the man who had been blind. "Give glory to God,[b]" they said. "We know this man is a sinner."

[25]He replied, "Whether he is a sinner or not, I don't know. One thing I do know. I was blind but now I see!"

[26]Then they asked him, "What did he do to you? How did he open your eyes?"

[27]He answered, "I have told you already and you did not listen. Why do you want to hear it again? Do you want to become his disciples, too?"

[28]Then they hurled insults at him and said, "You are this fellow's disciple! We are disciples of Moses! [29]We know that God spoke to Moses, but as for this fellow, we don't even know where he comes from."

[30]The man answered, "Now that is remarkable! You don't know where he comes from, yet he opened my eyes. [31]We know that God does not listen to sinners. He listens to the godly man who does his will. [32]Nobody has ever heard of opening the eyes of a man born blind. [33]If this man were not from God, he could do nothing."

[34]To this they replied, "You were steeped in sin at birth; how dare you lecture us!" And they threw him out.

Spiritual Blindness

[35]Jesus heard that they had thrown him out, and when he found him, he said, "Do you believe in the Son of Man?"

[36]"Who is he, sir?" the man asked. "Tell me so that I may believe in him."

[37]Jesus said, "You have now seen him; in fact, he is the one speaking with you."

[38]Then the man said, "Lord, I believe," and he worshiped him.

[39]Jesus said, "For judgment I have come into this world, so that the blind will see and those who see will become blind."

[40]Some Pharisees who were with him heard him say this and asked, "What? Are we blind too?"

[41]Jesus said, "If you were blind, you would not be guilty of sin; but now that you claim you can see, your guilt remains.

The Shepherd and His Flock

10 "I tell you the truth, the man who does not enter the sheep pen by the gate, but climbs in by some other way, is a thief and a robber. [2]The man who enters by the gate is the shepherd of his sheep. [3]The watchman opens the gate for him, and the sheep listen to his voice. He calls his own sheep by name and leads them out. [4]When he has brought out all his own, he goes on ahead of them, and his sheep follow him because they know his voice. [5]But they will never follow a stranger; in fact, they will run away from him because they do not recognize a stranger's voice." [6]Jesus used this figure of speech, but they did not understand what he was telling them.

[7]Therefore Jesus said again, "I tell you

---

[a]22 Or *Messiah*   [b]24 A solemn charge to tell the truth (see Joshua 7:19)

the truth, I am the gate for the sheep. **8**All who ever came before me were thieves and robbers, but the sheep did not listen to them. **9**I am the gate; whoever enters through me will be saved.*a* He will come in and go out, and find pasture. **10**The thief comes only to steal and kill and destroy; I have come that they may have life, and have it to the full.

11"I am the good shepherd. The good shepherd lays down his life for the sheep. **12**The hired hand is not the shepherd who owns the sheep. So when he sees the wolf coming, he abandons the sheep and runs away. Then the wolf attacks the flock and scatters it. **13**The man

a9 Or kept safe

WEDNESDAY

VERSE:	AUTHOR:	PASSAGE:
John 10:3	Edith Bajema	John 10:1–18

Called by Name

Ruth Veltkamp, a missionary in Africa, was stuck. She was experiencing tremendous resistance to the gospel among the Muslims with whom she worked. So she prayed, "God, break this impasse. Do something to teach them that Christianity is superior."

God answered by giving the religious leaders, one after the other, dreams and visions.

One leader, Ara, was a devout priest. He came to Ruth, asking her to explain a troubling vision. "In my dream, I see an ugly figure next to me, ready to tie me up with heavy chains. But on a hill farther away, I see a white-robed person tending sheep. That person calls to me. He calls my name three times!"

Ruth was delighted. She showed Ara the verse from John 10, explaining that Jesus is the good shepherd who calls his sheep by name. Pleased to find the explanation for his vision in the Bible, Ara became a follower of Jesus and founded eight churches.

When the good shepherd calls you by name, he is not only calling you by the name that your friends and family use. He is calling to your spirit, to the essence of who you are. As Psalm 139 says, "O LORD, you have searched me and you know me . . . For you created my inmost being" (Psalm 139:1, 13).

Who you are and who you will become, only Jesus knows. He says, "To him who overcomes, I will give . . . a white stone with a new name written on it, known only to him who receives it" (Revelation 2:17).

Jesus calls to you in the night, as you lie down to sleep. He calls to you in the morning when you awake. Let yourself hear him. Listen for the voice of the good shepherd, calling you by name.

ADDITIONAL SCRIPTURE READINGS:
1 Samuel 3:9–10; Luke 10:20; Revelation 21:27

Go to page 143 for your next devotional reading.

runs away because he is a hired hand and cares nothing for the sheep.

14"I am the good shepherd; I know my sheep and my sheep know me— **15**just as the Father knows me and I know the Father—and I lay down my life for the sheep. **16**I have other sheep that are not of this sheep pen. I must bring them also. They too will listen to my voice, and there shall be one flock and one shepherd. **17**The reason my Father loves me is that I lay down my life—only to take it up again. **18**No one takes it from me, but I lay it down of my own accord. I have authority to lay it down and authority to take it up again. This command I received from my Father."

19At these words the Jews were again divided. **20**Many of them said, "He is demon-possessed and raving mad. Why listen to him?"

21But others said, "These are not the sayings of a man possessed by a demon. Can a demon open the eyes of the blind?"

The Unbelief of the Jews

22Then came the Feast of Dedication[a] at Jerusalem. It was winter, **23**and Jesus was in the temple area walking in Solomon's Colonnade. **24**The Jews gathered around him, saying, "How long will you keep us in suspense? If you are the Christ,[b] tell us plainly."

25Jesus answered, "I did tell you, but you do not believe. The miracles I do in my Father's name speak for me, **26**but you do not believe because you are not my sheep. **27**My sheep listen to my voice; I know them, and they follow me. **28**I give them eternal life, and they shall never perish; no one can snatch them out of my hand. **29**My Father, who has given them to me, is greater than all[c]; no one can snatch them out of my Father's hand. **30**I and the Father are one."

31Again the Jews picked up stones to stone him, **32**but Jesus said to them, "I have shown you many great miracles from the Father. For which of these do you stone me?"

33"We are not stoning you for any of these," replied the Jews, "but for blasphemy, because you, a mere man, claim to be God."

34Jesus answered them, "Is it not written in your Law, 'I have said you are gods'[d]? **35**If he called them 'gods,' to whom the word of God came—and the Scripture cannot be broken— **36**what about the one whom the Father set apart as his very own and sent into the world? Why then do you accuse me of blasphemy because I said, 'I am God's Son'? **37**Do not believe me unless I do what my Father does. **38**But if I do it, even though you do not believe me, believe the miracles, that you may know and understand that the Father is in me, and I in the Father." **39**Again they tried to seize him, but he escaped their grasp.

40Then Jesus went back across the Jordan to the place where John had been baptizing in the early days. Here he stayed **41**and many people came to him. They said, "Though John never performed a miraculous sign, all that John said about this man was true." **42**And in that place many believed in Jesus.

The Death of Lazarus

11 Now a man named Lazarus was sick. He was from Bethany, the village of Mary and her sister Martha. **2**This Mary, whose brother Lazarus now lay sick, was the same one who poured perfume on the Lord and wiped his feet with her hair. **3**So the sisters sent word to Jesus, "Lord, the one you love is sick."

4When he heard this, Jesus said, "This sickness will not end in death. No, it is for God's glory so that God's Son may be glorified through it." **5**Jesus loved Martha and her sister and Lazarus. **6**Yet when he heard that Lazarus was sick, he stayed where he was two more days.

7Then he said to his disciples, "Let us go back to Judea."

8"But Rabbi," they said, "a short while ago the Jews tried to stone you, and yet you are going back there?"

9Jesus answered, "Are there not twelve hours of daylight? A man who walks by day will not stumble, for he sees by this world's light. **10**It is when he walks by night that he stumbles, for he has no light."

11After he had said this, he went on to tell them, "Our friend Lazarus has fallen

---

a22 That is, Hanukkah   b24 Or Messiah   c29 Many early manuscripts What my Father has given me is greater than all   d34 Psalm 82:6

asleep; but I am going there to wake him up."

¹²His disciples replied, "Lord, if he sleeps, he will get better." ¹³Jesus had been speaking of his death, but his disciples thought he meant natural sleep.

¹⁴So then he told them plainly, "Lazarus is dead, ¹⁵and for your sake I am glad I was not there, so that you may believe. But let us go to him."

¹⁶Then Thomas (called Didymus) said to the rest of the disciples, "Let us also go, that we may die with him."

Jesus Comforts the Sisters

¹⁷On his arrival, Jesus found that Lazarus had already been in the tomb for four days. ¹⁸Bethany was less than two miles[a] from Jerusalem, ¹⁹and many Jews had come to Martha and Mary to comfort them in the loss of their brother. ²⁰When Martha heard that Jesus was coming, she went out to meet him, but Mary stayed at home.

²¹"Lord," Martha said to Jesus, "if you had been here, my brother would not have died. ²²But I know that even now God will give you whatever you ask."

²³Jesus said to her, "Your brother will rise again."

²⁴Martha answered, "I know he will rise again in the resurrection at the last day."

²⁵Jesus said to her, "I am the resurrection and the life. He who believes in me will live, even though he dies; ²⁶and whoever lives and believes in me will never die. Do you believe this?"

²⁷"Yes, Lord," she told him, "I believe that you are the Christ,[b] the Son of God, who was to come into the world."

²⁸And after she had said this, she went back and called her sister Mary aside. "The Teacher is here," she said, "and is asking for you." ²⁹When Mary heard this, she got up quickly and went to him. ³⁰Now Jesus had not yet entered the village, but was still at the place where Martha had met him. ³¹When the Jews who had been with Mary in the house, comforting her, noticed how quickly she got up and went out, they followed her, supposing she was going to the tomb to mourn there.

³²When Mary reached the place where Jesus was and saw him, she fell at his feet and said, "Lord, if you had been here, my brother would not have died."

³³When Jesus saw her weeping, and the Jews who had come along with her also weeping, he was deeply moved in spirit and troubled. ³⁴"Where have you laid him?" he asked.

"Come and see, Lord," they replied.

³⁵Jesus wept.

³⁶Then the Jews said, "See how he loved him!"

³⁷But some of them said, "Could not he who opened the eyes of the blind man have kept this man from dying?"

Jesus Raises Lazarus From the Dead

³⁸Jesus, once more deeply moved, came to the tomb. It was a cave with a stone laid across the entrance. ³⁹"Take away the stone," he said.

"But, Lord," said Martha, the sister of the dead man, "by this time there is a bad odor, for he has been there four days."

⁴⁰Then Jesus said, "Did I not tell you that if you believed, you would see the glory of God?"

⁴¹So they took away the stone. Then Jesus looked up and said, "Father, I thank you that you have heard me. ⁴²I knew that you always hear me, but I said this for the benefit of the people standing here, that they may believe that you sent me."

⁴³When he had said this, Jesus called in a loud voice, "Lazarus, come out!" ⁴⁴The dead man came out, his hands and feet wrapped with strips of linen, and a cloth around his face.

Jesus said to them, "Take off the grave clothes and let him go."

The Plot to Kill Jesus

⁴⁵Therefore many of the Jews who had come to visit Mary, and had seen what Jesus did, put their faith in him. ⁴⁶But some of them went to the Pharisees and told them what Jesus had done. ⁴⁷Then the chief priests and the Pharisees called a meeting of the Sanhedrin.

"What are we accomplishing?" they asked. "Here is this man performing many miraculous signs. ⁴⁸If we let him go on like this, everyone will believe in him, and then the Romans will come and take away both our place[c] and our nation."

⁴⁹Then one of them, named Caiaphas,

---

[a]18 Greek *fifteen stadia* (about 3 kilometers)   [b]27 Or *Messiah*   [c]48 Or *temple*

who was high priest that year, spoke up, "You know nothing at all! ⁵⁰You do not realize that it is better for you that one man die for the people than that the whole nation perish."

⁵¹He did not say this on his own, but as high priest that year he prophesied that Jesus would die for the Jewish nation, ⁵²and not only for that nation but also for the scattered children of God, to bring them together and make them one. ⁵³So from that day on they plotted to take his life.

⁵⁴Therefore Jesus no longer moved about publicly among the Jews. Instead he withdrew to a region near the desert, to a village called Ephraim, where he stayed with his disciples.

⁵⁵When it was almost time for the Jewish Passover, many went up from the country to Jerusalem for their ceremonial cleansing before the Passover. ⁵⁶They kept looking for Jesus, and as they stood in the temple area they asked one another, "What do you think? Isn't he coming to the Feast at all?" ⁵⁷But the chief priests and Pharisees had given orders that if anyone found out where Jesus was, he should report it so that they might arrest him.

Jesus Anointed at Bethany

12 Six days before the Passover, Jesus arrived at Bethany, where Lazarus lived, whom Jesus had raised from the dead. ²Here a dinner was given in Jesus' honor. Martha served, while Lazarus was among those reclining at the table with him. ³Then Mary took about a pint*a* of pure nard, an expensive perfume; she poured it on Jesus' feet and wiped his feet with her hair. And the house was filled with the fragrance of the perfume.

⁴But one of his disciples, Judas Iscariot, who was later to betray him, objected, ⁵"Why wasn't this perfume sold and the money given to the poor? It was worth a year's wages.*b*" ⁶He did not say this because he cared about the poor but because he was a thief; as keeper of the money bag, he used to help himself to what was put into it.

⁷"Leave her alone," Jesus replied. "⌊It was intended⌋ that she should save this

perfume for the day of my burial. ⁸You will always have the poor among you, but you will not always have me."

⁹Meanwhile a large crowd of Jews found out that Jesus was there and came, not only because of him but also to see Lazarus, whom he had raised from the dead. ¹⁰So the chief priests made plans to kill Lazarus as well, ¹¹for on account of him many of the Jews were going over to Jesus and putting their faith in him.

The Triumphal Entry

¹²The next day the great crowd that had come for the Feast heard that Jesus was on his way to Jerusalem. ¹³They took palm branches and went out to meet him, shouting,

"Hosanna!*c*"

"Blessed is he who comes in the name of the Lord!"*d*

"Blessed is the King of Israel!"

¹⁴Jesus found a young donkey and sat upon it, as it is written,

¹⁵"Do not be afraid, O Daughter of Zion;
      see, your king is coming,
   seated on a donkey's colt."*e*

¹⁶At first his disciples did not understand all this. Only after Jesus was glorified did they realize that these things had been written about him and that they had done these things to him.

¹⁷Now the crowd that was with him when he called Lazarus from the tomb and raised him from the dead continued to spread the word. ¹⁸Many people, because they had heard that he had given this miraculous sign, went out to meet him. ¹⁹So the Pharisees said to one another, "See, this is getting us nowhere. Look how the whole world has gone after him!"

Jesus Predicts His Death

²⁰Now there were some Greeks among those who went up to worship at the Feast. ²¹They came to Philip, who was from Bethsaida in Galilee, with a request. "Sir," they said, "we would like to see Jesus." ²²Philip went to tell An-

---

*a*3 Greek *a litra* (probably about 0.5 liter)   *b*5 Greek *three hundred denarii*   *c*13 A Hebrew expression meaning "Save!" which became an exclamation of praise   *d*13 Psalm 118:25, 26   *e*15 Zech. 9:9

drew; Andrew and Philip in turn told Jesus.

[23] Jesus replied, "The hour has come for the Son of Man to be glorified. [24] I tell you the truth, unless a kernel of wheat falls to the ground and dies, it remains only a single seed. But if it dies, it produces many seeds. [25] The man who loves his life will lose it, while the man who hates his life in this world will keep it for eternal life. [26] Whoever serves me must follow me; and where I am, my servant also will be. My Father will honor the one who serves me.

[27] "Now my heart is troubled, and what shall I say? 'Father, save me from

---

THURSDAY

VERSE:	AUTHOR:	PASSAGE:
John 12:24	Gloria Gaither	John 12:23-38

And a Time to Die

[Dear Will—] As I am writing this, death and resurrection dance together today, not only in the death and resurrection of our Lord but also in spring's final battle with winter. Today, Will, I sit by the bedside of your great-grandmother, my dear mother. Alphas and omegas, beginnings and endings. They whirl and clash in such a blinding confusion that it is hard to tell them apart. It is obvious there is struggle in both dying and birthing, and though we tend to think something has to be born to die, the truth is, says the Word of the Lord, that something has to die to be born. "Unless a kernel of wheat falls to the ground and dies, it remains only a single seed. But if it dies, it produces many seeds" (v. 24).

This time last year, Will, we were helping your mother with some very hard days. Pain in the process and glory in the promise of you were dancing in her, and we all felt the conflict. This year we struggle with winter as the spirit that would be born fresh and new battles with the pull of earth and decay. It is a hard fight with much pain. Earth does not give up easily, and winter sometimes rages its final storms violently. But winter is doomed, nonetheless, and spring will win.

Now we wait long hours in a hospital room and struggle with death. Over and over death has reared its head and shaken its fist at life, but life doesn't give in easily. Yet this process will be completed because life—perfect life—will win, even over the love of human life. Death will be swallowed up in victory. And the ultimate irony is that in losing life—even as well as she's loved it—Grandma Sickal will be taken over by a life even better.

This process may flash and rage and look threatening. But death—though it will have its ugly moment—will itself die. Our Lord's resurrection is our proof and our promise.

ADDITIONAL SCRIPTURE READINGS:
Isaiah 25:8-9; Romans 8:37-39; 1 Corinthians 15:51-57

Go to page 146 for your next devotional reading.

this hour'? No, it was for this very reason I came to this hour. **28**Father, glorify your name!"

Then a voice came from heaven, "I have glorified it, and will glorify it again." **29**The crowd that was there and heard it said it had thundered; others said an angel had spoken to him.

30Jesus said, "This voice was for your benefit, not mine. **31**Now is the time for judgment on this world; now the prince of this world will be driven out. **32**But I, when I am lifted up from the earth, will draw all men to myself." **33**He said this to show the kind of death he was going to die.

34The crowd spoke up, "We have heard from the Law that the Christ*a* will remain forever, so how can you say, 'The Son of Man must be lifted up'? Who is this 'Son of Man'?"

35Then Jesus told them, "You are going to have the light just a little while longer. Walk while you have the light, before darkness overtakes you. The man who walks in the dark does not know where he is going. **36**Put your trust in the light while you have it, so that you may become sons of light." When he had finished speaking, Jesus left and hid himself from them.

The Jews Continue in Their Unbelief

37Even after Jesus had done all these miraculous signs in their presence, they still would not believe in him. **38**This was to fulfill the word of Isaiah the prophet:

"Lord, who has believed our
        message
    and to whom has the arm of the
        Lord been revealed?"*b*

39For this reason they could not believe, because, as Isaiah says elsewhere:

40"He has blinded their eyes
    and deadened their hearts,
so they can neither see with their
        eyes,
    nor understand with their hearts,
    nor turn—and I would heal
        them."*c*

41Isaiah said this because he saw Jesus' glory and spoke about him.

42Yet at the same time many even among the leaders believed in him. But because of the Pharisees they would not confess their faith for fear they would be put out of the synagogue; **43**for they loved praise from men more than praise from God.

44Then Jesus cried out, "When a man believes in me, he does not believe in me only, but in the one who sent me. **45**When he looks at me, he sees the one who sent me. **46**I have come into the world as a light, so that no one who believes in me should stay in darkness.

47"As for the person who hears my words but does not keep them, I do not judge him. For I did not come to judge the world, but to save it. **48**There is a judge for the one who rejects me and does not accept my words; that very word which I spoke will condemn him at the last day. **49**For I did not speak of my own accord, but the Father who sent me commanded me what to say and how to say it. **50**I know that his command leads to eternal life. So whatever I say is just what the Father has told me to say."

Jesus Washes His Disciples' Feet

13 It was just before the Passover Feast. Jesus knew that the time had come for him to leave this world and go to the Father. Having loved his own who were in the world, he now showed them the full extent of his love.*d*

2The evening meal was being served, and the devil had already prompted Judas Iscariot, son of Simon, to betray Jesus. **3**Jesus knew that the Father had put all things under his power, and that he had come from God and was returning to God; **4**so he got up from the meal, took off his outer clothing, and wrapped a towel around his waist. **5**After that, he poured water into a basin and began to wash his disciples' feet, drying them with the towel that was wrapped around him.

6He came to Simon Peter, who said to him, "Lord, are you going to wash my feet?"

7Jesus replied, "You do not realize now what I am doing, but later you will understand."

8"No," said Peter, "you shall never wash my feet."

---

a34 Or *Messiah*   *b38* Isaiah 53:1   *c40* Isaiah 6:10   *d1* Or *he loved them to the last*

Jesus answered, "Unless I wash you, you have no part with me."

⁹"Then, Lord," Simon Peter replied, "not just my feet but my hands and my head as well!"

¹⁰Jesus answered, "A person who has had a bath needs only to wash his feet; his whole body is clean. And you are clean, though not every one of you." ¹¹For he knew who was going to betray him, and that was why he said not every one was clean.

¹²When he had finished washing their feet, he put on his clothes and returned to his place. "Do you understand what I have done for you?" he asked them. ¹³"You call me 'Teacher' and 'Lord,' and rightly so, for that is what I am. ¹⁴Now that I, your Lord and Teacher, have washed your feet, you also should wash one another's feet. ¹⁵I have set you an example that you should do as I have done for you. ¹⁶I tell you the truth, no servant is greater than his master, nor is a messenger greater than the one who sent him. ¹⁷Now that you know these things, you will be blessed if you do them.

Jesus Predicts His Betrayal

¹⁸"I am not referring to all of you; I know those I have chosen. But this is to fulfill the scripture: 'He who shares my bread has lifted up his heel against me.'ᵃ

¹⁹"I am telling you now before it happens, so that when it does happen you will believe that I am He. ²⁰I tell you the truth, whoever accepts anyone I send accepts me; and whoever accepts me accepts the one who sent me."

²¹After he had said this, Jesus was troubled in spirit and testified, "I tell you the truth, one of you is going to betray me."

²²His disciples stared at one another, at a loss to know which of them he meant. ²³One of them, the disciple whom Jesus loved, was reclining next to him. ²⁴Simon Peter motioned to this disciple and said, "Ask him which one he means."

²⁵Leaning back against Jesus, he asked him, "Lord, who is it?"

²⁶Jesus answered, "It is the one to whom I will give this piece of bread when I have dipped it in the dish." Then, dipping the piece of bread, he gave it to Judas Iscariot, son of Simon. ²⁷As soon as Judas took the bread, Satan entered into him.

"What you are about to do, do quickly," Jesus told him, ²⁸but no one at the meal understood why Jesus said this to him. ²⁹Since Judas had charge of the money, some thought Jesus was telling him to buy what was needed for the Feast, or to give something to the poor. ³⁰As soon as Judas had taken the bread, he went out. And it was night.

Jesus Predicts Peter's Denial

³¹When he was gone, Jesus said, "Now is the Son of Man glorified and God is glorified in him. ³²If God is glorified in him,ᵇ God will glorify the Son in himself, and will glorify him at once. ³³"My children, I will be with you only a little longer. You will look for me, and just as I told the Jews, so I tell you now: Where I am going, you cannot come.

³⁴"A new command I give you: Love one another. As I have loved you, so you must love one another. ³⁵By this all men will know that you are my disciples, if you love one another."

³⁶Simon Peter asked him, "Lord, where are you going?"

Jesus replied, "Where I am going, you cannot follow now, but you will follow later."

³⁷Peter asked, "Lord, why can't I follow you now? I will lay down my life for you."

³⁸Then Jesus answered, "Will you really lay down your life for me? I tell you the truth, before the rooster crows, you will disown me three times!

Jesus Comforts His Disciples

14 "Do not let your hearts be troubled. Trust in God;ᶜ trust also in me. ²In my Father's house are many rooms; if it were not so, I would have told you. I am going there to prepare a place for you. ³And if I go and prepare a place for you, I will come back and take you to be with me that you also may be where I am. ⁴You know the way to the place where I am going."

ᵃ18 Psalm 41:9   ᵇ32 Many early manuscripts do not have *If God is glorified in him.*   ᶜ1 Or *You trust in God*

Jesus the Way to the Father

5Thomas said to him, "Lord, we don't know where you are going, so how can we know the way?"

6Jesus answered, "I am the way and the truth and the life. No one comes to the Father except through me. **7**If you really knew me, you would know[a] my Father as well. From now on, you do know him and have seen him."

8Philip said, "Lord, show us the Father and that will be enough for us."

9Jesus answered: "Don't you know me, Philip, even after I have been among you such a long time? Anyone who has seen me has seen the Father. How can you say, 'Show us the Father'? **10**Don't

a7 Some early manuscripts If you really have known me, you will know

---

FRIDAY

VERSE:	AUTHOR:	PASSAGE:
John 14:2	Kay Marshall Strom	John 14:1–14

Do Not Fear

At the age of twenty-five, Johanna Veenstra, a young woman who had grown up among the bright lights and social whirl of New York City, left her exciting life to live in an ant-infested mud hut in Nigeria. God had called her, she was certain of that, and she had joyfully accepted.

"There has been no sacrifice," she wrote, "because the Lord Jesus himself is my constant companion."

Despite the hardships and frustrations of living in [rather primitive] Africa, Johanna established an effective medical and educational ministry. Her work was successful and rewarding.

In a letter home, Johanna told about a particular African Christian who had died. "He went from a mud hut to a mansion," she wrote. But before her letter reached home, Johanna herself had died, suddenly and unexpectedly, at the age of thirty-nine. The words she had written of her African friend rang true for her, as well.

We will never experience the completeness of our ultimate selves in this life. Not until after death. For most people in this world, that would be a terrifying thought. But not for God's children. Rather than looking ahead with alarm or fear, the prospect of reaching our highest pinnacle when we are in our heavenly home in the company of our heavenly Father should fill our hearts with joyful anticipation. Especially when we understand that Jesus himself has gone on ahead to prepare for us a special place. He is looking forward to our coming.

Where do you live now? Whether shack or palace, it can never compare to the mansion that is awaiting you.

ADDITIONAL SCRIPTURE READINGS:
Job 19:25–26; 2 Corinthians 5:1–9; Philippians 1:20–21

Go to page 148 for your next devotional reading.

you believe that I am in the Father, and that the Father is in me? The words I say to you are not just my own. Rather, it is the Father, living in me, who is doing his work. [11]Believe me when I say that I am in the Father and the Father is in me; or at least believe on the evidence of the miracles themselves. [12]I tell you the truth, anyone who has faith in me will do what I have been doing. He will do even greater things than these, because I am going to the Father. [13]And I will do whatever you ask in my name, so that the Son may bring glory to the Father. [14]You may ask me for anything in my name, and I will do it.

Jesus Promises the Holy Spirit

[15]"If you love me, you will obey what I command. [16]And I will ask the Father, and he will give you another Counselor to be with you forever— [17]the Spirit of truth. The world cannot accept him, because it neither sees him nor knows him. But you know him, for he lives with you and will be[a] in you. [18]I will not leave you as orphans; I will come to you. [19]Before long, the world will not see me anymore, but you will see me. Because I live, you also will live. [20]On that day you will realize that I am in my Father, and you are in me, and I am in you. [21]Whoever has my commands and obeys them, he is the one who loves me. He who loves me will be loved by my Father, and I too will love him and show myself to him."

[22]Then Judas (not Judas Iscariot) said, "But, Lord, why do you intend to show yourself to us and not to the world?"

[23]Jesus replied, "If anyone loves me, he will obey my teaching. My Father will love him, and we will come to him and make our home with him. [24]He who does not love me will not obey my teaching. These words you hear are not my own; they belong to the Father who sent me.

[25]"All this I have spoken while still with you. [26]But the Counselor, the Holy Spirit, whom the Father will send in my name, will teach you all things and will remind you of everything I have said to you. [27]Peace I leave with you; my peace I give you. I do not give to you as the world gives. Do not let your hearts be troubled and do not be afraid.

[28]"You heard me say, 'I am going away and I am coming back to you.' If you loved me, you would be glad that I am going to the Father, for the Father is greater than I. [29]I have told you now before it happens, so that when it does happen you will believe. [30]I will not speak with you much longer, for the prince of this world is coming. He has no hold on me, [31]but the world must learn that I love the Father and that I do exactly what my Father has commanded me.

"Come now; let us leave.

The Vine and the Branches

15 "I am the true vine, and my Father is the gardener. [2]He cuts off every branch in me that bears no fruit, while every branch that does bear fruit he prunes[b] so that it will be even more fruitful. [3]You are already clean because of the word I have spoken to you. [4]Remain in me, and I will remain in you. No branch can bear fruit by itself; it must remain in the vine. Neither can you bear fruit unless you remain in me.

[5]"I am the vine; you are the branches. If a man remains in me and I in him, he will bear much fruit; apart from me you can do nothing. [6]If anyone does not remain in me, he is like a branch that is thrown away and withers; such branches are picked up, thrown into the fire and burned. [7]If you remain in me and my words remain in you, ask whatever you wish, and it will be given you. [8]This is to my Father's glory, that you bear much fruit, showing yourselves to be my disciples.

[9]"As the Father has loved me, so have I loved you. Now remain in my love. [10]If you obey my commands, you will remain in my love, just as I have obeyed my Father's commands and remain in his love. [11]I have told you this so that my joy may be in you and that your joy may be complete. [12]My command is this: Love each other as I have loved you. [13]Greater love has no one than this, that he lay down his life for his friends. [14]You are my friends if you do what I command. [15]I no longer call you servants, because a servant does not know

---

[a]17 Some early manuscripts and is   [b]2 The Greek for prunes also means cleans.

WEEKENDING

RECALL

Jesus himself was crucified because he would not, could not compromise what he knew truth to be. Every moment of his earthly life, he lived truth because he was truth. "I am the way and the truth and the life," Jesus declared. This was madness to those who lived bound by the rigidities of the "popular" religious concepts of his time. More than madness, his words were considered blasphemy. But the fact remained: He *was* the truth and the life, and so he spoke and so he lived. And because he did, so he died, leaving behind him men and women whom Paul described as being under the control of the *love* of Christ.

If we live truth . . . we live Christ, and the same power that raised him from the dead will give us the courage and the daring to love enough to speak the truth.

Eugenia Price

REFLECT

Saturday: John 14:5–14
Sunday: Ephesians 4:25

*Go to page 149 for your
next devotional reading.*

his master's business. Instead, I have called you friends, for everything that I learned from my Father I have made known to you. [16]You did not choose me, but I chose you and appointed you to go and bear fruit—fruit that will last. Then the Father will give you whatever you ask in my name. [17]This is my command: Love each other.

The World Hates the Disciples

[18]"If the world hates you, keep in mind that it hated me first. [19]If you belonged to the world, it would love you as its own. As it is, you do not belong to the world, but I have chosen you out of the world. That is why the world hates you. [20]Remember the words I spoke to you: 'No servant is greater than his

MONDAY

VERSE:
John 15:13

AUTHOR:
Doris W. Greig

PASSAGE:
John 15:1–17

Friends

As I think about friendship, I wonder if I had my life to live over, how differently I would live it.

Would I have invited more friends over for dinner, even if it were just for a hamburger fry or macaroni and cheese? Would I have sat on the lawn more often with my neighbors and visited while we watched the children play?

Would I have cried more often with them when appropriate, and laughed more often when that was in order? Would I have said, "I'm sorry," more often?

I want to be more like the kind of friend found in this acrostic:

F — Fun loving; Feeling of acceptance; Faithful
R — Risk being real, understood, even misunderstood
I — Interested in the welfare of others; Impartial
E — Expect the best of others; Empathetic
N — Natural relationship, a wholesome acceptance of others; Non-exclusive
D — Diplomatic; Delightful to be with; Durable in hard times
S — Sympathetic; Supportive with prayer and help; Stable
H — Helpful; Hopeful; Healing; Happy
I — Interdependent by helping others
P — Patient; Protective of reputation and confidences; Pleasant to be with; Personable

If I were given another opportunity at life and friendship, I would seize every minute of it! I would look at it and really see it and live it for Jesus.

ADDITIONAL SCRIPTURE READINGS:
1 Samuel 18:1–4; Hosea 10:12; Mark 2:1–5

Go to page 152 for your next devotional reading.

master.'[a] If they persecuted me, they will persecute you also. If they obeyed my teaching, they will obey yours also. [21]They will treat you this way because of my name, for they do not know the One who sent me. [22]If I had not come and spoken to them, they would not be guilty of sin. Now, however, they have no excuse for their sin. [23]He who hates me hates my Father as well. [24]If I had not done among them what no one else did, they would not be guilty of sin. But now they have seen these miracles, and yet they have hated both me and my Father. [25]But this is to fulfill what is written in their Law: 'They hated me without reason.'[b]

[26]"When the Counselor comes, whom I will send to you from the Father, the Spirit of truth who goes out from the Father, he will testify about me. [27]And you also must testify, for you have been with me from the beginning.

16 "All this I have told you so that you will not go astray. [2]They will put you out of the synagogue; in fact, a time is coming when anyone who kills you will think he is offering a service to God. [3]They will do such things because they have not known the Father or me. [4]I have told you this, so that when the time comes you will remember that I warned you. I did not tell you this at first because I was with you.

The Work of the Holy Spirit

[5]"Now I am going to him who sent me, yet none of you asks me, 'Where are you going?' [6]Because I have said these things, you are filled with grief. [7]But I tell you the truth: It is for your good that I am going away. Unless I go away, the Counselor will not come to you; but if I go, I will send him to you. [8]When he comes, he will convict the world of guilt[c] in regard to sin and righteousness and judgment: [9]in regard to sin, because men do not believe in me; [10]in regard to righteousness, because I am going to the Father, where you can see me no longer; [11]and in regard to judgment, because the prince of this world now stands condemned.

[12]"I have much more to say to you, more than you can now bear. [13]But when he, the Spirit of truth, comes, he will guide you into all truth. He will not speak on his own; he will speak only what he hears, and he will tell you what is yet to come. [14]He will bring glory to me by taking from what is mine and making it known to you. [15]All that belongs to the Father is mine. That is why I said the Spirit will take from what is mine and make it known to you.

[16]"In a little while you will see me no more, and then after a little while you will see me."

The Disciples' Grief Will Turn to Joy

[17]Some of his disciples said to one another, "What does he mean by saying, 'In a little while you will see me no more, and then after a little while you will see me,' and 'Because I am going to the Father'?" [18]They kept asking, "What does he mean by 'a little while'? We don't understand what he is saying."

[19]Jesus saw that they wanted to ask him about this, so he said to them, "Are you asking one another what I meant when I said, 'In a little while you will see me no more, and then after a little while you will see me'? [20]I tell you the truth, you will weep and mourn while the world rejoices. You will grieve, but your grief will turn to joy. [21]A woman giving birth to a child has pain because her time has come; but when her baby is born she forgets the anguish because of her joy that a child is born into the world. [22]So with you: Now is your time of grief, but I will see you again and you will rejoice, and no one will take away your joy. [23]In that day you will no longer ask me anything. I tell you the truth, my Father will give you whatever you ask in my name. [24]Until now you have not asked for anything in my name. Ask and you will receive, and your joy will be complete.

[25]"Though I have been speaking figuratively, a time is coming when I will no longer use this kind of language but will tell you plainly about my Father. [26]In that day you will ask in my name. I am not saying that I will ask the Father on your behalf. [27]No, the Father himself loves you because you have loved me and have believed that I came from God. [28]I came from the Father and entered the world; now I am leaving the world and going back to the Father."

[29]Then Jesus' disciples said, "Now

---

[a]20 John 13:16 [b]25 Psalms 35:19; 69:4 [c]8 Or will expose the guilt of the world

you are speaking clearly and without figures of speech. [30]Now we can see that you know all things and that you do not even need to have anyone ask you questions. This makes us believe that you came from God."

[31]"You believe at last!"[a] Jesus answered. [32]"But a time is coming, and has come, when you will be scattered, each to his own home. You will leave me all alone. Yet I am not alone, for my Father is with me.

[33]"I have told you these things, so that in me you may have peace. In this world you will have trouble. But take heart! I have overcome the world."

Jesus Prays for Himself

17 After Jesus said this, he looked toward heaven and prayed:

"Father, the time has come. Glorify your Son, that your Son may glorify you. [2]For you granted him authority over all people that he might give eternal life to all those you have given him. [3]Now this is eternal life: that they may know you, the only true God, and Jesus Christ, whom you have sent. [4]I have brought you glory on earth by completing the work you gave me to do. [5]And now, Father, glorify me in your presence with the glory I had with you before the world began.

Jesus Prays for His Disciples

[6]"I have revealed you[b] to those whom you gave me out of the world. They were yours; you gave them to me and they have obeyed your word. [7]Now they know that everything you have given me comes from you. [8]For I gave them the words you gave me and they accepted them. They knew with certainty that I came from you, and they believed that you sent me. [9]I pray for them. I am not praying for the world, but for those you have given me, for they are yours. [10]All I have is yours, and all you have is mine. And glory has come to me through them. [11]I will remain in the world no longer, but they are still in the world, and I am coming to you. Holy Father, protect them by the power of your name—the name you gave me—so that they may be one as we are one. [12]While I was with them, I protected them and kept them safe by that name you gave me. None has been lost except the one doomed to destruction so that Scripture would be fulfilled.

[13]"I am coming to you now, but I say these things while I am still in the world, so that they may have the full measure of my joy within them. [14]I have given them your word and the world has hated them, for they are not of the world any more than I am of the world. [15]My prayer is not that you take them out of the world but that you protect them from the evil one. [16]They are not of the world, even as I am not of it. [17]Sanctify[c] them by the truth; your word is truth. [18]As you sent me into the world, I have sent them into the world. [19]For them I sanctify myself, that they too may be truly sanctified.

Jesus Prays for All Believers

[20]"My prayer is not for them alone. I pray also for those who will believe in me through their message, [21]that all of them may be one, Father, just as you are in me and I am in you. May they also be in us so that the world may believe that you have sent me. [22]I have given them the glory that you gave me, that they may be one as we are one: [23]I in them and you in me. May they be brought to complete unity to let the world know that you sent me and have loved them even as you have loved me.

[24]"Father, I want those you have given me to be with me where I am, and to see my glory, the glory you have given me because you loved me before the creation of the world.

[25]"Righteous Father, though the world does not know you, I know you, and they know that you have sent me. [26]I have made you known to them, and will continue to make you known in order that the love you have for me may be in them and that I myself may be in them."

---

[a]31 Or "Do you now believe?" [b]6 Greek your name; also in verse 26 [c]17 Greek hagiazo (set apart for sacred use or make holy); also in verse 19

VERSE:
John 17:23

AUTHOR:
Edith Bajema

PASSAGE:
John 17:20–23

Becoming One

A married couple came to the counselor's office, seeking guidance. "We've been married only six months, but we're starting to fight all the time," said the husband. "She says I don't do enough to help her."

"You never look after my interests!" said the wife heatedly. "The only thing you care about is what you need."

After listening to this for half an hour, the counselor gave them one suggestion. "Each of you write down what you feel you need out of this marriage and out of your life."

The couple did this, and the counselor continued: "Exchange lists. Margaret, your job is to focus primarily on Tim's list and assist him in any way to meet his needs and goals. Tim, you do the same with Margaret's list. Forget your own list; let your spouse be the primary caretaker of your own needs and goals."

They agreed reluctantly and left. Two weeks later, they returned. After hearing what they had to say, the counselor told them, "You're on the right track. Call me if you need me."

That was twenty-five years ago. Now they are celebrating a very successful marriage and their anniversary with their four children and many friends.

The secret to their unity? Taking the other person's needs, feelings and desires into themselves. In a sense, a bit of Tim was "in" Margaret, and vice versa. Margaret gave of herself to help accomplish Tim's goals, and Tim did the same for her.

Unity in a marriage is wonderful when it happens, but it's often difficult to achieve. Unity among believers can be even more elusive. Believers differ, disagree, hurt each other's feelings, fight about issues and problems.

The key to becoming one lies in Jesus' prayer to his Father for all believers: "that they may be one as we are one: I in them and you in me" (vv. 22–23).

Do you willingly pledge yourself to put Jesus' plans and priorities first, making them your own? Then you have allowed Jesus to be "in" you.

And when you meet with other believers who have done the same, you can't help but become "like-minded, having the same love, being one in spirit and purpose" (Philippians 2:2).

ADDITIONAL SCRIPTURE READINGS:
Psalm 133:1–3; Ephesians 4:1–6; Philippians 2:1–4

Go to page 157 for your next devotional reading.

Jesus Arrested

18 When he had finished praying, Jesus left with his disciples and crossed the Kidron Valley. On the other side there was an olive grove, and he and his disciples went into it.

2Now Judas, who betrayed him, knew the place, because Jesus had often met there with his disciples. **3**So Judas came to the grove, guiding a detachment of soldiers and some officials from the chief priests and Pharisees. They were carrying torches, lanterns and weapons.

4Jesus, knowing all that was going to happen to him, went out and asked them, "Who is it you want?"

5"Jesus of Nazareth," they replied.

"I am he," Jesus said. (And Judas the traitor was standing there with them.) **6**When Jesus said, "I am he," they drew back and fell to the ground.

7Again he asked them, "Who is it you want?"

And they said, "Jesus of Nazareth."

8"I told you that I am he," Jesus answered. "If you are looking for me, then let these men go." **9**This happened so that the words he had spoken would be fulfilled: "I have not lost one of those you gave me."[a]

10Then Simon Peter, who had a sword, drew it and struck the high priest's servant, cutting off his right ear. (The servant's name was Malchus.)

11Jesus commanded Peter, "Put your sword away! Shall I not drink the cup the Father has given me?"

Jesus Taken to Annas

12Then the detachment of soldiers with its commander and the Jewish officials arrested Jesus. They bound him **13**and brought him first to Annas, who was the father-in-law of Caiaphas, the high priest that year. **14**Caiaphas was the one who had advised the Jews that it would be good if one man died for the people.

Peter's First Denial

15Simon Peter and another disciple were following Jesus. Because this disciple was known to the high priest, he went with Jesus into the high priest's courtyard, **16**but Peter had to wait outside at the door. The other disciple, who was known to the high priest, came back, spoke to the girl on duty there and brought Peter in.

17"You are not one of his disciples, are you?" the girl at the door asked Peter.

He replied, "I am not."

18It was cold, and the servants and officials stood around a fire they had made to keep warm. Peter also was standing with them, warming himself.

The High Priest Questions Jesus

19Meanwhile, the high priest questioned Jesus about his disciples and his teaching.

20"I have spoken openly to the world," Jesus replied. "I always taught in synagogues or at the temple, where all the Jews come together. I said nothing in secret. **21**Why question me? Ask those who heard me. Surely they know what I said."

22When Jesus said this, one of the officials nearby struck him in the face. "Is this the way you answer the high priest?" he demanded.

23"If I said something wrong," Jesus replied, "testify as to what is wrong. But if I spoke the truth, why did you strike me?" **24**Then Annas sent him, still bound, to Caiaphas the high priest.[b]

Peter's Second and Third Denials

25As Simon Peter stood warming himself, he was asked, "You are not one of his disciples, are you?"

He denied it, saying, "I am not."

26One of the high priest's servants, a relative of the man whose ear Peter had cut off, challenged him, "Didn't I see you with him in the olive grove?" **27**Again Peter denied it, and at that moment a rooster began to crow.

Jesus Before Pilate

28Then the Jews led Jesus from Caiaphas to the palace of the Roman governor. By now it was early morning, and to avoid ceremonial uncleanness the Jews did not enter the palace; they wanted to be able to eat the Passover. **29**So Pilate came out to them and asked, "What charges are you bringing against this man?"

30"If he were not a criminal," they replied, "we would not have handed him over to you."

---

[a]9 John 6:39   [b]24 Or (Now Annas had sent him, still bound, to Caiaphas the high priest.)

³¹Pilate said, "Take him yourselves and judge him by your own law."

"But we have no right to execute anyone," the Jews objected. ³²This happened so that the words Jesus had spoken indicating the kind of death he was going to die would be fulfilled.

³³Pilate then went back inside the palace, summoned Jesus and asked him, "Are you the king of the Jews?"

³⁴"Is that your own idea," Jesus asked, "or did others talk to you about me?"

³⁵"Am I a Jew?" Pilate replied. "It was your people and your chief priests who handed you over to me. What is it you have done?"

³⁶Jesus said, "My kingdom is not of this world. If it were, my servants would fight to prevent my arrest by the Jews. But now my kingdom is from another place."

³⁷"You are a king, then!" said Pilate.

Jesus answered, "You are right in saying I am a king. In fact, for this reason I was born, and for this I came into the world, to testify to the truth. Everyone on the side of truth listens to me."

³⁸"What is truth?" Pilate asked. With this he went out again to the Jews and said, "I find no basis for a charge against him. ³⁹But it is your custom for me to release to you one prisoner at the time of the Passover. Do you want me to release 'the king of the Jews'?"

⁴⁰They shouted back, "No, not him! Give us Barabbas!" Now Barabbas had taken part in a rebellion.

Jesus Sentenced to be Crucified

19 Then Pilate took Jesus and had him flogged. ²The soldiers twisted together a crown of thorns and put it on his head. They clothed him in a purple robe ³and went up to him again and again, saying, "Hail, king of the Jews!" And they struck him in the face.

⁴Once more Pilate came out and said to the Jews, "Look, I am bringing him out to you to let you know that I find no basis for a charge against him." ⁵When Jesus came out wearing the crown of thorns and the purple robe, Pilate said to them, "Here is the man!"

⁶As soon as the chief priests and their officials saw him, they shouted, "Crucify! Crucify!"

But Pilate answered, "You take him and crucify him. As for me, I find no basis for a charge against him."

⁷The Jews insisted, "We have a law, and according to that law he must die, because he claimed to be the Son of God."

⁸When Pilate heard this, he was even more afraid, ⁹and he went back inside the palace. "Where do you come from?" he asked Jesus, but Jesus gave him no answer. ¹⁰"Do you refuse to speak to me?" Pilate said. "Don't you realize I have power either to free you or to crucify you?"

¹¹Jesus answered, "You would have no power over me if it were not given to you from above. Therefore the one who handed me over to you is guilty of a greater sin."

¹²From then on, Pilate tried to set Jesus free, but the Jews kept shouting, "If you let this man go, you are no friend of Caesar. Anyone who claims to be a king opposes Caesar."

¹³When Pilate heard this, he brought Jesus out and sat down on the judge's seat at a place known as the Stone Pavement (which in Aramaic is Gabbatha). ¹⁴It was the day of Preparation of Passover Week, about the sixth hour.

"Here is your king," Pilate said to the Jews.

¹⁵But they shouted, "Take him away! Take him away! Crucify him!"

"Shall I crucify your king?" Pilate asked.

"We have no king but Caesar," the chief priests answered.

¹⁶Finally Pilate handed him over to them to be crucified.

The Crucifixion

So the soldiers took charge of Jesus. ¹⁷Carrying his own cross, he went out to the place of the Skull (which in Aramaic is called Golgotha). ¹⁸Here they crucified him, and with him two others—one on each side and Jesus in the middle.

¹⁹Pilate had a notice prepared and fastened to the cross. It read: JESUS OF NAZARETH, THE KING OF THE JEWS. ²⁰Many of the Jews read this sign, for the place where Jesus was crucified was near the city, and the sign was written in Aramaic, Latin and Greek. ²¹The chief priests of the Jews protested to Pilate, "Do not write 'The King of the Jews,' but that this man claimed to be king of the Jews."

22Pilate answered, "What I have written, I have written."

23When the soldiers crucified Jesus, they took his clothes, dividing them into four shares, one for each of them, with the undergarment remaining. This garment was seamless, woven in one piece from top to bottom.

24"Let's not tear it," they said to one another. "Let's decide by lot who will get it."

This happened that the scripture might be fulfilled which said,

"They divided my garments among
  them
and cast lots for my clothing."a

So this is what the soldiers did.

25Near the cross of Jesus stood his mother, his mother's sister, Mary the wife of Clopas, and Mary Magdalene. 26When Jesus saw his mother there, and the disciple whom he loved standing nearby, he said to his mother, "Dear woman, here is your son," 27and to the disciple, "Here is your mother." From that time on, this disciple took her into his home.

The Death of Jesus

28Later, knowing that all was now completed, and so that the Scripture would be fulfilled, Jesus said, "I am thirsty." 29A jar of wine vinegar was there, so they soaked a sponge in it, put the sponge on a stalk of the hyssop plant, and lifted it to Jesus' lips. 30When he had received the drink, Jesus said, "It is finished." With that, he bowed his head and gave up his spirit.

31Now it was the day of Preparation, and the next day was to be a special Sabbath. Because the Jews did not want the bodies left on the crosses during the Sabbath, they asked Pilate to have the legs broken and the bodies taken down. 32The soldiers therefore came and broke the legs of the first man who had been crucified with Jesus, and then those of the other. 33But when they came to Jesus and found that he was already dead, they did not break his legs. 34Instead, one of the soldiers pierced Jesus' side with a spear, bringing a sudden flow of blood and water. 35The man who saw it has given testimony, and his testimony is true. He knows that he tells the truth, and he testifies so that you also may believe. 36These things happened so that the scripture would be fulfilled: "Not one of his bones will be broken,"b 37and, as another scripture says, "They will look on the one they have pierced."c

The Burial of Jesus

38Later, Joseph of Arimathea asked Pilate for the body of Jesus. Now Joseph was a disciple of Jesus, but secretly because he feared the Jews. With Pilate's permission, he came and took the body away. 39He was accompanied by Nicodemus, the man who earlier had visited Jesus at night. Nicodemus brought a mixture of myrrh and aloes, about seventy-five pounds.d 40Taking Jesus' body, the two of them wrapped it, with the spices, in strips of linen. This was in accordance with Jewish burial customs. 41At the place where Jesus was crucified, there was a garden, and in the garden a new tomb, in which no one had ever been laid. 42Because it was the Jewish day of Preparation and since the tomb was nearby, they laid Jesus there.

The Empty Tomb

20 Early on the first day of the week, while it was still dark, Mary Magdalene went to the tomb and saw that the stone had been removed from the entrance. 2So she came running to Simon Peter and the other disciple, the one Jesus loved, and said, "They have taken the Lord out of the tomb, and we don't know where they have put him!"

3So Peter and the other disciple started for the tomb. 4Both were running, but the other disciple outran Peter and reached the tomb first. 5He bent over and looked in at the strips of linen lying there but did not go in. 6Then Simon Peter, who was behind him, arrived and went into the tomb. He saw the strips of linen lying there, 7as well as the burial cloth that had been around Jesus' head. The cloth was folded up by itself, separate from the linen. 8Finally the other disciple, who had reached the tomb first, also went inside. He saw and believed. 9(They still did not understand

a24 Psalm 22:18   b36 Exodus 12:46; Num. 9:12; Psalm 34:20   c37 Zech. 12:10   d39 Greek a hundred litrai (about 34 kilograms)

from Scripture that Jesus had to rise from the dead.)

Jesus Appears to Mary Magdalene

10Then the disciples went back to their homes, **11**but Mary stood outside the tomb crying. As she wept, she bent over to look into the tomb **12**and saw two angels in white, seated where Jesus' body had been, one at the head and the other at the foot.

13They asked her, "Woman, why are you crying?"

"They have taken my Lord away," she said, "and I don't know where they have put him." **14**At this, she turned around and saw Jesus standing there, but she did not realize that it was Jesus.

15"Woman," he said, "why are you crying? Who is it you are looking for?"

Thinking he was the gardener, she said, "Sir, if you have carried him away, tell me where you have put him, and I will get him."

16Jesus said to her, "Mary."

She turned toward him and cried out in Aramaic, "Rabboni!" (which means Teacher).

17Jesus said, "Do not hold on to me, for I have not yet returned to the Father. Go instead to my brothers and tell them, 'I am returning to my Father and your Father, to my God and your God.' "

18Mary Magdalene went to the disciples with the news: "I have seen the Lord!" And she told them that he had said these things to her.

Jesus Appears to His Disciples

19On the evening of that first day of the week, when the disciples were together, with the doors locked for fear of the Jews, Jesus came and stood among them and said, "Peace be with you!" **20**After he said this, he showed them his hands and side. The disciples were overjoyed when they saw the Lord.

21Again Jesus said, "Peace be with you! As the Father has sent me, I am sending you." **22**And with that he breathed on them and said, "Receive the Holy Spirit. **23**If you forgive anyone his sins, they are forgiven; if you do not forgive them, they are not forgiven."

Jesus Appears to Thomas

24Now Thomas (called Didymus), one of the Twelve, was not with the disciples when Jesus came. **25**So the other disciples told him, "We have seen the Lord!"

But he said to them, "Unless I see the nail marks in his hands and put my finger where the nails were, and put my hand into his side, I will not believe it."

26A week later his disciples were in the house again, and Thomas was with them. Though the doors were locked, Jesus came and stood among them and said, "Peace be with you!" **27**Then he said to Thomas, "Put your finger here; see my hands. Reach out your hand and put it into my side. Stop doubting and believe."

28Thomas said to him, "My Lord and my God!"

29Then Jesus told him, "Because you have seen me, you have believed; blessed are those who have not seen and yet have believed."

30Jesus did many other miraculous signs in the presence of his disciples, which are not recorded in this book. **31**But these are written that you may[a] believe that Jesus is the Christ, the Son of God, and that by believing you may have life in his name.

Jesus and the Miraculous Catch of Fish

21 Afterward Jesus appeared again to his disciples, by the Sea of Tiberias.[b] It happened this way: **2**Simon Peter, Thomas (called Didymus), Nathanael from Cana in Galilee, the sons of Zebedee, and two other disciples were together. **3**"I'm going out to fish," Simon Peter told them, and they said, "We'll go with you." So they went out and got into the boat, but that night they caught nothing.

4Early in the morning, Jesus stood on the shore, but the disciples did not realize that it was Jesus.

5He called out to them, "Friends, haven't you any fish?"

"No," they answered.

6He said, "Throw your net on the right side of the boat and you will find some." When they did, they were unable to haul the net in because of the large number of fish.

7Then the disciple whom Jesus loved said to Peter, "It is the Lord!" As soon as

Simon Peter heard him say, "It is the Lord," he wrapped his outer garment around him (for he had taken it off) and jumped into the water. [8]The other disciples followed in the boat, towing the net full of fish, for they were not far from shore, about a hundred yards.[a] [9]When they landed, they saw a fire of burning coals there with fish on it, and some bread.

[10]Jesus said to them, "Bring some of the fish you have just caught."

[11]Simon Peter climbed aboard and dragged the net ashore. It was full of large fish, 153, but even with so many the net was not torn. [12]Jesus said to them, "Come and have breakfast." None of the disciples dared ask him, "Who are you?" They knew it was the Lord. [13]Jesus came, took the bread and gave it to

[a]8 Greek *about two hundred cubits* (about 90 meters)

WEDNESDAY

VERSE:
John 20:29

AUTHOR:
Debra Klingsporn

PASSAGE:
John 20:24–31

Trusting in the Unseen

Sitting on my bookshelf is a book published several years ago called *The Myth of Certainty*. The title alone catches my eye and speaks to me with a ring of truth. How I long for a world of black and white, good and bad, yes and no; a world of clear-cut distinctions and effortless decisions because the good and bad can be easily identified. No blurring rationalizations. No complicating considerations.

But clear-cut distinctions and effortless choices aren't true to my experience of life. Between black and white are shades of gray. Between good and bad are confusing questions. Between yes and no is a strong maybe.

The fact of the matter is, no matter how black and white and absolute some defenders of the faith portray the gospel, I simply can't buy that line. My experience and the experience of people of faith throughout the centuries, is one of a God who meets us *in* the questions, who honors our seeking, and who created us to be intelligent beings. When it comes to faith, if we're looking for proof and certainty, we won't find it.

Living at the heart of faith is living with uncertainty, trusting in the unseen. Somewhere along the way, we have to leap the chasm between that which we know absolutely and that which calls us from within. Yet even in our uncertainty, we walk in the presence of the holy.

God is far more interested in our honesty than our piety. We have only to offer him a willing heart and truthful spirit and he'll take it from there, meeting us in the chasm as we make the leap.

ADDITIONAL SCRIPTURE READINGS:
Mark 9:24; 1 Corinthians 13:12; 2 Corinthians 4:16–18

Go to page 163 for your next devotional reading.

them, and did the same with the fish. [14]This was now the third time Jesus appeared to his disciples after he was raised from the dead.

Jesus Reinstates Peter

[15]When they had finished eating, Jesus said to Simon Peter, "Simon son of John, do you truly love me more than these?"

"Yes, Lord," he said, "you know that I love you."

Jesus said, "Feed my lambs."

[16]Again Jesus said, "Simon son of John, do you truly love me?"

He answered, "Yes, Lord, you know that I love you."

Jesus said, "Take care of my sheep."

[17]The third time he said to him, "Simon son of John, do you love me?"

Peter was hurt because Jesus asked him the third time, "Do you love me?" He said, "Lord, you know all things; you know that I love you."

Jesus said, "Feed my sheep. [18]I tell you the truth, when you were younger you dressed yourself and went where you wanted; but when you are old you will stretch out your hands, and some-

one else will dress you and lead you where you do not want to go." [19]Jesus said this to indicate the kind of death by which Peter would glorify God. Then he said to him, "Follow me!"

[20]Peter turned and saw that the disciple whom Jesus loved was following them. (This was the one who had leaned back against Jesus at the supper and had said, "Lord, who is going to betray you?") [21]When Peter saw him, he asked, "Lord, what about him?"

[22]Jesus answered, "If I want him to remain alive until I return, what is that to you? You must follow me." [23]Because of this, the rumor spread among the brothers that this disciple would not die. But Jesus did not say that he would not die; he only said, "If I want him to remain alive until I return, what is that to you?"

[24]This is the disciple who testifies to these things and who wrote them down. We know that his testimony is true.

[25]Jesus did many other things as well. If every one of them were written down, I suppose that even the whole world would not have room for the books that would be written.

LIKE *a sequel to a movie, Acts picks up the action begun in the Gospel of Luke. Some refer to the book of Acts as "The Acts of the Holy Spirit," because it focuses on the coming of the Spirit on God's people—the church—in a new and powerful way. In this book Luke records Christianity's amazing growth and shows that revival comes not by human effort but by the power of the Holy Spirit. The Spirit so active in Acts is the same Spirit at work in your life today.*

ACTS

Jesus Taken Up Into Heaven

1 In my former book, Theophilus, I wrote about all that Jesus began to do and to teach ²until the day he was taken up to heaven, after giving instructions through the Holy Spirit to the apostles he had chosen. ³After his suffering, he showed himself to these men and gave many convincing proofs that he was alive. He appeared to them over a period of forty days and spoke about the kingdom of God. ⁴On one occasion, while he was eating with them, he gave them this command: "Do not leave Jerusalem, but wait for the gift my Father promised, which you have heard me speak about. ⁵For John baptized with[a] water, but in a few days you will be baptized with the Holy Spirit."

⁶So when they met together, they asked him, "Lord, are you at this time going to restore the kingdom to Israel?"

⁷He said to them: "It is not for you to know the times or dates the Father has set by his own authority. ⁸But you will receive power when the Holy Spirit comes on you; and you will be my witnesses in Jerusalem, and in all Judea and Samaria, and to the ends of the earth."

⁹After he said this, he was taken up

before their very eyes, and a cloud hid him from their sight.

[10]They were looking intently up into the sky as he was going, when suddenly two men dressed in white stood beside them. [11]"Men of Galilee," they said, "why do you stand here looking into the sky? This same Jesus, who has been taken from you into heaven, will come back in the same way you have seen him go into heaven."

Matthias Chosen to Replace Judas

[12]Then they returned to Jerusalem from the hill called the Mount of Olives, a Sabbath day's walk[a] from the city. [13]When they arrived, they went upstairs to the room where they were staying. Those present were Peter, John, James and Andrew; Philip and Thomas, Bartholomew and Matthew; James son of Alphaeus and Simon the Zealot, and Judas son of James. [14]They all joined together constantly in prayer, along with the women and Mary the mother of Jesus, and with his brothers.

[15]In those days Peter stood up among the believers[b] (a group numbering about a hundred and twenty) [16]and said, "Brothers, the Scripture had to be fulfilled which the Holy Spirit spoke long ago through the mouth of David concerning Judas, who served as guide for those who arrested Jesus— [17]he was one of our number and shared in this ministry."

[18](With the reward he got for his wickedness, Judas bought a field; there he fell headlong, his body burst open and all his intestines spilled out. [19]Everyone in Jerusalem heard about this, so they called that field in their language Akeldama, that is, Field of Blood.)

[20]"For," said Peter, "it is written in the book of Psalms,

" 'May his place be deserted;
　let there be no one to dwell in
　　it,'[c]

and,

" 'May another take his place of
　leadership.'[d]

[21]Therefore it is necessary to choose one of the men who have been with us the whole time the Lord Jesus went in and out among us, [22]beginning from John's baptism to the time when Jesus was taken up from us. For one of these must become a witness with us of his resurrection."

[23]So they proposed two men: Joseph called Barsabbas (also known as Justus) and Matthias. [24]Then they prayed, "Lord, you know everyone's heart. Show us which of these two you have chosen [25]to take over this apostolic ministry, which Judas left to go where he belongs." [26]Then they cast lots, and the lot fell to Matthias; so he was added to the eleven apostles.

The Holy Spirit Comes at Pentecost

2 When the day of Pentecost came, they were all together in one place. [2]Suddenly a sound like the blowing of a violent wind came from heaven and filled the whole house where they were sitting. [3]They saw what seemed to be tongues of fire that separated and came to rest on each of them. [4]All of them were filled with the Holy Spirit and began to speak in other tongues[e] as the Spirit enabled them.

[5]Now there were staying in Jerusalem God-fearing Jews from every nation under heaven. [6]When they heard this sound, a crowd came together in bewilderment, because each one heard them speaking in his own language. [7]Utterly amazed, they asked: "Are not all these men who are speaking Galileans? [8]Then how is it that each of us hears them in his own native language? [9]Parthians, Medes and Elamites; residents of Mesopotamia, Judea and Cappadocia, Pontus and Asia, [10]Phrygia and Pamphylia, Egypt and the parts of Libya near Cyrene; visitors from Rome [11](both Jews and converts to Judaism); Cretans and Arabs—we hear them declaring the wonders of God in our own tongues!" [12]Amazed and perplexed, they asked one another, "What does this mean?"

[13]Some, however, made fun of them and said, "They have had too much wine.[f]"

Peter Addresses the Crowd

[14]Then Peter stood up with the Eleven, raised his voice and addressed the crowd: "Fellow Jews and all of you who

---

[a]12 That is, about 3/4 mile (about 1,100 meters)　　[b]15 Greek brothers　　[c]20 Psalm 69:25
[d]20 Psalm 109:8　　[e]4 Or languages; also in verse 11　　[f]13 Or sweet wine

live in Jerusalem, let me explain this to you; listen carefully to what I say. [15]These men are not drunk, as you suppose. It's only nine in the morning! [16]No, this is what was spoken by the prophet Joel:

[17]" 'In the last days, God says,
   I will pour out my Spirit on all
      people.
Your sons and daughters will
      prophesy,
   your young men will see visions,
   your old men will dream dreams.
[18]Even on my servants, both men and
      women,
   I will pour out my Spirit in those
      days,
   and they will prophesy
[19]I will show wonders in the heaven
      above
   and signs on the earth below,
   blood and fire and billows of
      smoke.
[20]The sun will be turned to darkness
   and the moon to blood
   before the coming of the great and
      glorious day of the Lord.
[21]And everyone who calls
   on the name of the Lord will be
      saved.' [a]

[22]"Men of Israel, listen to this: Jesus of Nazareth was a man accredited by God to you by miracles, wonders and signs, which God did among you through him, as you yourselves know. [23]This man was handed over to you by God's set purpose and foreknowledge; and you, with the help of wicked men,[b] put him to death by nailing him to the cross. [24]But God raised him from the dead, freeing him from the agony of death, because it was impossible for death to keep its hold on him. [25]David said about him:

" 'I saw the Lord always before me.
   Because he is at my right hand,
   I will not be shaken.
[26]Therefore my heart is glad and my
      tongue rejoices;
   my body also will live in hope,
[27]because you will not abandon me to
      the grave,

   nor will you let your Holy One see
      decay.
[28]You have made known to me the
      paths of life;
   you will fill me with joy in your
      presence.' [c]

[29]"Brothers, I can tell you confidently that the patriarch David died and was buried, and his tomb is here to this day. [30]But he was a prophet and knew that God had promised him on oath that he would place one of his descendants on his throne. [31]Seeing what was ahead, he spoke of the resurrection of the Christ,[d] that he was not abandoned to the grave, nor did his body see decay. [32]God has raised this Jesus to life, and we are all witnesses of the fact. [33]Exalted to the right hand of God, he has received from the Father the promised Holy Spirit and has poured out what you now see and hear. [34]For David did not ascend to heaven, and yet he said,

" 'The Lord said to my Lord:
   "Sit at my right hand
[35]until I make your enemies
   a footstool for your feet." ' [e]

[36]"Therefore let all Israel be assured of this: God has made this Jesus, whom you crucified, both Lord and Christ."

[37]When the people heard this, they were cut to the heart and said to Peter and the other apostles, "Brothers, what shall we do?"

[38]Peter replied, "Repent and be baptized, every one of you, in the name of Jesus Christ for the forgiveness of your sins. And you will receive the gift of the Holy Spirit. [39]The promise is for you and your children and for all who are far off—for all whom the Lord our God will call."

[40]With many other words he warned them; and he pleaded with them, "Save yourselves from this corrupt generation." [41]Those who accepted his message were baptized, and about three thousand were added to their number that day.

The Fellowship of the Believers

[42]They devoted themselves to the apostles' teaching and to the fellowship,

---

[a]21 Joel 2:28-32   [b]23 Or *of those not having the law* (that is, Gentiles)   [c]28 Psalm 16:8-11
[d]31 Or *Messiah*. "The Christ" (Greek) and "the Messiah" (Hebrew) both mean "the Anointed One";
also in verse 36.   [e]35 Psalm 110:1

to the breaking of bread and to prayer. [43]Everyone was filled with awe, and many wonders and miraculous signs were done by the apostles. [44]All the believers were together and had everything in common. [45]Selling their possessions and goods, they gave to anyone as he had need. [46]Every day they continued to meet together in the temple courts. They broke bread in their homes and ate together with glad and sincere hearts, [47]praising God and enjoying the favor of all the people. And the Lord added to their number daily those who were being saved.

Peter Heals the Crippled Beggar

3 One day Peter and John were going up to the temple at the time of prayer—at three in the afternoon. [2]Now a man crippled from birth was being carried to the temple gate called Beautiful, where he was put every day to beg from those going into the temple courts. [3]When he saw Peter and John about to enter, he asked them for money. [4]Peter looked straight at him, as did John. Then Peter said, "Look at us!" [5]So the man gave them his attention, expecting to get something from them.

[6]Then Peter said, "Silver or gold I do not have, but what I have I give you. In the name of Jesus Christ of Nazareth, walk." [7]Taking him by the right hand, he helped him up, and instantly the man's feet and ankles became strong. [8]He jumped to his feet and began to walk. Then he went with them into the temple courts, walking and jumping, and praising God. [9]When all the people saw him walking and praising God, [10]they recognized him as the same man who used to sit begging at the temple gate called Beautiful, and they were filled with wonder and amazement at what had happened to him.

Peter Speaks to the Onlookers

[11]While the beggar held on to Peter and John, all the people were astonished and came running to them in the place called Solomon's Colonnade. [12]When Peter saw this, he said to them: "Men of Israel, why does this surprise you? Why do you stare at us as if by our own power or godliness we had made this man walk? [13]The God of Abraham, Isaac and Jacob, the God of our fathers, has glorified his servant Jesus. You handed him over to be killed, and you disowned him before Pilate, though he had decided to let him go. [14]You disowned the Holy and Righteous One and asked that a murderer be released to you. [15]You killed the author of life, but God raised him from the dead. We are witnesses of this. [16]By faith in the name of Jesus, this man whom you see and know was made strong. It is Jesus' name and the faith that comes through him that has given this complete healing to him, as you can all see.

[17]"Now, brothers, I know that you acted in ignorance, as did your leaders. [18]But this is how God fulfilled what he had foretold through all the prophets, saying that his Christ[a] would suffer. [19]Repent, then, and turn to God, so that your sins may be wiped out, that times of refreshing may come from the Lord, [20]and that he may send the Christ, who has been appointed for you—even Jesus. [21]He must remain in heaven until the time comes for God to restore everything, as he promised long ago through his holy prophets. [22]For Moses said, 'The Lord your God will raise up for you a prophet like me from among your own people; you must listen to everything he tells you. [23]Anyone who does not listen to him will be completely cut off from among his people.'[b]

[24]"Indeed, all the prophets from Samuel on, as many as have spoken, have foretold these days. [25]And you are heirs of the prophets and of the covenant God made with your fathers. He said to Abraham, 'Through your offspring all peoples on earth will be blessed.'[c] [26]When God raised up his servant, he sent him first to you to bless you by turning each of you from your wicked ways."

Peter and John Before the Sanhedrin

4 The priests and the captain of the temple guard and the Sadducees came up to Peter and John while they were speaking to the people. [2]They were greatly disturbed because the apostles were teaching the people and proclaiming in Jesus the resurrection of the dead. [3]They seized Peter and John, and because it was evening, they put them in jail until the next day. [4]But many who

---

[a]18 Or *Messiah*; also in verse 20   [b]23 Deut. 18:15,18,19   [c]25 Gen. 22:18; 26:4

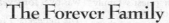
VERSE:	AUTHOR:	PASSAGE:
Acts 2:44	Jill Briscoe	Acts 2:42-47

The Forever Family

Pentecost resulted in a common binding together of God's forever family. Before his death and resurrection, Jesus himself had been the unifying factor, but this had been limiting because the Lord had been confined to his earthly body. Now the indwelling Spirit, given without measure, was to bring together all those who believed in him.

Once, while I was waiting for a flight at a Washington airport, my attention was drawn to a group of excited couples. All of them had strollers with them, and baby paraphernalia was all over the place, but there were no babies in sight. I discovered these eight couples had never met before that particular moment, and I watched them curiously as they made polite but restrained conversation.

Suddenly the plane they were waiting for arrived, and into the eager waiting arms of these couples were placed eight beautiful Korean orphans, all about three months old. What a transformation took place among those excited people—they suddenly became almost like one big family. Those of us watching from outside their experience laughed and cried with them at this marvelous gift of new life, but none of us could identify with them the way they suddenly seemed to identify with each other.

After all, these new parents had something very unique in common. They laughed—and cried a little, too—as they began to show off their babies to each other.

That same sort of "binding" quality comes about among human beings who stretch out their spiritual arms and accept God's gift of new life into their hearts. After I became a Christian, I couldn't get over this "family" feeling. I felt it whenever I met a bunch of believers. Even though we often had very little in common apart from our faith in Christ, I somehow felt we had known each other a very long time.

This sense of family crossed all barriers, so that the "oneness" operated even when I was introduced to a total stranger. This was really wonderful because I felt a true sense of belonging. I'd come home to the family of God. And today, years later, I still rejoice in being one of the family!

ADDITIONAL SCRIPTURE READINGS:
Luke 3:11; Acts 4:31-35; Galatians 6:10

Go to page 170 for your next devotional reading.

heard the message believed, and the number of men grew to about five thousand.

[5]The next day the rulers, elders and teachers of the law met in Jerusalem. [6]Annas the high priest was there, and so were Caiaphas, John, Alexander and the other men of the high priest's family. [7]They had Peter and John brought before them and began to question them: "By what power or what name did you do this?"

[8]Then Peter, filled with the Holy Spirit, said to them: "Rulers and elders of the people! [9]If we are being called to account today for an act of kindness shown to a cripple and are asked how he was healed, [10]then know this, you and all the people of Israel: It is by the name of Jesus Christ of Nazareth, whom you crucified but whom God raised from the dead, that this man stands before you healed. [11]He is

" 'the stone you builders rejected,
which has become the
capstone.[a][b]

[12]Salvation is found in no one else, for there is no other name under heaven given to men by which we must be saved."

[13]When they saw the courage of Peter and John and realized that they were unschooled, ordinary men, they were astonished and they took note that these men had been with Jesus. [14]But since they could see the man who had been healed standing there with them, there was nothing they could say. [15]So they ordered them to withdraw from the Sanhedrin and then conferred together. [16]"What are we going to do with these men?" they asked. "Everybody living in Jerusalem knows they have done an outstanding miracle, and we cannot deny it. [17]But to stop this thing from spreading any further among the people, we must warn these men to speak no longer to anyone in this name."

[18]Then they called them in again and commanded them not to speak or teach at all in the name of Jesus. [19]But Peter and John replied, "Judge for yourselves whether it is right in God's sight to obey you rather than God. [20]For we cannot help speaking about what we have seen and heard."

[21]After further threats they let them go. They could not decide how to punish them, because all the people were praising God for what had happened. [22]For the man who was miraculously healed was over forty years old.

The Believers' Prayer

[23]On their release, Peter and John went back to their own people and reported all that the chief priests and elders had said to them. [24]When they heard this, they raised their voices together in prayer to God. "Sovereign Lord," they said, "you made the heaven and the earth and the sea, and everything in them. [25]You spoke by the Holy Spirit through the mouth of your servant, our father David:

" 'Why do the nations rage
and the peoples plot in vain?
[26]The kings of the earth take their
stand
and the rulers gather together
against the Lord
and against his Anointed One.[c][d]

[27]Indeed Herod and Pontius Pilate met together with the Gentiles and the people[e] of Israel in this city to conspire against your holy servant Jesus, whom you anointed. [28]They did what your power and will had decided beforehand should happen. [29]Now, Lord, consider their threats and enable your servants to speak your word with great boldness. [30]Stretch out your hand to heal and perform miraculous signs and wonders through the name of your holy servant Jesus."

[31]After they prayed, the place where they were meeting was shaken. And they were all filled with the Holy Spirit and spoke the word of God boldly.

The Believers Share Their Possessions

[32]All the believers were one in heart and mind. No one claimed that any of his possessions was his own, but they shared everything they had. [33]With great power the apostles continued to testify to the resurrection of the Lord Jesus, and much grace was upon them all. [34]There were no needy persons among

---

[a]11 Or cornerstone   [b]11 Psalm 118:22   [c]26 That is, Christ or Messiah   [d]26 Psalm 2:1,2
[e]27 The Greek is plural.

them. For from time to time those who owned lands or houses sold them, brought the money from the sales ³⁵and put it at the apostles' feet, and it was distributed to anyone as he had need.

³⁶Joseph, a Levite from Cyprus, whom the apostles called Barnabas (which means Son of Encouragement), ³⁷sold a field he owned and brought the money and put it at the apostles' feet.

Ananias and Sapphira

5 Now a man named Ananias, together with his wife Sapphira, also sold a piece of property. ²With his wife's full knowledge he kept back part of the money for himself, but brought the rest and put it at the apostles' feet.

³Then Peter said, "Ananias, how is it that Satan has so filled your heart that you have lied to the Holy Spirit and have kept for yourself some of the money you received for the land? ⁴Didn't it belong to you before it was sold? And after it was sold, wasn't the money at your disposal? What made you think of doing such a thing? You have not lied to men but to God."

⁵When Ananias heard this, he fell down and died. And great fear seized all who heard what had happened. ⁶Then the young men came forward, wrapped up his body, and carried him out and buried him.

⁷About three hours later his wife came in, not knowing what had happened. ⁸Peter asked her, "Tell me, is this the price you and Ananias got for the land?"

"Yes," she said, "that is the price."

⁹Peter said to her, "How could you agree to test the Spirit of the Lord? Look! The feet of the men who buried your husband are at the door, and they will carry you out also."

¹⁰At that moment she fell down at his feet and died. Then the young men came in and, finding her dead, carried her out and buried her beside her husband. ¹¹Great fear seized the whole church and all who heard about these events.

The Apostles Heal Many

¹²The apostles performed many miraculous signs and wonders among the people. And all the believers used to meet together in Solomon's Colonnade. ¹³No one else dared join them, even though they were highly regarded by the people. ¹⁴Nevertheless, more and more men and women believed in the Lord and were added to their number. ¹⁵As a result, people brought the sick into the streets and laid them on beds and mats so that at least Peter's shadow might fall on some of them as he passed by. ¹⁶Crowds gathered also from the towns around Jerusalem, bringing their sick and those tormented by evilᵃ spirits, and all of them were healed.

The Apostles Persecuted

¹⁷Then the high priest and all his associates, who were members of the party of the Sadducees, were filled with jealousy. ¹⁸They arrested the apostles and put them in the public jail. ¹⁹But during the night an angel of the Lord opened the doors of the jail and brought them out. ²⁰"Go, stand in the temple courts," he said, "and tell the people the full message of this new life."

²¹At daybreak they entered the temple courts, as they had been told, and began to teach the people.

When the high priest and his associates arrived, they called together the Sanhedrin—the full assembly of the elders of Israel—and sent to the jail for the apostles. ²²But on arriving at the jail, the officers did not find them there. So they went back and reported, ²³"We found the jail securely locked, with the guards standing at the doors; but when we opened them, we found no one inside." ²⁴On hearing this report, the captain of the temple guard and the chief priests were puzzled, wondering what would come of this.

²⁵Then someone came and said, "Look! The men you put in jail are standing in the temple courts teaching the people." ²⁶At that, the captain went with his officers and brought the apostles. They did not use force, because they feared that the people would stone them.

²⁷Having brought the apostles, they made them appear before the Sanhedrin to be questioned by the high priest. ²⁸"We gave you strict orders not to teach in this name," he said. "Yet you have filled Jerusalem with your teaching and are determined to make us guilty of this man's blood."

ᵃ16 Greek unclean

[29]Peter and the other apostles replied: "We must obey God rather than men! [30]The God of our fathers raised Jesus from the dead—whom you had killed by hanging him on a tree. [31]God exalted him to his own right hand as Prince and Savior that he might give repentance and forgiveness of sins to Israel. [32]We are witnesses of these things, and so is the Holy Spirit, whom God has given to those who obey him."

[33]When they heard this, they were furious and wanted to put them to death. [34]But a Pharisee named Gamaliel, a teacher of the law, who was honored by all the people, stood up in the Sanhedrin and ordered that the men be put outside for a little while. [35]Then he addressed them: "Men of Israel, consider carefully what you intend to do to these men. [36]Some time ago Theudas appeared, claiming to be somebody, and about four hundred men rallied to him. He was killed, all his followers were dispersed, and it all came to nothing. [37]After him, Judas the Galilean appeared in the days of the census and led a band of people in revolt. He too was killed, and all his followers were scattered. [38]Therefore, in the present case I advise you: Leave these men alone! Let them go! For if their purpose or activity is of human origin, it will fail. [39]But if it is from God, you will not be able to stop these men; you will only find yourselves fighting against God."

[40]His speech persuaded them. They called the apostles in and had them flogged. Then they ordered them not to speak in the name of Jesus, and let them go.

[41]The apostles left the Sanhedrin, rejoicing because they had been counted worthy of suffering disgrace for the Name. [42]Day after day, in the temple courts and from house to house, they never stopped teaching and proclaiming the good news that Jesus is the Christ.[a]

The Choosing of the Seven

6 In those days when the number of disciples was increasing, the Grecian Jews among them complained against the Hebraic Jews because their widows were being overlooked in the daily distribution of food. [2]So the Twelve gathered all the disciples together and said, "It would not be right for us to neglect the ministry of the word of God in order to wait on tables. [3]Brothers, choose seven men from among you who are known to be full of the Spirit and wisdom. We will turn this responsibility over to them [4]and will give our attention to prayer and the ministry of the word."

[5]This proposal pleased the whole group. They chose Stephen, a man full of faith and of the Holy Spirit; also Philip, Procorus, Nicanor, Timon, Parmenas, and Nicolas from Antioch, a convert to Judaism. [6]They presented these men to the apostles, who prayed and laid their hands on them.

[7]So the word of God spread. The number of disciples in Jerusalem increased rapidly, and a large number of priests became obedient to the faith.

Stephen Seized

[8]Now Stephen, a man full of God's grace and power, did great wonders and miraculous signs among the people. [9]Opposition arose, however, from members of the Synagogue of the Freedmen (as it was called)—Jews of Cyrene and Alexandria as well as the provinces of Cilicia and Asia. These men began to argue with Stephen, [10]but they could not stand up against his wisdom or the Spirit by whom he spoke.

[11]Then they secretly persuaded some men to say, "We have heard Stephen speak words of blasphemy against Moses and against God."

[12]So they stirred up the people and the elders and the teachers of the law. They seized Stephen and brought him before the Sanhedrin. [13]They produced false witnesses, who testified, "This fellow never stops speaking against this holy place and against the law. [14]For we have heard him say that this Jesus of Nazareth will destroy this place and change the customs Moses handed down to us."

[15]All who were sitting in the Sanhedrin looked intently at Stephen, and they saw that his face was like the face of an angel.

Stephen's Speech to the Sanhedrin

7 Then the high priest asked him, "Are these charges true?"

[a]42 Or Messiah

²To this he replied: "Brothers and fathers, listen to me! The God of glory appeared to our father Abraham while he was still in Mesopotamia, before he lived in Haran. ³'Leave your country and your people,' God said, 'and go to the land I will show you.'ᵃ

⁴"So he left the land of the Chaldeans and settled in Haran. After the death of his father, God sent him to this land where you are now living. ⁵He gave him no inheritance here, not even a foot of ground. But God promised him that he and his descendants after him would possess the land, even though at that time Abraham had no child. ⁶God spoke to him in this way: 'Your descendants will be strangers in a country not their own, and they will be enslaved and mistreated four hundred years. ⁷But I will punish the nation they serve as slaves,' God said, 'and afterward they will come out of that country and worship me in this place.'ᵇ ⁸Then he gave Abraham the covenant of circumcision. And Abraham became the father of Isaac and circumcised him eight days after his birth. Later Isaac became the father of Jacob, and Jacob became the father of the twelve patriarchs.

⁹"Because the patriarchs were jealous of Joseph, they sold him as a slave into Egypt. But God was with him ¹⁰and rescued him from all his troubles. He gave Joseph wisdom and enabled him to gain the goodwill of Pharaoh king of Egypt; so he made him ruler over Egypt and all his palace.

¹¹"Then a famine struck all Egypt and Canaan, bringing great suffering, and our fathers could not find food. ¹²When Jacob heard that there was grain in Egypt, he sent our fathers on their first visit. ¹³On their second visit, Joseph told his brothers who he was, and Pharaoh learned about Joseph's family. ¹⁴After this, Joseph sent for his father Jacob and his whole family, seventy-five in all. ¹⁵Then Jacob went down to Egypt, where he and our fathers died. ¹⁶Their bodies were brought back to Shechem and placed in the tomb that Abraham had bought from the sons of Hamor at Shechem for a certain sum of money.

¹⁷"As the time drew near for God to fulfill his promise to Abraham, the number of our people in Egypt greatly increased. ¹⁸Then another king, who knew nothing about Joseph, became ruler of Egypt. ¹⁹He dealt treacherously with our people and oppressed our forefathers by forcing them to throw out their newborn babies so that they would die.

²⁰"At that time Moses was born, and he was no ordinary child.ᶜ For three months he was cared for in his father's house. ²¹When he was placed outside, Pharaoh's daughter took him and brought him up as her own son. ²²Moses was educated in all the wisdom of the Egyptians and was powerful in speech and action.

²³"When Moses was forty years old, he decided to visit his fellow Israelites. ²⁴He saw one of them being mistreated by an Egyptian, so he went to his defense and avenged him by killing the Egyptian. ²⁵Moses thought that his own people would realize that God was using him to rescue them, but they did not. ²⁶The next day Moses came upon two Israelites who were fighting. He tried to reconcile them by saying, 'Men, you are brothers; why do you want to hurt each other?'

²⁷"But the man who was mistreating the other pushed Moses aside and said, 'Who made you ruler and judge over us? ²⁸Do you want to kill me as you killed the Egyptian yesterday?'ᵈ ²⁹When Moses heard this, he fled to Midian, where he settled as a foreigner and had two sons.

³⁰"After forty years had passed, an angel appeared to Moses in the flames of a burning bush in the desert near Mount Sinai. ³¹When he saw this, he was amazed at the sight. As he went over to look more closely, he heard the Lord's voice: ³²'I am the God of your fathers, the God of Abraham, Isaac and Jacob.'ᵉ Moses trembled with fear and did not dare to look.

³³"Then the Lord said to him, 'Take off your sandals; the place where you are standing is holy ground. ³⁴I have indeed seen the oppression of my people in Egypt. I have heard their groaning and have come down to set them free. Now come, I will send you back to Egypt.'ᶠ

³⁵"This is the same Moses whom they

ᵃ3 Gen. 12:1   ᵇ7 Gen. 15:13,14   ᶜ20 Or was fair in the sight of God   ᵈ28 Exodus 2:14
ᵉ32 Exodus 3:6   ᶠ34 Exodus 3:5,7,8,10

had rejected with the words, 'Who made you ruler and judge?' He was sent to be their ruler and deliverer by God himself, through the angel who appeared to him in the bush. **36**He led them out of Egypt and did wonders and miraculous signs in Egypt, at the Red Sea*a* and for forty years in the desert.

37"This is that Moses who told the Israelites, 'God will send you a prophet like me from your own people.'*b* **38**He was in the assembly in the desert, with the angel who spoke to him on Mount Sinai, and with our fathers; and he received living words to pass on to us.

39"But our fathers refused to obey him. Instead, they rejected him and in their hearts turned back to Egypt. **40**They told Aaron, 'Make us gods who will go before us. As for this fellow Moses who led us out of Egypt—we don't know what has happened to him!'*c* **41**That was the time they made an idol in the form of a calf. They brought sacrifices to it and held a celebration in honor of what their hands had made. **42**But God turned away and gave them over to the worship of the heavenly bodies. This agrees with what is written in the book of the prophets:

" 'Did you bring me sacrifices and
　　offerings
　forty years in the desert, O house
　　of Israel?
43You have lifted up the shrine of
　　Molech
　and the star of your god Rephan,
　the idols you made to worship.
Therefore I will send you into exile'*d*
　beyond Babylon.

44"Our forefathers had the tabernacle of the Testimony with them in the desert. It had been made as God directed Moses, according to the pattern he had seen. **45**Having received the tabernacle, our fathers under Joshua brought it with them when they took the land from the nations God drove out before them. It remained in the land until the time of David, **46**who enjoyed God's favor and asked that he might provide a dwelling place for the God of Jacob.*e* **47**But it was Solomon who built the house for him.

48"However, the Most High does not live in houses made by men. As the prophet says:

49" 'Heaven is my throne,
　and the earth is my footstool.
What kind of house will you build
　　for me?
　　　　　　　　　says the Lord.
　Or where will my resting place be?
50Has not my hand made all these
　　things?'*f*

51"You stiff-necked people, with uncircumcised hearts and ears! You are just like your fathers: You always resist the Holy Spirit! **52**Was there ever a prophet your fathers did not persecute? They even killed those who predicted the coming of the Righteous One. And now you have betrayed and murdered him— **53**you who have received the law that was put into effect through angels but have not obeyed it."

The Stoning of Stephen

54When they heard this, they were furious and gnashed their teeth at him. **55**But Stephen, full of the Holy Spirit, looked up to heaven and saw the glory of God, and Jesus standing at the right hand of God. **56**"Look," he said, "I see heaven open and the Son of Man standing at the right hand of God."

57At this they covered their ears and, yelling at the top of their voices, they all rushed at him, **58**dragged him out of the city and began to stone him. Meanwhile, the witnesses laid their clothes at the feet of a young man named Saul.

59While they were stoning him, Stephen prayed, "Lord Jesus, receive my spirit." **60**Then he fell on his knees and cried out, "Lord, do not hold this sin against them." When he had said this, he fell asleep.

8 And Saul was there, giving approval to his death.

The Church Persecuted and Scattered

On that day a great persecution broke out against the church at Jerusalem, and all except the apostles were scattered throughout Judea and Samaria. **2**Godly men buried Stephen and mourned deeply for him. **3**But Saul began to destroy the church. Going from house to house,

---

a36 That is, Sea of Reeds　　*b37* Deut. 18:15　　*c40* Exodus 32:1　　*d43* Amos 5:25-27
e46 Some early manuscripts *the house of Jacob*　　*f50* Isaiah 66:1,2

he dragged off men and women and put them in prison.

Philip in Samaria

⁴Those who had been scattered preached the word wherever they went. ⁵Philip went down to a city in Samaria and proclaimed the Christ*a* there. ⁶When the crowds heard Philip and saw the miraculous signs he did, they all paid close attention to what he said. ⁷With shrieks, evil*b* spirits came out of many, and many paralytics and cripples were healed. ⁸So there was great joy in that city.

Simon the Sorcerer

⁹Now for some time a man named Simon had practiced sorcery in the city and amazed all the people of Samaria. He boasted that he was someone great, ¹⁰and all the people, both high and low, gave him their attention and exclaimed, "This man is the divine power known as the Great Power." ¹¹They followed him because he had amazed them for a long time with his magic. ¹²But when they believed Philip as he preached the good news of the kingdom of God and the name of Jesus Christ, they were baptized, both men and women. ¹³Simon himself believed and was baptized. And he followed Philip everywhere, astonished by the great signs and miracles he saw.

¹⁴When the apostles in Jerusalem heard that Samaria had accepted the word of God, they sent Peter and John to them. ¹⁵When they arrived, they prayed for them that they might receive the Holy Spirit, ¹⁶because the Holy Spirit had not yet come upon any of them; they had simply been baptized into*c* the name of the Lord Jesus. ¹⁷Then Peter and John placed their hands on them, and they received the Holy Spirit.

¹⁸When Simon saw that the Spirit was given at the laying on of the apostles' hands, he offered them money ¹⁹and said, "Give me also this ability so that everyone on whom I lay my hands may receive the Holy Spirit."

²⁰Peter answered: "May your money perish with you, because you thought you could buy the gift of God with money! ²¹You have no part or share in this ministry, because your heart is not right before God. ²²Repent of this wickedness and pray to the Lord. Perhaps he will forgive you for having such a thought in your heart. ²³For I see that you are full of bitterness and captive to sin."

²⁴Then Simon answered, "Pray to the Lord for me so that nothing you have said may happen to me."

²⁵When they had testified and proclaimed the word of the Lord, Peter and John returned to Jerusalem, preaching the gospel in many Samaritan villages.

Philip and the Ethiopian

²⁶Now an angel of the Lord said to Philip, "Go south to the road—the desert road—that goes down from Jerusalem to Gaza." ²⁷So he started out, and on his way he met an Ethiopian*d* eunuch, an important official in charge of all the treasury of Candace, queen of the Ethiopians. This man had gone to Jerusalem to worship, ²⁸and on his way home was sitting in his chariot reading the book of Isaiah the prophet. ²⁹The Spirit told Philip, "Go to that chariot and stay near it."

³⁰Then Philip ran up to the chariot and heard the man reading Isaiah the prophet. "Do you understand what you are reading?" Philip asked.

³¹"How can I," he said, "unless someone explains it to me?" So he invited Philip to come up and sit with him.

³²The eunuch was reading this passage of Scripture:

"He was led like a sheep to the
        slaughter,
    and as a lamb before the shearer
        is silent,
    so he did not open his mouth.
³³In his humiliation he was deprived
        of justice.
    Who can speak of his
        descendants?
    For his life was taken from the
        earth."*e*

³⁴The eunuch asked Philip, "Tell me, please, who is the prophet talking about, himself or someone else?" ³⁵Then Philip began with that very passage of Scripture and told him the good news about Jesus.

³⁶As they traveled along the road, they

---

*a*5 Or *Messiah*   *b*7 Greek *unclean*   *c*16 Or in   *d*27 That is, from the upper Nile region
*e*33 Isaiah 53:7,8

came to some water and the eunuch said, "Look, here is water. Why shouldn't I be baptized?"[a] ³⁸And he gave orders to stop the chariot. Then both Philip and the eunuch went down into the water and Philip baptized him. ³⁹When they came up out of the water, the Spirit of the Lord suddenly took Philip away, and the eunuch did not see him again, but went on his way rejoicing. ⁴⁰Philip, however, appeared at Azo-

tus and traveled about, preaching the gospel in all the towns until he reached Caesarea.

Saul's Conversion

9 Meanwhile, Saul was still breathing out murderous threats against the Lord's disciples. He went to the high priest ²and asked him for letters to the synagogues in Damascus, so that if he found any there who belonged to the

---

^a36 Some late manuscripts *baptized?" ³⁷Philip said, "If you believe with all your heart, you may." The eunuch answered, "I believe that Jesus Christ is the Son of God."*

FRIDAY

VERSE:	AUTHOR:	PASSAGE:
Acts 8:21	Jarena Lee	Acts 8:9–25

All Sins Swept Away

The man who was to speak in the afternoon of that day was the Reverend Richard Allen [1760–1831], since bishop of the African Methodist Episcopals in America. During the labors of this man that afternoon, I had come to the conclusion that this is the people to which my heart unites. And it so happened that, as soon as the service closed, he invited such as felt a desire to flee the wrath to come, to unite on trial with them—I embraced the opportunity.

Three weeks from that day, my soul was gloriously converted to God under preaching, at the very outset of the sermon. The text was barely pronounced, which was "You have no part or share in this ministry, because your heart is not right before God" (v. 21), when there appeared to *my* view, in the center of the heart, *one* sin, and this was *malice*—against one particular individual who had striven deeply to injure me, which I resented.

At this discovery I said, "*Lord*, I forgive *every* creature."

That instant it appeared to me as if a garment, which had entirely enveloped my whole person even to my fingers' ends, split at the crown of my head and was stripped away from me, passing like a shadow from my sight—the glory of God seemed to cover me in its stead. That moment, though hundreds were present, I did leap to my feet and declare that God, for Christ's sake, had pardoned the sins of my soul. Great was the ecstasy of my mind, for I felt that not only the sin of malice was pardoned, but all other sins were swept away together.

ADDITIONAL SCRIPTURE READINGS:
Isaiah 61:10; Luke 17:4; 2 Corinthians 5:17

Go to page 173 for your next devotional reading.

Way, whether men or women, he might take them as prisoners to Jerusalem. [3]As he neared Damascus on his journey, suddenly a light from heaven flashed around him. [4]He fell to the ground and heard a voice say to him, "Saul, Saul, why do you persecute me?"

[5]"Who are you, Lord?" Saul asked.

"I am Jesus, whom you are persecuting," he replied. [6]"Now get up and go into the city, and you will be told what you must do."

[7]The men traveling with Saul stood there speechless; they heard the sound but did not see anyone. [8]Saul got up from the ground, but when he opened his eyes he could see nothing. So they led him by the hand into Damascus. [9]For three days he was blind, and did not eat or drink anything.

[10]In Damascus there was a disciple named Ananias. The Lord called to him in a vision, "Ananias!"

"Yes, Lord," he answered.

[11]The Lord told him, "Go to the house of Judas on Straight Street and ask for a man from Tarsus named Saul, for he is praying. [12]In a vision he has seen a man named Ananias come and place his hands on him to restore his sight."

[13]"Lord," Ananias answered, "I have heard many reports about this man and all the harm he has done to your saints in Jerusalem. [14]And he has come here with authority from the chief priests to arrest all who call on your name."

[15]But the Lord said to Ananias, "Go! This man is my chosen instrument to carry my name before the Gentiles and their kings and before the people of Israel. [16]I will show him how much he must suffer for my name."

[17]Then Ananias went to the house and entered it. Placing his hands on Saul, he said, "Brother Saul, the Lord—Jesus, who appeared to you on the road as you were coming here—has sent me so that you may see again and be filled with the Holy Spirit." [18]Immediately, something like scales fell from Saul's eyes, and he could see again. He got up and was baptized, [19]and after taking some food, he regained his strength.

Saul in Damascus and Jerusalem

Saul spent several days with the disciples in Damascus. [20]At once he began to preach in the synagogues that Jesus is the Son of God. [21]All those who heard him were astonished and asked, "Isn't he the man who raised havoc in Jerusalem among those who call on this name? And hasn't he come here to take them as prisoners to the chief priests?" [22]Yet Saul grew more and more powerful and baffled the Jews living in Damascus by proving that Jesus is the Christ.[a]

[23]After many days had gone by, the Jews conspired to kill him, [24]but Saul learned of their plan. Day and night they kept close watch on the city gates in order to kill him. [25]But his followers took him by night and lowered him in a basket through an opening in the wall.

[26]When he came to Jerusalem, he tried to join the disciples, but they were all afraid of him, not believing that he really was a disciple. [27]But Barnabas took him and brought him to the apostles. He told them how Saul on his journey had seen the Lord and that the Lord had spoken to him, and how in Damascus he had preached fearlessly in the name of Jesus. [28]So Saul stayed with them and moved about freely in Jerusalem, speaking boldly in the name of the Lord. [29]He talked and debated with the Grecian Jews, but they tried to kill him. [30]When the brothers learned of this, they took him down to Caesarea and sent him off to Tarsus.

[31]Then the church throughout Judea, Galilee and Samaria enjoyed a time of peace. It was strengthened; and encouraged by the Holy Spirit, it grew in numbers, living in the fear of the Lord.

Aeneas and Dorcas

[32]As Peter traveled about the country, he went to visit the saints in Lydda. [33]There he found a man named Aeneas, a paralytic who had been bedridden for eight years. [34]"Aeneas," Peter said to him, "Jesus Christ heals you. Get up and take care of your mat." Immediately Aeneas got up. [35]All those who lived in Lydda and Sharon saw him and turned to the Lord.

[36]In Joppa there was a disciple named Tabitha (which, when translated, is Dorcas[b]), who was always doing good and helping the poor. [37]About that time she became sick and died, and her body was washed and placed in an upstairs room.

[a]22 Or Messiah   [b]36 Both Tabitha (Aramaic) and Dorcas (Greek) mean gazelle.

³⁸Lydda was near Joppa; so when the disciples heard that Peter was in Lydda, they sent two men to him and urged him, "Please come at once!"

³⁹Peter went with them, and when he arrived he was taken upstairs to the room. All the widows stood around him, crying and showing him the robes and other clothing that Dorcas had made while she was still with them.

⁴⁰Peter sent them all out of the room; then he got down on his knees and prayed. Turning toward the dead woman, he said, "Tabitha, get up." She opened her eyes, and seeing Peter she sat up. ⁴¹He took her by the hand and helped her to her feet. Then he called the believers and the widows and presented her to them alive. ⁴²This became known all over Joppa, and many people believed in the Lord. ⁴³Peter stayed in Joppa for some time with a tanner named Simon.

Cornelius Calls for Peter

10 At Caesarea there was a man named Cornelius, a centurion in what was known as the Italian Regiment. ²He and all his family were devout and God-fearing; he gave generously to those in need and prayed to God regularly. ³One day at about three in the afternoon he had a vision. He distinctly saw an angel of God, who came to him and said, "Cornelius!"

⁴Cornelius stared at him in fear. "What is it, Lord?" he asked.

The angel answered, "Your prayers and gifts to the poor have come up as a memorial offering before God. ⁵Now send men to Joppa to bring back a man named Simon who is called Peter. ⁶He is staying with Simon the tanner, whose house is by the sea."

⁷When the angel who spoke to him had gone, Cornelius called two of his servants and a devout soldier who was one of his attendants. ⁸He told them everything that had happened and sent them to Joppa.

Peter's Vision

⁹About noon the following day as they were on their journey and approaching the city, Peter went up on the roof to pray. ¹⁰He became hungry and wanted something to eat, and while the meal was being prepared, he fell into a trance. ¹¹He saw heaven opened and something like a large sheet being let down to earth by its four corners. ¹²It contained all kinds of four-footed animals, as well as reptiles of the earth and birds of the air. ¹³Then a voice told him, "Get up, Peter. Kill and eat."

¹⁴"Surely not, Lord!" Peter replied. "I have never eaten anything impure or unclean."

¹⁵The voice spoke to him a second time, "Do not call anything impure that God has made clean."

¹⁶This happened three times, and immediately the sheet was taken back to heaven.

¹⁷While Peter was wondering about the meaning of the vision, the men sent by Cornelius found out where Simon's house was and stopped at the gate. ¹⁸They called out, asking if Simon who was known as Peter was staying there.

¹⁹While Peter was still thinking about the vision, the Spirit said to him, "Simon, three*ᵃ* men are looking for you. ²⁰So get up and go downstairs. Do not hesitate to go with them, for I have sent them."

²¹Peter went down and said to the men, "I'm the one you're looking for. Why have you come?"

²²The men replied, "We have come from Cornelius the centurion. He is a righteous and God-fearing man, who is respected by all the Jewish people. A holy angel told him to have you come to his house so that he could hear what you have to say." ²³Then Peter invited the men into the house to be his guests.

Peter at Cornelius' House

The next day Peter started out with them, and some of the brothers from Joppa went along. ²⁴The following day he arrived in Caesarea. Cornelius was expecting them and had called together his relatives and close friends. ²⁵As Peter entered the house, Cornelius met him and fell at his feet in reverence. ²⁶But Peter made him get up. "Stand up," he said, "I am only a man myself."

²⁷Talking with him, Peter went inside and found a large gathering of people. ²⁸He said to them: "You are well aware that it is against our law for a Jew to associate with a Gentile or visit him. But

---

ᵃ 19 One early manuscript *two*; other manuscripts do not have the number.

WEEKENDING

RECONCILE

I am always troubled whenever I see injustice against any race of people. Growing up in the South, I saw so much of this that I feel deeply that no human being should ever be treated unjustly. I am concerned about any discrimination, of any people, regardless of race or other physical differences. We are all God's children and deserving of his rewards.

Rosa Parks

REFLECT

Saturday: Acts 10:34–43
Sunday: Colossians 3:1–17

*Go to page 175 for your
next devotional reading.*

God has shown me that I should not call any man impure or unclean. ²⁹So when I was sent for, I came without raising any objection. May I ask why you sent for me?"

³⁰Cornelius answered: "Four days ago I was in my house praying at this hour, at three in the afternoon. Suddenly a man in shining clothes stood before me ³¹and said, 'Cornelius, God has heard your prayer and remembered your gifts to the poor. ³²Send to Joppa for Simon who is called Peter. He is a guest in the home of Simon the tanner, who lives by the sea.' ³³So I sent for you immediately, and it was good of you to come. Now we are all here in the presence of God to listen to everything the Lord has commanded you to tell us."

³⁴Then Peter began to speak: "I now realize how true it is that God does not show favoritism ³⁵but accepts men from every nation who fear him and do what is right. ³⁶You know the message God sent to the people of Israel, telling the good news of peace through Jesus Christ, who is Lord of all. ³⁷You know what has happened throughout Judea, beginning in Galilee after the baptism that John preached— ³⁸how God anointed Jesus of Nazareth with the Holy Spirit and power, and how he went around doing good and healing all who were under the power of the devil, because God was with him.

³⁹"We are witnesses of everything he did in the country of the Jews and in Jerusalem. They killed him by hanging him on a tree, ⁴⁰but God raised him from the dead on the third day and caused him to be seen. ⁴¹He was not seen by all the people, but by witnesses whom God had already chosen—by us who ate and drank with him after he rose from the dead. ⁴²He commanded us to preach to the people and to testify that he is the one whom God appointed as judge of the living and the dead. ⁴³All the prophets testify about him that everyone who believes in him receives forgiveness of sins through his name."

⁴⁴While Peter was still speaking these words, the Holy Spirit came on all who heard the message. ⁴⁵The circumcised believers who had come with Peter were astonished that the gift of the Holy Spirit had been poured out even on the Gen-

tiles. ⁴⁶For they heard them speaking in tongues^a and praising God.

Then Peter said, ⁴⁷"Can anyone keep these people from being baptized with water? They have received the Holy Spirit just as we have." ⁴⁸So he ordered that they be baptized in the name of Jesus Christ. Then they asked Peter to stay with them for a few days.

Peter Explains His Actions

11 The apostles and the brothers throughout Judea heard that the Gentiles also had received the word of God. ²So when Peter went up to Jerusalem, the circumcised believers criticized him ³and said, "You went into the house of uncircumcised men and ate with them."

⁴Peter began and explained everything to them precisely as it had happened: ⁵"I was in the city of Joppa praying, and in a trance I saw a vision. I saw something like a large sheet being let down from heaven by its four corners, and it came down to where I was. ⁶I looked into it and saw four-footed animals of the earth, wild beasts, reptiles, and birds of the air. ⁷Then I heard a voice telling me, 'Get up, Peter. Kill and eat.'

⁸"I replied, 'Surely not, Lord! Nothing impure or unclean has ever entered my mouth.'

⁹"The voice spoke from heaven a second time, 'Do not call anything impure that God has made clean.' ¹⁰This happened three times, and then it was all pulled up to heaven again.

¹¹"Right then three men who had been sent to me from Caesarea stopped at the house where I was staying. ¹²The Spirit told me to have no hesitation about going with them. These six brothers also went with me, and we entered the man's house. ¹³He told us how he had seen an angel appear in his house and say, 'Send to Joppa for Simon who is called Peter. ¹⁴He will bring you a message through which you and all your household will be saved.'

¹⁵"As I began to speak, the Holy Spirit came on them as he had come on us at the beginning. ¹⁶Then I remembered what the Lord had said: 'John baptized with^b water, but you will be baptized with the Holy Spirit.' ¹⁷So if God gave them the same gift as he gave us, who

^a46 Or other languages   ^b16 Or in

believed in the Lord Jesus Christ, who was I to think that I could oppose God?"

[18]When they heard this, they had no further objections and praised God, saying, "So then, God has granted even the Gentiles repentance unto life."

The Church in Antioch

[19]Now those who had been scattered by the persecution in connection with Stephen traveled as far as Phoenicia, Cyprus and Antioch, telling the message only to Jews. [20]Some of them, however,

---

MONDAY

VERSE: Acts 10:34   **AUTHOR:** Jill Briscoe   **PASSAGE:** Acts 10:34–43

Christ Crosses Boundaries

I have found out you can't choose your friends, relatives or even your enemies if you follow Jesus. That's because he chooses them for you! And when that happens, as Peter discovered, there can be no room in your life for the pigs of prejudice!

Those of us who take pride in the fact that we are not prejudiced usually find out that we are! I used to think I was only prejudiced against people who were prejudiced. At the same time, true to my [British] upbringing, I believed that middle-class English people just didn't mix with "lower-class" English people; "It just isn't done," as we British folk would say.

Then I found the Lord—and discovered he kept strange company. Soon I was seeing my prejudices in a whole new light. Call it vision if you will—a vision of him that gave me a vision of them and a vision of me!

It is Christ, of course, who can make the difference! Referring to the literal barrier that the Jews erected in the temple courtyard to separate Jew from Gentile, Paul remarks, "For he himself is our peace, who has made the two one and has destroyed the barrier, the dividing wall of hostility" (Ephesians 2:14). It is only by understanding the universal plan of God and by asking humbly to be a part of bringing that plan into effect that the Christian can begin to understand his prejudices and work to overcome them.

If we look around for an example of someone who could have had reason to be prejudiced but wasn't, we would have to look at Jesus himself . . . He did not prejudge the woman at the well, as his disciples most certainly did. He ate with tax collectors and sinners such as Matthew (Matthew 9:9–13) and Zacchaeus (Luke 19:1–9), capturing their hearts and changing their behavior forever.

Jesus' example was radical. Over and over he tried to tell people to differentiate between tradition and truth—and called them to follow the truth, which abolishes prejudice.

ADDITIONAL SCRIPTURE READINGS:
Matthew 9:9–13; Luke 10:30–35; Ephesians 2

Go to page 176 for your next devotional reading.

men from Cyprus and Cyrene, went to Antioch and began to speak to Greeks also, telling them the good news about the Lord Jesus. ²¹The Lord's hand was with them, and a great number of people believed and turned to the Lord.

²²News of this reached the ears of the church at Jerusalem, and they sent Barnabas to Antioch. ²³When he arrived and saw the evidence of the grace of God, he was glad and encouraged them all to remain true to the Lord with all their hearts. ²⁴He was a good man, full of the Holy Spirit and faith, and a great number of people were brought to the Lord.

²⁵Then Barnabas went to Tarsus to look for Saul, ²⁶and when he found him, he brought him to Antioch. So for a whole year Barnabas and Saul met with the church and taught great numbers of people. The disciples were called Christians first at Antioch.

²⁷During this time some prophets came down from Jerusalem to Antioch. ²⁸One of them, named Agabus, stood up

---

TUESDAY

VERSE:	AUTHOR:	PASSAGE:
Acts 11:24	Jean E. Syswerda	Acts 11:19-30

A Good Man

My husband is one of the friendliest people I know. Whenever we have to wait in a restaurant line or attend a strange church, he immediately begins to get to know the people around him.

It embarrasses our kids at times. They produce the ritual groans, and they roll their eyes at each other whenever they hear him begin to engage a total stranger in conversation.

Before long the stranger is no longer a stranger but is found to have some relative in common or to have worked somewhere someone else we know worked or has read some book we've read. A bond, however tenuous, has been formed between two human beings.

When I think of my friendly husband I often also think of what one of Billy Graham's critics said of him after actually meeting him—that never had he seen friendliness have such a strong cutting edge. Not only by his evangelistic preaching, but by being friendly, Billy Graham has touched countless lives. By being friendly I'm sure my husband has also touched other people's lives in ways we will probably never know.

I really think friendliness is something of a spiritual gift. Acts 11:24 says Barnabas was "a good man," but I think if you could talk to some of the people of Antioch they'd tell you he was one of the friendliest guys they'd ever met.

Thank you, God, for all the friendly people in the world and for what they give to me when I'm the stranger.

ADDITIONAL SCRIPTURE READINGS:
Psalm 55:13-14; Proverbs 22:11; 2 Corinthians 2:14-15

Go to page 183 for your next devotional reading.

and through the Spirit predicted that a severe famine would spread over the entire Roman world. (This happened during the reign of Claudius.) ²⁹The disciples, each according to his ability, decided to provide help for the brothers living in Judea. ³⁰This they did, sending their gift to the elders by Barnabas and Saul.

Peter's Miraculous Escape From Prison

12 It was about this time that King Herod arrested some who belonged to the church, intending to persecute them. ²He had James, the brother of John, put to death with the sword. ³When he saw that this pleased the Jews, he proceeded to seize Peter also. This happened during the Feast of Unleavened Bread. ⁴After arresting him, he put him in prison, handing him over to be guarded by four squads of four soldiers each. Herod intended to bring him out for public trial after the Passover.

⁵So Peter was kept in prison, but the church was earnestly praying to God for him.

⁶The night before Herod was to bring him to trial, Peter was sleeping between two soldiers, bound with two chains, and sentries stood guard at the entrance. ⁷Suddenly an angel of the Lord appeared and a light shone in the cell. He struck Peter on the side and woke him up. "Quick, get up!" he said, and the chains fell off Peter's wrists.

⁸Then the angel said to him, "Put on your clothes and sandals." And Peter did so. "Wrap your cloak around you and follow me," the angel told him. ⁹Peter followed him out of the prison, but he had no idea that what the angel was doing was really happening; he thought he was seeing a vision. ¹⁰They passed the first and second guards and came to the iron gate leading to the city. It opened for them by itself, and they went through it. When they had walked the length of one street, suddenly the angel left him.

¹¹Then Peter came to himself and said, "Now I know without a doubt that the Lord sent his angel and rescued me from Herod's clutches and from everything the Jewish people were anticipating."

¹²When this had dawned on him, he went to the house of Mary the mother of John, also called Mark, where many people had gathered and were praying. ¹³Peter knocked at the outer entrance, and a servant girl named Rhoda came to answer the door. ¹⁴When she recognized Peter's voice, she was so overjoyed she ran back without opening it and exclaimed, "Peter is at the door!"

¹⁵"You're out of your mind," they told her. When she kept insisting that it was so, they said, "It must be his angel."

¹⁶But Peter kept on knocking, and when they opened the door and saw him, they were astonished. ¹⁷Peter motioned with his hand for them to be quiet and described how the Lord had brought him out of prison. "Tell James and the brothers about this," he said, and then he left for another place.

¹⁸In the morning, there was no small commotion among the soldiers as to what had become of Peter. ¹⁹After Herod had a thorough search made for him and did not find him, he cross-examined the guards and ordered that they be executed.

Herod's Death

Then Herod went from Judea to Caesarea and stayed there a while. ²⁰He had been quarreling with the people of Tyre and Sidon; they now joined together and sought an audience with him. Having secured the support of Blastus, a trusted personal servant of the king, they asked for peace, because they depended on the king's country for their food supply.

²¹On the appointed day Herod, wearing his royal robes, sat on his throne and delivered a public address to the people. ²²They shouted, "This is the voice of a god, not of a man." ²³Immediately, because Herod did not give praise to God, an angel of the Lord struck him down, and he was eaten by worms and died.

²⁴But the word of God continued to increase and spread.

²⁵When Barnabas and Saul had finished their mission, they returned from ᵃ Jerusalem, taking with them John, also called Mark.

Barnabas and Saul Sent Off

13 In the church at Antioch there were prophets and teachers:

ᵃ 25 Some manuscripts *to*

Barnabas, Simeon called Niger, Lucius of Cyrene, Manaen (who had been brought up with Herod the tetrarch) and Saul. **2**While they were worshiping the Lord and fasting, the Holy Spirit said, "Set apart for me Barnabas and Saul for the work to which I have called them." **3**So after they had fasted and prayed, they placed their hands on them and sent them off.

On Cyprus

4The two of them, sent on their way by the Holy Spirit, went down to Seleucia and sailed from there to Cyprus. **5**When they arrived at Salamis, they proclaimed the word of God in the Jewish synagogues. John was with them as their helper.

6They traveled through the whole island until they came to Paphos. There they met a Jewish sorcerer and false prophet named Bar-Jesus, **7**who was an attendant of the proconsul, Sergius Paulus. The proconsul, an intelligent man, sent for Barnabas and Saul because he wanted to hear the word of God. **8**But Elymas the sorcerer (for that is what his name means) opposed them and tried to turn the proconsul from the faith. **9**Then Saul, who was also called Paul, filled with the Holy Spirit, looked straight at Elymas and said, **10**"You are a child of the devil and an enemy of everything that is right! You are full of all kinds of deceit and trickery. Will you never stop perverting the right ways of the Lord? **11**Now the hand of the Lord is against you. You are going to be blind, and for a time you will be unable to see the light of the sun."

Immediately mist and darkness came over him, and he groped about, seeking someone to lead him by the hand. **12**When the proconsul saw what had happened, he believed, for he was amazed at the teaching about the Lord.

In Pisidian Antioch

13From Paphos, Paul and his companions sailed to Perga in Pamphylia, where John left them to return to Jerusalem. **14**From Perga they went on to Pisidian Antioch. On the Sabbath they entered the synagogue and sat down. **15**After the reading from the Law and the Prophets, the synagogue rulers sent word to them,

saying, "Brothers, if you have a message of encouragement for the people, please speak."

16Standing up, Paul motioned with his hand and said: "Men of Israel and you Gentiles who worship God, listen to me! **17**The God of the people of Israel chose our fathers; he made the people prosper during their stay in Egypt, with mighty power he led them out of that country, **18**he endured their conduct*a* for about forty years in the desert, **19**he overthrew seven nations in Canaan and gave their land to his people as their inheritance. **20**All this took about 450 years.

"After this, God gave them judges until the time of Samuel the prophet. **21**Then the people asked for a king, and he gave them Saul son of Kish, of the tribe of Benjamin, who ruled forty years. **22**After removing Saul, he made David their king. He testified concerning him: 'I have found David son of Jesse a man after my own heart; he will do everything I want him to do.'

23"From this man's descendants God has brought to Israel the Savior Jesus, as he promised. **24**Before the coming of Jesus, John preached repentance and baptism to all the people of Israel. **25**As John was completing his work, he said: 'Who do you think I am? I am not that one. No, but he is coming after me, whose sandals I am not worthy to untie.'

26"Brothers, children of Abraham, and you God-fearing Gentiles, it is to us that this message of salvation has been sent. **27**The people of Jerusalem and their rulers did not recognize Jesus, yet in condemning him they fulfilled the words of the prophets that are read every Sabbath. **28**Though they found no proper ground for a death sentence, they asked Pilate to have him executed. **29**When they had carried out all that was written about him, they took him down from the tree and laid him in a tomb. **30**But God raised him from the dead, **31**and for many days he was seen by those who had traveled with him from Galilee to Jerusalem. They are now his witnesses to our people.

32"We tell you the good news: What God promised our fathers **33**he has fulfilled for us, their children, by raising

a18 Some manuscripts *and cared for them*

up Jesus. As it is written in the second Psalm:

" 'You are my Son;
    today I have become your
        Father.[a' b]

34The fact that God raised him from the dead, never to decay, is stated in these words:

" 'I will give you the holy and sure
        blessings promised to
        David.'[c]

35So it is stated elsewhere:

" 'You will not let your Holy One
        see decay.'[d]

36"For when David had served God's purpose in his own generation, he fell asleep; he was buried with his fathers and his body decayed. **37**But the one whom God raised from the dead did not see decay.

38"Therefore, my brothers, I want you to know that through Jesus the forgiveness of sins is proclaimed to you. **39**Through him everyone who believes is justified from everything you could not be justified from by the law of Moses. **40**Take care that what the prophets have said does not happen to you:

41" 'Look, you scoffers,
    wonder and perish,
for I am going to do something in
        your days
    that you would never believe,
        even if someone told you.'[e"]

42As Paul and Barnabas were leaving the synagogue, the people invited them to speak further about these things on the next Sabbath. **43**When the congregation was dismissed, many of the Jews and devout converts to Judaism followed Paul and Barnabas, who talked with them and urged them to continue in the grace of God.

44On the next Sabbath almost the whole city gathered to hear the word of the Lord. **45**When the Jews saw the crowds, they were filled with jealousy and talked abusively against what Paul was saying.

46Then Paul and Barnabas answered them boldly: "We had to speak the word of God to you first. Since you reject it and do not consider yourselves worthy of eternal life, we now turn to the Gentiles. **47**For this is what the Lord has commanded us:

" 'I have made you[f] a light for the
        Gentiles,
    that you[f] may bring salvation to
        the ends of the earth.'[g"]

48When the Gentiles heard this, they were glad and honored the word of the Lord; and all who were appointed for eternal life believed.

49The word of the Lord spread through the whole region. **50**But the Jews incited the God-fearing women of high standing and the leading men of the city. They stirred up persecution against Paul and Barnabas, and expelled them from their region. **51**So they shook the dust from their feet in protest against them and went to Iconium. **52**And the disciples were filled with joy and with the Holy Spirit.

In Iconium

14 At Iconium Paul and Barnabas went as usual into the Jewish synagogue. There they spoke so effectively that a great number of Jews and Gentiles believed. **2**But the Jews who refused to believe stirred up the Gentiles and poisoned their minds against the brothers. **3**So Paul and Barnabas spent considerable time there, speaking boldly for the Lord, who confirmed the message of his grace by enabling them to do miraculous signs and wonders. **4**The people of the city were divided; some sided with the Jews, others with the apostles. **5**There was a plot afoot among the Gentiles and Jews, together with their leaders, to mistreat them and stone them. **6**But they found out about it and fled to the Lycaonian cities of Lystra and Derbe and to the surrounding country, **7**where they continued to preach the good news.

In Lystra and Derbe

8In Lystra there sat a man crippled in his feet, who was lame from birth and had never walked. **9**He listened to Paul as he was speaking. Paul looked directly at him, saw that he had faith to be healed **10**and called out, "Stand up on

---

a 33 Or *have begotten you*   *b* 33 Psalm 2:7   *c* 34 Isaiah 55:3   *d* 35 Psalm 16:10   *e* 41 Hab. 1:5   *f* 47 The Greek is singular.   *g* 47 Isaiah 49:6

your feet!" At that, the man jumped up and began to walk.

11When the crowd saw what Paul had done, they shouted in the Lycaonian language, "The gods have come down to us in human form!" 12Barnabas they called Zeus, and Paul they called Hermes because he was the chief speaker. 13The priest of Zeus, whose temple was just outside the city, brought bulls and wreaths to the city gates because he and the crowd wanted to offer sacrifices to them.

14But when the apostles Barnabas and Paul heard of this, they tore their clothes and rushed out into the crowd, shouting: 15"Men, why are you doing this? We too are only men, human like you. We are bringing you good news, telling you to turn from these worthless things to the living God, who made heaven and earth and sea and everything in them. 16In the past, he let all nations go their own way. 17Yet he has not left himself without testimony: He has shown kindness by giving you rain from heaven and crops in their seasons; he provides you with plenty of food and fills your hearts with joy." 18Even with these words, they had difficulty keeping the crowd from sacrificing to them.

19Then some Jews came from Antioch and Iconium and won the crowd over. They stoned Paul and dragged him outside the city, thinking he was dead. 20But after the disciples had gathered around him, he got up and went back into the city. The next day he and Barnabas left for Derbe.

The Return to Antioch in Syria

21They preached the good news in that city and won a large number of disciples. Then they returned to Lystra, Iconium and Antioch, 22strengthening the disciples and encouraging them to remain true to the faith. "We must go through many hardships to enter the kingdom of God," they said. 23Paul and Barnabas appointed elders*a* for them in each church and, with prayer and fasting, committed them to the Lord, in whom they had put their trust. 24After going through Pisidia, they came into Pamphylia, 25and when they had preached the word in Perga, they went down to Attalia.

26From Attalia they sailed back to Antioch, where they had been committed to the grace of God for the work they had now completed. 27On arriving there, they gathered the church together and reported all that God had done through them and how he had opened the door of faith to the Gentiles. 28And they stayed there a long time with the disciples.

The Council at Jerusalem

15 Some men came down from Judea to Antioch and were teaching the brothers: "Unless you are circumcised, according to the custom taught by Moses, you cannot be saved." 2This brought Paul and Barnabas into sharp dispute and debate with them. So Paul and Barnabas were appointed, along with some other believers, to go up to Jerusalem to see the apostles and elders about this question. 3The church sent them on their way, and as they traveled through Phoenicia and Samaria, they told how the Gentiles had been converted. This news made all the brothers very glad. 4When they came to Jerusalem, they were welcomed by the church and the apostles and elders, to whom they reported everything God had done through them.

5Then some of the believers who belonged to the party of the Pharisees stood up and said, "The Gentiles must be circumcised and required to obey the law of Moses."

6The apostles and elders met to consider this question. 7After much discussion, Peter got up and addressed them: "Brothers, you know that some time ago God made a choice among you that the Gentiles might hear from my lips the message of the gospel and believe. 8God, who knows the heart, showed that he accepted them by giving the Holy Spirit to them, just as he did to us. 9He made no distinction between us and them, for he purified their hearts by faith. 10Now then, why do you try to test God by putting on the necks of the disciples a yoke that neither we nor our fathers have been able to bear? 11No! We believe it is through the grace of our Lord Jesus that we are saved, just as they are."

12The whole assembly became silent

---

a 23 Or *Barnabas ordained elders; or Barnabas had elders elected*

as they listened to Barnabas and Paul telling about the miraculous signs and wonders God had done among the Gentiles through them. [13]When they finished, James spoke up: "Brothers, listen to me. [14]Simon[a] has described to us how God at first showed his concern by taking from the Gentiles a people for himself. [15]The words of the prophets are in agreement with this, as it is written:

[16]" 'After this I will return
    and rebuild David's fallen tent.
  Its ruins I will rebuild,
    and I will restore it,
[17]that the remnant of men may seek
    the Lord,
  and all the Gentiles who bear my
    name,
  says the Lord, who does these
    things'[b]
[18] that have been known for ages.[c]

[19]"It is my judgment, therefore, that we should not make it difficult for the Gentiles who are turning to God. [20]Instead we should write to them, telling them to abstain from food polluted by idols, from sexual immorality, from the meat of strangled animals and from blood. [21]For Moses has been preached in every city from the earliest times and is read in the synagogues on every Sabbath."

The Council's Letter to Gentile Believers

[22]Then the apostles and elders, with the whole church, decided to choose some of their own men and send them to Antioch with Paul and Barnabas. They chose Judas (called Barsabbas) and Silas, two men who were leaders among the brothers. [23]With them they sent the following letter:

The apostles and elders, your brothers,

To the Gentile believers in Antioch, Syria and Cilicia:

Greetings.

[24]We have heard that some went out from us without our authorization and disturbed you, troubling your minds by what they said. [25]So we all agreed to choose some men and send them to you with our dear friends Barnabas and Paul— [26]men who have risked their lives for the name of our Lord Jesus Christ. [27]Therefore we are sending Judas and Silas to confirm by word of mouth what we are writing. [28]It seemed good to the Holy Spirit and to us not to burden you with anything beyond the following requirements: [29]You are to abstain from food sacrificed to idols, from blood, from the meat of strangled animals and from sexual immorality. You will do well to avoid these things.

Farewell.

[30]The men were sent off and went down to Antioch, where they gathered the church together and delivered the letter. [31]The people read it and were glad for its encouraging message. [32]Judas and Silas, who themselves were prophets, said much to encourage and strengthen the brothers. [33]After spending some time there, they were sent off by the brothers with the blessing of peace to return to those who had sent them.[d] [35]But Paul and Barnabas remained in Antioch, where they and many others taught and preached the word of the Lord.

Disagreement Between Paul and Barnabas

[36]Some time later Paul said to Barnabas, "Let us go back and visit the brothers in all the towns where we preached the word of the Lord and see how they are doing." [37]Barnabas wanted to take John, also called Mark, with them, [38]but Paul did not think it wise to take him, because he had deserted them in Pamphylia and had not continued with them in the work. [39]They had such a sharp disagreement that they parted company. Barnabas took Mark and sailed for Cyprus, [40]but Paul chose Silas and left, commended by the brothers to the grace of the Lord. [41]He went through Syria and Cilicia, strengthening the churches.

---

[a]14 Greek *Simeon*, a variant of *Simon*; that is, Peter   [b]17 Amos 9:11,12   [c]17,18 Some
manuscripts *things'*— / [18]*known to the Lord for ages is his work*   [d]33 Some manuscripts *them*, [34]*but Silas*
decided to remain there

Timothy Joins Paul and Silas

16 He came to Derbe and then to Lystra, where a disciple named Timothy lived, whose mother was a Jewess and a believer, but whose father was a Greek. **2**The brothers at Lystra and Iconium spoke well of him. **3**Paul wanted to take him along on the journey, so he circumcised him because of the Jews who lived in that area, for they all knew that his father was a Greek. **4**As they traveled from town to town, they delivered the decisions reached by the apostles and elders in Jerusalem for the people to obey. **5**So the churches were strengthened in the faith and grew daily in numbers.

Paul's Vision of the Man of Macedonia

6Paul and his companions traveled throughout the region of Phrygia and Galatia, having been kept by the Holy Spirit from preaching the word in the province of Asia. **7**When they came to the border of Mysia, they tried to enter Bithynia, but the Spirit of Jesus would not allow them to. **8**So they passed by Mysia and went down to Troas. **9**During the night Paul had a vision of a man of Macedonia standing and begging him, "Come over to Macedonia and help us." **10**After Paul had seen the vision, we got ready at once to leave for Macedonia, concluding that God had called us to preach the gospel to them.

Lydia's Conversion in Philippi

11From Troas we put out to sea and sailed straight for Samothrace, and the next day on to Neapolis. **12**From there we traveled to Philippi, a Roman colony and the leading city of that district of Macedonia. And we stayed there several days.

13On the Sabbath we went outside the city gate to the river, where we expected to find a place of prayer. We sat down and began to speak to the women who had gathered there. **14**One of those listening was a woman named Lydia, a dealer in purple cloth from the city of Thyatira, who was a worshiper of God. The Lord opened her heart to respond to Paul's message. **15**When she and the members of her household were baptized, she invited us to her home. "If you consider me a believer in the Lord," she said, "come and stay at my house." And she persuaded us.

Paul and Silas in Prison

16Once when we were going to the place of prayer, we were met by a slave girl who had a spirit by which she predicted the future. She earned a great deal of money for her owners by fortune-telling. **17**This girl followed Paul and the rest of us, shouting, "These men are servants of the Most High God, who are telling you the way to be saved." **18**She kept this up for many days. Finally Paul became so troubled that he turned around and said to the spirit, "In the name of Jesus Christ I command you to come out of her!" At that moment the spirit left her.

19When the owners of the slave girl realized that their hope of making money was gone, they seized Paul and Silas and dragged them into the marketplace to face the authorities. **20**They brought them before the magistrates and said, "These men are Jews, and are throwing our city into an uproar **21**by advocating customs unlawful for us Romans to accept or practice."

22The crowd joined in the attack against Paul and Silas, and the magistrates ordered them to be stripped and beaten. **23**After they had been severely flogged, they were thrown into prison, and the jailer was commanded to guard them carefully. **24**Upon receiving such orders, he put them in the inner cell and fastened their feet in the stocks.

25About midnight Paul and Silas were praying and singing hymns to God, and the other prisoners were listening to them. **26**Suddenly there was such a violent earthquake that the foundations of the prison were shaken. At once all the prison doors flew open, and everybody's chains came loose. **27**The jailer woke up, and when he saw the prison doors open, he drew his sword and was about to kill himself because he thought the prisoners had escaped. **28**But Paul shouted, "Don't harm yourself! We are all here!"

29The jailer called for lights, rushed in and fell trembling before Paul and Silas. **30**He then brought them out and asked, "Sirs, what must I do to be saved?"

³¹They replied, "Believe in the Lord Jesus, and you will be saved—you and your household." ³²Then they spoke the word of the Lord to him and to all the others in his house. ³³At that hour the the night the jailer took them and washed their wounds; then immediately he and all his family were baptized. ³⁴The jailer brought them into his house and set a meal before them; he was filled with joy because he had come to believe in God—he and his whole family.

³⁵When it was daylight, the magistrates sent their officers to the jailer with the order: "Release those men." ³⁶The jailer told Paul, "The magistrates have ordered that you and Silas be released. Now you can leave. Go in peace."

³⁷But Paul said to the officers: "They beat us publicly without a trial, even though we are Roman citizens, and threw us into prison. And now do they want to get rid of us quietly? No! Let them come themselves and escort us out."

³⁸The officers reported this to the magistrates, and when they heard that Paul and Silas were Roman citizens, they were alarmed. ³⁹They came to appease them and escorted them from the prison, requesting them to leave the city. ⁴⁰After Paul and Silas came out of the prison, they went to Lydia's house, where they met with the brothers and encouraged them. Then they left.

In Thessalonica

17 When they had passed through Amphipolis and Apollonia, they came to Thessalonica, where there was a Jewish synagogue. ²As his custom was, Paul went into the synagogue, and on three Sabbath days he reasoned with them from the Scriptures, ³explaining and proving that the Christᵃ had to suffer and rise from the dead. "This Jesus I am proclaiming to you is the Christ,ᵃ " he said. ⁴Some of the Jews were persuaded and joined Paul and Silas, as did

ᵃ3 Or *Messiah*

WEDNESDAY

VERSE:
Acts 16:34

AUTHOR:
Anne Ortlund

PASSAGE:
Acts 16:16-40

Performance

"What must I do," asked the Philippian jailer, "to be saved?" (v. 30).

And Paul answered, "Believe. Just believe, and you'll be saved—that's all it takes. Don't 'do'; you'll just get in the way. Let God do the 'doing'!"

When we're itchy to "do," it's usually because we really *don't believe*, so we're trying to help God out. In Jesus' hometown, "he did not do many miracles there because of their lack of faith" (Matthew 13:58). They didn't take seriously his supernatural power so available for them, so he didn't use it! And when we don't understand his resurrection power within us, we develop an activist religion that crowds out the possibility of that giant, explosive power's working in our lives.

ADDITIONAL SCRIPTURE READINGS:
Psalm 147; Isaiah 55:1; Ephesians 2:8

Go to page 184 for your next devotional reading.

a large number of God-fearing Greeks and not a few prominent women.

⁵But the Jews were jealous; so they rounded up some bad characters from the marketplace, formed a mob and started a riot in the city. They rushed to Jason's house in search of Paul and Silas in order to bring them out to the crowd.ᵃ ⁶But when they did not find them, they dragged Jason and some other brothers before the city officials, shouting: "These men who have caused trouble all over the world have now come here, ⁷and Jason has welcomed them into his house. They are all defying Caesar's decrees, saying that there is another king, one called Jesus." ⁸When they heard this, the crowd and the city officials were thrown into turmoil. ⁹Then they made Jason and the others post bond and let them go.

a5 Or the assembly of the people

In Berea

¹⁰As soon as it was night, the brothers sent Paul and Silas away to Berea. On arriving there, they went to the Jewish synagogue. ¹¹Now the Bereans were of more noble character than the Thessalonians, for they received the message with great eagerness and examined the Scriptures every day to see if what Paul said was true. ¹²Many of the Jews believed, as did also a number of prominent Greek women and many Greek men.

¹³When the Jews in Thessalonica learned that Paul was preaching the word of God at Berea, they went there too, agitating the crowds and stirring them up. ¹⁴The brothers immediately sent Paul to the coast, but Silas and Timothy stayed at Berea. ¹⁵The men who escorted Paul brought him to Athens and

---

THURSDAY

VERSE:	AUTHOR:	PASSAGE:
Acts 17:11	**Phyllis Bennett**	Acts 17:10–15

A Word of Appreciation

In *The Hiding Place* Corrie ten Boom relates the story of her misery of being placed in a barracks infested with fleas in a concentration camp in World War II. Much to Corrie's disgust, her sister Betsie, upon first entering this particular barracks, began thanking the Lord for the fleas! Corrie could find no reason to thank God for these miserable little creatures. Corrie and Betsie did notice, however, that their particular barracks was rarely visited by the guards, allowing them great freedom to read portions of Scripture out loud to the women confined with them. It was weeks later when they discovered the miracle of their uninterrupted Bible study—the fleas! The guards didn't want to take a chance of getting personally infested!

How easy it is to take the Word of God for granted. Corrie and Betsie only had one copy of each of the four Gospels to share with these women who desperately needed hope. [We should] appreciate the availability of God's Word and all its richness.

ADDITIONAL SCRIPTURE READINGS:
Psalm 119:105–112; Acts 7:51—8:8; Hebrews 11:32–40

Go to page 189 for your next devotional reading.

then left with instructions for Silas and Timothy to join him as soon as possible.

In Athens

[16]While Paul was waiting for them in Athens, he was greatly distressed to see that the city was full of idols. [17]So he reasoned in the synagogue with the Jews and the God-fearing Greeks, as well as in the marketplace day by day with those who happened to be there. [18]A group of Epicurean and Stoic philosophers began to dispute with him. Some of them asked, "What is this babbler trying to say?" Others remarked, "He seems to be advocating foreign gods." They said this because Paul was preaching the good news about Jesus and the resurrection. [19]Then they took him and brought him to a meeting of the Areopagus, where they said to him, "May we know what this new teaching is that you are presenting? [20]You are bringing some strange ideas to our ears, and we want to know what they mean." [21](All the Athenians and the foreigners who lived there spent their time doing nothing but talking about and listening to the latest ideas.)

[22]Paul then stood up in the meeting of the Areopagus and said: "Men of Athens! I see that in every way you are very religious. [23]For as I walked around and looked carefully at your objects of worship, I even found an altar with this inscription: TO AN UNKNOWN GOD. Now what you worship as something unknown I am going to proclaim to you.

[24]"The God who made the world and everything in it is the Lord of heaven and earth and does not live in temples built by hands. [25]And he is not served by human hands, as if he needed anything, because he himself gives all men life and breath and everything else. [26]From one man he made every nation of men, that they should inhabit the whole earth; and he determined the times set for them and the exact places where they should live. [27]God did this so that men would seek him and perhaps reach out for him and find him, though he is not far from each one of us. [28]'For in him we live and move and have our being.' As some of your own poets have said, 'We are his offspring.'

[29]"Therefore since we are God's offspring, we should not think that the divine being is like gold or silver or stone—an image made by man's design and skill. [30]In the past God overlooked such ignorance, but now he commands all people everywhere to repent. [31]For he has set a day when he will judge the world with justice by the man he has appointed. He has given proof of this to all men by raising him from the dead."

[32]When they heard about the resurrection of the dead, some of them sneered, but others said, "We want to hear you again on this subject." [33]At that, Paul left the Council. [34]A few men became followers of Paul and believed. Among them was Dionysius, a member of the Areopagus, also a woman named Damaris, and a number of others.

In Corinth

18 After this, Paul left Athens and went to Corinth. [2]There he met a Jew named Aquila, a native of Pontus, who had recently come from Italy with his wife Priscilla, because Claudius had ordered all the Jews to leave Rome. Paul went to see them, [3]and because he was a tentmaker as they were, he stayed and worked with them. [4]Every Sabbath he reasoned in the synagogue, trying to persuade Jews and Greeks.

[5]When Silas and Timothy came from Macedonia, Paul devoted himself exclusively to preaching, testifying to the Jews that Jesus was the Christ.[a] [6]But when the Jews opposed Paul and became abusive, he shook out his clothes in protest and said to them, "Your blood be on your own heads! I am clear of my responsibility. From now on I will go to the Gentiles."

[7]Then Paul left the synagogue and went next door to the house of Titius Justus, a worshiper of God. [8]Crispus, the synagogue ruler, and his entire household believed in the Lord; and many of the Corinthians who heard him believed and were baptized.

[9]One night the Lord spoke to Paul in a vision: "Do not be afraid; keep on speaking, do not be silent. [10]For I am with you, and no one is going to attack and harm you, because I have many people in this city." [11]So Paul stayed for

---

[a]5 Or Messiah; also in verse 28

a year and a half, teaching them the word of God.

12While Gallio was proconsul of Achaia, the Jews made a united attack on Paul and brought him into court. 13"This man," they charged, "is persuading the people to worship God in ways contrary to the law."

14Just as Paul was about to speak, Gallio said to the Jews, "If you Jews were making a complaint about some misdemeanor or serious crime, it would be reasonable for me to listen to you. 15But since it involves questions about words and names and your own law—settle the matter yourselves. I will not be a judge of such things." 16So he had them ejected from the court. 17Then they all turned on Sosthenes the synagogue ruler and beat him in front of the court. But Gallio showed no concern whatever.

Priscilla, Aquila and Apollos

18Paul stayed on in Corinth for some time. Then he left the brothers and sailed for Syria, accompanied by Priscilla and Aquila. Before he sailed, he had his hair cut off at Cenchrea because of a vow he had taken. 19They arrived at Ephesus, where Paul left Priscilla and Aquila. He himself went into the synagogue and reasoned with the Jews. 20When they asked him to spend more time with them, he declined. 21But as he left, he promised, "I will come back if it is God's will." Then he set sail from Ephesus. 22When he landed at Caesarea, he went up and greeted the church and then went down to Antioch.

23After spending some time in Antioch, Paul set out from there and traveled from place to place throughout the region of Galatia and Phrygia, strengthening all the disciples.

24Meanwhile a Jew named Apollos, a native of Alexandria, came to Ephesus. He was a learned man, with a thorough knowledge of the Scriptures. 25He had been instructed in the way of the Lord, and he spoke with great fervor[a] and taught about Jesus accurately, though he knew only the baptism of John. 26He began to speak boldly in the synagogue. When Priscilla and Aquila heard him, they invited him to their home and explained to him the way of God more adequately.

27When Apollos wanted to go to Achaia, the brothers encouraged him and wrote to the disciples there to welcome him. On arriving, he was a great help to those who by grace had believed. 28For he vigorously refuted the Jews in public debate, proving from the Scriptures that Jesus was the Christ.

Paul in Ephesus

19 While Apollos was at Corinth, Paul took the road through the interior and arrived at Ephesus. There he found some disciples 2and asked them, "Did you receive the Holy Spirit when[b] you believed?"

They answered, "No, we have not even heard that there is a Holy Spirit."

3So Paul asked, "Then what baptism did you receive?"

"John's baptism," they replied.

4Paul said, "John's baptism was a baptism of repentance. He told the people to believe in the one coming after him, that is, in Jesus." 5On hearing this, they were baptized into[c] the name of the Lord Jesus. 6When Paul placed his hands on them, the Holy Spirit came on them, and they spoke in tongues[d] and prophesied. 7There were about twelve men in all.

8Paul entered the synagogue and spoke boldly there for three months, arguing persuasively about the kingdom of God. 9But some of them became obstinate; they refused to believe and publicly maligned the Way. So Paul left them. He took the disciples with him and had discussions daily in the lecture hall of Tyrannus. 10This went on for two years, so that all the Jews and Greeks who lived in the province of Asia heard the word of the Lord.

11God did extraordinary miracles through Paul, 12so that even handkerchiefs and aprons that had touched him were taken to the sick, and their illnesses were cured and the evil spirits left them.

13Some Jews who went around driving out evil spirits tried to invoke the name of the Lord Jesus over those who were demon-possessed. They would say, "In the name of Jesus, whom Paul preaches, I command you to come out." 14Seven sons of Sceva, a Jewish chief priest, were doing this. 15⌊One day⌋ the evil spirit an-

---

a25 Or with fervor in the Spirit   b2 Or after   c5 Or in   d6 Or other languages swered them, "Jesus I know, and I know about Paul, but who are you?" [16]Then the man who had the evil spirit jumped on them and overpowered them all. He gave them such a beating that they ran out of the house naked and bleeding.

[17]When this became known to the Jews and Greeks living in Ephesus, they were all seized with fear, and the name of the Lord Jesus was held in high honor. [18]Many of those who believed now came and openly confessed their evil deeds. [19]A number who had practiced sorcery brought their scrolls together and burned them publicly. When they calculated the value of the scrolls, the total came to fifty thousand drachmas.[a] [20]In this way the word of the Lord spread widely and grew in power.

[21]After all this had happened, Paul decided to go to Jerusalem, passing through Macedonia and Achaia. "After I have been there," he said, "I must visit Rome also." [22]He sent two of his helpers, Timothy and Erastus, to Macedonia, while he stayed in the province of Asia a little longer.

The Riot in Ephesus

[23]About that time there arose a great disturbance about the Way. [24]A silversmith named Demetrius, who made silver shrines of Artemis, brought in no little business for the craftsmen. [25]He called them together, along with the workmen in related trades, and said: "Men, you know we receive a good income from this business. [26]And you see and hear how this fellow Paul has convinced and led astray large numbers of people here in Ephesus and in practically the whole province of Asia. He says that man-made gods are no gods at all. [27]There is danger not only that our trade will lose its good name, but also that the temple of the great goddess Artemis will be discredited, and the goddess herself, who is worshiped throughout the province of Asia and the world, will be robbed of her divine majesty."

[28]When they heard this, they were furious and began shouting: "Great is Artemis of the Ephesians!" [29]Soon the whole city was in an uproar. The people seized Gaius and Aristarchus, Paul's traveling companions from Macedonia, and rushed as one man into the theater.

[30]Paul wanted to appear before the crowd, but the disciples would not let him. [31]Even some of the officials of the province, friends of Paul, sent him a message begging him not to venture into the theater.

[32]The assembly was in confusion: Some were shouting one thing, some another. Most of the people did not even know why they were there. [33]The Jews pushed Alexander to the front, and some of the crowd shouted instructions to him. He motioned for silence in order to make a defense before the people. [34]But when they realized he was a Jew, they all shouted in unison for about two hours: "Great is Artemis of the Ephesians!"

[35]The city clerk quieted the crowd and said: "Men of Ephesus, doesn't all the world know that the city of Ephesus is the guardian of the temple of the great Artemis and of her image, which fell from heaven? [36]Therefore, since these facts are undeniable, you ought to be quiet and not do anything rash. [37]You have brought these men here, though they have neither robbed temples nor blasphemed our goddess. [38]If, then, Demetrius and his fellow craftsmen have a grievance against anybody, the courts are open and there are proconsuls. They can press charges. [39]If there is anything further you want to bring up, it must be settled in a legal assembly. [40]As it is, we are in danger of being charged with rioting because of today's events. In that case we would not be able to account for this commotion, since there is no reason for it." [41]After he had said this, he dismissed the assembly.

Through Macedonia and Greece

20 When the uproar had ended, Paul sent for the disciples and, after encouraging them, said good-by and set out for Macedonia. [2]He traveled through that area, speaking many words of encouragement to the people, and finally arrived in Greece, [3]where he stayed three months. Because the Jews made a plot against him just as he was about to sail for Syria, he decided to go back through Macedonia. [4]He was accompanied by Sopater son of Pyrrhus from Berea, Aristarchus and Secundus from Thessalonica, Gaius from Derbe, Timo-

[a]19 A drachma was a silver coin worth about a day's wages.

thy also, and Tychicus and Trophimus from the province of Asia. **5**These men went on ahead and waited for us at Troas. **6**But we sailed from Philippi after the Feast of Unleavened Bread, and five days later joined the others at Troas, where we stayed seven days.

Eutychus Raised From the Dead at Troas

7On the first day of the week we came together to break bread. Paul spoke to the people and, because he intended to leave the next day, kept on talking until midnight. **8**There were many lamps in the upstairs room where we were meeting. **9**Seated in a window was a young man named Eutychus, who was sinking into a deep sleep as Paul talked on and on. When he was sound asleep, he fell to the ground from the third story and was picked up dead. **10**Paul went down, threw himself on the young man and put his arms around him. "Don't be alarmed," he said. "He's alive!" **11**Then he went upstairs again and broke bread and ate. After talking until daylight, he left. **12**The people took the young man home alive and were greatly comforted.

Paul's Farewell to the Ephesian Elders

13We went on ahead to the ship and sailed for Assos, where we were going to take Paul aboard. He had made this arrangement because he was going there on foot. **14**When he met us at Assos, we took him aboard and went on to Mitylene. **15**The next day we set sail from there and arrived off Kios. The day after that we crossed over to Samos, and on the following day arrived at Miletus. **16**Paul had decided to sail past Ephesus to avoid spending time in the province of Asia, for he was in a hurry to reach Jerusalem, if possible, by the day of Pentecost.

17From Miletus, Paul sent to Ephesus for the elders of the church. **18**When they arrived, he said to them: "You know how I lived the whole time I was with you, from the first day I came into the province of Asia. **19**I served the Lord with great humility and with tears, although I was severely tested by the plots of the Jews. **20**You know that I have not hesitated to preach anything that would be helpful to you but have taught you publicly and from house to house. **21**I have declared to both Jews and Greeks that they must turn to God in repentance and have faith in our Lord Jesus.

22"And now, compelled by the Spirit, I am going to Jerusalem, not knowing what will happen to me there. **23**I only know that in every city the Holy Spirit warns me that prison and hardships are facing me. **24**However, I consider my life worth nothing to me, if only I may finish the race and complete the task the Lord Jesus has given me—the task of testifying to the gospel of God's grace.

25"Now I know that none of you among whom I have gone about preaching the kingdom will ever see me again. **26**Therefore, I declare to you today that I am innocent of the blood of all men. **27**For I have not hesitated to proclaim to you the whole will of God. **28**Keep watch over yourselves and all the flock of which the Holy Spirit has made you overseers.*a* Be shepherds of the church of God,*b* which he bought with his own blood. **29**I know that after I leave, savage wolves will come in among you and will not spare the flock. **30**Even from your own number men will arise and distort the truth in order to draw away disciples after them. **31**So be on your guard! Remember that for three years I never stopped warning each of you night and day with tears.

32"Now I commit you to God and to the word of his grace, which can build you up and give you an inheritance among all those who are sanctified. **33**I have not coveted anyone's silver or gold or clothing. **34**You yourselves know that these hands of mine have supplied my own needs and the needs of my companions. **35**In everything I did, I showed you that by this kind of hard work we must help the weak, remembering the words the Lord Jesus himself said: 'It is more blessed to give than to receive.'"

36When he had said this, he knelt down with all of them and prayed. **37**They all wept as they embraced him and kissed him. **38**What grieved them most was his statement that they would never see his face again. Then they accompanied him to the ship.

---

a 28 Traditionally *bishops*　　*b 28* Many manuscripts *of the Lord*

On to Jerusalem

21 After we had torn ourselves away from them, we put out to sea and sailed straight to Cos. The next day we went to Rhodes and from there to Patara. ²We found a ship crossing over to Phoenicia, went on board and set sail. ³After sighting Cyprus and passing to the south of it, we sailed on to Syria. We landed at Tyre, where our ship was to unload its cargo. ⁴Finding the disciples there, we stayed with them seven days. Through the Spirit they urged Paul not to go on to Jerusalem. ⁵But when our time was up, we left and continued on our way. All the disciples and their wives and children accompanied us out of the city, and there on the beach we knelt to pray. ⁶After saying good-by to each other, we went aboard the ship, and they returned home.

⁷We continued our voyage from Tyre and landed at Ptolemais, where we greeted the brothers and stayed with them for a day. ⁸Leaving the next day, we reached Caesarea and stayed at the house of Philip the evangelist, one of the Seven. ⁹He had four unmarried daughters who prophesied.

¹⁰After we had been there a number of days, a prophet named Agabus came down from Judea. ¹¹Coming over to us, he took Paul's belt, tied his own hands and feet with it and said, "The Holy Spirit says, 'In this way the Jews of Jerusalem will bind the owner of this belt and will hand him over to the Gentiles.'"

¹²When we heard this, we and the people there pleaded with Paul not to go up to Jerusalem. ¹³Then Paul answered,

---

FRIDAY

VERSE: Acts 20:24   AUTHOR: Mother Teresa of Calcutta   PASSAGE: Acts 20:13–38

My Life and My Faith

The meaning of my life is the love of God.

It is Christ in his distressing disguise whom I love and serve. Jesus has said, "I was hungry and you gave me something to eat . . . I was a stranger and you invited me in, I needed clothes and you clothed me . . ." (Matthew 25:35–36).

Nobody can take my religion from me. Therefore, nobody can refuse me the right to practice it.

Nobody can take it away from me. It is something within me. If there is no alternative to persecution and if that is the only way that Christ wants to come among his people, by radiating his love for them through my actions, I would stay to serve them, but I wouldn't give up my faith.

I would be ready to give my life, but not my faith.

I am nothing. He is all. I do nothing of my own. He does it.

That is what I am, God's pencil. A tiny bit of pencil with which he writes what he likes.

God writes through us, and however imperfect instruments we may be, he writes beautifully.

ADDITIONAL SCRIPTURE READINGS:
Isaiah 64:8; John 3:30; Galatians 2:20

Go to page 194 for your next devotional reading.

"Why are you weeping and breaking my heart? I am ready not only to be bound, but also to die in Jerusalem for the name of the Lord Jesus." ¹⁴When he would not be dissuaded, we gave up and said, "The Lord's will be done."

¹⁵After this, we got ready and went up to Jerusalem. ¹⁶Some of the disciples from Caesarea accompanied us and brought us to the home of Mnason, where we were to stay. He was a man from Cyprus and one of the early disciples.

Paul's Arrival at Jerusalem

¹⁷When we arrived at Jerusalem, the brothers received us warmly. ¹⁸The next day Paul and the rest of us went to see James, and all the elders were present. ¹⁹Paul greeted them and reported in detail what God had done among the Gentiles through his ministry.

²⁰When they heard this, they praised God. Then they said to Paul: "You see, brother, how many thousands of Jews have believed, and all of them are zealous for the law. ²¹They have been informed that you teach all the Jews who live among the Gentiles to turn away from Moses, telling them not to circumcise their children or live according to our customs. ²²What shall we do? They will certainly hear that you have come, ²³so do what we tell you. There are four men with us who have made a vow. ²⁴Take these men, join in their purification rites and pay their expenses, so that they can have their heads shaved. Then everybody will know there is no truth in these reports about you, but that you yourself are living in obedience to the law. ²⁵As for the Gentile believers, we have written to them our decision that they should abstain from food sacrificed to idols, from blood, from the meat of strangled animals and from sexual immorality."

²⁶The next day Paul took the men and purified himself along with them. Then he went to the temple to give notice of the date when the days of purification would end and the offering would be made for each of them.

Paul Arrested

²⁷When the seven days were nearly over, some Jews from the province of Asia saw Paul at the temple. They stirred up the whole crowd and seized him, ²⁸shouting, "Men of Israel, help us! This is the man who teaches all men everywhere against our people and our law and this place. And besides, he has brought Greeks into the temple area and defiled this holy place." ²⁹(They had previously seen Trophimus the Ephesian in the city with Paul and assumed that Paul had brought him into the temple area.)

³⁰The whole city was aroused, and the people came running from all directions. Seizing Paul, they dragged him from the temple, and immediately the gates were shut. ³¹While they were trying to kill him, news reached the commander of the Roman troops that the whole city of Jerusalem was in an uproar. ³²He at once took some officers and soldiers and ran down to the crowd. When the rioters saw the commander and his soldiers, they stopped beating Paul.

³³The commander came up and arrested him and ordered him to be bound with two chains. Then he asked who he was and what he had done. ³⁴Some in the crowd shouted one thing and some another, and since the commander could not get at the truth because of the uproar, he ordered that Paul be taken into the barracks. ³⁵When Paul reached the steps, the violence of the mob was so great he had to be carried by the soldiers. ³⁶The crowd that followed kept shouting, "Away with him!"

Paul Speaks to the Crowd

³⁷As the soldiers were about to take Paul into the barracks, he asked the commander, "May I say something to you?"

"Do you speak Greek?" he replied. ³⁸"Aren't you the Egyptian who started a revolt and led four thousand terrorists out into the desert some time ago?"

³⁹Paul answered, "I am a Jew, from Tarsus in Cilicia, a citizen of no ordinary city. Please let me speak to the people."

⁴⁰Having received the commander's permission, Paul stood on the steps and motioned to the crowd. When they were all silent, he said to them in Aramaic[a]:

22

¹"Brothers and fathers, listen now to my defense."

²When they heard him speak to them in Aramaic, they became very quiet.

---

[a] 40 Or possibly *Hebrew*; also in 22:2

Then Paul said: **3**"I am a Jew, born in Tarsus of Cilicia, but brought up in this city. Under Gamaliel I was thoroughly trained in the law of our fathers and was just as zealous for God as any of you are today. **4**I persecuted the followers of this Way to their death, arresting both men and women and throwing them into prison, **5**as also the high priest and all the Council can testify. I even obtained letters from them to their brothers in Damascus, and went there to bring these people as prisoners to Jerusalem to be punished.

6"About noon as I came near Damascus, suddenly a bright light from heaven flashed around me. **7**I fell to the ground and heard a voice say to me, 'Saul! Saul! Why do you persecute me?'

8" 'Who are you, Lord?' I asked.

" 'I am Jesus of Nazareth, whom you are persecuting,' he replied. **9**My companions saw the light, but they did not understand the voice of him who was speaking to me.

10" 'What shall I do, Lord?' I asked.

" 'Get up,' the Lord said, 'and go into Damascus. There you will be told all that you have been assigned to do.' **11**My companions led me by the hand into Damascus, because the brilliance of the light had blinded me.

12"A man named Ananias came to see me. He was a devout observer of the law and highly respected by all the Jews living there. **13**He stood beside me and said, 'Brother Saul, receive your sight!' And at that very moment I was able to see him.

14"Then he said: 'The God of our fathers has chosen you to know his will and to see the Righteous One and to hear words from his mouth. **15**You will be his witness to all men of what you have seen and heard. **16**And now what are you waiting for? Get up, be baptized and wash your sins away, calling on his name.'

17"When I returned to Jerusalem and was praying at the temple, I fell into a trance **18**and saw the Lord speaking. 'Quick!' he said to me. 'Leave Jerusalem immediately, because they will not accept your testimony about me.'

19" 'Lord,' I replied, 'these men know that I went from one synagogue to another to imprison and beat those who

believe in you. **20**And when the blood of your martyr[a] Stephen was shed, I stood there giving my approval and guarding the clothes of those who were killing him.'

21"Then the Lord said to me, 'Go; I will send you far away to the Gentiles.' "

Paul the Roman Citizen

22The crowd listened to Paul until he said this. Then they raised their voices and shouted, "Rid the earth of him! He's not fit to live!"

23As they were shouting and throwing off their cloaks and flinging dust into the air, **24**the commander ordered Paul to be taken into the barracks. He directed that he be flogged and questioned in order to find out why the people were shouting at him like this. **25**As they stretched him out to flog him, Paul said to the centurion standing there, "Is it legal for you to flog a Roman citizen who hasn't even been found guilty?"

26When the centurion heard this, he went to the commander and reported it. "What are you going to do?" he asked. "This man is a Roman citizen."

27The commander went to Paul and asked, "Tell me, are you a Roman citizen?"

"Yes, I am," he answered.

28Then the commander said, "I had to pay a big price for my citizenship."

"But I was born a citizen," Paul replied.

29Those who were about to question him withdrew immediately. The commander himself was alarmed when he realized that he had put Paul, a Roman citizen, in chains.

Before the Sanhedrin

30The next day, since the commander wanted to find out exactly why Paul was being accused by the Jews, he released him and ordered the chief priests and all the Sanhedrin to assemble. Then he brought Paul and had him stand before them.

23 Paul looked straight at the Sanhedrin and said, "My brothers, I have fulfilled my duty to God in all good conscience to this day." **2**At this the high priest Ananias ordered those standing near Paul to strike him on the mouth. **3**Then Paul said to him, "God will strike you, you whitewashed wall! You sit there to judge me according to the law, yet you yourself violate the law by commanding that I be struck!"

[4]Those who were standing near Paul said, "You dare to insult God's high priest?"

[5]Paul replied, "Brothers, I did not realize that he was the high priest; for it is written: 'Do not speak evil about the ruler of your people.'[a]"

[6]Then Paul, knowing that some of them were Sadducees and the others Pharisees, called out in the Sanhedrin, "My brothers, I am a Pharisee, the son of a Pharisee. I stand on trial because of my hope in the resurrection of the dead." [7]When he said this, a dispute broke out between the Pharisees and the Sadducees, and the assembly was divided. [8](The Sadducees say that there is no resurrection, and that there are neither angels nor spirits, but the Pharisees acknowledge them all.)

[9]There was a great uproar, and some of the teachers of the law who were Pharisees stood up and argued vigorously. "We find nothing wrong with this man," they said. "What if a spirit or an angel has spoken to him?" [10]The dispute became so violent that the commander was afraid Paul would be torn to pieces by them. He ordered the troops to go down and take him away from them by force and bring him into the barracks.

[11]The following night the Lord stood near Paul and said, "Take courage! As you have testified about me in Jerusalem, so you must also testify in Rome."

The Plot to Kill Paul

[12]The next morning the Jews formed a conspiracy and bound themselves with an oath not to eat or drink until they had killed Paul. [13]More than forty men were involved in this plot. [14]They went to the chief priests and elders and said, "We have taken a solemn oath not to eat anything until we have killed Paul. [15]Now then, you and the Sanhedrin petition the commander to bring him before you on the pretext of wanting more accurate information about his case. We are ready to kill him before he gets here."

[16]But when the son of Paul's sister heard of this plot, he went into the barracks and told Paul.

[17]Then Paul called one of the centurions and said, "Take this young man to the commander; he has something to tell him." [18]So he took him to the commander.

The centurion said, "Paul, the prisoner, sent for me and asked me to bring this young man to you because he has something to tell you."

[19]The commander took the young man by the hand, drew him aside and asked, "What is it you want to tell me?"

[20]He said: "The Jews have agreed to ask you to bring Paul before the Sanhedrin tomorrow on the pretext of wanting more accurate information about him. [21]Don't give in to them, because more than forty of them are waiting in ambush for him. They have taken an oath not to eat or drink until they have killed him. They are ready now, waiting for your consent to their request."

[22]The commander dismissed the young man and cautioned him, "Don't tell anyone that you have reported this to me."

Paul Transferred to Caesarea

[23]Then he called two of his centurions and ordered them, "Get ready a detachment of two hundred soldiers, seventy horsemen and two hundred spearmen[b] to go to Caesarea at nine tonight. [24]Provide mounts for Paul so that he may be taken safely to Governor Felix."

[25]He wrote a letter as follows:

[26]Claudius Lysias,

To His Excellency, Governor Felix:

Greetings.

[27]This man was seized by the Jews and they were about to kill him, but I came with my troops and rescued him, for I had learned that he is a Roman citizen. [28]I wanted to know why they were accusing him, so I brought him to their Sanhedrin. [29]I found that the accusation had to do with questions about their law, but there was no charge against him that deserved death or imprisonment. [30]When I was informed of a plot to be carried out against the man, I sent him to you at once. I

a5 Exodus 22:28   b23 The meaning of the Greek for this word is uncertain.

also ordered his accusers to present to you their case against him.

[31]So the soldiers, carrying out their orders, took Paul with them during the night and brought him as far as Antipatris. [32]The next day they let the cavalry go on with him, while they returned to the barracks. [33]When the cavalry arrived in Caesarea, they delivered the letter to the governor and handed Paul over to him. [34]The governor read the letter and asked what province he was from. Learning that he was from Cilicia, [35]he said, "I will hear your case when your accusers get here." Then he ordered that Paul be kept under guard in Herod's palace.

The Trial Before Felix

24 Five days later the high priest Ananias went down to Caesarea with some of the elders and a lawyer named Tertullus, and they brought their charges against Paul before the governor. [2]When Paul was called in, Tertullus presented his case before Felix: "We have enjoyed a long period of peace under you, and your foresight has brought about reforms in this nation. [3]Everywhere and in every way, most excellent Felix, we acknowledge this with profound gratitude. [4]But in order not to weary you further, I would request that you be kind enough to hear us briefly.

[5]"We have found this man to be a troublemaker, stirring up riots among the Jews all over the world. He is a ringleader of the Nazarene sect [6]and even tried to desecrate the temple; so we seized him. [8]By[a] examining him yourself you will be able to learn the truth about all these charges we are bringing against him."

[9]The Jews joined in the accusation, asserting that these things were true.

[10]When the governor motioned for him to speak, Paul replied: "I know that for a number of years you have been a judge over this nation; so I gladly make my defense. [11]You can easily verify that no more than twelve days ago I went up to Jerusalem to worship. [12]My accusers did not find me arguing with anyone at the temple, or stirring up a crowd in the synagogues or anywhere else in the city. [13]And they cannot prove to you the charges they are now making against me. [14]However, I admit that I worship the God of our fathers as a follower of the Way, which they call a sect. I believe everything that agrees with the Law and that is written in the Prophets, [15]and I have the same hope in God as these men, that there will be a resurrection of both the righteous and the wicked. [16]So I strive always to keep my conscience clear before God and man.

[17]"After an absence of several years, I came to Jerusalem to bring my people gifts for the poor and to present offerings. [18]I was ceremonially clean when they found me in the temple courts doing this. There was no crowd with me, nor was I involved in any disturbance. [19]But there are some Jews from the province of Asia, who ought to be here before you and bring charges if they have anything against me. [20]Or these who are here should state what crime they found in me when I stood before the Sanhedrin— [21]unless it was this one thing I shouted as I stood in their presence: 'It is concerning the resurrection of the dead that I am on trial before you today.' "

[22]Then Felix, who was well acquainted with the Way, adjourned the proceedings. "When Lysias the commander comes," he said, "I will decide your case." [23]He ordered the centurion to keep Paul under guard but to give him some freedom and permit his friends to take care of his needs.

[24]Several days later Felix came with his wife Drusilla, who was a Jewess. He sent for Paul and listened to him as he spoke about faith in Christ Jesus. [25]As Paul discoursed on righteousness, self-control and the judgment to come, Felix was afraid and said, "That's enough for now! You may leave. When I find it convenient, I will send for you." [26]At the same time he was hoping that Paul would offer him a bribe, so he sent for him frequently and talked with him.

[27]When two years had passed, Felix was succeeded by Porcius Festus, but because Felix wanted to grant a favor to the Jews, he left Paul in prison.

---

[a]6-8 Some manuscripts *him and wanted to judge him according to our law. [7]But the commander, Lysias, came and with the use of much force snatched him from our hands [8]and ordered his accusers to come before you. By*

WEEKENDING

REMEMBER

Service and worship are inseparable.
Worship is a service of praise and ado-
ration, a recognition of priorities. The
acts of worship, whether formal or
informal, whether through singing
hymns or doing our best, say that we
know who is first, who's in charge,
who's the boss. This is why we can't
relegate worship to a once-a-week habit
. . . Only by living in worship will we get
away from promoting ourselves to head
[person].

Cheryl Forbes

REVIVE

Saturday: Psalm 100
Sunday: John 4:21–24

*Go to page 201 for your
next devotional reading.*

The Trial Before Festus

25 Three days after arriving in the province, Festus went up from Caesarea to Jerusalem, ²where the chief priests and Jewish leaders appeared before him and presented the charges against Paul. ³They urgently requested Festus, as a favor to them, to have Paul transferred to Jerusalem, for they were preparing an ambush to kill him along the way. ⁴Festus answered, "Paul is being held at Caesarea, and I myself am going there soon. ⁵Let some of your leaders come with me and press charges against the man there, if he has done anything wrong."

⁶After spending eight or ten days with them, he went down to Caesarea, and the next day he convened the court and ordered that Paul be brought before him. ⁷When Paul appeared, the Jews who had come down from Jerusalem stood around him, bringing many serious charges against him, which they could not prove.

⁸Then Paul made his defense: "I have done nothing wrong against the law of the Jews or against the temple or against Caesar."

⁹Festus, wishing to do the Jews a favor, said to Paul, "Are you willing to go up to Jerusalem and stand trial before me there on these charges?"

¹⁰Paul answered: "I am now standing before Caesar's court, where I ought to be tried. I have not done any wrong to the Jews, as you yourself know very well. ¹¹If, however, I am guilty of doing anything deserving death, I do not refuse to die. But if the charges brought against me by these Jews are not true, no one has the right to hand me over to them. I appeal to Caesar!"

¹²After Festus had conferred with his council, he declared: "You have appealed to Caesar. To Caesar you will go!"

Festus Consults King Agrippa

¹³A few days later King Agrippa and Bernice arrived at Caesarea to pay their respects to Festus. ¹⁴Since they were spending many days there, Festus discussed Paul's case with the king. He said: "There is a man here whom Felix left as a prisoner. ¹⁵When I went to Jerusalem, the chief priests and elders of the

Jews brought charges against him and asked that he be condemned.

¹⁶"I told them that it is not the Roman custom to hand over any man before he has faced his accusers and has had an opportunity to defend himself against their charges. ¹⁷When they came here with me, I did not delay the case, but convened the court the next day and ordered the man to be brought in. ¹⁸When his accusers got up to speak, they did not charge him with any of the crimes I had expected. ¹⁹Instead, they had some points of dispute with him about their own religion and about a dead man named Jesus who Paul claimed was alive. ²⁰I was at a loss how to investigate such matters; so I asked if he would be willing to go to Jerusalem and stand trial there on these charges. ²¹When Paul made his appeal to be held over for the Emperor's decision, I ordered him held until I could send him to Caesar."

²²Then Agrippa said to Festus, "I would like to hear this man myself."

He replied, "Tomorrow you will hear him."

Paul Before Agrippa

²³The next day Agrippa and Bernice came with great pomp and entered the audience room with the high ranking officers and the leading men of the city. At the command of Festus, Paul was brought in. ²⁴Festus said: "King Agrippa, and all who are present with us, you see this man! The whole Jewish community has petitioned me about him in Jerusalem and here in Caesarea, shouting that he ought not to live any longer. ²⁵I found he had done nothing deserving of death, but because he made his appeal to the Emperor I decided to send him to Rome. ²⁶But I have nothing definite to write to His Majesty about him. Therefore I have brought him before all of you, and especially before you, King Agrippa, so that as a result of this investigation I may have something to write. ²⁷For I think it is unreasonable to send on a prisoner without specifying the charges against him."

26 Then Agrippa said to Paul, "You have permission to speak for yourself."

So Paul motioned with his hand and began his defense: ²"King Agrippa, I consider myself fortunate to stand before you today as I make my defense against all the accusations of the Jews, **3**and especially so because you are well acquainted with all the Jewish customs and controversies. Therefore, I beg you to listen to me patiently.

4 "The Jews all know the way I have lived ever since I was a child, from the beginning of my life in my own country, and also in Jerusalem. **5**They have known me for a long time and can testify, if they are willing, that according to the strictest sect of our religion, I lived as a Pharisee. **6**And now it is because of my hope in what God has promised our fathers that I am on trial today. **7**This is the promise our twelve tribes are hoping to see fulfilled as they earnestly serve God day and night. O king, it is because of this hope that the Jews are accusing me. **8**Why should any of you consider it incredible that God raises the dead?

9 "I too was convinced that I ought to do all that was possible to oppose the name of Jesus of Nazareth. **10**And that is just what I did in Jerusalem. On the authority of the chief priests I put many of the saints in prison, and when they were put to death, I cast my vote against them. **11**Many a time I went from one synagogue to another to have them punished, and I tried to force them to blaspheme. In my obsession against them, I even went to foreign cities to persecute them.

12 "On one of these journeys I was going to Damascus with the authority and commission of the chief priests. **13**About noon, O king, as I was on the road, I saw a light from heaven, brighter than the sun, blazing around me and my companions. **14**We all fell to the ground, and I heard a voice saying to me in Aramaic,*a* 'Saul, Saul, why do you persecute me? It is hard for you to kick against the goads.'

15 "Then I asked, 'Who are you, Lord?'

" 'I am Jesus, whom you are persecuting,' the Lord replied. **16**'Now get up and stand on your feet. I have appeared to you to appoint you as a servant and as a witness of what you have seen of me and what I will show you. **17**I will rescue you from your own people and from the Gentiles. I am sending you to them **18**to open their eyes and turn them from darkness to light, and from the power of

Satan to God, so that they may receive forgiveness of sins and a place among those who are sanctified by faith in me.'

19 "So then, King Agrippa, I was not disobedient to the vision from heaven. **20**First to those in Damascus, then to those in Jerusalem and in all Judea, and to the Gentiles also, I preached that they should repent and turn to God and prove their repentance by their deeds. **21**That is why the Jews seized me in the temple courts and tried to kill me. **22**But I have had God's help to this very day, and so I stand here and testify to small and great alike. I am saying nothing beyond what the prophets and Moses said would happen— **23**that the Christ*b* would suffer and, as the first to rise from the dead, would proclaim light to his own people and to the Gentiles."

24At this point Festus interrupted Paul's defense. "You are out of your mind, Paul!" he shouted. "Your great learning is driving you insane."

25 "I am not insane, most excellent Festus," Paul replied. "What I am saying is true and reasonable. **26**The king is familiar with these things, and I can speak freely to him. I am convinced that none of this has escaped his notice, because it was not done in a corner. **27**King Agrippa, do you believe the prophets? I know you do."

28Then Agrippa said to Paul, "Do you think that in such a short time you can persuade me to be a Christian?"

29Paul replied, "Short time or long—I pray God that not only you but all who are listening to me today may become what I am, except for these chains."

30The king rose, and with him the governor and Bernice and those sitting with them. **31**They left the room, and while talking with one another, they said, "This man is not doing anything that deserves death or imprisonment."

32Agrippa said to Festus, "This man could have been set free if he had not appealed to Caesar."

Paul Sails for Rome

27 When it was decided that we would sail for Italy, Paul and some other prisoners were handed over to a centurion named Julius, who belonged to the Imperial Regiment. **2**We boarded a ship from Adramyttium about

a14 Or *Hebrew*   *b23* Or *Messiah*

to sail for ports along the coast of the province of Asia, and we put out to sea. Aristarchus, a Macedonian from Thessalonica, was with us.

³The next day we landed at Sidon; and Julius, in kindness to Paul, allowed him to go to his friends so they might provide for his needs. ⁴From there we put out to sea again and passed to the lee of Cyprus because the winds were against us. ⁵When we had sailed across the open sea off the coast of Cilicia and Pamphylia, we landed at Myra in Lycia. ⁶There the centurion found an Alexandrian ship sailing for Italy and put us on board. ⁷We made slow headway for many days and had difficulty arriving off Cnidus. When the wind did not allow us to hold our course, we sailed to the lee of Crete, opposite Salmone. ⁸We moved along the coast with difficulty and came to a place called Fair Havens, near the town of Lasea.

⁹Much time had been lost, and sailing had already become dangerous because by now it was after the Fast.ᵃ So Paul warned them, ¹⁰"Men, I can see that our voyage is going to be disastrous and bring great loss to ship and cargo, and to our own lives also." ¹¹But the centurion, instead of listening to what Paul said, followed the advice of the pilot and of the owner of the ship. ¹²Since the harbor was unsuitable to winter in, the majority decided that we should sail on, hoping to reach Phoenix and winter there. This was a harbor in Crete, facing both southwest and northwest.

The Storm

¹³When a gentle south wind began to blow, they thought they had obtained what they wanted; so they weighed anchor and sailed along the shore of Crete. ¹⁴Before very long, a wind of hurricane force, called the "northeaster," swept down from the island. ¹⁵The ship was caught by the storm and could not head into the wind; so we gave way to it and were driven along. ¹⁶As we passed to the lee of a small island called Cauda, we were hardly able to make the lifeboat secure. ¹⁷When the men had hoisted it aboard, they passed ropes under the ship itself to hold it together. Fearing

that they would run aground on the sandbars of Syrtis, they lowered the sea anchor and let the ship be driven along. ¹⁸We took such a violent battering from the storm that the next day they began to throw the cargo overboard. ¹⁹On the third day, they threw the ship's tackle overboard with their own hands. ²⁰When neither sun nor stars appeared for many days and the storm continued raging, we finally gave up all hope of being saved.

²¹After the men had gone a long time without food, Paul stood up before them and said: "Men, you should have taken my advice not to sail from Crete; then you would have spared yourselves this damage and loss. ²²But now I urge you to keep up your courage, because not one of you will be lost; only the ship will be destroyed. ²³Last night an angel of the God whose I am and whom I serve stood beside me ²⁴and said, 'Do not be afraid, Paul. You must stand trial before Caesar; and God has graciously given you the lives of all who sail with you.' ²⁵So keep up your courage, men, for I have faith in God that it will happen just as he told me. ²⁶Nevertheless, we must run aground on some island."

The Shipwreck

²⁷On the fourteenth night we were still being driven across the Adriaticᵇ Sea, when about midnight the sailors sensed they were approaching land. ²⁸They took soundings and found that the water was a hundred and twenty feetᶜ deep. A short time later they took soundings again and found it was ninety feetᵈ deep. ²⁹Fearing that we would be dashed against the rocks, they dropped four anchors from the stern and prayed for daylight. ³⁰In an attempt to escape from the ship, the sailors let the lifeboat down into the sea, pretending they were going to lower some anchors from the bow. ³¹Then Paul said to the centurion and the soldiers, "Unless these men stay with the ship, you cannot be saved." ³²So the soldiers cut the ropes that held the lifeboat and let it fall away.

³³Just before dawn Paul urged them all to eat. "For the last fourteen days," he

---

ᵃ9 That is, the Day of Atonement (Yom Kippur)   ᵇ27 In ancient times the name referred to an area extending well south of Italy.   ᶜ28 Greek *twenty orguias* (about 37 meters)   ᵈ28 Greek *fifteen orguias* (about 27 meters)

said, "you have been in constant suspense and have gone without food—you haven't eaten anything. ³⁴Now I urge you to take some food. You need it to survive. Not one of you will lose a single hair from his head." ³⁵After he said this, he took some bread and gave thanks to God in front of them all. Then he broke it and began to eat. ³⁶They were all encouraged and ate some food themselves. ³⁷Altogether there were 276 of us on board. ³⁸When they had eaten as much as they wanted, they lightened the ship by throwing the grain into the sea.

³⁹When daylight came, they did not recognize the land, but they saw a bay with a sandy beach, where they decided to run the ship aground if they could. ⁴⁰Cutting loose the anchors, they left them in the sea and at the same time untied the ropes that held the rudders. Then they hoisted the foresail to the wind and made for the beach. ⁴¹But the ship struck a sandbar and ran aground. The bow stuck fast and would not move, and the stern was broken to pieces by the pounding of the surf.

⁴²The soldiers planned to kill the prisoners to prevent any of them from swimming away and escaping. ⁴³But the centurion wanted to spare Paul's life and kept them from carrying out their plan. He ordered those who could swim to jump overboard first and get to land. ⁴⁴The rest were to get there on planks or on pieces of the ship. In this way everyone reached land in safety.

Ashore on Malta

28 Once safely on shore, we found out that the island was called Malta. ²The islanders showed us unusual kindness. They built a fire and welcomed us all because it was raining and cold. ³Paul gathered a pile of brushwood and, as he put it on the fire, a viper, driven out by the heat, fastened itself on his hand. ⁴When the islanders saw the snake hanging from his hand, they said to each other, "This man must be a murderer; for though he escaped from the sea, Justice has not allowed him to live." ⁵But Paul shook the snake off into the fire and suffered no ill effects. ⁶The people expected him to swell up or suddenly fall dead, but after waiting a long time and seeing nothing un-

usual happen to him, they changed their minds and said he was a god.

⁷There was an estate nearby that belonged to Publius, the chief official of the island. He welcomed us to his home and for three days entertained us hospitably. ⁸His father was sick in bed, suffering from fever and dysentery. Paul went in to see him and, after prayer, placed his hands on him and healed him. ⁹When this had happened, the rest of the sick on the island came and were cured. ¹⁰They honored us in many ways and when we were ready to sail, they furnished us with the supplies we needed.

Arrival at Rome

¹¹After three months we put out to sea in a ship that had wintered in the island. It was an Alexandrian ship with the figurehead of the twin gods Castor and Pollux. ¹²We put in at Syracuse and stayed there three days. ¹³From there we set sail and arrived at Rhegium. The next day the south wind came up, and on the following day we reached Puteoli. ¹⁴There we found some brothers who invited us to spend a week with them. And so we came to Rome. ¹⁵The brothers there had heard that we were coming, and they traveled as far as the Forum of Appius and the Three Taverns to meet us. At the sight of these men Paul thanked God and was encouraged. ¹⁶When we got to Rome, Paul was allowed to live by himself, with a soldier to guard him.

Paul Preaches at Rome Under Guard

¹⁷Three days later he called together the leaders of the Jews. When they had assembled, Paul said to them: "My brothers, although I have done nothing against our people or against the customs of our ancestors, I was arrested in Jerusalem and handed over to the Romans. ¹⁸They examined me and wanted to release me, because I was not guilty of any crime deserving death. ¹⁹But when the Jews objected, I was compelled to appeal to Caesar—not that I had any charge to bring against my own people. ²⁰For this reason I have asked to see you and talk with you. It is because of the hope of Israel that I am bound with this chain." ²¹They replied, "We have not received

any letters from Judea concerning you, and none of the brothers who have come from there has reported or said anything bad about you. [22]But we want to hear what your views are, for we know that people everywhere are talking against this sect."

[23]They arranged to meet Paul on a certain day, and came in even larger numbers to the place where he was staying. From morning till evening he explained and declared to them the kingdom of God and tried to convince them about Jesus from the Law of Moses and from the Prophets. [24]Some were convinced by what he said, but others would not believe. [25]They disagreed among themselves and began to leave after Paul had made this final statement: "The Holy Spirit spoke the truth to your forefathers when he said through Isaiah the prophet:

[26]" 'Go to this people and say,

"You will be ever hearing but never understanding;
you will be ever seeing but never perceiving."
[27]For this people's heart has become calloused;
they hardly hear with their ears,
and they have closed their eyes.
Otherwise they might see with their eyes,
hear with their ears,
understand with their hearts
and turn, and I would heal them.'[a]

[28]"Therefore I want you to know that God's salvation has been sent to the Gentiles, and they will listen!"[b]

[30]For two whole years Paul stayed there in his own rented house and welcomed all who came to see him. [31]Boldly and without hindrance he preached the kingdom of God and taught about the Lord Jesus Christ.

---

[a]27 Isaiah 6:9,10   [b]28 Some manuscripts listen!" [29]After he said this, the Jews left, arguing vigorously among themselves.

ROMANS *offers some of the most lively teaching on faith and life ever recorded. In this letter Paul tells of God's wonderful plan for redeeming his people and setting them free for service through the power of his Spirit. As you read about the riches of God's grace, be comforted that nothing "will be able to separate us from the love of God" (8:39) and respond to his love with a transformed life of service.*

ROMANS

1 Paul, a servant of Christ Jesus, called to be an apostle and set apart for the gospel of God— ²the gospel he promised beforehand through his prophets in the Holy Scriptures ³regarding his Son, who as to his human nature was a descendant of David, ⁴and who through the Spirit*ᵃ* of holiness was declared with power to be the Son of God*ᵇ* by his resurrection from the dead: Jesus Christ our Lord. ⁵Through him and for his name's sake, we received grace and apostleship to call people from among all the Gentiles to the obedience that comes from faith. ⁶And you also are among those who are called to belong to Jesus Christ.

⁷To all in Rome who are loved by God and called to be saints:

Grace and peace to you from God our Father and from the Lord Jesus Christ.

Paul's Longing to Visit Rome

⁸First, I thank my God through Jesus Christ for all of you, because your faith is being reported all over the world. ⁹God, whom I serve with my whole heart in preaching the gospel of his Son, is my witness how constantly I remember you ¹⁰in my prayers at all times; and I pray that now at last by God's will the way may be opened for me to come to you.

¹¹I long to see you so that I may impart to you some spiritual gift to make you strong— ¹²that is, that you and I may be mutually encouraged by each other's faith. ¹³I do not want you to be

---

*ᵃ*4 Or *who as to his spirit*   *ᵇ*4 Or *was appointed to be the Son of God with power*

unaware, brothers, that I planned many times to come to you (but have been prevented from doing so until now) in order that I might have a harvest among you, just as I have had among the other Gentiles.

[14] I am obligated both to Greeks and non-Greeks, both to the wise and the foolish. [15] That is why I am so eager to preach the gospel also to you who are at Rome.

[16] I am not ashamed of the gospel, because it is the power of God for the salvation of everyone who believes: first for the Jew, then for the Gentile. [17] For in the gospel a righteousness from God is revealed, a righteousness that is by faith from first to last,[a] just as it is written: "The righteous will live by faith."[b]

God's Wrath Against Mankind

[18] The wrath of God is being revealed from heaven against all the godlessness and wickedness of men who suppress the truth by their wickedness, [19] since what may be known about God is plain to them, because God has made it plain to them. [20] For since the creation of the world God's invisible qualities—his eternal power and divine nature—have been clearly seen, being understood from what has been made, so that men are without excuse.

[21] For although they knew God, they

[a]17 Or *is from faith to faith*   [b]17 Hab. 2:4

MONDAY

VERSE:	AUTHOR:	PASSAGE:
Romans 1:5	Marjorie Holmes	Romans 1:1-13

"Stop! Come Back!"

A friend and I were discussing permissiveness in raising children. And some of its seeming products . . . who swarm around Dupont Circle here in Washington, D.C.

"You know what terrible traffic there is up there," she said. "Well, one day I saw a [young man] starting to jaywalk right into it. And I couldn't stand it, so I yelled at him, 'Stop! Come back!' He turned with such a startled expression, I do believe it was the first time in his life he'd ever heard a direct command.

"Then, as if he couldn't believe his ears, he turned and headed right on. But I called again, 'You'll get killed, come back!'

"And he did. I don't know whether he realized he was being foolish, or whether he was simply obeying me. Anyway, he came, looking kind of sheepish and kind of glad. I think that may be three-fourths of the trouble with a lot of kids today. They've never had people who *cared* enough about them to order them, 'Stop! Come back!' "

The Bible is full of such commands for all of us, no matter what our age. They are the words of a loving Father who knows what can harm us and destroy the happiness we seek. He cares enough about us to order, "Don't do this. Stop, come back!"

ADDITIONAL SCRIPTURE READINGS:
Genesis 3:3; Deuteronomy 11; Hebrews 2:1-4

Go to page 206 for your next devotional reading.

neither glorified him as God nor gave thanks to him, but their thinking became futile and their foolish hearts were darkened. ²²Although they claimed to be wise, they became fools ²³and exchanged the glory of the immortal God for images made to look like mortal man and birds and animals and reptiles.

²⁴Therefore God gave them over in the sinful desires of their hearts to sexual impurity for the degrading of their bodies with one another. ²⁵They exchanged the truth of God for a lie, and worshiped and served created things rather than the Creator—who is forever praised. Amen.

²⁶Because of this, God gave them over to shameful lusts. Even their women exchanged natural relations for unnatural ones. ²⁷In the same way the men also abandoned natural relations with women and were inflamed with lust for one another. Men committed indecent acts with other men, and received in themselves the due penalty for their perversion.

²⁸Furthermore, since they did not think it worthwhile to retain the knowledge of God, he gave them over to a depraved mind, to do what ought not to be done. ²⁹They have become filled with every kind of wickedness, evil, greed and depravity. They are full of envy, murder, strife, deceit and malice. They are gossips, ³⁰slanderers, God-haters, insolent, arrogant and boastful; they invent ways of doing evil; they disobey their parents; ³¹they are senseless, faithless, heartless, ruthless. ³²Although they know God's righteous decree that those who do such things deserve death, they not only continue to do these very things but also approve of those who practice them.

God's Righteous Judgment

2 You, therefore, have no excuse, you who pass judgment on someone else, for at whatever point you judge the other, you are condemning yourself, because you who pass judgment do the same things. ²Now we know that God's judgment against those who do such things is based on truth. ³So when you, a mere man, pass judgment on them and yet do the same things, do you think you will escape God's judgment? ⁴Or do you show contempt for the riches of his kindness, tolerance and pa-

tience, not realizing that God's kindness leads you toward repentance?

⁵But because of your stubbornness and your unrepentant heart, you are storing up wrath against yourself for the day of God's wrath, when his righteous judgment will be revealed. ⁶God "will give to each person according to what he has done."ᵃ ⁷To those who by persistence in doing good seek glory, honor and immortality, he will give eternal life. ⁸But for those who are self-seeking and who reject the truth and follow evil, there will be wrath and anger. ⁹There will be trouble and distress for every human being who does evil: first for the Jew, then for the Gentile; ¹⁰but glory, honor and peace for everyone who does good: first for the Jew, then for the Gentile. ¹¹For God does not show favoritism.

¹²All who sin apart from the law will also perish apart from the law, and all who sin under the law will be judged by the law. ¹³For it is not those who hear the law who are righteous in God's sight, but it is those who obey the law who will be declared righteous. ¹⁴(Indeed, when Gentiles, who do not have the law, do by nature things required by the law, they are a law for themselves, even though they do not have the law, ¹⁵since they show that the requirements of the law are written on their hearts, their consciences also bearing witness, and their thoughts now accusing, now even defending them.) ¹⁶This will take place on the day when God will judge men's secrets through Jesus Christ, as my gospel declares.

The Jews and the Law

¹⁷Now you, if you call yourself a Jew; if you rely on the law and brag about your relationship to God; ¹⁸if you know his will and approve of what is superior because you are instructed by the law; ¹⁹if you are convinced that you are a guide for the blind, a light for those who are in the dark, ²⁰an instructor of the foolish, a teacher of infants, because you have in the law the embodiment of knowledge and truth— ²¹you, then, who teach others, do you not teach yourself? You who preach against stealing, do you steal? ²²You who say that people should not commit adultery, do you commit

---

ᵃ6 Psalm 62:12; Prov. 24:12

adultery? You who abhor idols, do you rob temples? [23]You who brag about the law, do you dishonor God by breaking the law? [24]As it is written: "God's name is blasphemed among the Gentiles because of you."[a]

[25]Circumcision has value if you observe the law, but if you break the law, you have become as though you had not been circumcised. [26]If those who are not circumcised keep the law's requirements, will they not be regarded as though they were circumcised? [27]The one who is not circumcised physically and yet obeys the law will condemn you who, even though you have the[b] written code and circumcision, are a lawbreaker.

[28]A man is not a Jew if he is only one outwardly, nor is circumcision merely outward and physical. [29]No, a man is a Jew if he is one inwardly; and circumcision is circumcision of the heart, by the Spirit, not by the written code. Such a man's praise is not from men, but from God.

God's Faithfulness

3 What advantage, then, is there in being a Jew, or what value is there in circumcision? [2]Much in every way! First of all, they have been entrusted with the very words of God.

[3]What if some did not have faith? Will their lack of faith nullify God's faithfulness? [4]Not at all! Let God be true, and every man a liar. As it is written:

"So that you may be proved right
    when you speak
and prevail when you judge."[c]

[5]But if our unrighteousness brings out God's righteousness more clearly, what shall we say? That God is unjust in bringing his wrath on us? (I am using a human argument.) [6]Certainly not! If that were so, how could God judge the world? [7]Someone might argue, "If my falsehood enhances God's truthfulness and so increases his glory, why am I still condemned as a sinner?" [8]Why not say—as we are being slanderously reported as saying and as some claim that we say—"Let us do evil that good may

result"? Their condemnation is deserved.

No One Is Righteous

[9]What shall we conclude then? Are we any better[d]? Not at all! We have already made the charge that Jews and Gentiles alike are all under sin. [10]As it is written:

"There is no one righteous, not even
    one;
[11]   there is no one who understands,
        no one who seeks God.
[12]All have turned away,
    they have together become
        worthless;
there is no one who does good,
    not even one."[e]
[13]"Their throats are open graves;
    their tongues practice deceit."[f]
"The poison of vipers is on their
    lips."[g]
[14]   "Their mouths are full of cursing
        and bitterness."[h]
[15]"Their feet are swift to shed blood;
[16]   ruin and misery mark their ways,
[17]and the way of peace they do not
    know."[i]
[18]   "There is no fear of God before
        their eyes."[j]

[19]Now we know that whatever the law says, it says to those who are under the law, so that every mouth may be silenced and the whole world held accountable to God. [20]Therefore no one will be declared righteous in his sight by observing the law; rather, through the law we become conscious of sin.

Righteousness Through Faith

[21]But now a righteousness from God, apart from law, has been made known, to which the Law and the Prophets testify. [22]This righteousness from God comes through faith in Jesus Christ to all who believe. There is no difference, [23]for all have sinned and fall short of the glory of God, [24]and are justified freely by his grace through the redemption that came by Christ Jesus. [25]God presented him as a sacrifice of atonement,[k] through faith in his blood. He did this to demonstrate his justice, because in his forbearance he had left the sins com-

---

[a]24 Isaiah 52:5; Ezek. 36:22   [b]27 Or who, by means of a   [c]4 Psalm 51:4   [d]9 Or worse
[e]12 Psalms 14:1-3; 53:1-3; Eccles. 7:20   [f]13 Psalm 5:9   [g]13 Psalm 140:3   [h]14 Psalm 10:7
[i]17 Isaiah 59:7,8   [j]18 Psalm 36:1   [k]25 Or as the one who would turn aside his wrath, taking away sin

mitted beforehand unpunished— [26]he did it to demonstrate his justice at the present time, so as to be just and the one who justifies those who have faith in Jesus.

[27]Where, then, is boasting? It is excluded. On what principle? On that of observing the law? No, but on that of faith. [28]For we maintain that a man is justified by faith apart from observing the law. [29]Is God the God of Jews only? Is he not the God of Gentiles too? Yes, of Gentiles too, [30]since there is only one God, who will justify the circumcised by faith and the uncircumcised through that same faith. [31]Do we, then, nullify the law by this faith? Not at all! Rather, we uphold the law.

Abraham Justified by Faith

4 What then shall we say that Abraham, our forefather, discovered in this matter? [2]If, in fact, Abraham was justified by works, he had something to boast about—but not before God. [3]What does the Scripture say? "Abraham believed God, and it was credited to him as righteousness."[a]

[4]Now when a man works, his wages are not credited to him as a gift, but as an obligation. [5]However, to the man who does not work but trusts God who justifies the wicked, his faith is credited as righteousness. [6]David says the same thing when he speaks of the blessedness of the man to whom God credits righteousness apart from works:

[7]"Blessed are they
    whose transgressions are forgiven,
    whose sins are covered.
[8]Blessed is the man
    whose sin the Lord will never
        count against him."[b]

[9]Is this blessedness only for the circumcised, or also for the uncircumcised? We have been saying that Abraham's faith was credited to him as righteousness. [10]Under what circumstances was it credited? Was it after he was circumcised, or before? It was not after, but before! [11]And he received the sign of circumcision, a seal of the righteousness that he had by faith while he was still uncircumcised. So then, he is the father of all who believe but have not

been circumcised, in order that righteousness might be credited to them. [12]And he is also the father of the circumcised who not only are circumcised but who also walk in the footsteps of the faith that our father Abraham had before he was circumcised.

[13]It was not through law that Abraham and his offspring received the promise that he would be heir of the world, but through the righteousness that comes by faith. [14]For if those who live by law are heirs, faith has no value and the promise is worthless, [15]because law brings wrath. And where there is no law there is no transgression.

[16]Therefore, the promise comes by faith, so that it may be by grace and may be guaranteed to all Abraham's offspring—not only to those who are of the law but also to those who are of the faith of Abraham. He is the father of us all. [17]As it is written: "I have made you a father of many nations."[c] He is our father in the sight of God, in whom he believed—the God who gives life to the dead and calls things that are not as though they were.

[18]Against all hope, Abraham in hope believed and so became the father of many nations, just as it had been said to him, "So shall your offspring be."[d] [19]Without weakening in his faith, he faced the fact that his body was as good as dead—since he was about a hundred years old—and that Sarah's womb was also dead. [20]Yet he did not waver through unbelief regarding the promise of God, but was strengthened in his faith and gave glory to God, [21]being fully persuaded that God had power to do what he had promised. [22]This is why "it was credited to him as righteousness." [23]The words "it was credited to him" were written not for him alone, [24]but also for us, to whom God will credit righteousness—for us who believe in him who raised Jesus our Lord from the dead. [25]He was delivered over to death for our sins and was raised to life for our justification.

Peace and Joy

5 Therefore, since we have been justified through faith, we[e] have peace with God through our Lord Jesus Christ,

a3 Gen. 15:6; also in verse 22   b8 Psalm 32:1,2   c17 Gen. 17:5   d18 Gen. 15:5   e1 Or let us

²through whom we have gained access by faith into this grace in which we now stand. And we*a* rejoice in the hope of the glory of God. ³Not only so, but we*a* also rejoice in our sufferings, because we know that suffering produces perseverance; ⁴perseverance, character; and character, hope. ⁵And hope does not disappoint us, because God has poured out his love into our hearts by the Holy Spirit, whom he has given us.

⁶You see, at just the right time, when we were still powerless, Christ died for the ungodly. ⁷Very rarely will anyone die for a righteous man, though for a good man someone might possibly dare to die. ⁸But God demonstrates his own love for us in this: While we were still sinners, Christ died for us.

⁹Since we have now been justified by his blood, how much more shall we be saved from God's wrath through him! ¹⁰For if, when we were God's enemies, we were reconciled to him through the death of his Son, how much more, having been reconciled, shall we be saved through his life! ¹¹Not only is this so, but we also rejoice in God through our Lord Jesus Christ, through whom we have now received reconciliation.

Death Through Adam, Life Through Christ

¹²Therefore, just as sin entered the world through one man, and death through sin, and in this way death came to all men, because all sinned— ¹³for before the law was given, sin was in the world. But sin is not taken into account when there is no law. ¹⁴Nevertheless, death reigned from the time of Adam to the time of Moses, even over those who did not sin by breaking a command, as did Adam, who was a pattern of the one to come.

¹⁵But the gift is not like the trespass. For if the many died by the trespass of the one man, how much more did God's grace and the gift that came by the grace of the one man, Jesus Christ, overflow to the many! ¹⁶Again, the gift of God is not like the result of the one man's sin: The judgment followed one sin and brought condemnation, but the gift followed many trespasses and brought justification. ¹⁷For if, by the trespass of

the one man, death reigned through that one man, how much more will those who receive God's abundant provision of grace and of the gift of righteousness reign in life through the one man, Jesus Christ.

¹⁸Consequently, just as the result of one trespass was condemnation for all men, so also the result of one act of righteousness was justification that brings life for all men. ¹⁹For just as through the disobedience of the one man the many were made sinners, so also through the obedience of the one man the many will be made righteous.

²⁰The law was added so that the trespass might increase. But where sin increased, grace increased all the more, ²¹so that, just as sin reigned in death, so also grace might reign through righteousness to bring eternal life through Jesus Christ our Lord.

Dead to Sin, Alive in Christ

6 What shall we say, then? Shall we go on sinning so that grace may increase? ²By no means! We died to sin; how can we live in it any longer? ³Or don't you know that all of us who were baptized into Christ Jesus were baptized into his death? ⁴We were therefore buried with him through baptism into death in order that, just as Christ was raised from the dead through the glory of the Father, we too may live a new life.

⁵If we have been united with him like this in his death, we will certainly also be united with him in his resurrection. ⁶For we know that our old self was crucified with him so that the body of sin might be done away with,*b* that we should no longer be slaves to sin— ⁷because anyone who has died has been freed from sin.

⁸Now if we died with Christ, we believe that we will also live with him. ⁹For we know that since Christ was raised from the dead, he cannot die again; death no longer has mastery over him. ¹⁰The death he died, he died to sin once for all; but the life he lives, he lives to God.

¹¹In the same way, count yourselves dead to sin but alive to God in Christ Jesus. ¹²Therefore do not let sin reign in your mortal body so that you obey its evil desires. ¹³Do not offer the parts of

a2,3 Or *let us*   *b6* Or *be rendered powerless*

VERSE:
Romans 5:3

AUTHOR:
Joni Eareckson Tada

PASSAGE:
Romans 5:1–5

Threshing

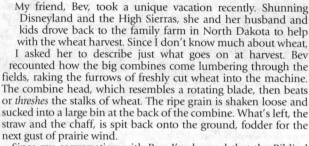

My friend, Bev, took a unique vacation recently. Shunning Disneyland and the High Sierras, she and her husband and kids drove back to the family farm in North Dakota to help with the wheat harvest. Since I don't know much about wheat, I asked her to describe just what goes on at harvest. Bev recounted how the big combines come lumbering through the fields, raking the furrows of freshly cut wheat into the machine. The combine head, which resembles a rotating blade, then beats or *threshes* the stalks of wheat. The ripe grain is shaken loose and sucked into a large bin at the back of the combine. What's left, the straw and the chaff, is spit back onto the ground, fodder for the next gust of prairie wind.

Since my conversation with Bev, I've learned that the Biblical word *tribulation* has its root meaning in the word "thresh." What I've just described to you, believe it or not, is a process that applies to believers as well as wheat. Have a few of those big combines lumbered across the field toward you within the past year . . . perhaps within the past *week*?

Tribulations. Those big unavoidable trials that threaten to cut you down and beat you back and forth. Being threshed is never easy. Never pleasant. But Paul in Romans 5 tells us that tribulation brings about perseverance and perseverance yields a crop of "character" (v. 4).

God is after something precious in your soul. Just like that North Dakota farmer, he's after a harvest . . . the golden grain of patience, perseverance and strong character. And how is that grain harvested? Only through threshing . . . through tribulation. The farmer doesn't thresh weeds, does he? He wouldn't waste his time. He threshes the wheat which yields grain from the chaff. That priceless, blessed grain.

I know it's hard to picture "results" or the "yield" when you're going through so much testing. It's hard to imagine how God might be pleased or how you might be benefited. But splendid spiritual grain is to be found only in the lives of those with noble character—character gleaned through threshing.

Somehow that makes the beating and the flailing of a threshing trial worthwhile.

ADDITIONAL SCRIPTURE READINGS:
2 Corinthians 12:7–10; 2 Timothy 1:7–12; James 1:3

Go to page 209 for your next devotional reading.

your body to sin, as instruments of wickedness, but rather offer yourselves to God, as those who have been brought from death to life; and offer the parts of your body to him as instruments of righteousness. [14]For sin shall not be your master, because you are not under law, but under grace.

Slaves to Righteousness

[15]What then? Shall we sin because we are not under law but under grace? By no means! [16]Don't you know that when you offer yourselves to someone to obey him as slaves, you are slaves to the one whom you obey—whether you are slaves to sin, which leads to death, or to obedience, which leads to righteousness? [17]But thanks be to God that, though you used to be slaves to sin, you wholeheartedly obeyed the form of teaching to which you were entrusted. [18]You have been set free from sin and have become slaves to righteousness.

[19]I put this in human terms because you are weak in your natural selves. Just as you used to offer the parts of your body in slavery to impurity and to ever-increasing wickedness, so now offer them in slavery to righteousness leading to holiness. [20]When you were slaves to sin, you were free from the control of righteousness. [21]What benefit did you reap at that time from the things you are now ashamed of? Those things result in death! [22]But now that you have been set free from sin and have become slaves to God, the benefit you reap leads to holiness, and the result is eternal life. [23]For the wages of sin is death, but the gift of God is eternal life in[a] Christ Jesus our Lord.

An Illustration From Marriage

7 Do you not know, brothers—for I am speaking to men who know the law—that the law has authority over a man only as long as he lives? [2]For example, by law a married woman is bound to her husband as long as he is alive, but if her husband dies, she is released from the law of marriage. [3]So then, if she marries another man while her husband is still alive, she is called an adulteress. But if her husband dies, she is released from that law and is not an adulteress, even though she marries another man.

[4]So, my brothers, you also died to the law through the body of Christ, that you might belong to another, to him who was raised from the dead, in order that we might bear fruit to God. [5]For when we were controlled by the sinful nature,[b] the sinful passions aroused by the law were at work in our bodies, so that we bore fruit for death. [6]But now, by dying to what once bound us, we have been released from the law so that we serve in the new way of the Spirit, and not in the old way of the written code.

Struggling With Sin

[7]What shall we say, then? Is the law sin? Certainly not! Indeed I would not have known what sin was except through the law. For I would not have known what coveting really was if the law had not said, "Do not covet."[c] [8]But sin, seizing the opportunity afforded by the commandment, produced in me every kind of covetous desire. For apart from law, sin is dead. [9]Once I was alive apart from law; but when the commandment came, sin sprang to life and I died. [10]I found that the very commandment that was intended to bring life actually brought death. [11]For sin, seizing the opportunity afforded by the commandment, deceived me, and through the commandment put me to death. [12]So then, the law is holy, and the commandment is holy, righteous and good.

[13]Did that which is good, then, become death to me? By no means! But in order that sin might be recognized as sin, it produced death in me through what was good, so that through the commandment sin might become utterly sinful.

[14]We know that the law is spiritual; but I am unspiritual, sold as a slave to sin. [15]I do not understand what I do. For what I want to do I do not do, but what I hate I do. [16]And if I do what I do not want to do, I agree that the law is good. [17]As it is, it is no longer I myself who do it, but it is sin living in me. [18]I know that nothing good lives in me, that is, in my sinful nature.[d] For I have the desire to do what is good, but I cannot carry it out. [19]For what I do is not the good I

---

[a]23 Or through flesh   [b]5 Or the flesh; also in verse 25   [c]7 Exodus 20:17; Deut. 5:21   [d]18 Or my

want to do; no, the evil I do not want to do—this I keep on doing. **20**Now if I do what I do not want to do, it is no longer I who do it, but it is sin living in me that does it.

21So I find this law at work: When I want to do good, evil is right there with me. **22**For in my inner being I delight in God's law; **23**but I see another law at work in the members of my body, waging war against the law of my mind and making me a prisoner of the law of sin at work within my members. **24**What a wretched man I am! Who will rescue me from this body of death? **25**Thanks be to God—through Jesus Christ our Lord!

So then, I myself in my mind am a slave to God's law, but in the sinful nature a slave to the law of sin.

Life Through the Spirit

8 Therefore, there is now no condemnation for those who are in Christ Jesus,*a* **2**because through Christ Jesus the law of the Spirit of life set me free from the law of sin and death. **3**For what the law was powerless to do in that it was weakened by the sinful nature,*b* God did by sending his own Son in the likeness of sinful man to be a sin offering.*c* And so he condemned sin in sinful man,*d* **4**in order that the righteous requirements of the law might be fully met in us, who do not live according to the sinful nature but according to the Spirit.

5Those who live according to the sinful nature have their minds set on what that nature desires; but those who live in accordance with the Spirit have their minds set on what the Spirit desires. **6**The mind of sinful man*e* is death, but the mind controlled by the Spirit is life and peace; **7**the sinful mind*f* is hostile to God. It does not submit to God's law, nor can it do so. **8**Those controlled by the sinful nature cannot please God.

9You, however, are controlled not by the sinful nature but by the Spirit, if the Spirit of God lives in you. And if anyone does not have the Spirit of Christ, he does not belong to Christ. **10**But if Christ is in you, your body is dead because of sin, yet your spirit is alive because of

righteousness. **11**And if the Spirit of him who raised Jesus from the dead is living in you, he who raised Christ from the dead will also give life to your mortal bodies through his Spirit, who lives in you.

12Therefore, brothers, we have an obligation—but it is not to the sinful nature, to live according to it. **13**For if you live according to the sinful nature, you will die; but if by the Spirit you put to death the misdeeds of the body, you will live, **14**because those who are led by the Spirit of God are sons of God. **15**For you did not receive a spirit that makes you a slave again to fear, but you received the Spirit of sonship.*g* And by him we cry, "*Abba,*h* Father." **16**The Spirit himself testifies with our spirit that we are God's children. **17**Now if we are children, then we are heirs—heirs of God and co-heirs with Christ, if indeed we share in his sufferings in order that we may also share in his glory.

Future Glory

18I consider that our present sufferings are not worth comparing with the glory that will be revealed in us. **19**The creation waits in eager expectation for the sons of God to be revealed. **20**For the creation was subjected to frustration, not by its own choice, but by the will of the one who subjected it, in hope **21**that*i* the creation itself will be liberated from its bondage to decay and brought into the glorious freedom of the children of God.

22We know that the whole creation has been groaning as in the pains of childbirth right up to the present time. **23**Not only so, but we ourselves, who have the firstfruits of the Spirit, groan inwardly as we wait eagerly for our adoption as sons, the redemption of our bodies. **24**For in this hope we were saved. But hope that is seen is no hope at all. Who hopes for what he already has? **25**But if we hope for what we do not yet have, we wait for it patiently.

26In the same way, the Spirit helps us in our weakness. We do not know what we ought to pray for, but the Spirit himself intercedes for us with groans that

---

a 1 Some later manuscripts *Jesus, who do not live according to the sinful nature but according to the Spirit,* *b 3* Or *the flesh;* also in verses 4, 5, 8, 9, 12 and 13 *c 3* Or *man, for sin* *d 3* Or *in the flesh* *e 6* Or *mind set on the flesh* *f 7* Or *The mind set on the flesh* *g 15* Or *adoption* *h 15* Aramaic for *Father* *i 20,21* Or *subjected it in hope. 21For*

words cannot express. ²⁷And he who searches our hearts knows the mind of the Spirit, because the Spirit intercedes for the saints in accordance with God's will.

More Than Conquerors

²⁸And we know that in all things God works for the good of those who love him,ᵃ whoᵇ have been called according to his purpose. ²⁹For those God foreknew he also predestined to be conformed to the likeness of his Son, that he might be the firstborn among many brothers. ³⁰And those he predestined, he also called; those he called, he also justified; those he justified, he also glorified.

³¹What, then, shall we say in response to this? If God is for us, who can be against us? ³²He who did not spare his own Son, but gave him up for us all—how will he not also, along with him, graciously give us all things? ³³Who will bring any charge against those whom God has chosen? It is God who justifies. ³⁴Who is he that condemns? Christ Jesus, who died—more

ᵃ28 Some manuscripts *And we know that all things work together for good to those who love God* *ᵇ28* Or *works together with those who love him to bring about what is good—with those who*

VERSE:	AUTHOR:	PASSAGE:
Romans 8:26	Anne Ortlund	Romans 8:26–27

Alongside Us

A mother once took her little boy to hear Paderewski, the great pianist. At the beginning there was simply a bare stage with a spotlight focused on the grand piano and bench. The mother and son had come half an hour early, and eventually the little boy got restless. Somehow, the mother got absorbed in reading the program, and when she finally looked up, his seat was empty! She looked everywhere around her, and he was nowhere to be seen.

Then—her heart was in her throat—suddenly she heard the sound of "Chopsticks." There he was on stage, in the spotlight, picking away on the long concert grand!

"Get him out of there!" came voices from the crowd.

"No!" cried a European accent from the wings, and the great Paderewski strode on stage. "Boy, keep going. I'll help you."

And he sat down on the bench next to the little fellow and began adding fabulous improvisations—chords, patterns, runs and additional melodies—as the two of them entranced the packed house with "Variations on Chopsticks"!

When we pick at our pathetic little prayers—when we live our pathetic little lives—suddenly we are not alone. Someone has come alongside us—none other than the Almighty Spirit of God!—and we have moved into a duet of greatness beyond our dreams.

ADDITIONAL SCRIPTURE READINGS:
1 Chronicles 29:10–12; John 15:4–5; 2 Corinthians 12:9–10

Go to page 211 for your next devotional reading.

than that, who was raised to life—is at the right hand of God and is also interceding for us. ³⁵Who shall separate us from the love of Christ? Shall trouble or hardship or persecution or famine or nakedness or danger or sword? ³⁶As it is written:

> "For your sake we face death all day
>   long;
>   we are considered as sheep to be
>   slaughtered."ᵃ

³⁷No, in all these things we are more than conquerors through him who loved us. ³⁸For I am convinced that neither death nor life, neither angels nor demons,ᵇ neither the present nor the future, nor any powers, ³⁹neither height nor depth, nor anything else in all creation, will be able to separate us from the love of God that is in Christ Jesus our Lord.

God's Sovereign Choice

9 I speak the truth in Christ—I am not lying, my conscience confirms it in the Holy Spirit— ²I have great sorrow and unceasing anguish in my heart. ³For I could wish that I myself were cursed and cut off from Christ for the sake of my brothers, those of my own race, ⁴the people of Israel. Theirs is the adoption as sons; theirs the divine glory, the covenants, the receiving of the law, the temple worship and the promises. ⁵Theirs are the patriarchs, and from them is traced the human ancestry of Christ, who is God over all, forever praised!ᶜ Amen.

⁶It is not as though God's word had failed. For not all who are descended from Israel are Israel. ⁷Nor because they are his descendants are they all Abraham's children. On the contrary, "It is through Isaac that your offspring will be reckoned."ᵈ ⁸In other words, it is not the natural children who are God's children, but it is the children of the promise who are regarded as Abraham's offspring. ⁹For this was how the promise was stated: "At the appointed time I will return, and Sarah will have a son."ᵉ

¹⁰Not only that, but Rebekah's children had one and the same father, our father Isaac. ¹¹Yet, before the twins were born or had done anything good or bad—in order that God's purpose in election might stand: ¹²not by works but by him who calls—she was told, "The older will serve the younger."ᶠ ¹³Just as it is written: "Jacob I loved, but Esau I hated."ᵍ

¹⁴What then shall we say? Is God unjust? Not at all! ¹⁵For he says to Moses,

> "I will have mercy on whom I have
>   mercy,
>   and I will have compassion on
>   whom I have compassion."ʰ

¹⁶It does not, therefore, depend on man's desire or effort, but on God's mercy. ¹⁷For the Scripture says to Pharaoh: "I raised you up for this very purpose, that I might display my power in you and that my name might be proclaimed in all the earth."ⁱ ¹⁸Therefore God has mercy on whom he wants to have mercy, and he hardens whom he wants to harden.

¹⁹One of you will say to me: "Then why does God still blame us? For who resists his will?" ²⁰But who are you, O man, to talk back to God? "Shall what is formed say to him who formed it, 'Why did you make me like this?'"ʲ ²¹Does not the potter have the right to make out of the same lump of clay some pottery for noble purposes and some for common use?

²²What if God, choosing to show his wrath and make his power known, bore with great patience the objects of his wrath—prepared for destruction? ²³What if he did this to make the riches of his glory known to the objects of his mercy, whom he prepared in advance for glory— ²⁴even us, whom he also called, not only from the Jews but also from the Gentiles? ²⁵As he says in Hosea:

> "I will call them 'my people' who are
>   not my people;
>   and I will call her 'my loved one'
>   who is not my loved one,"ᵏ

²⁶and,

> "It will happen that in the very place
>   where it was said to them,
>   'You are not my people,'

ᵃ36 Psalm 44:22   ᵇ38 Or *nor heavenly rulers*   ᶜ5 Or *Christ, who is over all. God be forever praised!* Or *Christ. God who is over all be forever praised!*   ᵈ7 Gen. 21:12   ᵉ9 Gen. 18:10,14   ᶠ12 Gen. 25:23   ᵍ13 Mal. 1:2,3   ʰ15 Exodus 33:19   ⁱ17 Exodus 9:16   ʲ20 Isaiah 29:16; 45:9   ᵏ25 Hosea 2:23

they will be called 'sons of the living God.' " [a]

27 Isaiah cries out concerning Israel:

"Though the number of the Israelites
    be like the sand by the sea,
    only the remnant will be saved.
28 For the Lord will carry out
    his sentence on earth with speed
        and finality." [b]

29 It is just as Isaiah said previously:

"Unless the Lord Almighty
    had left us descendants,
we would have become like Sodom,
    we would have been like
        Gomorrah." [c]

Israel's Unbelief

30 What then shall we say? That the Gentiles, who did not pursue righteousness, have obtained it, a righteousness that is by faith; 31 but Israel, who pursued a law of righteousness, has not attained it. 32 Why not? Because they pursued it not by faith but as if it were by works. They stumbled over the "stumbling stone." 33 As it is written:

"See, I lay in Zion a stone that
    causes men to stumble
and a rock that makes them fall,
    and the one who trusts in him will
        never be put to shame." [d]

10 Brothers, my heart's desire and prayer to God for the Israelites is that they may be saved. 2 For I can testify about them that they are zealous for God, but their zeal is not based on knowledge. 3 Since they did not know the righteousness that comes from God and sought to establish their own, they did not submit to God's righteousness. 4 Christ is the end of the law so that there may be righteousness for everyone who believes.

5 Moses describes in this way the righteousness that is by the law: "The man who does these things will live by them." [e] 6 But the righteousness that is

a26 Hosea 1:10   b28 Isaiah 10:22,23   c29 Isaiah 1:9   d33 Isaiah 8:14; 28:16
e5 Lev. 18:5

THURSDAY

VERSE:	AUTHOR:	PASSAGE:
Romans 9:21	Jan Johnson	Romans 9:1–29

Telling God What to Do

I've had great ideas over the years of how God could solve my problems. I listed solutions for him: Change my grouchy neighbor's heart; cure my friend of cancer; make my spouse as devoted as the ones described in the how-to books on marriage. Some of these things happened and some of them didn't. I felt that God disappointed me too many times.

I see now that I have been using prayer as a weapon of control. I have tried to control God—as if that were possible!

With a surrendered attitude, I can bring my requests to God in a different way. I'm still fervent and consistent, but I don't have to tell God what to do. Instead, I watch, wait and cooperate.

To accept God's sovereignty is one more necessary surrender.

ADDITIONAL SCRIPTURE READINGS:
2 Chronicles 7:14; Job 1:20–22; Mark 14:34–36

Go to page 214 for your next devotional reading.

by faith says: "Do not say in your heart, 'Who will ascend into heaven?'*a*" (that is, to bring Christ down) [7]"or 'Who will descend into the deep?'*b*" (that is, to bring Christ up from the dead). [8]But what does it say? "The word is near you; it is in your mouth and in your heart,"*c* that is, the word of faith we are proclaiming: [9]That if you confess with your mouth, "Jesus is Lord," and believe in your heart that God raised him from the dead, you will be saved. [10]For it is with your heart that you believe and are justified, and it is with your mouth that you confess and are saved. [11]As the Scripture says, "Anyone who trusts in him will never be put to shame."*d* [12]For there is no difference between Jew and Gentile—the same Lord is Lord of all and richly blesses all who call on him, [13]for, "Everyone who calls on the name of the Lord will be saved."*e*

[14]How, then, can they call on the one they have not believed in? And how can they believe in the one of whom they have not heard? And how can they hear without someone preaching to them? [15]And how can they preach unless they are sent? As it is written, "How beautiful are the feet of those who bring good news!"*f*

[16]But not all the Israelites accepted the good news. For Isaiah says, "Lord, who has believed our message?"*g* [17]Consequently, faith comes from hearing the message, and the message is heard through the word of Christ. [18]But I ask: Did they not hear? Of course they did:

"Their voice has gone out into all the earth,
    their words to the ends of the world."*h*

[19]Again I ask: Did Israel not understand? First, Moses says,

"I will make you envious by those who are not a nation;
    I will make you angry by a nation that has no understanding."*i*

[20]And Isaiah boldly says,

"I was found by those who did not seek me;

I revealed myself to those who did not ask for me."*j*

[21]But concerning Israel he says,

"All day long I have held out my hands
    to a disobedient and obstinate people."*k*

The Remnant of Israel

11 I ask then: Did God reject his people? By no means! I am an Israelite myself, a descendant of Abraham, from the tribe of Benjamin. [2]God did not reject his people, whom he foreknew. Don't you know what the Scripture says in the passage about Elijah—how he appealed to God against Israel: [3]"Lord, they have killed your prophets and torn down your altars; I am the only one left, and they are trying to kill me"*l*? [4]And what was God's answer to him? "I have reserved for myself seven thousand who have not bowed the knee to Baal."*m* [5]So too, at the present time there is a remnant chosen by grace. [6]And if by grace, then it is no longer by works; if it were, grace would no longer be grace.*n*

[7]What then? What Israel sought so earnestly it did not obtain, but the elect did. The others were hardened, [8]as it is written:

"God gave them a spirit of stupor,
    eyes so that they could not see
    and ears so that they could not hear,
to this very day."*o*

[9]And David says:

"May their table become a snare and a trap,
    a stumbling block and a retribution for them.
[10]May their eyes be darkened so they cannot see,
    and their backs be bent forever."*p*

Ingrafted Branches

[11]Again I ask: Did they stumble so as to fall beyond recovery? Not at all! Rather, because of their transgression, salvation has come to the Gentiles to make

---

a6 Deut. 30:12   *b7* Deut. 30:13   *c8* Deut. 30:14   *d11* Isaiah 28:16   *e13* Joel 2:32
f15 Isaiah 52:7   *g16* Isaiah 53:1   *h18* Psalm 19:4   *i19* Deut. 32:21   *j20* Isaiah 65:1
k21 Isaiah 65:2   *l3* 1 Kings 19:10,14   *m4* 1 Kings 19:18   *n6* Some manuscripts *by grace. But if by works, then it is no longer grace; if it were, grace would no longer be work.*   *o8* Deut. 29:4; Isaiah 29:10   *p10* Psalm 69:22,23

Israel envious. [12]But if their transgression means riches for the world, and their loss means riches for the Gentiles, how much greater riches will their fullness bring!

[13]I am talking to you Gentiles. Inasmuch as I am the apostle to the Gentiles, I make much of my ministry [14]in the hope that I may somehow arouse my own people to envy and save some of them. [15]For if their rejection is the reconciliation of the world, what will their acceptance be but life from the dead? [16]If the part of the dough offered as firstfruits is holy, then the whole batch is holy; if the root is holy, so are the branches.

[17]If some of the branches have been broken off, and you, though a wild olive shoot, have been grafted in among the others and now share in the nourishing sap from the olive root, [18]do not boast over those branches. If you do, consider this: You do not support the root, but the root supports you. [19]You will say then, "Branches were broken off so that I could be grafted in." [20]Granted. But they were broken off because of unbelief, and you stand by faith. Do not be arrogant, but be afraid. [21]For if God did not spare the natural branches, he will not spare you either.

[22]Consider therefore the kindness and sternness of God: sternness to those who fell, but kindness to you, provided that you continue in his kindness. Otherwise, you also will be cut off. [23]And if they do not persist in unbelief, they will be grafted in, for God is able to graft them in again. [24]After all, if you were cut out of an olive tree that is wild by nature, and contrary to nature were grafted into a cultivated olive tree, how much more readily will these, the natural branches, be grafted into their own olive tree!

All Israel Will Be Saved

[25]I do not want you to be ignorant of this mystery, brothers, so that you may not be conceited: Israel has experienced a hardening in part until the full number of the Gentiles has come in. [26]And so all Israel will be saved, as it is written:

"The deliverer will come from Zion;
   he will turn godlessness away
     from Jacob.
[27]And this is[a] my covenant with them
   when I take away their sins."[b]

[28]As far as the gospel is concerned, they are enemies on your account; but as far as election is concerned, they are loved on account of the patriarchs, [29]for God's gifts and his call are irrevocable. [30]Just as you who were at one time disobedient to God have now received mercy as a result of their disobedience, [31]so they too have now become disobedient in order that they too may now[c] receive mercy as a result of God's mercy to you. [32]For God has bound all men over to disobedience so that he may have mercy on them all.

Doxology

[33]Oh, the depth of the riches of the
   wisdom and[d] knowledge of
   God!
How unsearchable his judgments,
   and his paths beyond tracing out!
[34]"Who has known the mind of the
   Lord?
Or who has been his
   counselor?"[e]
[35]"Who has ever given to God,
   that God should repay him?"[f]
[36]For from him and through him and
   to him are all things.
To him be the glory forever!
   Amen.

Living Sacrifices

12 Therefore, I urge you, brothers, in view of God's mercy, to offer your bodies as living sacrifices, holy and pleasing to God—this is your spiritual[g] act of worship. [2]Do not conform any longer to the pattern of this world, but be transformed by the renewing of your mind. Then you will be able to test and approve what God's will is—his good, pleasing and perfect will.

[3]For by the grace given me I say to every one of you: Do not think of yourself more highly than you ought, but rather think of yourself with sober judgment, in accordance with the measure of faith God has given you. [4]Just as each of

[a]27 Or will be   [b]27 Isaiah 59:20,21; 27:9; Jer. 31:33,34   [c]31 Some manuscripts do not have now.   [d]33 Or riches and the wisdom and the   [e]34 Isaiah 40:13   [f]35 Job 41:11   [g]1 Or reasonable

us has one body with many members, and these members do not all have the same function, [5]so in Christ we who are many form one body, and each member belongs to all the others. [6]We have different gifts, according to the grace given us. If a man's gift is prophesying, let him use it in proportion to his[a] faith. [7]If it is serving, let him serve; if it is teaching, let him teach; [8]if it is encouraging, let him encourage; if it is contribut-ing to the needs of others, let him give generously; if it is leadership, let him govern diligently; if it is showing mercy, let him do it cheerfully.

Love

[9]Love must be sincere. Hate what is evil; cling to what is good. [10]Be devoted to one another in brotherly love. Honor one another above yourselves. [11]Never be lacking in zeal, but keep your spiritu-

[a]6 Or *in agreement with the*

FRIDAY

VERSE:
Romans 12:10

AUTHOR:
Anne Ortlund

PASSAGE:
Romans 12:9–16

The Bible's Kind of Love

The hunger for meaningful Christian togetherness has grown enormous in today's world. And I think the hunger is intensi-fied by the fact of our actual shyness, our inhibitions, our clumsiness in handling each other.

Think about your average married partners. In their minds are wild, wonderful dreams of how they'd like to treat each other, siz-zling straight off the pages of novels! But in reality? They'd be ter-rified of anything a cut above tepid and predictable.

Don't you think most of us Christians are the same? We love to talk and dream "relationships," but in actuality our own often seem to be self-serving, phony, disappointing or at least just unap-pealing.

We need to look hard at the Bible's kind of love.

It's realistic.
It's tender.
It's aggressive.
It's tenacious.
It's jealous.
It's forever.
It's emotional.
It's total.
It's unspeakably sweet.
It's tough!

God loves us with tough love . . . and that's the way we need to learn to love each other.

ADDITIONAL SCRIPTURE READINGS:
John 13:12–17; 1 Corinthians 13:4–9; Philippians 1:9–11

Go to page 216 for your next devotional reading.

al fervor, serving the Lord. [12]Be joyful in hope, patient in affliction, faithful in prayer. [13]Share with God's people who are in need. Practice hospitality.

[14]Bless those who persecute you; bless and do not curse. [15]Rejoice with those who rejoice; mourn with those who mourn. [16]Live in harmony with one another. Do not be proud, but be willing to associate with people of low position.[a] Do not be conceited.

[17]Do not repay anyone evil for evil. Be careful to do what is right in the eyes of everybody. [18]If it is possible, as far as it depends on you, live at peace with everyone. [19]Do not take revenge, my friends, but leave room for God's wrath, for it is written: "It is mine to avenge; I will repay,"[b] says the Lord. [20]On the contrary:

"If your enemy is hungry, feed him;
    if he is thirsty, give him something
    to drink.
In doing this, you will heap burning
    coals on his head."[c]

[21]Do not be overcome by evil, but overcome evil with good.

Submission to the Authorities

13 Everyone must submit himself to the governing authorities, for there is no authority except that which God has established. The authorities that exist have been established by God. [2]Consequently, he who rebels against the authority is rebelling against what God has instituted, and those who do so will bring judgment on themselves. [3]For rulers hold no terror for those who do right, but for those who do wrong. Do you want to be free from fear of the one in authority? Then do what is right and he will commend you. [4]For he is God's servant to do you good. But if you do wrong, be afraid, for he does not bear the sword for nothing. He is God's servant, an agent of wrath to bring punishment on the wrongdoer. [5]Therefore, it is necessary to submit to the authorities, not only because of possible punishment but also because of conscience.

[6]This is also why you pay taxes, for the authorities are God's servants, who give their full time to governing. [7]Give everyone what you owe him: If you owe taxes, pay taxes; if revenue, then revenue; if respect, then respect; if honor, then honor.

Love, for the Day Is Near

[8]Let no debt remain outstanding, except the continuing debt to love one another, for he who loves his fellowman has fulfilled the law. [9]The commandments, "Do not commit adultery," "Do not murder," "Do not steal," "Do not covet,"[d] and whatever other commandment there may be, are summed up in this one rule: "Love your neighbor as yourself."[e] [10]Love does no harm to its neighbor. Therefore love is the fulfillment of the law.

[11]And do this, understanding the present time. The hour has come for you to wake up from your slumber, because our salvation is nearer now than when we first believed. [12]The night is nearly over; the day is almost here. So let us put aside the deeds of darkness and put on the armor of light. [13]Let us behave decently, as in the daytime, not in orgies and drunkenness, not in sexual immorality and debauchery, not in dissension and jealousy. [14]Rather, clothe yourselves with the Lord Jesus Christ, and do not think about how to gratify the desires of the sinful nature.[f]

The Weak and the Strong

14 Accept him whose faith is weak, without passing judgment on disputable matters. [2]One man's faith allows him to eat everything, but another man, whose faith is weak, eats only vegetables. [3]The man who eats everything must not look down on him who does not, and the man who does not eat everything must not condemn the man who does, for God has accepted him. [4]Who are you to judge someone else's servant? To his own master he stands or falls. And he will stand, for the Lord is able to make him stand.

[5]One man considers one day more sacred than another; another man considers every day alike. Each one should be fully convinced in his own mind. [6]He who regards one day as special, does so to the Lord. He who eats meat, eats to the Lord, for he gives thanks to God; and he who abstains, does so to the

a16 Or willing to do menial work   b19 Deut. 32:35
Deut. 5:17-19,21   e9 Lev. 19:18   f14 Or the flesh   c20 Prov. 25:21,22   d9 Exodus 20:13-15,17

WEEKENDING

REALIZE

Jesus said that those who mourn, those who are poor and persecuted and have nothing are happy! How could he say such things? Only in light of another kingdom, another world, another way of seeing this world. He came to bring life—another kind of life altogether. And it is in terms of that life that we must learn to look at our suffering. I have found it possible, when I see suffering from that perspective, wholeheartedly to accept it. But it takes a steady fixing of my gaze on the cross.

If the cross is the place where the worst thing that could happen happened, it is also the place where the best thing that could happen happened. Ultimate hatred and ultimate love met on those two crosspieces of wood. Suffering and love were brought into harmony.

Elisabeth Elliot

REFLECT

Saturday: John 11:25–26
Sunday: Romans 5:1–11

Go to page 218 for your next devotional reading.

Lord and gives thanks to God. **7**For none of us lives to himself alone and none of us dies to himself alone. **8**If we live, we live to the Lord; and if we die, we die to the Lord. So, whether we live or die, we belong to the Lord.

9For this very reason, Christ died and returned to life so that he might be the Lord of both the dead and the living. **10**You, then, why do you judge your brother? Or why do you look down on your brother? For we will all stand before God's judgment seat. **11**It is written:

"'As surely as I live,' says the Lord,
  'every knee will bow before me;
    every tongue will confess to
      God.'" *a*

12So then, each of us will give an account of himself to God.

13Therefore let us stop passing judgment on one another. Instead, make up your mind not to put any stumbling block or obstacle in your brother's way. **14**As one who is in the Lord Jesus, I am fully convinced that no food *b* is unclean in itself. But if anyone regards something as unclean, then for him it is unclean. **15**If your brother is distressed because of what you eat, you are no longer acting in love. Do not by your eating destroy your brother for whom Christ died. **16**Do not allow what you consider good to be spoken of as evil. **17**For the kingdom of God is not a matter of eating and drinking, but of righteousness, peace and joy in the Holy Spirit, **18**because anyone who serves Christ in this way is pleasing to God and approved by men.

19Let us therefore make every effort to do what leads to peace and to mutual edification. **20**Do not destroy the work of God for the sake of food. All food is clean, but it is wrong for a man to eat anything that causes someone else to stumble. **21**It is better not to eat meat or drink wine or to do anything else that will cause your brother to fall.

22So whatever you believe about these things keep between yourself and God. Blessed is the man who does not condemn himself by what he approves. **23**But the man who has doubts is condemned if he eats, because his eating is not from faith; and everything that does not come from faith is sin.

15 We who are strong ought to bear with the failings of the weak and not to please ourselves. **2**Each of us should please his neighbor for his good, to build him up. **3**For even Christ did not please himself but, as it is written: "The insults of those who insult you have fallen on me." *c* **4**For everything that was written in the past was written to teach us, so that through endurance and the encouragement of the Scriptures we might have hope.

5May the God who gives endurance and encouragement give you a spirit of unity among yourselves as you follow Christ Jesus, **6**so that with one heart and mouth you may glorify the God and Father of our Lord Jesus Christ.

7Accept one another, then, just as Christ accepted you, in order to bring praise to God. **8**For I tell you that Christ has become a servant of the Jews *d* on behalf of God's truth, to confirm the promises made to the patriarchs **9**so that the Gentiles may glorify God for his mercy, as it is written:

"Therefore I will praise you among
    the Gentiles;
  I will sing hymns to your name." *e*

10Again, it says,

"Rejoice, O Gentiles, with his
    people." *f*

11And again,

"Praise the Lord, all you Gentiles,
  and sing praises to him, all you
    peoples." *g*

12And again, Isaiah says,

"The Root of Jesse will spring up,
  one who will arise to rule over the
    nations;
the Gentiles will hope in him." *h*

13May the God of hope fill you with all joy and peace as you trust in him, so that you may overflow with hope by the power of the Holy Spirit.

Paul the Minister to the Gentiles

14I myself am convinced, my brothers, that you yourselves are full of goodness,

---

a11 Isaiah 45:23 *b14* Or *that nothing* *c3* Psalm 69:9 *d8* Greek *circumcision*
e9 2 Samuel 22:50; Psalm 18:49 *f10* Deut. 32:43 *g11* Psalm 117:1 *h12* Isaiah 11:10

complete in knowledge and competent to instruct one another. ¹⁵I have written you quite boldly on some points, as if to remind you of them again, because of the grace God gave me ¹⁶to be a minister of Christ Jesus to the Gentiles with the priestly duty of proclaiming the gospel of God, so that the Gentiles might become an offering acceptable to God, sanctified by the Holy Spirit.

¹⁷Therefore I glory in Christ Jesus in my service to God. ¹⁸I will not venture to speak of anything except what Christ has accomplished through me in leading the Gentiles to obey God by what I have said and done— ¹⁹by the power of signs and miracles, through the power of the Spirit. So from Jerusalem all the way around to Illyricum, I have fully proclaimed the gospel of Christ. ²⁰It has always been my ambition to preach the gospel where Christ was not known, so that I would not be building on some-one else's foundation. ²¹Rather, as it is written:

> "Those who were not told about him
> will see,
> and those who have not heard will
> understand." ᵃ

²²This is why I have often been hindered from coming to you.

Paul's Plan to Visit Rome

²³But now that there is no more place for me to work in these regions, and since I have been longing for many years to see you, ²⁴I plan to do so when I go to Spain. I hope to visit you while passing through and to have you assist me on my journey there, after I have enjoyed your company for a while. ²⁵Now, however, I am on my way to Jerusalem in the service of the saints there. ²⁶For Macedonia and Achaia were pleased to make a contribution for the poor among

ᵃ21 Isaiah 52:15

⟨ MONDAY ⟩

VERSE:	AUTHOR:	PASSAGE:
Romans 14:19	Kathryn Hillen	Romans 14

Piece Work

She was just a dishwasher in a restaurant. Part of her duty was the shuttling of dirty dishes to the kitchen and the return of clean ones to the shelves under the counter. As she was busily arranging these, a man seated at the counter asked her, "Don't you wish your job was piecework?"

She looked up with a questioning look. The term was unfamiliar to her. Then, a jagged-toothed smile broke over her expressive face as she replied, "Brother, I'm makin' peace every chance I get! I'm doin' peace work!"

How wonderful! I wish people were more concerned with "peace work" than with "piecework." If he is our peace, then we should be peacemakers. An overemphasis on piecework to gain wages rather than peace work for an eternal inheritance can never bring satisfaction. Where is your life's emphasis?

ADDITIONAL SCRIPTURE READINGS:
Psalm 34:11–14; Matthew 5:9; Colossians 3:15

Go to page 220 for your next devotional reading.

the saints in Jerusalem. [27]They were pleased to do it, and indeed they owe it to them. For if the Gentiles have shared in the Jews' spiritual blessings, they owe it to the Jews to share with them their material blessings. [28]So after I have completed this task and have made sure that they have received this fruit, I will go to Spain and visit you on the way. [29]I know that when I come to you, I will come in the full measure of the blessing of Christ.

[30]I urge you, brothers, by our Lord Jesus Christ and by the love of the Spirit, to join me in my struggle by praying to God for me. [31]Pray that I may be rescued from the unbelievers in Judea and that my service in Jerusalem may be acceptable to the saints there, [32]so that by God's will I may come to you with joy and together with you be refreshed. [33]The God of peace be with you all. Amen.

Personal Greetings

16 I commend to you our sister Phoebe, a servant[a] of the church in Cenchrea. [2]I ask you to receive her in the Lord in a way worthy of the saints and to give her any help she may need from you, for she has been a great help to many people, including me.

[3]Greet Priscilla[b] and Aquila, my fellow workers in Christ Jesus. [4]They risked their lives for me. Not only I but all the churches of the Gentiles are grateful to them.

[5]Greet also the church that meets at their house.

Greet my dear friend Epenetus, who was the first convert to Christ in the province of Asia.

[6]Greet Mary, who worked very hard for you.

[7]Greet Andronicus and Junias, my relatives who have been in prison with me. They are outstanding among the apostles, and they were in Christ before I was.

[8]Greet Ampliatus, whom I love in the Lord.

[9]Greet Urbanus, our fellow worker in Christ, and my dear friend Stachys.

[10]Greet Apelles, tested and approved in Christ.

Greet those who belong to the household of Aristobulus.

[11]Greet Herodion, my relative.

Greet those in the household of Narcissus who are in the Lord.

[12]Greet Tryphena and Tryphosa, those women who work hard in the Lord.

Greet my dear friend Persis, another woman who has worked very hard in the Lord.

[13]Greet Rufus, chosen in the Lord, and his mother, who has been a mother to me, too.

[14]Greet Asyncritus, Phlegon, Hermes, Patrobas, Hermas and the brothers with them.

[15]Greet Philologus, Julia, Nereus and his sister, and Olympas and all the saints with them.

[16]Greet one another with a holy kiss.

All the churches of Christ send greetings.

[17]I urge you, brothers, to watch out for those who cause divisions and put obstacles in your way that are contrary to the teaching you have learned. Keep away from them. [18]For such people are not serving our Lord Christ, but their own appetites. By smooth talk and flattery they deceive the minds of naive people. [19]Everyone has heard about your obedience, so I am full of joy over you; but I want you to be wise about what is good, and innocent about what is evil.

[20]The God of peace will soon crush Satan under your feet.

The grace of our Lord Jesus be with you.

[21]Timothy, my fellow worker, sends his greetings to you, as do Lucius, Jason and Sosipater, my relatives.

[22]I, Tertius, who wrote down this letter, greet you in the Lord.

[23]Gaius, whose hospitality I and the whole church here enjoy, sends you his greetings.

Erastus, who is the city's director of public works, and our brother Quartus send you their greetings.[c]

[25]Now to him who is able to establish you by my gospel and the proclamation

---

[a]1 Or *deaconess*   [b]3 Greek *Prisca*, a variant of *Priscilla*   [c]23 Some manuscripts *their greetings.*
[24]*May the grace of our Lord Jesus Christ be with all of you. Amen.*

of Jesus Christ, according to the revelation of the mystery hidden for long ages past, [26]but now revealed and made known through the prophetic writings by the command of the eternal God, so that all nations might believe and obey him— [27]to the only wise God be glory forever through Jesus Christ! Amen.

TUESDAY

VERSE:
Romans 16:19

AUTHOR:
Cynthia Culp Allen

PASSAGE:
Romans 16:17–20

Obedient Children

Don't you love it when you ask one of your kids to do something and he or she actually does it?

If your children are like ours (normal), they have days when they just can't bring themselves to cheerfully obey.

Other days, it's "Okay, I'll do it. I'll be done playing in a minute."

Then there are those few glorious occasions when you call a request from the kitchen and you hear, "Yes, ma'am."

What? What did he say? Did I hear right? Yes, he said, "Yes, ma'am," and with such a sweet, respectful tone of voice. Oh, I love being a mother!

I especially love motherhood when my three-year-old is in this agreeable mood.

He'll answer me from his play with, "Yes, your Majesty!" (He heard that on a cartoon!)

Does my heavenly Father see me as an obedient child or as a willful one? When he asks me to do something, do I grumble and complain? Do I put off his request, making him wait on me?

There are times when I know God must smile because he asks me to do something and I answer immediately, "Yes, Sir." Or better yet, "Yes, your Majesty!" I am much happier when I respond to him that way.

ADDITIONAL SCRIPTURE READINGS:
Deuteronomy 30:1–6; 1 Samuel 15:22; Matthew 7:21

Go to page 222 for your next devotional reading.

PAUL *writes to the church he had started in Corinth (Acts 18:1–17), a church now struggling to live in obedience. In a letter marked by loving concern and a true pastor's heart, Paul addresses problems in Christian conduct and character. Look for practical information relevant to Christian living and relationships, as well as uplifting words about love (chapter 13) and the resurrection (chapter 15).*

1 CORINTHIANS

1 Paul, called to be an apostle of Christ Jesus by the will of God, and our brother Sosthenes,

²To the church of God in Corinth, to those sanctified in Christ Jesus and called to be holy, together with all those everywhere who call on the name of our Lord Jesus Christ—their Lord and ours:

³Grace and peace to you from God our Father and the Lord Jesus Christ.

Thanksgiving

⁴I always thank God for you because of his grace given you in Christ Jesus. ⁵For in him you have been enriched in every way—in all your speaking and in all your knowledge— ⁶because our testimony about Christ was confirmed in you. ⁷Therefore you do not lack any spiritual gift as you eagerly wait for our Lord Jesus Christ to be revealed. ⁸He will keep you strong to the end, so that you will be blameless on the day of our Lord Jesus Christ. ⁹God, who has called you into fellowship with his Son Jesus Christ our Lord, is faithful.

Divisions in the Church

¹⁰I appeal to you, brothers, in the name of our Lord Jesus Christ, that all of you agree with one another so that there may be no divisions among you and that you may be perfectly united in mind and thought. ¹¹My brothers, some from Chloe's household have informed me that there are quarrels among you. ¹²What I mean is this: One of you says, "I follow Paul"; another, "I follow Apol-

los"; another, "I follow Cephas[a]"; still another, "I follow Christ."

[13]Is Christ divided? Was Paul crucified for you? Were you baptized into[b] the name of Paul? [14]I am thankful that I did not baptize any of you except Crispus and Gaius, [15]so no one can say that you were baptized into my name. [16](Yes, I also baptized the household of Stephanas; beyond that, I don't remember if I baptized anyone else.) [17]For Christ did not send me to baptize, but to preach the gospel—not with words of human wisdom, lest the cross of Christ be emptied of its power.

Christ the Wisdom and Power of God

[18]For the message of the cross is foolishness to those who are perishing, but to us who are being saved it is the power of God. [19]For it is written:

> "I will destroy the wisdom of the
> wise;
> the intelligence of the intelligent I
> will frustrate."[c]

[20]Where is the wise man? Where is the scholar? Where is the philosopher of this age? Has not God made foolish the wisdom of the world? [21]For since in the wisdom of God the world through its wisdom did not know him, God was pleased through the foolishness of what was preached to save those who believe. [22]Jews demand miraculous signs and Greeks look for wisdom, [23]but we preach Christ crucified: a stumbling block to Jews and foolishness to Gentiles, [24]but to those whom God has called, both Jews and Greeks, Christ the power of God and the wisdom of God. [25]For the foolishness of God is wiser than man's wisdom, and the weakness

---

[a]12 That is, Peter　　　[b]13 Or *in*; also in verse 15　　　[c]19 Isaiah 29:14

WEDNESDAY

VERSE:	AUTHOR:	PASSAGE:
1 Corinthians 1:10	Babbie Mason	1 Corinthians 1:10–17

Together in Worship

Sometimes, I think one reason there's so much prejudice in the world is because we don't try to understand each other. And the church can be one of the most segregated institutions there is.

In the mid-eighties, I had church concerts canceled once the organizers learned I was black. Being black, you grow up with racism. You've cried enough already, so then you become angry. But I had to learn to forgive, because if I didn't, I knew it would be very easy for me to become bitter.

I try to do something positive to bring people together. Last November, I held two concerts in Mississippi, where black people and white people came together to worship. It was one of the most beautiful sights I've ever seen! We can learn so much from fellowshiping with each other. When different races come together, the worship experience takes on a whole new dimension. That's what I call the body of Christ personified.

ADDITIONAL SCRIPTURE READINGS:
Romans 12:9–16; Romans 15:5–6; Galatians 3:26–28

Go to page 224 for your next devotional reading.

of God is stronger than man's strength.

26Brothers, think of what you were when you were called. Not many of you were wise by human standards; not many were influential; not many were of noble birth. **27**But God chose the foolish things of the world to shame the wise; God chose the weak things of the world to shame the strong. **28**He chose the lowly things of this world and the despised things—and the things that are not—to nullify the things that are, **29**so that no one may boast before him. **30**It is because of him that you are in Christ Jesus, who has become for us wisdom from God—that is, our righteousness, holiness and redemption. **31**Therefore, as it is written: "Let him who boasts boast in the Lord."[a]

2 When I came to you, brothers, I did not come with eloquence or superior wisdom as I proclaimed to you the testimony about God.[b] **2**For I resolved to know nothing while I was with you except Jesus Christ and him crucified. **3**I came to you in weakness and fear, and with much trembling. **4**My message and my preaching were not with wise and persuasive words, but with a demonstration of the Spirit's power, **5**so that your faith might not rest on men's wisdom, but on God's power.

Wisdom From the Spirit

6We do, however, speak a message of wisdom among the mature, but not the wisdom of this age or of the rulers of this age, who are coming to nothing. **7**No, we speak of God's secret wisdom, a wisdom that has been hidden and that God destined for our glory before time began. **8**None of the rulers of this age understood it, for if they had, they would not have crucified the Lord of glory. **9**However, as it is written:

"No eye has seen,
   no ear has heard,
no mind has conceived
   what God has prepared for those
      who love him"[c]—

10but God has revealed it to us by his Spirit.

The Spirit searches all things, even the deep things of God. **11**For who among men knows the thoughts of a man ex-

cept the man's spirit within him? In the same way no one knows the thoughts of God except the Spirit of God. **12**We have not received the spirit of the world but the Spirit who is from God, that we may understand what God has freely given us. **13**This is what we speak, not in words taught us by human wisdom but in words taught by the Spirit, expressing spiritual truths in spiritual words.[d] **14**The man without the Spirit does not accept the things that come from the Spirit of God, for they are foolishness to him, and he cannot understand them, because they are spiritually discerned. **15**The spiritual man makes judgments about all things, but he himself is not subject to any man's judgment:

16"For who has known the mind of the
      Lord
   that he may instruct him?"[e]

But we have the mind of Christ.

On Divisions in the Church

3 Brothers, I could not address you as spiritual but as worldly—mere infants in Christ. **2**I gave you milk, not solid food, for you were not yet ready for it. Indeed, you are still not ready. **3**You are still worldly. For since there is jealousy and quarreling among you, are you not worldly? Are you not acting like mere men? **4**For when one says, "I follow Paul," and another, "I follow Apollos," are you not mere men?

5What, after all, is Apollos? And what is Paul? Only servants, through whom you came to believe—as the Lord has assigned to each his task. **6**I planted the seed, Apollos watered it, but God made it grow. **7**So neither he who plants nor he who waters is anything, but only God, who makes things grow. **8**The man who plants and the man who waters have one purpose, and each will be rewarded according to his own labor. **9**For we are God's fellow workers; you are God's field, God's building.

10By the grace God has given me, I laid a foundation as an expert builder, and someone else is building on it. But each one should be careful how he builds. **11**For no one can lay any foundation other than the one already laid, which is

---

[a]31 Jer. 9:24   [b]1 Some manuscripts *as I proclaimed to you God's mystery*   [c]9 Isaiah 64:4
[d]13 Or *Spirit, interpreting spiritual truths to spiritual men*   [e]16 Isaiah 40:13

Jesus Christ. ¹²If any man builds on this foundation using gold, silver, costly stones, wood, hay or straw, ¹³his work will be shown for what it is, because the Day will bring it to light. It will be revealed with fire, and the fire will test the quality of each man's work. ¹⁴If what he has built survives, he will receive his reward. ¹⁵If it is burned up, he will suffer loss; he himself will be saved, but only as one escaping through the flames.

¹⁶Don't you know that you yourselves are God's temple and that God's Spirit lives in you? ¹⁷If anyone destroys God's temple, God will destroy him; for God's temple is sacred, and you are that temple.

¹⁸Do not deceive yourselves. If any one of you thinks he is wise by the standards of this age, he should become a "fool" so that he may become wise. ¹⁹For the wisdom of this world is foolishness in God's sight. As it is written: "He catches the wise in their crafti-

---

THURSDAY

VERSE:	AUTHOR:	PASSAGE:
1 Corinthians 3:17	Barbara DeGrote-Sorensen and David Allen Sorensen	1 Corinthians 3

We're More Than Physical Creatures

Why are we in so much pain? Why don't we feel good?

Our bodies are created with a pace of their own. While disease, heredity or a physiological breakdown may throw that pace out of whack, more often than not our bodies are responding to the environment we create for them.

If we create a fast-talking, hard-working, overindulging, clock-watching environment for ourselves, overconsuming our physical and emotional resources, we can expect to feel lousy. It will become a way of life—the logical consequence. We are effectively choosing to create our pace of death.

Does making a space for God mean a healthy diet, exercise and good mental health? If we believe this is God's will for us, yes. "Do you not know that your body is a temple of the Holy Spirit, who is in you, whom you have received from God?" (1 Corinthians 6:19).

Are we out of pace with our eating habits? Was our last bit of exercise a walk to the [ice cream shop]? Do we find ourselves acting spiritually double-minded—saying we believe one thing about the care of our body and doing another?

Perhaps we need to move . . . beyond merely talking about the physical benefits of good diet, exercise and time management. Feeling good is not the ultimate objective; living in a healthy relationship with God is.

With that overarching goal we begin to make choices that help us stay in a right relationship with God. We can discover an environment in which worship and wellness become a way of life.

ADDITIONAL SCRIPTURE READINGS:
Psalm 37:1–5; Proverbs 23:1–8; Romans 8:11

Go to page 226 for your next devotional reading.

ness"[a]; [20]and again, "The Lord knows that the thoughts of the wise are futile."[b] [21]So then, no more boasting about men! All things are yours, [22]whether Paul or Apollos or Cephas[c] or the world or life or death or the present or the future—all are yours, [23]and you are of Christ, and Christ is of God.

Apostles of Christ

4 So then, men ought to regard us as servants of Christ and as those entrusted with the secret things of God. [2]Now it is required that those who have been given a trust must prove faithful. [3]I care very little if I am judged by you or by any human court; indeed, I do not even judge myself. [4]My conscience is clear, but that does not make me innocent. It is the Lord who judges me. [5]Therefore judge nothing before the appointed time; wait till the Lord comes. He will bring to light what is hidden in darkness and will expose the motives of men's hearts. At that time each will receive his praise from God.

[6]Now, brothers, I have applied these things to myself and Apollos for your benefit, so that you may learn from us the meaning of the saying, "Do not go beyond what is written." Then you will not take pride in one man over against another. [7]For who makes you different from anyone else? What do you have that you did not receive? And if you did receive it, why do you boast as though you did not?

[8]Already you have all you want! Already you have become rich! You have become kings—and that without us! How I wish that you really had become kings so that we might be kings with you! [9]For it seems to me that God has put us apostles on display at the end of the procession, like men condemned to die in the arena. We have been made a spectacle to the whole universe, to angels as well as to men. [10]We are fools for Christ, but you are so wise in Christ! We are weak, but you are strong! You are honored, we are dishonored! [11]To this very hour we go hungry and thirsty, we are in rags, we are brutally treated, we are homeless. [12]We work hard with our own hands. When we are cursed, we bless; when we are persecuted, we

endure it; [13]when we are slandered, we answer kindly. Up to this moment we have become the scum of the earth, the refuse of the world.

[14]I am not writing this to shame you, but to warn you, as my dear children. [15]Even though you have ten thousand guardians in Christ, you do not have many fathers, for in Christ Jesus I became your father through the gospel. [16]Therefore I urge you to imitate me. [17]For this reason I am sending to you Timothy, my son whom I love, who is faithful in the Lord. He will remind you of my way of life in Christ Jesus, which agrees with what I teach everywhere in every church.

[18]Some of you have become arrogant, as if I were not coming to you. [19]But I will come to you very soon, if the Lord is willing, and then I will find out not only how these arrogant people are talking, but what power they have. [20]For the kingdom of God is not a matter of talk but of power. [21]What do you prefer? Shall I come to you with a whip, or in love and with a gentle spirit?

Expel the Immoral Brother!

5 It is actually reported that there is sexual immorality among you, and of a kind that does not occur even among pagans: A man has his father's wife. [2]And you are proud! Shouldn't you rather have been filled with grief and have put out of your fellowship the man who did this? [3]Even though I am not physically present, I am with you in spirit. And I have already passed judgment on the one who did this, just as if I were present. [4]When you are assembled in the name of our Lord Jesus and I am with you in spirit, and the power of our Lord Jesus is present, [5]hand this man over to Satan, so that the sinful nature[d] may be destroyed and his spirit saved on the day of the Lord.

[6]Your boasting is not good. Don't you know that a little yeast works through the whole batch of dough? [7]Get rid of the old yeast that you may be a new batch without yeast—as you really are. For Christ, our Passover lamb, has been sacrificed. [8]Therefore let us keep the Festival, not with the old yeast, the yeast of malice and wickedness, but with

[a]19 Job 5:13   [b]20 Psalm 94:11   [c]22 That is, Peter   [d]5 Or that his body; or that the flesh

bread without yeast, the bread of sincerity and truth.

⁹I have written you in my letter not to associate with sexually immoral people— ¹⁰not at all meaning the people of this world who are immoral, or the greedy and swindlers, or idolaters. In that case you would have to leave this world. ¹¹But now I am writing you that you must not associate with anyone who calls himself a brother but is sexually immoral or greedy, an idolater or a

---

FRIDAY

VERSE:	AUTHOR:	PASSAGE:
1 Corinthians 4:7	Claire Cloninger	1 Corinthians 4

Learning to Share

Something begins to happen as we grow to acknowledge God's ownership and our "loanership" of our lives and possessions. Eventually we begin to ask, "Lord, how would you have me share this gift? What would you have me do with your money . . . your possessions . . . your home?" And once we've asked, we can be sure there will be an answer.

One early morning I got an SOS call from one of my prayer partners. She asked me if I would be willing to get together a box of clothes for a young woman who had fled from her abusive marriage without taking any of her own things. Picking through my closet, sensibly selecting the older garments and the things I was tired of, I was suddenly struck by the fact that every one of the dresses and skirts and blouses in my closet was nothing more than a loaner. None of them really belonged to me. Surely I could afford to be a little more extravagant with God's stuff.

I slowly and deliberately reached for my nearly new pink sweater and put it in the giveaway box. And that gave me another idea. Excitedly, I opened my dresser drawer and pulled out a new nightgown (with the tags still on it) and tucked that in also.

I guess I'll never know how that young, abused wife felt as she opened the box of clothes I sent her. But I know that while I was packing the clothes that morning, I experienced a wonderful surge of freedom and joy that far surpassed any excitement I could have felt buying something new for myself.

My very life is not my own. It is a "loaner," just like the car our dealership lets us drive while our car is in the shop. We can drive the loaner, but only so long as they say so. The dealership holds the papers on it; we don't.

The same thing is true of my life. God is the one who owns it, and he's just letting me "drive" it for him for awhile. My job is a loaner; my health, my talent and my ability to earn a living—all loaners! I can't boast about any of them.

ADDITIONAL SCRIPTURE READINGS:
Psalm 24:1; Proverbs 22:9; 1 Timothy 6:17–18; 1 Peter 4:8–11

Go to page 228 for your next devotional reading.

slanderer, a drunkard or a swindler. With such a man do not even eat.

[12]What business is it of mine to judge those outside the church? Are you not to judge those inside? [13]God will judge those outside. "Expel the wicked man from among you."[a]

Lawsuits Among Believers

6 If any of you has a dispute with another, dare he take it before the ungodly for judgment instead of before the saints? [2]Do you not know that the saints will judge the world? And if you are to judge the world, are you not competent to judge trivial cases? [3]Do you not know that we will judge angels? How much more the things of this life! [4]Therefore, if you have disputes about such matters, appoint as judges even men of little account in the church![b] [5]I say this to shame you. Is it possible that there is nobody among you wise enough to judge a dispute between believers? [6]But instead, one brother goes to law against another—and this in front of unbelievers!

[7]The very fact that you have lawsuits among you means you have been completely defeated already. Why not rather be wronged? Why not rather be cheated? [8]Instead, you yourselves cheat and do wrong, and you do this to your brothers.

[9]Do you not know that the wicked will not inherit the kingdom of God? Do not be deceived: Neither the sexually immoral nor idolaters nor adulterers nor male prostitutes nor homosexual offenders [10]nor thieves nor the greedy nor drunkards nor slanderers nor swindlers will inherit the kingdom of God. [11]And that is what some of you were. But you were washed, you were sanctified, you were justified in the name of the Lord Jesus Christ and by the Spirit of our God.

Sexual Immorality

[12]"Everything is permissible for me"—but not everything is beneficial. "Everything is permissible for me"—but I will not be mastered by anything. [13]"Food for the stomach and the stomach for food"—but God will destroy them both.

The body is not meant for sexual immorality, but for the Lord, and the Lord for the body. [14]By his power God raised the Lord from the dead, and he will raise us also. [15]Do you not know that your bodies are members of Christ himself? Shall I then take the members of Christ and unite them with a prostitute? Never! [16]Do you not know that he who unites himself with a prostitute is one with her in body? For it is said, "The two will become one flesh."[c] [17]But he who unites himself with the Lord is one with him in spirit.

[18]Flee from sexual immorality. All other sins a man commits are outside his body, but he who sins sexually sins against his own body. [19]Do you not know that your body is a temple of the Holy Spirit, who is in you, whom you have received from God? You are not your own; [20]you were bought at a price. Therefore honor God with your body.

Marriage

7 Now for the matters you wrote about: It is good for a man not to marry.[d] [2]But since there is so much immorality, each man should have his own wife, and each woman her own husband. [3]The husband should fulfill his marital duty to his wife, and likewise the wife to her husband. [4]The wife's body does not belong to her alone but also to her husband. In the same way, the husband's body does not belong to him alone but also to his wife. [5]Do not deprive each other except by mutual consent and for a time, so that you may devote yourselves to prayer. Then come together again so that Satan will not tempt you because of your lack of self-control. [6]I say this as a concession, not as a command. [7]I wish that all men were as I am. But each man has his own gift from God; one has this gift, another has that.

[8]Now to the unmarried and the widows I say: It is good for them to stay unmarried, as I am. [9]But if they cannot control themselves, they should marry, for it is better to marry than to burn with passion.

[10]To the married I give this command

---

[a]13 Deut. 17:7; 19:19; 21:21; 22:21,24; 24:7 account in the church?   [c]16 Gen. 2:24   [b]4 Or matters, do you appoint as judges men of little   [d]1 Or "It is good for a man not to have sexual relations with a woman."

WEEKENDING

REKINDLE

We have often said we would not choose to go back to some of those early days of our marriage. Too often, early love is a mirage built on daydreams. Love deepens with understanding, and varying viewpoints expand and challenge one another. So many things improve with age. A recent advertisement read, "Things of true quality need not fear the years. [Time] only improves them." So it is with marriage.

Those who abandon ship the first time it enters a storm miss the calm beyond. And the rougher the storms weathered together, the deeper and stronger real love grows.

Ruth Bell Graham

REVIEW

Saturday: Song of Songs 8:6–7
Sunday: 1 Corinthians 13

Go to page 229 for your next devotional reading.

(not I, but the Lord): A wife must not separate from her husband. **11**But if she does, she must remain unmarried or else be reconciled to her husband. And a husband must not divorce his wife.

12To the rest I say this (I, not the Lord): If any brother has a wife who is not a believer and she is willing to live with him, he must not divorce her. **13**And if a woman has a husband who is not a believer and he is willing to live with her, she must not divorce him. **14**For the unbelieving husband has been sanctified through his wife, and the unbelieving wife has been sanctified through her believing husband. Otherwise your children would be unclean, but as it is, they are holy.

15But if the unbeliever leaves, let him do so. A believing man or woman is not bound in such circumstances; God has called us to live in peace. **16**How do you know, wife, whether you will save your husband? Or, how do you know, husband, whether you will save your wife?

17Nevertheless, each one should retain the place in life that the Lord assigned to him and to which God has called him. This is the rule I lay down in all the churches. **18**Was a man already circumcised when he was called? He should not become uncircumcised. Was a man uncircumcised when he was called? He should not be circumcised. **19**Circumcision is nothing and uncircumcision is nothing. Keeping God's commands is what counts. **20**Each one should remain in the situation which he was in when God called him. **21**Were you a slave when you were called? Don't let it trouble you—although if you can gain your freedom, do so. **22**For he who was a slave when he was called by the Lord is the Lord's freedman; similarly, he who was a free man when he was called is Christ's slave. **23**You were bought at a price; do not become slaves of men. **24**Brothers, each man, as responsible to God, should remain in the situation God called him to.

25Now about virgins: I have no command from the Lord, but I give a judg-

---

⟨ MONDAY ⟩

VERSE:	AUTHOR:	PASSAGE:
1 Corinthians 7:17	Marjorie Holmes	1 Corinthians 7:1–17

A Psalm for Marriage

I am married, I am married, and my heart is glad.

I will give thanks unto the Lord for the love and protection of my husband. I will give thanks for the blessed protection and satisfaction of my home. I will give thanks that I have someone of my own to help and comfort and even to worry about, someone to encourage and to love.

My husband is beside me wherever I need to go. My husband is behind me supporting me in whatever I need to do. I need not face the world alone. I need not face my family alone.

I need face only myself and my God alone. And this is good. This is very good.

Whatever our differences, whatever our trials, I will give thanks unto the Lord for my husband and my marriage.

ADDITIONAL SCRIPTURE READINGS:
Genesis 2:18; Proverbs 5:18–20; Song of Songs 8:6–7

Go to page 234 for your next devotional reading.

ment as one who by the Lord's mercy is trustworthy. [26]Because of the present crisis, I think that it is good for you to remain as you are. [27]Are you married? Do not seek a divorce. Are you unmarried? Do not look for a wife. [28]But if you do marry, you have not sinned; and if a virgin marries, she has not sinned. But those who marry will face many troubles in this life, and I want to spare you this.

[29]What I mean, brothers, is that the time is short. From now on those who have wives should live as if they had none; [30]those who mourn, as if they did not; those who are happy, as if they were not; those who buy something, as if it were not theirs to keep; [31]those who use the things of the world, as if not engrossed in them. For this world in its present form is passing away.

[32]I would like you to be free from concern. An unmarried man is concerned about the Lord's affairs—how he can please the Lord. [33]But a married man is concerned about the affairs of this world—how he can please his wife—[34]and his interests are divided. An unmarried woman or virgin is concerned about the Lord's affairs: Her aim is to be devoted to the Lord in both body and spirit. But a married woman is concerned about the affairs of this world—how she can please her husband. [35]I am saying this for your own good, not to restrict you, but that you may live in a right way in undivided devotion to the Lord.

[36]If anyone thinks he is acting improperly toward the virgin he is engaged to, and if she is getting along in years and he feels he ought to marry, he should do as he wants. He is not sinning. They should get married. [37]But the man who has settled the matter in his own mind, who is under no compulsion but has control over his own will, and who has made up his mind not to marry the virgin—this man also does the right thing. [38]So then, he who marries the virgin does right, but he who does not marry her does even better.[a]

[39]A woman is bound to her husband as long as he lives. But if her husband dies, she is free to marry anyone she wishes, but he must belong to the Lord. [40]In my judgment, she is happier if she stays as she is—and I think that I too have the Spirit of God.

Food Sacrificed to Idols

8 Now about food sacrificed to idols: We know that we all possess knowledge.[b] Knowledge puffs up, but love builds up. [2]The man who thinks he knows something does not yet know as he ought to know. [3]But the man who loves God is known by God.

[4]So then, about eating food sacrificed to idols: We know that an idol is nothing at all in the world and that there is no God but one. [5]For even if there are so-called gods, whether in heaven or on earth (as indeed there are many "gods" and many "lords"), [6]yet for us there is but one God, the Father, from whom all things came and for whom we live; and there is but one Lord, Jesus Christ, through whom all things came and through whom we live.

[7]But not everyone knows this. Some people are still so accustomed to idols that when they eat such food they think of it as having been sacrificed to an idol, and since their conscience is weak, it is defiled. [8]But food does not bring us near to God; we are no worse if we do not eat, and no better if we do.

[9]Be careful, however, that the exercise of your freedom does not become a stumbling block to the weak. [10]For if anyone with a weak conscience sees you who have this knowledge eating in an idol's temple, won't he be emboldened to eat what has been sacrificed to idols? [11]So this weak brother, for whom Christ died, is destroyed by your knowledge. [12]When you sin against your brothers in this way and wound their weak conscience, you sin against Christ. [13]Therefore, if what I eat causes my brother to fall into sin, I will never eat meat again, so that I will not cause him to fall.

[a]36-38 Or [36]If anyone thinks he is not treating his daughter properly, and if she is getting along in years, and he feels she ought to marry, he should do as he wants. He is not sinning. He should let her get married. [37]But the man who has settled the matter in his own mind, who is under no compulsion but has control over his own will, and who has made up his mind to keep the virgin unmarried—this man also does the right thing. [38]So then, he who gives his virgin in marriage does right, but he who does not give her in marriage does even better.
[b]1 Or "We all possess knowledge," as you say

The Rights of an Apostle

9 Am I not free? Am I not an apostle? Have I not seen Jesus our Lord? Are you not the result of my work in the Lord? ²Even though I may not be an apostle to others, surely I am to you! For you are the seal of my apostleship in the Lord.

³This is my defense to those who sit in judgment on me. ⁴Don't we have the right to food and drink? ⁵Don't we have the right to take a believing wife along with us, as do the other apostles and the Lord's brothers and Cephas[a]? ⁶Or is it only I and Barnabas who must work for a living?

⁷Who serves as a soldier at his own expense? Who plants a vineyard and does not eat of its grapes? Who tends a flock and does not drink of the milk? ⁸Do I say this merely from a human point of view? Doesn't the Law say the same thing? ⁹For it is written in the Law of Moses: "Do not muzzle an ox while it is treading out the grain."[b] Is it about oxen that God is concerned? ¹⁰Surely he says this for us, doesn't he? Yes, this was written for us, because when the plowman plows and the thresher threshes, they ought to do so in the hope of sharing in the harvest. ¹¹If we have sown spiritual seed among you, is it too much if we reap a material harvest from you? ¹²If others have this right of support from you, shouldn't we have it all the more?

But we did not use this right. On the contrary, we put up with anything rather than hinder the gospel of Christ. ¹³Don't you know that those who work in the temple get their food from the temple, and those who serve at the altar share in what is offered on the altar? ¹⁴In the same way, the Lord has commanded that those who preach the gospel should receive their living from the gospel.

¹⁵But I have not used any of these rights. And I am not writing this in the hope that you will do such things for me. I would rather die than have anyone deprive me of this boast. ¹⁶Yet when I preach the gospel, I cannot boast, for I am compelled to preach. Woe to me if I do not preach the gospel! ¹⁷If I preach voluntarily, I have a reward; if not volun-

tarily, I am simply discharging the trust committed to me. ¹⁸What then is my reward? Just this: that in preaching the gospel I may offer it free of charge, and so not make use of my rights in preaching it.

¹⁹Though I am free and belong to no man, I make myself a slave to everyone, to win as many as possible. ²⁰To the Jews I became like a Jew, to win the Jews. To those under the law I became like one under the law (though I myself am not under the law), so as to win those under the law. ²¹To those not having the law I became like one not having the law (though I am not free from God's law but am under Christ's law), so as to win those not having the law. ²²To the weak I became weak, to win the weak. I have become all things to all men so that by all possible means I might save some. ²³I do all this for the sake of the gospel, that I may share in its blessings.

²⁴Do you not know that in a race all the runners run, but only one gets the prize? Run in such a way as to get the prize. ²⁵Everyone who competes in the games goes into strict training. They do it to get a crown that will not last; but we do it to get a crown that will last forever. ²⁶Therefore I do not run like a man running aimlessly; I do not fight like a man beating the air. ²⁷No, I beat my body and make it my slave so that after I have preached to others, I myself will not be disqualified for the prize.

Warnings From Israel's History

10 For I do not want you to be ignorant of the fact, brothers, that our forefathers were all under the cloud and that they all passed through the sea. ²They were all baptized into Moses in the cloud and in the sea. ³They all ate the same spiritual food ⁴and drank the same spiritual drink; for they drank from the spiritual rock that accompanied them, and that rock was Christ. ⁵Nevertheless, God was not pleased with most of them; their bodies were scattered over the desert.

⁶Now these things occurred as examples[c] to keep us from setting our hearts on evil things as they did. ⁷Do not be idolaters, as some of them were; as it is written: "The people sat down to eat and

---

[a]5 That is, Peter   [b]9 Deut. 25:4   [c]6 Or *types*; also in verse 11

drink and got up to indulge in pagan revelry."[a] [8]We should not commit sexual immorality, as some of them did—and in one day twenty-three thousand of them died. [9]We should not test the Lord, as some of them did—and were killed by snakes. [10]And do not grumble, as some of them did—and were killed by the destroying angel.

[11]These things happened to them as examples and were written down as warnings for us, on whom the fulfillment of the ages has come. [12]So, if you think you are standing firm, be careful that you don't fall! [13]No temptation has seized you except what is common to man. And God is faithful; he will not let you be tempted beyond what you can bear. But when you are tempted, he will also provide a way out so that you can stand up under it.

Idol Feasts and the Lord's Supper

[14]Therefore, my dear friends, flee from idolatry. [15]I speak to sensible people; judge for yourselves what I say. [16]Is not the cup of thanksgiving for which we give thanks a participation in the blood of Christ? And is not the bread that we break a participation in the body of Christ? [17]Because there is one loaf, we, who are many, are one body, for we all partake of the one loaf.

[18]Consider the people of Israel: Do not those who eat the sacrifices participate in the altar? [19]Do I mean then that a sacrifice offered to an idol is anything, or that an idol is anything? [20]No, but the sacrifices of pagans are offered to demons, not to God, and I do not want you to be participants with demons. [21]You cannot drink the cup of the Lord and the cup of demons too; you cannot have a part in both the Lord's table and the table of demons. [22]Are we trying to arouse the Lord's jealousy? Are we stronger than he?

The Believer's Freedom

[23]"Everything is permissible"—but not everything is beneficial. "Everything is permissible"—but not everything is constructive. [24]Nobody should seek his own good, but the good of others.

[25]Eat anything sold in the meat market without raising questions of conscience, [26]for, "The earth is the Lord's, and everything in it."[b]

[27]If some unbeliever invites you to a meal and you want to go, eat whatever is put before you without raising questions of conscience. [28]But if anyone says to you, "This has been offered in sacrifice," then do not eat it, both for the sake of the man who told you and for conscience' sake[c]— [29]the other man's conscience, I mean, not yours. For why should my freedom be judged by another's conscience? [30]If I take part in the meal with thankfulness, why am I denounced because of something I thank God for?

[31]So whether you eat or drink or whatever you do, do it all for the glory of God. [32]Do not cause anyone to stumble, whether Jews, Greeks or the church of God— [33]even as I try to please everybody in every way. For I am not seeking my own good but the good of many, so that they may be saved. [11][1]Follow my example, as I follow the example of Christ.

Propriety in Worship

[2]I praise you for remembering me in everything and for holding to the teachings,[d] just as I passed them on to you.

[3]Now I want you to realize that the head of every man is Christ, and the head of the woman is man, and the head of Christ is God. [4]Every man who prays or prophesies with his head covered dishonors his head. [5]And every woman who prays or prophesies with her head uncovered dishonors her head—it is just as though her head were shaved. [6]If a woman does not cover her head, she should have her hair cut off; and if it is a disgrace for a woman to have her hair cut or shaved off, she should cover her head. [7]A man ought not to cover his head,[e] since he is the image and glory of God; but the woman is the glory of man. [8]For man did not come from wom-

---

[a]7 Exodus 32:6　[b]26 Psalm 24:1　[c]28 Some manuscripts conscience' sake, for "the earth is the Lord's and everything in it"　[d]2 Or traditions　[e]4-7 Or [4]Every man who prays or prophesies with long hair dishonors his head. [5]And every woman who prays or prophesies with no covering of hair, on her head dishonors her head—she is just like one of the "shorn women." [6]If a woman has no covering, let her be for now with short hair, but since it is a disgrace for a woman to have her hair shorn or shaved, she should grow it again. [7]A man ought not to have long hair

an, but woman from man; [9]neither was man created for woman, but woman for man. [10]For this reason, and because of the angels, the woman ought to have a sign of authority on her head.

[11]In the Lord, however, woman is not independent of man, nor is man independent of woman. [12]For as woman came from man, so also man is born of woman. But everything comes from God. [13]Judge for yourselves: Is it proper for a woman to pray to God with her head uncovered? [14]Does not the very nature of things teach you that if a man has long hair, it is a disgrace to him, [15]but that if a woman has long hair, it is her glory? For long hair is given to her as a covering. [16]If anyone wants to be contentious about this, we have no other practice—nor do the churches of God.

The Lord's Supper

[17]In the following directives I have no praise for you, for your meetings do more harm than good. [18]In the first place, I hear that when you come together as a church, there are divisions among you, and to some extent I believe it. [19]No doubt there have to be differences among you to show which of you have God's approval. [20]When you come together, it is not the Lord's Supper you eat, [21]for as you eat, each of you goes ahead without waiting for anybody else. One remains hungry, another gets drunk. [22]Don't you have homes to eat and drink in? Or do you despise the church of God and humiliate those who have nothing? What shall I say to you? Shall I praise you for this? Certainly not!

[23]For I received from the Lord what I also passed on to you: The Lord Jesus, on the night he was betrayed, took bread, [24]and when he had given thanks, he broke it and said, "This is my body, which is for you; do this in remembrance of me." [25]In the same way, after supper he took the cup, saying, "This cup is the new covenant in my blood; do this, whenever you drink it, in remembrance of me." [26]For whenever you eat this bread and drink this cup, you proclaim the Lord's death until he comes.

[27]Therefore, whoever eats the bread or drinks the cup of the Lord in an unworthy manner will be guilty of sinning against the body and blood of the Lord.

[28]A man ought to examine himself before he eats of the bread and drinks of the cup. [29]For anyone who eats and drinks without recognizing the body of the Lord eats and drinks judgment on himself. [30]That is why many among you are weak and sick, and a number of you have fallen asleep. [31]But if we judged ourselves, we would not come under judgment. [32]When we are judged by the Lord, we are being disciplined so that we will not be condemned with the world.

[33]So then, my brothers, when you come together to eat, wait for each other. [34]If anyone is hungry, he should eat at home, so that when you meet together it may not result in judgment.

And when I come I will give further directions.

Spiritual Gifts

12 Now about spiritual gifts, brothers, I do not want you to be ignorant. [2]You know that when you were pagans, somehow or other you were influenced and led astray to mute idols. [3]Therefore I tell you that no one who is speaking by the Spirit of God says, "Jesus be cursed," and no one can say, "Jesus is Lord," except by the Holy Spirit.

[4]There are different kinds of gifts, but the same Spirit. [5]There are different kinds of service, but the same Lord. [6]There are different kinds of working, but the same God works all of them in all men.

[7]Now to each one the manifestation of the Spirit is given for the common good. [8]To one there is given through the Spirit the message of wisdom, to another the message of knowledge by means of the same Spirit, [9]to another faith by the same Spirit, to another gifts of healing by that one Spirit, [10]to another miraculous powers, to another prophecy, to another distinguishing between spirits, to another speaking in different kinds of tongues,[a] and to still another the interpretation of tongues.[a] [11]All these are the work of one and the same Spirit, and he gives them to each one, just as he determines.

One Body, Many Parts

[12]The body is a unit, though it is made up of many parts; and though all its

parts are many, they form one body. So it is with Christ. [13]For we were all baptized by[a] one Spirit into one body—whether Jews or Greeks, slave or free—and we were all given the one Spirit to drink.

[14]Now the body is not made up of one part but of many. [15]If the foot should say, "Because I am not a hand, I do not belong to the body," it would not for that reason cease to be part of the body. [16]And if the ear should say, "Because I am not an eye, I do not belong to the body," it would not for that reason cease to be part of the body. [17]If the whole body were an eye, where would the sense of hearing be? If the whole body were an ear, where would the sense of smell be? [18]But in fact God has arranged the parts in the body, every one of them, just as he wanted them to be. [19]If they were all one part, where would the body be? [20]As it is, there are many parts, but one body.

[21]The eye cannot say to the hand, "I don't need you!" And the head cannot say to the feet, "I don't need you!" [22]On the contrary, those parts of the body that seem to be weaker are indispensable, [23]and the parts that we think are less

[a]13 Or *with*; or *in*

TUESDAY

VERSE:	AUTHOR:	PASSAGE:
1 Corinthians 12:18	ann kiemel anderson	1 Corinthians 12

Being Our Best

for most of life, i think we fight God. we keep trying to show him what we were made for. we keep giving him better ideas. we keep working for something bigger & greater than anything he seems to have in mind. for many of us, by the time we are in mid-life, we feel we somehow have missed out on some of the great things we were born for. we fight with God over this.

God made me with special ideas in mind, but i wish i could have been in on the planning. my skin would have been more olive-colored, & flawless. my hair more coarse, with some curl in it. my shoulders broader. my eyes wider-spaced. i would have completely removed the lazy part in me that i have to fight with all the time.

i come to you, however, knowing God made me not to impress you. not to be on book covers. not to be an authority. not to be perfect or a genius. not to make a million dollars!

God made me to be uncomplicated in my faith. to watch children & kites & sunsets & rainbows & enjoy them. to take your hand regardless of who you are or how you look. to listen to you. to accept you right where you are. to love you unconditionally.

God made me to be real. to be honest. to be open. to never compare myself to you, but to strive to become my own best person. to have character & dignity.

ADDITIONAL SCRIPTURE READINGS:
Job 5:6–9; Psalm 8:4; Psalm 139; 1 Peter 1:22–25

Go to page 236 for your next devotional reading.

honorable we treat with special honor. And the parts that are unpresentable are treated with special modesty, **24**while our presentable parts need no special treatment. But God has combined the members of the body and has given greater honor to the parts that lacked it, **25**so that there should be no division in the body, but that its parts should have equal concern for each other. **26**If one part suffers, every part suffers with it; if one part is honored, every part rejoices with it.

27Now you are the body of Christ, and each one of you is a part of it. **28**And in the church God has appointed first of all apostles, second prophets, third teachers, then workers of miracles, also those having gifts of healing, those able to help others, those with gifts of administration, and those speaking in different kinds of tongues. **29**Are all apostles? Are all prophets? Are all teachers? Do all work miracles? **30**Do all have gifts of healing? Do all speak in tongues*a*? Do all interpret? **31**But eagerly desire*b* the greater gifts.

Love

And now I will show you the most excellent way.

13 If I speak in the tongues*c* of men and of angels, but have not love, I am only a resounding gong or a clanging cymbal. **2**If I have the gift of prophecy and can fathom all mysteries and all knowledge, and if I have a faith that can move mountains, but have not love, I am nothing. **3**If I give all I possess to the poor and surrender my body to the flames,*d* but have not love, I gain nothing.

4Love is patient, love is kind. It does not envy, it does not boast, it is not proud. **5**It is not rude, it is not self-seeking, it is not easily angered, it keeps no record of wrongs. **6**Love does not delight in evil but rejoices with the truth. **7**It always protects, always trusts, always hopes, always perseveres.

8Love never fails. But where there are prophecies, they will cease; where there are tongues, they will be stilled; where there is knowledge, it will pass away.

9For we know in part and we prophesy in part, **10**but when perfection comes, the imperfect disappears. **11**When I was a child, I talked like a child, I thought like a child, I reasoned like a child. When I became a man, I put childish ways behind me. **12**Now we see but a poor reflection as in a mirror; then we shall see face to face. Now I know in part; then I shall know fully, even as I am fully known.

13And now these three remain: faith, hope and love. But the greatest of these is love.

Gifts of Prophecy and Tongues

14 Follow the way of love and eagerly desire spiritual gifts, especially the gift of prophecy. **2**For anyone who speaks in a tongue*e* does not speak to men but to God. Indeed, no one understands him; he utters mysteries with his spirit.*f* **3**But everyone who prophesies speaks to men for their strengthening, encouragement and comfort. **4**He who speaks in a tongue edifies himself, but he who prophesies edifies the church. **5**I would like every one of you to speak in tongues,*g* but I would rather have you prophesy. He who prophesies is greater than one who speaks in tongues,*g* unless he interprets, so that the church may be edified.

6Now, brothers, if I come to you and speak in tongues, what good will I be to you, unless I bring you some revelation or knowledge or prophecy or word of instruction? **7**Even in the case of lifeless things that make sounds, such as the flute or harp, how will anyone know what tune is being played unless there is a distinction in the notes? **8**Again, if the trumpet does not sound a clear call, who will get ready for battle? **9**So it is with you. Unless you speak intelligible words with your tongue, how will anyone know what you are saying? You will just be speaking into the air. **10**Undoubtedly there are all sorts of languages in the world, yet none of them is without meaning. **11**If then I do not grasp the meaning of what someone is saying, I am a foreigner to the speaker, and he is a foreigner to me. **12**So it is with you.

---

a30 Or *other languages*   *b31* Or *But you are eagerly desiring*   *c1* Or *languages*   *d3* Some early manuscripts *body that I may boast*   *e2* Or *another language*; also in verses 4, 13, 14, 19, 26 and 27   *f2* Or *by the Spirit*   *g5* Or *other languages*; also in verses 6, 18, 22, 23 and 39

Since you are eager to have spiritual gifts, try to excel in gifts that build up the church.

¹³For this reason anyone who speaks in a tongue should pray that he may interpret what he says. ¹⁴For if I pray in a tongue, my spirit prays, but my mind is unfruitful. ¹⁵So what shall I do? I will pray with my spirit, but I will also pray with my mind; I will sing with my spirit, but I will also sing with my mind. ¹⁶If you are praising God with your spirit, how can one who finds himself among those who do not understand*

say "Amen" to your thanksgiving, since he does not know what you are saying? ¹⁷You may be giving thanks well enough, but the other man is not edified.

¹⁸I thank God that I speak in tongues more than all of you. ¹⁹But in the church I would rather speak five intelligible words to instruct others than ten thousand words in a tongue.

²⁰Brothers, stop thinking like children. In regard to evil be infants, but in your thinking be adults. ²¹In the Law it is written:

ᵃ16 Or among the inquirers

WEDNESDAY

VERSE: AUTHOR: PASSAGE:
1 Corinthians 13:6   Shirley Pope Waite   1 Corinthians 13:4–6

Disarming Love

Virginia Randolph was a pioneer in black education. She began teaching in a southern rural school in 1892. As she tried to instill high ethical standards along with the "Three *R*s," many parents resented it.

In fact, one mother bragged about whipping every teacher at that school. She vowed Miss Randolph would be next.

One day, Virginia saw the woman standing on the porch with a long stick. She'd just finished reading 1 Corinthians 13 to her class.

"Children," she began, keeping her voice steady, "this morning I'm going to pray, 'Lord, have mercy on the dear mother that came to school.' So glad to see you, dear mother." Virginia then led the boys and girls in singing, "I Need Thee Every Hour."

She continued, "Now, students, this has been the first mother to visit school. She has two lovely children, and you know the hand that rocks the cradle rules the world. Don't you feel proud? I'll ask her to speak to us."

That mother was so touched, her eyes filled with tears.

"I came for one thing and found another," she said. "I will never disturb the classroom again." She kept her promise and became a willing school worker.

Isn't it amazing how love disarms hostility? It was true in 1892 and is just as true [more than] one hundred years later.

ADDITIONAL SCRIPTURE READINGS:
Proverbs 10:12; Romans 12:18–21; 2 Corinthians 5:18–19

Go to page 239 for your next devotional reading.

"Through men of strange tongues
and through the lips of foreigners
I will speak to this people,
but even then they will not listen
to me,"[a]
says the Lord.

22Tongues, then, are a sign, not for believers but for unbelievers; prophecy, however, is for believers, not for unbelievers. 23So if the whole church comes together and everyone speaks in tongues, and some who do not understand[b] or some unbelievers come in, will they not say that you are out of your mind? 24But if an unbeliever or someone who does not understand[c] comes in while everybody is prophesying, he will be convinced by all that he is a sinner and will be judged by all, 25and the secrets of his heart will be laid bare. So he will fall down and worship God, exclaiming, "God is really among you!"

Orderly Worship

26What then shall we say, brothers? When you come together, everyone has a hymn, or a word of instruction, a revelation, a tongue or an interpretation. All of these must be done for the strengthening of the church. 27If anyone speaks in a tongue, two—or at the most three—should speak, one at a time, and someone must interpret. 28If there is no interpreter, the speaker should keep quiet in the church and speak to himself and God.

29Two or three prophets should speak, and the others should weigh carefully what is said. 30And if a revelation comes to someone who is sitting down, the first speaker should stop. 31For you can all prophesy in turn so that everyone may be instructed and encouraged. 32The spirits of prophets are subject to the control of prophets. 33For God is not a God of disorder but of peace.

As in all the congregations of the saints, 34women should remain silent in the churches. They are not allowed to speak, but must be in submission, as the Law says. 35If they want to inquire about something, they should ask their own husbands at home; for it is disgraceful for a woman to speak in the church.

36Did the word of God originate with you? Or are you the only people it has reached? 37If anybody thinks he is a prophet or spiritually gifted, let him acknowledge that what I am writing to you is the Lord's command. 38If he ignores this, he himself will be ignored.[d]

39Therefore, my brothers, be eager to prophesy, and do not forbid speaking in tongues. 40But everything should be done in a fitting and orderly way.

The Resurrection of Christ

15 Now, brothers, I want to remind you of the gospel I preached to you, which you received and on which you have taken your stand. 2By this gospel you are saved, if you hold firmly to the word I preached to you. Otherwise, you have believed in vain.

3For what I received I passed on to you as of first importance[e]: that Christ died for our sins according to the Scriptures, 4that he was buried, that he was raised on the third day according to the Scriptures, 5and that he appeared to Peter,[f] and then to the Twelve. 6After that, he appeared to more than five hundred of the brothers at the same time, most of whom are still living, though some have fallen asleep. 7Then he appeared to James, then to all the apostles, 8and last of all he appeared to me also, as to one abnormally born.

9For I am the least of the apostles and do not even deserve to be called an apostle, because I persecuted the church of God. 10But by the grace of God I am what I am, and his grace to me was not without effect. No, I worked harder than all of them—yet not I, but the grace of God that was with me. 11Whether, then, it was I or they, this is what we preach, and this is what you believed.

The Resurrection of the Dead

12But if it is preached that Christ has been raised from the dead, how can some of you say that there is no resurrection of the dead? 13If there is no resurrection of the dead, then not even Christ has been raised. 14And if Christ has not been raised, our preaching is useless and so is your faith. 15More

---

*a*21 Isaiah 28:11,12   *b*23 Or *some inquirers*   *c*24 Or *or some inquirer*   *d*38 Some manuscripts
If he is ignorant of this, let him be ignorant   *e*3 Or *you at the first*   *f*5 Greek *Cephas*

than that, we are then found to be false witnesses about God, for we have testified about God that he raised Christ from the dead. But he did not raise him if in fact the dead are not raised. ¹⁶For if the dead are not raised, then Christ has not been raised either. ¹⁷And if Christ has not been raised, your faith is futile; you are still in your sins. ¹⁸Then those also who have fallen asleep in Christ are lost. ¹⁹If only for this life we have hope in Christ, we are to be pitied more than all men.

²⁰But Christ has indeed been raised from the dead, the firstfruits of those who have fallen asleep. ²¹For since death came through a man, the resurrection of the dead comes also through a man. ²²For as in Adam all die, so in Christ all will be made alive. ²³But each in his own turn: Christ, the firstfruits; then, when he comes, those who belong to him. ²⁴Then the end will come, when he hands over the kingdom to God the Father after he has destroyed all dominion, authority and power. ²⁵For he must reign until he has put all his enemies under his feet. ²⁶The last enemy to be destroyed is death. ²⁷For he "has put everything under his feet." *a* Now when it says that "everything" has been put under him, it is clear that this does not include God himself, who put everything under Christ. ²⁸When he has done this, then the Son himself will be made subject to him who put everything under him, so that God may be all in all.

²⁹Now if there is no resurrection, what will those do who are baptized for the dead? If the dead are not raised at all, why are people baptized for them? ³⁰And as for us, why do we endanger ourselves every hour? ³¹I die every day— I mean that, brothers—just as surely as I glory over you in Christ Jesus our Lord. ³²If I fought wild beasts in Ephesus for merely human reasons, what have I gained? If the dead are not raised,

"Let us eat and drink,
    for tomorrow we die." *b*

³³Do not be misled: "Bad company corrupts good character." ³⁴Come back to your senses as you ought, and stop sinning; for there are some who are ignorant of God—I say this to your shame.

The Resurrection Body

³⁵But someone may ask, "How are the dead raised? With what kind of body will they come?" ³⁶How foolish! What you sow does not come to life unless it dies. ³⁷When you sow, you do not plant the body that will be, but just a seed, perhaps of wheat or of something else. ³⁸But God gives it a body as he has determined, and to each kind of seed he gives its own body. ³⁹All flesh is not the same: Men have one kind of flesh, animals have another, birds another and fish another. ⁴⁰There are also heavenly bodies and there are earthly bodies; but the splendor of the heavenly bodies is one kind, and the splendor of the earthly bodies is another. ⁴¹The sun has one kind of splendor, the moon another and the stars another; and star differs from star in splendor.

⁴²So will it be with the resurrection of the dead. The body that is sown is perishable, it is raised imperishable; ⁴³it is sown in dishonor, it is raised in glory; it is sown in weakness, it is raised in power; ⁴⁴it is sown a natural body, it is raised a spiritual body.

If there is a natural body, there is also a spiritual body. ⁴⁵So it is written: "The first man Adam became a living being" *c*; the last Adam, a life-giving spirit. ⁴⁶The spiritual did not come first, but the natural, and after that the spiritual. ⁴⁷The first man was of the dust of the earth, the second man from heaven. ⁴⁸As was the earthly man, so are those who are of the earth; and as is the man from heaven, so also are those who are of heaven. ⁴⁹And just as we have borne the likeness of the earthly man, so shall we*d* bear the likeness of the man from heaven.

⁵⁰I declare to you, brothers, that flesh and blood cannot inherit the kingdom of God, nor does the perishable inherit the imperishable. ⁵¹Listen, I tell you a mystery: We will not all sleep, but we will all be changed— ⁵²in a flash, in the twinkling of an eye, at the last trumpet. For the trumpet will sound, the dead will be raised imperishable, and we will be changed. ⁵³For the perishable must clothe itself with the imperishable, and the mortal with immortality. ⁵⁴When the perishable has been clothed with the

a27 Psalm 8:6   *b32* Isaiah 22:13   *c45* Gen. 2:7   *d49* Some early manuscripts *so let us*

imperishable, and the mortal with immortality, then the saying that is written will come true: "Death has been swallowed up in victory."[a]

⁵⁵"Where, O death, is your victory?
    Where, O death, is your sting?"[b]

⁵⁶The sting of death is sin, and the power of sin is the law. ⁵⁷But thanks be to God! He gives us the victory through our Lord Jesus Christ.

⁵⁸Therefore, my dear brothers, stand firm. Let nothing move you. Always give yourselves fully to the work of the Lord, because you know that your labor in the Lord is not in vain.

The Collection for God's People

16 Now about the collection for God's people: Do what I told the Galatian churches to do. ²On the first day of every week, each one of you should set aside a sum of money in keeping with his income, saving it up, so that when I come no collections will have to be made. ³Then, when I arrive, I will give letters of introduction to the men you approve and send them with

---

a54 Isaiah 25:8   *b55* Hosea 13:14

‹ THURSDAY ›

VERSE:	AUTHOR:	PASSAGE:
1 Corinthians 15:57	Catherine Doherty	1 Corinthians 15:35–58

Christ Is Risen!

Alleluia! Christ is risen! Verily he is risen! Because he has, darkness has been conquered by light, death by life and hate by love.

Now the world lives in the resurrected Christ. Whether men and women know it or not, the world has changed; it and the cosmos are now living, existing in the Lord of history, of eternity, of time and of love. And not only the church is on a pilgrimage toward the . . . second coming, but so are all men and women and all the world, and all that surrounds God's world.

The resurrection of Christ brought love among us, and it is the very principle of our existence. If we recognize this, we can transform the world. It's such a simple thing that requires only faith in the resurrected Christ. It is so simple, it is overlooked by many who write heavy treatises about abolishing poverty and stopping wars. But human beings are not satiated with bread alone. They desperately need love, almost more than the air they breathe.

Why not start the fire of love by loving—one by one—all whom we meet and deal with during the day? Then indeed the resurrection of Christ will become meaningful and our pilgrimage to him will become joyous and we will restore the world to him, and we will eat the fruit of love daily—peace and happiness, the like of which we never dreamed existed. Let's begin now.

Alleluia! Christ is risen! Verily he is risen!

ADDITIONAL SCRIPTURE READINGS:
Romans 5:9–18; Ephesians 1:15–20; 1 Peter 1:3

Go to page 242 for your next devotional reading.

your gift to Jerusalem. [4]If it seems advisable for me to go also, they will accompany me.

Personal Requests

[5]After I go through Macedonia, I will come to you—for I will be going through Macedonia. [6]Perhaps I will stay with you awhile, or even spend the winter, so that you can help me on my journey, wherever I go. [7]I do not want to see you now and make only a passing visit; I hope to spend some time with you, if the Lord permits. [8]But I will stay on at Ephesus until Pentecost, [9]because a great door for effective work has opened to me, and there are many who oppose me.

[10]If Timothy comes, see to it that he has nothing to fear while he is with you, for he is carrying on the work of the Lord, just as I am. [11]No one, then, should refuse to accept him. Send him on his way in peace so that he may return to me. I am expecting him along with the brothers.

[12]Now about our brother Apollos: I strongly urged him to go to you with the brothers. He was quite unwilling to go now, but he will go when he has the opportunity.

[13]Be on your guard; stand firm in the faith; be men of courage; be strong. [14]Do everything in love.

[15]You know that the household of Stephanas were the first converts in Achaia, and they have devoted themselves to the service of the saints. I urge you, brothers, [16]to submit to such as these and to everyone who joins in the work, and labors at it. [17]I was glad when Stephanas, Fortunatus and Achaicus arrived, because they have supplied what was lacking from you. [18]For they refreshed my spirit and yours also. Such men deserve recognition.

Final Greetings

[19]The churches in the province of Asia send you greetings. Aquila and Priscilla[a] greet you warmly in the Lord, and so does the church that meets at their house. [20]All the brothers here send you greetings. Greet one another with a holy kiss.

[21]I, Paul, write this greeting in my own hand.

[22]If anyone does not love the Lord—a curse be on him. Come, O Lord[b]!

[23]The grace of the Lord Jesus be with you.

[24]My love to all of you in Christ Jesus. Amen.[c]

---

[a]19   Greek *Prisca*, a variant of *Priscilla*   [b]22   In Aramaic the expression *Come, O Lord* is *Marana tha.*
[c]24   Some manuscripts do not have *Amen.*

PAUL *writes this second letter to the Corinthians a few months after the first letter. The divisions and problems addressed in 1 Corinthians are still present in the church, and false teachers are challenging Paul's integrity and his authority as an apostle. With passionate emotion, Paul moves back and forth between despair and ecstatic joy. Watch for practical advice on resolving conflict within the church and providing financial support for the church and for the poor.*

2 CORINTHIANS

1 Paul, an apostle of Christ Jesus by the will of God, and Timothy our brother,

To the church of God in Corinth, together with all the saints throughout Achaia:

²Grace and peace to you from God our Father and the Lord Jesus Christ.

The God of All Comfort

³Praise be to the God and Father of our Lord Jesus Christ, the Father of compassion and the God of all comfort, ⁴who comforts us in all our troubles, so that we can comfort those in any trouble with the comfort we ourselves have received from God. ⁵For just as the suffer-

ings of Christ flow over into our lives, so also through Christ our comfort overflows. ⁶If we are distressed, it is for your comfort and salvation; if we are comforted, it is for your comfort, which produces in you patient endurance of the same sufferings we suffer. ⁷And our hope for you is firm, because we know that just as you share in our sufferings, so also you share in our comfort.

⁸We do not want you to be uninformed, brothers, about the hardships we suffered in the province of Asia. We were under great pressure, far beyond our ability to endure, so that we despaired even of life. ⁹Indeed, in our hearts we felt the sentence of death. But this happened that we might not rely on

VERSE:
2 Corinthians 1:4

AUTHOR:
Deforia Lane

PASSAGE:
2 Corinthians 1:3–11

The Harmony of Faith and Suffering

Suffering, and the sin that breeds it, is a reality so great, so overpowering, so menacing, that God seemed forced to resort to desperate measures to deal with it. No magic wand, no thunderous word, no angels, no prophet, no society in the world could eliminate sin and suffering.

God's answer . . . was Jesus Christ, God in human flesh. God the Father would send God the Son, clothed in human flesh, into the world to suffer and accept the consequences of sin.

Sin and pain seem to prevail. Babies die of cancer. Puppies are hit on the road. Hitler rises to power. We yell at our children. The power of suffering is that great. So what, in the end, does the cross really mean? What good is an escape route, really, if it does not open until the end of time? I think that the answer, in part, is that the cross never promises to free us from pain and suffering, not at least in the present. The cross, in fact, promises just the opposite: the certainty of pain and suffering.

Here is the mystery: The path of joy runs straight through the heart of pain and suffering. Christianity, alone among the world's religions, does not run from pain but embraces it, and then and only then does it move through it. Jesus Christ is our example of faith: "For the joy set before him endured the cross, scorning its shame, and sat down at the right hand of the throne of God" (Hebrews 12:2). Faith, at the very least, asks us to believe this: The path to heaven runs through suffering. *Through* the sorrow of the world, *through* that certain fog of doubt and pain, we have faith: sure of what we hope for, certain of what we do not see. God is love. God is in control. God will wipe away every tear and replace it with a river of joy.

Faith carries with it movement—from what we know to what we long for, from suffering to joy, from earth to heaven. That movement, that song, is always driven and graced by the choice we make to love.

ADDITIONAL SCRIPTURE READINGS:
Romans 8:18; Colossians 1:26–29; Hebrews 11:1

Go to page 244 for your next devotional reading.

ourselves but on God, who raises the dead. [10]He has delivered us from such a deadly peril, and he will deliver us. On him we have set our hope that he will continue to deliver us, [11]as you help us by your prayers. Then many will give thanks on our[a] behalf for the gracious favor granted us in answer to the prayers of many.

Paul's Change of Plans

[12]Now this is our boast: Our conscience testifies that we have conducted ourselves in the world, and especially in our relations with you, in the holiness and sincerity that are from God. We have done so not according to worldly wisdom but according to God's grace. [13]For we do not write you anything you cannot read or understand. And I hope that, [14]as you have understood us in part, you will come to understand fully that you can boast of us just as we will boast of you in the day of the Lord Jesus.

[15]Because I was confident of this, I planned to visit you first so that you might benefit twice. [16]I planned to visit you on my way to Macedonia and to come back to you from Macedonia, and then to have you send me on my way to Judea. [17]When I planned this, did I do it lightly? Or do I make my plans in a worldly manner so that in the same breath I say, "Yes, yes" and "No, no"?

[18]But as surely as God is faithful, our message to you is not "Yes" and "No." [19]For the Son of God, Jesus Christ, who was preached among you by me and Silas[b] and Timothy, was not "Yes" and "No," but in him it has always been "Yes." [20]For no matter how many promises God has made, they are "Yes" in Christ. And so through him the "Amen" is spoken by us to the glory of God. [21]Now it is God who makes both us and you stand firm in Christ. He anointed us, [22]set his seal of ownership on us, and put his Spirit in our hearts as a deposit, guaranteeing what is to come.

[23]I call God as my witness that it was in order to spare you that I did not return to Corinth. [24]Not that we lord it over your faith, but we work with you for your joy, because it is by faith you stand firm. [1]So I made up my mind that I would not make another painful visit to you. [2]For if I grieve you, who is left to make me glad but you whom I have grieved? [3]I wrote as I did so that when I came I should not be distressed by those who ought to make me rejoice. I had confidence in all of you, that you would all share my joy. [4]For I wrote you out of great distress and anguish of heart and with many tears, not to grieve you but to let you know the depth of my love for you.

Forgiveness for the Sinner

[5]If anyone has caused grief, he has not so much grieved me as he has grieved all of you, to some extent—not to put it too severely. [6]The punishment inflicted on him by the majority is sufficient for him. [7]Now instead, you ought to forgive and comfort him, so that he will not be overwhelmed by excessive sorrow. [8]I urge you, therefore, to reaffirm your love for him. [9]The reason I wrote you was to see if you would stand the test and be obedient in everything. [10]If you forgive anyone, I also forgive him. And what I have forgiven—if there was anything to forgive—I have forgiven in the sight of Christ for your sake, [11]in order that Satan might not outwit us. For we are not unaware of his schemes.

Ministers of the New Covenant

[12]Now when I went to Troas to preach the gospel of Christ and found that the Lord had opened a door for me, [13]I still had no peace of mind, because I did not find my brother Titus there. So I said good-by to them and went on to Macedonia.

[14]But thanks be to God, who always leads us in triumphal procession in Christ and through us spreads everywhere the fragrance of the knowledge of him. [15]For we are to God the aroma of Christ among those who are being saved and those who are perishing. [16]To the one we are the smell of death; to the other, the fragrance of life. And who is equal to such a task? [17]Unlike so many, we do not peddle the word of God for profit. On the contrary, in Christ we speak before God with sincerity, like men sent from God.

[3] Are we beginning to commend ourselves again? Or do we need, like some people, letters of recommendation

---

[a]11 Many manuscripts *your*   [b]19 Greek *Silvanus*, a variant of *Silas*

WEEKENDING

REVIVE

Life is a struggle . . . The beauty is, we do not have to toss and turn alone. We are not trapped by circumstances. We are creatures drawn upward by God's transforming love, by touches of tender mercy . . . These miracles of transformation happen every day.

A mother takes in stride her teenager's outburst of anger and serves her a cup of tea. A nurse looks beyond a needle-pocked arm to a sick spirit that needs a hug more than a sleeping pill. A teacher refuses to believe that a slow learner is on the borderline of retardation and finds out that dyslexia is the problem.

In myriad ways, the image of God is disclosed by people who are foolish enough to love without affixing any price to their self-gift. Every day someone on earth sees the face of God in a suffering person. Every day in jars of clay treasure untold is revealed.

Susan Muto

REFLECT

Saturday: 2 Corinthians 4:1–12
Sunday: Matthew 25:31–46

*Go to page 246 for your
next devotional reading.*

to you or from you? **2**You yourselves are our letter, written on our hearts, known and read by everybody. **3**You show that you are a letter from Christ, the result of our ministry, written not with ink but with the Spirit of the living God, not on tablets of stone but on tablets of human hearts.

4Such confidence as this is ours through Christ before God. **5**Not that we are competent in ourselves to claim anything for ourselves, but our competence comes from God. **6**He has made us competent as ministers of a new covenant—not of the letter but of the Spirit; for the letter kills, but the Spirit gives life.

The Glory of the New Covenant

7Now if the ministry that brought death, which was engraved in letters on stone, came with glory, so that the Israelites could not look steadily at the face of Moses because of its glory, fading though it was, **8**will not the ministry of the Spirit be even more glorious? **9**If the ministry that condemns men is glorious, how much more glorious is the ministry that brings righteousness! **10**For what was glorious has no glory now in comparison with the surpassing glory. **11**And if what was fading away came with glory, how much greater is the glory of that which lasts!

12Therefore, since we have such a hope, we are very bold. **13**We are not like Moses, who would put a veil over his face to keep the Israelites from gazing at it while the radiance was fading away. **14**But their minds were made dull, for to this day the same veil remains when the old covenant is read. It has not been removed, because only in Christ is it taken away. **15**Even to this day when Moses is read, a veil covers their hearts. **16**But whenever anyone turns to the Lord, the veil is taken away. **17**Now the Lord is the Spirit, and where the Spirit of the Lord is, there is freedom. **18**And we, who with unveiled faces all reflect[a] the Lord's glory, are being transformed into his likeness with ever-increasing glory, which comes from the Lord, who is the Spirit.

Treasures in Jars of Clay

4 Therefore, since through God's mercy we have this ministry, we do not lose heart. **2**Rather, we have renounced secret and shameful ways; we do not use deception, nor do we distort the word of God. On the contrary, by setting forth the truth plainly we commend ourselves to every man's conscience in the sight of God. **3**And even if our gospel is veiled, it is veiled to those who are perishing. **4**The god of this age has blinded the minds of unbelievers, so that they cannot see the light of the gospel of the glory of Christ, who is the image of God. **5**For we do not preach ourselves, but Jesus Christ as Lord, and ourselves as your servants for Jesus' sake. **6**For God, who said, "Let light shine out of darkness,"[b] made his light shine in our hearts to give us the light of the knowledge of the glory of God in the face of Christ.

7But we have this treasure in jars of clay to show that this all-surpassing power is from God and not from us. **8**We are hard pressed on every side, but not crushed; perplexed, but not in despair; **9**persecuted, but not abandoned; struck down, but not destroyed. **10**We always carry around in our body the death of Jesus, so that the life of Jesus may also be revealed in our body. **11**For we who are alive are always being given over to death for Jesus' sake, so that his life may be revealed in our mortal body. **12**So then, death is at work in us, but life is at work in you.

13It is written: "I believed; therefore I have spoken."[c] With that same spirit of faith we also believe and therefore speak, **14**because we know that the one who raised the Lord Jesus from the dead will also raise us with Jesus and present us with you in his presence. **15**All this is for your benefit, so that the grace that is reaching more and more people may cause thanksgiving to overflow to the glory of God.

16Therefore we do not lose heart. Though outwardly we are wasting away, yet inwardly we are being renewed day by day. **17**For our light and momentary troubles are achieving for us an eternal glory that far outweighs them all. **18**So we fix our eyes not on what is seen, but on what is unseen. For what is seen is temporary, but what is unseen is eternal.

---

*a*18 Or *contemplate*   *b*6 Gen. 1:3   *c*13 Psalm 116:10

VERSE:
2 Corinthians 2:15

AUTHOR:
Alma Barkman

PASSAGE:
2 Corinthians 2:12–17

A Rare Perfume

Every so often you get a whiff of something that triggers off a whole chain of reminiscences. I walked into the bathroom a few minutes ago and the lingering traces of air freshener reminded me of Lifebuoy soap—the original orange-pink bar with the hexagon corners that graced the old washstand in farm kitchens. Everybody who crossed paths with a bar of Lifebuoy came away feeling cleaner, and smelling it, too. At one point it seemed the entire rural population was a walking billboard. Suddenly the soap tycoons switched perfumes, and we had to pay for more sophisticated but less effective forms of advertising.

Hair tonic seemed to hold its own a bit longer, despite the fact that it smelled like perfumed chicken fat, rancid at that. When the spring winds beckoned, many a young man with hair slicked down shiny went courting a girl friend who sprouted a frizzy home permanent, traces of which, when exposed to warm sunshine, faintly resembled a skunk.

What I find peculiar is that people seem to interpret odors differently. What is perfumy to one person is pungent to another. [My husband] detests brushing against geranium leaves, while I think their scent is rather invigorating.

The apostle Paul reminds us that, as believers, we represent the "aroma" (sweet savor) of Christ (v. 15). Not everyone, however, will interpret our behavior as sweet (and sometimes for valid reasons!), nor will they savor our presence if it means embarrassment to them in an uncomfortable situation.

We should remember that rare perfumes have subtle appeal, and a dab behind each ear is about all that is required. Instead of gently attracting people toward Christ, however, some Christians feel they must "come on strong." Overwhelmed by such a bold confrontation with the gospel, unbelievers may actually find it repulsive.

Just as we use perfume with discretion, so we must use discernment in approaching people about salvation. It is reassuring to know that even so humble an effort as a life daily committed to Christ leaves lingering traces of testimony wherever we go, and "through us spreads everywhere the fragrance of the knowledge of him" (v. 14).

ADDITIONAL SCRIPTURE READINGS:
Ezekiel 20:41–42; Ephesians 5:1–2

Go to page 249 for your next devotional reading.

Our Heavenly Dwelling

5 Now we know that if the earthly tent we live in is destroyed, we have a building from God, an eternal house in heaven, not built by human hands. ²Meanwhile we groan, longing to be clothed with our heavenly dwelling, ³because when we are clothed, we will not be found naked. ⁴For while we are in this tent, we groan and are burdened, because we do not wish to be unclothed but to be clothed with our heavenly dwelling, so that what is mortal may be swallowed up by life. ⁵Now it is God who has made us for this very purpose and has given us the Spirit as a deposit, guaranteeing what is to come.

⁶Therefore we are always confident and know that as long as we are at home in the body we are away from the Lord. ⁷We live by faith, not by sight. ⁸We are confident, I say, and would prefer to be away from the body and at home with the Lord. ⁹So we make it our goal to please him, whether we are at home in the body or away from it. ¹⁰For we must all appear before the judgment seat of Christ, that each one may receive what is due him for the things done while in the body, whether good or bad.

The Ministry of Reconciliation

¹¹Since, then, we know what it is to fear the Lord, we try to persuade men. What we are is plain to God, and I hope it is also plain to your conscience. ¹²We are not trying to commend ourselves to you again, but are giving you an opportunity to take pride in us, so that you can answer those who take pride in what is seen rather than in what is in the heart. ¹³If we are out of our mind, it is for the sake of God; if we are in our right mind, it is for you. ¹⁴For Christ's love compels us, because we are convinced that one died for all, and therefore all died. ¹⁵And he died for all, that those who live should no longer live for themselves but for him who died for them and was raised again.

¹⁶So from now on we regard no one from a worldly point of view. Though we once regarded Christ in this way, we do so no longer. ¹⁷Therefore, if anyone is in Christ, he is a new creation; the old has gone, the new has come! ¹⁸All this is from God, who reconciled us to himself through Christ and gave us the ministry of reconciliation: ¹⁹that God was reconciling the world to himself in Christ, not counting men's sins against them. And he has committed to us the message of reconciliation. ²⁰We are therefore Christ's ambassadors, as though God were making his appeal through us. We implore you on Christ's behalf: Be reconciled to God. ²¹God made him who had no sin to be sin*a* for us, so that in him we might become the righteousness of God.

6 As God's fellow workers we urge you not to receive God's grace in vain. ²For he says,

"In the time of my favor I heard you,
　and in the day of salvation I
　　helped you."*b*

I tell you, now is the time of God's favor, now is the day of salvation.

Paul's Hardships

³We put no stumbling block in anyone's path, so that our ministry will not be discredited. ⁴Rather, as servants of God we commend ourselves in every way: in great endurance; in troubles, hardships and distresses; ⁵in beatings, imprisonments and riots; in hard work, sleepless nights and hunger; ⁶in purity, understanding, patience and kindness; in the Holy Spirit and in sincere love; ⁷in truthful speech and in the power of God; with weapons of righteousness in the right hand and in the left; ⁸through glory and dishonor, bad report and good report; genuine, yet regarded as impostors; ⁹known, yet regarded as unknown; dying, and yet we live on; beaten, and yet not killed; ¹⁰sorrowful, yet always rejoicing; poor, yet making many rich; having nothing, and yet possessing everything.

¹¹We have spoken freely to you, Corinthians, and opened wide our hearts to you. ¹²We are not withholding our affection from you, but you are withholding yours from us. ¹³As a fair exchange— I speak as to my children—open wide your hearts also.

Do Not Be Yoked With Unbelievers

¹⁴Do not be yoked together with unbelievers. For what do righteousness and wickedness have in common? Or

---

*a*21 Or *be a sin offering*　　*b*2 Isaiah 49:8

what fellowship can light have with darkness? 15What harmony is there between Christ and Belial*a*? What does a believer have in common with an unbeliever? 16What agreement is there between the temple of God and idols? For we are the temple of the living God. As God has said: "I will live with them and walk among them, and I will be their God, and they will be my people."*b*

17"Therefore come out from them
    and be separate,
                        says the Lord.
  Touch no unclean thing,
    and I will receive you."*c*
18"I will be a Father to you,
    and you will be my sons and
        daughters,
            says the Lord Almighty."*d*

7 Since we have these promises, dear friends, let us purify ourselves from everything that contaminates body and spirit, perfecting holiness out of reverence for God.

Paul's Joy

2Make room for us in your hearts. We have wronged no one, we have corrupted no one, we have exploited no one. 3I do not say this to condemn you; I have said before that you have such a place in our hearts that we would live or die with you. 4I have great confidence in you; I take great pride in you. I am greatly encouraged; in all our troubles my joy knows no bounds.

5For when we came into Macedonia, this body of ours had no rest, but we were harassed at every turn—conflicts on the outside, fears within. 6But God, who comforts the downcast, comforted us by the coming of Titus, 7and not only by his coming but also by the comfort you had given him. He told us about your longing for me, your deep sorrow, your ardent concern for me, so that my joy was greater than ever.

8Even if I caused you sorrow by my letter, I do not regret it. Though I did regret it—I see that my letter hurt you, but only for a little while— 9yet now I am happy, not because you were made sorry, but because your sorrow led you to repentance. For you became sorrowful as God intended and so were not

harmed in any way by us. 10Godly sorrow brings repentance that leads to salvation and leaves no regret, but worldly sorrow brings death. 11See what this godly sorrow has produced in you: what earnestness, what eagerness to clear yourselves, what indignation, what alarm, what longing, what concern, what readiness to see justice done. At every point you have proved yourselves to be innocent in this matter. 12So even though I wrote to you, it was not on account of the one who did the wrong or of the injured party, but rather that before God you could see for yourselves how devoted to us you are. 13By all this we are encouraged.

In addition to our own encouragement, we were especially delighted to see how happy Titus was, because his spirit has been refreshed by all of you. 14I had boasted to him about you, and you have not embarrassed me. But just as everything we said to you was true, so our boasting about you to Titus has proved to be true as well. 15And his affection for you is all the greater when he remembers that you were all obedient, receiving him with fear and trembling. 16I am glad I can have complete confidence in you.

Generosity Encouraged

8 And now, brothers, we want you to know about the grace that God has given the Macedonian churches. 2Out of the most severe trial, their overflowing joy and their extreme poverty welled up in rich generosity. 3For I testify that they gave as much as they were able, and even beyond their ability. Entirely on their own, 4they urgently pleaded with us for the privilege of sharing in this service to the saints. 5And they did not do as we expected, but they gave themselves first to the Lord and then to us in keeping with God's will. 6So we urged Titus, since he had earlier made a beginning, to bring also to completion this act of grace on your part. 7But just as you excel in everything—in faith, in speech, in knowledge, in complete earnestness and in your love for us*e*—see that you also excel in this grace of giving.

8I am not commanding you, but I want to test the sincerity of your love by

---

*a15 Greek *Beliar*, a variant of *Belial*   *b16 Lev. 26:12; Jer. 32:38; Ezek. 37:27   *c17 Isaiah 52:11; Ezek. 20:34,41   *d18 2 Samuel 7:14; 7:8   *e7 Some manuscripts *in our love for you*

VERSE:
2 Corinthians 7:2

AUTHOR:
Susan Lenzkes

PASSAGE:
2 Corinthians 7:2–4

Feeling at Home

Certain friends have a way of
setting up residence in us.
They march into some
barren room of our heart and
hang cheery curtains,
scatter soft rugs,
dot the walls with framed prints of
tender and whimsical moments,
then set about building a
cozy fire beside two
sink-back-and-stay-awhile chairs.
We may not always know exactly when
such friends moved in,
but we're so very glad they did!

Some people have a way of making themselves at home. They
don't ring the front doorbell. They slip in the back with a freshly
plucked daisy or two. No formalities. Just, "How wonderful to see
you!"

They don't care if there's clutter on the floor. They'll either help
you pick it up, or step over it to pour you each a cup of coffee. "A
penny for your thoughts," they say. "No, a nickel; your thoughts
are always worth more."

How do these people do it? Perhaps the key to the back door of
our hearts is simply acceptance—the kind of love that would just
as soon hug you in a tattered bathrobe as in your Sunday best.
Such people leave behind their expectations of how others should
be and what they should do. To them, every person is buried treasure to be discovered and enjoyed. Differences are a source of
delight. Evaluations, judgments and makeovers are not their job.
Loving acceptance is.

When such a person takes me into her heart, it is certain that she
cannot stay long out of mine.

ADDITIONAL SCRIPTURE READINGS:
1 Samuel 18:1–4; Proverbs 18:24; John 15:13–15; Romans 15:7

Go to page 251 for your next devotional reading.

comparing it with the earnestness of others. ⁹For you know the grace of our Lord Jesus Christ, that though he was rich, yet for your sakes he became poor, so that you through his poverty might become rich.

¹⁰And here is my advice about what is best for you in this matter: Last year you were the first not only to give but also to have the desire to do so. ¹¹Now finish the work, so that your eager willingness to do it may be matched by your completion of it, according to your means. ¹²For if the willingness is there, the gift is acceptable according to what one has, not according to what he does not have.

¹³Our desire is not that others might be relieved while you are hard pressed, but that there might be equality. ¹⁴At the present time your plenty will supply what they need, so that in turn their plenty will supply what you need. Then there will be equality, ¹⁵as it is written: "He who gathered much did not have too much, and he who gathered little did not have too little."ᵃ

Titus Sent to Corinth

¹⁶I thank God, who put into the heart of Titus the same concern I have for you. ¹⁷For Titus not only welcomed our appeal, but he is coming to you with much enthusiasm and on his own initiative. ¹⁸And we are sending along with him the brother who is praised by all the churches for his service to the gospel. ¹⁹What is more, he was chosen by the churches to accompany us as we carry the offering, which we administer in order to honor the Lord himself and to show our eagerness to help. ²⁰We want to avoid any criticism of the way we administer this liberal gift. ²¹For we are taking pains to do what is right, not only in the eyes of the Lord but also in the eyes of men.

²²In addition, we are sending with them our brother who has often proved to us in many ways that he is zealous, and now even more so because of his great confidence in you. ²³As for Titus, he is my partner and fellow worker among you; as for our brothers, they are representatives of the churches and an honor to Christ. ²⁴Therefore show these men the proof of your love and the rea-

son for our pride in you, so that the churches can see it.

9 There is no need for me to write to you about this service to the saints. ²For I know your eagerness to help, and I have been boasting about it to the Macedonians, telling them that since last year you in Achaia were ready to give; and your enthusiasm has stirred most of them to action. ³But I am sending the brothers in order that our boasting about you in this matter should not prove hollow, but that you may be ready, as I said you would be. ⁴For if any Macedonians come with me and find you unprepared, we—not to say anything about you—would be ashamed of having been so confident. ⁵So I thought it necessary to urge the brothers to visit you in advance and finish the arrangements for the generous gift you had promised. Then it will be ready as a generous gift, not as one grudgingly given.

Sowing Generously

⁶Remember this: Whoever sows sparingly will also reap sparingly, and whoever sows generously will also reap generously. ⁷Each man should give what he has decided in his heart to give, not reluctantly or under compulsion, for God loves a cheerful giver. ⁸And God is able to make all grace abound to you, so that in all things at all times, having all that you need, you will abound in every good work. ⁹As it is written:

"He has scattered abroad his gifts to
    the poor;
  his righteousness endures
    forever."ᵇ

¹⁰Now he who supplies seed to the sower and bread for food will also supply and increase your store of seed and will enlarge the harvest of your righteousness. ¹¹You will be made rich in every way so that you can be generous on every occasion, and through us your generosity will result in thanksgiving to God.

¹²This service that you perform is not only supplying the needs of God's people but is also overflowing in many expressions of thanks to God. ¹³Because of the service by which you have proved yourselves, men will praise God for the obedience that accompanies your con-

---

ᵃ15 Exodus 16:18   ᵇ9 Psalm 112:9

fession of the gospel of Christ, and for your generosity in sharing with them and with everyone else. **14**And in their prayers for you their hearts will go out to you, because of the surpassing grace God has given you. **15**Thanks be to God for his indescribable gift!

Paul's Defense of His Ministry

10 By the meekness and gentleness of Christ, I appeal to you—I, Paul, who am "timid" when face to face with you, but "bold" when away! **2**I beg you that when I come I may not have to be as bold as I expect to be toward some people who think that we live by the standards of this world. **3**For though we live in the world, we do not wage war as the world does. **4**The weapons we fight with are not the weapons of the world. On the contrary, they have divine power to demolish strongholds. **5**We demolish arguments and every pretension that sets itself up against the knowledge of God, and we take captive every thought to make it obedient to Christ. **6**And we will be ready to punish every act of disobedience, once your obedience is complete.

7You are looking only on the surface of things.*a* If anyone is confident that he belongs to Christ, he should consider again that we belong to Christ just as much as he. **8**For even if I boast somewhat freely about the authority the Lord gave us for building you up rather than pulling you down, I will not be ashamed of it. **9**I do not want to seem to be trying to frighten you with my letters. **10**For some say, "His letters are weighty and forceful, but in person he is unimpressive and his speaking amounts to nothing." **11**Such people should realize that what we are in our letters when we are absent, we will be in our actions when we are present.

12We do not dare to classify or compare ourselves with some who commend themselves. When they measure themselves by themselves and compare themselves with themselves, they are not wise. **13**We, however, will not boast beyond proper limits, but will confine our boasting to the field God has assigned to us, a field that reaches even to you. **14**We are not going too far in our boasting, as would be the case if we had not come to you, for we did get as far as you with the gospel of Christ. **15**Neither do we go beyond our limits by boasting

a 7 Or *Look at the obvious facts*

> ⟨ **WEDNESDAY** ⟩
>
> | VERSE: | AUTHOR: | PASSAGE: |
> |---|---|---|
> | 2 Corinthians 9:8 | Mother Teresa of Calcutta | 2 Corinthians 9:6–15 |
>
> ## Joy
>
> Joy is prayer. Joy is strength. Joy is love. Joy is a net of love by which you can catch souls. God loves a cheerful giver. One gives most who gives with joy. The best way to show our gratitude to God and people is to accept everything with joy. A joyful heart is the normal result of a heart burning with love. Never let anything so fill you with sorrow as to make you forget the joy of Christ risen.
>
> This I tell my sisters. This I tell to you.
>
> ---
>
> **ADDITIONAL SCRIPTURE READINGS:**
> **Proverbs 17:22; Galatians 5:22–23; Philippians 4:4**
>
> *Go to page 254 for your next devotional reading.*

of work done by others.[a] Our hope is that, as your faith continues to grow, our area of activity among you will greatly expand, [16]so that we can preach the gospel in the regions beyond you. For we do not want to boast about work already done in another man's territory. [17]But, "Let him who boasts boast in the Lord."[b] [18]For it is not the one who commends himself who is approved, but the one whom the Lord commends.

Paul and the False Apostles

11 I hope you will put up with a little of my foolishness; but you are already doing that. [2]I am jealous for you with a godly jealousy. I promised you to one husband, to Christ, so that I might present you as a pure virgin to him. [3]But I am afraid that just as Eve was deceived by the serpent's cunning, your minds may somehow be led astray from your sincere and pure devotion to Christ. [4]For if someone comes to you and preaches a Jesus other than the Jesus we preached, or if you receive a different spirit from the one you received, or a different gospel from the one you accepted, you put up with it easily enough. [5]But I do not think I am in the least inferior to those "super-apostles." [6]I may not be a trained speaker, but I do have knowledge. We have made this perfectly clear to you in every way.

[7]Was it a sin for me to lower myself in order to elevate you by preaching the gospel of God to you free of charge? [8]I robbed other churches by receiving support from them so as to serve you. [9]And when I was with you and needed something, I was not a burden to anyone, for the brothers who came from Macedonia supplied what I needed. I have kept myself from being a burden to you in any way, and will continue to do so. [10]As surely as the truth of Christ is in me, nobody in the regions of Achaia will stop this boasting of mine. [11]Why? Because I do not love you? God knows I do! [12]And I will keep on doing what I am doing in order to cut the ground from under those who want an opportunity to be considered equal with us in the things they boast about.

[13]For such men are false apostles, deceitful workmen, masquerading as apostles of Christ. [14]And no wonder, for Satan himself masquerades as an angel of light. [15]It is not surprising, then, if his servants masquerade as servants of righteousness. Their end will be what their actions deserve.

Paul Boasts About His Sufferings

[16]I repeat: Let no one take me for a fool. But if you do, then receive me just as you would a fool, so that I may do a little boasting. [17]In this self-confident boasting I am not talking as the Lord would, but as a fool. [18]Since many are boasting in the way the world does, I too will boast. [19]You gladly put up with fools since you are so wise! [20]In fact, you even put up with anyone who enslaves you or exploits you or takes advantage of you or pushes himself forward or slaps you in the face. [21]To my shame I admit that we were too weak for that!

What anyone else dares to boast about—I am speaking as a fool—I also dare to boast about. [22]Are they Hebrews? So am I. Are they Israelites? So am I. Are they Abraham's descendants? So am I. [23]Are they servants of Christ? (I am out of my mind to talk like this.) I am more. I have worked much harder, been in prison more frequently, been flogged more severely, and been exposed to death again and again. [24]Five times I received from the Jews the forty lashes minus one. [25]Three times I was beaten with rods, once I was stoned, three times I was shipwrecked, I spent a night and a day in the open sea, [26]I have been constantly on the move. I have been in danger from rivers, in danger from bandits, in danger from my own countrymen, in danger from Gentiles; in danger in the city, in danger in the country, in danger at sea; and in danger from false brothers. [27]I have labored and toiled and have often gone without sleep; I have known hunger and thirst and have often gone without food; I have been cold and naked. [28]Besides everything else, I face daily the pressure of my concern for all the churches. [29]Who

---

[a]13-15 Or [13]We, however, will not boast about things that cannot be measured, but we will boast according to the standard of measurement that the God of measure has assigned us—a measurement that relates even to you. [14] . . . . [15]Neither do we boast about things that cannot be measured in regard to the work done by others.
[b]17 Jer. 9:24

is weak, and I do not feel weak? Who is led into sin, and I do not inwardly burn? [30]If I must boast, I will boast of the things that show my weakness. [31]The God and Father of the Lord Jesus, who is to be praised forever, knows that I am not lying. [32]In Damascus the governor under King Aretas had the city of the Damascenes guarded in order to arrest me. [33]But I was lowered in a basket from a window in the wall and slipped through his hands.

Paul's Vision and His Thorn

12 I must go on boasting. Although there is nothing to be gained, I will go on to visions and revelations from the Lord. [2]I know a man in Christ who fourteen years ago was caught up to the third heaven. Whether it was in the body or out of the body I do not know—God knows. [3]And I know that this man—whether in the body or apart from the body I do not know, but God knows— [4]was caught up to paradise. He heard inexpressible things, things that man is not permitted to tell. [5]I will boast about a man like that, but I will not boast about myself, except about my weaknesses. [6]Even if I should choose to boast, I would not be a fool, because I would be speaking the truth. But I refrain, so no one will think more of me than is warranted by what I do or say.

[7]To keep me from becoming conceited because of these surpassingly great revelations, there was given me a thorn in my flesh, a messenger of Satan, to torment me. [8]Three times I pleaded with the Lord to take it away from me. [9]But he said to me, "My grace is sufficient for you, for my power is made perfect in weakness." Therefore I will boast all the more gladly about my weaknesses, so that Christ's power may rest on me. [10]That is why, for Christ's sake, I delight in weaknesses, in insults, in hardships, in persecutions, in difficulties. For when I am weak, then I am strong.

Paul's Concern for the Corinthians

[11]I have made a fool of myself, but you drove me to it. I ought to have been commended by you, for I am not in the least inferior to the "super-apostles," even though I am nothing. [12]The things that mark an apostle—signs, wonders and miracles—were done among you with great perseverance. [13]How were you inferior to the other churches, except that I was never a burden to you? Forgive me this wrong!

[14]Now I am ready to visit you for the third time, and I will not be a burden to you, because what I want is not your possessions but you. After all, children should not have to save up for their parents, but parents for their children. [15]So I will very gladly spend for you everything I have and expend myself as well. If I love you more, will you love me less? [16]Be that as it may, I have not been a burden to you. Yet, crafty fellow that I am, I caught you by trickery! [17]Did I exploit you through any of the men I sent you? [18]I urged Titus to go to you and I sent our brother with him. Titus did not exploit you, did he? Did we not act in the same spirit and follow the same course?

[19]Have you been thinking all along that we have been defending ourselves to you? We have been speaking in the sight of God as those in Christ; and everything we do, dear friends, is for your strengthening. [20]For I am afraid that when I come I may not find you as I want you to be, and you may not find me as you want me to be. I fear that there may be quarreling, jealousy, outbursts of anger, factions, slander, gossip, arrogance and disorder. [21]I am afraid that when I come again my God will humble me before you, and I will be grieved over many who have sinned earlier and have not repented of the impurity, sexual sin and debauchery in which they have indulged.

Final Warnings

13 This will be my third visit to you. "Every matter must be established by the testimony of two or three witnesses."[a] [2]I already gave you a warning when I was with you the second time. I now repeat it while absent: On my return I will not spare those who sinned earlier or any of the others, [3]since you are demanding proof that Christ is speaking through me. He is not weak in dealing with you, but is powerful among you. [4]For to be sure, he was crucified in weakness, yet he lives by

[a]1 Deut. 19:15

God's power. Likewise, we are weak in him, yet by God's power we will live with him to serve you.

⁵Examine yourselves to see whether you are in the faith; test yourselves. Do you not realize that Christ Jesus is in you—unless, of course, you fail the test? ⁶And I trust that you will discover that we have not failed the test. ⁷Now we pray to God that you will not do anything wrong. Not that people will see that we have stood the test but that you

---

THURSDAY

VERSE:
2 Corinthians 12:9

AUTHOR:
Paula Michelsen

PASSAGE:
2 Corinthians 12:8-9

Bagels and Swiss Cheese

Do you ever feel cheated when you bite into a Swiss cheese sandwich and come up with a mouthful of holes? I do. I wonder why I'm willing to pay full price for a sandwich that's half air. But, then, why do I prefer drinking a can of sugarless, caffeine-free fizz with no nutritive value?

This year it seems I've acquired an unusual taste for nothingness—for emptiness, fatigue and discouragement. From my outward appearance you'd never guess I've felt more like "Swiss cheese" than the usual "sharp cheddar." I've met the deadlines at work, and I've made all the soccer and ballet lessons, and even found time to volunteer for extracurricular activities at church.

But inside I've often felt like the middle of a bagel—empty. I've just been rolling along, admitting "I can do it!" If ever I felt like a candidate for supermom, it's not now. Instead, I've learned a lot about humility, like being able to say, "I'm sorry, I blew it!" or "I goofed—I shouldn't have said that!"

At work, with my employees, I've had to repeatedly admit shortcomings. At home, my husband and children know Mom's not perfect. I feel more like a "blow-out" than a "burn-out," since I can't blame hormones—I'm too young to be in a mid-life crisis!

I found myself wanting to quit my job, go on vacation, sleep for days. But these are all unrealistic escapes—or escapades—that wouldn't honor God. No; instead, I want to bring him glory by getting up every day and taking my family and job seriously, no matter how inadequate I feel.

The whistling wind of the Holy Spirit has found a way to breathe through the nothingness of my human nature. I can see God's strength reaching through my "hole-iness" to touch others around me. I've come to the humiliating conclusion that God wants me weak and wobbly, so he can be more visible.

Maybe that's why I've come to savor Swiss cheese this year; I've learned to develop an appetite for the unseen.

ADDITIONAL SCRIPTURE READINGS:
1 Kings 19:3-9; Romans 8:5-11; 2 Corinthians 4:8-11

Go to page 257 for your next devotional reading.

will do what is right even though we may seem to have failed. **8**For we cannot do anything against the truth, but only for the truth. **9**We are glad whenever we are weak but you are strong; and our prayer is for your perfection. **10**This is why I write these things when I am absent, that when I come I may not have to be harsh in my use of authority—the authority the Lord gave me for building you up, not for tearing you down.

Final Greetings

11Finally, brothers, good-by. Aim for perfection, listen to my appeal, be of one mind, live in peace. And the God of love and peace will be with you.

12Greet one another with a holy kiss. **13**All the saints send their greetings.

14May the grace of the Lord Jesus Christ, and the love of God, and the fellowship of the Holy Spirit be with you all.

PAUL'S *letter to the churches he established in Galatia (Acts 13:13–14:28) contains his classic statement of the foundational Biblical truth that a person is justified by faith in Christ. After warning the Galatians not to desert the gospel, Paul encourages them to live out the freedom they have in Christ. As you read this letter, ask God to help you enjoy the freedom you have in Christ as you live a Spirit-filled life (5:22–23).*

GALATIANS

1 Paul, an apostle—sent not from men nor by man, but by Jesus Christ and God the Father, who raised him from the dead— ²and all the brothers with me,

To the churches in Galatia:

³Grace and peace to you from God our Father and the Lord Jesus Christ, ⁴who gave himself for our sins to rescue us from the present evil age, according to the will of our God and Father, ⁵to whom be glory for ever and ever. Amen.

No Other Gospel

⁶I am astonished that you are so quickly deserting the one who called you by the grace of Christ and are turning to a different gospel— ⁷which is really no gospel at all. Evidently some people are throwing you into confusion and are trying to pervert the gospel of Christ. ⁸But even if we or an angel from heaven should preach a gospel other than the one we preached to you, let him be eternally condemned! ⁹As we have already said, so now I say again: If anybody is preaching to you a gospel other than what you accepted, let him be eternally condemned!

¹⁰Am I now trying to win the approval of men, or of God? Or am I trying to please men? If I were still trying to please men, I would not be a servant of Christ.

Paul Called by God

¹¹I want you to know, brothers, that the gospel I preached is not something that man made up. ¹²I did not receive it from any man, nor was I taught it; rath-

er, I received it by revelation from Jesus Christ.

[13]For you have heard of my previous way of life in Judaism, how intensely I persecuted the church of God and tried to destroy it. [14]I was advancing in Judaism beyond many Jews of my own age and was extremely zealous for the traditions of my fathers. [15]But when God, who set me apart from birth[a] and called me by his grace, was pleased [16]to reveal his Son in me so that I might preach him among the Gentiles, I did not consult any man, [17]nor did I go up to Jerusalem to see those who were apostles before I was, but I went immediately into Arabia and later returned to Damascus.

[18]Then after three years, I went up to Jerusalem to get acquainted with Peter[b] and stayed with him fifteen days. [19]I saw none of the other apostles—only James, the Lord's brother. [20]I assure you

before God that what I am writing you is no lie. [21]Later I went to Syria and Cilicia. [22]I was personally unknown to the churches of Judea that are in Christ. [23]They only heard the report: "The man who formerly persecuted us is now preaching the faith he once tried to destroy." [24]And they praised God because of me.

Paul Accepted by the Apostles

2 Fourteen years later I went up again to Jerusalem, this time with Barnabas. I took Titus along also. [2]I went in response to a revelation and set before them the gospel that I preach among the Gentiles. But I did this privately to those who seemed to be leaders, for fear that I was running or had run my race in vain. [3]Yet not even Titus, who was with me, was compelled to be circumcised, even though he was a Greek. [4]This matter

[a]15 Or *from my mother's womb*   [b]18 Greek *Cephas*

FRIDAY

VERSE:	AUTHOR:	PASSAGE:
Galatians 1:10	Cynthia Heald	Galatians 1:1–10

Freedom From Perfectionism

A lingering weight I carry from my past is wanting to be perfect in order to be accepted by God and other people. Whenever I fail, I tend to want to disappear from the planet. I berate myself and renew my vow never to let it happen again!

It encourages me to hear Paul say that he was not perfect and that he would not allow his past to dictate his present behavior (see Philippians 3:12–16). God certainly does not expect me to be perfect; in a sense he is pleased when I do something right! It has been freeing to me to know that God can break destructive patterns. He can guide us into confronting the deep wounds of our past by giving us wise counselors, faithful friends and his Spirit. He, and only he, can take away our sin and guilt.

God is in the business of freedom and newness, and it is when I acknowledge my past and confess my sin that I can begin to experience his liberty. He gives new lives for old.

ADDITIONAL SCRIPTURE READINGS:
Psalm 119:45; Romans 3:24; Romans 8:12–17

Go to page 258 for your next devotional reading.

WEEKENDING

REKINDLE

O, God, give me grace for this day.
   Not for a lifetime, nor for next week,
nor for tomorrow, just for this day.
   Direct my thoughts and bless them.
   Direct my work and bless it.
   Direct the things I say, and give them
     blessing too.
   Direct and bless everything that I
     think and speak and do.
So for this one day, just this one day, I
have the gift of grace that comes from
your presence.
   O, God, for this day, just this one
day, let me live generously, kindly, in a
state of grace and goodness that denies
my many imperfections and makes me
more like you.

Marjorie Holmes

RESTORE

Saturday: Ephesians 4:13
Sunday: 2 Corinthians 13:11–14

*Go to page 260 for your
next devotional reading.*

arose, because some false brothers had infiltrated our ranks to spy on the freedom we have in Christ Jesus and to make us slaves. [5]We did not give in to them for a moment, so that the truth of the gospel might remain with you.

[6]As for those who seemed to be important—whatever they were makes no difference to me; God does not judge by external appearance—those men added nothing to my message. [7]On the contrary, they saw that I had been entrusted with the task of preaching the gospel to the Gentiles,[a] just as Peter had been to the Jews.[b] [8]For God, who was at work in the ministry of Peter as an apostle to the Jews, was also at work in my ministry as an apostle to the Gentiles. [9]James, Peter[c] and John, those reputed to be pillars, gave me and Barnabas the right hand of fellowship when they recognized the grace given to me. They agreed that we should go to the Gentiles, and they to the Jews. [10]All they asked was that we should continue to remember the poor, the very thing I was eager to do.

Paul Opposes Peter

[11]When Peter came to Antioch, I opposed him to his face, because he was clearly in the wrong. [12]Before certain men came from James, he used to eat with the Gentiles. But when they arrived, he began to draw back and separate himself from the Gentiles because he was afraid of those who belonged to the circumcision group. [13]The other Jews joined him in his hypocrisy, so that by their hypocrisy even Barnabas was led astray.

[14]When I saw that they were not acting in line with the truth of the gospel, I said to Peter in front of them all, "You are a Jew, yet you live like a Gentile and not like a Jew. How is it, then, that you force Gentiles to follow Jewish customs?

[15]"We who are Jews by birth and not 'Gentile sinners' [16]know that a man is not justified by observing the law, but by faith in Jesus Christ. So we, too, have put our faith in Christ Jesus that we may be justified by faith in Christ and not by observing the law, because by observing the law no one will be justified.

[17]"If, while we seek to be justified in Christ, it becomes evident that we ourselves are sinners, does that mean that Christ promotes sin? Absolutely not! [18]If I rebuild what I destroyed, I prove that I am a lawbreaker. [19]For through the law I died to the law so that I might live for God. [20]I have been crucified with Christ and I no longer live, but Christ lives in me. The life I live in the body, I live by faith in the Son of God, who loved me and gave himself for me. [21]I do not set aside the grace of God, for if righteousness could be gained through the law, Christ died for nothing!"[d]

Faith or Observance of the Law

3 You foolish Galatians! Who has bewitched you? Before your very eyes Jesus Christ was clearly portrayed as crucified. [2]I would like to learn just one thing from you: Did you receive the Spirit by observing the law, or by believing what you heard? [3]Are you so foolish? After beginning with the Spirit, are you now trying to attain your goal by human effort? [4]Have you suffered so much for nothing—if it really was for nothing? [5]Does God give you his Spirit and work miracles among you because you observe the law, or because you believe what you heard?

[6]Consider Abraham: "He believed God, and it was credited to him as righteousness."[e] [7]Understand, then, that those who believe are children of Abraham. [8]The Scripture foresaw that God would justify the Gentiles by faith, and announced the gospel in advance to Abraham: "All nations will be blessed through you."[f] [9]So those who have faith are blessed along with Abraham, the man of faith.

[10]All who rely on observing the law are under a curse, for it is written: "Cursed is everyone who does not continue to do everything written in the Book of the Law."[g] [11]Clearly no one is justified before God by the law, because, "The righteous will live by faith."[h] [12]The law is not based on faith; on the

---

[a]7 Greek *uncircumcised*   [b]7 Greek *circumcised*; also in verses 8 and 9   [c]9 Greek *Cephas*; also in verses 11 and 14   [d]21 Some interpreters end the quotation after verse 14.   [e]6 Gen. 15:6   [f]8 Gen. 12:3; 18:18; 22:18   [g]10 Deut. 27:26   [h]11 Hab. 2:4

contrary, "The man who does these things will live by them."[a] [13]Christ redeemed us from the curse of the law by becoming a curse for us, for it is written: "Cursed is everyone who is hung on a tree."[b] [14]He redeemed us in order that the blessing given to Abraham might come to the Gentiles through Christ Jesus, so that by faith we might receive the promise of the Spirit.

[a]12 Lev. 18:5   [b]13 Deut. 21:23

MONDAY

VERSE:
Galatians 3:9

AUTHOR:
Paula Rinehart

PASSAGE:
Galatians 3:1–14

Open-Handed Faith

I suspect that much of what I formerly called faith is little better than having invited God into the parlor of my life while I checked his references. I was not sure that I could risk giving him the full run of the place. Sometimes I have felt frustrated with his apparent absence, wondering why he seldom seemed present in a more immediate way. And at other times I have wanted him to go away and leave me be.

God is moving me toward something qualitatively different. It is a faith that looks more like an open hand than a clenched fist—a faith that is wide and free and at ease with uncertainty.

This kind of open-ended trust always seems to come unexpectedly. It comes only after you've been disillusioned with what seemed like faith, only after some stinging disappointment causes your box to collapse. The paradox is that this kind of trust begins in those unlikely moments when there is no experiential reason to believe. Only then is there room for real faith to take root. It is born in the fearlessness that comes when you've already lost a good portion of what you were so afraid of losing in the first place. It sprouts at a point of contradiction.

The movement toward genuine faith is marked by choosing to trust God even when we know the outcome may be different than we had ever imagined. We let go of our preconceived notions of how things ought to be. If life is a river, we jump right out into the middle and let it take us where it will.

That kind of faith is new to me. I hardly know how to make my way around in it yet. Spiritual prescriptions and techniques on how to live the Christian life—I have a whole repertoire of those. But I am just now moving beyond the simple answers into a place where I can enjoy a relationship with a Person, sometimes elliptical, full of ebb and flow, desert and garden. I am learning to let the dissonance feed my newfound trust.

ADDITIONAL SCRIPTURE READINGS:
Psalm 37:5–7; Psalm 40:3–5; Proverbs 3:5–6

Go to page 263 for your next devotional reading.

The Law and the Promise

[15]Brothers, let me take an example from everyday life. Just as no one can set aside or add to a human covenant that has been duly established, so it is in this case. [16]The promises were spoken to Abraham and to his seed. The Scripture does not say "and to seeds," meaning many people, but "and to your seed,"[a] meaning one person, who is Christ. [17]What I mean is this: The law, introduced 430 years later, does not set aside the covenant previously established by God and thus do away with the promise. [18]For if the inheritance depends on the law, then it no longer depends on a promise; but God in his grace gave it to Abraham through a promise.

[19]What, then, was the purpose of the law? It was added because of transgressions until the Seed to whom the promise referred had come. The law was put into effect through angels by a mediator. [20]A mediator, however, does not represent just one party; but God is one.

[21]Is the law, therefore, opposed to the promises of God? Absolutely not! For if a law had been given that could impart life, then righteousness would certainly have come by the law. [22]But the Scripture declares that the whole world is a prisoner of sin, so that what was promised, being given through faith in Jesus Christ, might be given to those who believe.

[23]Before this faith came, we were held prisoners by the law, locked up until faith should be revealed. [24]So the law was put in charge to lead us to Christ[b] that we might be justified by faith. [25]Now that faith has come, we are no longer under the supervision of the law.

Sons of God

[26]You are all sons of God through faith in Christ Jesus, [27]for all of you who were baptized into Christ have clothed yourselves with Christ. [28]There is neither Jew nor Greek, slave nor free, male nor female, for you are all one in Christ Jesus. [29]If you belong to Christ, then you are Abraham's seed, and heirs according to the promise.

4 What I am saying is that as long as the heir is a child, he is no different from a slave, although he owns the whole estate. [2]He is subject to guardians and trustees until the time set by his father. [3]So also, when we were children, we were in slavery under the basic principles of the world. [4]But when the time had fully come, God sent his Son, born of a woman, born under law, [5]to redeem those under law, that we might receive the full rights of sons. [6]Because you are sons, God sent the Spirit of his Son into our hearts, the Spirit who calls out, "Abba,[c] Father." [7]So you are no longer a slave, but a son; and since you are a son, God has made you also an heir.

Paul's Concern for the Galatians

[8]Formerly, when you did not know God, you were slaves to those who by nature are not gods. [9]But now that you know God—or rather are known by God—how is it that you are turning back to those weak and miserable principles? Do you wish to be enslaved by them all over again? [10]You are observing special days and months and seasons and years! [11]I fear for you, that somehow I have wasted my efforts on you.

[12]I plead with you, brothers, become like me, for I became like you. You have done me no wrong. [13]As you know, it was because of an illness that I first preached the gospel to you. [14]Even though my illness was a trial to you, you did not treat me with contempt or scorn. Instead, you welcomed me as if I were an angel of God, as if I were Christ Jesus himself. [15]What has happened to all your joy? I can testify that, if you could have done so, you would have torn out your eyes and given them to me. [16]Have I now become your enemy by telling you the truth?

[17]Those people are zealous to win you over, but for no good. What they want is to alienate you ⌊from us⌋ so that you may be zealous for them. [18]It is fine to be zealous, provided the purpose is good, and to be so always and not just when I am with you. [19]My dear children, for whom I am again in the pains of childbirth until Christ is formed in you, [20]how I wish I could be with you now and change my tone, because I am perplexed about you!

---

[a]16 Gen. 12:7; 13:15; 24:7   [b]24 Or charge until Christ came   [c]6 Aramaic for Father

Hagar and Sarah

[21]Tell me, you who want to be under the law, are you not aware of what the law says? [22]For it is written that Abraham had two sons, one by the slave woman and the other by the free woman. [23]His son by the slave woman was born in the ordinary way; but his son by the free woman was born as the result of a promise.

[24]These things may be taken figuratively, for the women represent two covenants. One covenant is from Mount Sinai and bears children who are to be slaves: This is Hagar. [25]Now Hagar stands for Mount Sinai in Arabia and corresponds to the present city of Jerusalem, because she is in slavery with her children. [26]But the Jerusalem that is above is free, and she is our mother. [27]For it is written:

"Be glad, O barren woman,
   who bears no children;
break forth and cry aloud,
   you who have no labor pains;
because more are the children of the
     desolate woman
   than of her who has a husband."[a]

[28]Now you, brothers, like Isaac, are children of promise. [29]At that time the son born in the ordinary way persecuted the son born by the power of the Spirit. It is the same now. [30]But what does the Scripture say? "Get rid of the slave woman and her son, for the slave woman's son will never share in the inheritance with the free woman's son."[b] [31]Therefore, brothers, we are not children of the slave woman, but of the free woman.

Freedom in Christ

5 It is for freedom that Christ has set us free. Stand firm, then, and do not let yourselves be burdened again by a yoke of slavery.

[2]Mark my words! I, Paul, tell you that if you let yourselves be circumcised, Christ will be of no value to you at all. [3]Again I declare to every man who lets himself be circumcised that he is obligated to obey the whole law. [4]You who are trying to be justified by law have been alienated from Christ; you have fallen away from grace. [5]But by faith we eagerly await through the Spirit the righteousness for which we hope. [6]For in Christ Jesus neither circumcision nor uncircumcision has any value. The only thing that counts is faith expressing itself through love.

[7]You were running a good race. Who cut in on you and kept you from obeying the truth? [8]That kind of persuasion does not come from the one who calls you. [9]"A little yeast works through the whole batch of dough." [10]I am confident in the Lord that you will take no other view. The one who is throwing you into confusion will pay the penalty, whoever he may be. [11]Brothers, if I am still preaching circumcision, why am I still being persecuted? In that case the offense of the cross has been abolished. [12]As for those agitators, I wish they would go the whole way and emasculate themselves!

[13]You, my brothers, were called to be free. But do not use your freedom to indulge the sinful nature[c]; rather, serve one another in love. [14]The entire law is summed up in a single command: "Love your neighbor as yourself."[d] [15]If you keep on biting and devouring each other, watch out or you will be destroyed by each other.

Life by the Spirit

[16]So I say, live by the Spirit, and you will not gratify the desires of the sinful nature. [17]For the sinful nature desires what is contrary to the Spirit, and the Spirit what is contrary to the sinful nature. They are in conflict with each other, so that you do not do what you want. [18]But if you are led by the Spirit, you are not under law.

[19]The acts of the sinful nature are obvious: sexual immorality, impurity and debauchery; [20]idolatry and witchcraft; hatred, discord, jealousy, fits of rage, selfish ambition, dissensions, factions [21]and envy; drunkenness, orgies, and the like. I warn you, as I did before, that those who live like this will not inherit the kingdom of God.

[22]But the fruit of the Spirit is love, joy, peace, patience, kindness, goodness, faithfulness, [23]gentleness and self-control. Against such things there is no law. [24]Those who belong to Christ Jesus have crucified the sinful nature with its

---

[a]27 Isaiah 54:1   [b]30 Gen. 21:10   [c]13 Or *the flesh*; also in verses 16, 17, 19 and 24   [d]14 Lev. 19:18

passions and desires. ²⁵Since we live by the Spirit, let us keep in step with the Spirit. ²⁶Let us not become conceited, provoking and envying each other.

Doing Good to All

6 Brothers, if someone is caught in a sin, you who are spiritual should restore him gently. But watch yourself, or you also may be tempted. ²Carry each other's burdens, and in this way you will fulfill the law of Christ. ³If anyone thinks he is something when he is noth-

ing, he deceives himself. ⁴Each one should test his own actions. Then he can take pride in himself, without comparing himself to somebody else, ⁵for each one should carry his own load.

⁶Anyone who receives instruction in the word must share all good things with his instructor.

⁷Do not be deceived: God cannot be mocked. A man reaps what he sows. ⁸The one who sows to please his sinful nature, from that nature*ᵃ* will reap destruction; the one who sows to please

ᵃ8 Or his flesh, from the flesh

◁ **TUESDAY** ▷

VERSE:
Galatians 5:1

AUTHOR:
Cynthia Heald

PASSAGE:
Galatians 5:1–15

Freedom in Christ

I have heard of slaves who were given freedom by the Emancipation Proclamation who still chose to live in slavery. For them, freedom was a frightening unknown. I think of the Israelites who were freed from their slavery in Egypt, yet longed for the food they received while in captivity (Exodus 16:3; Numbers 11:5). They were willing to become slaves again just to satisfy their appetites.

Freedom can be overwhelming, and it may seem that we are really sacrificing the "good life" to be set free by Christ. To truly understand the weight of sin and self is to begin to grasp the preciousness of our freedom in Christ. This understanding is a continuing process for me. I give up my freedom when I insist on being in control, demanding my own happiness and building walls of protection. All of these behaviors seem right and feel comfortable, but they ultimately become heavy burdens.

God clearly calls us to "give up" this cumbersome, defeating "old self." I think more than anything this means grasping the truth that I have the power to lay aside these encumbrances. I don't have to be a slave to sin, to myself or to others in order to feel good about who I am. I don't have to have the world tell me what will make me happy. True freedom is realizing that apart from Christ, I am not free. If I really want to experience this "addictive aliveness," then I will throw off everything that hinders me from being truly alive.

ADDITIONAL SCRIPTURE READINGS:
Exodus 16:3; John 8:36; Romans 8:2

Go to page 266 for your next devotional reading.

the Spirit, from the Spirit will reap eternal life. [9]Let us not become weary in doing good, for at the proper time we will reap a harvest if we do not give up. [10]Therefore, as we have opportunity, let us do good to all people, especially to those who belong to the family of believers.

Not Circumcision but a New Creation

[11]See what large letters I use as I write to you with my own hand!

[12]Those who want to make a good impression outwardly are trying to compel you to be circumcised. The only reason they do this is to avoid being persecuted for the cross of Christ. [13]Not even those who are circumcised obey the law, yet they want you to be circumcised that they may boast about your flesh. [14]May I never boast except in the cross of our Lord Jesus Christ, through which[a] the world has been crucified to me, and I to the world. [15]Neither circumcision nor uncircumcision means anything; what counts is a new creation. [16]Peace and mercy to all who follow this rule, even to the Israel of God.

[17]Finally, let no one cause me trouble, for I bear on my body the marks of Jesus.

[18]The grace of our Lord Jesus Christ be with your spirit, brothers. Amen.

---

[a] 14 Or whom

PAUL *writes this letter so that his readers might better understand God's eternal purposes for the church. One of those purposes is to reconcile people to God and to each other through the work of Jesus on the cross. Think about your own relationship with God and others and your own need for reconciliation. Look for Paul's practical advice on how to live in unity with God and one another.*

EPHESIANS

1 Paul, an apostle of Christ Jesus by the will of God,

To the saints in Ephesus,*a* the faithful*b* in Christ Jesus:

2Grace and peace to you from God our Father and the Lord Jesus Christ.

Spiritual Blessings in Christ

3Praise be to the God and Father of our Lord Jesus Christ, who has blessed us in the heavenly realms with every spiritual blessing in Christ. **4**For he chose us in him before the creation of the world to be holy and blameless in his sight. In love **5**he*c* predestined us to be adopted as his sons through Jesus Christ, in accordance with his pleasure and will— **6**to the praise of his glorious

grace, which he has freely given us in the One he loves. **7**In him we have redemption through his blood, the forgiveness of sins, in accordance with the riches of God's grace **8**that he lavished on us with all wisdom and understanding. **9**And he*d* made known to us the mystery of his will according to his good pleasure, which he purposed in Christ, **10**to be put into effect when the times will have reached their fulfillment—to bring all things in heaven and on earth together under one head, even Christ.

11In him we were also chosen,*e* having been predestined according to the plan of him who works out everything in conformity with the purpose of his will, **12**in order that we, who were the first to hope in Christ, might be for the

---

a1 Some early manuscripts do not have *in Ephesus.*   *b1* Or *believers who are*   *c4,5* Or *sight in love.*
5He   *d8,9* Or *us. With all wisdom and understanding,* *9he*   *e11* Or *were made heirs*

praise of his glory. ¹³And you also were included in Christ when you heard the word of truth, the gospel of your salvation. Having believed, you were marked in him with a seal, the promised Holy Spirit, ¹⁴who is a deposit guaranteeing our inheritance until the redemption of those who are God's possession—to the praise of his glory.

Thanksgiving and Prayer

¹⁵For this reason, ever since I heard about your faith in the Lord Jesus and your love for all the saints, ¹⁶I have not stopped giving thanks for you, remembering you in my prayers. ¹⁷I keep asking that the God of our Lord Jesus Christ, the glorious Father, may give you the Spirit*a* of wisdom and revelation, so that you may know him better. ¹⁸I pray also that the eyes of your heart may be enlightened in order that you may know the hope to which he has called you, the riches of his glorious inheritance in the saints, ¹⁹and his incomparably great power for us who believe. That power is like the working of his mighty strength, ²⁰which he exerted in Christ when he

a 17 Or a spirit

WEDNESDAY

VERSE:	AUTHOR:	PASSAGE:
Ephesians 1:5	Kay Marshall Strom	Ephesians 1:3-5

Abba, Father

If you are a believer who has trusted in Jesus Christ, you cannot truly see yourself as God sees you unless you first understand your position with Christ. Do you realize how wonderful that position is? Do you comprehend the astounding things that are true of you? Here is a list just to get you started.
If you are a child of God you:

- are blessed with every spiritual blessing
- were chosen before the foundation of the world
- are holy and without blame before God
- were predestined to be adopted by God
- have been made accepted by God
- are redeemed through Christ's blood
- have been forgiven for your sins

There's more. The relationship you have with your Father God is truly intimate and special. You can call him "Abba, Father." Abba is equivalent to our word for daddy. That means you can come before God and call him Daddy!

Because of God's sovereign and gracious act in providing for your salvation by adopting you, there is a blessed climate of intimate love and trust between you. How infinitely precious and worthwhile you must be to him!

ADDITIONAL SCRIPTURE READINGS:
Jeremiah 31:9; Matthew 6; 1 John 3:1

Go to page 268 for your next devotional reading.

raised him from the dead and seated him at his right hand in the heavenly realms, [21]far above all rule and authority, power and dominion, and every title that can be given, not only in the present age but also in the one to come. [22]And God placed all things under his feet and appointed him to be head over everything for the church, [23]which is his body, the fullness of him who fills everything in every way.

Made Alive in Christ

2 As for you, you were dead in your transgressions and sins, [2]in which you used to live when you followed the ways of this world and of the ruler of the kingdom of the air, the spirit who is now at work in those who are disobedient. [3]All of us also lived among them at one time, gratifying the cravings of our sinful nature[a] and following its desires and thoughts. Like the rest, we were by nature objects of wrath. [4]But because of his great love for us, God, who is rich in mercy, [5]made us alive with Christ even when we were dead in transgressions— it is by grace you have been saved. [6]And God raised us up with Christ and seated us with him in the heavenly realms in Christ Jesus, [7]in order that in the coming ages he might show the incomparable riches of his grace, expressed in his kindness to us in Christ Jesus. [8]For it is by grace you have been saved, through faith—and this not from yourselves, it is the gift of God— [9]not by works, so that no one can boast. [10]For we are God's workmanship, created in Christ Jesus to do good works, which God prepared in advance for us to do.

One in Christ

[11]Therefore, remember that formerly you who are Gentiles by birth and called "uncircumcised" by those who call themselves "the circumcision" (that done in the body by the hands of men)— [12]remember that at that time you were separate from Christ, excluded from citizenship in Israel and foreigners to the covenants of the promise, without hope and without God in the world. [13]But now in Christ Jesus you who once were far away have been brought near through the blood of Christ.

[14]For he himself is our peace, who has made the two one and has destroyed the barrier, the dividing wall of hostility, [15]by abolishing in his flesh the law with its commandments and regulations. His purpose was to create in himself one new man out of the two, thus making peace, [16]and in this one body to reconcile both of them to God through the cross, by which he put to death their hostility. [17]He came and preached peace to you who were far away and peace to those who were near. [18]For through him we both have access to the Father by one Spirit.

[19]Consequently, you are no longer foreigners and aliens, but fellow citizens with God's people and members of God's household, [20]built on the foundation of the apostles and prophets, with Christ Jesus himself as the chief cornerstone. [21]In him the whole building is joined together and rises to become a holy temple in the Lord. [22]And in him you too are being built together to become a dwelling in which God lives by his Spirit.

Paul the Preacher to the Gentiles

3 For this reason I, Paul, the prisoner of Christ Jesus for the sake of you Gentiles—

[2]Surely you have heard about the administration of God's grace that was given to me for you, [3]that is, the mystery made known to me by revelation, as I have already written briefly. [4]In reading this, then, you will be able to understand my insight into the mystery of Christ, [5]which was not made known to men in other generations as it has now been revealed by the Spirit to God's holy apostles and prophets. [6]This mystery is that through the gospel the Gentiles are heirs together with Israel, members together of one body, and sharers together in the promise in Christ Jesus.

[7]I became a servant of this gospel by the gift of God's grace given me through the working of his power. [8]Although I am less than the least of all God's people, this grace was given me: to preach to the Gentiles the unsearchable riches of Christ, [9]and to make plain to everyone the administration of this mystery,

---

[a]3 Or *our flesh*

which for ages past was kept hidden in God, who created all things. **10**His intent was that now, through the church, the manifold wisdom of God should be made known to the rulers and authorities in the heavenly realms, **11**according to his eternal purpose which he accomplished in Christ Jesus our Lord. **12**In him and through faith in him we may approach God with freedom and confidence. **13**I ask you, therefore, not to be discouraged because of my sufferings for you, which are your glory.

A Prayer for the Ephesians

14For this reason I kneel before the Father, **15**from whom his whole family*a* in heaven and on earth derives its name. **16**I pray that out of his glorious riches he may strengthen you with power through his Spirit in your inner being, **17**so that Christ may dwell in your hearts through faith. And I pray that you, being rooted and established in love, **18**may have power, together with all the saints, to grasp how wide and long and high and deep is the love of Christ, **19**and to know

a 15 Or whom all fatherhood

THURSDAY

VERSE: | AUTHOR: | PASSAGE:
Ephesians 2:14 | **Debra Klingsporn** | **Ephesians 2:14–22**

A Time for Peace

Snowbirds. That's what we always called them. They were folks from the North who sought the milder temperatures of the Sunbelt in the harshest months of winter. Some locals resented their annual migratory invasion, while others welcomed their business. But almost everybody considered them different. One of "them," not one of "us."

Distinctions. Differences. Categories.

How tempting is the universal tendency to categorize people we meet. We place them safely in little boxes in our minds labeled "familiar" or "unfamiliar" while denying our prejudices. Blue collar or white collar; white or black; educated or underprivileged. Labels become boxes in our minds into which we can admit or reject the people we encounter from day to day.

But differences aside, we really are more alike than different. And we never know through whom God may want to speak to us, get our attention or touch our hearts.

The person who most aggravates me is quite possibly a reflection of my own shadow side, that part of me that I most dislike, struggle with or find embarrassing. Before too quickly casting judgment on another, perhaps I need to ask God to help me turn the spotlight back on myself. Perhaps I could begin by praying for the person I find it difficult to deal with, and in doing so, I may be surprised by who experiences the greatest change in attitude—it just might be me.

ADDITIONAL SCRIPTURE READINGS:
Psalm 133; Acts 10:24–48; Ephesians 4:3–6

Go to page 269 for your next devotional reading.

this love that surpasses knowledge—that you may be filled to the measure of all the fullness of God.

20Now to him who is able to do immeasurably more than all we ask or imagine, according to his power that is at work within us, **21**to him be glory in the church and in Christ Jesus throughout all generations, for ever and ever! Amen.

FRIDAY

VERSE:	AUTHOR:	PASSAGE:
Ephesians 3:18	Claire Cloninger	Ephesians 3:14–21

Original Self-Worth

Adam and Eve lost the clear, simple sense of their own identity. That picture of themselves that they had found reflected in the loving eyes of the one who designed them was blurred and distorted when they rebelled against him. Suddenly they were ashamed of the bodies they had felt so good about. Suddenly they were scrambling for fig leaves and a good hideout.

Many of us carry in us the destructive payoff for Eden's wrong choice. We find our image in the eyes of imperfect others (parents, peers, teachers, etc.) and develop a faulty sense of self.

An unhealthy and unrealistic sense of self can make our lives miserable and even ruin our health. I have known more than one anorexic teen who has stubbornly tried to starve herself because she saw her thin body as fat. I have another gorgeous friend who has won major beauty competitions, yet she sees her flaws far more clearly than she sees her strong points.

Our loss of identity often goes deeper than our looks. We try to acquire a feeling of significance in many other areas as well: our work, our achievements, our bank accounts, our social standing, our "connections." Adam and Eve in the garden did not need any of these things to prove their value. But our chaotic culture has us running around in circles trying to find our worth in doing.

The year I worked in the advertising industry, I saw firsthand that fortunes are made and empires built on the shaky self-images of prospective consumers. Every ad I wrote was aimed at convincing buyers that purchasing this car or shopping at that store or dining at this restaurant would finally make them feel whole and happy and fulfilled—that with one simple purchase they would magically possess the self-confidence they had been lacking.

But the truth is, no amount of money can buy back for us that true, balanced, sense of self-worth that was left behind in Eden. It can only be found where Adam and Eve found it, in the eyes of the one who made us.

ADDITIONAL SCRIPTURE READINGS:
Genesis 3; 2 Corinthians 5:1–5

Go to page 271 for your next devotional reading.

Unity in the Body of Christ

4 As a prisoner for the Lord, then, I urge you to live a life worthy of the calling you have received. **2**Be completely humble and gentle; be patient, bearing with one another in love. **3**Make every effort to keep the unity of the Spirit through the bond of peace. **4**There is one body and one Spirit— just as you were called to one hope when you were called— **5**one Lord, one faith, one baptism; **6**one God and Father of all, who is over all and through all and in all.

7But to each one of us grace has been given as Christ apportioned it. **8**This is why it[a] says:

"When he ascended on high,
  he led captives in his train
  and gave gifts to men."[b]

9(What does "he ascended" mean except that he also descended to the lower, earthly regions[c]? **10**He who descended is the very one who ascended higher than all the heavens, in order to fill the whole universe.) **11**It was he who gave some to be apostles, some to be prophets, some to be evangelists, and some to be pastors and teachers, **12**to prepare God's people for works of service, so that the body of Christ may be built up **13**until we all reach unity in the faith and in the knowledge of the Son of God and become mature, attaining to the whole measure of the fullness of Christ.

14Then we will no longer be infants, tossed back and forth by the waves, and blown here and there by every wind of teaching and by the cunning and craftiness of men in their deceitful scheming. **15**Instead, speaking the truth in love, we will in all things grow up into him who is the Head, that is, Christ. **16**From him the whole body, joined and held together by every supporting ligament, grows and builds itself up in love, as each part does its work.

Living as Children of Light

17So I tell you this, and insist on it in the Lord, that you must no longer live as the Gentiles do, in the futility of their thinking. **18**They are darkened in their understanding and separated from the life of God because of the ignorance that is in them due to the hardening of their hearts. **19**Having lost all sensitivity, they have given themselves over to sensuality so as to indulge in every kind of impurity, with a continual lust for more.

20You, however, did not come to know Christ that way. **21**Surely you heard of him and were taught in him in accordance with the truth that is in Jesus. **22**You were taught, with regard to your former way of life, to put off your old self, which is being corrupted by its deceitful desires; **23**to be made new in the attitude of your minds; **24**and to put on the new self, created to be like God in true righteousness and holiness.

25Therefore each of you must put off falsehood and speak truthfully to his neighbor, for we are all members of one body. **26**"In your anger do not sin"[d]: Do not let the sun go down while you are still angry, **27**and do not give the devil a foothold. **28**He who has been stealing must steal no longer, but must work, doing something useful with his own hands, that he may have something to share with those in need.

29Do not let any unwholesome talk come out of your mouths, but only what is helpful for building others up according to their needs, that it may benefit those who listen. **30**And do not grieve the Holy Spirit of God, with whom you were sealed for the day of redemption. **31**Get rid of all bitterness, rage and anger, brawling and slander, along with every form of malice. **32**Be kind and compassionate to one another, forgiving each other, just as in Christ God forgave you.

5 Be imitators of God, therefore, as dearly loved children **2**and live a life of love, just as Christ loved us and gave himself up for us as a fragrant offering and sacrifice to God.

3But among you there must not be even a hint of sexual immorality, or of any kind of impurity, or of greed, because these are improper for God's holy people. **4**Nor should there be obscenity, foolish talk or coarse joking, which are out of place, but rather thanksgiving. **5**For of this you can be sure: No immoral, impure or greedy person—such a man is an idolater—has any inheritance in the kingdom of Christ and of God.[e]

---

[a]8 Or *God*   [b]8 Psalm 68:18   [c]9 Or *the depths of the earth*   [d]26 Psalm 4:4   [e]5 Or *kingdom of the Christ and God*

WEEKENDING

REFLECT

May the mind of Christ, my Savior,
Live in me from day to day,
By his love and power controlling
All I do and say.

May the word of God dwell richly
In my heart from hour to hour,
So that all may see I triumph
Only through his power.

May the peace of God, my Father,
Rule my life in everything,
That I may be calm to comfort
Sick and sorrowing.

May the love of Jesus fill me
As the waters fill the sea.
Him exalting, self abasing:
This is victory.

Kate B. Wilkinson

REVIVE

Saturday: Ephesians 3:14–21
Sunday: Philippians 2:5–10

*Go to page 273 for your
next devotional reading.*

[6]Let no one deceive you with empty words, for because of such things God's wrath comes on those who are disobedient. [7]Therefore do not be partners with them.

[8]For you were once darkness, but now you are light in the Lord. Live as children of light [9](for the fruit of the light consists in all goodness, righteousness and truth) [10]and find out what pleases the Lord. [11]Have nothing to do with the fruitless deeds of darkness, but rather expose them. [12]For it is shameful even to mention what the disobedient do in secret. [13]But everything exposed by the light becomes visible, [14]for it is light that makes everything visible. This is why it is said:

"Wake up, O sleeper,
    rise from the dead,
and Christ will shine on you."

[15]Be very careful, then, how you live—not as unwise but as wise, [16]making the most of every opportunity, because the days are evil. [17]Therefore do not be foolish, but understand what the Lord's will is. [18]Do not get drunk on wine, which leads to debauchery. Instead, be filled with the Spirit. [19]Speak to one another with psalms, hymns and spiritual songs. Sing and make music in your heart to the Lord, [20]always giving thanks to God the Father for everything, in the name of our Lord Jesus Christ.

[21]Submit to one another out of reverence for Christ.

Wives and Husbands

[22]Wives, submit to your husbands as to the Lord. [23]For the husband is the head of the wife as Christ is the head of the church, his body, of which he is the Savior. [24]Now as the church submits to Christ, so also wives should submit to their husbands in everything.

[25]Husbands, love your wives, just as Christ loved the church and gave himself up for her [26]to make her holy, cleansing[a] her by the washing with water through the word, [27]and to present her to himself as a radiant church, without stain or wrinkle or any other blemish, but holy and blameless. [28]In this same way, husbands ought to love their wives as their own bodies. He who loves his wife loves himself. [29]After all,

no one ever hated his own body, but he feeds and cares for it, just as Christ does the church— [30]for we are members of his body. [31]"For this reason a man will leave his father and mother and be united to his wife, and the two will become one flesh."[b] [32]This is a profound mystery—but I am talking about Christ and the church. [33]However, each one of you also must love his wife as he loves himself, and the wife must respect her husband.

Children and Parents

6 Children, obey your parents in the Lord, for this is right. [2]"Honor your father and mother"—which is the first commandment with a promise— [3]"that it may go well with you and that you may enjoy long life on the earth."[c]

[4]Fathers, do not exasperate your children; instead, bring them up in the training and instruction of the Lord.

Slaves and Masters

[5]Slaves, obey your earthly masters with respect and fear, and with sincerity of heart, just as you would obey Christ. [6]Obey them not only to win their favor when their eye is on you, but like slaves of Christ, doing the will of God from your heart. [7]Serve wholeheartedly, as if you were serving the Lord, not men, [8]because you know that the Lord will reward everyone for whatever good he does, whether he is slave or free.

[9]And masters, treat your slaves in the same way. Do not threaten them, since you know that he who is both their Master and yours is in heaven, and there is no favoritism with him.

The Armor of God

[10]Finally, be strong in the Lord and in his mighty power. [11]Put on the full armor of God so that you can take your stand against the devil's schemes. [12]For our struggle is not against flesh and blood, but against the rulers, against the authorities, against the powers of this dark world and against the spiritual forces of evil in the heavenly realms. [13]Therefore put on the full armor of God, so that when the day of evil comes, you may be able to stand your ground, and after you have done everything, to stand. [14]Stand firm then, with the belt of

---

[a]26 Or *having cleansed*   [b]31 Gen. 2:24   [c]3 Deut. 5:16

truth buckled around your waist, with the breastplate of righteousness in place, [15]and with your feet fitted with the readiness that comes from the gospel of peace. [16]In addition to all this, take up the shield of faith, with which you can extinguish all the flaming arrows of the evil one. [17]Take the helmet of salvation and the sword of the Spirit, which is the word of God. [18]And pray in the Spirit on all occasions with all kinds of prayers and requests. With this in mind, be alert and always keep on praying for all the saints.

[19]Pray also for me, that whenever I open my mouth, words may be given me so that I will fearlessly make known the mystery of the gospel, [20]for which I am an ambassador in chains. Pray that I may declare it fearlessly, as I should.

Final Greetings

[21]Tychicus, the dear brother and faithful servant in the Lord, will tell you everything, so that you also may know how I am and what I am doing. [22]I am sending him to you for this very purpose, that you may know how we are, and that he may encourage you.

[23]Peace to the brothers, and love with faith from God the Father and the Lord Jesus Christ. [24]Grace to all who love our Lord Jesus Christ with an undying love.

⟨ MONDAY ⟩

VERSE:	AUTHOR:	PASSAGE:
Ephesians 5:25	Teresa & David Ferguson, Holly & Chris Thurman	Ephesians 5:22–33

Love Is Forever

I watched him look into the window and check his reflection. He carefully combed his hair and straightened his tie. He had to be seventy years old, yet he acted as eager as a schoolboy. He was a regular visitor to the nursing home. He was meeting his wife, a victim of Alzheimer's. His wife never spoke much. But it didn't seem to matter to him that he got no response from his wife. He made cheery conversation, read letters from family, sang to her, fed her or just held her hand.

Love, a rare commitment to care for another regardless of the response. Christ took human form to give us that love—at the cross. Mr. Lacy is pitied but a privileged man, who loves his wife in such a way that the world may look on with a deep sense of longing. He paints a beautiful picture for the rest of us to see and enjoy what Christ's love for us looks like.

ADDITIONAL SCRIPTURE READINGS:
John 15:13; Romans 5:8; 1 Corinthians 13:4–7

Go to page 275 for your next devotional reading.

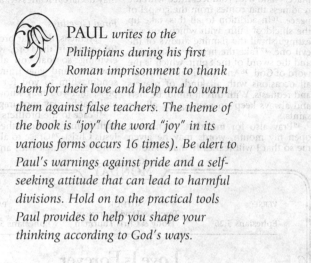

PAUL *writes to the Philippians during his first Roman imprisonment to thank them for their love and help and to warn them against false teachers. The theme of the book is "joy" (the word "joy" in its various forms occurs 16 times). Be alert to Paul's warnings against pride and a self-seeking attitude that can lead to harmful divisions. Hold on to the practical tools Paul provides to help you shape your thinking according to God's ways.*

PHILIPPIANS

1 Paul and Timothy, servants of Christ Jesus,

To all the saints in Christ Jesus at Philippi, together with the overseers*a* and deacons:

²Grace and peace to you from God our Father and the Lord Jesus Christ.

Thanksgiving and Prayer

³I thank my God every time I remember you. ⁴In all my prayers for all of you, I always pray with joy ⁵because of your partnership in the gospel from the first day until now, ⁶being confident of this, that he who began a good work in you will carry it on to completion until the day of Christ Jesus.

⁷It is right for me to feel this way about all of you, since I have you in my heart; for whether I am in chains or defending and confirming the gospel, all of you share in God's grace with me. ⁸God can testify how I long for all of you with the affection of Christ Jesus.

⁹And this is my prayer: that your love may abound more and more in knowledge and depth of insight, ¹⁰so that you may be able to discern what is best and may be pure and blameless until the day of Christ, ¹¹filled with the fruit of righteousness that comes through Jesus Christ—to the glory and praise of God.

Paul's Chains Advance the Gospel

¹²Now I want you to know, brothers,

that what has happened to me has really served to advance the gospel. [13]As a result, it has become clear throughout the whole palace guard[a] and to everyone else that I am in chains for Christ. [14]Because of my chains, most of the brothers in the Lord have been encouraged to speak the word of God more courageously and fearlessly.

[15]It is true that some preach Christ out of envy and rivalry, but others out of goodwill. [16]The latter do so in love, knowing that I am put here for the defense of the gospel. [17]The former preach Christ out of selfish ambition, not sincerely, supposing that they can stir up trouble for me while I am in chains.[b] [18]But what does it matter? The important thing is that in every way, whether from false motives or true, Christ is preached. And because of this I rejoice.

Yes, and I will continue to rejoice, [19]for I know that through your prayers and the help given by the Spirit of Jesus Christ, what has happened to me will turn out for my deliverance.[c] [20]I eagerly expect and hope that I will in no way be ashamed, but will have sufficient courage so that now as always Christ will be exalted in my body, whether by life or by death. [21]For to me, to live is Christ and to die is gain. [22]If I am to go on living in the body, this will mean fruitful labor for me. Yet what shall I choose? I do not know! [23]I am torn between the two: I desire to depart and be with Christ, which is better by far; [24]but it is more necessary for you that I remain in the

---

[a]13 Or *whole palace*   [b]16,17 Some late manuscripts have verses 16 and 17 in reverse order.
[c]19 Or *salvation*

TUESDAY

VERSE:
Philippians 1:6

AUTHOR:
Kay Marshall Strom

PASSAGE:
Philippians 1:3-6

The Best Is Yet to Come

We know that however satisfying our life is here on earth, the best is yet to come. Consider these comparisons:

- Here on earth, you can be sure of God's love. In heaven, you will constantly be basking in that love.
- Here on earth, you can know you are accepted by God. In heaven, you will hold an honored place as God's child, sister of Christ.
- Here on earth, you can strive to be Christlike. In heaven, you will be perfect.
- Here on earth, you live by faith. In heaven, you will understand it all and thank God for his wisdom in every little thing.
- Here on earth, your treasure is pitiful and shabby and falling apart. In heaven, the treasure you stored up is priceless and indestructible.

Hallelujah! The best really is yet to come!

ADDITIONAL SCRIPTURE READINGS:
Isaiah 65:25; 2 Peter 3:13; Revelation 21:1-5

Go to page 277 for your next devotional reading.

body. 25Convinced of this, I know that I will remain, and I will continue with all of you for your progress and joy in the faith, 26so that through my being with you again your joy in Christ Jesus will overflow on account of me.

27Whatever happens, conduct yourselves in a manner worthy of the gospel of Christ. Then, whether I come and see you or only hear about you in my absence, I will know that you stand firm in one spirit, contending as one man for the faith of the gospel 28without being frightened in any way by those who oppose you. This is a sign to them that they will be destroyed, but that you will be saved—and that by God. 29For it has been granted to you on behalf of Christ not only to believe on him, but also to suffer for him, 30since you are going through the same struggle you saw I had, and now hear that I still have.

Imitating Christ's Humility

2 If you have any encouragement from being united with Christ, if any comfort from his love, if any fellowship with the Spirit, if any tenderness and compassion, 2then make my joy complete by being like-minded, having the same love, being one in spirit and purpose. 3Do nothing out of selfish ambition or vain conceit, but in humility consider others better than yourselves. 4Each of you should look not only to your own interests, but also to the interests of others.

5Your attitude should be the same as that of Christ Jesus:

6Who, being in very nature*a* God,
　　did not consider equality with God
　　　　something to be grasped,
7but made himself nothing,
　　taking the very nature*b* of a
　　　　servant,
　　being made in human likeness.
8And being found in appearance as a
　　man,
　　he humbled himself
　　and became obedient to death—
　　　　even death on a cross!
9Therefore God exalted him to the
　　highest place
　　and gave him the name that is
　　　　above every name,

10that at the name of Jesus every knee
　　should bow,
　　in heaven and on earth and under
　　　　the earth,
11and every tongue confess that Jesus
　　Christ is Lord,
　　to the glory of God the Father.

Shining as Stars

12Therefore, my dear friends, as you have always obeyed—not only in my presence, but now much more in my absence—continue to work out your salvation with fear and trembling, 13for it is God who works in you to will and to act according to his good purpose.

14Do everything without complaining or arguing, 15so that you may become blameless and pure, children of God without fault in a crooked and depraved generation, in which you shine like stars in the universe 16as you hold out*c* the word of life—in order that I may boast on the day of Christ that I did not run or labor for nothing. 17But even if I am being poured out like a drink offering on the sacrifice and service coming from your faith, I am glad and rejoice with all of you. 18So you too should be glad and rejoice with me.

Timothy and Epaphroditus

19I hope in the Lord Jesus to send Timothy to you soon, that I also may be cheered when I receive news about you. 20I have no one else like him, who takes a genuine interest in your welfare. 21For everyone looks out for his own interests, not those of Jesus Christ. 22But you know that Timothy has proved himself, because as a son with his father he has served with me in the work of the gospel. 23I hope, therefore, to send him as soon as I see how things go with me. 24And I am confident in the Lord that I myself will come soon.

25But I think it is necessary to send back to you Epaphroditus, my brother, fellow worker and fellow soldier, who is also your messenger, whom you sent to take care of my needs. 26For he longs for all of you and is distressed because you heard he was ill. 27Indeed he was ill, and almost died. But God had mercy on him, and not on him only but also on me, to spare me sorrow upon sorrow. 28Therefore I am all the more eager to send him,

*a*6 Or in the form of　　*b*7 Or the form　　*c*16 Or hold on to

so that when you see him again you may be glad and I may have less anxiety. ²⁹Welcome him in the Lord with great joy, and honor men like him, ³⁰because he almost died for the work of Christ, risking his life to make up for the help you could not give me.

No Confidence in the Flesh

3 Finally, my brothers, rejoice in the Lord! It is no trouble for me to write the same things to you again, and it is a safeguard for you.

²Watch out for those dogs, those men who do evil, those mutilators of the flesh. ³For it is we who are the circumcision, we who worship by the Spirit of God, who glory in Christ Jesus, and who put no confidence in the flesh— ⁴though I myself have reasons for such confidence.

If anyone else thinks he has reasons to put confidence in the flesh, I have more: ⁵circumcised on the eighth day, of the people of Israel, of the tribe of Benjamin, a Hebrew of Hebrews; in regard to the law, a Pharisee; ⁶as for zeal, persecuting the church; as for legalistic righteousness, faultless.

⁷But whatever was to my profit I now consider loss for the sake of Christ. ⁸What is more, I consider everything a loss compared to the surpassing greatness of knowing Christ Jesus my Lord,

WEDNESDAY

VERSE:	AUTHOR:	PASSAGE:
Philippians 2:15	Elisa Morgan and Carol Kuykendall	Philippians 2:12-18

Dare to Dream

Dreams make the difference between living a life and really *living* a life. But some of us, caught up in the busyness of life, have forgotten how to dream. Here are some suggestions:

Identify where you want to grow and then start dreaming about possibilities for getting there. Writer Gary Hardaway comments, "We must dream, because we are made in the image of him who sees things that are not and wills them to be." *

Find a quiet spot. Sit back and let your thoughts roam. What has God already done in your life? What might he still do? Consider, just for a moment, what isn't but could be. Dream beyond where you are.

Dreams begin with asking such questions as, "If you could do anything you wanted with an extra hour today, what would it be?" Sometimes dreams have their roots in the past. "When you think back over your childhood, what did you do with your spare time?" Dreams also peer around the corners of our lives and right into the places where we live, [giving us] clues as to how we can grow.

Identify where you want to grow. Then start dreaming a dream for your life and make a plan.

* "When Dreams Die," *Moody Monthly* (June 1986): 20.

ADDITIONAL SCRIPTURE READINGS:
Psalm 35:9; 1 Thessalonians 5:23; 1 Peter 2:2

Go to page 279 for your next devotional reading.

for whose sake I have lost all things. I consider them rubbish, that I may gain Christ [9]and be found in him, not having a righteousness of my own that comes from the law, but that which is through faith in Christ—the righteousness that comes from God and is by faith. [10]I want to know Christ and the power of his resurrection and the fellowship of sharing in his sufferings, becoming like him in his death, [11]and so, somehow, to attain to the resurrection from the dead.

Pressing on Toward the Goal

[12]Not that I have already obtained all this, or have already been made perfect, but I press on to take hold of that for which Christ Jesus took hold of me. [13]Brothers, I do not consider myself yet to have taken hold of it. But one thing I do: Forgetting what is behind and straining toward what is ahead, [14]I press on toward the goal to win the prize for which God has called me heavenward in Christ Jesus.

[15]All of us who are mature should take such a view of things. And if on some point you think differently, that too God will make clear to you. [16]Only let us live up to what we have already attained.

[17]Join with others in following my example, brothers, and take note of those who live according to the pattern we gave you. [18]For, as I have often told you before and now say again even with tears, many live as enemies of the cross of Christ. [19]Their destiny is destruction, their god is their stomach, and their glory is in their shame. Their mind is on earthly things. [20]But our citizenship is in heaven. And we eagerly await a Savior from there, the Lord Jesus Christ, [21]who, by the power that enables him to bring everything under his control, will transform our lowly bodies so that they will be like his glorious body.

4 Therefore, my brothers, you whom I love and long for, my joy and crown, that is how you should stand firm in the Lord, dear friends!

Exhortations

[2]I plead with Euodia and I plead with Syntyche to agree with each other in the Lord. [3]Yes, and I ask you, loyal yokefellow,[a] help these women who have contended at my side in the cause of the gospel, along with Clement and the rest of my fellow workers, whose names are in the book of life.

[4]Rejoice in the Lord always. I will say it again: Rejoice! [5]Let your gentleness be evident to all. The Lord is near. [6]Do not be anxious about anything, but in everything, by prayer and petition, with thanksgiving, present your requests to God. [7]And the peace of God, which transcends all understanding, will guard your hearts and your minds in Christ Jesus.

[8]Finally, brothers, whatever is true, whatever is noble, whatever is right, whatever is pure, whatever is lovely, whatever is admirable—if anything is excellent or praiseworthy—think about such things. [9]Whatever you have learned or received or heard from me, or seen in me—put it into practice. And the God of peace will be with you.

Thanks for Their Gifts

[10]I rejoice greatly in the Lord that at last you have renewed your concern for me. Indeed, you have been concerned, but you had no opportunity to show it. [11]I am not saying this because I am in need, for I have learned to be content whatever the circumstances. [12]I know what it is to be in need, and I know what it is to have plenty. I have learned the secret of being content in any and every situation, whether well fed or hungry, whether living in plenty or in want. [13]I can do everything through him who gives me strength.

[14]Yet it was good of you to share in my troubles. [15]Moreover, as you Philippians know, in the early days of your acquaintance with the gospel, when I set out from Macedonia, not one church shared with me in the matter of giving and receiving, except you only; [16]for even when I was in Thessalonica, you sent me aid again and again when I was in need. [17]Not that I am looking for a gift, but I am looking for what may be credited to your account. [18]I have received full payment and even more; I am amply supplied, now that I have re-

ceived from Epaphroditus the gifts you sent. They are a fragrant offering, an acceptable sacrifice, pleasing to God. ¹⁹And my God will meet all your needs according to his glorious riches in Christ Jesus.

²⁰To our God and Father be glory for ever and ever. Amen.

Final Greetings

²¹Greet all the saints in Christ Jesus. The brothers who are with me send greetings. ²²All the saints send you greetings, especially those who belong to Caesar's household.

²³The grace of the Lord Jesus Christ be with your spirit. Amen.ᵃ

ᵃ23 Some manuscripts do not have *Amen*.

THURSDAY

VERSE:
Philippians 3:13

AUTHOR:
Shirley Pope Waite

PASSAGE:
Philippians 3:12–21

Delight in the Day

My husband and I were taking our first bike ride of the season. After years of biking, I still feel like a beginner on my first outing each spring.

Approaching an intersection, I heard a car behind me. I glanced back. My bike veered to the right, and the wheel scraped the curbing. Over I went. Luckily, my only damage was a skinned knee, a broken finger nail and total embarrassment.

"What happened?" Kyle asked.

I meekly replied, "I looked back."

It's so easy to look back on past mistakes, such as those I made while raising my children. And when an older relative criticized my maternal efforts, anger hitchhiked along with guilt. For years, these destructive emotions kept me from a closer walk with God.

What a lesson Paul teaches me! He refused to dwell on past ugly mistakes or unfair criticism. He put those things behind him, and kept his eye on what was ahead, saying "I press on toward the goal to win the prize for which God has called me heavenward in Christ Jesus" (v. 14).

ADDITIONAL SCRIPTURE READINGS:
Romans 5:15–18; 1 Timothy 6:12; Hebrews 12:1–2

Go to page 281 for your next devotional reading.

DURING *Paul's three-year ministry in Ephesus, Epaphras is converted and carries the gospel to Colosse. The young church that results then becomes the target of heretical attack. Paul's purpose in writing this letter is to refute the false teachers by asserting the supremacy of Christ and examining what that means for everyday living. As you read this letter, look for insights on ways to form attitudes and carry out actions that honor the Lord.*

COLOSSIANS

1 Paul, an apostle of Christ Jesus by the will of God, and Timothy our brother,

²To the holy and faithful*ᵃ* brothers in Christ at Colosse:

Grace and peace to you from God our Father.*ᵇ*

Thanksgiving and Prayer

³We always thank God, the Father of our Lord Jesus Christ, when we pray for you, ⁴because we have heard of your faith in Christ Jesus and of the love you have for all the saints— ⁵the faith and love that spring from the hope that is stored up for you in heaven and that you have already heard about in the word of truth, the gospel ⁶that has come to you. All over the world this gospel is bearing fruit and growing, just as it has been doing among you since the day you heard it and understood God's grace in all its truth. ⁷You learned it from Epaphras, our dear fellow servant, who is a faithful minister of Christ on our*ᶜ* behalf, ⁸and who also told us of your love in the Spirit.

⁹For this reason, since the day we heard about you, we have not stopped praying for you and asking God to fill you with the knowledge of his will through all spiritual wisdom and understanding. ¹⁰And we pray this in order that you may live a life worthy of the

ᵃ2 Or *believing*   *ᵇ2* Some manuscripts *Father and the Lord Jesus Christ*   *ᶜ7* Some manuscripts *your*

Lord and may please him in every way: bearing fruit in every good work, growing in the knowledge of God, **11**being strengthened with all power according to his glorious might so that you may have great endurance and patience, and joyfully **12**giving thanks to the Father, who has qualified you[a] to share in the inheritance of the saints in the kingdom of light. **13**For he has rescued us from the dominion of darkness and brought us into the kingdom of the Son he loves, **14**in whom we have redemption,[b] the forgiveness of sins.

[a]12 Some manuscripts *us*   [b]14 A few late manuscripts *redemption through his blood*

FRIDAY

VERSE: AUTHOR: PASSAGE:
Colossians 1:27   Claire Cloninger   Colossians 1:24–29

The Glorious Mystery: God Within Us

Jesus desires to be even closer to us than a brother or a friend. He is not only the God who is above us and the God who has come among us; he is also the God who desires to dwell within us. This is the fact that the apostle Paul described in Colossians 1:27 as "the glorious riches of this mystery, which is Christ in you, the hope of glory." It is the wonder he describes in Galatians 2:20 when he says, "I have been crucified with Christ and I no longer live, but Christ lives in me."

This is the mystery we were made to contain: the very life of Jesus. He means to live out the reality of who he is right here within the reality of who we are. He means to be our lives—the breath in our lungs, the thoughts in our heads, the energy and creativity in our jobs, the love in our hearts. He means to take on the stress and unravel the inner complications so that we can move through our lives just as he did, in gentleness and simplicity and harmony.

We were never intended to be more than containers: temples to contain his glory (1 Corinthians 3:16–17), branches to contain the sap of his life (John 15:1–8), vessels to contain the new wine of his Spirit (Romans 9:20–21). We are the glove; he is the hand. We are the cup; he is the coffee. We are the lamp; he is the light.

This is what we were made for. This is the intended purpose of the human person and personality; not to be gods, but to contain God. This is the kind of unity that was present in the garden but that is sadly missing in this world. It is the sheer simplicity of God's design that was shattered by humanity's sin. And it is the reason that Jesus came and cared and was tortured and killed and laid in a tomb and raised to life again . . . so that he could give us another shot at being what we were intended to be.

ADDITIONAL SCRIPTURE READINGS:
John 14:15; Galatians 2:20

Go to page 282 for your next devotional reading.

WEEKENDING

REVIEW

Who can explain God? It takes all of
Jesus Christ to explain him. There are
hundreds of functions and facets and
names of Jesus: the Light, the Ancient
of Days, the I Am, Wonderful
Counselor, the Light of Israel, the
Branch, the Rock, the Lord, the chief
Cornerstone, the Way, the Truth, the
Life and on and on and on. He is the
express image of God's Person, but it
takes every facet of him to reveal fully
the glories of the Godhead.

REFLECT

This is the Christ in whom you've
been placed. This is the Christ who surrounds you—above you, beneath you,
around you, before you, behind you,
within you. This is the Christ who is all,
and in all. You are complete, "running
over," in him!

Anne Ortlund

RESTORE

Saturday: Colossians 1:19
Sunday: Colossians 2:7

*Go to page 284 for your
next devotional reading.*

The Supremacy of Christ

15He is the image of the invisible God, the firstborn over all creation. **16**For by him all things were created: things in heaven and on earth, visible and invisible, whether thrones or powers or rulers or authorities; all things were created by him and for him. **17**He is before all things, and in him all things hold together. **18**And he is the head of the body, the church; he is the beginning and the firstborn from among the dead, so that in everything he might have the supremacy. **19**For God was pleased to have all his fullness dwell in him, **20**and through him to reconcile to himself all things, whether things on earth or things in heaven, by making peace through his blood, shed on the cross.

21Once you were alienated from God and were enemies in your minds because of[a] your evil behavior. **22**But now he has reconciled you by Christ's physical body through death to present you holy in his sight, without blemish and free from accusation— **23**if you continue in your faith, established and firm, not moved from the hope held out in the gospel. This is the gospel that you heard and that has been proclaimed to every creature under heaven, and of which I, Paul, have become a servant.

Paul's Labor for the Church

24Now I rejoice in what was suffered for you, and I fill up in my flesh what is still lacking in regard to Christ's afflictions, for the sake of his body, which is the church. **25**I have become its servant by the commission God gave me to present to you the word of God in its fullness— **26**the mystery that has been kept hidden for ages and generations, but is now disclosed to the saints. **27**To them God has chosen to make known among the Gentiles the glorious riches of this mystery, which is Christ in you, the hope of glory.

28We proclaim him, admonishing and teaching everyone with all wisdom, so that we may present everyone perfect in Christ. **29**To this end I labor, struggling with all his energy, which so powerfully works in me.

2 I want you to know how much I am struggling for you and for those at Laodicea, and for all who have not met me personally. **2**My purpose is that they may be encouraged in heart and united in love, so that they may have the full riches of complete understanding, in order that they may know the mystery of God, namely, Christ, **3**in whom are hidden all the treasures of wisdom and knowledge. **4**I tell you this so that no one may deceive you by fine-sounding arguments. **5**For though I am absent from you in body, I am present with you in spirit and delight to see how orderly you are and how firm your faith in Christ is.

Freedom From Human Regulations Through Life With Christ

6So then, just as you received Christ Jesus as Lord, continue to live in him, **7**rooted and built up in him, strengthened in the faith as you were taught, and overflowing with thankfulness.

8See to it that no one takes you captive through hollow and deceptive philosophy, which depends on human tradition and the basic principles of this world rather than on Christ.

9For in Christ all the fullness of the Deity lives in bodily form, **10**and you have been given fullness in Christ, who is the head over every power and authority. **11**In him you were also circumcised, in the putting off of the sinful nature,[b] not with a circumcision done by the hands of men but with the circumcision done by Christ, **12**having been buried with him in baptism and raised with him through your faith in the power of God, who raised him from the dead.

13When you were dead in your sins and in the uncircumcision of your sinful nature,[c] God made you[d] alive with Christ. He forgave us all our sins, **14**having canceled the written code, with its regulations, that was against us and that stood opposed to us; he took it away, nailing it to the cross. **15**And having disarmed the powers and authorities, he made a public spectacle of them, triumphing over them by the cross.[e]

16Therefore do not let anyone judge

a21 Or *minds, as shown by*   *b11* Or *the flesh*   *c13* Or *your flesh*   *d13* Some manuscripts *us*
e15 Or *them in him*

you by what you eat or drink, or with regard to a religious festival, a New Moon celebration or a Sabbath day. **17**These are a shadow of the things that were to come; the reality, however, is found in Christ. **18**Do not let anyone who delights in false humility and the worship of angels disqualify you for the prize. Such a person goes into great detail about what he has seen, and his unspiritual mind puffs him up with idle notions. **19**He has lost connection with the Head, from whom the whole body, supported and held together by its ligaments and sinews, grows as God causes it to grow.

❮ MONDAY ❯

VERSE:	AUTHOR:	PASSAGE:
Colossians 2:5	Emilie Barnes	Colossians 2:1–5

A Sense of Order

A home [filled with a welcoming spirit] has a sense of order about it. A sense that people, not possessions, are in charge of the household . . . that life is proceeding with a purpose and according to an overall plan.

Most of us respond positively to that kind of order in our lives because we are made in the image of God, and because God organized the whole universe to proceed in an orderly fashion. Think of the creation, when God created a beautiful, populated globe out of darkness and chaos. He is the ultimate organizer, and the results of his ordering Spirit are always good. We automatically feel more comfortable and more welcome when we sense his kind of order in our lives.

In a truly welcoming home, organization takes its proper place in the overall scheme of the universe. The daily chores of maintenance become something we can glory in, partly because they don't overwhelm us or define our whole existence.

Don't let this talk of order and organization make you feel guilty or panicked. Even if chaos and clutter in your home and life are wearing you down, the solution is not a whirlwind effort to "get organized." Unless you begin with the heart, the most complete reorganization of house and home will just give you a clean slate for chaos—and may drive you and everyone else crazy in the process.

We humans weren't made to "get organized." We were made to live as God's children, worshiping him and delighting in him. As we open our hearts and attitudes to God, putting him first in our lives and looking to him for guidance, he will show us little ways to organize the chaos and lead a more peaceful, ordered existence.

And it doesn't have to happen all at once. It has taken me thirty years to develop the systems that help me maintain order . . . in my life—and I'm still learning.

ADDITIONAL SCRIPTURE READINGS:
Genesis 1; 1 Corinthians 14:40

Go to page 286 for your next devotional reading.

20 Since you died with Christ to the basic principles of this world, why, as though you still belonged to it, do you submit to its rules: **21** "Do not handle! Do not taste! Do not touch!"? **22** These are all destined to perish with use, because they are based on human commands and teachings. **23** Such regulations indeed have an appearance of wisdom, with their self-imposed worship, their false humility and their harsh treatment of the body, but they lack any value in restraining sensual indulgence.

Rules for Holy Living

3 Since, then, you have been raised with Christ, set your hearts on things above, where Christ is seated at the right hand of God. **2** Set your minds on things above, not on earthly things. **3** For you died, and your life is now hidden with Christ in God. **4** When Christ, who is your*a* life, appears, then you also will appear with him in glory.

5 Put to death, therefore, whatever belongs to your earthly nature: sexual immorality, impurity, lust, evil desires and greed, which is idolatry. **6** Because of these, the wrath of God is coming.*b* **7** You used to walk in these ways, in the life you once lived. **8** But now you must rid yourselves of all such things as these: anger, rage, malice, slander, and filthy language from your lips. **9** Do not lie to each other, since you have taken off your old self with its practices **10** and have put on the new self, which is being renewed in knowledge in the image of its Creator. **11** Here there is no Greek or Jew, circumcised or uncircumcised, barbarian, Scythian, slave or free, but Christ is all, and is in all.

12 Therefore, as God's chosen people, holy and dearly loved, clothe yourselves with compassion, kindness, humility, gentleness and patience. **13** Bear with each other and forgive whatever grievances you may have against one another. Forgive as the Lord forgave you. **14** And over all these virtues put on love, which binds them all together in perfect unity.

15 Let the peace of Christ rule in your hearts, since as members of one body you were called to peace. And be thankful. **16** Let the word of Christ dwell in you richly as you teach and admonish one another with all wisdom, and as you sing psalms, hymns and spiritual songs with gratitude in your hearts to God. **17** And whatever you do, whether in word or deed, do it all in the name of the Lord Jesus, giving thanks to God the Father through him.

Rules for Christian Households

18 Wives, submit to your husbands, as is fitting in the Lord.

19 Husbands, love your wives and do not be harsh with them.

20 Children, obey your parents in everything, for this pleases the Lord.

21 Fathers, do not embitter your children, or they will become discouraged.

22 Slaves, obey your earthly masters in everything; and do it, not only when their eye is on you and to win their favor, but with sincerity of heart and reverence for the Lord. **23** Whatever you do, work at it with all your heart, as working for the Lord, not for men, **24** since you know that you will receive an inheritance from the Lord as a reward. It is the Lord Christ you are serving. **25** Anyone who does wrong will be repaid for his wrong, and there is no favoritism.

4 Masters, provide your slaves with what is right and fair, because you know that you also have a Master in heaven.

Further Instructions

2 Devote yourselves to prayer, being watchful and thankful. **3** And pray for us, too, that God may open a door for our message, so that we may proclaim the mystery of Christ, for which I am in chains. **4** Pray that I may proclaim it clearly, as I should. **5** Be wise in the way you act toward outsiders; make the most of every opportunity. **6** Let your conversation be always full of grace, seasoned with salt, so that you may know how to answer everyone.

Final Greetings

7 Tychicus will tell you all the news about me. He is a dear brother, a faithful minister and fellow servant in the Lord. **8** I am sending him to you for the

---

a4 Some manuscripts *our*   *b6* Some early manuscripts *coming on those who are disobedient*

express purpose that you may know about our*a* circumstances and that he may encourage your hearts. **9**He is coming with Onesimus, our faithful and dear brother, who is one of you. They will tell you everything that is happening here.

10My fellow prisoner Aristarchus sends you his greetings, as does Mark, the cousin of Barnabas. (You have received instructions about him; if he comes to you, welcome him.) **11**Jesus, who is called Justus, also sends greetings. These are the only Jews among my fellow workers for the kingdom of God, and they have proved a comfort to me. **12**Epaphras, who is one of you and a servant of Christ Jesus, sends greetings. He is always wrestling in prayer for you, that you may stand firm in all the will of God, mature and fully assured. **13**I vouch for him that he is working hard for you and for those at Laodicea and Hierapolis. **14**Our dear friend Luke, the doctor, and Demas send greetings. **15**Give my greetings to the brothers at Laodicea, and to Nympha and the church in her house.

a8 Some manuscripts *that he may know about your*

TUESDAY

VERSE:	AUTHOR:	PASSAGE:
Colossians 3:17	Kay Marshall Strom	Colossians 3

Do It As to the Lord

My grandmother told me many stories about my grandfather whom I hardly remember. He had been a circuit riding preacher in the Ozark mountains of Missouri. On Sundays he would ride a trail from one tiny town nestled in the hills to another hidden in a hollow to another tucked away beside a small stream. He would get to each town once a month.

Everyone came to church early to wait for Grandpa, and they begged him to stay and stay. They would bring fried chicken and freshly baked pies, and they'd sing and eat and listen to him preach well into the afternoon. They were poor folks, so they would pay him with whatever they had. One time grandfather came home dragging a load of freshly chopped firewood.

"That was pretty crummy pay for working all day!" I sniffed.

"Oh, no!" Grandma told me. "Those people worked hard just to keep body and soul together. They gave your grandfather everything they had, just as if they were giving it to Jesus himself."

I wish I had gotten to know them. Those people in the hills and hollows of the Ozark mountains were living out Paul's admonition in Colossians 3:16–17. They longed for God's word to dwell in them. They loved to hear teaching, and they praised God with psalms and hymns and spiritual songs. And they responded to the message, giving in the name of Jesus as if they were giving to Jesus himself.

ADDITIONAL SCRIPTURE READINGS:
Psalm 37:25–26; Psalm 112:5–9; 2 Corinthians 9:12–15

Go to page 289 for your next devotional reading.

¹⁶After this letter has been read to you, see that it is also read in the church of the Laodiceans and that you in turn read the letter from Laodicea.

¹⁷Tell Archippus: "See to it that you complete the work you have received in the Lord."

¹⁸I, Paul, write this greeting in my own hand. Remember my chains. Grace be with you.

PAUL *founds the church at Thessalonica during his second missionary journey. Paul writes to commend believers for growing in the Lord and to encourage them to correct some misunderstandings. The subject of Christ's second coming permeates this letter, with almost every chapter referring to it. As you live in a culture hostile to Christian values, look in this letter for guidelines on relationships and for perspectives on life shaped by eternity.*

1 THESSALONIANS

1 Paul, Silas[a] and Timothy,

To the church of the Thessalonians in God the Father and the Lord Jesus Christ:

Grace and peace to you.[b]

Thanksgiving for the Thessalonians' Faith

2 We always thank God for all of you, mentioning you in our prayers. 3 We continually remember before our God and Father your work produced by faith, your labor prompted by love, and your endurance inspired by hope in our Lord Jesus Christ.

4 For we know, brothers loved by God, that he has chosen you, 5 because our gospel came to you not simply with words, but also with power, with the Holy Spirit and with deep conviction. You know how we lived among you for your sake. 6 You became imitators of us and of the Lord; in spite of severe suffering, you welcomed the message with the joy given by the Holy Spirit. 7 And so you became a model to all the believers in Macedonia and Achaia. 8 The Lord's message rang out from you not only in Macedonia and Achaia—your faith in God has become known everywhere. Therefore we do not need to say anything about it, 9 for they themselves re-

---

a 1 Greek *Silvanus,* a variant of *Silas*
Jesus Christ
b 1 Some early manuscripts *you from God our Father and the Lord*

port what kind of reception you gave us. They tell how you turned to God from idols to serve the living and true God, [10]and to wait for his Son from heaven, whom he raised from the dead—Jesus, who rescues us from the coming wrath.

Paul's Ministry in Thessalonica

2 You know, brothers, that our visit to you was not a failure. [2]We had previously suffered and been insulted in Philippi, as you know, but with the help of our God we dared to tell you his gospel in spite of strong opposition. [3]For the appeal we make does not spring from error or impure motives, nor are we trying to trick you. [4]On the contrary, we speak as men approved by God to be entrusted with the gospel. We are not trying to please men but God, who tests our hearts. [5]You know we never used flattery, nor did we put on a mask to cover up greed—God is our witness.

[6]We were not looking for praise from men, not from you or anyone else.

As apostles of Christ we could have been a burden to you, [7]but we were gentle among you, like a mother caring for her little children. [8]We loved you so much that we were delighted to share with you not only the gospel of God but our lives as well, because you had become so dear to us. [9]Surely you remember, brothers, our toil and hardship; we worked night and day in order not to be a burden to anyone while we preached the gospel of God to you.

[10]You are witnesses, and so is God, of how holy, righteous and blameless we were among you who believed. [11]For you know that we dealt with each of you as a father deals with his own children, [12]encouraging, comforting and urging you to live lives worthy of God, who calls you into his kingdom and glory.

[13]And we also thank God continually because, when you received the word of

---

WEDNESDAY

VERSE:	AUTHOR:	PASSAGE:
1 Thessalonians 2:11	Kathryn Hillen	1 Thessalonians 2:1–16

My Heritage

I grew up with five lively brothers who often excluded me from their plans. At times my feeling of rejection brought tears. When that happened, my father, his dark brown eyes twinkling, would call me to his side and whisper some future plan or a comforting thought, calling it our "secret." Sometimes the secret was riding along with him on an errand or helping him with some task for which I was eminently unqualified. The secret was never particularly exciting, but I was happy to be doing something with my father. When he wanted to be with me, I knew that he cared about me.

In retrospect I realize how fortunate I was to have a father who gave me a good example of the care and concern of the heavenly Father. My father was not wealthy, but his gift to me is priceless, for it helps me to trust God with assurance that he will never leave or forsake me.

ADDITIONAL SCRIPTURE READINGS:
Deuteronomy 31:6; Hebrews 13:5; 1 Peter 5:7

Go to page 291 for your next devotional reading.

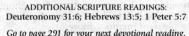

God, which you heard from us, you accepted it not as the word of men, but as it actually is, the word of God, which is at work in you who believe. ¹⁴For you, brothers, became imitators of God's churches in Judea, which are in Christ Jesus: You suffered from your own countrymen the same things those churches suffered from the Jews, ¹⁵who killed the Lord Jesus and the prophets and also drove us out. They displease God and are hostile to all men ¹⁶in their effort to keep us from speaking to the Gentiles so that they may be saved. In this way they always heap up their sins to the limit. The wrath of God has come upon them at last.ᵃ

Paul's Longing to See the Thessalonians

¹⁷But, brothers, when we were torn away from you for a short time (in person, not in thought), out of our intense longing we made every effort to see you. ¹⁸For we wanted to come to you—certainly I, Paul, did, again and again—but Satan stopped us. ¹⁹For what is our hope, our joy, or the crown in which we will glory in the presence of our Lord Jesus when he comes? Is it not you? ²⁰Indeed, you are our glory and joy.

3 So when we could stand it no longer, we thought it best to be left by ourselves in Athens. ²We sent Timothy, who is our brother and God's fellow workerᵇ in spreading the gospel of Christ, to strengthen and encourage you in your faith, ³so that no one would be unsettled by these trials. You know quite well that we were destined for them. ⁴In fact, when we were with you, we kept telling you that we would be persecuted. And it turned out that way, as you well know. ⁵For this reason, when I could stand it no longer, I sent to find out about your faith. I was afraid that in some way the tempter might have tempted you and our efforts might have been useless.

Timothy's Encouraging Report

⁶But Timothy has just now come to us from you and has brought good news about your faith and love. He has told us that you always have pleasant memo-

ries of us and that you long to see us, just as we also long to see you. ⁷Therefore, brothers, in all our distress and persecution we were encouraged about you because of your faith. ⁸For now we really live, since you are standing firm in the Lord. ⁹How can we thank God enough for you in return for all the joy we have in the presence of our God because of you? ¹⁰Night and day we pray most earnestly that we may see you again and supply what is lacking in your faith.

¹¹Now may our God and Father himself and our Lord Jesus clear the way for us to come to you. ¹²May the Lord make your love increase and overflow for each other and for everyone else, just as ours does for you. ¹³May he strengthen your hearts so that you will be blameless and holy in the presence of our God and Father when our Lord Jesus comes with all his holy ones.

Living to Please God

4 Finally, brothers, we instructed you how to live in order to please God, as in fact you are living. Now we ask you and urge you in the Lord Jesus to do this more and more. ²For you know what instructions we gave you by the authority of the Lord Jesus.

³It is God's will that you should be sanctified: that you should avoid sexual immorality; ⁴that each of you should learn to control his own bodyᶜ in a way that is holy and honorable, ⁵not in passionate lust like the heathen, who do not know God; ⁶and that in this matter no one should wrong his brother or take advantage of him. The Lord will punish men for all such sins, as we have already told you and warned you. ⁷For God did not call us to be impure, but to live a holy life. ⁸Therefore, he who rejects this instruction does not reject man but God, who gives you his Holy Spirit.

⁹Now about brotherly love we do not need to write to you, for you yourselves have been taught by God to love each other. ¹⁰And in fact, you do love all the brothers throughout Macedonia. Yet we urge you, brothers, to do so more and more.

ᵃ16 Or them fully   ᵇ2 Some manuscripts brother and fellow worker; other manuscripts brother and God's servant   ᶜ4 Or learn to live with his own wife; or learn to acquire a wife

¹¹Make it your ambition to lead a quiet life, to mind your own business and to work with your hands, just as we told you, ¹²so that your daily life may win the respect of outsiders and so that you will not be dependent on anybody.

The Coming of the Lord

¹³Brothers, we do not want you to be ignorant about those who fall asleep, or to grieve like the rest of men, who have no hope. ¹⁴We believe that Jesus died

THURSDAY

VERSE:
1 Thessalonians
4:14

AUTHOR:
Gigi Graham Tchividjian

PASSAGE:
1 Thessalonians
4:13–18

The Kiss

As soon as we heard the news that LaoNaing had suffered a stroke, we caught a plane to North Carolina. Arriving in Asheville, we went directly to the hospital, where we found my maternal grandmother lying frail and helpless, attached to life-sustaining tubes and machines. We could sense her frustration and agitation. Although she could not speak, she made it known in no uncertain terms that she wished to go home.

After consulting with the doctor, we decided to comply with her wishes. As soon as she saw the familiar surroundings and was tucked safely in her own bed, she relaxed, and a peaceful expression replaced the one of strain and concern. We kept her as comfortable as possible and, knowing she enjoyed our presence, someone always kept her company as well.

Since LaoNaing had loved music all her life, Mother had a special tape made for her—hymns that would especially bless and encourage. Since my grandmother was aware she was dying, the hymn she wished to hear over and over again was "The King Is Coming."

Each day she grew weaker. It was hard to see her fading slowly away, but she was ready and eager to meet her Lord and to rejoin loved ones who had gone before.

She died early one November morning—quietly and peacefully. When I went to tell the children, little Tullian said, "Mama, LaoNaing had a hurt, and Jesus came and kissed it away." This two-year-old understood better than I the "homegoing" of a child of God. Thinking I was offering comfort, I found myself comforted.

I do not know when the Lord will come for me. I may live to a ripe old age like my grandmother, or he may choose to complete my life early. But I do know that he has provided for my eternal security through Jesus Christ and that until that day, he provides for my daily life through the power of the Holy Spirit.

ADDITIONAL SCRIPTURE READINGS:
Psalm 116:15; Isaiah 25:8; 1 Corinthians 15:55

Go to page 292 for your next devotional reading.

VERSE:
1 Thessalonians 5:11

AUTHOR:
Sharon Mahoe

PASSAGE:
1 Thessalonians 5

Gravity at Work

The tears rolled out of my eyes and down into my ears. I was lying on my back, you see. Gravity was at work. (The other kind of gravity was at work, too. Nothing was funny. Nothing at all.)

I reached for my Bible. It fell open (honest) at Lamentations. Through blurring tears I read [from] chapter 3: "I have been deprived of peace; I have forgotten what prosperity is . . . Yet this I call to mind and therefore I have hope: Because of the LORD's great love we are not consumed, for his compassions never fail" (vv. 17, 21–22).

So many times in the past few weeks I had come home to hear a message of encouragement on my answering machine: "Thinking of you"; "I love you"; even a couple of "Who loves ya, baby?"

Day after day, when hysteria and raw emotions were my constant companions during my divorce, I found the incredible support and concern of friends every time I needed someone.

On one of those particularly fragile days, I came into my office to find a large rectangular box on my desk. Mystified, I opened it to find—carefully arranged amidst hills of white tissue—fragrant soaps, shampoo, lotions and bubble bath. The note said, "For the times when things get bad. When you use these I'm thinking of you. I love you, Kathleen."

Kathleen Mary. Her dear gesture that day gave me peace in the midst of swirling clouds of panic. Each bubble bath, every time I smelled the fragrant soaps on my skin, I felt her love and concern for me. She gave me a token of her support and encouragement, the warmth of which has lasted for years.

Encouragement has never filled a flat tire. Encouragement has never made a car payment, nor fixed a broken washing machine. But encouragement from another gives us the strength to do what we feel we cannot do, hold on when we feel we cannot hold on, and try what we might not dare to try.

Encouragement. Doesn't sound like much, but it's everything. Send some encouragement today. You'll be part of someone's memories for a long, long time.

ADDITIONAL SCRIPTURE READINGS:
Isaiah 1:17; 1 Thessalonians 4:18; Hebrews 3:13

Go to page 294 for your next devotional reading.

and rose again and so we believe that God will bring with Jesus those who have fallen asleep in him. **15**According to the Lord's own word, we tell you that we who are still alive, who are left till the coming of the Lord, will certainly not precede those who have fallen asleep. **16**For the Lord himself will come down from heaven, with a loud command, with the voice of the archangel and with the trumpet call of God, and the dead in Christ will rise first. **17**After that, we who are still alive and are left will be caught up together with them in the clouds to meet the Lord in the air. And so we will be with the Lord forever. **18**Therefore encourage each other with these words.

5 Now, brothers, about times and dates we do not need to write to you, **2**for you know very well that the day of the Lord will come like a thief in the night. **3**While people are saying, "Peace and safety," destruction will come on them suddenly, as labor pains on a pregnant woman, and they will not escape.

4But you, brothers, are not in darkness so that this day should surprise you like a thief. **5**You are all sons of the light and sons of the day. We do not belong to the night or to the darkness. **6**So then, let us not be like others, who are asleep, but let us be alert and self-controlled. **7**For those who sleep, sleep at night, and those who get drunk, get drunk at night. **8**But since we belong to the day, let us be self-controlled, putting on faith and love as a breastplate, and the hope of salvation as a helmet. **9**For God did not appoint us to suffer wrath but to receive salvation through our Lord Jesus Christ. **10**He died for us so that, whether we are awake or asleep, we may live together with him. **11**Therefore encourage one another and build each other up, just as in fact you are doing.

Final Instructions

12Now we ask you, brothers, to respect those who work hard among you, who are over you in the Lord and who admonish you. **13**Hold them in the highest regard in love because of their work. Live in peace with each other. **14**And we urge you, brothers, warn those who are idle, encourage the timid, help the weak, be patient with everyone. **15**Make sure that nobody pays back wrong for wrong, but always try to be kind to each other and to everyone else.

16Be joyful always; **17**pray continually; **18**give thanks in all circumstances, for this is God's will for you in Christ Jesus.

19Do not put out the Spirit's fire; **20**do not treat prophecies with contempt. **21**Test everything. Hold on to the good. **22**Avoid every kind of evil.

23May God himself, the God of peace, sanctify you through and through. May your whole spirit, soul and body be kept blameless at the coming of our Lord Jesus Christ. **24**The one who calls you is faithful and he will do it.

25Brothers, pray for us. **26**Greet all the brothers with a holy kiss. **27**I charge you before the Lord to have this letter read to all the brothers.

28The grace of our Lord Jesus Christ be with you.

WEEKENDING

REALIZE

If you want to be respected for your actions, then your behavior must be above reproach. I learned from my grandmother and mother that one should always respect oneself and live right. This is how you gain the respect of others. If our lives demonstrate that we are peaceful, humble and trusted, this is recognized by others. If our lives demonstrate something else, that will be noticed too.

Rosa Parks

REVIVE

Saturday: 1 Thessalonians 1:3–10
Sunday: 2 Timothy 1:3–7

*Go to page 296 for your
next devotional reading.*

PAUL *writes this second letter to believers at Thessalonica who need clarification on the advice given in his first letter. Some people have misunderstood Paul and are so sure Jesus is coming soon that they stop working. While assuring the Thessalonians that Jesus is in fact coming again, Paul urges his readers to concentrate on living and working with what he has given them for today.*

2 THESSALONIANS

1 Paul, Silas[a] and Timothy,

To the church of the Thessalonians in God our Father and the Lord Jesus Christ:

²Grace and peace to you from God the Father and the Lord Jesus Christ.

Thanksgiving and Prayer

³We ought always to thank God for you, brothers, and rightly so, because your faith is growing more and more, and the love every one of you has for each other is increasing. ⁴Therefore, among God's churches we boast about your perseverance and faith in all the persecutions and trials you are enduring.

⁵All this is evidence that God's judgment is right, and as a result you will be counted worthy of the kingdom of God, for which you are suffering. ⁶God is just: He will pay back trouble to those who trouble you ⁷and give relief to you who are troubled, and to us as well. This will happen when the Lord Jesus is revealed from heaven in blazing fire with his powerful angels. ⁸He will punish those who do not know God and do not obey the gospel of our Lord Jesus. ⁹They will be punished with everlasting destruction and shut out from the presence of the Lord and from the majesty of his power ¹⁰on the day he comes to be glorified in his holy people and to be marveled at among all those who have believed. This includes you, because you believed our testimony to you.

¹¹With this in mind, we constantly

pray for you, that our God may count you worthy of his calling, and that by his power he may fulfill every good purpose of yours and every act prompted by your faith. [12]We pray this so that the name of our Lord Jesus may be glorified in you, and you in him, according to the grace of our God and the Lord Jesus Christ.[a]

The Man of Lawlessness

2 Concerning the coming of our Lord Jesus Christ and our being gathered to him, we ask you, brothers, [2]not to become easily unsettled or alarmed by some prophecy, report or letter supposed to have come from us, saying that the day of the Lord has already come. [3]Don't let anyone deceive you in any way, for ˌthat day will not comeˌ until the rebellion occurs and the man of lawlessness[b] is revealed, the man doomed to destruction. [4]He will oppose and will exalt himself over everything that is called God or is worshiped, so that he sets himself up in God's temple, proclaiming himself to be God.

[5]Don't you remember that when I was with you I used to tell you these things? [6]And now you know what is holding him back, so that he may be revealed at the proper time. [7]For the secret power of lawlessness is already at work; but the one who now holds it back will continue to do so till he is taken out of the way. [8]And then the lawless one will be revealed, whom the Lord Jesus will overthrow with the breath of his mouth and destroy by the splendor of his coming. [9]The coming of the lawless one will be in accordance with the work of Satan displayed in all kinds of counterfeit miracles, signs and wonders, [10]and in every sort of evil that deceives those who are perishing. They perish because they refused to love the truth and so be saved. [11]For this reason God sends them a powerful delusion so that they will be-

[a]12 Or God and Lord, Jesus Christ   [b]3 Some manuscripts sin

---

MONDAY

VERSE:	AUTHOR:	PASSAGE:
2 Thessalonians 1:11	Susanna Wesley	2 Thessalonians 1

Prayer for Diligence

Be pleased, O God, to grant to me that great freedom of mind that will enable me to follow and attend on Jesus with a pure heart; to be ever prepared and disposed to observe his example and obey his precepts. And do thou further help me to achieve that consummate prudence, great purity, great separation from the world, much liberty and a firm and steadfast faith in the Lord Jesus that will enable me to manage the common affairs of life in such a way as not to misemploy or neglect the improvement of my talents; to be industrious without covetousness; diligent without anxiety; as exact in each detail of action as if success were dependent on it, and yet so resigned as to leave all events to thee and still attributing to thee the praise of every good work. *Amen.*

ADDITIONAL SCRIPTURE READINGS:
Proverbs 12:4; Proverbs 16:3; Hebrews 11:9–10

Go to page 297 for your next devotional reading.

VERSE:
2 Thessalonians 2:13

AUTHOR:
Deneese L. Jones

PASSAGE:
2 Thessalonians 2:13–17

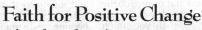

Faith for Positive Change

After that day of transformation seventeen years ago . . . I began to step into the world expecting good things to happen. I learned that "without faith it is impossible to please God" (Hebrews 11:6).

As the [African-American] mother of two daughters, I have experienced that having this kind of faith means being active, not sitting back bemoaning life and waiting for change. It means loving and believing in ourselves and using the transforming power of God's Holy Spirit to move our lives forward. The truth seems simple, but living it is not so simple. As time has gone by, I have seen the work of the Holy Spirit in my life as well as his saving grace in my husband. Times have been difficult financially, physically, mentally and spiritually, but faith in God has begun a revolution in my life.

During the difficult years of child-rearing, the most revolutionary thing that African-American women can do is to have faith. Faith will allow us to hold a positive vision of what we want for ourselves and for our children and to put the energy behind that vision to make it a reality. Our enemy is not the system or those who foster it. Our enemy is fear that blinds us to truth, fear that keeps us bitter with anger and fear that leaves us without power. This is the kind of fear that keeps us focused on what we do not want rather than on what we need to lead us and our families toward a harmonious, abundant way of life as promised by Jesus Christ.

However, with renewed faith, we are never alone. We realize that in Christ we have everything we need to overcome any of life's challenges. There may have been countless times when we have felt the earth shake beneath us, or the weight of life pressing in on us. This is happening to our people today and to people throughout the world. It is one of the many ways in which the Holy Spirit speaks to us and encourages us to change.

ADDITIONAL SCRIPTURE READINGS:
2 Corinthians 3:18; Ephesians 2:6–8; Colossians 1:23

Go to page 300 for your next devotional reading.

lieve the lie [12]and so that all will be condemned who have not believed the truth but have delighted in wickedness.

Stand Firm

[13]But we ought always to thank God for you, brothers loved by the Lord, because from the beginning God chose you[a] to be saved through the sanctifying work of the Spirit and through belief in the truth. [14]He called you to this through our gospel, that you might share in the glory of our Lord Jesus Christ. [15]So then, brothers, stand firm and hold to the teachings[b] we passed on to you, whether by word of mouth or by letter.

[16]May our Lord Jesus Christ himself and God our Father, who loved us and by his grace gave us eternal encouragement and good hope, [17]encourage your hearts and strengthen you in every good deed and word.

Request for Prayer

3 Finally, brothers, pray for us that the message of the Lord may spread rapidly and be honored, just as it was with you. [2]And pray that we may be delivered from wicked and evil men, for not everyone has faith. [3]But the Lord is faithful, and he will strengthen and protect you from the evil one. [4]We have confidence in the Lord that you are doing and will continue to do the things we command. [5]May the Lord direct your hearts into God's love and Christ's perseverance.

Warning Against Idleness

[6]In the name of the Lord Jesus Christ, we command you, brothers, to keep away from every brother who is idle and does not live according to the teaching[c] you received from us. [7]For you yourselves know how you ought to follow our example. We were not idle when we were with you, [8]nor did we eat anyone's food without paying for it. On the contrary, we worked night and day, laboring and toiling so that we would not be a burden to any of you. [9]We did this, not because we do not have the right to such help, but in order to make ourselves a model for you to follow. [10]For even when we were with you, we gave you this rule: "If a man will not work, he shall not eat."

[11]We hear that some among you are idle. They are not busy; they are busybodies. [12]Such people we command and urge in the Lord Jesus Christ to settle down and earn the bread they eat. [13]And as for you, brothers, never tire of doing what is right.

[14]If anyone does not obey our instruction in this letter, take special note of him. Do not associate with him, in order that he may feel ashamed. [15]Yet do not regard him as an enemy, but warn him as a brother.

Final Greetings

[16]Now may the Lord of peace himself give you peace at all times and in every way. The Lord be with all of you.

[17]I, Paul, write this greeting in my own hand, which is the distinguishing mark in all my letters. This is how I write.

[18]The grace of our Lord Jesus Christ be with you all.

---

[a]13 Some manuscripts *because God chose you as his firstfruits*　　[b]15 Or *traditions*　　[c]6 Or *tradition*

PAUL *writes to Timothy with affirmation and advice on how to lead the church at Ephesus. Here you will find guidelines for running a church, practical help for believers in their relationships with others and advice on dealing with false teachers. Look for the underlying principles you can apply in your everyday life as you seek to be true to the faith.*

1 TIMOTHY

1 Paul, an apostle of Christ Jesus by the command of God our Savior and of Christ Jesus our hope,

²To Timothy my true son in the faith:

Grace, mercy and peace from God the Father and Christ Jesus our Lord.

Warning Against False Teachers of the Law

³As I urged you when I went into Macedonia, stay there in Ephesus so that you may command certain men not to teach false doctrines any longer ⁴nor to devote themselves to myths and endless genealogies. These promote controversies rather than God's work—which is by faith. ⁵The goal of this command is love, which comes from a pure heart and a good conscience and a sincere faith. ⁶Some have wandered away from these and turned to meaningless talk. ⁷They want to be teachers of the law, but they do not know what they are talking about or what they so confidently affirm.

⁸We know that the law is good if one uses it properly. ⁹We also know that law*a* is made not for the righteous but for lawbreakers and rebels, the ungodly and sinful, the unholy and irreligious; for those who kill their fathers or mothers, for murderers, ¹⁰for adulterers and perverts, for slave traders and liars and perjurers—and for whatever else is contrary to the sound doctrine ¹¹that conforms to the glorious gospel of the blessed God, which he entrusted to me.

The Lord's Grace to Paul

¹²I thank Christ Jesus our Lord, who has given me strength, that he considered me faithful, appointing me to his

a 9 Or *that the law*

service. ¹³Even though I was once a blasphemer and a persecutor and a violent man, I was shown mercy because I acted in ignorance and unbelief. ¹⁴The grace of our Lord was poured out on me abundantly, along with the faith and love that are in Christ Jesus.

¹⁵Here is a trustworthy saying that deserves full acceptance: Christ Jesus came into the world to save sinners—of whom I am the worst. ¹⁶But for that very reason I was shown mercy so that in me, the worst of sinners, Christ Jesus might display his unlimited patience as an example for those who would believe on him and receive eternal life. ¹⁷Now to the King eternal, immortal, invisible, the only God, be honor and glory for ever and ever. Amen.

¹⁸Timothy, my son, I give you this instruction in keeping with the prophecies once made about you, so that by following them you may fight the good fight, ¹⁹holding on to faith and a good conscience. Some have rejected these and so have shipwrecked their faith. ²⁰Among them are Hymenaeus and Alexander, whom I have handed over to Satan to be taught not to blaspheme.

Instructions on Worship

2 I urge, then, first of all, that requests, prayers, intercession and thanksgiving be made for everyone—

◁ WEDNESDAY ▷

VERSE:
1 Timothy 1:12

AUTHOR:
Author Unknown

PASSAGE:
1 Timothy 1:12—2:7

Climbing the Musical Scale

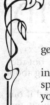

DO—Do not worry over things that may never happen, and even if they happen, worry will not help. Do count your blessings before you count cares.

RE—Radiate good will and a spirit of benevolence. Like laughter, it . . . makes yourself, as well as others, feel better.

ME—Mete kindness, understanding, tolerance and forgiveness generously. You reap as you mete.

FA—Far-reaching are the therapeutic benefits of spiritual thinking. You become as you habitually think. Resentment, hatred, spite, envy and vengeance pack radioactive fallout that gnaws at your vitals. They are self-consuming.

SO—Sow the seeds of love, friendship, empathy and helpfulness. These hardy seeds take root in the crustiest ground.

LA—Laugh at yourself now and then. You who can laugh at yourself are less apt to be at war with yourself. Laugh at yourself, even if you don't feel like laughing.

TI—Teach yourself awareness and appreciation of all the wonders of nature. Thank God daily for the precious gift of life. Genuine gratitude and discontent are never found together.

DO—Do not expect someone else to open the door to happiness for you. You must do it yourself. You alone have the key. Turn it.

ADDITIONAL SCRIPTURE READINGS:
Galatians 5:22–23; Ephesians 5:1; 1 Thessalonians 4:7

Go to page 302 for your next devotional reading.

[2]for kings and all those in authority, that we may live peaceful and quiet lives in all godliness and holiness. [3]This is good, and pleases God our Savior, [4]who wants all men to be saved and to come to a knowledge of the truth. [5]For there is one God and one mediator between God and men, the man Christ Jesus, [6]who gave himself as a ransom for all men—the testimony given in its proper time. [7]And for this purpose I was appointed a herald and an apostle—I am telling the truth, I am not lying—and a teacher of the true faith to the Gentiles.

[8]I want men everywhere to lift up holy hands in prayer, without anger or disputing.

[9]I also want women to dress modestly, with decency and propriety, not with braided hair or gold or pearls or expensive clothes, [10]but with good deeds, appropriate for women who profess to worship God.

[11]A woman should learn in quietness and full submission. [12]I do not permit a woman to teach or to have authority over a man; she must be silent. [13]For Adam was formed first, then Eve. [14]And Adam was not the one deceived; it was the woman who was deceived and became a sinner. [15]But women[a] will be saved[b] through childbearing—if they continue in faith, love and holiness with propriety.

Overseers and Deacons

3 Here is a trustworthy saying: If anyone sets his heart on being an overseer,[c] he desires a noble task. [2]Now the overseer must be above reproach, the husband of but one wife, temperate, self-controlled, respectable, hospitable, able to teach, [3]not given to drunkenness, not violent but gentle, not quarrelsome, not a lover of money. [4]He must manage his own family well and see that his children obey him with proper respect. [5](If anyone does not know how to manage his own family, how can he take care of God's church?) [6]He must not be a recent convert, or he may become conceited and fall under the same judgment as the devil. [7]He must also have a good reputation with outsiders, so that he will not fall into disgrace and into the devil's trap.

[8]Deacons, likewise, are to be men worthy of respect, sincere, not indulging in much wine, and not pursuing dishonest gain. [9]They must keep hold of the deep truths of the faith with a clear conscience. [10]They must first be tested; and then if there is nothing against them, let them serve as deacons.

[11]In the same way, their wives[d] are to be women worthy of respect, not malicious talkers but temperate and trustworthy in everything.

[12]A deacon must be the husband of but one wife and must manage his children and his household well. [13]Those who have served well gain an excellent standing and great assurance in their faith in Christ Jesus.

[14]Although I hope to come to you soon, I am writing you these instructions so that, [15]if I am delayed, you will know how people ought to conduct themselves in God's household, which is the church of the living God, the pillar and foundation of the truth. [16]Beyond all question, the mystery of godliness is great:

> He[e] appeared in a body,[f]
> was vindicated by the Spirit,
> was seen by angels,
> was preached among the nations,
> was believed on in the world,
> was taken up in glory.

Instructions to Timothy

4 The Spirit clearly says that in later times some will abandon the faith and follow deceiving spirits and things taught by demons. [2]Such teachings come through hypocritical liars, whose consciences have been seared as with a hot iron. [3]They forbid people to marry and order them to abstain from certain foods, which God created to be received with thanksgiving by those who believe and who know the truth. [4]For everything God created is good, and nothing is to be rejected if it is received with thanksgiving, [5]because it is consecrated by the word of God and prayer.

[6]If you point these things out to the brothers, you will be a good minister of Christ Jesus, brought up in the truths of the faith and of the good teaching that you have followed. [7]Have nothing to do

---

[a]15 Greek *she*   [b]15 Or *restored*   [c]1 Traditionally *bishop;* also in verse 2   [d]11 Or *way,*
deaconesses   [e]16 Some manuscripts *God*   [f]16 Or *in the flesh*

with godless myths and old wives' tales; rather, train yourself to be godly. **⁸**For physical training is of some value, but godliness has value for all things, holding promise for both the present life and the life to come.

⁹This is a trustworthy saying that deserves full acceptance **¹⁰**(and for this we labor and strive), that we have put our hope in the living God, who is the Savior of all men, and especially of those who believe.

¹¹Command and teach these things. **¹²**Don't let anyone look down on you because you are young, but set an example for the believers in speech, in life, in love, in faith and in purity. **¹³**Until I come, devote yourself to the public reading of Scripture, to preaching and to teaching. **¹⁴**Do not neglect your gift, which was given you through a prophetic message when the body of elders laid their hands on you.

¹⁵Be diligent in these matters; give yourself wholly to them, so that everyone may see your progress. **¹⁶**Watch your life and doctrine closely. Persevere in them, because if you do, you will save both yourself and your hearers.

Advice About Widows, Elders and Slaves

5 Do not rebuke an older man harshly, but exhort him as if he were your father. Treat younger men as brothers, **²**older women as mothers, and younger women as sisters, with absolute purity.

³Give proper recognition to those widows who are really in need. **⁴**But if a widow has children or grandchildren, these should learn first of all to put their religion into practice by caring for their own family and so repaying their parents and grandparents, for this is pleasing to God. **⁵**The widow who is really in need and left all alone puts her hope in God and continues night and day to pray and to ask God for help. **⁶**But the widow who lives for pleasure is dead even while she lives. **⁷**Give the people these instructions, too, so that no one may be open to blame. **⁸**If anyone does not provide for his relatives, and especially for his immediate family, he has denied the faith and is worse than an unbeliever.

⁹No widow may be put on the list of widows unless she is over sixty, has

---

⟨ THURSDAY ⟩

VERSE:	AUTHOR:	PASSAGE:
1 Timothy 4:16	Hannah Whitall Smith	1 Timothy 4

A Living Faith

I attribute my discovery of my heavenly Father largely to what I had known of the goodness of my earthly parents. They never said much about religion, for the Quaker fear of meddling between a soul and its maker had created a habit of reserve that could not easily be broken through. But they showed plainly that their lives were lived in a region of profound faith in an ever-present God. We could not but see that he was to them a reality beyond all other realities. Of religious teaching we had but little, but of religious example and influence we had a never-failing supply. Not by talking, but by daily living, were impressions made on our childish hearts.

ADDITIONAL SCRIPTURE READINGS:
Colossians 3:17; 2 Timothy 1:5; James 2:14–26

Go to page 304 for your next devotional reading.

been faithful to her husband,[a] [10]and is well known for her good deeds, such as bringing up children, showing hospitality, washing the feet of the saints, helping those in trouble and devoting herself to all kinds of good deeds.

[11]As for younger widows, do not put them on such a list. For when their sensual desires overcome their dedication to Christ, they want to marry. [12]Thus they bring judgment on themselves, because they have broken their first pledge. [13]Besides, they get into the habit of being idle and going about from house to house. And not only do they become idlers, but also gossips and busybodies, saying things they ought not to. [14]So I counsel younger widows to marry, to have children, to manage their homes and to give the enemy no opportunity for slander. [15]Some have in fact already turned away to follow Satan.

[16]If any woman who is a believer has widows in her family, she should help them and not let the church be burdened with them, so that the church can help those widows who are really in need.

[17]The elders who direct the affairs of the church well are worthy of double honor, especially those whose work is preaching and teaching. [18]For the Scripture says, "Do not muzzle the ox while it is treading out the grain,"[b] and "The worker deserves his wages."[c] [19]Do not entertain an accusation against an elder unless it is brought by two or three witnesses. [20]Those who sin are to be rebuked publicly, so that the others may take warning.

[21]I charge you, in the sight of God and Christ Jesus and the elect angels, to keep these instructions without partiality, and to do nothing out of favoritism.

[22]Do not be hasty in the laying on of hands, and do not share in the sins of others. Keep yourself pure.

[23]Stop drinking only water, and use a little wine because of your stomach and your frequent illnesses.

[24]The sins of some men are obvious, reaching the place of judgment ahead of them; the sins of others trail behind them. [25]In the same way, good deeds are obvious, and even those that are not cannot be hidden.

6 All who are under the yoke of slavery should consider their masters worthy of full respect, so that God's name and our teaching may not be slandered. [2]Those who have believing masters are not to show less respect for them because they are brothers. Instead, they are to serve them even better, because those who benefit from their service are believers, and dear to them. These are the things you are to teach and urge on them.

Love of Money

[3]If anyone teaches false doctrines and does not agree to the sound instruction of our Lord Jesus Christ and to godly teaching, [4]he is conceited and understands nothing. He has an unhealthy interest in controversies and quarrels about words that result in envy, strife, malicious talk, evil suspicions [5]and constant friction between men of corrupt mind, who have been robbed of the truth and who think that godliness is a means to financial gain.

[6]But godliness with contentment is great gain. [7]For we brought nothing into the world, and we can take nothing out of it. [8]But if we have food and clothing, we will be content with that. [9]People who want to get rich fall into temptation and a trap and into many foolish and harmful desires that plunge men into ruin and destruction. [10]For the love of money is a root of all kinds of evil. Some people, eager for money, have wandered from the faith and pierced themselves with many griefs.

Paul's Charge to Timothy

[11]But you, man of God, flee from all this, and pursue righteousness, godliness, faith, love, endurance and gentleness. [12]Fight the good fight of the faith. Take hold of the eternal life to which you were called when you made your good confession in the presence of many witnesses. [13]In the sight of God, who gives life to everything, and of Christ Jesus, who while testifying before Pontius Pilate made the good confession, I charge you [14]to keep this command without spot or blame until the appearing of our Lord Jesus Christ, [15]which God will bring about in his own time—God, the blessed and only Ruler, the King of kings and Lord of lords, [16]who alone is

---

[a]9 Or has had but one husband   [b]18 Deut. 25:4   [c]18 Luke 10:7

immortal and who lives in unapproachable light, whom no one has seen or can see. To him be honor and might forever. Amen.

17Command those who are rich in this present world not to be arrogant nor to put their hope in wealth, which is so uncertain, but to put their hope in God, who richly provides us with everything for our enjoyment. 18Command them to do good, to be rich in good deeds, and to be generous and willing to share. 19In this way they will lay up treasure for themselves as a firm foundation for the coming age, so that they may take hold of the life that is truly life.

20Timothy, guard what has been entrusted to your care. Turn away from godless chatter and the opposing ideas of what is falsely called knowledge, 21which some have professed and in so doing have wandered from the faith.

Grace be with you.

⟨ FRIDAY ⟩

VERSE:	AUTHOR:	PASSAGE:
1 Timothy 6:18	Colleen Townsend Evans	1 Timothy 6:18–21

Happy Are the Generous

I have learned a lot about receiving from the women in the congregations we have served, for they have been such beautiful givers in my times of need. I have learned still more from a good friend, a woman my mother's age. For some wonderful, unknown reason, God must have put me "in her basket," because she has done so many generous, kind and truly helpful things for me that I've lost count. And that's the way she wants it.

At first it was hard for me to accept so much generosity. My independent streak got in the way and I began to feel uncomfortably indebted to my friend. I wanted to return her love in tangible ways, and of course I couldn't. Being a sensitive person, she realized how I felt and one day she had a talk with me.

"Colleen, I get a lot of pleasure out of doing things for you," she said. "If only I didn't have to worry about your feeling of indebtedness . . . think of the fun I could have!" I couldn't believe it. She made me feel that I'd be doing her a favor by accepting her deeds of love.

I did a little thinking and a little praying, and gradually my attitude began to change. I put myself in my friend's place and realized how I would have felt if someone accepted my generosity with a frown on her face. And if a friend returned my favor tit for tat—like some kind of duty—it would make my generosity look like a pompous gesture done just for show. No—since my friend gave freely and lavishly of herself, responding to my needs as she saw them, the best way for me to be generous was to become a good receiver.

ADDITIONAL SCRIPTURE READINGS:
Psalm 112:5; Proverbs 11:25; 2 Corinthians 9:11–13

Go to page 305 for your next devotional reading.

WEEKENDING

REALIZE

Thou mighty God of Sea and Land,
I here resigne into thy hand
The Son of Prayers, of vowes, of teares,
The child I stay'd for many yeares.
Thou heard'st me then, and gav'st him me;
Hear me again, I give him Thee.
He's mine, but more, O Lord, thine own,
For sure thy Grace on him is shown.
No freind I have like Thee to trust,
For mortall helpes are brittle Dust.
Preserve, O Lord, from stormes and wrack,
Protect him there, and bring him back;
And if thou shalt spare me a space,
That I again may see his face,
Then shall I celebrate thy Praise,
And Blesse thee for't even all my Dayes.
If otherwise I goe to Rest,
Thy Will bee done, for that is best;
Perswade my heart I shall him see
For ever happefy'd with Thee.

Anne Bradstreet

Upon My Son Samuel
His Goeing For England, November 6, 1657

REFLECT

Saturday: 1 Samuel 1:21–28
Sunday: 2 Thessalonians 3:3

Go to page 307 for your
next devotional reading.

PAUL'S *second letter to Timothy, written shortly before Paul's death, represents the advice of someone who knows he is at the end of his life. Languishing in a cold dungeon, chained like a common criminal, Paul knows that his work is done. He challenges Timothy to a more effective ministry and encourages him to persevere in his walk with God. Ask God to give you daily strength to keep walking with him, secure in the hope that is yours in Christ.*

2 TIMOTHY

1 Paul, an apostle of Christ Jesus by the will of God, according to the promise of life that is in Christ Jesus,

²To Timothy, my dear son:

Grace, mercy and peace from God the Father and Christ Jesus our Lord.

Encouragement to Be Faithful

³I thank God, whom I serve, as my forefathers did, with a clear conscience, as night and day I constantly remember you in my prayers. ⁴Recalling your tears, I long to see you, so that I may be filled with joy. ⁵I have been reminded of your sincere faith, which first lived in your grandmother Lois and in your mother Eunice and, I am persuaded, now lives in you also. ⁶For this reason I remind you to fan into flame the gift of God, which is in you through the laying on of my hands. ⁷For God did not give us a spirit of timidity, but a spirit of power, of love and of self-discipline.

⁸So do not be ashamed to testify about our Lord, or ashamed of me his prisoner. But join with me in suffering for the gospel, by the power of God, ⁹who has saved us and called us to a holy life—not because of anything we have done but because of his own purpose and grace. This grace was given us in Christ Jesus before the beginning of time, ¹⁰but it has now been revealed through the appearing of our Savior, Christ Jesus, who has destroyed death and has brought life and immortality to light through the gospel. ¹¹And of this gospel I was appointed a herald and an

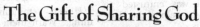
VERSE:	AUTHOR:	PASSAGE:
2 Timothy 1:5	Jan Stoop and Betty Southard	2 Timothy 1

The Gift of Sharing God

As Betty listened to her little two-year-old granddaughter happily playing and singing a medley of songs in the background, joyful memories flooded her thoughts: her own grandmother working in the kitchen while little Betty played happily and sang those very same songs, songs her own grandma had sung to her.

"I stopped to think about Grandma and how she shared her love of God with me," Betty said. "Grandma didn't have much education, and she knew nothing about theology, but she sure knew how to love. For more than fifty years she taught Sunday school to two-year-olds."

Every Saturday Betty's grandparents would go over to the church to make sure the Sunday school room was ready for the children. All the fresh juice and animal crackers Grandma served. The special little things she always had ready to illustrate the Bible story—construction-paper flowers with the words "He careth for you" carefully printed by hand; or small bags of rice to represent the bags of grain Joseph gave his brothers. The flannel boards, the piles of crayons and paper. The open, welcoming arms of Grandma.

"When Grandma died at eighty-five, the church was filled for her funeral," Betty recalls. "Many stood to pay tribute to her living demonstration of God's love. A lot of people have personal relationships with God because Grandma loved their little children."

Betty never recalls her grandmother preaching about God. She doesn't remember her judging or condemning others. Those around her saw in her a God who really cared for people, a God to whom each person was important, however small or insignificant that one might be. They saw a God who could be trusted to always be there, ready to welcome each person with open arms. "Hers was a simple faith—childlike, really," Betty said. "Yet I wonder if Grandma, in all her simplicity, wasn't a more effective evangelist than the world's greatest preachers."

ADDITIONAL SCRIPTURE READINGS:
Psalm 102:12; Proverbs 11:30; 1 Corinthians 15:3

Go to page 309 for your next devotional reading.

apostle and a teacher. [12]That is why I am suffering as I am. Yet I am not ashamed, because I know whom I have believed, and am convinced that he is able to guard what I have entrusted to him for that day.

[13]What you heard from me, keep as the pattern of sound teaching, with faith and love in Christ Jesus. [14]Guard the good deposit that was entrusted to you—guard it with the help of the Holy Spirit who lives in us.

[15]You know that everyone in the province of Asia has deserted me, including Phygelus and Hermogenes.

[16]May the Lord show mercy to the household of Onesiphorus, because he often refreshed me and was not ashamed of my chains. [17]On the contrary, when he was in Rome, he searched hard for me until he found me. [18]May the Lord grant that he will find mercy from the Lord on that day! You know very well in how many ways he helped me in Ephesus.

2 You then, my son, be strong in the grace that is in Christ Jesus. [2]And the things you have heard me say in the presence of many witnesses entrust to reliable men who will also be qualified to teach others. [3]Endure hardship with us like a good soldier of Christ Jesus. [4]No one serving as a soldier gets involved in civilian affairs—he wants to please his commanding officer. [5]Similarly, if anyone competes as an athlete, he does not receive the victor's crown unless he competes according to the rules. [6]The hardworking farmer should be the first to receive a share of the crops. [7]Reflect on what I am saying, for the Lord will give you insight into all this.

[8]Remember Jesus Christ, raised from the dead, descended from David. This is my gospel, [9]for which I am suffering even to the point of being chained like a criminal. But God's word is not chained. [10]Therefore I endure everything for the sake of the elect, that they too may obtain the salvation that is in Christ Jesus, with eternal glory.

[11]Here is a trustworthy saying:

If we died with him,
  we will also live with him;
[12]if we endure,
  we will also reign with him.
If we disown him,
  he will also disown us;
[13]if we are faithless,
  he will remain faithful,
  for he cannot disown himself.

A Workman Approved by God

[14]Keep reminding them of these things. Warn them before God against quarreling about words; it is of no value, and only ruins those who listen. [15]Do your best to present yourself to God as one approved, a workman who does not need to be ashamed and who correctly handles the word of truth. [16]Avoid godless chatter, because those who indulge in it will become more and more ungodly. [17]Their teaching will spread like gangrene. Among them are Hymenaeus and Philetus, [18]who have wandered away from the truth. They say that the resurrection has already taken place, and they destroy the faith of some. [19]Nevertheless, God's solid foundation stands firm, sealed with this inscription: "The Lord knows those who are his,"[a] and, "Everyone who confesses the name of the Lord must turn away from wickedness."

[20]In a large house there are articles not only of gold and silver, but also of wood and clay; some are for noble purposes and some for ignoble. [21]If a man cleanses himself from the latter, he will be an instrument for noble purposes, made holy, useful to the Master and prepared to do any good work.

[22]Flee the evil desires of youth, and pursue righteousness, faith, love and peace, along with those who call on the Lord out of a pure heart. [23]Don't have anything to do with foolish and stupid arguments, because you know they produce quarrels. [24]And the Lord's servant must not quarrel; instead, he must be kind to everyone, able to teach, not resentful. [25]Those who oppose him he must gently instruct, in the hope that God will grant them repentance leading them to a knowledge of the truth, [26]and that they will come to their senses and escape from the trap of the devil, who has taken them captive to do his will.

[a]19 Num. 16:5 (see Septuagint)

Godlessness in the Last Days

3 But mark this: There will be terrible times in the last days. ²People will be lovers of themselves, lovers of money, boastful, proud, abusive, disobedient to their parents, ungrateful, unholy, ³without love, unforgiving, slanderous, without self-control, brutal, not lovers of the good, ⁴treacherous, rash, conceit-ed, lovers of pleasure rather than lovers of God— ⁵having a form of godliness but denying its power. Have nothing to do with them.

⁶They are the kind who worm their way into homes and gain control over weak-willed women, who are loaded down with sins and are swayed by all kinds of evil desires, ⁷always learning but never able to acknowledge the truth.

TUESDAY

VERSE:	AUTHOR:	PASSAGE:
2 Timothy 4:7–8	Paula Rinehart	2 Timothy 4:1–8

A Realistic Hope

We said we'd never grow up and we'd never grow old; we'd never trust anyone over thirty. And now [some] of us have long since passed that tender age and are in the midst of giving each other black fortieth birthday parties. Who knows? We may yet grow old.

For [this] generation, more than any other in the twentieth century, the twenty-five years between youth and middle-age have been marked by unmet expectations. We found many of our dreams unreachable. Growing up has been less about realizing our dreams and more about making our dreams subject to reality.

In one sense, when we tied our faith to our cultural expectations, we succumbed to the illusion that we could experience heaven in the here and now. It is true that one day our dreams and longings will be fulfilled beyond our wildest imaginations. Life will happen the way it's supposed to, the way we always wanted it to—some-day—*but not now.* Now we plow through time, groping, learning, hurting, struggling, failing and sometimes succeeding. God can help us and strengthen us, but he never promised to keep us from pain. "Our Father refreshes us with some pleasant inns on the journey, but [he] will not encourage us to mistake them for home," wrote C.S. Lewis. No matter what the song says, heaven is not a place on earth.

Perhaps disappointed dreams are our best opportunities to transfer hope to its rightful place. Heaven is where our biggest dreams belong. Realizing that can help us make it through the here and now without placing a burden on the present that it was never meant to bear. That's hope—realistic hope—which may yet serve to carry us through the rest of the journey.

ADDITIONAL SCRIPTURE READINGS:
Isaiah 40:31; Romans 12:12; Titus 1:2

Go to page 312 for your next devotional reading.

⁸Just as Jannes and Jambres opposed Moses, so also these men oppose the truth—men of depraved minds, who, as far as the faith is concerned, are rejected. ⁹But they will not get very far because, as in the case of those men, their folly will be clear to everyone.

Paul's Charge to Timothy

¹⁰You, however, know all about my teaching, my way of life, my purpose, faith, patience, love, endurance, ¹¹persecutions, sufferings—what kinds of things happened to me in Antioch, Iconium and Lystra, the persecutions I endured. Yet the Lord rescued me from all of them. ¹²In fact, everyone who wants to live a godly life in Christ Jesus will be persecuted, ¹³while evil men and impostors will go from bad to worse, deceiving and being deceived. ¹⁴But as for you, continue in what you have learned and have become convinced of, because you know those from whom you learned it, ¹⁵and how from infancy you have known the holy Scriptures, which are able to make you wise for salvation through faith in Christ Jesus. ¹⁶All Scripture is God-breathed and is useful for teaching, rebuking, correcting and training in righteousness, ¹⁷so that the man of God may be thoroughly equipped for every good work.

4 In the presence of God and of Christ Jesus, who will judge the living and the dead, and in view of his appearing and his kingdom, I give you this charge: ²Preach the Word; be prepared in season and out of season; correct, rebuke and encourage—with great patience and careful instruction. ³For the time will come when men will not put up with sound doctrine. Instead, to suit their own desires, they will gather around them a great number of teachers to say what their itching ears want to hear. ⁴They will turn their ears away from the truth and turn aside to myths. ⁵But you, keep your head in all situations, endure hardship, do the work of an evangelist, discharge all the duties of your ministry.

⁶For I am already being poured out like a drink offering, and the time has come for my departure. ⁷I have fought the good fight, I have finished the race, I have kept the faith. ⁸Now there is in store for me the crown of righteousness, which the Lord, the righteous Judge, will award to me on that day—and not only to me, but also to all who have longed for his appearing.

Personal Remarks

⁹Do your best to come to me quickly, ¹⁰for Demas, because he loved this world, has deserted me and has gone to Thessalonica. Crescens has gone to Galatia, and Titus to Dalmatia. ¹¹Only Luke is with me. Get Mark and bring him with you, because he is helpful to me in my ministry. ¹²I sent Tychicus to Ephesus. ¹³When you come, bring the cloak that I left with Carpus at Troas, and my scrolls, especially the parchments.

¹⁴Alexander the metalworker did me a great deal of harm. The Lord will repay him for what he has done. ¹⁵You too should be on your guard against him, because he strongly opposed our message.

¹⁶At my first defense, no one came to my support, but everyone deserted me. May it not be held against them. ¹⁷But the Lord stood at my side and gave me strength, so that through me the message might be fully proclaimed and all the Gentiles might hear it. And I was delivered from the lion's mouth. ¹⁸The Lord will rescue me from every evil attack and will bring me safely to his heavenly kingdom. To him be glory for ever and ever. Amen.

Final Greetings

¹⁹Greet Priscilla[a] and Aquila and the household of Onesiphorus. ²⁰Erastus stayed in Corinth, and I left Trophimus sick in Miletus. ²¹Do your best to get here before winter. Eubulus greets you, and so do Pudens, Linus, Claudia and all the brothers.

²²The Lord be with your spirit. Grace be with you.

---

[a]19 Greek Prisca, a variant of Priscilla

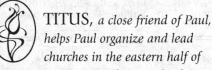

TITUS, *a close friend of Paul, helps Paul organize and lead churches in the eastern half of the Roman empire. Paul writes this letter to Titus to help him lead the troubled church on the island of Crete. Paul covers such matters as qualifications of church leaders, guidelines for a godly life and an emphasis on faith that overcomes division among believers.*

TITUS

1 Paul, a servant of God and an apostle of Jesus Christ for the faith of God's elect and the knowledge of the truth that leads to godliness— ²a faith and knowledge resting on the hope of eternal life, which God, who does not lie, promised before the beginning of time, ³and at his appointed season he brought his word to light through the preaching entrusted to me by the command of God our Savior,

⁴To Titus, my true son in our common faith:

Grace and peace from God the Father and Christ Jesus our Savior.

Titus' Task on Crete

⁵The reason I left you in Crete was that you might straighten out what was left unfinished and appoint*ᵃ* elders in every town, as I directed you. ⁶An elder must be blameless, the husband of but one wife, a man whose children believe and are not open to the charge of being wild and disobedient. ⁷Since an overseer*ᵇ* is entrusted with God's work, he must be blameless—not overbearing, not quick-tempered, not given to drunkenness, not violent, not pursuing dishonest gain. ⁸Rather he must be hospitable, one who loves what is good, who is self-controlled, upright, holy and disciplined. ⁹He must hold firmly to the trustworthy message as it has been taught, so that he can encourage others by sound doctrine and refute those who oppose it.

¹⁰For there are many rebellious people, mere talkers and deceivers, especially those of the circumcision group. ¹¹They must be silenced, because they

ᵃ5 Or *ordain*   *ᵇ7* Traditionally *bishop*

are ruining whole households by teaching things they ought not to teach—and that for the sake of dishonest gain. [12]Even one of their own prophets has said, "Cretans are always liars, evil brutes, lazy gluttons." [13]This testimony is true. Therefore, rebuke them sharply, so that they will be sound in the faith [14]and will pay no attention to Jewish myths or to the commands of those who reject the truth. [15]To the pure, all things are pure, but to those who are

---

WEDNESDAY

VERSE: Titus 2:3	AUTHOR: Elisa Morgan and Carol Kuykendall	PASSAGE: Titus 2

What Every Mom Needs

In the local MOPS [Mothers of Preschoolers] group, mentors are modeled on the "Titus woman" principle, found in Titus 2:3–5: "Teach the older women to be reverent in the way they live . . . to teach what is good. Then they can train the younger women to love their husbands and children, to be self-controlled and pure, to be busy at home, to be kind, and to be subject to their husbands, so that no one will malign the word of God." They are "mothering mentors."

A mothering mentor is a woman who has scaled the mountain you intend to climb. She's gone before you. She knows the path. She knows the toeholds. She comes alongside you and offers encouragement that you, too, can make it. From her own life experience, she can teach on such subjects as how to mother, how to organize life, how to develop your abilities and character. For a young mother who has never seen good mothering in practice before, [the mentor] might model mothering. She might give a glimpse of what marriage looks like down the road or how to hurdle difficult spots in friendship.

Mentors are all around us. They are in churches, in families, in cross-generational friendships. If you're eager to find a mentoring mother, look for qualities like honesty, wisdom, discernment and encouragement. Watch from a distance before pursuing a relationship. Then, work up your courage and ask if you can poke around a bit to see how she does what she does with her kids. Mentoring doesn't have to be a formal arrangement, nor will you always learn everything you need to know from one single person.

A mothering mentor is not a know-it-all. She's not an expert with degrees and credentials trailing after her name, although she might possess formal training. She's simply a mom who's made it through some of the most challenging years of mothering. She's learned from her mistakes, enjoyed a few successes and can now share her insights with those of us who are coming along behind.

ADDITIONAL SCRIPTURE READINGS:
Leviticus 19:32; Titus 3:14; Hebrews 13:7

Go to page 313 for your next devotional reading.

corrupted and do not believe, nothing is pure. In fact, both their minds and consciences are corrupted. [16]They claim to know God, but by their actions they deny him. They are detestable, disobedient and unfit for doing anything good.

What Must Be Taught to Various Groups

2 You must teach what is in accord with sound doctrine. [2]Teach the older men to be temperate, worthy of respect, self-controlled, and sound in faith, in love and in endurance.

[3]Likewise, teach the older women to be reverent in the way they live, not to be slanderers or addicted to much wine, but to teach what is good. [4]Then they can train the younger women to love their husbands and children, [5]to be self-controlled and pure, to be busy at home, to be kind, and to be subject to their husbands, so that no one will malign the word of God.

[6]Similarly, encourage the young men to be self-controlled. [7]In everything set them an example by doing what is good. In your teaching show integrity, seriousness [8]and soundness of speech that cannot be condemned, so that those

THURSDAY

VERSE:	AUTHOR:	PASSAGE:
Titus 2:13	Gigi Graham Tchividjian	Titus 2:11–3:11

He Is Coming!

"Mama, come quick!" my young son called excitedly, the cold winter air rushing past the small snow-suited frame silhouetted in the open doorway.

I ran to see what he wanted. He grabbed my hand and pulled me into the fresh snow just beginning to melt in the warm sunshine.

"There! *There!* Up in the sky!" he cried, pointing to a bright object. With anticipation in his blue eyes and hope in his voice, he asked, "Mama, is that Jesus coming back?"

Oh, how I wished I could have shouted a resounding yes. Instead, I took the little fellow in my arms and explained that it was just an airplane, reflecting the afternoon sun. Together we watched as the plane continued its flight across the sky and over the mountain peaks.

As I rearranged his cap and adjusted his mittens, I sensed a gentle rebuke in his disappointed face. I remembered how I, too, had thrilled at the thought of the imminent return of the Lord Jesus. But I had become so caught up with the business of everyday living that I had lost my awareness of the reality that he could come back at any time.

Scripture teaches that there is a special crown—a crown of righteousness—set aside for those who look forward to and love his appearing.

ADDITIONAL SCRIPTURE READINGS:
Matthew 24:42–44; John 11:25; Acts 1:10–11; 2 Timothy 4:8

Go to page 316 for your next devotional reading.

who oppose you may be ashamed because they have nothing bad to say about us.

[9]Teach slaves to be subject to their masters in everything, to try to please them, not to talk back to them, [10]and not to steal from them, but to show that they can be fully trusted, so that in every way they will make the teaching about God our Savior attractive.

[11]For the grace of God that brings salvation has appeared to all men. [12]It teaches us to say "No" to ungodliness and worldly passions, and to live self-controlled, upright and godly lives in this present age, [13]while we wait for the blessed hope—the glorious appearing of our great God and Savior, Jesus Christ, [14]who gave himself for us to redeem us from all wickedness and to purify for himself a people that are his very own, eager to do what is good.

[15]These, then, are the things you should teach. Encourage and rebuke with all authority. Do not let anyone despise you.

Doing What Is Good

3 Remind the people to be subject to rulers and authorities, to be obedient, to be ready to do whatever is good, [2]to slander no one, to be peaceable and considerate, and to show true humility toward all men.

[3]At one time we too were foolish, disobedient, deceived and enslaved by all kinds of passions and pleasures. We lived in malice and envy, being hated and hating one another. [4]But when the kindness and love of God our Savior appeared, [5]he saved us, not because of righteous things we had done, but because of his mercy. He saved us through the washing of rebirth and renewal by the Holy Spirit, [6]whom he poured out on us generously through Jesus Christ our Savior, [7]so that, having been justified by his grace, we might become heirs having the hope of eternal life. [8]This is a trustworthy saying. And I want you to stress these things, so that those who have trusted in God may be careful to devote themselves to doing what is good. These things are excellent and profitable for everyone.

[9]But avoid foolish controversies and genealogies and arguments and quarrels about the law, because these are unprofitable and useless. [10]Warn a divisive person once, and then warn him a second time. After that, have nothing to do with him. [11]You may be sure that such a man is warped and sinful; he is self-condemned.

Final Remarks

[12]As soon as I send Artemas or Tychicus to you, do your best to come to me at Nicopolis, because I have decided to winter there. [13]Do everything you can to help Zenas the lawyer and Apollos on their way and see that they have everything they need. [14]Our people must learn to devote themselves to doing what is good, in order that they may provide for daily necessities and not live unproductive lives.

[15]Everyone with me sends you greetings. Greet those who love us in the faith.

Grace be with you all.

PHILEMON, *a believer in Colosse, owns a slave named Onesimus who steals from his owner and then runs away. But Onesimus meets Paul and through his ministry becomes a Christian. Now he is willing to return to his master. Paul writes this personal appeal to ask Philemon to accept Onesimus as a Christian brother, not as a slave. Read this letter as a case study in the cost of asking for forgiveness and of granting it.*

PHILEMON

¹Paul, a prisoner of Christ Jesus, and Timothy our brother,

To Philemon our dear friend and fellow worker, ²to Apphia our sister, to Archippus our fellow soldier and to the church that meets in your home:

³Grace to you and peace from God our Father and the Lord Jesus Christ.

Thanksgiving and Prayer

⁴I always thank my God as I remember you in my prayers, ⁵because I hear about your faith in the Lord Jesus and your love for all the saints. ⁶I pray that you may be active in sharing your faith, so that you will have a full understanding of every good thing we have in Christ. ⁷Your love has given me great joy and encouragement, because you, brother, have refreshed the hearts of the saints.

Paul's Plea for Onesimus

⁸Therefore, although in Christ I could be bold and order you to do what you ought to do, ⁹yet I appeal to you on the basis of love. I then, as Paul—an old man and now also a prisoner of Christ Jesus— ¹⁰I appeal to you for my son Onesimus,[a] who became my son while I was in chains. ¹¹Formerly he was useless to you, but now he has become useful both to you and to me.

¹²I am sending him—who is my very heart—back to you. ¹³I would have liked

---

[a]10 *Onesimus* means *useful.*

to keep him with me so that he could take your place in helping me while I am in chains for the gospel. [14]But I did not want to do anything without your consent, so that any favor you do will be spontaneous and not forced. [15]Perhaps the reason he was separated from you for a little while was that you might have him back for good— [16]no longer as a slave, but better than a slave, as a dear brother. He is very dear to me but even dearer to you, both as a man and as a brother in the Lord.

[17]So if you consider me a partner, welcome him as you would welcome me. [18]If he has done you any wrong or owes you anything, charge it to me. [19]I, Paul, am writing this with my own hand. I will pay it back—not to mention that you owe me your very self. [20]I do wish, brother, that I may have some benefit from you in the Lord; refresh my heart in Christ. [21]Confident of your obedience, I write to you, knowing that you will do even more than I ask.

[22]And one thing more: Prepare a guest room for me, because I hope to be restored to you in answer to your prayers.

[23]Epaphras, my fellow prisoner in Christ Jesus, sends you greetings. [24]And so do Mark, Aristarchus, Demas and Luke, my fellow workers.

[25]The grace of the Lord Jesus Christ be with your spirit.

FRIDAY

VERSE:
Philemon 11

AUTHOR:
Susan Lenzkes

PASSAGE:
Philemon

Increase in Value

Onesimus was a slave, quite possibly a renegade, who had stolen from his master, Philemon. He seemed to be of little worth—until the apostle Paul befriended him. From his prison cell Paul shared the good news of the love of Christ with this runaway, and God's love dramatically increased his value. Suddenly this slave became "my son . . . very dear to me . . . useful . . . a dear brother . . . my very heart" (vv. 10–16).

Do you know people who feel and act as though they aren't worth much . . . people enslaved by sin, bad habits, weakness or self-loathing? We who carry the love of God within us have the power to increase their value from useless to useful, from slave to dear brother or sister. This is the joyous privilege of friendship in Christ.

ADDITIONAL SCRIPTURE READINGS:
2 Chronicles 7:14; John 1:29; Colossians 1:13–14

Go to page 317 for your next devotional reading.

WEEKENDING

REFLECT

"But where are you going to, Helen? Can you see? Do you know?"

"I believe: I have faith: I am going to God."

"Where is God? What is God?"

"My Maker and yours, who will never destroy what he created. I rely implicitly on his power, and confide wholly in his goodness: I count the hours till that eventful one arrives which shall restore me to him, reveal him to me . . . I believe God is good; I can resign my immortal part to him without any misgiving. God is my father; God is my friend: I love him; I believe he loves me."

"And shall I see you again, Helen, when I die?"

"You will come to the same region of happiness: be received by the same mighty, universal Parent, no doubt, dear Jane."

Charlotte Bronte, Jane Eyre

RESTORE

Saturday: Psalm 34
Sunday: 1 John 2:28–3:10

Go to page 319 for your next devotional reading.

THE *first-century church suffered severe persecution, and this letter is written in that setting. The intended readers seem to be Jewish Christians who are thinking of abandoning their faith and of lapsing back into Judaism. The author exhorts them to hold fast to their confession of Christ as Savior and Lord. The theme of Hebrews is the absolute supremacy and sufficiency of Jesus Christ as revealer and as mediator of God's grace. As you read this book, look for the inspiration to keep going in the faith.*

HEBREWS

The Son Superior to Angels

1 In the past God spoke to our forefathers through the prophets at many times and in various ways, ²but in these last days he has spoken to us by his Son, whom he appointed heir of all things, and through whom he made the universe. ³The Son is the radiance of God's glory and the exact representation of his being, sustaining all things by his powerful word. After he had provided purification for sins, he sat down at the right hand of the Majesty in heaven. ⁴So he became as much superior to the angels as the name he has inherited is superior to theirs.

⁵For to which of the angels did God ever say,

"You are my Son;
    today I have become your
        Father*a" b*?

Or again,

"I will be his Father,
    and he will be my Son"*c*?

⁶And again, when God brings his firstborn into the world, he says,

---

"Let all God's angels worship
   him."[a]

[7]In speaking of the angels he says,

"He makes his angels winds,
   his servants flames of fire."[b]

[8]But about the Son he says,

"Your throne, O God, will last for
   ever and ever,

[a]6 Deut. 32:43 (see Dead Sea Scrolls and Septuagint)

and righteousness will be the
   scepter of your kingdom.
[9]You have loved righteousness and
   hated wickedness;
therefore God, your God, has set
   you above your companions
by anointing you with the oil of
   joy."[c]

[10]He also says,

[b]7 Psalm 104:4   [c]9 Psalm 45:6,7

MONDAY

VERSE:
Hebrews 1:14

AUTHOR:
Basilea Schlink

PASSAGE:
Hebrews 1

Angels That Serve

"The heavens declare the glory of God"(Psalm 19:1). Yes, the
heavenly realm, the realm of the angels, where the Almighty
reigns, giving them commands concerning the administration of the entire creation, tells us what God is like in his
omnipotence. It tells us about the throne of God, exalted above
all worlds. From there the perfect rule of God goes forth into all
the universe.

How deeply comforting is the knowledge that in the end times
when the elements such as fire, water and nuclear energy are let
loose, it is the angels who have control of these forces! When
through the agency of his angels the Lord unleashes the elements,
turning them into destructive forces, his own will experience miracles. The angels will command the elements not to cause any
harm to those who truly love and fear God.

Protecting, judging, battling, supervising—every service rendered
by these thousands of angels to nations, individuals and the kingdom of God, however awe-inspiring, pales in comparison with the
dealings of God. The ministry of angels is but a dim reflection of
the way God watches over everything and how his heart throbs
with love and sorrow for us, the nations and his creation in the fervent desire to help us.

The activity of the angels, the extent of their authority and their
devoted service all proclaim, "Who is like God!" How he must love
the [children of humankind] to send to their aid and service his
mighty ones from the heavenly hosts!

ADDITIONAL SCRIPTURE READINGS:
Psalms 91:11-12; Matthew 13:40-41

Go to page 322 for your next devotional reading.

"In the beginning, O Lord, you laid
    the foundations of the earth,
and the heavens are the work of
    your hands.
[11]They will perish, but you remain;
    they will all wear out like a
    garment.
[12]You will roll them up like a robe;
    like a garment they will be
    changed.
But you remain the same,
    and your years will never end."[a]

[13]To which of the angels did God ever
say,

"Sit at my right hand
until I make your enemies
    a footstool for your feet"[b]?

[14]Are not all angels ministering spirits
sent to serve those who will inherit salvation?

Warning to Pay Attention

2 We must pay more careful attention, therefore, to what we have
heard, so that we do not drift away. [2]For
if the message spoken by angels was
binding, and every violation and disobedience received its just punishment,
[3]how shall we escape if we ignore such
a great salvation? This salvation, which
was first announced by the Lord, was
confirmed to us by those who heard
him. [4]God also testified to it by signs,
wonders and various miracles, and gifts
of the Holy Spirit distributed according
to his will.

Jesus Made Like His Brothers

[5]It is not to angels that he has subjected the world to come, about which we
are speaking. [6]But there is a place where
someone has testified:

"What is man that you are mindful
    of him,
    the son of man that you care for
        him?
[7]You made him a little[c] lower than
    the angels;
    you crowned him with glory and
        honor
[8]   and put everything under his
        feet."[d]

In putting everything under him, God
left nothing that is not subject to him.
Yet at present we do not see everything
subject to him. [9]But we see Jesus, who
was made a little lower than the angels,
now crowned with glory and honor because he suffered death, so that by the
grace of God he might taste death for
everyone.

[10]In bringing many sons to glory, it
was fitting that God, for whom and
through whom everything exists, should
make the author of their salvation perfect through suffering. [11]Both the one
who makes men holy and those who are
made holy are of the same family. So
Jesus is not ashamed to call them brothers. [12]He says,

"I will declare your name to my
    brothers;
    in the presence of the congregation
        I will sing your praises."[e]

[13]And again,

"I will put my trust in him."[f]

And again he says,

"Here am I, and the children God
    has given me."[g]

[14]Since the children have flesh and
blood, he too shared in their humanity
so that by his death he might destroy
him who holds the power of death—that
is, the devil— [15]and free those who all
their lives were held in slavery by their
fear of death. [16]For surely it is not angels
he helps, but Abraham's descendants.
[17]For this reason he had to be made like
his brothers in every way, in order that
he might become a merciful and faithful
high priest in service to God, and that he
might make atonement for[h] the sins of
the people. [18]Because he himself suffered when he was tempted, he is able to
help those who are being tempted.

Jesus Greater Than Moses

3 Therefore, holy brothers, who share
in the heavenly calling, fix your
thoughts on Jesus, the apostle and high
priest whom we confess. [2]He was faithful to the one who appointed him, just
as Moses was faithful in all God's
house. [3]Jesus has been found worthy of

---

[a]12 Psalm 102:25-27   [b]13 Psalm 110:1   [c]7 Or him for a little while; also in verse 9
[d]8 Psalm 8:4-6   [e]12 Psalm 22:22   [f]13 Isaiah 8:17   [g]13 Isaiah 8:18   [h]17 Or and that he
might turn aside God's wrath, taking away

greater honor than Moses, just as the builder of a house has greater honor than the house itself. **4**For every house is built by someone, but God is the builder of everything. **5**Moses was faithful as a servant in all God's house, testifying to what would be said in the future. **6**But Christ is faithful as a son over God's house. And we are his house, if we hold on to our courage and the hope of which we boast.

Warning Against Unbelief

7So, as the Holy Spirit says:

"Today, if you hear his voice,
8 do not harden your hearts
as you did in the rebellion,
during the time of testing in the
desert,
9where your fathers tested and tried
me
and for forty years saw what I did.
10That is why I was angry with that
generation,
and I said, 'Their hearts are
always going astray,
and they have not known my
ways.'
11So I declared on oath in my anger,
'They shall never enter my
rest.' " *a*

12See to it, brothers, that none of you has a sinful, unbelieving heart that turns away from the living God. **13**But encourage one another daily, as long as it is called Today, so that none of you may be hardened by sin's deceitfulness. **14**We have come to share in Christ if we hold firmly till the end the confidence we had at first. **15**As has just been said:

"Today, if you hear his voice,
do not harden your hearts
as you did in the rebellion." *b*

16Who were they who heard and rebelled? Were they not all those Moses led out of Egypt? **17**And with whom was he angry for forty years? Was it not with those who sinned, whose bodies fell in the desert? **18**And to whom did God swear that they would never enter his rest if not to those who disobeyed *c*? **19**So we see that they were not able to enter, because of their unbelief.

A Sabbath-Rest for the People of God

4 Therefore, since the promise of entering his rest still stands, let us be careful that none of you be found to have fallen short of it. **2**For we also have had the gospel preached to us, just as they did; but the message they heard was of no value to them, because those who heard did not combine it with faith. *d* **3**Now we who have believed enter that rest, just as God has said,

"So I declared on oath in my anger,
'They shall never enter my
rest.' " *e*

And yet his work has been finished since the creation of the world. **4**For somewhere he has spoken about the seventh day in these words: "And on the seventh day God rested from all his work." *f* **5**And again in the passage above he says, "They shall never enter my rest."

6It still remains that some will enter that rest, and those who formerly had the gospel preached to them did not go in, because of their disobedience. **7**Therefore God again set a certain day, calling it Today, when a long time later he spoke through David, as was said before:

"Today, if you hear his voice,
do not harden your hearts." *b*

8For if Joshua had given them rest, God would not have spoken later about another day. **9**There remains, then, a Sabbath-rest for the people of God; **10**for anyone who enters God's rest also rests from his own work, just as God did from his. **11**Let us, therefore, make every effort to enter that rest, so that no one will fall by following their example of disobedience.

12For the word of God is living and active. Sharper than any double-edged sword, it penetrates even to dividing soul and spirit, joints and marrow; it judges the thoughts and attitudes of the heart. **13**Nothing in all creation is hidden from God's sight. Everything is uncovered and laid bare before the eyes of him to whom we must give account.

---

a11 Psalm 95:7-11   *b15,7* Psalm 95:7,8
they did not share in the faith of those who obeyed   *c18* Or *disbelieved*   *d2* Many manuscripts *because*
e3 Psalm 95:11; also in verse 5   *f4* Gen. 2:2

Jesus the Great High Priest

14Therefore, since we have a great high priest who has gone through the heavens,[a] Jesus the Son of God, let us hold firmly to the faith we profess. **15**For we do not have a high priest who is unable to sympathize with our weaknesses, but we have one who has been tempted in

[a]14 Or *gone into heaven*

◁ **TUESDAY** ▷

VERSE: AUTHOR: PASSAGE:
Hebrews 3:13   Carol Van Klompenburg   Hebrews 3

The Future Is Now

[Sometimes] we think we will start to live at some future date . . . Our drive to the mythical future prevents our savoring the present. It becomes simply a step . . . with no meaning of its own. I do the dishes so I can get to the laundry . . . I read to my children to augment their verbal skills.

But said Sophie Kerr, "The future is now!" . . . We shape our future by how we handle the present . . . In each moment the real future for the real me is now. What does this mean? The "future is now" means you are seated in the presence of God. Knowing that the future is now . . . that each moment is the Lord's, frees us from seeing all of life as work.

A theatre professor at a college I attended demonstrated what it means to know the future is now. He arrived on campus before 7:00 each morning . . . He was often on campus until 10:00 at night. He was hard-working and creative.

But religiously he refused to enter a single meeting or conference in the late afternoon. At 3:30 he went home for a coffee break. Then he took his long-eared hound for a walk in the country. They ambled outdoors in any season. They crunched through fallen leaves and sogged through drizzle.

He called his dog "Piphy." He had shortened the unlikely word "epiphany" and christened his lop-eared hound with it. As a college student I thought it was a preposterous choice of names. But looking back now, I approve.

An epiphany is a sudden grasp of the essential nature of something. It is also a manifestation of a divine being. Our knowledge of God, our sense of his presence often comes . . . when we stop work and "walk our dog"—whatever form that walk may take for us. We can be touched again by the eternal, and the future can be now.

To be touched by those epiphany moments is to live, not just in the three dimensions of space and the fourth dimension of time, but also in a fifth dimension that extends toward our God.

ADDITIONAL SCRIPTURE READINGS:
Psalm 100:1–2; 1 Corinthians 3:7–9; Colossians 1:10

Go to page 325 for your next devotional reading.

every way, just as we are—yet was without sin. [16]Let us then approach the throne of grace with confidence, so that we may receive mercy and find grace to help us in our time of need.

5 Every high priest is selected from among men and is appointed to represent them in matters related to God, to offer gifts and sacrifices for sins. [2]He is able to deal gently with those who are ignorant and are going astray, since he himself is subject to weakness. [3]This is why he has to offer sacrifices for his own sins, as well as for the sins of the people.

[4]No one takes this honor upon himself; he must be called by God, just as Aaron was. [5]So Christ also did not take upon himself the glory of becoming a high priest. But God said to him,

"You are my Son;
    today I have become your
        Father."[a]"[b]

[6]And he says in another place,

"You are a priest forever,
    in the order of Melchizedek."[c]

[7]During the days of Jesus' life on earth, he offered up prayers and petitions with loud cries and tears to the one who could save him from death, and he was heard because of his reverent submission. [8]Although he was a son, he learned obedience from what he suffered [9]and, once made perfect, he became the source of eternal salvation for all who obey him [10]and was designated by God to be high priest in the order of Melchizedek.

Warning Against Falling Away

[11]We have much to say about this, but it is hard to explain because you are slow to learn. [12]In fact, though by this time you ought to be teachers, you need someone to teach you the elementary truths of God's word all over again. You need milk, not solid food! [13]Anyone who lives on milk, being still an infant, is not acquainted with the teaching about righteousness. [14]But solid food is for the mature, who by constant use have trained themselves to distinguish good from evil.

6 Therefore let us leave the elementary teachings about Christ and go on to maturity, not laying again the foundation of repentance from acts that lead to death,[d] and of faith in God, [2]instruction about baptisms, the laying on of hands, the resurrection of the dead, and eternal judgment. [3]And God permitting, we will do so.

[4]It is impossible for those who have once been enlightened, who have tasted the heavenly gift, who have shared in the Holy Spirit, [5]who have tasted the goodness of the word of God and the powers of the coming age, [6]if they fall away, to be brought back to repentance, because[e] to their loss they are crucifying the Son of God all over again and subjecting him to public disgrace.

[7]Land that drinks in the rain often falling on it and that produces a crop useful to those for whom it is farmed receives the blessing of God. [8]But land that produces thorns and thistles is worthless and is in danger of being cursed. In the end it will be burned.

[9]Even though we speak like this, dear friends, we are confident of better things in your case—things that accompany salvation. [10]God is not unjust; he will not forget your work and the love you have shown him as you have helped his people and continue to help them. [11]We want each of you to show this same diligence to the very end, in order to make your hope sure. [12]We do not want you to become lazy, but to imitate those who through faith and patience inherit what has been promised.

The Certainty of God's Promise

[13]When God made his promise to Abraham, since there was no one greater for him to swear by, he swore by himself, [14]saying, "I will surely bless you and give you many descendants."[f] [15]And so after waiting patiently, Abraham received what was promised.

[16]Men swear by someone greater than themselves, and the oath confirms what is said and puts an end to all argument. [17]Because God wanted to make the unchanging nature of his purpose very clear to the heirs of what was promised, he confirmed it with an oath. [18]God did this so that, by two unchangeable things

---

[a]5 Or have begotten you   [b]5 Psalm 2:7   [c]6 Psalm 110:4   [d]1 Or from useless rituals   [e]6 Or
repentance while   [f]14 Gen. 22:17

in which it is impossible for God to lie, we who have fled to take hold of the hope offered to us may be greatly encouraged. ¹⁹We have this hope as an anchor for the soul, firm and secure. It enters the inner sanctuary behind the curtain, ²⁰where Jesus, who went before us, has entered on our behalf. He has become a high priest forever, in the order of Melchizedek.

Melchizedek the Priest

7 This Melchizedek was king of Salem and priest of God Most High. He met Abraham returning from the defeat of the kings and blessed him, ²and Abraham gave him a tenth of everything. First, his name means "king of righteousness"; then also, "king of Salem" means "king of peace." ³Without father or mother, without genealogy, without beginning of days or end of life, like the Son of God he remains a priest forever.

⁴Just think how great he was: Even the patriarch Abraham gave him a tenth of the plunder! ⁵Now the law requires the descendants of Levi who become priests to collect a tenth from the people—that is, their brothers—even though their brothers are descended from Abraham. ⁶This man, however, did not trace his descent from Levi, yet he collected a tenth from Abraham and blessed him who had the promises. ⁷And without doubt the lesser person is blessed by the greater. ⁸In the one case, the tenth is collected by men who die; but in the other case, by him who is declared to be living. ⁹One might even say that Levi, who collects the tenth, paid the tenth through Abraham, ¹⁰because when Melchizedek met Abraham, Levi was still in the body of his ancestor.

Jesus Like Melchizedek

¹¹If perfection could have been attained through the Levitical priesthood (for on the basis of it the law was given to the people), why was there still need for another priest to come—one in the order of Melchizedek, not in the order of Aaron? ¹²For when there is a change of the priesthood, there must also be a change of the law. ¹³He of whom these things are said belonged to a different tribe, and no one from that tribe has ever served at the altar. ¹⁴For it is clear that our Lord descended from Judah, and in regard to that tribe Moses said nothing about priests. ¹⁵And what we have said is even more clear if another priest like Melchizedek appears, ¹⁶one who has become a priest not on the basis of a regulation as to his ancestry but on the basis of the power of an indestructible life. ¹⁷For it is declared:

"You are a priest forever,
    in the order of Melchizedek." ᵃ

¹⁸The former regulation is set aside because it was weak and useless ¹⁹(for the law made nothing perfect), and a better hope is introduced, by which we draw near to God.

²⁰And it was not without an oath! Others became priests without any oath, ²¹but he became a priest with an oath when God said to him:

"The Lord has sworn
    and will not change his mind:
'You are a priest forever.' " ᵃ

²²Because of this oath, Jesus has become the guarantee of a better covenant.

²³Now there have been many of those priests, since death prevented them from continuing in office; ²⁴but because Jesus lives forever, he has a permanent priesthood. ²⁵Therefore he is able to save completely ᵇ those who come to God through him, because he always lives to intercede for them.

²⁶Such a high priest meets our need—one who is holy, blameless, pure, set apart from sinners, exalted above the heavens. ²⁷Unlike the other high priests, he does not need to offer sacrifices day after day, first for his own sins, and then for the sins of the people. He sacrificed for their sins once for all when he offered himself. ²⁸For the law appoints as high priests men who are weak; but the oath, which came after the law, appointed the Son, who has been made perfect forever.

The High Priest of a New Covenant

8 The point of what we are saying is this: We do have such a high priest, who sat down at the right hand of the throne of the Majesty in heaven, ²and who serves in the sanctuary, the true tabernacle set up by the Lord, not by man.

ᵃ 17,21 Psalm 110:4   ᵇ 25 Or forever

VERSE:
Hebrews 6:19

AUTHOR:
Deforia Lane

PASSAGE:
Hebrews 6:13–20

His Grace Is Sufficient

God *and* I. That was it. Fresh out of miracles it seemed. God *and* I. In the face of death, it's either that or nothing at all. There was no one to blame, no sign, no job, no certainty, no cure in sight, and no telling what God had in mind. I was alone with God, holy in his determined, unpredictable will. That was it, a place of both alarming aloneness and tender communion.

I don't want this to sound too pious or sentimentally spiritual; whatever this process entailed, it was certainly not devout or sweet. I was really frightened. These days were filled with the peculiar and strangling frenzy of waiting. I cried a lot, worried a lot, questioned a lot, felt lost, slept little, and beyond all of that, God began to touch me deeply.

I started being honest, dreadfully honest. I felt the freedom to do not just the right thing, but the *real* thing. I didn't like the idea of death. Death is, for me, the great intruder.

I was angry with God that he would ask me even to consider it.

I had questions for which I didn't think God had the answers, or if he did, he wasn't willing to share them with me. And when I asked those questions, a surprising thing happened: what was meant as confrontation became release. Far from resenting my questions, God welcomed them. He bore the pain in the questions just as Christ bore the cross. In my confusion, I may have wanted to wound him, but he only bled for me. In expressing what was really going on inside me — the anger, hurt, the rage against dying — he comprehended my pain and translated my helplessness into certain strength. I don't know how. I don't know much about such grace.

God and I. And in the dropping of I, just God. That was it, no answers, no specifics on a night beach, no concluding refrain. Just of letting go of it, all of it, and in the release, in the dying itself, the seed of hope. I know it sounds backward, but I have found that the deepest moments in my life have always been the least contrived. In the release of control, I have found humbling power. In the chaos, I have found moments of sustaining peace.

God gave no answers, then, just his presence. Just that. And his grace was sufficient.

ADDITIONAL SCRIPTURE READINGS:
1 Peter 4:1–2, 12–13; Hebrews 10:35—11:2

Go to page 327 for your next devotional reading.

[3]Every high priest is appointed to offer both gifts and sacrifices, and so it was necessary for this one also to have something to offer. [4]If he were on earth, he would not be a priest, for there are already men who offer the gifts prescribed by the law. [5]They serve at a sanctuary that is a copy and shadow of what is in heaven. This is why Moses was warned when he was about to build the tabernacle: "See to it that you make everything according to the pattern shown you on the mountain."[a] [6]But the ministry Jesus has received is as superior to theirs as the covenant of which he is mediator is superior to the old one, and it is founded on better promises.

[7]For if there had been nothing wrong with that first covenant, no place would have been sought for another. [8]But God found fault with the people and said[b]:

"The time is coming, declares the
    Lord,
  when I will make a new covenant
with the house of Israel
  and with the house of Judah.
[9]It will not be like the covenant
  I made with their forefathers
when I took them by the hand
  to lead them out of Egypt,
because they did not remain faithful
    to my covenant,
  and I turned away from them,
            declares the Lord.
[10]This is the covenant I will make with
    the house of Israel
  after that time, declares the Lord.
I will put my laws in their minds
  and write them on their hearts.
I will be their God,
  and they will be my people.
[11]No longer will a man teach his
    neighbor,
  or a man his brother, saying,
    'Know the Lord,'
because they will all know me,
  from the least of them to the
    greatest.
[12]For I will forgive their wickedness
  and will remember their sins no
    more."[c]

[13]By calling this covenant "new," he has made the first one obsolete; and what is obsolete and aging will soon disappear.

Worship in the Earthly Tabernacle

9 Now the first covenant had regulations for worship and also an earthly sanctuary. [2]A tabernacle was set up. In its first room were the lampstand, the table and the consecrated bread; this was called the Holy Place. [3]Behind the second curtain was a room called the Most Holy Place, [4]which had the golden altar of incense and the gold-covered ark of the covenant. This ark contained the gold jar of manna, Aaron's staff that had budded, and the stone tablets of the covenant. [5]Above the ark were the cherubim of the Glory, overshadowing the atonement cover.[d] But we cannot discuss these things in detail now.

[6]When everything had been arranged like this, the priests entered regularly into the outer room to carry on their ministry. [7]But only the high priest entered the inner room, and that only once a year, and never without blood, which he offered for himself and for the sins the people had committed in ignorance. [8]The Holy Spirit was showing by this that the way into the Most Holy Place had not yet been disclosed as long as the first tabernacle was still standing. [9]This is an illustration for the present time, indicating that the gifts and sacrifices being offered were not able to clear the conscience of the worshiper. [10]They are only a matter of food and drink and various ceremonial washings—external regulations applying until the time of the new order.

The Blood of Christ

[11]When Christ came as high priest of the good things that are already here,[e] he went through the greater and more perfect tabernacle that is not man-made, that is to say, not a part of this creation. [12]He did not enter by means of the blood of goats and calves; but he entered the Most Holy Place once for all by his own blood, having obtained eternal redemption. [13]The blood of goats and bulls and the ashes of a heifer sprinkled on those who are ceremonially unclean sanctify them so that they are outwardly clean. [14]How much more, then, will the blood of Christ, who through the eternal Spirit offered himself unblemished to

---

[a]5 Exodus 25:40   [b]8 Some manuscripts may be translated *fault and said to the people.*
[c]12 Jer. 31:31-34   [d]5 Traditionally *the mercy seat*   [e]11 Some early manuscripts *are to come*

God, cleanse our consciences from acts that lead to death,[a] so that we may serve the living God! [15]For this reason Christ is the mediator of a new covenant, that those who are called may receive the promised eternal inheritance—now that he has died as a ransom to set them free from the sins committed under the first covenant.

[16]In the case of a will,[b] it is necessary to prove the death of the one who made it, [17]because a will is in force only when somebody has died; it never takes effect while the one who made it is living. [18]This is why even the first covenant was not put into effect without blood. [19]When Moses had proclaimed every commandment of the law to all the people, he took the blood of calves, together with water, scarlet wool and branches of hyssop, and sprinkled the scroll and all the people. [20]He said, "This is the blood of the covenant, which God has commanded you to keep."[c] [21]In the same way, he sprinkled with the blood both the tabernacle and everything used in its ceremonies. [22]In fact, the law requires that nearly everything be cleansed with blood, and without the shedding of blood there is no forgiveness.

[23]It was necessary, then, for the copies of the heavenly things to be purified with these sacrifices, but the heavenly things themselves with better sacrifices

[a]14 Or *from useless rituals*   [b]16 Same Greek word as *covenant*; also in verse 17   [c]20 Exodus 24:8

THURSDAY

VERSE:
Hebrews 9:14

AUTHOR:
Zoe B. Metzger

PASSAGE:
Hebrews 9:11–28

What Wrinkles?

Little Zoe, our granddaughter, was coming home with us for overnight. Buckled between us in the front seat of the car, she looked up through the windshield at a sky studded with stars.

"I wonder how God keeps the stars up there," she said. "Do you think he uses white glue?"

Grandpa chuckled, and I gave Zoe a squeeze. "I don't know how he does it, honey, but I do know you are a precious baby."

"I'm not a baby," she corrected me. "I'm four. I'm getting old."

"Oh, no!" I replied. "I'm the one who's getting old."

"Grammy, you're not old." She reached up to touch my face. "You don't have any wrinkles!"

Now, I've left sixty behind and I do have wrinkles. But Zoe looks at me with love; she doesn't see them.

And that's the wonderful way in which God looks at me—with love. Through the eyes of love, he sees me without blemish, made perfect by the sacrifice of his Son, Jesus. He chose me to be a "a jewel in a crown," and fastens me there, not with white glue, but with his promises.

God loves me, and he loves you. Because of Jesus, he doesn't see our wrinkles!

ADDITIONAL SCRIPTURE READINGS:
Romans 5:10; Colossians 1:22

Go to page 330 for your next devotional reading.

than these. [24]For Christ did not enter a man-made sanctuary that was only a copy of the true one; he entered heaven itself, now to appear for us in God's presence. [25]Nor did he enter heaven to offer himself again and again, the way the high priest enters the Most Holy Place every year with blood that is not his own. [26]Then Christ would have had to suffer many times since the creation of the world. But now he has appeared once for all at the end of the ages to do away with sin by the sacrifice of himself. [27]Just as man is destined to die once, and after that to face judgment, [28]so Christ was sacrificed once to take away the sins of many people; and he will appear a second time, not to bear sin, but to bring salvation to those who are waiting for him.

Christ's Sacrifice Once for All

10 The law is only a shadow of the good things that are coming— not the realities themselves. For this reason it can never, by the same sacrifices repeated endlessly year after year, make perfect those who draw near to worship. [2]If it could, would they not have stopped being offered? For the worshipers would have been cleansed once for all, and would no longer have felt guilty for their sins. [3]But those sacrifices are an annual reminder of sins, [4]because it is impossible for the blood of bulls and goats to take away sins.

[5]Therefore, when Christ came into the world, he said:

"Sacrifice and offering you did not
　　desire,
　　but a body you prepared for me;
[6]with burnt offerings and sin
　　offerings
　　you were not pleased.
[7]Then I said, 'Here I am—it is written
　　about me in the scroll—
　　I have come to do your will,
　　　O God.'"[a]

[8]First he said, "Sacrifices and offerings, burnt offerings and sin offerings you did not desire, nor were you pleased with them" (although the law required them to be made). [9]Then he said, "Here I am, I have come to do your will." He sets aside the first to establish the second. [10]And by that will, we have been

made holy through the sacrifice of the body of Jesus Christ once for all.

[11]Day after day every priest stands and performs his religious duties; again and again he offers the same sacrifices, which can never take away sins. [12]But when this priest had offered for all time one sacrifice for sins, he sat down at the right hand of God. [13]Since that time he waits for his enemies to be made his footstool, [14]because by one sacrifice he has made perfect forever those who are being made holy.

[15]The Holy Spirit also testifies to us about this. First he says:

[16]"This is the covenant I will make
　　with them
　　after that time, says the Lord.
I will put my laws in their hearts,
　　and I will write them on their
　　　minds."[b]

[17]Then he adds:

"Their sins and lawless acts
　　I will remember no more."[c]

[18]And where these have been forgiven, there is no longer any sacrifice for sin.

A Call to Persevere

[19]Therefore, brothers, since we have confidence to enter the Most Holy Place by the blood of Jesus, [20]by a new and living way opened for us through the curtain, that is, his body, [21]and since we have a great priest over the house of God, [22]let us draw near to God with a sincere heart in full assurance of faith, having our hearts sprinkled to cleanse us from a guilty conscience and having our bodies washed with pure water. [23]Let us hold unswervingly to the hope we profess, for he who promised is faithful. [24]And let us consider how we may spur one another on toward love and good deeds. [25]Let us not give up meeting together, as some are in the habit of doing, but let us encourage one another—and all the more as you see the Day approaching.

[26]If we deliberately keep on sinning after we have received the knowledge of the truth, no sacrifice for sins is left, [27]but only a fearful expectation of judgment and of raging fire that will consume the enemies of God. [28]Anyone who rejected the law of Moses died

---

[a]7 Psalm 40:6-8 (see Septuagint)　　　[b]16 Jer. 31:33　　　[c]17 Jer. 31:34

without mercy on the testimony of two or three witnesses. ²⁹How much more severely do you think a man deserves to be punished who has trampled the Son of God under foot, who has treated as an unholy thing the blood of the covenant that sanctified him, and who has insulted the Spirit of grace? ³⁰For we know him who said, "It is mine to avenge; I will repay,"ᵃ and again, "The Lord will judge his people."ᵇ ³¹It is a dreadful thing to fall into the hands of the living God.

³²Remember those earlier days after you had received the light, when you stood your ground in a great contest in the face of suffering. ³³Sometimes you were publicly exposed to insult and persecution; at other times you stood side by side with those who were so treated. ³⁴You sympathized with those in prison and joyfully accepted the confiscation of your property, because you knew that you yourselves had better and lasting possessions.

³⁵So do not throw away your confidence; it will be richly rewarded. ³⁶You need to persevere so that when you have done the will of God, you will receive what he has promised. ³⁷For in just a very little while,

"He who is coming will come and
    will not delay.
³⁸ But my righteous oneᶜ will live by
    faith.
And if he shrinks back,
    I will not be pleased with him."ᵈ

³⁹But we are not of those who shrink back and are destroyed, but of those who believe and are saved.

By Faith

11 Now faith is being sure of what we hope for and certain of what we do not see. ²This is what the ancients were commended for.

³By faith we understand that the universe was formed at God's command, so that what is seen was not made out of what was visible.

⁴By faith Abel offered God a better sacrifice than Cain did. By faith he was commended as a righteous man, when God spoke well of his offerings. And by

faith he still speaks, even though he is dead.

⁵By faith Enoch was taken from this life, so that he did not experience death; he could not be found, because God had taken him away. For before he was taken, he was commended as one who pleased God. ⁶And without faith it is impossible to please God, because anyone who comes to him must believe that he exists and that he rewards those who earnestly seek him.

⁷By faith Noah, when warned about things not yet seen, in holy fear built an ark to save his family. By his faith he condemned the world and became heir of the righteousness that comes by faith.

⁸By faith Abraham, when called to go to a place he would later receive as his inheritance, obeyed and went, even though he did not know where he was going. ⁹By faith he made his home in the promised land like a stranger in a foreign country; he lived in tents, as did Isaac and Jacob, who were heirs with him of the same promise. ¹⁰For he was looking forward to the city with foundations, whose architect and builder is God.

¹¹By faith Abraham, even though he was past age—and Sarah herself was barren—was enabled to become a father because heᵉ considered him faithful who had made the promise. ¹²And so from this one man, and he as good as dead, came descendants as numerous as the stars in the sky and as countless as the sand on the seashore.

¹³All these people were still living by faith when they died. They did not receive the things promised; they only saw them and welcomed them from a distance. And they admitted that they were aliens and strangers on earth. ¹⁴People who say such things show that they are looking for a country of their own. ¹⁵If they had been thinking of the country they had left, they would have had opportunity to return. ¹⁶Instead, they were longing for a better country—a heavenly one. Therefore God is not ashamed to be called their God, for he has prepared a city for them.

¹⁷By faith Abraham, when God tested him, offered Isaac as a sacrifice. He who

---

ᵃ30 Deut. 32:35   ᵇ30 Deut. 32:36; Psalm 135:14   ᶜ38 One early manuscript *But the righteous*
ᵈ38 Hab. 2:3,4   ᵉ11 Or *By faith even Sarah, who was past age, was enabled to bear children because she*

had received the promises was about to sacrifice his one and only son, **18**even though God had said to him, "It is through Isaac that your offspring*a* will be reckoned."*b* **19**Abraham reasoned that God could raise the dead, and figuratively speaking, he did receive Isaac back from death.

20By faith Isaac blessed Jacob and Esau in regard to their future.

21By faith Jacob, when he was dying, blessed each of Joseph's sons, and worshiped as he leaned on the top of his staff.

22By faith Joseph, when his end was near, spoke about the exodus of the Is-

a18 Greek *seed*   *b18* Gen. 21:12

FRIDAY

VERSE:	AUTHOR:	PASSAGE:
Hebrews 11:13	Carole Mayhall	Hebrews 11:11–16

Winning . . . Long Term

I find myself little different than the impatient "instant" world around me. Our world wants it—and often *has* it—now. Instant credit cards, instant meals, instant entertainment.

But as I reflect, I don't see "instant" as one of God's goals. Long-term gains, in God's economy, beat instant every time.

The examples God gives us of Biblical heroes—Abel, Enoch, Noah, Abraham—looked at things in a way we seldom do. Of course they wanted to see God's promises fulfilled quickly, but somehow they also kept firmly in mind the "long-term" aspect of the promises as well.

The fulfillment of the short-term promises encouraged them: Abel's sacrifice was accepted; Enoch was translated to heaven; Noah survived the flood and experienced rebuilding the land; Abraham had Isaac and lived to see him reproduce.

But the stability of their lives was firmly secured by their future focus, their eternal perspective. They were "still living by faith" (in the long-term promises) when they died (v. 13).

I'm grateful that God usually doesn't make me wait too long to experience what he says he will do. I'm sure he is aware of my impatience! But I am thinking more these days of promises for the future, which are *so much bigger*!

I need balance and wisdom between the here and now and the forever future, between praying for the fulfillment of short-term promises and keeping my heart, thoughts, and desires rooted in God's long-term promises.

Here I see the short term only. But when the long-term promises are a reality instead of a hope, I'm confident that the short-term ones, which give my life joy now, will fade into *insignificance*.

ADDITIONAL SCRIPTURE READINGS:
Genesis 18:15–19; Psalm 119:162; 2 Corinthians 1:18,20

Go to page 332 for your next devotional reading.

raelites from Egypt and gave instructions about his bones.

²³By faith Moses' parents hid him for three months after he was born, because they saw he was no ordinary child, and they were not afraid of the king's edict.

²⁴By faith Moses, when he had grown up, refused to be known as the son of Pharaoh's daughter. ²⁵He chose to be mistreated along with the people of God rather than to enjoy the pleasures of sin for a short time. ²⁶He regarded disgrace for the sake of Christ as of greater value than the treasures of Egypt, because he was looking ahead to his reward. ²⁷By faith he left Egypt, not fearing the king's anger; he persevered because he saw him who is invisible. ²⁸By faith he kept the Passover and the sprinkling of blood, so that the destroyer of the firstborn would not touch the firstborn of Israel.

²⁹By faith the people passed through the Red Sea[a] as on dry land; but when the Egyptians tried to do so, they were drowned.

³⁰By faith the walls of Jericho fell, after the people had marched around them for seven days.

³¹By faith the prostitute Rahab, because she welcomed the spies, was not killed with those who were disobedient.[b]

³²And what more shall I say? I do not have time to tell about Gideon, Barak, Samson, Jephthah, David, Samuel and the prophets, ³³who through faith conquered kingdoms, administered justice, and gained what was promised; who shut the mouths of lions, ³⁴quenched the fury of the flames, and escaped the edge of the sword; whose weakness was turned to strength; and who became powerful in battle and routed foreign armies. ³⁵Women received back their dead, raised to life again. Others were tortured and refused to be released, so that they might gain a better resurrection. ³⁶Some faced jeers and flogging, while still others were chained and put in prison. ³⁷They were stoned[c]; they were sawed in two; they were put to death by the sword. They went about in sheepskins and goatskins, destitute, persecuted and mistreated— ³⁸the world was not worthy of them. They wandered in deserts and mountains, and in caves and holes in the ground.

³⁹These were all commended for their faith, yet none of them received what had been promised. ⁴⁰God had planned something better for us so that only together with us would they be made perfect.

God Disciplines His Sons

12 Therefore, since we are surrounded by such a great cloud of witnesses, let us throw off everything that hinders and the sin that so easily entangles, and let us run with perseverance the race marked out for us. ²Let us fix our eyes on Jesus, the author and perfecter of our faith, who for the joy set before him endured the cross, scorning its shame, and sat down at the right hand of the throne of God. ³Consider him who endured such opposition from sinful men, so that you will not grow weary and lose heart.

⁴In your struggle against sin, you have not yet resisted to the point of shedding your blood. ⁵And you have forgotten that word of encouragement that addresses you as sons:

"My son, do not make light of the
　　Lord's discipline,
　and do not lose heart when he
　　rebukes you,
⁶because the Lord disciplines those
　　he loves,
　and he punishes everyone he
　　accepts as a son."[d]

⁷Endure hardship as discipline; God is treating you as sons. For what son is not disciplined by his father? ⁸If you are not disciplined (and everyone undergoes discipline), then you are illegitimate children and not true sons. ⁹Moreover, we have all had human fathers who disciplined us and we respected them for it. How much more should we submit to the Father of our spirits and live! ¹⁰Our fathers disciplined us for a little while as they thought best; but God disciplines us for our good, that we may share in his holiness. ¹¹No discipline seems pleasant at the time, but painful. Later on, however, it produces a harvest of righteousness and peace for those who have been trained by it.

---

[a]29 That is, Sea of Reeds　　[b]31 Or *unbelieving*　　[c]37 Some early manuscripts *stoned; they were put to the test;*　　[d]6 Prov. 3:11,12

WEEKENDING

REFLECT

Tell me, did Cinderella live happily ever
after without a struggle? Did Sleeping
Beauty live happily ever after without a
trauma? Did Rapunzel live happily ever
after without grief? Did Hansel and
Gretel live happily ever after without
deprivation? Did Jack and the beanstalk
live happily ever after without risk? Did
Thumbelina live happily ever after
without sacrifice? Are there any fairy
tales without *any* dragons?

Where in the world, then, did we
ever get the notion that to live happily
ever after means to live without trouble? For when we look at fairy tales we
find it's not the absence of dragons—
but the *taming* of dragons—that ushers
in happily ever after.

Brenda Wilbee

RESTORE

Saturday: James 1:1–18
Sunday: 1 Peter 1:3–9

*Go to page 333 for your
next devotional reading.*

[12]Therefore, strengthen your feeble arms and weak knees. [13]"Make level paths for your feet,"[a] so that the lame may not be disabled, but rather healed.

Warning Against Refusing God

[14]Make every effort to live in peace with all men and to be holy; without holiness no one will see the Lord. [15]See to it that no one misses the grace of God and that no bitter root grows up to cause trouble and defile many. [16]See that no one is sexually immoral, or is godless like Esau, who for a single meal sold his inheritance rights as the oldest son. [17]Afterward, as you know, when he wanted to inherit this blessing, he was rejected. He could bring about no change of mind, though he sought the blessing with tears.

[18]You have not come to a mountain that can be touched and that is burning with fire; to darkness, gloom and storm; [19]to a trumpet blast or to such a voice speaking words that those who heard it begged that no further word be spoken to them, [20]because they could not bear what was commanded: "If even an animal touches the mountain, it must be stoned."[b] [21]The sight was so terrifying that Moses said, "I am trembling with fear."[c]

[22]But you have come to Mount Zion, to the heavenly Jerusalem, the city of the living God. You have come to thousands upon thousands of angels in joyful as-

[a]13 Prov. 4:26   [b]20 Exodus 19:12,13   [c]21 Deut. 9:19

MONDAY

VERSE:	AUTHOR:	PASSAGE:
Hebrews 12:2	Mary Foxwell Loeks	Hebrews 12:1–13

Author and Editor [Perfecter]

There isn't a human author who doesn't, or wouldn't, benefit from a good editor. The author conceives and births the idea, but a second pair of eyes sees it in a different way and with a fresh perspective.

A case can also be made for the idea that human editors—those who perfect, polish and put on the finishing touches, those who see the work through to completion—need authors.

As our author, Jesus Christ conceived the very idea of us before the foundation of the world. He made possible both our birth and our new birth.

But he hasn't stopped there. He has the will, the ability and the authority to see us—his workmanship, his poem (Ephesians 2:10)—through to completion. Paul tells the Philippians that he is confident that "he who began a good work in you will carry it on to completion until the day of Christ Jesus" (Philippians 1:6).

Sometimes we question or chafe at all the editing that is prescribed for us. But ours is not an editor capable of error or capriciousness. Unlikely as it may seem at times, we will someday be all that he means for us to be, his masterpiece.

ADDITIONAL SCRIPTURE READINGS:
Ephesians 2:1–10; Philippians 1:3–11

Go to page 334 for your next devotional reading.

sembly, ²³to the church of the firstborn, whose names are written in heaven. You have come to God, the judge of all men, to the spirits of righteous men made perfect, ²⁴to Jesus the mediator of a new covenant, and to the sprinkled blood that speaks a better word than the blood of Abel.

²⁵See to it that you do not refuse him who speaks. If they did not escape when they refused him who warned them on earth, how much less will we, if we turn away from him who warns us from heaven? ²⁶At that time his voice shook the earth, but now he has promised, "Once more I will shake not only the

TUESDAY

VERSE:
Hebrews 13:1

AUTHOR:
Mary C. Crowley

PASSAGE:
Hebrews 13

Never Give Up

The great Russian writer, Solzhenitsyn, tells the bravest story I've ever heard to encourage us not to give up. In the Russian prison where he was, no one was allowed to speak. There was nothing to read, and no encouragement of any kind to sustain life. He said the strain and repression from this atmosphere had set in so badly that he thought, "I will never get out of here." So he considered taking his own life. He knew that if he tried to escape he would be shot, but he thought, "At least, that will be the end of that!"

His faith would not allow him to do that, though. When day came, he was taken out early in the morning to work and when a break in the work day came, he sat under a tree. He even placed his hand behind him, up against the tree he leaned against, ready to push off and run. Just then a shadow came across the grass and a fellow prisoner sat down beside him. They could speak no words, but he looked into the eyes of the new man who had recently come as a prisoner and saw something he had never seen in any face in prison before—a message of love and concern.

As their eyes locked in silence, they started communicating in their souls and the prisoner took a step forward and drew a cross on the ground with a stick.

Solzhenitsyn said new hope surged within him at that moment. Jesus does love me. He is in command. It is not hopeless!

Three days later he was released from that prison. At his release he learned that many people had been praying for him. He knew with powerful certainty that God is sovereign and there is still hope.

We mustn't give up! We might be the one to communicate hope to someone else, maybe by a gesture, maybe without words. We must love and pray and hold one another up.

ADDITIONAL SCRIPTURE READINGS:
Psalm 121:3–8; Isaiah 1:17; 1 Peter 1:4–5

Go to page 337 for your next devotional reading.

earth but also the heavens." [a] [27]The words "once more" indicate the removing of what can be shaken—that is, created things—so that what cannot be shaken may remain.

[28]Therefore, since we are receiving a kingdom that cannot be shaken, let us be thankful, and so worship God acceptably with reverence and awe, [29]for our "God is a consuming fire." [b]

Concluding Exhortations

13 Keep on loving each other as brothers. [2]Do not forget to entertain strangers, for by so doing some people have entertained angels without knowing it. [3]Remember those in prison as if you were their fellow prisoners, and those who are mistreated as if you yourselves were suffering.

[4]Marriage should be honored by all, and the marriage bed kept pure, for God will judge the adulterer and all the sexually immoral. [5]Keep your lives free from the love of money and be content with what you have, because God has said,

"Never will I leave you;
    never will I forsake you." [c]

[6]So we say with confidence,

"The Lord is my helper; I will not be
    afraid.
What can man do to me?" [d]

[7]Remember your leaders, who spoke the word of God to you. Consider the outcome of their way of life and imitate their faith. [8]Jesus Christ is the same yesterday and today and forever.

[9]Do not be carried away by all kinds of strange teachings. It is good for our hearts to be strengthened by grace, not by ceremonial foods, which are of no value to those who eat them. [10]We have an altar from which those who minister at the tabernacle have no right to eat. [11]The high priest carries the blood of animals into the Most Holy Place as a sin offering, but the bodies are burned outside the camp. [12]And so Jesus also suffered outside the city gate to make the people holy through his own blood. [13]Let us, then, go to him outside the camp, bearing the disgrace he bore. [14]For here we do not have an enduring city, but we are looking for the city that is to come.

[15]Through Jesus, therefore, let us continually offer to God a sacrifice of praise—the fruit of lips that confess his name. [16]And do not forget to do good and to share with others, for with such sacrifices God is pleased.

[17]Obey your leaders and submit to their authority. They keep watch over you as men who must give an account. Obey them so that their work will be a joy, not a burden, for that would be of no advantage to you.

[18]Pray for us. We are sure that we have a clear conscience and desire to live honorably in every way. [19]I particularly urge you to pray so that I may be restored to you soon.

[20]May the God of peace, who through the blood of the eternal covenant brought back from the dead our Lord Jesus, that great Shepherd of the sheep, [21]equip you with everything good for doing his will, and may he work in us what is pleasing to him, through Jesus Christ, to whom be glory for ever and ever. Amen.

[22]Brothers, I urge you to bear with my word of exhortation, for I have written you only a short letter.

[23]I want you to know that our brother Timothy has been released. If he arrives soon, I will come with him to see you.

[24]Greet all your leaders and all God's people. Those from Italy send you their greetings.

[25]Grace be with you all.

[a]26 Haggai 2:6   [b]29 Deut. 4:24   [c]5 Deut. 31:6   [d]6 Psalm 118:6,7

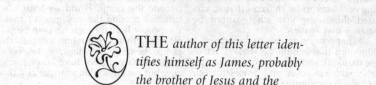

THE author of this letter identifies himself as James, probably the brother of Jesus and the leader of the Jerusalem council. The book of James has a distinctively Jewish nature that suggests it was composed when the church was still predominantly Jewish. The letter deals primarily with the practical aspects of the Christian faith, consisting of hard-hitting counsel for everyday conduct.

JAMES

1 James, a servant of God and of the Lord Jesus Christ,

To the twelve tribes scattered among the nations:

Greetings.

Trials and Temptations

²Consider it pure joy, my brothers, whenever you face trials of many kinds, ³because you know that the testing of your faith develops perseverance. ⁴Perseverance must finish its work so that you may be mature and complete, not lacking anything. ⁵If any of you lacks wisdom, he should ask God, who gives generously to all without finding fault, and it will be given to him. ⁶But when he asks, he must believe and not doubt, because he who doubts is like a wave of the sea, blown and tossed by the wind.

⁷That man should not think he will receive anything from the Lord; ⁸he is a double-minded man, unstable in all he does.

⁹The brother in humble circumstances ought to take pride in his high position. ¹⁰But the one who is rich should take pride in his low position, because he will pass away like a wild flower. ¹¹For the sun rises with scorching heat and withers the plant; its blossom falls and its beauty is destroyed. In the same way, the rich man will fade away even while he goes about his business.

¹²Blessed is the man who perseveres under trial, because when he has stood the test, he will receive the crown of life that God has promised to those who love him.

¹³When tempted, no one should say,

"God is tempting me." For God cannot be tempted by evil, nor does he tempt anyone; **14**but each one is tempted when, by his own evil desire, he is dragged away and enticed. **15**Then, after desire has conceived, it gives birth to sin; and sin, when it is full-grown, gives birth to death.

16Don't be deceived, my dear brothers. **17**Every good and perfect gift is from above, coming down from the Father of the heavenly lights, who does not change like shifting shadows. **18**He chose to give us birth through the word of truth, that we might be a kind of first-fruits of all he created.

Listening and Doing

19My dear brothers, take note of this: Everyone should be quick to listen, slow to speak and slow to become angry, **20**for man's anger does not bring about the righteous life that God desires.

21Therefore, get rid of all moral filth and the evil that is so prevalent and humbly accept the word planted in you, which can save you.

22Do not merely listen to the word, and so deceive yourselves. Do what it says. **23**Anyone who listens to the word but does not do what it says is like a man who looks at his face in a mirror **24**and, after looking at himself, goes away and immediately forgets what he looks like. **25**But the man who looks intently into the perfect law that gives freedom, and continues to do this, not forgetting what he has heard, but doing it—he will be blessed in what he does.

26If anyone considers himself religious and yet does not keep a tight rein on his tongue, he deceives himself and his religion is worthless. **27**Religion that God our Father accepts as pure and faultless is this: to look after orphans and widows in their distress and to keep

---

WEDNESDAY

VERSE:	AUTHOR:	PASSAGE:
James 1:19	Susan Lenzkes	James 1

Lend Me an Ear

Ears are busy these days. A listening, caring, available ear is increasingly difficult to find. Many seem permanently encased in the headphones of their own private interests. Others are busy vying for equal time with other parts of the body—such as an eye on the clock or a nose to the grindstone.

Even a free ear isn't necessarily free just to listen. When people come to us with their troubles, many of us discover we have a birth defect; our earbone is connected to our mouthbone. When patience, understanding and encouragement are most needed, we give advice, platitudes and "My experience can top *that*" stories.

The burdened who come to us needing to unburden are looking for an earbone connected to a heartbone.

It's good to remember that "listen" and "silent" are made of the same six letters.

Lend every man thy ear, but few thy voice. —Shakespeare

ADDITIONAL SCRIPTURE READINGS:
Proverbs 17:27; James 1:19; Revelation 13:9

Go to page 338 for your next devotional reading.

oneself from being polluted by the world.

Favoritism Forbidden

2 My brothers, as believers in our glorious Lord Jesus Christ, don't show favoritism. ²Suppose a man comes into your meeting wearing a gold ring and fine clothes, and a poor man in shabby clothes also comes in. ³If you show special attention to the man wearing fine clothes and say, "Here's a good seat for you," but say to the poor man, "You stand there" or "Sit on the floor by my feet," ⁴have you not discriminated among yourselves and become judges with evil thoughts?

⁵Listen, my dear brothers: Has not

THURSDAY

VERSE:	AUTHOR:	PASSAGE:
James 2:1	Shirley Pope Waite	James 2:1–13

It's What's Inside That Counts

We'd been traveling in the British Isles for almost three weeks. The little rented Ford Escort had become our close friend as we maneuvered it down narrow roads, constantly reminding ourselves, "Left side! Left side!"

"What day is this?" I asked my husband. He glanced at his watch.

"Sunday." He paused, and with emphasis, added, "A *sun* day!" We'd been so deluged with rain the few days before that we hadn't even caught a glimpse of Loch Lomond. But today the sun was shining brightly.

I was about to say how I missed attending church services, when we rounded a corner and there at the top of a hill stood a small church.

"I think that church is about to begin. Let's go!"

My husband was less than enthusiastic. "Look at us. We're not dressed properly. Besides, it's almost 11:30."

But people were headed toward the church. Seeing my glint of determination, he found a parking spot.

As we trudged up the hill, I mentally rehearsed how to explain our appearance. Sure enough, there was a greeter at the door. I mumbled something about being travelers.

"Ah, lass, the good Lord dain't care how ye are dressed!"

How grateful I was for that! As I listened to the delightful sermon on Colossians 1:27, "Christ in you, the hope of glory," and participated in Holy Communion, I had the assurance that it's what's inside that counts.

That brief hour set the tone for the rest of the day as we left the tiny church refreshed, renewed and ready to continue on toward Edinburgh.

ADDITIONAL SCRIPTURE READINGS:
1 Samuel 16:1-7; Galatians 2:6; Hebrews 10:25

Go to page 340 for your next devotional reading.

God chosen those who are poor in the eyes of the world to be rich in faith and to inherit the kingdom he promised those who love him? **6**But you have insulted the poor. Is it not the rich who are exploiting you? Are they not the ones who are dragging you into court? **7**Are they not the ones who are slandering the noble name of him to whom you belong?

8If you really keep the royal law found in Scripture, "Love your neighbor as yourself,"*a* you are doing right. **9**But if you show favoritism, you sin and are convicted by the law as lawbreakers. **10**For whoever keeps the whole law and yet stumbles at just one point is guilty of breaking all of it. **11**For he who said, "Do not commit adultery,"*b* also said, "Do not murder."*c* If you do not commit adultery but do commit murder, you have become a lawbreaker.

12Speak and act as those who are going to be judged by the law that gives freedom, **13**because judgment without mercy will be shown to anyone who has not been merciful. Mercy triumphs over judgment!

Faith and Deeds

14What good is it, my brothers, if a man claims to have faith but has no deeds? Can such faith save him? **15**Suppose a brother or sister is without clothes and daily food. **16**If one of you says to him, "Go, I wish you well; keep warm and well fed," but does nothing about his physical needs, what good is it? **17**In the same way, faith by itself, if it is not accompanied by action, is dead.

18But someone will say, "You have faith; I have deeds."

Show me your faith without deeds, and I will show you my faith by what I do. **19**You believe that there is one God. Good! Even the demons believe that— and shudder.

20You foolish man, do you want evidence that faith without deeds is useless*d*? **21**Was not our ancestor Abraham considered righteous for what he did when he offered his son Isaac on the altar? **22**You see that his faith and his actions were working together, and his faith was made complete by what he did. **23**And the scripture was fulfilled

that says, "Abraham believed God, and it was credited to him as righteousness,"*e* and he was called God's friend. **24**You see that a person is justified by what he does and not by faith alone.

25In the same way, was not even Rahab the prostitute considered righteous for what she did when she gave lodging to the spies and sent them off in a different direction? **26**As the body without the spirit is dead, so faith without deeds is dead.

Taming the Tongue

3 Not many of you should presume to be teachers, my brothers, because you know that we who teach will be judged more strictly. **2**We all stumble in many ways. If anyone is never at fault in what he says, he is a perfect man, able to keep his whole body in check.

3When we put bits into the mouths of horses to make them obey us, we can turn the whole animal. **4**Or take ships as an example. Although they are so large and are driven by strong winds, they are steered by a very small rudder wherever the pilot wants to go. **5**Likewise the tongue is a small part of the body, but it makes great boasts. Consider what a great forest is set on fire by a small spark. **6**The tongue also is a fire, a world of evil among the parts of the body. It corrupts the whole person, sets the whole course of his life on fire, and is itself set on fire by hell.

7All kinds of animals, birds, reptiles and creatures of the sea are being tamed and have been tamed by man, **8**but no man can tame the tongue. It is a restless evil, full of deadly poison.

9With the tongue we praise our Lord and Father, and with it we curse men, who have been made in God's likeness. **10**Out of the same mouth come praise and cursing. My brothers, this should not be. **11**Can both fresh water and salt*f* water flow from the same spring? **12**My brothers, can a fig tree bear olives, or a grapevine bear figs? Neither can a salt spring produce fresh water.

Two Kinds of Wisdom

13Who is wise and understanding among you? Let him show it by his good life, by deeds done in the humility that

---

a8 Lev. 19:18   *b11* Exodus 20:14; Deut. 5:18   *c11* Exodus 20:13; Deut. 5:17   *d20* Some early manuscripts *dead*   *e23* Gen. 15:6   *f11* Greek *bitter* (see also verse 14)

comes from wisdom. ¹⁴But if you harbor bitter envy and selfish ambition in your hearts, do not boast about it or deny the truth. ¹⁵Such "wisdom" does not come down from heaven but is earthly, unspiritual, of the devil. ¹⁶For where you have envy and selfish ambition, there you find disorder and every evil practice.

¹⁷But the wisdom that comes from heaven is first of all pure; then peaceloving, considerate, submissive, full of mercy and good fruit, impartial and sincere. ¹⁸Peacemakers who sow in peace raise a harvest of righteousness.

Submit Yourselves to God

4 What causes fights and quarrels among you? Don't they come from your desires that battle within you? ²You want something but don't get it. You kill and covet, but you cannot have what you want. You quarrel and fight. You do not have, because you do not ask God. ³When you ask, you do not receive, be-

---

FRIDAY

VERSE:
James 4:6

AUTHOR:
June Hunt

PASSAGE:
James 4:1–12

The Grace of God

The ninth grade algebra class was my all-time favorite. Because I loved puzzles, algebra was actually fun. Since other subjects were hard for me, my A's in algebra helped soothe my suffering self-image. In math class, I faced each test with confidence! Tuesday's test would be no different.

But while taking the test, I suddenly found that I couldn't remember the formula for number one . . . number two, or three, four, five . . . I had gone blank! I could only solve the last two problems. Stunned, I handed my paper to the teacher. After a long pensive pause, she asked, "When do you have study hall tomorrow?" "At 10:00," I nervously replied. The next day at 10:00 sharp, I was sitting in my algebra classroom with a second chance. I was given a gift called "grace."

Before even knowing what the word "grace" meant, I knew what it was like to be impacted by it. I was awed that a teacher would extend *undeserved favor* toward me. That's what the Greek work for grace means: "undeserved care, unearned favor."

Your God is a God of grace who not only saves you from eternal death but also saves you from a defeated life. He saves you by putting his life in you. If you focus only on what it's like to fail in certain areas of your life, you could be drawn into the downward spiral of dejection. However, Jesus said, "I have come that they may have life, and have it to the full" (John 10:10).

How blessed you are to know the God of grace who saves you from your failures. He is the God of the second chance . . . and the third . . . and the fourth.

ADDITIONAL SCRIPTURE READINGS:
Psalm 84:11–12; John 10:7–10; Hebrews 4:14–16

Go to page 342 for your next devotional reading.

cause you ask with wrong motives, that you may spend what you get on your pleasures.

[4]You adulterous people, don't you know that friendship with the world is hatred toward God? Anyone who chooses to be a friend of the world becomes an enemy of God. [5]Or do you think Scripture says without reason that the spirit he caused to live in us envies intensely?[a] [6]But he gives us more grace. That is why Scripture says:

"God opposes the proud
   but gives grace to the humble."[b]

[7]Submit yourselves, then, to God. Resist the devil, and he will flee from you. [8]Come near to God and he will come near to you. Wash your hands, you sinners, and purify your hearts, you double-minded. [9]Grieve, mourn and wail. Change your laughter to mourning and your joy to gloom. [10]Humble yourselves before the Lord, and he will lift you up.

[11]Brothers, do not slander one another. Anyone who speaks against his brother or judges him speaks against the law and judges it. When you judge the law, you are not keeping it, but sitting in judgment on it. [12]There is only one Lawgiver and Judge, the one who is able to save and destroy. But you—who are you to judge your neighbor?

Boasting About Tomorrow

[13]Now listen, you who say, "Today or tomorrow we will go to this or that city, spend a year there, carry on business and make money." [14]Why, you do not even know what will happen tomorrow. What is your life? You are a mist that appears for a little while and then vanishes. [15]Instead, you ought to say, "If it is the Lord's will, we will live and do this or that." [16]As it is, you boast and brag. All such boasting is evil. [17]Anyone, then, who knows the good he ought to do and doesn't do it, sins.

Warning to Rich Oppressors

5 Now listen, you rich people, weep and wail because of the misery that is coming upon you. [2]Your wealth has rotted, and moths have eaten your clothes. [3]Your gold and silver are corroded. Their corrosion will testify against you and eat your flesh like fire. You have hoarded wealth in the last days. [4]Look! The wages you failed to pay the workmen who mowed your fields are crying out against you. The cries of the harvesters have reached the ears of the Lord Almighty. [5]You have lived on earth in luxury and self-indulgence. You have fattened yourselves in the day of slaughter.[c] [6]You have condemned and murdered innocent men, who were not opposing you.

Patience in Suffering

[7]Be patient, then, brothers, until the Lord's coming. See how the farmer waits for the land to yield its valuable crop and how patient he is for the autumn and spring rains. [8]You too, be patient and stand firm, because the Lord's coming is near. [9]Don't grumble against each other, brothers, or you will be judged. The Judge is standing at the door!

[10]Brothers, as an example of patience in the face of suffering, take the prophets who spoke in the name of the Lord. [11]As you know, we consider blessed those who have persevered. You have heard of Job's perseverance and have seen what the Lord finally brought about. The Lord is full of compassion and mercy.

[12]Above all, my brothers, do not swear—not by heaven or by earth or by anything else. Let your "Yes" be yes, and your "No," no, or you will be condemned.

The Prayer of Faith

[13]Is any one of you in trouble? He should pray. Is anyone happy? Let him sing songs of praise. [14]Is any one of you sick? He should call the elders of the church to pray over him and anoint him with oil in the name of the Lord. [15]And the prayer offered in faith will make the sick person well; the Lord will raise him up. If he has sinned, he will be forgiven. [16]Therefore confess your sins to each other and pray for each other so that you may be healed. The prayer of a righteous man is powerful and effective.

[17]Elijah was a man just like us. He prayed earnestly that it would not rain, and it did not rain on the land for three

---

[a]5 Or *that God jealously longs for the spirit that he made to live in us*; or *that the Spirit he caused to live in us longs jealously*   [b]6 Prov. 3:34   [c]5 Or *yourselves as in a day of feasting*

WEEKENDING

REJOICE

Becky and Ephraim's youngest child, Annie, was born with a severe physical handicap. "Annie . . . Annie," they squealed as everyone in the family touched and hugged her, never treating her as a hothouse flower, always as a normal healthy child. It was a laying-on-of-hands, a healing going on every moment.

I wasn't sure I could have stayed focused on the joy, but Becky was also realistic, understanding that something could go wrong and "Annie might be taken away from us." For now, God had given them a gift. Annie was their treasure, their miracle.

Sue Bender

REVIVE

Saturday: Psalm 139
Sunday: Matthew 19:13–15

Go to page 343 for your next devotional reading.

and a half years. ¹⁸Again he prayed, and the heavens gave rain, and the earth produced its crops.

¹⁹My brothers, if one of you should wander from the truth and someone should bring him back, ²⁰remember this: Whoever turns a sinner from the error of his way will save him from death and cover over a multitude of sins.

MONDAY

VERSE:
James 5:16

AUTHOR:
Juanita and Dale Ryan

PASSAGE:
James 5:13–19

Admitting Our Wrongs

"I always kept everything in," Sue began. "It was like I had two lives. One that everyone saw, and one that only I knew about. Because of the secrets, I was full of shame and confusion. I expected it to be very painful to admit my wrongs. But, when I finally told everything to another human being, it was very different from what I expected. The person I told was not shocked; she did not shame me; she accepted me and told me she respected my courage and honesty. I felt like I would never be the same. Something changed inside."

Admitting our wrongs is a threefold process of confession. First, we admit our wrongs to God, then we admit our wrongs to ourselves, and then we admit our wrongs to another human being. This process can be a powerful, life-changing experience. We all long to be known; to share the secrets that are so toxic to our souls; to experience the grace of being loved and accepted—sins and all. The spiritual discipline of confession provides the structure within which we can experience this grace in practical ways.

God invites us to the spiritual discipline of confession. "Confess your sins to each other and pray for each other so that you may be healed" (v. 16). Confession is an act of obedience to this Biblical imperative. It is an imperative with a promise of healing.

ADDITIONAL SCRIPTURE READINGS:
Psalm 32:2–7; Psalm 51; 1 John 1:5–10

Go to page 345 for your next devotional reading.

THE *recipients of this letter
had been suffering various trials
and afflictions, along with a
very real threat of more severe difficulties
to come. Peter touches on various doctrines
and has much to say about Christian life
and duties. 1 Peter has been characterized
as a letter of suffering and persecution, of
suffering and glory, of hope and courage.
No other New Testament book so reflects
the real nature and effect of God's love in
Jesus Christ.*

1 PETER

1 Peter, an apostle of Jesus Christ,

To God's elect, strangers in the world,
scattered throughout Pontus, Galatia,
Cappadocia, Asia and Bithynia, ²who
have been chosen according to the foreknowledge of God the Father, through
the sanctifying work of the Spirit, for
obedience to Jesus Christ and sprinkling by his blood:

Grace and peace be yours in abundance.

Praise to God for a Living Hope

³Praise be to the God and Father of
our Lord Jesus Christ! In his great mercy
he has given us new birth into a living
hope through the resurrection of Jesus
Christ from the dead, ⁴and into an inheritance that can never perish, spoil or
fade—kept in heaven for you, ⁵who
through faith are shielded by God's
power until the coming of the salvation
that is ready to be revealed in the last
time. ⁶In this you greatly rejoice, though
now for a little while you may have had
to suffer grief in all kinds of trials.
⁷These have come so that your faith—of
greater worth than gold, which perishes
even though refined by fire—may be
proved genuine and may result in
praise, glory and honor when Jesus
Christ is revealed. ⁸Though you have
not seen him, you love him; and even
though you do not see him now, you
believe in him and are filled with an inexpressible and glorious joy, ⁹for you

are receiving the goal of your faith, the salvation of your souls.

¹⁰Concerning this salvation, the prophets, who spoke of the grace that was to come to you, searched intently and with the greatest care, ¹¹trying to find out the time and circumstances to which the Spirit of Christ in them was pointing when he predicted the sufferings of Christ and the glories that would follow. ¹²It was revealed to them that they were not serving themselves but you, when they spoke of the things that have now been told you by those who have preached the gospel to you by the Holy Spirit sent from heaven. Even angels long to look into these things.

Be Holy

¹³Therefore, prepare your minds for action; be self-controlled; set your hope fully on the grace to be given you when Jesus Christ is revealed. ¹⁴As obedient children, do not conform to the evil desires you had when you lived in ignorance. ¹⁵But just as he who called you is

---

TUESDAY

VERSE:	AUTHOR:	PASSAGE:
1 Peter 1:7	Elisabeth Elliot	1 Peter 1:3–12

A Flower From a Thorn

Here it is—in the gorse blossoming from thorns, in the harvest of wheat from the solitary grain—the *gospel*, the Good News of life out of death, a gospel for every individual, every need, every hopeless and helpless situation.

"It'll never work for mine," someone is tempted to say. Are you sure that your problems baffle the one who since the world began has been bringing flowers from thorns? Your thorns are a different story, are they? You have been brought to a place of self-despair, nothingness. It is hard even to think of any good reason for going on. You live in most unfavorable conditions, with intractable people, you are up against impossible odds. Is this something new? The people of Israel were up against impossible odds when they found themselves between the chariots of Egypt and the Red Sea. Their God is our God. The God of Israel. . . looks down on us with love and says, "Nothing has happened to you which is not common to all. I can manage it. Trust me."

He wants to transform every form of human suffering into something glorious. He can redeem it. He can bring life out of death. Every event of our lives provides opportunity to learn the deepest lesson anyone can learn on earth: "I have been crucified with Christ and I no longer live, but Christ lives in me" (Galatians 2:20). When our souls lie barren in a winter which seems hopeless and endless, God has not abandoned us. His work goes on. He asks our acceptance of the painful process and our trust that he will indeed give resurrection life.

ADDITIONAL SCRIPTURE READINGS:
Psalm 28:7–9 Romans 6:4; 2 Corinthians 4:8-10

Go to page 347 for your next devotional reading.

holy, so be holy in all you do; [16]for it is written: "Be holy, because I am holy." [a]

[17]Since you call on a Father who judges each man's work impartially, live your lives as strangers here in reverent fear. [18]For you know that it was not with perishable things such as silver or gold that you were redeemed from the empty way of life handed down to you from your forefathers, [19]but with the precious blood of Christ, a lamb without blemish or defect. [20]He was chosen before the creation of the world, but was revealed in these last times for your sake. [21]Through him you believe in God, who raised him from the dead and glorified him, and so your faith and hope are in God.

[22]Now that you have purified yourselves by obeying the truth so that you have sincere love for your brothers, love one another deeply, from the heart. [b] [23]For you have been born again, not of perishable seed, but of imperishable, through the living and enduring word of God. [24]For,

"All men are like grass,
    and all their glory is like the
       flowers of the field;
the grass withers and the flowers
       fall,
[25]   but the word of the Lord stands
       forever." [c]

And this is the word that was preached to you.

2 Therefore, rid yourselves of all malice and all deceit, hypocrisy, envy, and slander of every kind. [2]Like newborn babies, crave pure spiritual milk, so that by it you may grow up in your salvation, [3]now that you have tasted that the Lord is good.

The Living Stone and a Chosen People

[4]As you come to him, the living Stone—rejected by men but chosen by God and precious to him— [5]you also, like living stones, are being built into a spiritual house to be a holy priesthood, offering spiritual sacrifices acceptable to God through Jesus Christ. [6]For in Scripture it says:

"See, I lay a stone in Zion,

    a chosen and precious
       cornerstone,
and the one who trusts in him
    will never be put to shame." [d]

[7]Now to you who believe, this stone is precious. But to those who do not believe,

"The stone the builders rejected
    has become the capstone, [e] [f]

[8]and,

"A stone that causes men to stumble
    and a rock that makes them fall." [g]

They stumble because they disobey the message—which is also what they were destined for.

[9]But you are a chosen people, a royal priesthood, a holy nation, a people belonging to God, that you may declare the praises of him who called you out of darkness into his wonderful light. [10]Once you were not a people, but now you are the people of God; once you had not received mercy, but now you have received mercy.

[11]Dear friends, I urge you, as aliens and strangers in the world, to abstain from sinful desires, which war against your soul. [12]Live such good lives among the pagans that, though they accuse you of doing wrong, they may see your good deeds and glorify God on the day he visits us.

Submission to Rulers and Masters

[13]Submit yourselves for the Lord's sake to every authority instituted among men: whether to the king, as the supreme authority, [14]or to governors, who are sent by him to punish those who do wrong and to commend those who do right. [15]For it is God's will that by doing good you should silence the ignorant talk of foolish men. [16]Live as free men, but do not use your freedom as a coverup for evil; live as servants of God. [17]Show proper respect to everyone: Love the brotherhood of believers, fear God, honor the king.

[18]Slaves, submit yourselves to your masters with all respect, not only to those who are good and considerate, but also to those who are harsh. [19]For it is commendable if a man bears up un-

---

[a]16 Lev. 11:44,45; 19:2; 20:7   [b]22 Some early manuscripts *from a pure heart*   [c]25 Isaiah 40:6-8   [d]6 Isaiah 28:16   [e]7 Or *cornerstone*   [f]7 Psalm 118:22   [g]8 Isaiah 8:14

der the pain of unjust suffering because he is conscious of God. **20**But how is it to your credit if you receive a beating for doing wrong and endure it? But if you suffer for doing good and you endure it, this is commendable before God. **21**To this you were called, because Christ suffered for you, leaving you an example, that you should follow in his steps.

22"He committed no sin,
and no deceit was found in his
mouth."*a*

*a*22 Isaiah 53:9

23When they hurled their insults at him, he did not retaliate; when he suffered, he made no threats. Instead, he entrusted himself to him who judges justly. **24**He himself bore our sins in his body on the tree, so that we might die to sins and live for righteousness; by his wounds you have been healed. **25**For you were like sheep going astray, but now you have returned to the Shepherd and Overseer of your souls.

WEDNESDAY

VERSE:	AUTHOR:	PASSAGE:
1 Peter 2:9	Connie Neal	1 Peter 2:4–10

A Royal Princess

While every woman's life story is unique, there *are* longings of the heart that seem to be universal: the desire to find true love, the desire that someone will affirm our inherent value regardless of our situation, the hope that we can change. In this regard, we each need a Cinderella story of our own. God finds each of us in the cinders of a less than perfect world, held back from the life we dream of living. He longs to raise us up to a high position, transform us and grant us his power, so he seeks us out, inviting each of us to dance with him. And yet each of us needs someone to affirm our inherent value and encourage our transformation. We each need a Cinderella story of our own. Each woman's relationship with God is such that he finds her in the ashes, held back from the life she dreams of living. He seeks her, invites her to dance with him, transforms her by revealing the beauty hidden beneath the ashes, then confers on her his power and position.

Dancing in the arms of God is a relationship between you and God that is based on love and mutual respect. The two of you communicate in a close, intimate setting. He holds you, but his embrace is the embrace of a lover, not the restraint of an oppressor. As partners in this dance, God leads, and you let him, moving with the flow of his leading. You are not enveloped in God, losing your identity as a unique person; you are who you are, retaining your freedom and individuality at every turn.

ADDITIONAL SCRIPTURE READINGS:
Romans 8:28–30; 2 Corinthians 3:16–18; 2 Thessalonians 2:13

Go to page 349 for your next devotional reading.

Wives and Husbands

3 Wives, in the same way be submissive to your husbands so that, if any of them do not believe the word, they may be won over without words by the behavior of their wives, ²when they see the purity and reverence of your lives. ³Your beauty should not come from outward adornment, such as braided hair and the wearing of gold jewelry and fine clothes. ⁴Instead, it should be that of your inner self, the unfading beauty of a gentle and quiet spirit, which is of great worth in God's sight. ⁵For this is the way the holy women of the past who put their hope in God used to make themselves beautiful. They were submissive to their own husbands, ⁶like Sarah, who obeyed Abraham and called him her master. You are her daughters if you do what is right and do not give way to fear.

⁷Husbands, in the same way be considerate as you live with your wives, and treat them with respect as the weaker partner and as heirs with you of the gracious gift of life, so that nothing will hinder your prayers.

Suffering for Doing Good

⁸Finally, all of you, live in harmony with one another; be sympathetic, love as brothers, be compassionate and humble. ⁹Do not repay evil with evil or insult with insult, but with blessing, because to this you were called so that you may inherit a blessing. ¹⁰For,

"Whoever would love life
    and see good days
must keep his tongue from evil
    and his lips from deceitful speech.
¹¹He must turn from evil and do good;
    he must seek peace and pursue it.
¹²For the eyes of the Lord are on the
        righteous
    and his ears are attentive to their
        prayer,
but the face of the Lord is against
        those who do evil."[a]

¹³Who is going to harm you if you are eager to do good? ¹⁴But even if you should suffer for what is right, you are blessed. "Do not fear what they fear[b];

do not be frightened."[c] ¹⁵But in your hearts set apart Christ as Lord. Always be prepared to give an answer to everyone who asks you to give the reason for the hope that you have. But do this with gentleness and respect, ¹⁶keeping a clear conscience, so that those who speak maliciously against your good behavior in Christ may be ashamed of their slander. ¹⁷It is better, if it is God's will, to suffer for doing good than for doing evil. ¹⁸For Christ died for sins once for all, the righteous for the unrighteous, to bring you to God. He was put to death in the body but made alive by the Spirit, ¹⁹through whom[d] also he went and preached to the spirits in prison ²⁰who disobeyed long ago when God waited patiently in the days of Noah while the ark was being built. In it only a few people, eight in all, were saved through water, ²¹and this water symbolizes baptism that now saves you also—not the removal of dirt from the body but the pledge[e] of a good conscience toward God. It saves you by the resurrection of Jesus Christ, ²²who has gone into heaven and is at God's right hand—with angels, authorities and powers in submission to him.

Living for God

4 Therefore, since Christ suffered in his body, arm yourselves also with the same attitude, because he who has suffered in his body is done with sin. ²As a result, he does not live the rest of his earthly life for evil human desires, but rather for the will of God. ³For you have spent enough time in the past doing what pagans choose to do—living in debauchery, lust, drunkenness, orgies, carousing and detestable idolatry. ⁴They think it strange that you do not plunge with them into the same flood of dissipation, and they heap abuse on you. ⁵But they will have to give account to him who is ready to judge the living and the dead. ⁶For this is the reason the gospel was preached even to those who are now dead, so that they might be judged according to men in regard to the body, but live according to God in regard to the spirit.

⁷The end of all things is near. Therefore be clear minded and self-controlled

---

a12 Psalm 34:12-16   *b14* Or *not fear their threats*   *c14* Isaiah 8:12   *d18,19* Or *alive in the*
spirit, *19through which*   *e21* Or *response*

so that you can pray. **8**Above all, love each other deeply, because love covers over a multitude of sins. **9**Offer hospitality to one another without grumbling. **10**Each one should use whatever gift he has received to serve others, faithfully administering God's grace in its various forms. **11**If anyone speaks, he should do it as one speaking the very words of God. If anyone serves, he should do it with the strength God provides, so that in all things God may be praised through Jesus Christ. To him be the glo-ry and the power for ever and ever. Amen.

Suffering for Being a Christian

12Dear friends, do not be surprised at the painful trial you are suffering, as though something strange were happening to you. **13**But rejoice that you participate in the sufferings of Christ, so that you may be overjoyed when his glory is revealed. **14**If you are insulted because of the name of Christ, you are blessed, for the Spirit of glory and of God rests on

---

THURSDAY

VERSE:	AUTHOR:	PASSAGE:
1 Peter 4:12	Deforia Lane	1 Peter 4:12–19

God's Comfort

I wandered, like Israel in the desert, between faith and hunger, emancipation and fear, the odd need to go back and the hesitancy to move forward.

I remember one tear-filled day spent pacing side to side, back and forth, like a Bengal in a zoo. I finally sat down at the piano to calm myself. I opened the hymnbook to a song I had not heard before.

The music flowed, words to eyes to mind to heart to soul to fingers, like the river in an artery, fluid and pulsing, laced with what was necessary. It was an odd movement, the way the music connected with me; even though I had never seen the notes before and was not particularly good at sight reading. In the music, in the way my faith danced, Jesus was there, marking more than my time.

It was in this ebb and flow, the tension between what was and what might be, that I died my little deaths. In a sense, I had no choice; that was the demanding and terrible grace of it. Die to fear or go insane. Die to a need for a future or start living in the agony of sentences passed. Die to power and position, for what strength is there in an underground plot? Die to selfish desires, for what could be more selfish, more desperate, than demanding to live? The choices were both quite simple and exceedingly difficult. It was only as I moved in faith, one tiny step, that I found the grace to move again, another tiny step. I had to die so that I could live.

I was, through all the kicking and screaming, finally willing. That was it. God arranged the rest.

ADDITIONAL SCRIPTURE READINGS:
John 12:24–26; 2 Corinthians 5:15; 1 Peter 2:24

Go to page 352 for your next devotional reading.

you. [15]If you suffer, it should not be as a murderer or thief or any other kind of criminal, or even as a meddler. [16]However, if you suffer as a Christian, do not be ashamed, but praise God that you bear that name. [17]For it is time for judgment to begin with the family of God; and if it begins with us, what will the outcome be for those who do not obey the gospel of God? [18]And,

> "If it is hard for the righteous to be saved,
>   what will become of the ungodly and the sinner?"[a]

[19]So then, those who suffer according to God's will should commit themselves to their faithful Creator and continue to do good.

To Elders and Young Men

5 To the elders among you, I appeal as a fellow elder, a witness of Christ's sufferings and one who also will share in the glory to be revealed: [2]Be shepherds of God's flock that is under your care, serving as overseers—not because you must, but because you are willing, as God wants you to be; not greedy for money, but eager to serve; [3]not lording it over those entrusted to you, but being examples to the flock. [4]And when the Chief Shepherd appears, you will receive the crown of glory that will never fade away.

[5]Young men, in the same way be sub-missive to those who are older. All of you, clothe yourselves with humility toward one another, because,

> "God opposes the proud
>   but gives grace to the humble."[b]

[6]Humble yourselves, therefore, under God's mighty hand, that he may lift you up in due time. [7]Cast all your anxiety on him because he cares for you.

[8]Be self-controlled and alert. Your enemy the devil prowls around like a roaring lion looking for someone to devour. [9]Resist him, standing firm in the faith, because you know that your brothers throughout the world are undergoing the same kind of sufferings.

[10]And the God of all grace, who called you to his eternal glory in Christ, after you have suffered a little while, will himself restore you and make you strong, firm and steadfast. [11]To him be the power for ever and ever. Amen.

Final Greetings

[12]With the help of Silas,[c] whom I regard as a faithful brother, I have written to you briefly, encouraging you and testifying that this is the true grace of God. Stand fast in it.

[13]She who is in Babylon, chosen together with you, sends you her greetings, and so does my son Mark. [14]Greet one another with a kiss of love.

Peace to all of you who are in Christ.

---

[a]18 Prov. 11:31   [b]5 Prov. 3:34   [c]12 Greek *Silvanus*, a variant of *Silas*

THE *same group of Christians addressed in Peter's first letter are now in danger of being misled by false teachers. Peter, as a "shepherd" of Christ's sheep, not only teaches the church how to deal with these false teachers but also seeks to commend to his readers a wholesome combination of Christian faith and practice. Look for guidelines on developing Christian character and admonitions on how to live in view of the Lord's return.*

2 PETER

1 Simon Peter, a servant and apostle of Jesus Christ,

To those who through the righteousness of our God and Savior Jesus Christ have received a faith as precious as ours:

2Grace and peace be yours in abundance through the knowledge of God and of Jesus our Lord.

Making One's Calling and Election Sure

3His divine power has given us everything we need for life and godliness through our knowledge of him who called us by his own glory and goodness. 4Through these he has given us his very great and precious promises, so that through them you may participate in the divine nature and escape the corruption in the world caused by evil desires.

5For this very reason, make every effort to add to your faith goodness; and to goodness, knowledge; 6and to knowledge, self-control; and to self-control, perseverance; and to perseverance, godliness; 7and to godliness, brotherly kindness; and to brotherly kindness, love. 8For if you possess these qualities in increasing measure, they will keep you from being ineffective and unproductive in your knowledge of our Lord Jesus Christ. 9But if anyone does not have them, he is nearsighted and blind, and has forgotten that he has been cleansed from his past sins.

10Therefore, my brothers, be all the

more eager to make your calling and election sure. For if you do these things, you will never fall, ¹¹and you will receive a rich welcome into the eternal kingdom of our Lord and Savior Jesus Christ.

Prophecy of Scripture

¹²So I will always remind you of these things, even though you know them and are firmly established in the truth you now have. ¹³I think it is right to refresh your memory as long as I live in the tent of this body, ¹⁴because I know that I will soon put it aside, as our Lord Jesus Christ has made clear to me. ¹⁵And I will make every effort to see that after my departure you will always be able to remember these things.

¹⁶We did not follow cleverly invented stories when we told you about the power and coming of our Lord Jesus Christ, but we were eyewitnesses of his majesty. ¹⁷For he received honor and glory from God the Father when the

---

FRIDAY

VERSE:	AUTHOR:	PASSAGE:
2 Peter 1:7	Karen Burton Mains	2 Peter 1:3–11

Hospitality

In Webster's dictionary, the definition for hospitable is wedged between the word "hospice," which is a shelter, and the word "hospital" which is a place of healing. Ultimately, this is what we offer when we open our home in the true spirit of hospitality. We offer shelter; we offer healing.

When we give, having put away our pride, then Christ sanctifies the simple gift. He makes it holy, useful. My three-dollar oak table has become an altar where hungry hearts have been nourished with the bread of life, where thirsty spirits have received the living water. Our living room has been made a sanctuary where sacraments of comfort and communion have been offered, where we have shared in the fellowship of human suffering and human delight. More perfect to me than the praise, "You entertain beautifully!" is the whisper of the young girl who had just come to know Christ, "Thank you for having me. God is here in this home."

This really is the essence of hospitality, a heart open to God, with room prepared for the guest of the Holy Spirit, which welcomes the presence of Christ. This is what we share with those to whom we open our doors. We give to them him and think nothing of what we give of ourselves.

If Christians, corporately, would begin to practice hospitality, we could play significant roles in redeeming our society. There is no better place to be about the redemption of society than in the Christian servant's home; and the more we deal with the captive, the blind, the downtrodden, the more we realize that in this inhospitable world, a Christian home is a miracle to be shared.

ADDITIONAL SCRIPTURE READINGS:
Romans 12:13; 1 Timothy 5:10; 3 John 8

Go to page 354 for your next devotional reading.

voice came to him from the Majestic Glory, saying, "This is my Son, whom I love; with him I am well pleased."[a] [18]We ourselves heard this voice that came from heaven when we were with him on the sacred mountain.

[19]And we have the word of the prophets made more certain, and you will do well to pay attention to it, as to a light shining in a dark place, until the day dawns and the morning star rises in your hearts. [20]Above all, you must understand that no prophecy of Scripture came about by the prophet's own interpretation. [21]For prophecy never had its origin in the will of man, but men spoke from God as they were carried along by the Holy Spirit.

False Teachers and Their Destruction

2 But there were also false prophets among the people, just as there will be false teachers among you. They will secretly introduce destructive heresies, even denying the sovereign Lord who bought them—bringing swift destruction on themselves. [2]Many will follow their shameful ways and will bring the way of truth into disrepute. [3]In their greed these teachers will exploit you with stories they have made up. Their condemnation has long been hanging over them, and their destruction has not been sleeping.

[4]For if God did not spare angels when they sinned, but sent them to hell,[b] putting them into gloomy dungeons[c] to be held for judgment; [5]if he did not spare the ancient world when he brought the flood on its ungodly people, but protected Noah, a preacher of righteousness, and seven others; [6]if he condemned the cities of Sodom and Gomorrah by burning them to ashes, and made them an example of what is going to happen to the ungodly; [7]and if he rescued Lot, a righteous man, who was distressed by the filthy lives of lawless men [8](for that righteous man, living among them day after day, was tormented in his righteous soul by the lawless deeds he saw and heard)— [9]if this is so, then the Lord knows how to rescue godly men from trials and to hold the unrighteous for the day of judgment, while continuing

their punishment.[d] [10]This is especially true of those who follow the corrupt desire of the sinful nature[e] and despise authority.

Bold and arrogant, these men are not afraid to slander celestial beings; [11]yet even angels, although they are stronger and more powerful, do not bring slanderous accusations against such beings in the presence of the Lord. [12]But these men blaspheme in matters they do not understand. They are like brute beasts, creatures of instinct, born only to be caught and destroyed, and like beasts they too will perish.

[13]They will be paid back with harm for the harm they have done. Their idea of pleasure is to carouse in broad daylight. They are blots and blemishes, reveling in their pleasures while they feast with you.[f] [14]With eyes full of adultery, they never stop sinning; they seduce the unstable; they are experts in greed—an accursed brood! [15]They have left the straight way and wandered off to follow the way of Balaam son of Beor, who loved the wages of wickedness. [16]But he was rebuked for his wrongdoing by a donkey—a beast without speech—who spoke with a man's voice and restrained the prophet's madness.

[17]These men are springs without water and mists driven by a storm. Blackest darkness is reserved for them. [18]For they mouth empty, boastful words and, by appealing to the lustful desires of sinful human nature, they entice people who are just escaping from those who live in error. [19]They promise them freedom, while they themselves are slaves of depravity—for a man is a slave to whatever has mastered him. [20]If they have escaped the corruption of the world by knowing our Lord and Savior Jesus Christ and are again entangled in it and overcome, they are worse off at the end than they were at the beginning. [21]It would have been better for them not to have known the way of righteousness, than to have known it and then to turn their backs on the sacred command that was passed on to them. [22]Of them the proverbs are true: "A dog returns to its vomit,"[g] and, "A sow that

---

[a]17 Matt. 17:5; Mark 9:7; Luke 9:35   [b]4 Greek *Tartarus*   [c]4 Some manuscripts *into chains of darkness*   [d]9 Or *unrighteous for punishment until the day of judgment*   [e]10 Or *the flesh*   [f]13 Some manuscripts *in their love feasts*   [g]22 Prov. 26:11

WEEKENDING

REFLECT

Soul of Jesus sanctify me
Blood of Jesus wash me
Passion of Jesus comfort me
Wounds of Jesus hide me
Heart of Jesus receive me
Spirit of Jesus enliven me
Goodness of Jesus pardon me
Beauty of Jesus draw me
Humility of Jesus humble me
Peace of Jesus inflame me
Kingdom of Jesus come to me
Grace of Jesus pity me
Sanctity of Jesus sanctify me
Purity of Jesus purify me
Cross of Jesus support me
Nails of Jesus hold me
Mouth of Jesus bless me

In life, in death—in time and
Eternity—in the hour of Death defend
Me, call me to come to thee, receive me
with thy Saints in glory everlasting.

Elizabeth Seton

REVIVE

Saturday: 1 Peter 1:2–4
Sunday: 2 Peter 3:11–14

*Go to page 355 for your
next devotional reading.*

is washed goes back to her wallowing in the mud."

The Day of the Lord

3 Dear friends, this is now my second letter to you. I have written both of them as reminders to stimulate you to wholesome thinking. ²I want you to recall the words spoken in the past by the holy prophets and the command given by our Lord and Savior through your apostles.

³First of all, you must understand that in the last days scoffers will come, scoffing and following their own evil desires. ⁴They will say, "Where is this 'coming' he promised? Ever since our fathers died, everything goes on as it has since the beginning of creation." ⁵But they deliberately forget that long ago by God's word the heavens existed and the earth was formed out of water and by water. ⁶By these waters also the world of that time was deluged and destroyed. ⁷By the same word the present heavens and earth are reserved for fire, being kept for

---

MONDAY

VERSE:	AUTHOR:	PASSAGE:
2 Peter 3:13	Mary Lou Carney	2 Peter 3

The Language of Love

The story is told of Bozo, the circus elephant, who was scheduled for execution in the center ring. It seems that Bozo had changed from a well-behaved performer to a vicious animal, trying three times to kill his trainer.

Rifles were stacked along the side of the ring. Bozo trudged in a circle inside the steel cage, raising his trunk to trumpet his rage. But just as the ringmaster lifted his arm to give the fatal signal, a small man stepped forward.

"Let me in the cage," he pleaded. "In two minutes I will show you that Bozo is not a bad elephant." Surprised, but anxious to salvage his investment if possible, the ringmaster opened the cage, and the stranger stepped inside.

Bozo whirled around and glared through blood-shot eyes at the intruder. Softly, the man began to speak. Bozo stopped pacing and listened. His massive body quivered into relaxation. A small, childlike cry echoed from his huge trunk. Astonished, the crowd broke into applause.

That man was Rudyard Kipling. He had spoken to the elephant in Hindustani, knowing that the Indian beast was simply homesick. Kipling's words had made Bozo feel at peace again.

Sometimes we Christians, too, become homesick. Surrounded by the wickedness and misery of this world, we are tempted to despondency. We long for our heavenly home. That's when we need to hear again Christ's promise of peace (John 14:27), a promise spoken in the language of divine love.

ADDITIONAL SCRIPTURE READINGS:
John 14:23–27; Philippians 3:20–21; Colossians 3:1

Go to page 358 for your next devotional reading.

the day of judgment and destruction of ungodly men.

⁸But do not forget this one thing, dear friends: With the Lord a day is like a thousand years, and a thousand years are like a day. ⁹The Lord is not slow in keeping his promise, as some understand slowness. He is patient with you, not wanting anyone to perish, but everyone to come to repentance.

¹⁰But the day of the Lord will come like a thief. The heavens will disappear with a roar; the elements will be destroyed by fire, and the earth and everything in it will be laid bare.ᵃ

¹¹Since everything will be destroyed in this way, what kind of people ought you to be? You ought to live holy and godly lives ¹²as you look forward to the day of God and speed its coming.ᵇ That day will bring about the destruction of the heavens by fire, and the elements will melt in the heat. ¹³But in keeping with his promise we are looking forward to a new heaven and a new earth, the home of righteousness.

¹⁴So then, dear friends, since you are looking forward to this, make every effort to be found spotless, blameless and at peace with him. ¹⁵Bear in mind that our Lord's patience means salvation, just as our dear brother Paul also wrote you with the wisdom that God gave him. ¹⁶He writes the same way in all his letters, speaking in them of these matters. His letters contain some things that are hard to understand, which ignorant and unstable people distort, as they do the other Scriptures, to their own destruction.

¹⁷Therefore, dear friends, since you already know this, be on your guard so that you may not be carried away by the error of lawless men and fall from your secure position. ¹⁸But grow in the grace and knowledge of our Lord and Savior Jesus Christ. To him be the glory both now and forever! Amen.

ᵃ10 Some manuscripts be burned up   ᵇ12 Or as you wait eagerly for the day of God to come

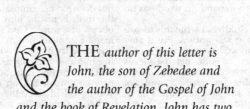

THE *author of this letter is John, the son of Zebedee and the author of the Gospel of John and the book of Revelation. John has two basic purposes in mind in this letter: (1) to expose false teachers who deny, among other things, Jesus' humanity, and (2) to give believers assurance of salvation. John stresses God's love as an example for us to follow in our relationships with each other. He encourages believers to live right and to maintain truth by maintaining fellowship with the Lord.*

1 JOHN

The Word of Life

1 That which was from the beginning, which we have heard, which we have seen with our eyes, which we have looked at and our hands have touched— this we proclaim concerning the Word of life. ²The life appeared; we have seen it and testify to it, and we proclaim to you the eternal life, which was with the Father and has appeared to us. ³We proclaim to you what we have seen and heard, so that you also may have fellowship with us. And our fellowship is with the Father and with his Son, Jesus Christ. ⁴We write this to make our*ᵃ* joy complete.

Walking in the Light

⁵This is the message we have heard from him and declare to you: God is light; in him there is no darkness at all. ⁶If we claim to have fellowship with him yet walk in the darkness, we lie and do not live by the truth. ⁷But if we walk in the light, as he is in the light, we have fellowship with one another, and the blood of Jesus, his Son, purifies us from all*ᵇ* sin.

⁸If we claim to be without sin, we deceive ourselves and the truth is not in us. ⁹If we confess our sins, he is faithful and just and will forgive us our sins and purify us from all unrighteousness. ¹⁰If

we claim we have not sinned, we make him out to be a liar and his word has no place in our lives.

2 My dear children, I write this to you so that you will not sin. But if anybody does sin, we have one who speaks to the Father in our defense—Jesus Christ, the Righteous One. ²He is the atoning sacrifice for our sins, and not only for ours but also for*a* the sins of the whole world.

³We know that we have come to know him if we obey his commands. ⁴The man who says, "I know him," but does not do what he commands is a liar, and the truth is not in him. ⁵But if anyone obeys his word, God's love*b* is truly made complete in him. This is how we know we are in him: ⁶Whoever claims to live in him must walk as Jesus did.

⁷Dear friends, I am not writing you a new command but an old one, which you have had since the beginning. This old command is the message you have heard. ⁸Yet I am writing you a new command; its truth is seen in him and you,

a2 Or *He is the one who turns aside God's wrath, taking away our sins, and not only ours but also word, love for God*   *b5* Or

---

TUESDAY

VERSE: 1 John 1:9	AUTHOR: Rebecca Manley Pippert	PASSAGE: 1 John 1

It's Tough and It Takes Time

We can lose our perspective while we are dealing with what is wrong with us. So we need to remember that it is not God's desire that we live in perpetual pain, morbidly focused on what is wrong. That tactic is the enemy's, not God's. God convicts us of sin only so we may be forgiven and enabled to walk in freedom.

Confession is not a list of petty blemishes drawn up grudgingly for the sake of an overbearing God. It is a facing up to those cancerous vices that sap vitality, cripple freedom and eventually kill. We are the ones who suffer if we sin.

To work to see the victory of God's grace over sin is not something we can knock off in a weekend. Though we live in a culture that is always in a hurry, and demands instant results, the Bible admonishes us to wait, to work at it and never to lose heart. I have discovered no magic key that enables us to lock out suffering or the painful and often slow process of growth. I have found no shortcuts, no gimmicks to becoming the person God desires. Evil never has the last word. God does. But while we wait, we need to ask for the grace of tenacity, so that we can hang on—and on and on—while he works his excellent purpose in us.

We shouldn't underestimate the pain that will be involved. But neither must we forget what is happening to us: We are being changed into the likeness of God.

ADDITIONAL SCRIPTURE READINGS:
Romans 6:19–23; Titus 2:11; Hebrews 9:15

Go to page 359 for your next devotional reading.

because the darkness is passing and the true light is already shining.

⁹Anyone who claims to be in the light but hates his brother is still in the darkness. ¹⁰Whoever loves his brother lives in the light, and there is nothing in him[a] to make him stumble. ¹¹But whoever hates his brother is in the darkness and walks around in the darkness; he does not know where he is going, because the darkness has blinded him.

¹²I write to you, dear children,

---

because your sins have been
    forgiven on account of his
    name.
¹³I write to you, fathers,
    because you have known him who
    is from the beginning.
I write to you, young men,
    because you have overcome the
    evil one.
I write to you, dear children,
    because you have known the
    Father.

[a]10 Or it

WEDNESDAY

VERSE:	AUTHOR:	PASSAGE:
1 John 2:6	Cynthia Culp Allen	1 John 2:1–6

Art 101

I love it when my children bring their artwork to me. Their proud smiles tell me how they feel about their finished piece before I even see it. Then I take the "masterpiece" and form my own "unbiased" opinion.

"What a wonderful drawing!" I say. "Let me hang it on the fridge where everyone can enjoy it."

Artistic talent requires practice and a good example to follow. I once took a tole painting class, and while I was painting I kept one eye on the teacher, the other eye on my work. I watched the teacher's every move and tried to imitate her. I studied her finished pieces and tried to paint mine exactly like hers. Actually, I copied her.

No, my painted pieces never looked just like the teacher's. They never could—even if I were as good as she was! My personality comes out in my painting (sometimes that is unfortunate!). But little by little, stroke by stroke, as I tried to copy my teacher, my paintings got more and more like hers.

In my relationship with Christ I'm taking a lifetime class in the art of being Christlike. As he teaches me, I keep one eye glued on him. I try to imitate him. Studying his Word helps me know his thoughts and actions in different situations. Jesus painted the whole New Testament with a broad sweep of love, forgiveness and mercy. My prayer is that my life will be the same as his.

ADDITIONAL SCRIPTURE READINGS:
Matthew 11:29; Romans 15:5; Philippians 2:1–11

Go to page 362 for your next devotional reading.

[14]I write to you, fathers,
  because you have known him who
    is from the beginning.
I write to you, young men,
  because you are strong,
  and the word of God lives in you,
  and you have overcome the evil one.

Do Not Love the World

[15]Do not love the world or anything in the world. If anyone loves the world, the love of the Father is not in him. [16]For everything in the world—the cravings of sinful man, the lust of his eyes and the boasting of what he has and does—comes not from the Father but from the world. [17]The world and its desires pass away, but the man who does the will of God lives forever.

Warning Against Antichrists

[18]Dear children, this is the last hour; and as you have heard that the antichrist is coming, even now many antichrists have come. This is how we know it is the last hour. [19]They went out from us, but they did not really belong to us. For if they had belonged to us, they would have remained with us; but their going showed that none of them belonged to us.

[20]But you have an anointing from the Holy One, and all of you know the truth.[a] [21]I do not write to you because you do not know the truth, but because you do know it and because no lie comes from the truth. [22]Who is the liar? It is the man who denies that Jesus is the Christ. Such a man is the antichrist—he denies the Father and the Son. [23]No one who denies the Son has the Father; whoever acknowledges the Son has the Father also.

[24]See that what you have heard from the beginning remains in you. If it does, you also will remain in the Son and in the Father. [25]And this is what he promised us—even eternal life.

[26]I am writing these things to you about those who are trying to lead you astray. [27]As for you, the anointing you received from him remains in you, and you do not need anyone to teach you. But as his anointing teaches you about all things and as that anointing is real, not counterfeit—just as it has taught you, remain in him.

Children of God

[28]And now, dear children, continue in him, so that when he appears we may be confident and unashamed before him at his coming. [29]If you know that he is righteous, you know that everyone who does what is right has been born of him.

3 How great is the love the Father has lavished on us, that we should be called children of God! And that is what we are! The reason the world does not know us is that it did not know him. [2]Dear friends, now we are children of God, and what we will be has not yet been made known. But we know that when he appears,[b] we shall be like him, for we shall see him as he is. [3]Everyone who has this hope in him purifies himself, just as he is pure.

[4]Everyone who sins breaks the law; in fact, sin is lawlessness. [5]But you know that he appeared so that he might take away our sins. And in him is no sin. [6]No one who lives in him keeps on sinning. No one who continues to sin has either seen him or known him.

[7]Dear children, do not let anyone lead you astray. He who does what is right is righteous, just as he is righteous. [8]He who does what is sinful is of the devil, because the devil has been sinning from the beginning. The reason the Son of God appeared was to destroy the devil's work. [9]No one who is born of God will continue to sin, because God's seed remains in him; he cannot go on sinning, because he has been born of God. [10]This is how we know who the children of God are and who the children of the devil are: Anyone who does not do what is right is not a child of God; nor is anyone who does not love his brother.

Love One Another

[11]This is the message you heard from the beginning: We should love one another. [12]Do not be like Cain, who belonged to the evil one and murdered his brother. And why did he murder him? Because his own actions were evil and his brother's were righteous. [13]Do not be surprised, my brothers, if the world hates you. [14]We know that we have passed from death to life, because we

---

[a]20 Some manuscripts *and you know all things*   [b]2 Or *when it is made known*

love our brothers. Anyone who does not love remains in death. **15**Anyone who hates his brother is a murderer, and you know that no murderer has eternal life in him.

16This is how we know what love is: Jesus Christ laid down his life for us. And we ought to lay down our lives for our brothers. **17**If anyone has material possessions and sees his brother in need but has no pity on him, how can the love of God be in him? **18**Dear children, let us not love with words or tongue but with actions and in truth. **19**This then is how we know that we belong to the truth, and how we set our hearts at rest in his presence **20**whenever our hearts condemn us. For God is greater than our hearts, and he knows everything.

21Dear friends, if our hearts do not condemn us, we have confidence before God **22**and receive from him anything we ask, because we obey his commands and do what pleases him. **23**And this is his command: to believe in the name of his Son, Jesus Christ, and to love one another as he commanded us. **24**Those who obey his commands live in him, and he in them. And this is how we know that he lives in us: We know it by the Spirit he gave us.

Test the Spirits

4 Dear friends, do not believe every spirit, but test the spirits to see whether they are from God, because many false prophets have gone out into the world. **2**This is how you can recognize the Spirit of God: Every spirit that acknowledges that Jesus Christ has come in the flesh is from God, **3**but every spirit that does not acknowledge Jesus is not from God. This is the spirit of the antichrist, which you have heard is coming and even now is already in the world.

4You, dear children, are from God and have overcome them, because the one who is in you is greater than the one who is in the world. **5**They are from the world and therefore speak from the viewpoint of the world, and the world listens to them. **6**We are from God, and whoever knows God listens to us; but whoever is not from God does not listen to us. This is how we recognize the Spirit[a] of truth and the spirit of falsehood.

God's Love and Ours

7Dear friends, let us love one another, for love comes from God. Everyone who loves has been born of God and knows God. **8**Whoever does not love does not know God, because God is love. **9**This is how God showed his love among us: He sent his one and only Son[b] into the world that we might live through him. **10**This is love: not that we loved God, but that he loved us and sent his Son as an atoning sacrifice for[c] our sins. **11**Dear friends, since God so loved us, we also ought to love one another. **12**No one has ever seen God; but if we love one another, God lives in us and his love is made complete in us.

13We know that we live in him and he in us, because he has given us of his Spirit. **14**And we have seen and testify that the Father has sent his Son to be the Savior of the world. **15**If anyone acknowledges that Jesus is the Son of God, God lives in him and he in God. **16**And so we know and rely on the love God has for us.

God is love. Whoever lives in love lives in God, and God in him. **17**In this way, love is made complete among us so that we will have confidence on the day of judgment, because in this world we are like him. **18**There is no fear in love. But perfect love drives out fear, because fear has to do with punishment. The one who fears is not made perfect in love.

19We love because he first loved us. **20**If anyone says, "I love God," yet hates his brother, he is a liar. For anyone who does not love his brother, whom he has seen, cannot love God, whom he has not seen. **21**And he has given us this command: Whoever loves God must also love his brother.

Faith in the Son of God

5 Everyone who believes that Jesus is the Christ is born of God, and everyone who loves the father loves his child as well. **2**This is how we know that we love the children of God: by loving

---

a6 Or *spirit*   *b9* Or *his only begotten Son*   *c10* Or *as the one who would turn aside his wrath,*
taking away

God and carrying out his commands. ³This is love for God: to obey his commands. And his commands are not burdensome, ⁴for everyone born of God overcomes the world. This is the victory that has overcome the world, even our faith. ⁵Who is it that overcomes the world? Only he who believes that Jesus is the Son of God.

⁶This is the one who came by water and blood—Jesus Christ. He did not come by water only, but by water and blood. And it is the Spirit who testifies, because the Spirit is the truth. ⁷For there are three that testify: ⁸the[a] Spirit, the water and the blood; and the three are in agreement. ⁹We accept man's testimony, but God's testimony is greater because it is the testimony of God, which he has given about his Son. ¹⁰Anyone who believes in the Son of God has this testimony in his heart. Anyone who does not believe God has made him out to be a liar, because he has not believed the testimony God has given about his Son. ¹¹And this is the testimony: God has given us eternal life, and this life is in his Son. ¹²He who has the Son has life; he who does not have the Son of God does not have life.

[a] 7,8 Late manuscripts of the Vulgate *testify in heaven: the Father, the Word and the Holy Spirit, and these three are one. ⁸And there are three that testify on earth: the* (not found in any Greek manuscript before the sixteenth century)

THURSDAY

VERSE:
1 John 4:18

AUTHOR:
Henrietta Mears

PASSAGE:
1 John 4:7–21

Have No Fear

One day in the mountain region of Scotland, a gigantic eagle snatched a little baby out of his crib and flew away with him. The people of the village ran out after the big bird, but the eagle perched itself upon a nearby mountain crag. Could the child possibly be rescued? A sailor tried to climb the ascent, but he was at last obliged to give up the attempt. A robust Highlander, accustomed to climbing those mountains, tried next and even his strength failed. At last a poor peasant woman came forward. She put her feet upon one shelf on the rock, then on the second, then on the third and in this manner she rose to the very top of the cliff. While all below held their breath for sheer fright, she came down step by step until she stood at the bottom of the rock with the child safely in her arms. Immediately shouts of praise arose from the crowd that had gathered.

Why did that woman succeed when the strong sailor and the experienced mountain climber had failed? Because that woman was the mother of the baby. Her love for her baby had given her the courage to do what the others had failed to do.

If the love of Christ is in your heart, you, too, will find that you will have the courage to do whatever he directs you to do.

ADDITIONAL SCRIPTURE READINGS:
Deuteronomy 31:6; Psalm 56:13; Isaiah 54:14

Go to page 365 for your next devotional reading.

Concluding Remarks

¹³I write these things to you who believe in the name of the Son of God so that you may know that you have eternal life. ¹⁴This is the confidence we have in approaching God: that if we ask anything according to his will, he hears us. ¹⁵And if we know that he hears us—whatever we ask—we know that we have what we asked of him.

¹⁶If anyone sees his brother commit a sin that does not lead to death, he should pray and God will give him life. I refer to those whose sin does not lead to death. There is a sin that leads to death. I am not saying that he should

pray about that. ¹⁷All wrongdoing is sin, and there is sin that does not lead to death.

¹⁸We know that anyone born of God does not continue to sin; the one who was born of God keeps him safe, and the evil one cannot harm him. ¹⁹We know that we are children of God, and that the whole world is under the control of the evil one. ²⁰We know also that the Son of God has come and has given us understanding, so that we may know him who is true. And we are in him who is true—even in his Son Jesus Christ. He is the true God and eternal life.

²¹Dear children, keep yourselves from idols.

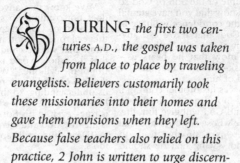

DURING *the first two centuries* A.D., *the gospel was taken from place to place by traveling evangelists. Believers customarily took these missionaries into their homes and gave them provisions when they left. Because false teachers also relied on this practice, 2 John is written to urge discernment in supporting traveling teachers. Look for the challenge to be certain about what you believe and how you live.*

2 JOHN

¹The elder,

To the chosen lady and her children, whom I love in the truth—and not I only, but also all who know the truth—²because of the truth, which lives in us and will be with us forever:

³Grace, mercy and peace from God the Father and from Jesus Christ, the Father's Son, will be with us in truth and love.

⁴It has given me great joy to find some of your children walking in the truth, just as the Father commanded us. ⁵And now, dear lady, I am not writing you a new command but one we have had from the beginning. I ask that we love one another. ⁶And this is love: that we walk in obedience to his commands. As you have heard from the beginning, his command is that you walk in love.

⁷Many deceivers, who do not acknowledge Jesus Christ as coming in the flesh, have gone out into the world. Any such person is the deceiver and the antichrist. ⁸Watch out that you do not lose what you have worked for, but that you may be rewarded fully. ⁹Anyone who runs ahead and does not continue in the teaching of Christ does not have God; whoever continues in the teaching has both the Father and the Son. ¹⁰If anyone comes to you and does not bring this teaching, do not take him into

your house or welcome him. **11**Anyone who welcomes him shares in his wicked work.

12I have much to write to you, but I do not want to use paper and ink. Instead, I hope to visit you and talk with you face to face, so that our joy may be complete.

13The children of your chosen sister send their greetings.

FRIDAY

VERSE:
2 John 5

AUTHOR:
Jean E. Syswerda

PASSAGE:
2 John

Love Is All We Can Give

I watched as the teens began to arrive for our weekly youth meeting. We gathered each Wednesday evening in a local gym, a more relaxed and less threatening spot than our church's fellowship hall.

J. came up, gave me a hug and described her latest argument with her parents. T. arrived; his eyes met mine only briefly, but I knew he needed to be sure I had noticed his arrival. R. came in looking like she wanted to pick a fight with anyone who got too close. She was one of the most unhappy teens I had ever met.

My eyes scanned the crowd of seventy or so teenagers. Such a diverse bunch. From drug users to clean, from promiscuous to chaste, from angry to contented, from unloved to loved.

I'd been working with our youth program for about six years. When I entered I fully expected to enjoy myself. I fully expected to like the kids. But I never, ever expected to love them like I did. With all their silliness and anger and insight and lack of self-confidence, they pulled at my heart and made me love them.

But I guess love is all we really have to give them. We can't whisk away years of abuse or neglect. We can't bypass angry parents. We can't magically change rebellion into compliance. But we can love them. And in doing so, maybe we can ease the hurt for a while or turn the direction taken or make one teen stop to consider what we offer through Jesus: our love and his.

ADDITIONAL SCRIPTURE READINGS:
Leviticus 19:18; Matthew 22:39; John 15:12

Go to page 367 for your next devotional reading.

ITINERANT *teachers sent out by John were rejected in one of the churches in the province of Asia by a dictatorial leader, Diotrephes. John writes to Gaius, his friend and a leader in the church, to thank Gaius for his help and to encourage him in his support of legitimate teachers. He also reproves Diotrephes for not cooperating and for rebelling against John's leadership.*

3 JOHN

[1]The elder,

To my dear friend Gaius, whom I love in the truth.

[2]Dear friend, I pray that you may enjoy good health and that all may go well with you, even as your soul is getting along well. [3]It gave me great joy to have some brothers come and tell about your faithfulness to the truth and how you continue to walk in the truth. [4]I have no greater joy than to hear that my children are walking in the truth.

[5]Dear friend, you are faithful in what you are doing for the brothers, even though they are strangers to you. [6]They have told the church about your love. You will do well to send them on their way in a manner worthy of God. [7]It was for the sake of the Name that they went out, receiving no help from the pagans. [8]We ought therefore to show hospitality to such men so that we may work together for the truth.

[9]I wrote to the church, but Diotrephes, who loves to be first, will have nothing to do with us. [10]So if I come, I will call attention to what he is doing, gossiping maliciously about us. Not satisfied with that, he refuses to welcome the brothers. He also stops those who want to do so and puts them out of the church.

[11]Dear friend, do not imitate what is evil but what is good. Anyone who does what is good is from God. Anyone who does what is evil has not seen God.

WEEKENDING

REMEMBER

I am convinced that God's Holy Spirit orchestrates our lives to touch others—strangers, friends, work-related people, service-industry workers and more—if we would just open up and be ourselves. How? Be free to be in love with Jesus in front of people. Be an ambassador through whom he can introduce himself. There is a world out there hungry and searching for Jesus and his love. Don't keep him to yourself.

Would you reject a friendly, caring individual, especially if you happened to be needy, hurting, lonely, dissatisfied with life—or actually searching for God?

Becky Tirabassi

REVIVE

Saturday: 3 John
Sunday: Acts 2:41–42

Go to page 370 for your next devotional reading.

[12]Demetrius is well spoken of by everyone—and even by the truth itself. We also speak well of him, and you know that our testimony is true.

[13]I have much to write you, but I do not want to do so with pen and ink. [14]I hope to see you soon, and we will talk face to face.

Peace to you. The friends here send their greetings. Greet the friends there by name.

JUDE *is a personal letter to one or more of the congregations dispersed throughout the Roman empire. The dangers facing the church at this time are not those of outright persecution but of heretics and distorters of the faith. Although Jude is eager to write about salvation, he must instead warn his readers about immoral men who are perverting God's grace. The letter advises believers to strengthen their relationship to God with prayer and mutual support.*

JUDE

¹Jude, a servant of Jesus Christ and a brother of James,

To those who have been called, who are loved by God the Father and kept by*a* Jesus Christ:

²Mercy, peace and love be yours in abundance.

The Sin and Doom of Godless Men

³Dear friends, although I was very eager to write to you about the salvation we share, I felt I had to write and urge you to contend for the faith that was once for all entrusted to the saints. ⁴For certain men whose condemnation was written about*b* long ago have secretly slipped in among you. They are godless men, who change the grace of our God into a license for immorality and deny Jesus Christ our only Sovereign and Lord.

⁵Though you already know all this, I want to remind you that the Lord*c* delivered his people out of Egypt, but later destroyed those who did not believe. ⁶And the angels who did not keep their positions of authority but abandoned their own home—these he has kept in darkness, bound with everlasting chains for judgment on the great Day. ⁷In a similar way, Sodom and Gomorrah and the surrounding towns gave themselves up to sexual immorality and perversion.

*a*1 Or *for; or in Jesus*   *b*4 Or *men who were marked out for condemnation*   *c*5 Some early manuscripts

They serve as an example of those who suffer the punishment of eternal fire.

⁸In the very same way, these dreamers pollute their own bodies, reject authority and slander celestial beings. ⁹But even the archangel Michael, when he was disputing with the devil about the body of Moses, did not dare to bring a slanderous accusation against him, but said, "The Lord rebuke you!" ¹⁰Yet these men speak abusively against whatever they do not understand; and what things they do understand by instinct, like unreasoning animals—these are the very things that destroy them.

¹¹Woe to them! They have taken the way of Cain; they have rushed for profit into Balaam's error; they have been destroyed in Korah's rebellion.

¹²These men are blemishes at your love feasts, eating with you without the slightest qualm—shepherds who feed only themselves. They are clouds without rain, blown along by the wind; autumn trees, without fruit and uprooted—twice dead. ¹³They are wild waves of the sea, foaming up their shame; wandering stars, for whom blackest darkness has been reserved forever.

¹⁴Enoch, the seventh from Adam, prophesied about these men: "See, the Lord is coming with thousands upon thousands of his holy ones ¹⁵to judge everyone, and to convict all the ungodly of all the ungodly acts they have done in the ungodly way, and of all the harsh words ungodly sinners have spoken against him." ¹⁶These men are grumblers and faultfinders; they follow their own evil desires; they boast about themselves and flatter others for their own advantage.

MONDAY

VERSE:
Jude 10

AUTHOR:
Catherine DeVries

PASSAGE:
Jude

Quest for Truth

Radio and television talk shows are becoming information sources for many of us. But as we listen, how many times have we wondered, "Is this really true? Am I hearing correct information?"

The quest for truth is getting more and more difficult. We live in an era that inundates us with information. How tempting it is to become exasperated and exclaim, "Information overload! Enough is enough!" Or perhaps it is tempting to stereotype, or take another person's analysis as our own. But in shutting out or simplifying issues, we run the risk of speaking "abusively against whatever [we] do not understand" (v. 10). We need to learn to think critically in order to glean the truth and leave the rest. But how?

The book of Jude—written for a time not unlike today, where truth is hidden and false teachers abound—encourages us to ground ourselves in faith and prayer. For it is God who guides us into truth (Psalm 25:5) and who reveals his truth in his son Jesus (John 1:17) and in his Word, which is truth (John 17:17).

ADDITIONAL SCRIPTURE READINGS:
Psalm 119:105; Proverbs 22:17–19; Philippians 4:8

Go to page 373 for your next devotional reading.

A Call to Persevere

[17]But, dear friends, remember what the apostles of our Lord Jesus Christ foretold. [18]They said to you, "In the last times there will be scoffers who will follow their own ungodly desires." [19]These are the men who divide you, who follow mere natural instincts and do not have the Spirit.

[20]But you, dear friends, build yourselves up in your most holy faith and pray in the Holy Spirit. [21]Keep yourselves in God's love as you wait for the mercy of our Lord Jesus Christ to bring you to eternal life.

[22]Be merciful to those who doubt; [23]snatch others from the fire and save them; to others show mercy, mixed with fear—hating even the clothing stained by corrupted flesh.

Doxology

[24]To him who is able to keep you from falling and to present you before his glorious presence without fault and with great joy— [25]to the only God our Savior be glory, majesty, power and authority, through Jesus Christ our Lord, before all ages, now and forevermore! Amen.

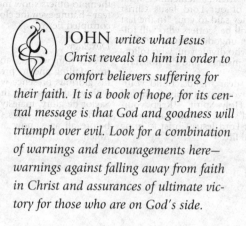

JOHN *writes what Jesus Christ reveals to him in order to comfort believers suffering for their faith. It is a book of hope, for its central message is that God and goodness will triumph over evil. Look for a combination of warnings and encouragements here—warnings against falling away from faith in Christ and assurances of ultimate victory for those who are on God's side.*

REVELATION

Prologue

1 The revelation of Jesus Christ, which God gave him to show his servants what must soon take place. He made it known by sending his angel to his servant John, ²who testifies to everything he saw—that is, the word of God and the testimony of Jesus Christ. ³Blessed is the one who reads the words of this prophecy, and blessed are those who hear it and take to heart what is written in it, because the time is near.

Greetings and Doxology

⁴John,

To the seven churches in the province of Asia:

Grace and peace to you from him who is, and who was, and who is to come, and from the seven spirits*ᵃ* before his throne, ⁵and from Jesus Christ, who is the faithful witness, the firstborn from the dead, and the ruler of the kings of the earth.

To him who loves us and has freed us from our sins by his blood, ⁶and has made us to be a kingdom and priests to serve his God and Father—to him be glory and power for ever and ever! Amen.

⁷Look, he is coming with the clouds,
and every eye will see him,
even those who pierced him;
and all the peoples of the earth
will mourn because of him.
So shall it be! Amen.

⁸"I am the Alpha and the Omega," says the Lord God, "who is, and who was, and who is to come, the Almighty."

ᵃ4 Or *the sevenfold Spirit*

One Like a Son of Man

9I, John, your brother and companion in the suffering and kingdom and patient endurance that are ours in Jesus, was on the island of Patmos because of the word of God and the testimony of Jesus. **10**On the Lord's Day I was in the Spirit, and I heard behind me a loud voice like a trumpet, **11**which said: "Write on a scroll what you see and send it to the seven churches: to Ephesus, Smyrna, Pergamum, Thyatira, Sardis, Philadelphia and Laodicea."

12I turned around to see the voice that was speaking to me. And when I turned I saw seven golden lampstands, **13**and among the lampstands was someone "like a son of man,"*a* dressed in a robe reaching down to his feet and with a golden sash around his chest. **14**His head and hair were white like wool, as white as snow, and his eyes were like blazing fire. **15**His feet were like bronze glowing in a furnace, and his voice was like the sound of rushing waters. **16**In his right hand he held seven stars, and out of his mouth came a sharp double-edged sword. His face was like the sun shining in all its brilliance.

17When I saw him, I fell at his feet as though dead. Then he placed his right hand on me and said: "Do not be afraid. I am the First and the Last. **18**I am the Living One; I was dead, and behold I am alive for ever and ever! And I hold the keys of death and Hades.

19"Write, therefore, what you have seen, what is now and what will take place later. **20**The mystery of the seven stars that you saw in my right hand and of the seven golden lampstands is this: The seven stars are the angels*b* of the seven churches, and the seven lampstands are the seven churches.

a13 Daniel 7:13   *b20* Or *messengers*

TUESDAY

VERSE:
Revelation 1:18

AUTHOR:
Rebecca Manley Pippert

PASSAGE:
Revelation 1

Living the Resurrection

The resurrection shows us that God is alive. He is really there. He speaks and out of nothing calls reality into being. His mighty acts in history are unquestionable. The common word for this in the Bible is the "living God." The ancient Hebrews who used this term were not interested merely in whether God existed, as if he were simply a prime mover or the last step in a philosopher's syllogism. What mattered to them was that he was alive and personal. He was involved in the affairs of this planet. His presence made a real difference.

Life in the Bible as a whole means something that is vibrant and dynamic. To speak of God as the "living God" is to make the claim that God is actively present, here and now. He is a person who has qualities: he loves, hates, pities, has compassion. We in return can ignore him, hate him, argue with him, reject him, know him, only because he is alive!

ADDITIONAL SCRIPTURE READINGS:
John 11:25–26; 1 Corinthians 15:57; Philippians 3:10–11

Go to page 377 for your next devotional reading.

To the Church in Ephesus

2 "To the angel[a] of the church in Ephesus write:

These are the words of him who holds the seven stars in his right hand and walks among the seven golden lampstands: ²I know your deeds, your hard work and your perseverance. I know that you cannot tolerate wicked men, that you have tested those who claim to be apostles but are not, and have found them false. ³You have persevered and have endured hardships for my name, and have not grown weary.

⁴Yet I hold this against you: You have forsaken your first love. ⁵Remember the height from which you have fallen! Repent and do the things you did at first. If you do not repent, I will come to you and remove your lampstand from its place. ⁶But you have this in your favor: You hate the practices of the Nicolaitans, which I also hate.

⁷He who has an ear, let him hear what the Spirit says to the churches. To him who overcomes, I will give the right to eat from the tree of life, which is in the paradise of God.

To the Church in Smyrna

⁸"To the angel of the church in Smyrna write:

These are the words of him who is the First and the Last, who died and came to life again. ⁹I know your afflictions and your poverty—yet you are rich! I know the slander of those who say they are Jews and are not, but are a synagogue of Satan. ¹⁰Do not be afraid of what you are about to suffer. I tell you, the devil will put some of you in prison to test you, and you will suffer persecution for ten days. Be faithful, even to the point of death, and I will give you the crown of life.

¹¹He who has an ear, let him hear what the Spirit says to the churches. He who overcomes will not be hurt at all by the second death.

To the Church in Pergamum

¹²"To the angel of the church in Pergamum write:

These are the words of him who has the sharp, double-edged sword. ¹³I know where you live—where Satan has his throne. Yet you remain true to my name. You did not renounce your faith in me, even in the days of Antipas, my faithful witness, who was put to death in your city—where Satan lives.

¹⁴Nevertheless, I have a few things against you: You have people there who hold to the teaching of Balaam, who taught Balak to entice the Israelites to sin by eating food sacrificed to idols and by committing sexual immorality. ¹⁵Likewise you also have those who hold to the teaching of the Nicolaitans. ¹⁶Repent therefore! Otherwise, I will soon come to you and will fight against them with the sword of my mouth.

¹⁷He who has an ear, let him hear what the Spirit says to the churches. To him who overcomes, I will give some of the hidden manna. I will also give him a white stone with a new name written on it, known only to him who receives it.

To the Church in Thyatira

¹⁸"To the angel of the church in Thyatira write:

These are the words of the Son of God, whose eyes are like blazing fire and whose feet are like burnished bronze. ¹⁹I know your deeds, your love and faith, your service and perseverance, and that you are now doing more than you did at first.

²⁰Nevertheless, I have this against you: You tolerate that woman Jezebel, who calls herself a prophetess. By her teaching she misleads my servants into sexual immorality and the eating of food sacrificed to idols. ²¹I have given her time to repent of her immorality, but she is unwilling. ²²So I will cast her on a bed of suffering, and I will make those who commit adul-

a 1 Or *messenger*; also in verses 8, 12 and 18

tery with her suffer intensely, unless they repent of her ways. ²³I will strike her children dead. Then all the churches will know that I am he who searches hearts and minds, and I will repay each of you according to your deeds. ²⁴Now I say to the rest of you in Thyatira, to you who do not hold to her teaching and have not learned Satan's so-called deep secrets (I will not impose any other burden on you): ²⁵Only hold on to what you have until I come.

²⁶To him who overcomes and does my will to the end, I will give authority over the nations—

²⁷'He will rule them with an iron scepter;
    he will dash them to pieces like pottery'ᵃ—

just as I have received authority from my Father. ²⁸I will also give him the morning star. ²⁹He who has an ear, let him hear what the Spirit says to the churches.

To the Church in Sardis

3 "To the angelᵇ of the church in Sardis write:

These are the words of him who holds the seven spiritsᶜ of God and the seven stars. I know your deeds; you have a reputation of being alive, but you are dead. ²Wake up! Strengthen what remains and is about to die, for I have not found your deeds complete in the sight of my God. ³Remember, therefore, what you have received and heard; obey it, and repent. But if you do not wake up, I will come like a thief, and you will not know at what time I will come to you.

⁴Yet you have a few people in Sardis who have not soiled their clothes. They will walk with me, dressed in white, for they are worthy. ⁵He who overcomes will, like them, be dressed in white. I will never blot out his name from the book of life, but will acknowledge his name before my Father and his angels. ⁶He who has an ear, let him

hear what the Spirit says to the churches.

To the Church in Philadelphia

⁷"To the angel of the church in Philadelphia write:

These are the words of him who is holy and true, who holds the key of David. What he opens no one can shut, and what he shuts no one can open. ⁸I know your deeds. See, I have placed before you an open door that no one can shut. I know that you have little strength, yet you have kept my word and have not denied my name. ⁹I will make those who are of the synagogue of Satan, who claim to be Jews though they are not, but are liars—I will make them come and fall down at your feet and acknowledge that I have loved you. ¹⁰Since you have kept my command to endure patiently, I will also keep you from the hour of trial that is going to come upon the whole world to test those who live on the earth.

¹¹I am coming soon. Hold on to what you have, so that no one will take your crown. ¹²Him who overcomes I will make a pillar in the temple of my God. Never again will he leave it. I will write on him the name of my God and the name of the city of my God, the new Jerusalem, which is coming down out of heaven from my God; and I will also write on him my new name. ¹³He who has an ear, let him hear what the Spirit says to the churches.

To the Church in Laodicea

¹⁴"To the angel of the church in Laodicea write:

These are the words of the Amen, the faithful and true witness, the ruler of God's creation. ¹⁵I know your deeds, that you are neither cold nor hot. I wish you were either one or the other! ¹⁶So, because you are lukewarm—neither hot nor cold—I am about to spit you out of my mouth. ¹⁷You say, 'I am rich; I have acquired wealth and do not need a thing.' But you do not realize that you are wretched, pitiful, poor,

---

ᵃ27 Psalm 2:9   ᵇ1 Or *messenger*; also in verses 7 and 14   ᶜ1 Or *the sevenfold Spirit*

blind and naked. [18]I counsel you to buy from me gold refined in the fire, so you can become rich; and white clothes to wear, so you can cover your shameful nakedness; and salve to put on your eyes, so you can see.

[19]Those whom I love I rebuke and discipline. So be earnest, and repent. [20]Here I am! I stand at the door and knock. If anyone hears my voice and opens the door, I will come in and eat with him, and he with me.

[21]To him who overcomes, I will give the right to sit with me on my throne, just as I overcame and sat down with my Father on his throne. [22]He who has an ear, let him hear what the Spirit says to the churches."

The Throne in Heaven

4 After this I looked, and there before me was a door standing open in heaven. And the voice I had first heard speaking to me like a trumpet said, "Come up here, and I will show you what must take place after this." [2]At once I was in the Spirit, and there before me was a throne in heaven with someone sitting on it. [3]And the one who sat there had the appearance of jasper and carnelian. A rainbow, resembling an emerald, encircled the throne. [4]Surrounding the throne were twenty-four other thrones, and seated on them were twenty-four elders. They were dressed in white and had crowns of gold on their heads. [5]From the throne came flashes of lightning, rumblings and peals of thunder. Before the throne, seven lamps were blazing. These are the seven spirits[a] of God. [6]Also before the throne there was what looked like a sea of glass, clear as crystal.

In the center, around the throne, were four living creatures, and they were covered with eyes, in front and in back. [7]The first living creature was like a lion, the second was like an ox, the third had a face like a man, the fourth was like a flying eagle. [8]Each of the four living creatures had six wings and was covered with eyes all around, even under his wings. Day and night they never stop saying:

"Holy, holy, holy
is the Lord God Almighty,
who was, and is, and is to come."

[9]Whenever the living creatures give glory, honor and thanks to him who sits on the throne and who lives for ever and ever, [10]the twenty-four elders fall down before him who sits on the throne, and worship him who lives for ever and ever. They lay their crowns before the throne and say:

[11]"You are worthy, our Lord and God,
to receive glory and honor and
power,
for you created all things,
and by your will they were created
and have their being."

The Scroll and the Lamb

5 Then I saw in the right hand of him who sat on the throne a scroll with writing on both sides and sealed with seven seals. [2]And I saw a mighty angel proclaiming in a loud voice, "Who is worthy to break the seals and open the scroll?" [3]But no one in heaven or on earth or under the earth could open the scroll or even look inside it. [4]I wept and wept because no one was found who was worthy to open the scroll or look inside. [5]Then one of the elders said to me, "Do not weep! See, the Lion of the tribe of Judah, the Root of David, has triumphed. He is able to open the scroll and its seven seals."

[6]Then I saw a Lamb, looking as if it had been slain, standing in the center of the throne, encircled by the four living creatures and the elders. He had seven horns and seven eyes, which are the seven spirits[a] of God sent out into all the earth. [7]He came and took the scroll from the right hand of him who sat on the throne. [8]And when he had taken it, the four living creatures and the twenty-four elders fell down before the Lamb. Each one had a harp and they were holding golden bowls full of incense, which are the prayers of the saints. [9]And they sang a new song:

"You are worthy to take the scroll
and to open its seals,
because you were slain,
and with your blood you
purchased men for God

---

[a]5,6 Or the sevenfold Spirit

from every tribe and language and people and nation.

[10] You have made them to be a
kingdom and priests to serve our God,
and they will reign on the earth."

[11] Then I looked and heard the voice of many angels, numbering thousands upon thousands, and ten thousand times ten thousand. They encircled the throne and the living creatures and the elders. [12] In a loud voice they sang:

"Worthy is the Lamb, who was slain,
to receive power and wealth and wisdom and strength
and honor and glory and praise!"

[13] Then I heard every creature in heaven and on earth and under the earth and on the sea, and all that is in them, singing:

"To him who sits on the throne and to the Lamb
be praise and honor and glory and power,
for ever and ever!"

[14] The four living creatures said, "Amen," and the elders fell down and worshiped.

The Seals

6 I watched as the Lamb opened the first of the seven seals. Then I heard one of the four living creatures say in a voice like thunder, "Come!" [2] I looked, and there before me was a white horse! Its rider held a bow, and he was

---

WEDNESDAY

VERSE:	AUTHOR:	PASSAGE:
Revelation 4:8	Gien Karssen	Revelation 4

Heavenly Restlessness

Human history clearly does not end in destruction and chaos, but in the glorification of God. This heavenly vision recorded in Revelation reveals him as the pivotal point of all of creation and world history. In the verses quoted above we find holy, heavenly restlessness. The heavenly creatures cannot keep their mouths—indeed, their very beings—from exalting the glory of God.

There is restlessness in heaven because the holiness of the triune God—Father, Son and Holy Spirit—has to be proclaimed without interruption. He is the Almighty, Creator and keeper of the universe and every living thing. He is the unchangeable, the eternal, who was and who is and who is to come: the Lord! Therefore, he is worthy to receive honor without ceasing. This eternal Lord is the Savior, who transformed sinful people into children of God.

People of every race and nationality will not stop thanking and worshiping Christ in eternity. He who humbled himself in the deepest hell is now exalted in the highest heaven. Therefore, all that is heard in heaven is, "Glory be to God."

We cannot do better than, by faith, to join this future heavenly host and exclaim joyfully, "Glory, Yes, Glory Be to God!"

ADDITIONAL SCRIPTURE READINGS:
Psalm 96; Psalm 150; Ephesians 1:6

Go to page 382 for your next devotional reading.

given a crown, and he rode out as a conqueror bent on conquest.

³When the Lamb opened the second seal, I heard the second living creature say, "Come!" ⁴Then another horse came out, a fiery red one. Its rider was given power to take peace from the earth and to make men slay each other. To him was given a large sword.

⁵When the Lamb opened the third seal, I heard the third living creature say, "Come!" I looked, and there before me was a black horse! Its rider was holding a pair of scales in his hand. ⁶Then I heard what sounded like a voice among the four living creatures, saying, "A quart*a* of wheat for a day's wages,*b* and three quarts of barley for a day's wages,*b* and do not damage the oil and the wine!"

⁷When the Lamb opened the fourth seal, I heard the voice of the fourth living creature say, "Come!" ⁸I looked, and there before me was a pale horse! Its rider was named Death, and Hades was following close behind him. They were given power over a fourth of the earth to kill by sword, famine and plague, and by the wild beasts of the earth.

⁹When he opened the fifth seal, I saw under the altar the souls of those who had been slain because of the word of God and the testimony they had maintained. ¹⁰They called out in a loud voice, "How long, Sovereign Lord, holy and true, until you judge the inhabitants of the earth and avenge our blood?" ¹¹Then each of them was given a white robe, and they were told to wait a little longer, until the number of their fellow servants and brothers who were to be killed as they had been was completed.

¹²I watched as he opened the sixth seal. There was a great earthquake. The sun turned black like sackcloth made of goat hair, the whole moon turned blood red, ¹³and the stars in the sky fell to earth, as late figs drop from a fig tree when shaken by a strong wind. ¹⁴The sky receded like a scroll, rolling up, and every mountain and island was removed from its place.

¹⁵Then the kings of the earth, the princes, the generals, the rich, the mighty, and every slave and every free man hid in caves and among the rocks of the mountains. ¹⁶They called to the mountains and the rocks, "Fall on us and hide us from the face of him who sits on the throne and from the wrath of the Lamb! ¹⁷For the great day of their wrath has come, and who can stand?"

144,000 Sealed

7 After this I saw four angels standing at the four corners of the earth, holding back the four winds of the earth to prevent any wind from blowing on the land or on the sea or on any tree. ²Then I saw another angel coming up from the east, having the seal of the living God. He called out in a loud voice to the four angels who had been given power to harm the land and the sea: ³"Do not harm the land or the sea or the trees until we put a seal on the foreheads of the servants of our God." ⁴Then I heard the number of those who were sealed: 144,000 from all the tribes of Israel.

⁵From the tribe of Judah 12,000
  were sealed,
 from the tribe of Reuben 12,000,
 from the tribe of Gad 12,000,
⁶from the tribe of Asher 12,000,
 from the tribe of Naphtali 12,000,
 from the tribe of Manasseh
  12,000,
⁷from the tribe of Simeon 12,000,
 from the tribe of Levi 12,000,
 from the tribe of Issachar 12,000,
⁸from the tribe of Zebulun 12,000,
 from the tribe of Joseph 12,000,
 from the tribe of Benjamin 12,000.

The Great Multitude in White Robes

⁹After this I looked and there before me was a great multitude that no one could count, from every nation, tribe, people and language, standing before the throne and in front of the Lamb. They were wearing white robes and were holding palm branches in their hands. ¹⁰And they cried out in a loud voice:

"Salvation belongs to our God,
 who sits on the throne,
 and to the Lamb."

¹¹All the angels were standing around the throne and around the elders and the four living creatures. They fell down on their faces before the throne and worshiped God, ¹²saying:

---

*a*6 Greek *a choinix* (probably about a liter)   *b*6 Greek *a denarius*

"Amen!
Praise and glory
and wisdom and thanks and honor
and power and strength
be to our God for ever and ever.
Amen!"

13Then one of the elders asked me, "These in white robes—who are they, and where did they come from?"

14I answered, "Sir, you know."

And he said, "These are they who have come out of the great tribulation; they have washed their robes and made them white in the blood of the Lamb. **15**Therefore,

"they are before the throne of God
    and serve him day and night in
        his temple;
and he who sits on the throne will
        spread his tent over them.
16Never again will they hunger;
    never again will they thirst.
The sun will not beat upon them,
    nor any scorching heat.
17For the Lamb at the center of the
        throne will be their shepherd;
    he will lead them to springs of
        living water.
And God will wipe away every tear
    from their eyes."

The Seventh Seal and the Golden Censer

8 When he opened the seventh seal, there was silence in heaven for about half an hour.

2And I saw the seven angels who stand before God, and to them were given seven trumpets.

3Another angel, who had a golden censer, came and stood at the altar. He was given much incense to offer, with the prayers of all the saints, on the golden altar before the throne. **4**The smoke of the incense, together with the prayers of the saints, went up before God from the angel's hand. **5**Then the angel took the censer, filled it with fire from the altar, and hurled it on the earth; and there came peals of thunder, rumblings, flashes of lightning and an earthquake.

The Trumpets

6Then the seven angels who had the seven trumpets prepared to sound them.

7The first angel sounded his trumpet, and there came hail and fire mixed with blood, and it was hurled down upon the earth. A third of the earth was burned up, a third of the trees were burned up, and all the green grass was burned up.

8The second angel sounded his trumpet, and something like a huge mountain, all ablaze, was thrown into the sea. A third of the sea turned into blood, **9**a third of the living creatures in the sea died, and a third of the ships were destroyed.

10The third angel sounded his trumpet, and a great star, blazing like a torch, fell from the sky on a third of the rivers and on the springs of water— **11**the name of the star is Wormwood.[a] A third of the waters turned bitter, and many people died from the waters that had become bitter.

12The fourth angel sounded his trumpet, and a third of the sun was struck, a third of the moon, and a third of the stars, so that a third of them turned dark. A third of the day was without light, and also a third of the night.

13As I watched, I heard an eagle that was flying in midair call out in a loud voice: "Woe! Woe! Woe to the inhabitants of the earth, because of the trumpet blasts about to be sounded by the other three angels!"

9 The fifth angel sounded his trumpet, and I saw a star that had fallen from the sky to the earth. The star was given the key to the shaft of the Abyss. **2**When he opened the Abyss, smoke rose from it like the smoke from a gigantic furnace. The sun and sky were darkened by the smoke from the Abyss. **3**And out of the smoke locusts came down upon the earth and were given power like that of scorpions of the earth. **4**They were told not to harm the grass of the earth or any plant or tree, but only those people who did not have the seal of God on their foreheads. **5**They were not given power to kill them, but only to torture them for five months. And the agony they suffered was like that of the sting of a scorpion when it strikes a man. **6**During those days men will seek death, but will not find it; they will long to die, but death will elude them.

---

a 11 That is, Bitterness

[7]The locusts looked like horses prepared for battle. On their heads they wore something like crowns of gold, and their faces resembled human faces. [8]Their hair was like women's hair, and their teeth were like lions' teeth. [9]They had breastplates like breastplates of iron, and the sound of their wings was like the thundering of many horses and chariots rushing into battle. [10]They had tails and stings like scorpions, and in their tails they had power to torment people for five months. [11]They had as king over them the angel of the Abyss, whose name in Hebrew is Abaddon, and in Greek, Apollyon.[a]

[12]The first woe is past; two other woes are yet to come.

[13]The sixth angel sounded his trumpet, and I heard a voice coming from the horns[b] of the golden altar that is before God. [14]It said to the sixth angel who had the trumpet, "Release the four angels who are bound at the great river Euphrates." [15]And the four angels who had been kept ready for this very hour and day and month and year were released to kill a third of mankind. [16]The number of the mounted troops was two hundred million. I heard their number.

[17]The horses and riders I saw in my vision looked like this: Their breastplates were fiery red, dark blue, and yellow as sulfur. The heads of the horses resembled the heads of lions, and out of their mouths came fire, smoke and sulfur. [18]A third of mankind was killed by the three plagues of fire, smoke and sulfur that came out of their mouths. [19]The power of the horses was in their mouths and in their tails; for their tails were like snakes, having heads with which they inflict injury.

[20]The rest of mankind that were not killed by these plagues still did not repent of the work of their hands; they did not stop worshiping demons, and idols of gold, silver, bronze, stone and wood—idols that cannot see or hear or walk. [21]Nor did they repent of their murders, their magic arts, their sexual immorality or their thefts.

The Angel and the Little Scroll

10 Then I saw another mighty angel coming down from heaven. He was robed in a cloud, with a rainbow above his head; his face was like the sun, and his legs were like fiery pillars. [2]He was holding a little scroll, which lay open in his hand. He planted his right foot on the sea and his left foot on the land, [3]and he gave a loud shout like the roar of a lion. When he shouted, the voices of the seven thunders spoke. [4]And when the seven thunders spoke, I was about to write; but I heard a voice from heaven say, "Seal up what the seven thunders have said and do not write it down."

[5]Then the angel I had seen standing on the sea and on the land raised his right hand to heaven. [6]And he swore by him who lives for ever and ever, who created the heavens and all that is in them, the earth and all that is in it, and the sea and all that is in it, and said, "There will be no more delay! [7]But in the days when the seventh angel is about to sound his trumpet, the mystery of God will be accomplished, just as he announced to his servants the prophets."

[8]Then the voice that I had heard from heaven spoke to me once more: "Go, take the scroll that lies open in the hand of the angel who is standing on the sea and on the land."

[9]So I went to the angel and asked him to give me the little scroll. He said to me, "Take it and eat it. It will turn your stomach sour, but in your mouth it will be as sweet as honey." [10]I took the little scroll from the angel's hand and ate it. It tasted as sweet as honey in my mouth, but when I had eaten it, my stomach turned sour. [11]Then I was told, "You must prophesy again about many peoples, nations, languages and kings."

The Two Witnesses

11 I was given a reed like a measuring rod and was told, "Go and measure the temple of God and the altar, and count the worshipers there. [2]But exclude the outer court; do not measure it, because it has been given to the Gentiles. They will trample on the holy city for 42 months. [3]And I will give power to my two witnesses, and they will prophesy for 1,260 days, clothed in sackcloth." [4]These are the two olive trees and the two lampstands that stand before the Lord of the earth. [5]If anyone tries to harm them, fire comes from their

---

[a] 11 Abaddon and Apollyon mean Destroyer.   [b] 13 That is, projections

mouths and devours their enemies. This is how anyone who wants to harm them must die. **6**These men have power to shut up the sky so that it will not rain during the time they are prophesying; and they have power to turn the waters into blood and to strike the earth with every kind of plague as often as they want.

7Now when they have finished their testimony, the beast that comes up from the Abyss will attack them, and overpower and kill them. **8**Their bodies will lie in the street of the great city, which is figuratively called Sodom and Egypt, where also their Lord was crucified. **9**For three and a half days men from every people, tribe, language and nation will gaze on their bodies and refuse them burial. **10**The inhabitants of the earth will gloat over them and will celebrate by sending each other gifts, because these two prophets had tormented those who live on the earth.

11But after the three and a half days a breath of life from God entered them, and they stood on their feet, and terror struck those who saw them. **12**Then they heard a loud voice from heaven saying to them, "Come up here." And they went up to heaven in a cloud, while their enemies looked on.

13At that very hour there was a severe earthquake and a tenth of the city collapsed. Seven thousand people were killed in the earthquake, and the survivors were terrified and gave glory to the God of heaven.

14The second woe has passed; the third woe is coming soon.

The Seventh Trumpet

15The seventh angel sounded his trumpet, and there were loud voices in heaven, which said:

"The kingdom of the world has
        become the kingdom of our
        Lord and of his Christ,
    and he will reign for ever and
        ever."

16And the twenty-four elders, who were seated on their thrones before God, fell on their faces and worshiped God, **17**saying:

"We give thanks to you, Lord God
        Almighty,
    the One who is and who was,

because you have taken your great
        power
    and have begun to reign.
18The nations were angry;
    and your wrath has come.
The time has come for judging the
        dead,
    and for rewarding your servants
        the prophets
and your saints and those who
        reverence your name,
    both small and great—
and for destroying those who
        destroy the earth."

19Then God's temple in heaven was opened, and within his temple was seen the ark of his covenant. And there came flashes of lightning, rumblings, peals of thunder, an earthquake and a great hailstorm.

The Woman and the Dragon

12 A great and wondrous sign appeared in heaven: a woman clothed with the sun, with the moon under her feet and a crown of twelve stars on her head. **2**She was pregnant and cried out in pain as she was about to give birth. **3**Then another sign appeared in heaven: an enormous red dragon with seven heads and ten horns and seven crowns on his heads. **4**His tail swept a third of the stars out of the sky and flung them to the earth. The dragon stood in front of the woman who was about to give birth, so that he might devour her child the moment it was born. **5**She gave birth to a son, a male child, who will rule all the nations with an iron scepter. And her child was snatched up to God and to his throne. **6**The woman fled into the desert to a place prepared for her by God, where she might be taken care of for 1,260 days.

7And there was war in heaven. Michael and his angels fought against the dragon, and the dragon and his angels fought back. **8**But he was not strong enough, and they lost their place in heaven. **9**The great dragon was hurled down—that ancient serpent called the devil, or Satan, who leads the whole world astray. He was hurled to the earth, and his angels with him.

10Then I heard a loud voice in heaven say:

"Now have come the salvation and
　　the power and the kingdom of
　　our God,
and the authority of his Christ.
For the accuser of our brothers,
　　who accuses them before our God
　　day and night,
has been hurled down.
¹¹They overcame him
　　by the blood of the Lamb
　　and by the word of their
　　testimony;
they did not love their lives so
　　much

as to shrink from death.
¹²Therefore rejoice, you heavens
　　and you who dwell in them!
But woe to the earth and the sea,
　　because the devil has gone down
　　to you!
He is filled with fury,
　　because he knows that his time is
　　short."

¹³When the dragon saw that he had
been hurled to the earth, he pursued the
woman who had given birth to the male
child. ¹⁴The woman was given the two

THURSDAY

VERSE:	AUTHOR:	PASSAGE:
Revelation 12:7–9	Ann Spangler	Revelation 12:7–17

When the Devil Lives Next Door

I don't know about you, but I have been tempted to utter a sarcastic "thanks a lot" to Michael and his angels for ejecting Satan and his cohorts from the heavenly realms. Couldn't they have tossed him into an unpopulated region of the universe? In a sense, the devil is now everyone's neighbor.

Knowing that the devil is on the loose is a sobering matter. But the Scriptures tell us how to engage in spiritual combat so that we needn't be afraid of Satan, "because the one who is in you is greater than the one who is in the world" (1 John 4:4). We need to arm ourselves with the tactics and weapons of heaven, rather than the strategies of this world. The more the gospel penetrates our lives, the more we will perceive that the weapons of Christ are humility, obedience to the Father, trust and faith, truth, right living and the Word of God, which is the "sword of the Spirit" (Ephesians 6:17).

We are not to let the neighborhood go to the devil, but we are to claim this earth for God's kingdom. As Scripture says, "The earth is the LORD's and everything in it" (Psalm 24:1). Jesus is in the business of recapturing territory for God, and we are enlisted in his army . . . As we fight the enemy, let us remember the prayer that Jesus taught us: "Our Father, in heaven, hallowed be your name, your kingdom come, your will be done on earth as it is in heaven" (Matthew 6:9–10). Let's bring the kingdom into our own neighborhoods. The more that heaven encroaches upon the earth, the less our enemy will like it here.

ADDITIONAL SCRIPTURE READINGS:
Ephesians 6:16–17; 1 John 2:13; Revelation 20:10–14

Go to page 390 for your next devotional reading.

wings of a great eagle, so that she might fly to the place prepared for her in the desert, where she would be taken care of for a time, times and half a time, out of the serpent's reach. **15**Then from his mouth the serpent spewed water like a river, to overtake the woman and sweep her away with the torrent. **16**But the earth helped the woman by opening its mouth and swallowing the river that the dragon had spewed out of his mouth. **17**Then the dragon was enraged at the woman and went off to make war against the rest of her offspring—those who obey God's commandments and hold to the testimony of Jesus. **1**And the dragon*a* stood on the shore of the sea.

13

The Beast out of the Sea

And I saw a beast coming out of the sea. He had ten horns and seven heads, with ten crowns on his horns, and on each head a blasphemous name. **2**The beast I saw resembled a leopard, but had feet like those of a bear and a mouth like that of a lion. The dragon gave the beast his power and his throne and great authority. **3**One of the heads of the beast seemed to have had a fatal wound, but the fatal wound had been healed. The whole world was astonished and followed the beast. **4**Men worshiped the dragon because he had given authority to the beast, and they also worshiped the beast and asked, "Who is like the beast? Who can make war against him?"

5The beast was given a mouth to utter proud words and blasphemies and to exercise his authority for forty-two months. **6**He opened his mouth to blaspheme God, and to slander his name and his dwelling place and those who live in heaven. **7**He was given power to make war against the saints and to conquer them. And he was given authority over every tribe, people, language and nation. **8**All inhabitants of the earth will worship the beast—all whose names have not been written in the book of life belonging to the Lamb that was slain from the creation of the world.*b*

9He who has an ear, let him hear.

10If anyone is to go into captivity,
    into captivity he will go.
If anyone is to be killed*c* with the
    sword,
    with the sword he will be killed.

This calls for patient endurance and faithfulness on the part of the saints.

The Beast out of the Earth

11Then I saw another beast, coming out of the earth. He had two horns like a lamb, but he spoke like a dragon. **12**He exercised all the authority of the first beast on his behalf, and made the earth and its inhabitants worship the first beast, whose fatal wound had been healed. **13**And he performed great and miraculous signs, even causing fire to come down from heaven to earth in full view of men. **14**Because of the signs he was given power to do on behalf of the first beast, he deceived the inhabitants of the earth. He ordered them to set up an image in honor of the beast who was wounded by the sword and yet lived. **15**He was given power to give breath to the image of the first beast, so that it could speak and cause all who refused to worship the image to be killed. **16**He also forced everyone, small and great, rich and poor, free and slave, to receive a mark on his right hand or on his forehead, **17**so that no one could buy or sell unless he had the mark, which is the name of the beast or the number of his name.

18This calls for wisdom. If anyone has insight, let him calculate the number of the beast, for it is man's number. His number is 666.

The Lamb and the 144,000

14 Then I looked, and there before me was the Lamb, standing on Mount Zion, and with him 144,000 who had his name and his Father's name written on their foreheads. **2**And I heard a sound from heaven like the roar of rushing waters and like a loud peal of thunder. The sound I heard was like that of harpists playing their harps. **3**And they sang a new song before the throne and before the four living creatures and the elders. No one could learn the song except the 144,000 who had been redeemed from the earth. **4**These are those who did not defile themselves with

---

a1 Some late manuscripts *And I belonging to the Lamb that was slain*   *b8* Or *written from the creation of the world in the book of life*   *c10* Some manuscripts *anyone kills*

women, for they kept themselves pure. They follow the Lamb wherever he goes. They were purchased from among men and offered as firstfruits to God and the Lamb. **5**No lie was found in their mouths; they are blameless.

The Three Angels

6Then I saw another angel flying in midair, and he had the eternal gospel to proclaim to those who live on the earth—to every nation, tribe, language and people. **7**He said in a loud voice, "Fear God and give him glory, because the hour of his judgment has come. Worship him who made the heavens, the earth, the sea and the springs of water."

8A second angel followed and said, "Fallen! Fallen is Babylon the Great, which made all the nations drink the maddening wine of her adulteries."

9A third angel followed them and said in a loud voice: "If anyone worships the beast and his image and receives his mark on the forehead or on the hand, **10**he, too, will drink of the wine of God's fury, which has been poured full strength into the cup of his wrath. He will be tormented with burning sulfur in the presence of the holy angels and of the Lamb. **11**And the smoke of their torment rises for ever and ever. There is no rest day or night for those who worship the beast and his image, or for anyone who receives the mark of his name." **12**This calls for patient endurance on the part of the saints who obey God's commandments and remain faithful to Jesus.

13Then I heard a voice from heaven say, "Write: Blessed are the dead who die in the Lord from now on."

"Yes," says the Spirit, "they will rest from their labor, for their deeds will follow them."

The Harvest of the Earth

14I looked, and there before me was a white cloud, and seated on the cloud was one "like a son of man"[a] with a crown of gold on his head and a sharp sickle in his hand. **15**Then another angel came out of the temple and called in a loud voice to him who was sitting on the cloud, "Take your sickle and reap, because the time to reap has come, for the harvest of the earth is ripe." **16**So he who was seated on the cloud swung his sickle over the earth, and the earth was harvested.

17Another angel came out of the temple in heaven, and he too had a sharp sickle. **18**Still another angel, who had charge of the fire, came from the altar and called in a loud voice to him who had the sharp sickle, "Take your sharp sickle and gather the clusters of grapes from the earth's vine, because its grapes are ripe." **19**The angel swung his sickle on the earth, gathered its grapes and threw them into the great winepress of God's wrath. **20**They were trampled in the winepress outside the city, and blood flowed out of the press, rising as high as the horses' bridles for a distance of 1,600 stadia.[b]

Seven Angels With Seven Plagues

15 I saw in heaven another great and marvelous sign: seven angels with the seven last plagues—last, because with them God's wrath is completed. **2**And I saw what looked like a sea of glass mixed with fire and, standing beside the sea, those who had been victorious over the beast and his image and over the number of his name. They held harps given them by God **3**and sang the song of Moses the servant of God and the song of the Lamb:

"Great and marvelous are your
       deeds,
    Lord God Almighty.
Just and true are your ways,
    King of the ages.
4Who will not fear you, O Lord,
    and bring glory to your name?
For you alone are holy.
All nations will come
    and worship before you,
for your righteous acts have been
       revealed."

5After this I looked and in heaven the temple, that is, the tabernacle of the Testimony, was opened. **6**Out of the temple came the seven angels with the seven plagues. They were dressed in clean, shining linen and wore golden sashes around their chests. **7**Then one of the four living creatures gave to the seven angels seven golden bowls filled with the wrath of God, who lives for ever and

---

a 14 Daniel 7:13   *b 20* That is, about 180 miles (about 300 kilometers)

ever. **8**And the temple was filled with smoke from the glory of God and from his power, and no one could enter the temple until the seven plagues of the seven angels were completed.

The Seven Bowls of God's Wrath

16 Then I heard a loud voice from the temple saying to the seven angels, "Go, pour out the seven bowls of God's wrath on the earth."

2The first angel went and poured out his bowl on the land, and ugly and painful sores broke out on the people who had the mark of the beast and worshiped his image.

3The second angel poured out his bowl on the sea, and it turned into blood like that of a dead man, and every living thing in the sea died.

4The third angel poured out his bowl on the rivers and springs of water, and they became blood. **5**Then I heard the angel in charge of the waters say:

"You are just in these judgments,
   you who are and who were, the
      Holy One,
   because you have so judged;
6for they have shed the blood of your
      saints and prophets,
   and you have given them blood to
      drink as they deserve."

7And I heard the altar respond:

"Yes, Lord God Almighty,
   true and just are your judgments."

8The fourth angel poured out his bowl on the sun, and the sun was given power to scorch people with fire. **9**They were seared by the intense heat and they cursed the name of God, who had control over these plagues, but they refused to repent and glorify him.

10The fifth angel poured out his bowl on the throne of the beast, and his kingdom was plunged into darkness. Men gnawed their tongues in agony **11**and cursed the God of heaven because of their pains and their sores, but they refused to repent of what they had done.

12The sixth angel poured out his bowl on the great river Euphrates, and its water was dried up to prepare the way for the kings from the East. **13**Then I saw three evil*a* spirits that looked like frogs;

they came out of the mouth of the dragon, out of the mouth of the beast and out of the mouth of the false prophet. **14**They are spirits of demons performing miraculous signs, and they go out to the kings of the whole world, to gather them for the battle on the great day of God Almighty.

15"Behold, I come like a thief! Blessed is he who stays awake and keeps his clothes with him, so that he may not go naked and be shamefully exposed."

16Then they gathered the kings together to the place that in Hebrew is called Armageddon.

17The seventh angel poured out his bowl into the air, and out of the temple came a loud voice from the throne, saying, "It is done!" **18**Then there came flashes of lightning, rumblings, peals of thunder and a severe earthquake. No earthquake like it has ever occurred since man has been on earth, so tremendous was the quake. **19**The great city split into three parts, and the cities of the nations collapsed. God remembered Babylon the Great and gave her the cup filled with the wine of the fury of his wrath. **20**Every island fled away and the mountains could not be found. **21**From the sky huge hailstones of about a hundred pounds each fell upon men. And they cursed God on account of the plague of hail, because the plague was so terrible.

The Woman on the Beast

17 One of the seven angels who had the seven bowls came and said to me, "Come, I will show you the punishment of the great prostitute, who sits on many waters. **2**With her the kings of the earth committed adultery and the inhabitants of the earth were intoxicated with the wine of her adulteries."

3Then the angel carried me away in the Spirit into a desert. There I saw a woman sitting on a scarlet beast that was covered with blasphemous names and had seven heads and ten horns. **4**The woman was dressed in purple and scarlet, and was glittering with gold, precious stones and pearls. She held a golden cup in her hand, filled with abominable things and the filth of her adulteries. **5**This title was written on her forehead:

a13 Greek *unclean*

MYSTERY
BABYLON THE GREAT
THE MOTHER OF PROSTITUTES
AND OF THE ABOMINATIONS OF THE EARTH.

⁶I saw that the woman was drunk with the blood of the saints, the blood of those who bore testimony to Jesus.

When I saw her, I was greatly astonished. ⁷Then the angel said to me: "Why are you astonished? I will explain to you the mystery of the woman and of the beast she rides, which has the seven heads and ten horns. ⁸The beast, which you saw, once was, now is not, and will come up out of the Abyss and go to his destruction. The inhabitants of the earth whose names have not been written in the book of life from the creation of the world will be astonished when they see the beast, because he once was, now is not, and yet will come.

⁹"This calls for a mind with wisdom. The seven heads are seven hills on which the woman sits. ¹⁰They are also seven kings. Five have fallen, one is, the other has not yet come; but when he does come, he must remain for a little while. ¹¹The beast who once was, and now is not, is an eighth king. He belongs to the seven and is going to his destruction.

¹²"The ten horns you saw are ten kings who have not yet received a kingdom, but who for one hour will receive authority as kings along with the beast. ¹³They have one purpose and will give their power and authority to the beast. ¹⁴They will make war against the Lamb, but the Lamb will overcome them because he is Lord of lords and King of kings—and with him will be his called, chosen and faithful followers."

¹⁵Then the angel said to me, "The waters you saw, where the prostitute sits, are peoples, multitudes, nations and languages. ¹⁶The beast and the ten horns you saw will hate the prostitute. They will bring her to ruin and leave her naked; they will eat her flesh and burn her with fire. ¹⁷For God has put it into their hearts to accomplish his purpose by agreeing to give the beast their power to rule, until God's words are fulfilled. ¹⁸The woman you saw is the great city that rules over the kings of the earth."

The Fall of Babylon

18 After this I saw another angel coming down from heaven. He had great authority, and the earth was illuminated by his splendor. ²With a mighty voice he shouted:

"Fallen! Fallen is Babylon the Great!
She has become a home for demons
and a haunt for every evil*a* spirit,
a haunt for every unclean and detestable bird.
³For all the nations have drunk
the maddening wine of her adulteries.
The kings of the earth committed adultery with her,
and the merchants of the earth grew rich from her excessive luxuries."

⁴Then I heard another voice from heaven say:

"Come out of her, my people,
so that you will not share in her sins,
so that you will not receive any of her plagues;
⁵for her sins are piled up to heaven,
and God has remembered her crimes.
⁶Give back to her as she has given;
pay her back double for what she has done.
Mix her a double portion from her own cup.
⁷Give her as much torture and grief
as the glory and luxury she gave herself.
In her heart she boasts,
'I sit as queen; I am not a widow,
and I will never mourn.'
⁸Therefore in one day her plagues will overtake her:
death, mourning and famine.
She will be consumed by fire,
for mighty is the Lord God who judges her.

⁹"When the kings of the earth who committed adultery with her and shared her luxury see the smoke of her burning, they will weep and mourn over her. ¹⁰Terrified at her torment, they will stand far off and cry:

" 'Woe! Woe, O great city,

---

*a*2 Greek *unclean*

O Babylon, city of power!
In one hour your doom has come!'

11 "The merchants of the earth will weep and mourn over her because no one buys their cargoes any more— **12** cargoes of gold, silver, precious stones and pearls; fine linen, purple, silk and scarlet cloth; every sort of citron wood, and articles of every kind made of ivory, costly wood, bronze, iron and marble; **13** cargoes of cinnamon and spice, of incense, myrrh and frankincense, of wine and olive oil, of fine flour and wheat; cattle and sheep; horses and carriages; and bodies and souls of men.

14 "They will say, 'The fruit you longed for is gone from you. All your riches and splendor have vanished, never to be recovered.' **15** The merchants who sold these things and gained their wealth from her will stand far off, terrified at her torment. They will weep and mourn **16** and cry out:

" 'Woe! Woe, O great city,
dressed in fine linen, purple and
scarlet,
and glittering with gold, precious
stones and pearls!
17 In one hour such great wealth has
been brought to ruin!'

"Every sea captain, and all who travel by ship, the sailors, and all who earn their living from the sea, will stand far off. **18** When they see the smoke of her burning, they will exclaim, 'Was there ever a city like this great city?' **19** They will throw dust on their heads, and with weeping and mourning cry out:

" 'Woe! Woe, O great city,
where all who had ships on the
sea
became rich through her wealth!
In one hour she has been brought to
ruin!
20 Rejoice over her, O heaven!
Rejoice, saints and apostles and
prophets!
God has judged her for the way she
treated you.' "

21 Then a mighty angel picked up a boulder the size of a large millstone and threw it into the sea, and said:

"With such violence
the great city of Babylon will be
thrown down,

never to be found again.
22 The music of harpists and
musicians, flute players and
trumpeters,
will never be heard in you again.
No workman of any trade
will ever be found in you again.
The sound of a millstone
will never be heard in you again.
23 The light of a lamp
will never shine in you again.
The voice of bridegroom and bride
will never be heard in you again.
Your merchants were the world's
great men.
By your magic spell all the nations
were led astray.
24 In her was found the blood of
prophets and of the saints,
and of all who have been killed on
the earth."

Hallelujah!

19 After this I heard what sounded like the roar of a great multitude in heaven shouting:

"Hallelujah!
Salvation and glory and power
belong to our God,
2 for true and just are his
judgments.
He has condemned the great
prostitute
who corrupted the earth by her
adulteries.
He has avenged on her the blood of
his servants."

3 And again they shouted:

"Hallelujah!
The smoke from her goes up for ever
and ever."

4 The twenty-four elders and the four living creatures fell down and worshiped God, who was seated on the throne. And they cried:

"Amen, Hallelujah!"

5 Then a voice came from the throne, saying:

"Praise our God,
all you his servants,
you who fear him,
both small and great!"

6 Then I heard what sounded like a great multitude, like the roar of rushing waters and like loud peals of thunder, shouting:

"Hallelujah!
  For our Lord God Almighty reigns.
[7]Let us rejoice and be glad
  and give him glory!
For the wedding of the Lamb has
  come,
  and his bride has made herself
  ready.
[8]Fine linen, bright and clean,
  was given her to wear."

(Fine linen stands for the righteous acts of the saints.)

[9]Then the angel said to me, "Write: 'Blessed are those who are invited to the wedding supper of the Lamb!' " And he added, "These are the true words of God."

[10]At this I fell at his feet to worship him. But he said to me, "Do not do it! I am a fellow servant with you and with your brothers who hold to the testimony of Jesus. Worship God! For the testimony of Jesus is the spirit of prophecy."

The Rider on the White Horse

[11]I saw heaven standing open and there before me was a white horse, whose rider is called Faithful and True. With justice he judges and makes war. [12]His eyes are like blazing fire, and on his head are many crowns. He has a name written on him that no one knows but he himself. [13]He is dressed in a robe dipped in blood, and his name is the Word of God. [14]The armies of heaven were following him, riding on white horses and dressed in fine linen, white and clean. [15]Out of his mouth comes a sharp sword with which to strike down the nations. "He will rule them with an iron scepter."[a] He treads the winepress of the fury of the wrath of God Almighty. [16]On his robe and on his thigh he has this name written:

KING OF KINGS AND LORD OF LORDS.

[17]And I saw an angel standing in the sun, who cried in a loud voice to all the birds flying in midair, "Come, gather together for the great supper of God, [18]so that you may eat the flesh of kings, generals, and mighty men, of horses and their riders, and the flesh of all people, free and slave, small and great."

[19]Then I saw the beast and the kings of the earth and their armies gathered together to make war against the rider on the horse and his army. [20]But the beast was captured, and with him the false prophet who had performed the miraculous signs on his behalf. With these signs he had deluded those who had received the mark of the beast and worshiped his image. The two of them were thrown alive into the fiery lake of burning sulfur. [21]The rest of them were killed with the sword that came out of the mouth of the rider on the horse, and all the birds gorged themselves on their flesh.

The Thousand Years

20 And I saw an angel coming down out of heaven, having the key to the Abyss and holding in his hand a great chain. [2]He seized the dragon, that ancient serpent, who is the devil, or Satan, and bound him for a thousand years. [3]He threw him into the Abyss, and locked and sealed it over him, to keep him from deceiving the nations anymore until the thousand years were ended. After that, he must be set free for a short time.

[4]I saw thrones on which were seated those who had been given authority to judge. And I saw the souls of those who had been beheaded because of their testimony for Jesus and because of the word of God. They had not worshiped the beast or his image and had not received his mark on their foreheads or their hands. They came to life and reigned with Christ a thousand years. [5](The rest of the dead did not come to life until the thousand years were ended.) This is the first resurrection. [6]Blessed and holy are those who have part in the first resurrection. The second death has no power over them, but they will be priests of God and of Christ and will reign with him for a thousand years.

Satan's Doom

[7]When the thousand years are over, Satan will be released from his prison [8]and will go out to deceive the nations in the four corners of the earth—Gog and Magog—to gather them for battle. In

number they are like the sand on the seashore. **9**They marched across the breadth of the earth and surrounded the camp of God's people, the city he loves. But fire came down from heaven and devoured them. **10**And the devil, who deceived them, was thrown into the lake of burning sulfur, where the beast and the false prophet had been thrown. They will be tormented day and night for ever and ever.

The Dead Are Judged

11Then I saw a great white throne and him who was seated on it. Earth and sky fled from his presence, and there was no place for them. **12**And I saw the dead, great and small, standing before the throne, and books were opened. Another book was opened, which is the book of life. The dead were judged according to what they had done as recorded in the books. **13**The sea gave up the dead that were in it, and death and Hades gave up the dead that were in them, and each person was judged according to what he had done. **14**Then death and Hades were thrown into the lake of fire. The lake of fire is the second death. **15**If anyone's name was not found written in the book of life, he was thrown into the lake of fire.

The New Jerusalem

21 Then I saw a new heaven and a new earth, for the first heaven and the first earth had passed away, and there was no longer any sea. **2**I saw the Holy City, the new Jerusalem, coming down out of heaven from God, prepared as a bride beautifully dressed for her husband. **3**And I heard a loud voice from the throne saying, "Now the dwelling of God is with men, and he will live with them. They will be his people, and God himself will be with them and be their God. **4**He will wipe every tear from their eyes. There will be no more death or mourning or crying or pain, for the old order of things has passed away."

5He who was seated on the throne said, "I am making everything new!" Then he said, "Write this down, for these words are trustworthy and true."

6He said to me: "It is done. I am the Alpha and the Omega, the Beginning and the End. To him who is thirsty I will give to drink without cost from the spring of the water of life. **7**He who overcomes will inherit all this, and I will be his God and he will be my son. **8**But the cowardly, the unbelieving, the vile, the murderers, the sexually immoral, those who practice magic arts, the idolaters and all liars—their place will be in the fiery lake of burning sulfur. This is the second death."

9One of the seven angels who had the seven bowls full of the seven last plagues came and said to me, "Come, I will show you the bride, the wife of the Lamb." **10**And he carried me away in the Spirit to a mountain great and high, and showed me the Holy City, Jerusalem, coming down out of heaven from God. **11**It shone with the glory of God, and its brilliance was like that of a very precious jewel, like a jasper, clear as crystal. **12**It had a great, high wall with twelve gates, and with twelve angels at the gates. On the gates were written the names of the twelve tribes of Israel. **13**There were three gates on the east, three on the north, three on the south and three on the west. **14**The wall of the city had twelve foundations, and on them were the names of the twelve apostles of the Lamb.

15The angel who talked with me had a measuring rod of gold to measure the city, its gates and its walls. **16**The city was laid out like a square, as long as it was wide. He measured the city with the rod and found it to be 12,000 stadia*a* in length, and as wide and high as it is long. **17**He measured its wall and it was 144 cubits*b* thick,*c* by man's measurement, which the angel was using. **18**The wall was made of jasper, and the city of pure gold, as pure as glass. **19**The foundations of the city walls were decorated with every kind of precious stone. The first foundation was jasper, the second sapphire, the third chalcedony, the fourth emerald, **20**the fifth sardonyx, the sixth carnelian, the seventh chrysolite, the eighth beryl, the ninth topaz, the tenth chrysoprase, the eleventh jacinth, and the twelfth amethyst.*d* **21**The twelve gates were twelve pearls, each gate made

---

a16 That is, about 1,400 miles (about 2,200 kilometers)   *b17* That is, about 200 feet (about 65 meters)   *c17* Or *high*   *d20* The precise identification of some of these precious stones is uncertain.

of a single pearl. The great street of the city was of pure gold, like transparent glass.

²¹I did not see a temple in the city, because the Lord God Almighty and the Lamb are its temple. ²³The city does not need the sun or the moon to shine on it, for the glory of God gives it light, and the Lamb is its lamp. ²⁴The nations will walk by its light, and the kings of the earth will bring their splendor into it. ²⁵On no day will its gates ever be shut,

---

FRIDAY

VERSE:	AUTHOR:	PASSAGE:
Revelation 21:20	Georgalyn Wilkinson	Revelation 21

Insignificantly Significant

My thirty-sixth birthday had been special. David, my wonderful husband, had seen to that. But just twelve days later, I stood by his hospital bed watching him fade into eternity.

Life had been so full. What more could I have wanted than to be missionaries to a desperately needy country like Japan? We were excited with our assignment there. Never could I have dreamed that on a mission trip to Korea David would have encountered physical problems which would in three short days take his life.

I stood beside his bed—numb and totally alone. I didn't know another woman in Korea. My precious daughters, six and eight years old, were at home where loving neighbors reached out to them in my place. They read to them about where their daddy had just gone to live. The girls had never thought so much about heaven before.

The thing I least wanted to do on this trip was to shop—for anything. But I hated to return home with no gift for my girls. On my way out of my hotel to the airport, I passed the gift shop. Not a toy or child's item was in sight. But there was a display of a very inexpensive, [and] typical, souvenir of Korea—the topaz stone. Quickly, I purchased two tiny necklaces and tucked them into my bag.

Our reunion was tearful, but wonderful. I gave them the insignificant gifts I'd found just before leaving. My eight-year-old burst out, "Mom, have you ever read Revelation?!"

"Well, yes, as a matter of fact, many times."

But before I could say more, she jumped with delight, for there in her hands she actually held a topaz, a piece of the place where her daddy was now standing. "It's the ninth layer, Mom!"

I could have given her no greater gift, for a chunk of heaven was hers that day—and would always be.

ADDITIONAL SCRIPTURE READINGS:
1 Corinthians 15:20–28; 1 Thessalonians 4:13–18; 1 Peter 1:3–6

Go to page 391 for your next devotional reading.

WEEKENDING

REJOICE

O Jesus Christ, the Bridegroom
Thou spotless Lamb of God
How all creation praises
How man and angels laud;
The heavenly hall is sounding
Redemption's antiphon
Bright majesty and glory
Stream from Thy glorious throne.

And how the heart is raptured
With songs unto the Lamb
Upon the throne of heaven
Beside the great I Am;
His countenance of beauty
The raptured saint shall see
And never more grow weary
Through all eternity.

My soul within is longing
God's heav'n above to see
The home of all the Blessed
The dwelling of the free;
The Father, Son and Spirit
Invite the Bride to come
To that fair spotless Kingdom
Where love shall make all one.

Basilea Schlink

REKINDLE

Saturday: Revelation 4
Sunday: Revelation 19:1–10

*Go to page 396 for your
next devotional reading.*

for there will be no night there. ²⁶The glory and honor of the nations will be brought into it. ²⁷Nothing impure will ever enter it, nor will anyone who does what is shameful or deceitful, but only those whose names are written in the Lamb's book of life.

The River of Life

22 Then the angel showed me the river of the water of life, as clear as crystal, flowing from the throne of God and of the Lamb ²down the middle of the great street of the city. On each side of the river stood the tree of life, bearing twelve crops of fruit, yielding its fruit every month. And the leaves of the tree are for the healing of the nations. ³No longer will there be any curse. The throne of God and of the Lamb will be in the city, and his servants will serve him. ⁴They will see his face, and his name will be on their foreheads. ⁵There will be no more night. They will not need the light of a lamp or the light of the sun, for the Lord God will give them light. And they will reign for ever and ever.

⁶The angel said to me, "These words are trustworthy and true. The Lord, the God of the spirits of the prophets, sent his angel to show his servants the things that must soon take place."

Jesus Is Coming

⁷"Behold, I am coming soon! Blessed is he who keeps the words of the prophecy in this book."

⁸I, John, am the one who heard and saw these things. And when I had heard and seen them, I fell down to worship at the feet of the angel who had been showing them to me. ⁹But he said to me, "Do not do it! I am a fellow servant with you and with your brothers the prophets and of all who keep the words of this book. Worship God!"

¹⁰Then he told me, "Do not seal up the words of the prophecy of this book, because the time is near. ¹¹Let him who does wrong continue to do wrong; let him who is vile continue to be vile; let him who does right continue to do right; and let him who is holy continue to be holy."

¹²"Behold, I am coming soon! My reward is with me, and I will give to everyone according to what he has done. ¹³I am the Alpha and the Omega, the First and the Last, the Beginning and the End.

¹⁴"Blessed are those who wash their robes, that they may have the right to the tree of life and may go through the gates into the city. ¹⁵Outside are the dogs, those who practice magic arts, the sexually immoral, the murderers, the idolaters and everyone who loves and practices falsehood.

¹⁶"I, Jesus, have sent my angel to give you*a* this testimony for the churches. I am the Root and the Offspring of David, and the bright Morning Star."

¹⁷The Spirit and the bride say, "Come!" And let him who hears say, "Come!" Whoever is thirsty, let him come; and whoever wishes, let him take the free gift of the water of life.

¹⁸I warn everyone who hears the words of the prophecy of this book: If anyone adds anything to them, God will add to him the plagues described in this book. ¹⁹And if anyone takes words away from this book of prophecy, God will take away from him his share in the tree of life and in the holy city, which are described in this book.

²⁰He who testifies to these things says, "Yes, I am coming soon."

Amen. Come, Lord Jesus.

²¹The grace of the Lord Jesus be with God's people. Amen.

---

a16 The Greek is plural.

PSALMS & PROVERBS

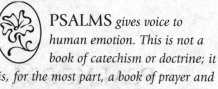

PSALMS *gives voice to human emotion. This is not a book of catechism or doctrine; it is, for the most part, a book of prayer and praise. It speaks to God in prayer and of God in praise and professions of faith and trust. Think of the psalms as entries in a diary, reflecting people's most intimate dealings with God. You will find comfort and strength here when you identify with the Old Testament saints who wrote these prayers and songs.*

PSALMS

BOOK I
Psalms 1–41

Psalm 1

1Blessed is the man
   who does not walk in the counsel
      of the wicked
 or stand in the way of sinners
   or sit in the seat of mockers.
2But his delight is in the law of the
      LORD,
   and on his law he meditates day
      and night.
3He is like a tree planted by streams
   of water,

   which yields its fruit in season
 and whose leaf does not wither.
   Whatever he does prospers.

4Not so the wicked!
   They are like chaff
   that the wind blows away.
5Therefore the wicked will not stand
      in the judgment,
   nor sinners in the assembly of the
      righteous.

6For the LORD watches over the way of
      the righteous,
   but the way of the wicked will
      perish.

Psalm 2

[1] Why do the nations conspire[a]
  and the peoples plot in vain?
[2] The kings of the earth take their
    stand
  and the rulers gather together
against the LORD
  and against his Anointed One.[b]
[3] "Let us break their chains," they say,
  "and throw off their fetters."

[4] The One enthroned in heaven
    laughs;
  the Lord scoffs at them.
[5] Then he rebukes them in his anger
  and terrifies them in his wrath,
    saying,
[6] "I have installed my King[c]
  on Zion, my holy hill."

[7] I will proclaim the decree of the LORD:

He said to me, "You are my Son[d];
  today I have become your Father.[e]
[8] Ask of me,
  and I will make the nations your
    inheritance,
  the ends of the earth your
    possession.
[9] You will rule them with an iron
    scepter[f];
  you will dash them to pieces like
    pottery."

[10] Therefore, you kings, be wise;
  be warned, you rulers of the earth.
[11] Serve the LORD with fear
  and rejoice with trembling.
[12] Kiss the Son, lest he be angry
  and you be destroyed in your way,
  for his wrath can flare up in a
    moment.
  Blessed are all who take refuge in
    him.

Psalm 3

A psalm of David. When he fled from
his son Absalom.

[1] O LORD, how many are my foes!
  How many rise up against me!
[2] Many are saying of me,
  "God will not deliver him."   Selah[g]

[3] But you are a shield around me,
    O LORD;
  you bestow glory on me and lift[h]
    up my head.
[4] To the LORD I cry aloud,
  and he answers me from his holy
    hill.   Selah

[5] I lie down and sleep;
  I wake again, because the LORD
    sustains me.
[6] I will not fear the tens of thousands
  drawn up against me on every
    side.

[7] Arise, O LORD!
  Deliver me, O my God!
Strike all my enemies on the jaw;
  break the teeth of the wicked.

[8] From the LORD comes deliverance.
  May your blessing be on your
    people.   Selah

Psalm 4

For the director of music. With stringed
instruments. A psalm of David.

[1] Answer me when I call to you,
    O my righteous God.
  Give me relief from my distress;
  be merciful to me and hear my
    prayer.

[2] How long, O men, will you turn my
    glory into shame[i]?
  How long will you love delusions
    and seek false gods[j]?   Selah
[3] Know that the LORD has set apart the
    godly for himself;
  the LORD will hear when I call to
    him.

[4] In your anger do not sin;
  when you are on your beds,
  search your hearts and be silent.
                Selah
[5] Offer right sacrifices
  and trust in the LORD.

[6] Many are asking, "Who can show us
    any good?"
  Let the light of your face shine
    upon us, O LORD.
[7] You have filled my heart with greater
    joy

---

[a]1 Hebrew; Septuagint *rage*   [b]2 Or *anointed one*   [c]6 Or *king*   [d]7 Or *son*; also in verse 12
[e]7 Or *have begotten you*   [f]9 Or *will break them with a rod of iron*   [g]2 A word of uncertain
meaning, occurring frequently in the Psalms; possibly a musical term   [h]3 Or LORD, / *my Glorious*
One, who lifts   [i]2 Or *you dishonor my Glorious One*   [j]2 Or *seek lies*

than when their grain and new
wine abound.
⁸I will lie down and sleep in peace,
for you alone, O LORD,
make me dwell in safety.

Psalm 5

*For the director of music. For flutes.
A psalm of David.*

¹Give ear to my words, O LORD,
consider my sighing.
²Listen to my cry for help,

my King and my God,
for to you I pray.
³In the morning, O LORD, you hear my
voice;
in the morning I lay my requests
before you
and wait in expectation.

⁴You are not a God who takes
pleasure in evil;
with you the wicked cannot dwell.
⁵The arrogant cannot stand in your
presence;
you hate all who do wrong.

MONDAY

VERSE: AUTHOR: PASSAGE:
Psalm 3:3   Kate Convissor   Psalm 3:1–8

A Shield Around Me

"You know I'm not very intuitive," my friend Dee said, breaking the silent prayer of the women's Bible study. "I don't see
visions or anything, but just now I saw the Lord standing guard
over you. Behind him were shadowy figures of things like anger
and depression. His arms were outspread, holding them back
and protecting you so nothing could harm you."

It was the week after Richard's funeral and I was on shaky, newborn legs. I was really too raw and unsteady to be out but had
always enjoyed the common sense and strength of these women.
I knew Dee's words were true. I felt that protection.

I had done what was necessary: contacted a lawyer, begun hundreds of thank-you notes, applied for Social Security. Now there
was just pain and all of life ahead. Pain, fierce and cleansing in its
intensity, still without anger, guilt or depression—all that would
come later.

The grace I felt didn't blunt the pain, didn't even keep the difficulties at bay. The cars still ran out of oil, fuses still blew, the grass
needed mowing and our machine was too cantankerous for the
job. These daily irritations were drips in an overflowing cup.

Grace was a sense of presence, of stillness, that was always there
just below the surface. Perhaps grace had always been there, but
my life had been too hurried, my mind too cluttered, to notice it.
Perhaps a feeling of unworthiness had blocked the presence of
God. All that fell away now. God was my Father, giving me each
day the ticket for the journey, and I clung to that grace like a child.

ADDITIONAL SCRIPTURE READINGS:
Psalm 18:1–6; Psalm 91:1–4; Philippians 4:7

Go to page 399 for your next devotional reading.

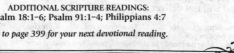

[6]You destroy those who tell lies;
　　bloodthirsty and deceitful men
　　the LORD abhors.

[7]But I, by your great mercy,
　　will come into your house;
　in reverence will I bow down
　　toward your holy temple.
[8]Lead me, O LORD, in your
　　righteousness
　　because of my enemies—
　make straight your way before me.

[9]Not a word from their mouth can be
　　trusted;
　　their heart is filled with
　　destruction.
Their throat is an open grave;
　　with their tongue they speak
　　deceit.
[10]Declare them guilty, O God!
　　Let their intrigues be their
　　downfall.
Banish them for their many sins,
　　for they have rebelled against you.

[11]But let all who take refuge in you be
　　glad;
　　let them ever sing for joy.
Spread your protection over them,
　　that those who love your name
　　may rejoice in you.
[12]For surely, O LORD, you bless the
　　righteous;
　　you surround them with your
　　favor as with a shield.

Psalm 6

For the director of music. With stringed
instruments. According to *sheminith.*[a]
A psalm of David.

[1]O LORD, do not rebuke me in your
　　anger
　　or discipline me in your wrath.
[2]Be merciful to me, LORD, for I am
　　faint;
　O LORD, heal me, for my bones are
　　in agony.
[3]My soul is in anguish.
　　How long, O LORD, how long?

[4]Turn, O LORD, and deliver me;
　　save me because of your unfailing
　　love.
[5]No one remembers you when he is
　　dead.
　Who praises you from the grave[b]?

[6]I am worn out from groaning;
　all night long I flood my bed with
　　weeping
　　and drench my couch with tears.
[7]My eyes grow weak with sorrow;
　　they fail because of all my foes.

[8]Away from me, all you who do evil,
　　for the LORD has heard my
　　weeping.
[9]The LORD has heard my cry for
　　mercy;
　　the LORD accepts my prayer.
[10]All my enemies will be ashamed and
　　dismayed;
　　they will turn back in sudden
　　disgrace.

Psalm 7

A *shiggaion*[c] of David, which he sang
to the LORD concerning Cush,
a Benjamite.

[1]O LORD my God, I take refuge in you;
　　save and deliver me from all who
　　pursue me,
[2]or they will tear me like a lion
　　and rip me to pieces with no one
　　to rescue me.

[3]O LORD my God, if I have done this
　　and there is guilt on my hands—
[4]if I have done evil to him who is at
　　peace with me
　or without cause have robbed my
　　foe—
[5]then let my enemy pursue and
　　overtake me;
　　let him trample my life to the
　　ground
　　and make me sleep in the dust.
　　　　　　　　　　　　　　　　Selah

[6]Arise, O LORD, in your anger;
　　rise up against the rage of my
　　enemies.
　Awake, my God; decree justice.
[7]Let the assembled peoples gather
　　around you.
　Rule over them from on high;
[8]　let the LORD judge the peoples.
Judge me, O LORD, according to my
　　righteousness,
　according to my integrity, O Most
　　High.
[9]O righteous God,
　　who searches minds and hearts,

---

[a]Title: Probably a musical term   [b]5 Hebrew *Sheol*   [c]Title: Probably a literary or musical term

bring to an end the violence of the
wicked
and make the righteous secure.

[10]My shield[a] is God Most High,
who saves the upright in heart.
[11]God is a righteous judge,
a God who expresses his wrath
every day.
[12]If he does not relent,
he[b] will sharpen his sword;
he will bend and string his bow.
[13]He has prepared his deadly
weapons;
he makes ready his flaming
arrows.

[14]He who is pregnant with evil
and conceives trouble gives birth
to disillusionment.
[15]He who digs a hole and scoops it
out
falls into the pit he has made.
[16]The trouble he causes recoils on
himself;
his violence comes down on his
own head.

[17]I will give thanks to the LORD because
of his righteousness
and will sing praise to the name of
the LORD Most High.

Psalm 8

For the director of music. According to
gittith.[c] A psalm of David.

[1]O LORD, our Lord,
how majestic is your name in all
the earth!

You have set your glory
above the heavens.
[2]From the lips of children and infants
you have ordained praise[d]
because of your enemies,
to silence the foe and the avenger.

[3]When I consider your heavens,
the work of your fingers,
the moon and the stars,
which you have set in place,
[4]what is man that you are mindful of
him,
the son of man that you care for
him?

[5]You made him a little lower than the
heavenly beings[e]
and crowned him with glory and
honor.

[6]You made him ruler over the works
of your hands;
you put everything under his feet:
[7]all flocks and herds,
and the beasts of the field,
[8]the birds of the air,
and the fish of the sea,
all that swim the paths of the
seas.

[9]O LORD, our Lord,
how majestic is your name in all
the earth!

Psalm 9[f]

For the director of music. To ⌊the tune
of⌋ "The Death of the Son." A psalm
of David.

[1]I will praise you, O LORD, with all my
heart;
I will tell of all your wonders.
[2]I will be glad and rejoice in you;
I will sing praise to your name,
O Most High.

[3]My enemies turn back;
they stumble and perish before
you.
[4]For you have upheld my right and
my cause;
you have sat on your throne,
judging righteously.
[5]You have rebuked the nations and
destroyed the wicked;
you have blotted out their name
for ever and ever.
[6]Endless ruin has overtaken the
enemy,
you have uprooted their cities;
even the memory of them has
perished.

[7]The LORD reigns forever;
he has established his throne for
judgment.
[8]He will judge the world in
righteousness;
he will govern the peoples with
justice.

---

[a]10 Or *sovereign*   [b]12 Or *If a man does not repent, / God*   [c]Title: Probably a musical term
[d]2 Or *strength*   [e]5 Or *than God*   [f]Psalms 9 and 10 may have been originally a single acrostic
poem, the stanzas of which begin with the successive letters of the Hebrew alphabet. In the Septuagint
they constitute one psalm.

⁹The LORD is a refuge for the
    oppressed,
  a stronghold in times of
    trouble.
¹⁰Those who know your name
    will trust in you,
  for you, LORD, have never forsaken
    those who seek you.
¹¹Sing praises to the LORD, enthroned
    in Zion;
  proclaim among the nations what
    he has done.
¹²For he who avenges blood
    remembers;

he does not ignore the cry of the
    afflicted.
¹³O LORD, see how my enemies
    persecute me!
  Have mercy and lift me up from
    the gates of death,
¹⁴that I may declare your praises
    in the gates of the Daughter of
    Zion
  and there rejoice in your salvation.
¹⁵The nations have fallen into the pit
    they have dug;
  their feet are caught in the net they
    have hidden.

⟨ TUESDAY ⟩

VERSE:	AUTHOR:	PASSAGE:
Psalm 9:7	Amy Carmichael	Psalm 9:7–10

Clouds

This evening the clouds lay low on the mountains so that
sometimes we could hardly see the familiar peaks. Sometimes
the stars, too, were nearly all covered. But always, just when it
seemed as though the mountains were going to be quite lost in
the mist, the higher peaks pushed out, and whereas the dimmer
stars were veiled, the brighter ones shone through.

Even supposing the clouds had wholly covered the face of the
mountains, and not a star shone through the piled-up masses, the
mountains would *still* have stood steadfast and the stars would not
have ceased to shine. I thought of this and found it very comforting, simple as it is.

Just so, our feelings do not affect God's facts. They may blow up,
like clouds, and cover the eternal things that we do most truly
believe. We may not see the shining of the promises—but still they
shine! And the strength of the hills that is his also, is not for one
moment less because of our human weakness.

Heaven is no dream. Feelings go and come, like clouds. But the
"hills" and "stars" abide.

*My Father, I will anchor my self, my thoughts and my will, in these
facts:*

You are.

You rule in heaven and on the earth.

You call me "righteous" because I am in Jesus, your Son.

No matter what it may seem, I will stand firm forever.

ADDITIONAL SCRIPTURE READINGS:
Proverbs 10:25; Isaiah 32:17

Go to page 408 for your next devotional reading.

¹⁶The LORD is known by his justice;
  the wicked are ensnared by the
  work of their hands.
                    Higgaion.^a *Selah*
¹⁷The wicked return to the grave,^b
  all the nations that forget God.
¹⁸But the needy will not always be
  forgotten,
  nor the hope of the afflicted ever
  perish.

¹⁹Arise, O LORD, let not man triumph;
  let the nations be judged in your
  presence.
²⁰Strike them with terror, O LORD;
  let the nations know they are but
  men.   *Selah*

Psalm 10^c

¹Why, O LORD, do you stand far off?
  Why do you hide yourself in times
  of trouble?

²In his arrogance the wicked man
  hunts down the weak,
  who are caught in the schemes he
  devises.
³He boasts of the cravings of his
  heart;
  he blesses the greedy and reviles
  the LORD.
⁴In his pride the wicked does not
  seek him;
  in all his thoughts there is no
  room for God.
⁵His ways are always prosperous;
  he is haughty and your laws are
  far from him;
  he sneers at all his enemies.
⁶He says to himself, "Nothing will
  shake me;
  I'll always be happy and never
  have trouble."
⁷His mouth is full of curses and lies
  and threats;
  trouble and evil are under his
  tongue.
⁸He lies in wait near the villages;
  from ambush he murders the
  innocent,
  watching in secret for his victims.
⁹He lies in wait like a lion in cover;
  he lies in wait to catch the
  helpless;

he catches the helpless and drags
  them off in his net.
¹⁰His victims are crushed, they
  collapse;
  they fall under his strength.
¹¹He says to himself, "God has
  forgotten;
  he covers his face and never sees."

¹²Arise, LORD! Lift up your hand,
  O God.
  Do not forget the helpless.
¹³Why does the wicked man revile
  God?
  Why does he say to himself,
  "He won't call me to account"?
¹⁴But you, O God, do see trouble and
  grief;
  you consider it to take it in hand.
The victim commits himself to you;
  you are the helper of the
  fatherless.
¹⁵Break the arm of the wicked and evil
  man;
  call him to account for his
  wickedness
  that would not be found out.

¹⁶The LORD is King for ever and ever;
  the nations will perish from his
  land.
¹⁷You hear, O LORD, the desire of the
  afflicted;
  you encourage them, and you
  listen to their cry,
¹⁸defending the fatherless and the
  oppressed,
  in order that man, who is of the
  earth, may terrify no more.

Psalm 11

For the director of music. Of David.

¹In the LORD I take refuge.
  How then can you say to me:
  "Flee like a bird to your mountain.
²For look, the wicked bend their
  bows;
  they set their arrows against the
  strings
to shoot from the shadows
  at the upright in heart.

---

^a16 Or *Meditation*; possibly a musical notation   ^b17 Hebrew *Sheol*   ^cPsalms 9 and 10 may have
been originally a single acrostic poem, the stanzas of which begin with the successive letters of the
Hebrew alphabet. In the Septuagint they constitute one psalm.

[3]When the foundations are being
        destroyed,
    what can the righteous do[a]?"

[4]The LORD is in his holy temple;
    the LORD is on his heavenly throne.
He observes the sons of men;
    his eyes examine them.
[5]The LORD examines the righteous,
    but the wicked[b] and those who
        love violence
    his soul hates.
[6]On the wicked he will rain
    fiery coals and burning sulfur;
    a scorching wind will be their lot.

[7]For the LORD is righteous,
    he loves justice;
    upright men will see his face.

Psalm 12

For the director of music. According to
sheminith.[c] A psalm of David.

[1]Help, LORD, for the godly are no
        more;
    the faithful have vanished from
        among men.
[2]Everyone lies to his neighbor;
    their flattering lips speak with
        deception.

[3]May the LORD cut off all flattering lips
    and every boastful tongue
[4]that says, "We will triumph with our
        tongues;
    we own our lips[d]—who is our
        master?"

[5]"Because of the oppression of the
        weak
    and the groaning of the needy,
I will now arise," says the LORD.
    "I will protect them from those
        who malign them."
[6]And the words of the LORD are
        flawless,
    like silver refined in a furnace of
        clay,
    purified seven times.

[7]O LORD, you will keep us safe
    and protect us from such people
        forever.
[8]The wicked freely strut about
    when what is vile is honored
        among men.

Psalm 13

For the director of music. A psalm
of David.

[1]How long, O LORD? Will you forget
        me forever?
    How long will you hide your face
        from me?
[2]How long must I wrestle with my
        thoughts
    and every day have sorrow in my
        heart?
    How long will my enemy triumph
        over me?

[3]Look on me and answer, O LORD my
        God.
    Give light to my eyes, or I will
        sleep in death,
[4]my enemy will say, "I have overcome
        him,"
    and my foes will rejoice when I
        fall.

[5]But I trust in your unfailing love;
    my heart rejoices in your salvation.
[6]I will sing to the LORD,
    for he has been good to me.

Psalm 14

For the director of music. Of David.

[1]The fool[e] says in his heart,
    "There is no God."
They are corrupt, their deeds are vile;
    there is no one who does good.

[2]The LORD looks down from heaven
        on the sons of men
to see if there are any who
        understand,
    any who seek God.
[3]All have turned aside,
    they have together become corrupt;
there is no one who does good,
    not even one.

[4]Will evildoers never learn—
    those who devour my people as
        men eat bread
    and who do not call on the LORD?
[5]There they are, overwhelmed with
        dread,
    for God is present in the company
        of the righteous.

[a]3 Or what is the Righteous One doing   [b]5 Or The LORD, the Righteous One, examines the wicked, /
[c]Title: Probably a musical term   [d]4 Or / our lips are our plowshares   [e]1 The Hebrew words
rendered fool in Psalms denote one who is morally deficient.

⁶You evildoers frustrate the plans of
 the poor,
  but the LORD is their refuge.

⁷Oh, that salvation for Israel would
  come out of Zion!
 When the LORD restores the
  fortunes of his people,
 let Jacob rejoice and Israel be glad!

Psalm 15

A psalm of David.

¹LORD, who may dwell in your
  sanctuary?
 Who may live on your holy hill?

²He whose walk is blameless
  and who does what is righteous,
 who speaks the truth from his heart
³ and has no slander on his tongue,
 who does his neighbor no wrong
  and casts no slur on his
   fellowman,
⁴who despises a vile man
  but honors those who fear the
   LORD,
 who keeps his oath
  even when it hurts,
⁵who lends his money without usury
  and does not accept a bribe
   against the innocent.

He who does these things
  will never be shaken.

Psalm 16

A miktam[a] of David.

¹Keep me safe, O God,
  for in you I take refuge.

²I said to the LORD, "You are my Lord;
  apart from you I have no good
   thing."
³As for the saints who are in the
  land,
 they are the glorious ones in
  whom is all my delight.[b]
⁴The sorrows of those will increase
  who run after other gods.
 I will not pour out their libations of
  blood
 or take up their names on my lips.

⁵LORD, you have assigned me my
  portion and my cup;
 you have made my lot secure.
⁶The boundary lines have fallen for
  me in pleasant places;
 surely I have a delightful
  inheritance.

⁷I will praise the LORD, who counsels
  me;
 even at night my heart instructs
  me.
⁸I have set the LORD always before me.
 Because he is at my right hand,
 I will not be shaken.

⁹Therefore my heart is glad and my
  tongue rejoices;
 my body also will rest secure,
¹⁰because you will not abandon me to
  the grave,[c]
 nor will you let your Holy One[d]
  see decay.
¹¹You have made[e] known to me the
  path of life;
 you will fill me with joy in your
  presence,
 with eternal pleasures at your right
  hand.

Psalm 17

A prayer of David.

¹Hear, O LORD, my righteous plea;
  listen to my cry.
 Give ear to my prayer—
  it does not rise from deceitful lips.
²May my vindication come from you;
  may your eyes see what is right.

³Though you probe my heart and
  examine me at night,
 though you test me, you will find
  nothing;
 I have resolved that my mouth will
  not sin.
⁴As for the deeds of men—
  by the word of your lips
 I have kept myself
  from the ways of the violent.
⁵My steps have held to your paths;
  my feet have not slipped.

⁶I call on you, O God, for you will
  answer me;
 give ear to me and hear my prayer.

---

[a]Title: Probably a literary or musical term   [b]3 Or As for the pagan priests who are in the land / and the
nobles in whom all delight, I said: [c]10 Hebrew Sheol   [d]10 Or your faithful one   [e]11 Or You will
make

⁷Show the wonder of your great love,
  you who save by your right hand
    those who take refuge in you from
      their foes.
⁸Keep me as the apple of your eye;
  hide me in the shadow of your
    wings
⁹from the wicked who assail me,
  from my mortal enemies who
    surround me.

¹⁰They close up their callous hearts,
  and their mouths speak with
    arrogance.
¹¹They have tracked me down, they
    now surround me,
  with eyes alert, to throw me to the
    ground.
¹²They are like a lion hungry for prey,
  like a great lion crouching in cover.

¹³Rise up, O LORD, confront them,
    bring them down;
  rescue me from the wicked by
    your sword.
¹⁴O LORD, by your hand save me from
    such men,
  from men of this world whose
    reward is in this life.

You still the hunger of those you
    cherish;
  their sons have plenty,
  and they store up wealth for their
    children.
¹⁵And I—in righteousness I will see
    your face;
  when I awake, I will be satisfied
    with seeing your likeness.

Psalm 18

For the director of music. Of David the
servant of the LORD. He sang to the
LORD the words of this song when the
LORD delivered him from the hand of
all his enemies and from the hand of
Saul. He said:

¹I love you, O LORD, my strength.

²The LORD is my rock, my fortress and
    my deliverer;
  my God is my rock, in whom I
    take refuge.
  He is my shield and the horn*a* of
    my salvation, my stronghold.

³I call to the LORD, who is worthy of
    praise,
  and I am saved from my enemies.

⁴The cords of death entangled me;
  the torrents of destruction
    overwhelmed me.
⁵The cords of the grave*b* coiled
    around me;
  the snares of death confronted me.
⁶In my distress I called to the LORD;
  I cried to my God for help.
  From his temple he heard my voice;
  my cry came before him, into his
    ears.

⁷The earth trembled and quaked,
  and the foundations of the
    mountains shook;
  they trembled because he was
    angry.
⁸Smoke rose from his nostrils;
  consuming fire came from his
    mouth,
  burning coals blazed out of it.
⁹He parted the heavens and came
    down;
  dark clouds were under his feet.
¹⁰He mounted the cherubim and flew;
  he soared on the wings of the
    wind.
¹¹He made darkness his covering, his
    canopy around him—
  the dark rain clouds of the sky.
¹²Out of the brightness of his presence
    clouds advanced,
  with hailstones and bolts of
    lightning.
¹³The LORD thundered from heaven;
  the voice of the Most High
    resounded.*c*
¹⁴He shot his arrows and scattered
    ⌊the enemies⌋,
  great bolts of lightning and routed
    them.
¹⁵The valleys of the sea were exposed
  and the foundations of the earth
    laid bare
  at your rebuke, O LORD,
  at the blast of breath from your
    nostrils.

¹⁶He reached down from on high and
    took hold of me;
  he drew me out of deep waters.

---

a2 *Horn* here symbolizes strength.   *b5* Hebrew *Sheol*   *c13* Some Hebrew manuscripts and
Septuagint (see also 2 Samuel 22:14); most Hebrew manuscripts *resounded, / amid hailstones and bolts of
lightning*

¹⁷He rescued me from my powerful
enemy,
from my foes, who were too
strong for me.
¹⁸They confronted me in the day of my
disaster,
but the LORD was my support.
¹⁹He brought me out into a spacious
place;
he rescued me because he
delighted in me.

²⁰The LORD has dealt with me
according to my
righteousness;
according to the cleanness of my
hands he has rewarded me.
²¹For I have kept the ways of the LORD;
I have not done evil by turning
from my God.
²²All his laws are before me;
I have not turned away from his
decrees.
²³I have been blameless before him
and have kept myself from sin.
²⁴The LORD has rewarded me according
to my righteousness,
according to the cleanness of my
hands in his sight.

²⁵To the faithful you show yourself
faithful,
to the blameless you show
yourself blameless,
²⁶to the pure you show yourself
pure,
but to the crooked you show
yourself shrewd.
²⁷You save the humble
but bring low those whose eyes
are haughty.
²⁸You, O LORD, keep my lamp burning;
my God turns my darkness into
light.
²⁹With your help I can advance against
a troop*a*;
with my God I can scale a wall.

³⁰As for God, his way is perfect;
the word of the LORD is flawless.
He is a shield
for all who take refuge in him.
³¹For who is God besides the LORD?
And who is the Rock except our
God?
³²It is God who arms me with strength
and makes my way perfect.

³³He makes my feet like the feet of a
deer;
he enables me to stand on the
heights.
³⁴He trains my hands for battle;
my arms can bend a bow of
bronze.
³⁵You give me your shield of victory,
and your right hand sustains me;
you stoop down to make me great.
³⁶You broaden the path beneath me,
so that my ankles do not turn.

³⁷I pursued my enemies and overtook
them;
I did not turn back till they were
destroyed.
³⁸I crushed them so that they could
not rise;
they fell beneath my feet.
³⁹You armed me with strength for
battle;
you made my adversaries bow at
my feet.
⁴⁰You made my enemies turn their
backs in flight,
and I destroyed my foes.
⁴¹They cried for help, but there was no
one to save them—
to the LORD, but he did not answer.
⁴²I beat them as fine as dust borne on
the wind;
I poured them out like mud in the
streets.

⁴³You have delivered me from the
attacks of the people;
you have made me the head of
nations;
people I did not know are subject
to me.
⁴⁴As soon as they hear me, they obey
me;
foreigners cringe before me.
⁴⁵They all lose heart;
they come trembling from their
strongholds.

⁴⁶The LORD lives! Praise be to my
Rock!
Exalted be God my Savior!
⁴⁷He is the God who avenges me,
who subdues nations under me,
⁴⁸   who saves me from my enemies.
You exalted me above my foes;
from violent men you rescued
me.

---

*a*29 Or *can run through a barricade*

⁴⁹Therefore I will praise you among
    the nations, O LORD;
    I will sing praises to your name.
⁵⁰He gives his king great victories;
    he shows unfailing kindness to
        his anointed,
    to David and his descendants
        forever.

Psalm 19

For the director of music. A psalm
of David.

¹The heavens declare the glory of
    God;
    the skies proclaim the work of his
        hands.
²Day after day they pour forth speech;
    night after night they display
        knowledge.
³There is no speech or language
    where their voice is not heard.ᵃ
⁴Their voiceᵇ goes out into all the
    earth,
    their words to the ends of the
        world.

In the heavens he has pitched a tent
    for the sun,
⁵   which is like a bridegroom coming
        forth from his pavilion,
    like a champion rejoicing to run
        his course.
⁶It rises at one end of the heavens
    and makes its circuit to the other;
    nothing is hidden from its heat.

⁷The law of the LORD is perfect,
    reviving the soul.
The statutes of the LORD are
        trustworthy,
    making wise the simple.
⁸The precepts of the LORD are right,
    giving joy to the heart.
The commands of the LORD are
        radiant,
    giving light to the eyes.
⁹The fear of the LORD is pure,
    enduring forever.
The ordinances of the LORD are sure
    and altogether righteous.
¹⁰They are more precious than gold,
    than much pure gold;
    they are sweeter than honey,
        than honey from the comb.
¹¹By them is your servant warned;

in keeping them there is great
    reward.

¹²Who can discern his errors?
    Forgive my hidden faults.
¹³Keep your servant also from willful
    sins;
    may they not rule over me.
Then will I be blameless,
    innocent of great transgression.

¹⁴May the words of my mouth and the
    meditation of my heart
    be pleasing in your sight,
    O LORD, my Rock and my
        Redeemer.

Psalm 20

For the director of music. A psalm
of David.

¹May the LORD answer you when you
    are in distress;
    may the name of the God of Jacob
        protect you.
²May he send you help from the
    sanctuary
    and grant you support from Zion.
³May he remember all your sacrifices
    and accept your burnt offerings.
                                    Selah
⁴May he give you the desire of your
    heart
    and make all your plans succeed.
⁵We will shout for joy when you are
    victorious
    and will lift up our banners in the
        name of our God.
May the LORD grant all your requests.

⁶Now I know that the LORD saves his
    anointed;
    he answers him from his holy
        heaven
    with the saving power of his right
        hand.
⁷Some trust in chariots and some in
    horses,
    but we trust in the name of the
        LORD our God.
⁸They are brought to their knees and
    fall,
    but we rise up and stand firm.

⁹O LORD, save the king!
    Answerᶜ us when we call!

ᵃ3 Or They have no speech, there are no words; / no sound is heard from them   ᵇ4 Septuagint, Jerome
and Syriac; Hebrew line   ᶜ9 Or save! / O King, answer

Psalm 21

For the director of music. A psalm
of David.

¹O LORD, the king rejoices in your
   strength.
  How great is his joy in the
     victories you give!
²You have granted him the desire of
   his heart
  and have not withheld the request
     of his lips.   *Selah*
³You welcomed him with rich
   blessings
  and placed a crown of pure gold
     on his head.
⁴He asked you for life, and you gave
   it to him—
  length of days, for ever and ever.
⁵Through the victories you gave, his
   glory is great;
  you have bestowed on him
     splendor and majesty.
⁶Surely you have granted him eternal
   blessings
  and made him glad with the joy of
     your presence.
⁷For the king trusts in the LORD;
  through the unfailing love of the
     Most High
  he will not be shaken.

⁸Your hand will lay hold on all your
   enemies;
  your right hand will seize your
     foes.
⁹At the time of your appearing
  you will make them like a fiery
     furnace.
  In his wrath the LORD will swallow
     them up,
  and his fire will consume them.
¹⁰You will destroy their descendants
   from the earth,
  their posterity from mankind.
¹¹Though they plot evil against you
  and devise wicked schemes, they
     cannot succeed;
¹²for you will make them turn their
   backs
  when you aim at them with drawn
     bow.

¹³Be exalted, O LORD, in your strength;
  we will sing and praise your
     might.

Psalm 22

For the director of music. To the tune
of "The Doe of the Morning." A psalm
of David.

¹My God, my God, why have you
   forsaken me?
  Why are you so far from saving
     me,
  so far from the words of my
     groaning?
²O my God, I cry out by day, but you
   do not answer,
  by night, and am not silent.

³Yet you are enthroned as the Holy
   One;
  you are the praise of Israel.ᵃ
⁴In you our fathers put their trust;
  they trusted and you delivered
     them.
⁵They cried to you and were saved;
  in you they trusted and were not
     disappointed.

⁶But I am a worm and not a man,
  scorned by men and despised by
     the people.
⁷All who see me mock me;
  they hurl insults, shaking their
     heads:
⁸"He trusts in the LORD;
  let the LORD rescue him.
  Let him deliver him,
   since he delights in him."

⁹Yet you brought me out of the
   womb;
  you made me trust in you
   even at my mother's breast.
¹⁰From birth I was cast upon you;
  from my mother's womb you have
     been my God.
¹¹Do not be far from me,
  for trouble is near
  and there is no one to help.

¹²Many bulls surround me;
  strong bulls of Bashan encircle
     me.
¹³Roaring lions tearing their prey
  open their mouths wide against
     me.
¹⁴I am poured out like water,
  and all my bones are out of joint.
  My heart has turned to wax;
   it has melted away within me.

ᵃ3 Or *Yet you are holy, / enthroned on the praises of Israel*

15My strength is dried up like a
potsherd,
and my tongue sticks to the roof
of my mouth;
you lay me*a* in the dust of death.
16Dogs have surrounded me;
a band of evil men has encircled
me,
they have pierced*b* my hands and
my feet.
17I can count all my bones;
people stare and gloat over me.
18They divide my garments among
them
and cast lots for my clothing.

19But you, O LORD, be not far off;
O my Strength, come quickly to
help me.
20Deliver my life from the sword,
my precious life from the power of
the dogs.
21Rescue me from the mouth of the
lions;
save*c* me from the horns of the
wild oxen.

22I will declare your name to my
brothers;
in the congregation I will praise
you.
23You who fear the LORD, praise him!
All you descendants of Jacob,
honor him!
Revere him, all you descendants of
Israel!
24For he has not despised or
disdained
the suffering of the afflicted one;
he has not hidden his face from him
but has listened to his cry for
help.

25From you comes the theme of my
praise in the great assembly;
before those who fear you*d* will I
fulfill my vows.
26The poor will eat and be satisfied;
they who seek the LORD will praise
him—
may your hearts live forever!
27All the ends of the earth
will remember and turn to the
LORD,
and all the families of the nations
will bow down before him,

28for dominion belongs to the LORD
and he rules over the nations.

29All the rich of the earth will feast and
worship;
all who go down to the dust will
kneel before him—
those who cannot keep themselves
alive.
30Posterity will serve him;
future generations will be told
about the Lord.
31They will proclaim his righteousness
to a people yet unborn—
for he has done it.

Psalm 23

A psalm of David.

1The LORD is my shepherd, I shall not
be in want.
2   He makes me lie down in green
pastures,
he leads me beside quiet waters,
3   he restores my soul.
He guides me in paths of
righteousness
for his name's sake.
4Even though I walk
through the valley of the shadow
of death,*e*
I will fear no evil,
for you are with me;
your rod and your staff,
they comfort me.

5You prepare a table before me
in the presence of my enemies.
You anoint my head with oil;
my cup overflows.
6Surely goodness and love will follow
me
all the days of my life,
and I will dwell in the house of the
LORD
forever.

Psalm 24

Of David. A psalm.

1The earth is the LORD's, and
everything in it,
the world, and all who live in it;
2for he founded it upon the seas

---

a15 Or / *I am laid*   *b16* Some Hebrew manuscripts, Septuagint and Syriac; most Hebrew
manuscripts / *like the lion,*   *c21* Or / *you have heard*   *d25* Hebrew *him*   *e4* Or *through the
darkest valley*

and established it upon the
waters.

³Who may ascend the hill of the
LORD?
Who may stand in his holy place?
⁴He who has clean hands and a pure
heart,
who does not lift up his soul to
an idol
or swear by what is false.ᵃ
⁵He will receive blessing from the
LORD
and vindication from God his
Savior.
⁶Such is the generation of those who
seek him,
who seek your face, O God of
Jacob.ᵇ   Selah

⁷Lift up your heads, O you gates;
be lifted up, you ancient doors,
that the King of glory may come
in.
⁸Who is this King of glory?
The LORD strong and mighty,
the LORD mighty in battle.
⁹Lift up your heads, O you gates;
lift them up, you ancient doors,
that the King of glory may come
in.
¹⁰Who is he, this King of glory?
The LORD Almighty—
he is the King of glory.   Selah

ᵃ4 Or *swear falsely*   ᵇ6 Two Hebrew manuscripts and Syriac (see also Septuagint); most Hebrew manuscripts *face, Jacob*

WEDNESDAY

VERSE:	AUTHOR:	PASSAGE:
Psalm 23:2-3	Jean E. Syswerda	Psalm 23:1-6

Cathedral

I go to church almost every evening. Not the large, stained-glass church of my childhood nor the simple country church of my present experience, but it's church just the same.

Most evenings, when the day winds down to an end, sometimes early, sometimes very late, I spend a few minutes at the door looking over my backyard. The holy hush of my wooded backyard is my cathedral.

After spending a day in an office of plastic and steel and computer screens, I need—no, more than that—I crave the realness of God's creation. In my backyard church I worship. The tree toads preach sermons of peace. The crickets chirp a song that sounds like praise. The incense is of damp earth and fresh grass. And the wind whispers to me of a God who is there.

In my doorway I move beyond myself. The hassles of the day and the pressures of modern life are eclipsed by a sense of God's presence and the peace it brings. In my green sanctuary I worship, and my soul is restored.

O Lord, my shepherd, thanks for my green pasture and for my restored soul.

ADDITIONAL SCRIPTURE READINGS:
John 10:11; 2 Corinthians 4:6-18

Go to page 410 for your next devotional reading.

Psalm 25[a]

Of David.

[1]To you, O LORD, I lift up my soul;
[2] in you I trust, O my God.
Do not let me be put to shame,
nor let my enemies triumph over
me.
[3]No one whose hope is in you
will ever be put to shame,
but they will be put to shame
who are treacherous without
excuse.

[4]Show me your ways, O LORD,
teach me your paths;
[5]guide me in your truth and teach me,
for you are God my Savior,
and my hope is in you all day
long.
[6]Remember, O LORD, your great mercy
and love,
for they are from of old.
[7]Remember not the sins of my youth
and my rebellious ways;
according to your love remember me,
for you are good, O LORD.

[8]Good and upright is the LORD;
therefore he instructs sinners in
his ways.
[9]He guides the humble in what is
right
and teaches them his way.
[10]All the ways of the LORD are loving
and faithful
for those who keep the demands
of his covenant.
[11]For the sake of your name, O LORD,
forgive my iniquity, though it is
great.
[12]Who, then, is the man that fears the
LORD?
He will instruct him in the way
chosen for him.
[13]He will spend his days in prosperity,
and his descendants will inherit
the land.
[14]The LORD confides in those who fear
him;
he makes his covenant known to
them.
[15]My eyes are ever on the LORD,
for only he will release my feet
from the snare.

[16]Turn to me and be gracious to me,
for I am lonely and afflicted.
[17]The troubles of my heart have
multiplied;
free me from my anguish.
[18]Look upon my affliction and my
distress
and take away all my sins.
[19]See how my enemies have increased
and how fiercely they hate me!
[20]Guard my life and rescue me;
let me not be put to shame,
for I take refuge in you.
[21]May integrity and uprightness protect
me,
because my hope is in you.

[22]Redeem Israel, O God,
from all their troubles!

Psalm 26

Of David.

[1]Vindicate me, O LORD,
for I have led a blameless life;
I have trusted in the LORD
without wavering.
[2]Test me, O LORD, and try me,
examine my heart and my mind;
[3]for your love is ever before me,
and I walk continually in your
truth.
[4]I do not sit with deceitful men,
nor do I consort with hypocrites;
[5]I abhor the assembly of evildoers
and refuse to sit with the wicked.
[6]I wash my hands in innocence,
and go about your altar, O LORD,
[7]proclaiming aloud your praise
and telling of all your wonderful
deeds.
[8]I love the house where you live,
O LORD,
the place where your glory dwells.

[9]Do not take away my soul along
with sinners,
my life with bloodthirsty men,
[10]in whose hands are wicked schemes,
whose right hands are full of
bribes.
[11]But I lead a blameless life;
redeem me and be merciful to me.
[12]My feet stand on level ground;
in the great assembly I will praise
the LORD.

[a]This psalm is an acrostic poem, the verses of which begin with the successive letters of the Hebrew alphabet.

Psalm 27

Of David.

¹The LORD is my light and my
salvation—
whom shall I fear?
The LORD is the stronghold of my
life—
of whom shall I be afraid?
²When evil men advance against me
to devour my flesh,ᵃ

when my enemies and my foes
attack me,
they will stumble and fall.
³Though an army besiege me,
my heart will not fear;
though war break out against me,
even then will I be confident.

⁴One thing I ask of the LORD,
this is what I seek:
that I may dwell in the house of the
LORD

ᵃ2 Or to slander me

THURSDAY

VERSE:	AUTHOR:	PASSAGE:
Psalm 27:1	Rosa Parks	Psalm 27:1–14

Sitting Down Without Fear

As a child, I learned from the Bible to trust in God and not be afraid. I have always felt comforted by reading the Psalms, especially Psalm 23 and 27.

I saw and heard so much as a child growing up with hate and injustice against black people. I learned to put my trust in God and to seek him as my strength. Long ago I set my mind to be a free person and not to give in to fear. I always felt that it was my right to defend myself if I could.

I have learned over the years that when one's mind is made up, this diminishes fear; knowing what must be done does away with fear. When I sat down on the bus the day I was arrested, I was thinking of going home. I had made up my mind quickly about what it was that I had to do, what I felt was right to do. I did not think of being physically tired or fearful. After so many years of oppression and being a victim of the mistreatment that my people had suffered, not giving up my seat—and whatever I had to face after not giving it up—was not important. I did not feel any fear at sitting in the seat I was sitting in. All I felt was tired. Tired of being pushed around. Tired of seeing the bad treatment and disrespect of children, women and men just because of the color of their skin. Tired of the Jim Crow laws. Tired of being oppressed. I was just plain tired.

I felt the Lord would give me the strength to endure whatever I had to face. God did away with all my fear. It was time for someone to stand up—or in my case, sit down. I refused to move.

ADDITIONAL SCRIPTURE READINGS:
Jeremiah 17:7–8; Ephesians 3:16–19

Go to page 412 for your next devotional reading.

all the days of my life,
to gaze upon the beauty of the LORD
and to seek him in his temple.
[5] For in the day of trouble
he will keep me safe in his
dwelling;
he will hide me in the shelter of his
tabernacle
and set me high upon a rock.
[6] Then my head will be exalted
above the enemies who surround
me;
at his tabernacle will I sacrifice with
shouts of joy;
I will sing and make music to the
LORD.

[7] Hear my voice when I call, O LORD;
be merciful to me and answer me.
[8] My heart says of you, "Seek his[a]
face!"
Your face, LORD, I will seek.
[9] Do not hide your face from me,
do not turn your servant away in
anger;
you have been my helper.
Do not reject me or forsake me,
O God my Savior.
[10] Though my father and mother
forsake me,
the LORD will receive me.
[11] Teach me your way, O LORD;
lead me in a straight path
because of my oppressors.
[12] Do not turn me over to the desire of
my foes,
for false witnesses rise up against
me,
breathing out violence.

[13] I am still confident of this:
I will see the goodness of the LORD
in the land of the living.
[14] Wait for the LORD;
be strong and take heart
and wait for the LORD.

Psalm 28

Of David.

[1] To you I call, O LORD my Rock;
do not turn a deaf ear to me.
For if you remain silent,
I will be like those who have gone
down to the pit.
[2] Hear my cry for mercy
as I call to you for help,

as I lift up my hands
toward your Most Holy Place.

[3] Do not drag me away with the
wicked,
with those who do evil,
who speak cordially with their
neighbors
but harbor malice in their hearts.
[4] Repay them for their deeds
and for their evil work;
repay them for what their hands
have done
and bring back upon them what
they deserve.
[5] Since they show no regard for the
works of the LORD
and what his hands have done,
he will tear them down
and never build them up again.

[6] Praise be to the LORD,
for he has heard my cry for mercy.
[7] The LORD is my strength and my
shield;
my heart trusts in him, and I am
helped.
My heart leaps for joy
and I will give thanks to him in
song.

[8] The LORD is the strength of his
people,
a fortress of salvation for his
anointed one.
[9] Save your people and bless your
inheritance;
be their shepherd and carry them
forever.

Psalm 29

A psalm of David.

[1] Ascribe to the LORD, O mighty ones,
ascribe to the LORD glory and
strength.
[2] Ascribe to the LORD the glory due his
name;
worship the LORD in the splendor
of his[b] holiness.

[3] The voice of the LORD is over the
waters;
the God of glory thunders,
the LORD thunders over the mighty
waters.
[4] The voice of the LORD is powerful;
the voice of the LORD is majestic.

---

[a] 8 Or To you, O my heart, he has said, "Seek my   [b] 2 Or LORD with the splendor of

⁵The voice of the LORD breaks the
   cedars;
   the LORD breaks in pieces the
   cedars of Lebanon.
⁶He makes Lebanon skip like a calf,
   Sirion*a* like a young wild ox.

a6 That is, Mount Hermon

⁷The voice of the LORD strikes
   with flashes of lightning.
⁸The voice of the LORD shakes the
   desert;
   the LORD shakes the Desert of
   Kadesh.

⟨ FRIDAY ⟩

VERSE: AUTHOR: PASSAGE:
Psalm 28:7   Debra Klingsporn   Psalm 28:6–9

Dancing Leaves

Another gray, dreary day. Wind, rain, sleet, snow. Ah, the variety of ways the weather can dampen my spirits. The overcast
skies rob the color from my world and I feel alone. Gray days
feel like Mondays—days full of too much to do and too little
time. Days with responsibilities crowding in and joy crowded
out. Gray days.

Yet in the road are dancing leaves. Leaves swirling in circular patterns across the street. Dancing leaves, you dance in circles, going
nowhere in particular. Don't you know today is bitter and cold?
Don't you realize the wind is making your world an unfriendly
place? Under gray skies and nasty weather, today is a day of over-
coats pulled tight and hats pulled low.

Still you dance. Crusty brown leaves, wrinkled and lifeless, you
dance. Yet this dance is not your own. Left to your own volition,
you'd be sitting in the nearest compost pile. No, this dance of
yours comes from a source completely other than your ring of
swirling leaves. This dance of yours is a defiant one, a dance which
laughs at the melancholy gray.

Dancing leaves, your defiance is contagious.

> Spirit of the living God,
> Surround my dreary world today
> And set my feet to dancing.
> The silent song of days gone gray,
> A heart that's heavy laden,
> Won't have the last, the final say.
> I know a song of dancing leaves,
> They swirl and twirl despite the gray.
> Spirit of the living God,
> Set my feet to dancing.

ADDITIONAL SCRIPTURE READINGS:
Psalm 30:11–12; Isaiah 40:4, 29–31

Go to page 414 for your next devotional reading.

⁹The voice of the LORD twists the
　　oaksᵃ
　　and strips the forests bare.
And in his temple all cry, "Glory!"

¹⁰The LORD sitsᵇ enthroned over the
　　flood;
　　the LORD is enthroned as King
　　　forever.
¹¹The LORD gives strength to his
　　people;
　　the LORD blesses his people with
　　　peace.

Psalm 30

A psalm. A song. For the dedication of
the temple.ᶜ Of David.

¹I will exalt you, O LORD,
　　for you lifted me out of the depths
　　and did not let my enemies gloat
　　　over me.
²O LORD my God, I called to you for
　　help
　　and you healed me.
³O LORD, you brought me up from the
　　graveᵈ;
　　you spared me from going down
　　　into the pit.

⁴Sing to the LORD, you saints of his;
　　praise his holy name.
⁵For his anger lasts only a moment,
　　but his favor lasts a lifetime;
weeping may remain for a night,
　　but rejoicing comes in the
　　　morning.

⁶When I felt secure, I said,
　　"I will never be shaken."
⁷O LORD, when you favored me,
　　you made my mountainᵉ stand
　　　firm;
but when you hid your face,
　　I was dismayed.

⁸To you, O LORD, I called;
　　to the Lord I cried for mercy:
⁹"What gain is there in my
　　destruction,ᶠ
　　in my going down into the pit?
Will the dust praise you?
　　Will it proclaim your faithfulness?
¹⁰Hear, O LORD, and be merciful to me;
　　O LORD, be my help."

¹¹You turned my wailing into dancing;

you removed my sackcloth and
　　clothed me with joy,
¹²that my heart may sing to you and
　　not be silent.
O LORD my God, I will give you
　　thanks forever.

Psalm 31

For the director of music. A psalm
of David.

¹In you, O LORD, I have taken refuge;
　　let me never be put to shame;
　　deliver me in your righteousness.
²Turn your ear to me,
　　come quickly to my rescue;
be my rock of refuge,
　　a strong fortress to save me.
³Since you are my rock and my
　　fortress,
　　for the sake of your name lead
　　　and guide me.
⁴Free me from the trap that is set for
　　me,
　　for you are my refuge.
⁵Into your hands I commit my spirit;
　　redeem me, O LORD, the God of
　　　truth.

⁶I hate those who cling to worthless
　　idols;
　　I trust in the LORD.
⁷I will be glad and rejoice in your
　　love,
　　for you saw my affliction
　　and knew the anguish of my soul.
⁸You have not handed me over to the
　　enemy
　　but have set my feet in a spacious
　　　place.

⁹Be merciful to me, O LORD, for I am
　　in distress;
　　my eyes grow weak with sorrow,
　　my soul and my body with grief.
¹⁰My life is consumed by anguish
　　and my years by groaning;
my strength fails because of my
　　affliction,ᵍ
　　and my bones grow weak.
¹¹Because of all my enemies,
　　I am the utter contempt of my
　　　neighbors;
I am a dread to my friends—
　　those who see me on the street
　　　flee from me.

ᵃ9 Or LORD makes the deer give birth　　　ᵇ10 Or sat　　　ᶜTitle: Or palace　　　ᵈ3 Hebrew Sheol
ᵉ7 Or hill country　　　ᶠ9 Or there if I am silenced　　　ᵍ10 Or guilt

WEEKENDING

REMEMBER

A warm letter from a friend. A compliment from my boss. An unexpected refund. A comforting Scripture. These arrive as God's good gifts to me. But they usually get overlooked while I'm focusing on what feels like—at least to me—insurmountable trouble. Always, it's trouble that God hasn't solved yet. Often, I complain about his delayed response. But really, my myopic vision isn't fair to him. If I lift my eyes off the problem, I can spot God's gifts all around me. They may not be the answer I'm searching for at the moment, but they're good and continuous gifts that say, "I still love you, my child." They remind me that God doesn't stop caring for me, even though I live with unfulfilled expectations. Now during the hard times, I remind myself to hunt for God's small surprises while I'm waiting for his big solution. It takes my mind off the problem. It helps me to trust him . . . It encourages me to know that God still cares.

Judith Couchman

REVIVE

Saturday: Psalm 36
Sunday: 1 Peter 5:5–7

Go to page 416 for your next devotional reading.

12I am forgotten by them as though I
    were dead;
  I have become like broken pottery.
13For I hear the slander of many;
    there is terror on every side;
  they conspire against me
    and plot to take my life.

14But I trust in you, O LORD;
    I say, "You are my God."
15My times are in your hands;
    deliver me from my enemies
    and from those who pursue me.
16Let your face shine on your servant;
    save me in your unfailing love.
17Let me not be put to shame, O LORD,
    for I have cried out to you;
  but let the wicked be put to shame
    and lie silent in the grave.a
18Let their lying lips be silenced,
    for with pride and contempt
    they speak arrogantly against the
      righteous.

19How great is your goodness,
    which you have stored up for
      those who fear you,
  which you bestow in the sight of
      men
    on those who take refuge in you.
20In the shelter of your presence you
    hide them
    from the intrigues of men;
  in your dwelling you keep them safe
    from accusing tongues.

21Praise be to the LORD,
    for he showed his wonderful love
      to me
    when I was in a besieged city.
22In my alarm I said,
    "I am cut off from your sight!"
  Yet you heard my cry for mercy
    when I called to you for help.

23Love the LORD, all his saints!
    The LORD preserves the faithful,
    but the proud he pays back in full.
24Be strong and take heart,
    all you who hope in the LORD.

Psalm 32

Of David. A *maskil.*b

1Blessed is he
    whose transgressions are forgiven,

  whose sins are covered.
2Blessed is the man
    whose sin the LORD does not count
      against him
    and in whose spirit is no deceit.

3When I kept silent,
    my bones wasted away
    through my groaning all day
      long.
4For day and night
    your hand was heavy upon me;
  my strength was sapped
    as in the heat of summer.   *Selah*
5Then I acknowledged my sin to
      you
    and did not cover up my iniquity.
  I said, "I will confess
    my transgressions to the LORD"—
  and you forgave
    the guilt of my sin.   *Selah*

6Therefore let everyone who is godly
      pray to you
    while you may be found;
  surely when the mighty waters rise,
    they will not reach him.
7You are my hiding place;
    you will protect me from trouble
    and surround me with songs of
      deliverance.   *Selah*

8I will instruct you and teach you in
      the way you should go;
    I will counsel you and watch over
      you.
9Do not be like the horse or the mule,
    which have no understanding
  but must be controlled by bit and
    bridle
    or they will not come to you.
10Many are the woes of the wicked,
    but the LORD's unfailing love
    surrounds the man who trusts in
      him.

11Rejoice in the LORD and be glad, you
      righteous;
    sing, all you who are upright in
      heart!

Psalm 33

1Sing joyfully to the LORD, you
    righteous;

---

a17 Hebrew *Sheol*   bTitle: Probably a literary or musical term

it is fitting for the upright to praise
  him.
²Praise the LORD with the harp;
  make music to him on the
    ten-stringed lyre.
³Sing to him a new song;
  play skillfully, and shout for joy.

⁴For the word of the LORD is right and
  true;
  he is faithful in all he does.
⁵The LORD loves righteousness and
  justice;
  the earth is full of his unfailing
    love.

MONDAY

VERSE: AUTHOR: PASSAGE:
Psalm 32:7   June Hunt   Psalm 32

I Am Hidden With Christ

The Nazis wielded terror over all who were not like them in
race, religion or rule. During World War II, the primary hate
targets were the Jews: their power stripped, property confis-
cated, people confined—and killed—in concentration camps. In
fact, in Nazi-dominated Holland, the ten Boom family had carefully hidden thousands of Jews in their "hiding place"—the secret
place behind their watch shop.

Then on February 28, 1944, that which was most feared happened—the hiding place was discovered! The Gestapo arrested the
ten Boom family. Their crime? Hiding Jews. Their punishment?
Immediate transport to a concentration camp.

As the two sisters waited in line to be searched, Corrie ten Boom
asked God if he would keep the Bible that was tucked inside her
clothing hidden from view. "Dear God, you have given me this
precious Book, you have kept it hidden through checkpoints and
inspections." The woman in front of Corrie was searched three
times. Beloved sister Betsie standing behind her was also searched.
Miraculously, the officer never touched Corrie. Her Bible now had
a hiding place in a German concentration camp!

Filth, disease, beating and rape became a part of their struggle
for survival. But as Corrie read the Bible's truths, she knew his
word would keep hatred from her heart. "I have hidden your word
in my heart that I might not sin against you" (Psalm 119:11).

Is there a hiding place for you? A place of healing for your dam-
aged emotions? When you have been treated harshly, you can be
free of hatred. Because he hides his truth in you, you are protected
from wrong thoughts and wrong choices. The adversary of your
life has no power to trap you . . . as long as you stay hidden in the
shelter of God's wings where you are safe from emotional destruction, hidden from emotional ruin.

ADDITIONAL SCRIPTURE READINGS:
Psalm 91; Colossians 3:3

Go to page 420 for your next devotional reading.

⁶By the word of the LORD were the
　　heavens made,
　　their starry host by the breath of
　　　his mouth.
⁷He gathers the waters of the sea into
　　jars*ᵃ*;
　　he puts the deep into storehouses.
⁸Let all the earth fear the LORD;
　　let all the people of the world
　　　revere him.
⁹For he spoke, and it came to be;
　　he commanded, and it stood
　　　firm.
¹⁰The LORD foils the plans of the
　　nations;
　　he thwarts the purposes of the
　　　peoples.
¹¹But the plans of the LORD stand firm
　　forever,
　　the purposes of his heart through
　　　all generations.

¹²Blessed is the nation whose God is
　　the LORD,
　　the people he chose for his
　　　inheritance.
¹³From heaven the LORD looks down
　　and sees all mankind;
¹⁴from his dwelling place he watches
　　all who live on earth—
¹⁵he who forms the hearts of all,
　　who considers everything they
　　　do.
¹⁶No king is saved by the size of his
　　army;
　　no warrior escapes by his great
　　　strength.
¹⁷A horse is a vain hope for
　　deliverance;
　　despite all its great strength it
　　　cannot save.
¹⁸But the eyes of the LORD are on those
　　who fear him,
　　on those whose hope is in his
　　　unfailing love,
¹⁹to deliver them from death
　　and keep them alive in famine.

²⁰We wait in hope for the LORD;
　　he is our help and our shield.
²¹In him our hearts rejoice,
　　for we trust in his holy name.
²²May your unfailing love rest
　　upon us, O LORD,
　　even as we put our hope in
　　　you.

Psalm 34*ᵇ*

Of David. When he pretended to be
insane before Abimelech, who drove
him away, and he left.

¹I will extol the LORD at all times;
　　his praise will always be on my
　　　lips.
²My soul will boast in the LORD;
　　let the afflicted hear and rejoice.
³Glorify the LORD with me;
　　let us exalt his name together.

⁴I sought the LORD, and he answered
　　me;
　　he delivered me from all my fears.
⁵Those who look to him are radiant;
　　their faces are never covered with
　　　shame.
⁶This poor man called, and the LORD
　　heard him;
　　he saved him out of all his
　　　troubles.
⁷The angel of the LORD encamps
　　around those who fear him,
　　and he delivers them.

⁸Taste and see that the LORD is good;
　　blessed is the man who takes
　　　refuge in him.
⁹Fear the LORD, you his saints,
　　for those who fear him lack
　　　nothing.
¹⁰The lions may grow weak and
　　hungry,
　　but those who seek the LORD lack
　　　no good thing.

¹¹Come, my children, listen to me;
　　I will teach you the fear of the
　　　LORD.
¹²Whoever of you loves life
　　and desires to see many good
　　　days,
¹³keep your tongue from evil
　　and your lips from speaking lies.
¹⁴Turn from evil and do good;
　　seek peace and pursue it.

¹⁵The eyes of the LORD are on the
　　righteous
　　and his ears are attentive to their
　　　cry;
¹⁶the face of the LORD is against those
　　who do evil,
　　to cut off the memory of them
　　　from the earth.

*ᵃ*7 Or *sea as into a heap*　　*ᵇ*This psalm is an acrostic poem, the verses of which begin with the
successive letters of the Hebrew alphabet.

17The righteous cry out, and the LORD
hears them;
he delivers them from all their
troubles.
18The LORD is close to the
brokenhearted
and saves those who are crushed
in spirit.

19A righteous man may have many
troubles,
but the LORD delivers him from
them all;
20he protects all his bones,
not one of them will be broken.

21Evil will slay the wicked;
the foes of the righteous will be
condemned.
22The LORD redeems his servants;
no one will be condemned who
takes refuge in him.

Psalm 35

Of David.

1Contend, O LORD, with those who
contend with me;
fight against those who fight
against me.
2Take up shield and buckler;
arise and come to my aid.
3Brandish spear and javelin[a]
against those who pursue me.
Say to my soul,
"I am your salvation."

4May those who seek my life
be disgraced and put to shame;
may those who plot my ruin
be turned back in dismay.
5May they be like chaff before the
wind,
with the angel of the LORD driving
them away;
6may their path be dark and slippery,
with the angel of the LORD
pursuing them.
7Since they hid their net for me
without cause
and without cause dug a pit for
me,
8may ruin overtake them by
surprise—
may the net they hid entangle
them,

may they fall into the pit, to their
ruin.
9Then my soul will rejoice in the LORD
and delight in his salvation.
10My whole being will exclaim,
"Who is like you, O LORD?
You rescue the poor from those too
strong for them,
the poor and needy from those
who rob them."

11Ruthless witnesses come forward;
they question me on things I
know nothing about.
12They repay me evil for good
and leave my soul forlorn.
13Yet when they were ill, I put on
sackcloth
and humbled myself with fasting.
When my prayers returned to me
unanswered,
14   I went about mourning
as though for my friend or
brother.
I bowed my head in grief
as though weeping for my mother.
15But when I stumbled, they gathered
in glee;
attackers gathered against me
when I was unaware.
They slandered me without
ceasing.
16Like the ungodly they maliciously
mocked[b];
they gnashed their teeth at me.
17O Lord, how long will you look on?
Rescue my life from their ravages,
my precious life from these lions.
18I will give you thanks in the great
assembly;
among throngs of people I will
praise you.

19Let not those gloat over me
who are my enemies without
cause;
let not those who hate me without
reason
maliciously wink the eye.
20They do not speak peaceably,
but devise false accusations
against those who live quietly in
the land.
21They gape at me and say, "Aha! Aha!
With our own eyes we have seen
it."

a 3 Or *and block the way*   *b* 16 Septuagint; Hebrew may mean *ungodly circle of mockers.*

²²O LORD, you have seen this; be not
    silent.
  Do not be far from me, O Lord.
²³Awake, and rise to my defense!
  Contend for me, my God and
    Lord.
²⁴Vindicate me in your righteousness,
    O LORD my God;
  do not let them gloat over me.
²⁵Do not let them think, "Aha, just
    what we wanted!"
  or say, "We have swallowed him
    up."

²⁶May all who gloat over my distress
    be put to shame and confusion;
  may all who exalt themselves over
    me
    be clothed with shame and
      disgrace.
²⁷May those who delight in my
    vindication
  shout for joy and gladness;
  may they always say, "The LORD be
    exalted,
  who delights in the well-being of
    his servant."
²⁸My tongue will speak of your
    righteousness
  and of your praises all day long.

Psalm 36

For the director of music. Of David the
servant of the LORD.

¹An oracle is within my heart
  concerning the sinfulness of the
    wicked:[a]
There is no fear of God
  before his eyes.
²For in his own eyes he flatters
    himself
  too much to detect or hate his sin.
³The words of his mouth are wicked
    and deceitful;
  he has ceased to be wise and to
    do good.
⁴Even on his bed he plots evil;
  he commits himself to a sinful
    course
  and does not reject what is wrong.

⁵Your love, O LORD, reaches to the
    heavens,
  your faithfulness to the skies.

⁶Your righteousness is like the mighty
    mountains,
  your justice like the great deep.
  O LORD, you preserve both man and
    beast.
⁷   How priceless is your unfailing
    love!
  Both high and low among men
    find[b] refuge in the shadow of
      your wings.
⁸They feast on the abundance of your
    house;
  you give them drink from your
    river of delights.
⁹For with you is the fountain of life;
  in your light we see light.

¹⁰Continue your love to those who
    know you,
  your righteousness to the upright
    in heart.
¹¹May the foot of the proud not come
    against me,
  nor the hand of the wicked drive
    me away.
¹²See how the evildoers lie fallen—
  thrown down, not able to rise!

Psalm 37[c]

Of David.

¹Do not fret because of evil men
  or be envious of those who do
    wrong;
²for like the grass they will soon
    wither,
  like green plants they will soon die
    away.

³Trust in the LORD and do good;
  dwell in the land and enjoy safe
    pasture.
⁴Delight yourself in the LORD
  and he will give you the desires of
    your heart.

⁵Commit your way to the LORD;
  trust in him and he will do this:
⁶He will make your righteousness
    shine like the dawn,
  the justice of your cause like the
    noonday sun.

⁷Be still before the LORD and wait
    patiently for him;

---

*a 1 Or heart: / Sin proceeds from the wicked.   b 7 Or love, O God! / Men find; or love! / Both heavenly
beings and men / find   c This psalm is an acrostic poem, the stanzas of which begin with the
successive letters of the Hebrew alphabet.*

do not fret when men succeed in
their ways,
when they carry out their wicked
schemes.

⁸Refrain from anger and turn from
wrath;
do not fret—it leads only to evil.
⁹For evil men will be cut off,
but those who hope in the LORD
will inherit the land.

¹⁰A little while, and the wicked will be
no more;
though you look for them, they
will not be found.
¹¹But the meek will inherit the land
and enjoy great peace.

¹²The wicked plot against the righteous
and gnash their teeth at them;
¹³but the Lord laughs at the wicked,
for he knows their day is coming.

¹⁴The wicked draw the sword
and bend the bow
to bring down the poor and needy,
to slay those whose ways are
upright.

¹⁵But their swords will pierce their
own hearts,
and their bows will be broken.

¹⁶Better the little that the righteous
have
than the wealth of many wicked;
¹⁷for the power of the wicked will be
broken,
but the LORD upholds the
righteous.

¹⁸The days of the blameless are known
to the LORD,
and their inheritance will endure
forever.
¹⁹In times of disaster they will not
wither;
in days of famine they will enjoy
plenty.

²⁰But the wicked will perish:
The LORD's enemies will be like the
beauty of the fields,
they will vanish—vanish like
smoke.

²¹The wicked borrow and do not repay,
but the righteous give generously;

⟨ TUESDAY ⟩

VERSE:
Psalm 37:5

AUTHOR:
Judith Lechman

PASSAGE:
Psalm 37:3–6

No Secrets

We are trying to enter into a relationship with God, and as is
true with any relationship, we must bring a vulnerable open-
ness to it. We cannot partition off from him certain frustrations
or disappointments, our happy plans for the evening or our
schedule for the workweek ahead. We are our ideas and
thoughts, hopes, ambitions, feelings and dreams. To begin a relationship and allow it to deepen, each of these aspects of our life
must not be hidden, but be ready to be presented to God.

This open sense of sharing is another way of saying that we truly
trust God. We are not afraid to rely upon him. We do so willingly,
with no hidden secrets. With such trust, we till the soil of our soul
for devotion.

ADDITIONAL SCRIPTURE READINGS:
Psalm 139:23; 2 Timothy 2:15

Go to page 424 for your next devotional reading.

²²those the LORD blesses will inherit
        the land,
    but those he curses will be cut off.

²³If the LORD delights in a man's way,
    he makes his steps firm;
²⁴though he stumble, he will not fall,
    for the LORD upholds him with his
        hand.

²⁵I was young and now I am old,
    yet I have never seen the righteous
        forsaken
    or their children begging bread.
²⁶They are always generous and lend
        freely;
    their children will be blessed.

²⁷Turn from evil and do good;
    then you will dwell in the land
        forever.
²⁸For the LORD loves the just
    and will not forsake his faithful
        ones.

    They will be protected forever,
        but the offspring of the wicked
            will be cut off;
²⁹the righteous will inherit the land
    and dwell in it forever.

³⁰The mouth of the righteous man
        utters wisdom,
    and his tongue speaks what is
        just.
³¹The law of his God is in his heart;
    his feet do not slip.

³²The wicked lie in wait for the
        righteous,
    seeking their very lives;
³³but the LORD will not leave them in
        their power
    or let them be condemned when
        brought to trial.

³⁴Wait for the LORD
    and keep his way.
    He will exalt you to inherit the land;
        when the wicked are cut off, you
            will see it.

³⁵I have seen a wicked and ruthless
        man
    flourishing like a green tree in its
        native soil,
³⁶but he soon passed away and was
        no more;
    though I looked for him, he could
        not be found.

³⁷Consider the blameless, observe the
        upright;
    there is a future[a] for the man of
        peace.
³⁸But all sinners will be destroyed;
    the future[b] of the wicked will be
        cut off.

³⁹The salvation of the righteous comes
        from the LORD;
    he is their stronghold in time of
        trouble.
⁴⁰The LORD helps them and delivers
        them;
    he delivers them from the wicked
        and saves them,
    because they take refuge in him.

Psalm 38

A psalm of David. A petition.

¹O LORD, do not rebuke me in your
        anger
    or discipline me in your wrath.
²For your arrows have pierced me,
    and your hand has come down
        upon me.
³Because of your wrath there is no
        health in my body;
    my bones have no soundness
        because of my sin.
⁴My guilt has overwhelmed me
    like a burden too heavy to bear.

⁵My wounds fester and are loathsome
    because of my sinful folly.
⁶I am bowed down and brought very
        low;
    all day long I go about mourning.
⁷My back is filled with searing pain;
    there is no health in my body.
⁸I am feeble and utterly crushed;
    I groan in anguish of heart.

⁹All my longings lie open before you,
        O Lord;
    my sighing is not hidden from
        you.
¹⁰My heart pounds, my strength fails
        me;
    even the light has gone from my
        eyes.
¹¹My friends and companions avoid
        me because of my wounds;
    my neighbors stay far away.
¹²Those who seek my life set their
        traps,

a37 Or there will be posterity   b38 Or posterity

those who would harm me talk of
my ruin;
all day long they plot deception.

¹³I am like a deaf man, who cannot
hear,
like a mute, who cannot open his
mouth;
¹⁴I have become like a man who does
not hear,
whose mouth can offer no reply.
¹⁵I wait for you, O LORD;
you will answer, O Lord my God.
¹⁶For I said, "Do not let them gloat
or exalt themselves over me when
my foot slips."

¹⁷For I am about to fall,
and my pain is ever with me.
¹⁸I confess my iniquity;
I am troubled by my sin.
¹⁹Many are those who are my vigorous
enemies;
those who hate me without reason
are numerous.
²⁰Those who repay my good with evil
slander me when I pursue what is
good.

²¹O LORD, do not forsake me;
be not far from me, O my God.
²²Come quickly to help me,
O Lord my Savior.

Psalm 39

For the director of music. For Jeduthun.
A psalm of David.

¹I said, "I will watch my ways
and keep my tongue from sin;
I will put a muzzle on my mouth
as long as the wicked are in my
presence."
²But when I was silent and still,
not even saying anything good,
my anguish increased.
³My heart grew hot within me,
and as I meditated, the fire
burned;
then I spoke with my tongue:

⁴"Show me, O LORD, my life's end
and the number of my days;
let me know how fleeting is my
life.
⁵You have made my days a mere
handbreadth;

the span of my years is as nothing
before you.
Each man's life is but a breath.
                                          Selah
⁶Man is a mere phantom as he goes
to and fro:
He bustles about, but only in vain;
he heaps up wealth, not knowing
who will get it.

⁷"But now, Lord, what do I look for?
My hope is in you.
⁸Save me from all my transgressions;
do not make me the scorn of
fools.
⁹I was silent; I would not open my
mouth,
for you are the one who has done
this.
¹⁰Remove your scourge from me;
I am overcome by the blow of
your hand.
¹¹You rebuke and discipline men for
their sin;
you consume their wealth like a
moth—
each man is but a breath.   *Selah*

¹²"Hear my prayer, O LORD,
listen to my cry for help;
be not deaf to my weeping.
For I dwell with you as an alien,
a stranger, as all my fathers were.
¹³Look away from me, that I may
rejoice again
before I depart and am no more."

Psalm 40

For the director of music. Of David.
A psalm.

¹I waited patiently for the LORD;
he turned to me and heard my cry.
²He lifted me out of the slimy pit,
out of the mud and mire;
he set my feet on a rock
and gave me a firm place to stand.
³He put a new song in my mouth,
a hymn of praise to our God.
Many will see and fear
and put their trust in the LORD.

⁴Blessed is the man
who makes the LORD his trust,
who does not look to the proud,
to those who turn aside to false
gods.ᵃ

ᵃ4 Or *to falsehood*

[5]Many, O LORD my God,
    are the wonders you have done.
The things you planned for us
    no one can recount to you;
were I to speak and tell of them,
    they would be too many to
        declare.

[6]Sacrifice and offering you did not
    desire,
    but my ears you have pierced[a,b];
burnt offerings and sin offerings
    you did not require.
[7]Then I said, "Here I am, I have
    come—
    it is written about me in the
        scroll.[c]
[8]I desire to do your will, O my God;
    your law is within my heart."

[9]I proclaim righteousness in the great
    assembly;
    I do not seal my lips,
    as you know, O LORD.
[10]I do not hide your righteousness in
    my heart;
    I speak of your faithfulness and
        salvation.
I do not conceal your love and your
    truth
    from the great assembly.

[11]Do not withhold your mercy from
    me, O LORD;
    may your love and your truth
        always protect me.
[12]For troubles without number
    surround me,
    my sins have overtaken me, and I
        cannot see.
They are more than the hairs of my
    head,
    and my heart fails within me.

[13]Be pleased, O LORD, to save me;
    O LORD, come quickly to help me.
[14]May all who seek to take my life
    be put to shame and confusion;
may all who desire my ruin
    be turned back in disgrace.
[15]May those who say to me, "Aha!
    Aha!"
    be appalled at their own shame.
[16]But may all who seek you
    rejoice and be glad in you;
may those who love your salvation
    always say,
    "The LORD be exalted!"

[17]Yet I am poor and needy;
    may the Lord think of me.
You are my help and my deliverer;
    O my God, do not delay.

Psalm 41

For the director of music. A psalm
of David.

[1]Blessed is he who has regard for the
    weak;
    the LORD delivers him in times of
        trouble.
[2]The LORD will protect him and
    preserve his life;
he will bless him in the land
    and not surrender him to the
        desire of his foes.
[3]The LORD will sustain him on his
    sickbed
    and restore him from his bed of
        illness.

[4]I said, "O LORD, have mercy on me;
    heal me, for I have sinned against
        you."
[5]My enemies say of me in malice,
    "When will he die and his name
        perish?"
[6]Whenever one comes to see me,
    he speaks falsely, while his heart
        gathers slander;
then he goes out and spreads it
    abroad.

[7]All my enemies whisper together
    against me;
    they imagine the worst for me,
        saying,
[8]"A vile disease has beset him;
    he will never get up from the place
        where he lies."
[9]Even my close friend, whom I
    trusted,
    he who shared my bread,
    has lifted up his heel against me.

[10]But you, O LORD, have mercy on me;
    raise me up, that I may repay
        them.
[11]I know that you are pleased with me,
    for my enemy does not triumph
        over me.
[12]In my integrity you uphold me
    and set me in your presence
        forever.

---

[a]6 Hebrew; Septuagint *but a body you have prepared for me* (see also Symmachus and Theodotion)
[b]6 Or *opened*   [c]7 Or *come / with the scroll written for me*

¹³Praise be to the LORD, the God of
Israel,
from everlasting to everlasting.
Amen and Amen.

BOOK II

Psalms 42–72

Psalm 42^a

For the director of music. A *maskil*^b of
the Sons of Korah.

¹As the deer pants for streams of
water,

so my soul pants for you,
O God.
²My soul thirsts for God, for
the living God.
When can I go and meet with
God?
³My tears have been my food
day and night,
while men say to me all day long,
"Where is your God?"
⁴These things I remember
as I pour out my soul:
how I used to go with the multitude,
leading the procession to the
house of God,

^aIn many Hebrew manuscripts Psalms 42 and 43 constitute one psalm.   ^bTitle: Probably a literary
or musical term

WEDNESDAY

VERSE: AUTHOR: PASSAGE:
Psalm 42:1   Elisa Morgan and Carol Kuykendall   Psalm 42

Feed Your Spirit

During the days when we are giving on demand, we need a
constant source of nourishment for ourselves as well.

Psalm 42:1–4 provides a mental picture of the many moms
who'd love to spend time with God but can't seem to fit it into
their hectic days: "As the deer pants for streams of water, so my
soul pants for you, O God. My soul thirsts for God, for the living
God. When can I go and meet with God?" (vv. 1-2).

There are many days when our spirits feel parched and we wonder when—or if—we'll ever "meet with God" again. Even getting to
church once a week is often difficult.

Instead of waiting to go to the house of the Lord, why not invite
him to your house? Sit down during a child's naptime and read a
few verses from the Gospel of John. Use a mealtime blessing to
really pray about what's happened that day. Leave your Bible open
on the table and grab a phrase from one of the psalms as you walk
by. Graze on Scripture morsels throughout the day from a flip-
book on the kitchen counter. Listen to a tape of the New
Testament in the car. Take a prayer walk through the neighborhood and talk to God about the details of your day.

When you think of taking a break, include a practice that will
feed your spirit.

ADDITIONAL SCRIPTURE READINGS:
Psalm 84; Isaiah 55:1; Matthew 5:6

Go to page 428 for your next devotional reading.

with shouts of joy and thanksgiving
  among the festive throng.

5Why are you downcast, O my soul?
  Why so disturbed within me?
Put your hope in God,
  for I will yet praise him,
  my Savior and 6my God.

My*a* soul is downcast within me;
  therefore I will remember you
from the land of the Jordan,
  the heights of Hermon—from
    Mount Mizar.
7Deep calls to deep
  in the roar of your waterfalls;
all your waves and breakers
  have swept over me.

8By day the LORD directs his love,
  at night his song is with me—
  a prayer to the God of my life.

9I say to God my Rock,
  "Why have you forgotten me?
Why must I go about mourning,
  oppressed by the enemy?"
10My bones suffer mortal agony
  as my foes taunt me,
saying to me all day long,
  "Where is your God?"

11Why are you downcast, O my soul?
  Why so disturbed within me?
Put your hope in God,
  for I will yet praise him,
  my Savior and my God.

Psalm 43*b*

1Vindicate me, O God,
  and plead my cause against an
    ungodly nation;
  rescue me from deceitful and
    wicked men.
2You are God my stronghold.
  Why have you rejected me?
Why must I go about mourning,
  oppressed by the enemy?
3Send forth your light and your truth,
  let them guide me;
let them bring me to your holy
    mountain,
  to the place where you dwell.
4Then will I go to the altar of God,
  to God, my joy and my delight.

I will praise you with the harp,
  O God, my God.

5Why are you downcast, O my soul?
  Why so disturbed within me?
Put your hope in God,
  for I will yet praise him,
  my Savior and my God.

Psalm 44

For the director of music. Of the Sons
    of Korah. A *maskil.c*

1We have heard with our ears, O God;
  our fathers have told us
what you did in their days,
  in days long ago.
2With your hand you drove out the
    nations
  and planted our fathers;
you crushed the peoples
  and made our fathers flourish.
3It was not by their sword that they
    won the land,
  nor did their arm bring them
    victory;
it was your right hand, your arm,
  and the light of your face, for you
    loved them.

4You are my King and my God,
  who decrees*d* victories for Jacob.
5Through you we push back our
    enemies;
  through your name we trample our
    foes.
6I do not trust in my bow,
  my sword does not bring me
    victory;
7but you give us victory over our
    enemies,
  you put our adversaries to shame.
8In God we make our boast all day
    long,
  and we will praise your name
    forever.   *Selah*

9But now you have rejected and
    humbled us;
  you no longer go out with our
    armies.
10You made us retreat before the
    enemy,
  and our adversaries have
    plundered us.

---

*a5,6 A few Hebrew manuscripts, Septuagint and Syriac; most Hebrew manuscripts praise him for his
saving help. / 6O my God, my   bIn many Hebrew manuscripts Psalms 42 and 43 constitute one
psalm.   cTitle: Probably a literary or musical term   d4 Septuagint, Aquila and Syriac; Hebrew
King, O God; / command*

11You gave us up to be devoured like
      sheep
   and have scattered us among the
      nations.
12You sold your people for a pittance,
   gaining nothing from their sale.

13You have made us a reproach to our
      neighbors,
   the scorn and derision of those
      around us.
14You have made us a byword among
      the nations;
   the peoples shake their heads at
      us.
15My disgrace is before me all day
      long,
   and my face is covered with
      shame
16at the taunts of those who reproach
      and revile me,
   because of the enemy, who is bent
      on revenge.

17All this happened to us,
   though we had not forgotten you
   or been false to your covenant.
18Our hearts had not turned back;
   our feet had not strayed from your
      path.
19But you crushed us and made us a
      haunt for jackals
   and covered us over with deep
      darkness.

20If we had forgotten the name of our
      God
   or spread out our hands to a
      foreign god,
21would not God have discovered it,
   since he knows the secrets of the
      heart?
22Yet for your sake we face death all
      day long;
   we are considered as sheep to be
      slaughtered.

23Awake, O Lord! Why do you sleep?
   Rouse yourself! Do not reject us
      forever.
24Why do you hide your face
   and forget our misery and
      oppression?

25We are brought down to the dust;
   our bodies cling to the ground.
26Rise up and help us;
   redeem us because of your
      unfailing love.

Psalm 45

For the director of music. To ⌊the tune
of⌋ "Lilies." Of the Sons of Korah. A
maskil.[a] A wedding song.

1My heart is stirred by a noble theme
   as I recite my verses for the king;
   my tongue is the pen of a skillful
      writer.

2You are the most excellent of men
   and your lips have been anointed
      with grace,
   since God has blessed you forever.
3Gird your sword upon your side,
      O mighty one;
   clothe yourself with splendor and
      majesty.
4In your majesty ride forth
      victoriously
   in behalf of truth, humility and
      righteousness;
   let your right hand display
      awesome deeds.
5Let your sharp arrows pierce the
      hearts of the king's enemies;
   let the nations fall beneath your
      feet.
6Your throne, O God, will last for ever
      and ever;
   a scepter of justice will be the
      scepter of your kingdom.
7You love righteousness and hate
      wickedness;
   therefore God, your God, has set
      you above your companions
   by anointing you with the oil of
      joy.
8All your robes are fragrant with
      myrrh and aloes and cassia;
   from palaces adorned with ivory
   the music of the strings makes
      you glad.
9Daughters of kings are among your
      honored women;
   at your right hand is the royal
      bride in gold of Ophir.

10Listen, O daughter, consider and give
      ear:
   Forget your people and your
      father's house.
11The king is enthralled by your
      beauty;
   honor him, for he is your lord.
12The Daughter of Tyre will come with
      a gift,[b]

aTitle: Probably a literary or musical term   b12 Or *A Tyrian robe is among the gifts*

men of wealth will seek your
favor.

13All glorious is the princess within
⌞her chamber⌟;
her gown is interwoven with gold.
14In embroidered garments she is led
to the king;
her virgin companions follow her
and are brought to you.
15They are led in with joy and
gladness;
they enter the palace of the king.

16Your sons will take the place of your
fathers;
you will make them princes
throughout the land.
17I will perpetuate your memory
through all generations,
therefore the nations will praise
you for ever and ever.

Psalm 46

For the director of music. Of the Sons
of Korah. According to *alamoth.*[a]
A song.

1God is our refuge and strength,
an ever-present help in trouble.
2Therefore we will not fear, though
the earth give way
and the mountains fall into the
heart of the sea,
3though its waters roar and foam
and the mountains quake with
their surging.   *Selah*

4There is a river whose streams make
glad the city of God,
the holy place where the Most
High dwells.
5God is within her, she will not fall;
God will help her at break of day.
6Nations are in uproar, kingdoms fall;
he lifts his voice, the earth melts.

7The LORD Almighty is with us;
the God of Jacob is our fortress.
Selah

8Come and see the works of the LORD,
the desolations he has brought on
the earth.
9He makes wars cease to the ends of
the earth;
he breaks the bow and shatters
the spear,

he burns the shields[b] with fire.
10"Be still, and know that I am God;
I will be exalted among the
nations,
I will be exalted in the earth."

11The LORD Almighty is with us;
the God of Jacob is our fortress.
Selah

Psalm 47

For the director of music. Of the Sons
of Korah. A psalm.

1Clap your hands, all you nations;
shout to God with cries of joy.
2How awesome is the LORD Most
High,
the great King over all the earth!
3He subdued nations under us,
peoples under our feet.
4He chose our inheritance for us,
the pride of Jacob, whom he loved.
Selah

5God has ascended amid shouts of
joy,
the LORD amid the sounding of
trumpets.
6Sing praises to God, sing praises;
sing praises to our King, sing
praises.

7For God is the King of all the earth;
sing to him a psalm[c] of praise.
8God reigns over the nations;
God is seated on his holy throne.
9The nobles of the nations assemble
as the people of the God of
Abraham,
for the kings[d] of the earth belong to
God;
he is greatly exalted.

Psalm 48

A song. A psalm of the Sons of Korah.

1Great is the LORD, and most worthy
of praise,
in the city of our God, his holy
mountain.
2It is beautiful in its loftiness,
the joy of the whole earth.
Like the utmost heights of Zaphon[e]
is Mount Zion,

---

[a]Title: Probably a musical term   [b]9 Or *chariots*   [c]7 Or *a maskil* (probably a literary or musical
term)   [d]9 Or *shields*   [e]2 *Zaphon* can refer to a sacred mountain or the direction north.

the*a* city of the Great King.
³God is in her citadels;
  he has shown himself to be her
    fortress.

⁴When the kings joined forces,
  when they advanced together,
⁵they saw ⌊her⌋ and were astounded;
  they fled in terror.
⁶Trembling seized them there,
  pain like that of a woman in labor.

⁷You destroyed them like ships of
    Tarshish
  shattered by an east wind.

⁸As we have heard,
  so have we seen
in the city of the LORD Almighty,
  in the city of our God:
  God makes her secure forever.

Selah

⁹Within your temple, O God,

---

*a*2 Or *earth, / Mount Zion, on the northern side / of the*

⟨ THURSDAY ⟩

VERSE:	AUTHOR:	PASSAGE:
Psalm 46:10	Gloria Gaither	Psalm 46

Quiet Earth

Stillness is more audible than any sound, not tinny like so many sounds I hear these days.

The silence is full and rich, insistent . . . demanding that I listen and suggesting always that I'd be foolish not to. Only fools refuse the counsel of the wise, and this silence seems to know everything. It seems I've been a prodigal, traipsing along behind the band just like a thoughtless gypsy anywhere the living was easy, stealing morsels when I could have had the loaf.

Maybe it's the oaks and beeches. These oaks have housed a thousand generations of owls and jays, and have withstood abuse from countless woodpeckers and people. They've seen the fleet-footed native children tossing pebbles at their roots and chasing little fawns around between them. They've stood and heard the council casting lots for war or peace while fragrant pipe smoke wafted through their branches.

Perhaps it is the brook, whispering of its secret travels, nurturing the earth along its way, or maybe it's the earth, the pregnant fertile earth, pulling me like influential kin back to my moorings and my heritage.

The earth is calling me home to the simple and eternal things. It persistently calls me to reject the glitter of the transient and return to Father's house.

The silence—a voice asking one pointed and unavoidable question: Will I return and inherit the earth? And here in the silence, the only sound to be heard is the whisper of my own answer.

ADDITIONAL SCRIPTURE READINGS:
1 Kings 19:12; Zechariah 2:13

Go to page 431 for your next devotional reading.

we meditate on your unfailing
  love.
[10]Like your name, O God,
    your praise reaches to the ends of
      the earth;
    your right hand is filled with
      righteousness.
[11]Mount Zion rejoices,
    the villages of Judah are glad
      because of your judgments.

[12]Walk about Zion, go around her,
    count her towers,
[13]consider well her ramparts,
    view her citadels,
    that you may tell of them to the
      next generation.
[14]For this God is our God for ever and
    ever;
    he will be our guide even to the
      end.

Psalm 49

For the director of music. Of the Sons
    of Korah. A psalm.

[1]Hear this, all you peoples;
    listen, all who live in this world,
[2]both low and high,
    rich and poor alike:
[3]My mouth will speak words of
      wisdom;
    the utterance from my heart will
      give understanding.
[4]I will turn my ear to a proverb;
    with the harp I will expound my
      riddle:

[5]Why should I fear when evil days
      come,
    when wicked deceivers surround
      me—
[6]those who trust in their wealth
    and boast of their great riches?
[7]No man can redeem the life of
      another
    or give to God a ransom for him—
[8]the ransom for a life is costly,
    no payment is ever enough—
[9]that he should live on forever
    and not see decay.

[10]For all can see that wise men die;
    the foolish and the senseless alike
      perish
    and leave their wealth to others.

[11]Their tombs will remain their
      houses[a] forever,
    their dwellings for endless
      generations,
    though they had[b] named lands
      after themselves.

[12]But man, despite his riches, does not
      endure;
    he is[c] like the beasts that perish.

[13]This is the fate of those who trust in
      themselves,
    and of their followers, who
      approve their sayings.   Selah
[14]Like sheep they are destined for the
      grave,[d]
    and death will feed on them.
  The upright will rule over them in
      the morning;
    their forms will decay in the
      grave,[d]
    far from their princely mansions.
[15]But God will redeem my life[e] from
      the grave;
    he will surely take me to himself.
                                        Selah

[16]Do not be overawed when a man
      grows rich,
    when the splendor of his house
      increases;
[17]for he will take nothing with him
      when he dies,
    his splendor will not descend with
      him.
[18]Though while he lived he counted
      himself blessed—
    and men praise you when you
      prosper—
[19]he will join the generation of his
      fathers,
    who will never see the light ⌊of
      life⌋.

[20]A man who has riches without
      understanding
    is like the beasts that perish.

Psalm 50

A psalm of Asaph.

[1]The Mighty One, God, the LORD,
    speaks and summons the earth
    from the rising of the sun to the
      place where it sets.

---

[a]11 Septuagint and Syriac; Hebrew *In their thoughts their houses will remain*   [b]11 Or */ for they have*
[c]12 Hebrew; Septuagint and Syriac read verse 12 the same as verse 20.   [d]14 Hebrew *Sheol*; also in
verse 15   [e]15 Or *soul*

²From Zion, perfect in beauty,
    God shines forth.
³Our God comes and will not be
        silent;
    a fire devours before him,
    and around him a tempest rages.
⁴He summons the heavens above,
    and the earth, that he may judge
        his people:
⁵"Gather to me my consecrated ones,
    who made a covenant with me by
        sacrifice."
⁶And the heavens proclaim his
        righteousness,
    for God himself is judge.   *Selah*

⁷"Hear, O my people, and I will
        speak,
    O Israel, and I will testify against
        you:
    I am God, your God.
⁸I do not rebuke you for your
        sacrifices
    or your burnt offerings, which are
        ever before me.
⁹I have no need of a bull from your
        stall
    or of goats from your pens,
¹⁰for every animal of the forest is
        mine,
    and the cattle on a thousand hills.
¹¹I know every bird in the mountains,
    and the creatures of the field are
        mine.
¹²If I were hungry I would not tell you,
    for the world is mine, and all that
        is in it.
¹³Do I eat the flesh of bulls
    or drink the blood of goats?
¹⁴Sacrifice thank offerings to God,
    fulfill your vows to the Most High,
¹⁵and call upon me in the day of
        trouble;
    I will deliver you, and you will
        honor me."

¹⁶But to the wicked, God says:

"What right have you to recite my
        laws
    or take my covenant on your lips?
¹⁷You hate my instruction
    and cast my words behind you.
¹⁸When you see a thief, you join with
        him;
    you throw in your lot with
        adulterers.

¹⁹You use your mouth for evil
    and harness your tongue to deceit.
²⁰You speak continually against your
        brother
    and slander your own mother's
        son.
²¹These things you have done and I
        kept silent;
    you thought I was altogether[a] like
        you.
But I will rebuke you
    and accuse you to your face.

²²"Consider this, you who forget God,
    or I will tear you to pieces, with
        none to rescue:
²³He who sacrifices thank offerings
        honors me,
    and he prepares the way
    so that I may show him[b] the
        salvation of God."

Psalm 51

*For the director of music. A psalm of
David. When the prophet Nathan came
to him after David had committed
adultery with Bathsheba.*

¹Have mercy on me, O God,
    according to your unfailing love;
    according to your great compassion
        blot out my transgressions.
²Wash away all my iniquity
    and cleanse me from my sin.

³For I know my transgressions,
    and my sin is always before me.
⁴Against you, you only, have I sinned
    and done what is evil in your
        sight,
    so that you are proved right when
        you speak
    and justified when you judge.
⁵Surely I was sinful at birth,
    sinful from the time my mother
        conceived me.
⁶Surely you desire truth in the inner
        parts[c];
    you teach[d] me wisdom in the
        inmost place.

⁷Cleanse me with hyssop, and I will
        be clean;
    wash me, and I will be whiter than
        snow.
⁸Let me hear joy and gladness;

---

[a] 21 Or *thought the 'I AM' was*   [b] 23 Or *and to him who considers his way / I will show*   [c] 6 The
meaning of the Hebrew for this phrase is uncertain.   [d] 6 Or *you desired . . . ; / you taught*

let the bones you have crushed
    rejoice.
⁹Hide your face from my sins
    and blot out all my iniquity.

¹⁰Create in me a pure heart, O God,
    and renew a steadfast spirit within
    me.
¹¹Do not cast me from your presence
    or take your Holy Spirit from me.
¹²Restore to me the joy of your
    salvation

and grant me a willing spirit, to
    sustain me.

¹³Then I will teach transgressors your
    ways,
    and sinners will turn back to
    you.
¹⁴Save me from bloodguilt, O God,
    the God who saves me,
    and my tongue will sing of your
    righteousness.
¹⁵O Lord, open my lips,

FRIDAY

VERSE: AUTHOR: PASSAGE:
Psalm 51:12   Gladis and Gordon DePree   Psalm 51

I Need Some Help

God,
I need some outside help tonight.
I want so much to be free,
But I don't feel free.

>   I know it all in my head
>   that your life is living in me,
>   that my life is a miracle,
>   But in my heart
>   It seems as if life is pressing in on me
>   And squeezing me,
>   Until I feel empty and limp.

Free . . .
What can that word mean
When my life belongs to so many other
    people,
When I get squeezed between the
    generation gap
And the tax bill,
And I want to walk out of the door and
    keep on walking and never stop . . .
Then what does it mean to be free?
God,
I need some help outside myself tonight.

ADDITIONAL SCRIPTURE READINGS:
Psalm 46; Colossians 2:10; Hebrews 13:6–7

Go to page 433 for your next devotional reading.

and my mouth will declare your
  praise.
[16]You do not delight in sacrifice, or I
    would bring it;
  you do not take pleasure in burnt
    offerings.
[17]The sacrifices of God are[a] a broken
    spirit;
  a broken and contrite heart,
  O God, you will not despise.

[18]In your good pleasure make Zion
    prosper;
  build up the walls of Jerusalem.
[19]Then there will be righteous
    sacrifices,
  whole burnt offerings to delight
    you;
  then bulls will be offered on your
    altar.

Psalm 52

  For the director of music. A maskil[b]
  of David. When Doeg the Edomite had
  gone to Saul and told him: "David has
  gone to the house of Ahimelech."

[1]Why do you boast of evil, you
    mighty man?
  Why do you boast all day long,
  you who are a disgrace in the eyes
    of God?
[2]Your tongue plots destruction;
  it is like a sharpened razor,
  you who practice deceit.
[3]You love evil rather than good,
  falsehood rather than speaking the
    truth.   Selah
[4]You love every harmful word,
  O you deceitful tongue!

[5]Surely God will bring you down to
    everlasting ruin:
  He will snatch you up and tear
    you from your tent;
  he will uproot you from the land
    of the living.   Selah
[6]The righteous will see and fear;
  they will laugh at him, saying,
[7]"Here now is the man
  who did not make God his
    stronghold
  but trusted in his great wealth
  and grew strong by destroying
    others!"

[8]But I am like an olive tree

flourishing in the house of God;
  I trust in God's unfailing love
  for ever and ever.
[9]I will praise you forever for what you
    have done;
  in your name I will hope, for your
    name is good.
  I will praise you in the presence of
    your saints.

Psalm 53

  For the director of music. According to
  mahalath.[c] A maskil[b] of David.

[1]The fool says in his heart,
  "There is no God."
They are corrupt, and their ways are
    vile;
  there is no one who does good.

[2]God looks down from heaven
    on the sons of men
  to see if there are any who
    understand,
  any who seek God.
[3]Everyone has turned away,
  they have together become corrupt;
there is no one who does good,
    not even one.

[4]Will the evildoers never learn—
  those who devour my people as
    men eat bread
  and who do not call on God?
[5]There they were, overwhelmed with
    dread,
  where there was nothing to dread.
God scattered the bones of those
    who attacked you;
  you put them to shame, for God
    despised them.
[6]Oh, that salvation for Israel would
    come out of Zion!
  When God restores the fortunes of
    his people,
  let Jacob rejoice and Israel be glad!

Psalm 54

For the director of music. With stringed
instruments. A maskil[b] of David. When
the Ziphites had gone to Saul and said,
  "Is not David hiding among us?"

[1]Save me, O God, by your name;
  vindicate me by your might.

---

[a]17 Or My sacrifice, O God, is   [b]Title: Probably a literary or musical term   [c]Title: Probably a
musical term

WEEKENDING

REJOICE

Practice sainthood—stand in silent awe
before your God. Practice sainthood
sing a song of praise in the shower.
Practice sainthood—smell a lilac.
Practice sainthood—jog through the
snow. Practice sainthood—laugh with
your toddler till your sides ache.
Practice sainthood—revel in God's revelation all around.

Enjoy the moment. Enjoy the second
tree from the corner, just as it stands. It
was placed there by your loving Father
to whom you, and this whole world,
belongs.

Carol VanKlompenburg

RENEW

Saturday: Psalm 52:8–9
Sunday: Psalm 149

*Go to page 435 for your
next devotional reading.*

²Hear my prayer, O God;
   listen to the words of my mouth.

³Strangers are attacking me;
   ruthless men seek my life—
   men without regard for God.   *Selah*

⁴Surely God is my help;
   the Lord is the one who sustains
   me.

⁵Let evil recoil on those who slander
   me;
   in your faithfulness destroy them.

⁶I will sacrifice a freewill offering to
   you;
   I will praise your name, O LORD,
   for it is good.
⁷For he has delivered me from all my
   troubles,
   and my eyes have looked in
   triumph on my foes.

Psalm 55

For the director of music. With stringed
instruments. A *maskil*ᵃ of David.

¹Listen to my prayer, O God,
   do not ignore my plea;
²   hear me and answer me.
My thoughts trouble me and I am
   distraught
³   at the voice of the enemy,
   at the stares of the wicked;
for they bring down suffering upon
   me
and revile me in their anger.

⁴My heart is in anguish within
   me;
   the terrors of death assail me.
⁵Fear and trembling have beset
   me;
   horror has overwhelmed me.
⁶I said, "Oh, that I had the wings of a
   dove!
   I would fly away and be at rest—
⁷I would flee far away
   and stay in the desert;   *Selah*
⁸I would hurry to my place of shelter,
   far from the tempest and storm."

⁹Confuse the wicked, O Lord,
   confound their speech,
   for I see violence and strife in the
   city.

¹⁰Day and night they prowl about on
   its walls;
   malice and abuse are within it.
¹¹Destructive forces are at work in the
   city;
   threats and lies never leave its
   streets.

¹²If an enemy were insulting me,
   I could endure it;
if a foe were raising himself against
   me,
   I could hide from him.
¹³But it is you, a man like myself,
   my companion, my close friend,
¹⁴with whom I once enjoyed sweet
   fellowship
as we walked with the throng at
   the house of God.

¹⁵Let death take my enemies by
   surprise;
   let them go down alive to the
   grave,ᵇ
   for evil finds lodging among them.

¹⁶But I call to God,
   and the LORD saves me.
¹⁷Evening, morning and noon
   I cry out in distress,
   and he hears my voice.
¹⁸He ransoms me unharmed
   from the battle waged against
   me,
   even though many oppose me.
¹⁹God, who is enthroned forever,
   will hear them and afflict them—
             Selah
men who never change their ways
   and have no fear of God.

²⁰My companion attacks his friends;
   he violates his covenant.
²¹His speech is smooth as butter,
   yet war is in his heart;
his words are more soothing than
   oil,
   yet they are drawn swords.

²²Cast your cares on the LORD
   and he will sustain you;
   he will never let the righteous fall.
²³But you, O God, will bring down the
   wicked
   into the pit of corruption;
bloodthirsty and deceitful men
   will not live out half their days.

But as for me, I trust in you.

ᵃTitle: Probably a literary or musical term   ᵇ15 Hebrew *Sheol*

Psalm 56

For the director of music. To ₁the tune
of₁ "A Dove on Distant Oaks." Of
David. A *miktam*. *a* When the
Philistines had seized him in Gath.

¹Be merciful to me, O God, for men
   hotly pursue me;
 all day long they press their attack.
²My slanderers pursue me all day
   long;
 many are attacking me in their
   pride.

³When I am afraid,
   I will trust in you.
⁴In God, whose word I praise,
   in God I trust; I will not be afraid.
 What can mortal man do to me?

⁵All day long they twist my words;
   they are always plotting to harm
   me.
⁶They conspire, they lurk,
   they watch my steps,
 eager to take my life.

⁷On no account let them escape;
   in your anger, O God, bring down
   the nations.
⁸Record my lament;
   list my tears on your scroll *b*—
 are they not in your record?

⁹Then my enemies will turn back
   when I call for help.
 By this I will know that God is for
   me.
¹⁰In God, whose word I praise,
   in the LORD, whose word I praise—

*a*Title: Probably a literary or musical term   *b*8 Or / *put my tears in your wineskin*

MONDAY

VERSE:	AUTHOR:	PASSAGE:
Psalm 55:4	Joan C. Webb	Psalm 55

Accepting Our Feelings

Many of us have the idea that in order to be mature, respected
adults we must renounce all our feelings. We may think that if
we are to be real men or women of God we must never admit
a need. We must always have an answer and always appear in
total control. Perhaps as children we were taught that it was
weak or cowardly to admit to disappointment, hurt, sadness, discouragement, anger or even happiness. But what we learned is a
misconception.

King David led his people to victory many times. Nations looked
up to him. But he made mistakes. He experienced the rejection of
trusted co-workers. He felt angry, jealous and hurt. David was a
truthful man who allowed himself to think and feel and be. In the
Psalms he often expressed sadness, discouragement and confusion. His acceptance of reality and the resulting feelings of disappointment and pain led him again and again to God. And God
called him "a man after my own heart" (Acts 13:22). Like David
we can think, feel and share, as responsible, mature men and
women of God.

ADDITIONAL SCRIPTURE READINGS:
2 Samuel 6:1–8; Lamentations 3:22–24; 1 Peter 5:7; Jude 24–25

Go to page 449 for your next devotional reading.

11in God I trust; I will not be afraid.
What can man do to me?

12I am under vows to you, O God;
I will present my thank offerings
to you.
13For you have delivered me*a* from
death
and my feet from stumbling,
that I may walk before God
in the light of life.*b*

Psalm 57

For the director of music. ⌊To the tune
of⌋ "Do Not Destroy." Of David. A
*miktam.*c When he had fled from Saul
into the cave.

1Have mercy on me, O God, have
mercy on me,
for in you my soul takes refuge.
I will take refuge in the shadow of
your wings
until the disaster has passed.

2I cry out to God Most High,
to God, who fulfills ⌊his purpose⌋
for me.
3He sends from heaven and saves
me,
rebuking those who hotly pursue
me;   *Selah*
God sends his love and his
faithfulness.

4I am in the midst of lions;
I lie among ravenous beasts—
men whose teeth are spears and
arrows,
whose tongues are sharp swords.

5Be exalted, O God, above the
heavens;
let your glory be over all the earth.

6They spread a net for my feet—
I was bowed down in distress.
They dug a pit in my path—
but they have fallen into it
themselves.   *Selah*

7My heart is steadfast, O God,
my heart is steadfast;
I will sing and make music.
8Awake, my soul!
Awake, harp and lyre!
I will awaken the dawn.

9I will praise you, O Lord, among the
nations;
I will sing of you among the
peoples.
10For great is your love, reaching to the
heavens;
your faithfulness reaches to the
skies.

11Be exalted, O God, above the
heavens;
let your glory be over all the earth.

Psalm 58

For the director of music. ⌊To the tune
of⌋ "Do Not Destroy." Of David.
A *miktam.*c

1Do you rulers indeed speak justly?
Do you judge uprightly among
men?
2No, in your heart you devise
injustice,
and your hands mete out violence
on the earth.
3Even from birth the wicked go astray;
from the womb they are wayward
and speak lies.
4Their venom is like the venom of a
snake,
like that of a cobra that has
stopped its ears,
5that will not heed the tune of the
charmer,
however skillful the enchanter may
be.

6Break the teeth in their mouths,
O God;
tear out, O LORD, the fangs of the
lions!
7Let them vanish like water that flows
away;
when they draw the bow, let their
arrows be blunted.
8Like a slug melting away as it moves
along,
like a stillborn child, may they not
see the sun.

9Before your pots can feel ⌊the heat
of⌋ the thorns—
whether they be green or dry—the
wicked will be swept away.*d*
10The righteous will be glad when they
are avenged,

---

*a*13 Or *my soul*   *b*13 Or *the land of the living*   *c*Title: Probably a literary or musical term
*d*9 The meaning of the Hebrew for this verse is uncertain.

when they bathe their feet in the
blood of the wicked.
¹¹Then men will say,
"Surely the righteous still are
rewarded;
surely there is a God who judges
the earth."

Psalm 59

For the director of music. ⌊To the tune
of⌋ "Do Not Destroy." Of David. A
miktam. [a] When Saul had sent men to
watch David's house in order to kill
him.

¹Deliver me from my enemies,
O God;
protect me from those who rise up
against me.
²Deliver me from evildoers
and save me from bloodthirsty
men.

³See how they lie in wait for me!
Fierce men conspire against me
for no offense or sin of mine,
O LORD.
⁴I have done no wrong, yet they are
ready to attack me.
Arise to help me; look on my
plight!
⁵O LORD God Almighty, the God of
Israel,
rouse yourself to punish all the
nations;
show no mercy to wicked traitors.
Selah

⁶They return at evening,
snarling like dogs,
and prowl about the city.
⁷See what they spew from their
mouths—
they spew out swords from their
lips,
and they say, "Who can hear us?"
⁸But you, O LORD, laugh at them;
you scoff at all those nations.

⁹O my Strength, I watch for you;
you, O God, are my fortress, ¹⁰my
loving God.

God will go before me
and will let me gloat over those
who slander me.

¹¹But do not kill them, O Lord our
shield, [b]
or my people will forget.
In your might make them wander
about,
and bring them down.
¹²For the sins of their mouths,
for the words of their lips,
let them be caught in their pride.
For the curses and lies they utter,
13   consume them in wrath,
consume them till they are no
more.
Then it will be known to the ends of
the earth
that God rules over Jacob.   *Selah*

¹⁴They return at evening,
snarling like dogs,
and prowl about the city.
¹⁵They wander about for food
and howl if not satisfied.
¹⁶But I will sing of your strength,
in the morning I will sing of your
love;
for you are my fortress,
my refuge in times of trouble.

¹⁷O my Strength, I sing praise to you;
you, O God, are my fortress, my
loving God.

Psalm 60

For the director of music. To ⌊the tune
of⌋ "The Lily of the Covenant." A
miktam [a] of David. For teaching. When
he fought Aram Naharaim [c] and Aram
Zobah, [d] and when Joab returned and
struck down twelve thousand Edomites
in the Valley of Salt.

¹You have rejected us, O God, and
burst forth upon us;
you have been angry—now restore
us!
²You have shaken the land and torn it
open;
mend its fractures, for it is
quaking.
³You have shown your people
desperate times;
you have given us wine that makes
us stagger.

⁴But for those who fear you, you have
raised a banner

to be unfurled against the bow.
                                    Selah

⁵Save us and help us with your right
    hand,
  that those you love may be
    delivered.
⁶God has spoken from his sanctuary:
  "In triumph I will parcel out
    Shechem
  and measure off the Valley of
    Succoth.
⁷Gilead is mine, and Manasseh is
    mine;
  Ephraim is my helmet,
  Judah my scepter.
⁸Moab is my washbasin,
  upon Edom I toss my sandal;
  over Philistia I shout in triumph."

⁹Who will bring me to the fortified
    city?
  Who will lead me to Edom?
¹⁰Is it not you, O God, you who have
    rejected us
  and no longer go out with our
    armies?
¹¹Give us aid against the enemy,
  for the help of man is worthless.
¹²With God we will gain the victory,
  and he will trample down our
    enemies.

Psalm 61

For the director of music. With stringed
instruments. Of David.

¹Hear my cry, O God;
  listen to my prayer.

²From the ends of the earth I call to
    you,
  I call as my heart grows faint;
  lead me to the rock that is higher
    than I.
³For you have been my refuge,
  a strong tower against the foe.

⁴I long to dwell in your tent forever
  and take refuge in the shelter of
    your wings.   *Selah*
⁵For you have heard my vows,
    O God;
  you have given me the heritage of
    those who fear your name.

⁶Increase the days of the king's life,
  his years for many generations.

⁷May he be enthroned in God's
    presence forever;
  appoint your love and faithfulness
    to protect him.

⁸Then will I ever sing praise to your
    name
  and fulfill my vows day after day.

Psalm 62

For the director of music. For Jeduthun.
A psalm of David.

¹My soul finds rest in God alone;
  my salvation comes from him.
²He alone is my rock and my
    salvation;
  he is my fortress, I will never be
    shaken.

³How long will you assault a man?
  Would all of you throw him
    down—
  this leaning wall, this tottering
    fence?
⁴They fully intend to topple him
  from his lofty place;
  they take delight in lies.
 With their mouths they bless,
  but in their hearts they curse.   *Selah*

⁵Find rest, O my soul, in God alone;
  my hope comes from him.
⁶He alone is my rock and my
    salvation;
  he is my fortress, I will not be
    shaken.
⁷My salvation and my honor depend
    on God[a];
  he is my mighty rock, my refuge.
⁸Trust in him at all times, O people;
  pour out your hearts to him,
  for God is our refuge.   *Selah*

⁹Lowborn men are but a breath,
  the highborn are but a lie;
 if weighed on a balance, they are
    nothing;
  together they are only a breath.
¹⁰Do not trust in extortion
  or take pride in stolen goods;
 though your riches increase,
  do not set your heart on them.

¹¹One thing God has spoken,
  two things have I heard:
 that you, O God, are strong,
¹² and that you, O Lord, are loving.

---

[a]7 Or / *God Most High is my salvation and my honor*

Surely you will reward each person
   according to what he has done.

Psalm 63

*A psalm of David. When he was in the
Desert of Judah.*

[1]O God, you are my God,
   earnestly I seek you;
my soul thirsts for you,
   my body longs for you,
in a dry and weary land
   where there is no water.

[2]I have seen you in the sanctuary
   and beheld your power and your
      glory.
[3]Because your love is better than life,
   my lips will glorify you.
[4]I will praise you as long as I live,
   and in your name I will lift up my
      hands.
[5]My soul will be satisfied as with the
      richest of foods;
   with singing lips my mouth will
      praise you.

[6]On my bed I remember you;
   I think of you through the watches
      of the night.
[7]Because you are my help,
   I sing in the shadow of your
      wings.
[8]My soul clings to you;
   your right hand upholds me.

[9]They who seek my life will be
      destroyed;
   they will go down to the depths of
      the earth.
[10]They will be given over to the sword
   and become food for jackals.

[11]But the king will rejoice in God;
   all who swear by God's name will
      praise him,
while the mouths of liars will be
      silenced.

Psalm 64

*For the director of music. A psalm
of David.*

[1]Hear me, O God, as I voice my
      complaint;
   protect my life from the threat of
      the enemy.

[2]Hide me from the conspiracy of the
      wicked,
   from that noisy crowd of
      evildoers.
[3]They sharpen their tongues like
      swords
   and aim their words like deadly
      arrows.
[4]They shoot from ambush at the
      innocent man;
   they shoot at him suddenly,
      without fear.

[5]They encourage each other in evil
      plans,
   they talk about hiding their snares;
   they say, "Who will see them[a]?"
[6]They plot injustice and say,
   "We have devised a perfect plan!"
   Surely the mind and heart of man
      are cunning.

[7]But God will shoot them with
      arrows;
   suddenly they will be struck down.
[8]He will turn their own tongues
      against them
   and bring them to ruin;
   all who see them will shake their
      heads in scorn.

[9]All mankind will fear;
   they will proclaim the works of
      God
   and ponder what he has done.
[10]Let the righteous rejoice in the LORD
   and take refuge in him;
   let all the upright in heart praise
      him!

Psalm 65

*For the director of music. A psalm
of David. A song.*

[1]Praise awaits[b] you, O God, in Zion;
   to you our vows will be fulfilled.
[2]O you who hear prayer,
   to you all men will come.
[3]When we were overwhelmed by sins,
   you forgave[c] our transgressions.
[4]Blessed are those you choose
   and bring near to live in your
      courts!
We are filled with the good things of
      your house,
   of your holy temple.

---

[a]5 Or *us*   [b]1 Or *befits*; the meaning of the Hebrew for this word is uncertain.   [c]3 Or *made*
atonement for

⁵You answer us with awesome deeds
        of righteousness,
    O God our Savior,
the hope of all the ends of the earth
    and of the farthest seas,
⁶who formed the mountains by your
        power,
    having armed yourself with
        strength,
⁷who stilled the roaring of the seas,
    the roaring of their waves,
    and the turmoil of the nations.
⁸Those living far away fear your
        wonders;
    where morning dawns and evening
        fades
    you call forth songs of joy.

⁹You care for the land and water it;
    you enrich it abundantly.
The streams of God are filled with
        water
    to provide the people with grain,
    for so you have ordained it.*ᵃ*
¹⁰You drench its furrows
    and level its ridges;
    you soften it with showers
    and bless its crops.
¹¹You crown the year with your
        bounty,
    and your carts overflow with
        abundance.
¹²The grasslands of the desert
        overflow;
    the hills are clothed with gladness.
¹³The meadows are covered with flocks
    and the valleys are mantled with
        grain;
    they shout for joy and sing.

Psalm 66

For the director of music. A song.
A psalm.

¹Shout with joy to God, all the earth!
² Sing the glory of his name;
    make his praise glorious!
³Say to God, "How awesome are your
        deeds!
    So great is your power
    that your enemies cringe before
        you.
⁴All the earth bows down to you;
    they sing praise to you,
    they sing praise to your name."
                                              Selah

⁵Come and see what God has done,
    how awesome his works in man's
        behalf!
⁶He turned the sea into dry land,
    they passed through the waters on
        foot—
    come, let us rejoice in him.
⁷He rules forever by his power,
    his eyes watch the nations—
    let not the rebellious rise up
        against him.   *Selah*

⁸Praise our God, O peoples,
    let the sound of his praise be
        heard;
⁹he has preserved our lives
    and kept our feet from slipping.
¹⁰For you, O God, tested us;
    you refined us like silver.
¹¹You brought us into prison
    and laid burdens on our backs.
¹²You let men ride over our heads;
    we went through fire and water,
    but you brought us to a place of
        abundance.

¹³I will come to your temple with
        burnt offerings
    and fulfill my vows to you—
¹⁴vows my lips promised and my
        mouth spoke
    when I was in trouble.
¹⁵I will sacrifice fat animals to you
    and an offering of rams;
    I will offer bulls and goats.   *Selah*

¹⁶Come and listen, all you who fear
        God;
    let me tell you what he has done
        for me.
¹⁷I cried out to him with my mouth;
    his praise was on my tongue.
¹⁸If I had cherished sin in my heart,
    the Lord would not have listened;
¹⁹but God has surely listened
    and heard my voice in prayer.
²⁰Praise be to God,
    who has not rejected my prayer
    or withheld his love from me!

Psalm 67

For the director of music. With stringed
instruments. A psalm. A song.

¹May God be gracious to us and
        bless us

ᵃ9 Or for that is how you prepare the land

and make his face shine upon us,
Selah

²that your ways may be known on
earth,
your salvation among all nations.

³May the peoples praise you, O God;
may all the peoples praise you.
⁴May the nations be glad and sing for
joy,
for you rule the peoples justly
and guide the nations of the earth.
Selah

⁵May the peoples praise you, O God;
may all the peoples praise you.

⁶Then the land will yield its harvest,
and God, our God, will bless us.
⁷God will bless us,
and all the ends of the earth will
fear him.

Psalm 68

For the director of music. Of David.
A psalm. A song.

¹May God arise, may his enemies be
scattered;
may his foes flee before him.
²As smoke is blown away by the
wind,
may you blow them away;
as wax melts before the fire,
may the wicked perish before God.
³But may the righteous be glad
and rejoice before God;
may they be happy and joyful.

⁴Sing to God, sing praise to his name,
extol him who rides on the
clouds*ᵃ*—
his name is the LORD—
and rejoice before him.
⁵A father to the fatherless, a defender
of widows,
is God in his holy dwelling.
⁶God sets the lonely in families,*ᵇ*
he leads forth the prisoners with
singing;
but the rebellious live in a
sun-scorched land.

⁷When you went out before your
people, O God,
when you marched through the
wasteland,   *Selah*
⁸the earth shook,

the heavens poured down rain,
before God, the One of Sinai,
before God, the God of Israel.
⁹You gave abundant showers, O God;
you refreshed your weary
inheritance.
¹⁰Your people settled in it,
and from your bounty, O God,
you provided for the poor.

¹¹The Lord announced the word,
and great was the company of
those who proclaimed it:
¹²"Kings and armies flee in haste;
in the camps men divide the
plunder.
¹³Even while you sleep among the
campfires,*ᶜ*
the wings of ˻my˼ dove are
sheathed with silver,
its feathers with shining gold."
¹⁴When the Almighty*ᵈ* scattered the
kings in the land,
it was like snow fallen on Zalmon.

¹⁵The mountains of Bashan are
majestic mountains;
rugged are the mountains of
Bashan.
¹⁶Why gaze in envy, O rugged
mountains,
at the mountain where God
chooses to reign,
where the LORD himself will dwell
forever?
¹⁷The chariots of God are tens of
thousands
and thousands of thousands;
the Lord ˻has come˼ from Sinai
into his sanctuary.
¹⁸When you ascended on high,
you led captives in your train;
you received gifts from men,
even from*ᵉ* the rebellious—
that you,*ᶠ* O LORD God, might
dwell there.

¹⁹Praise be to the Lord, to God our
Savior,
who daily bears our burdens.   *Selah*
²⁰Our God is a God who saves;
from the Sovereign LORD comes
escape from death.

²¹Surely God will crush the heads of
his enemies,
the hairy crowns of those who go
on in their sins.

ᵃ4 Or / *prepare the way for him who rides through the deserts*   *ᵇ6* Or *The desolate in a homeland*
ᶜ13 Or *saddlebags*   *ᵈ14* Hebrew *Shaddai*   *ᵉ18* Or *gifts for men, / even*   *ᶠ18* Or *they*

²²The Lord says, "I will bring them
  from Bashan;
  I will bring them from the depths
    of the sea,
²³that you may plunge your feet in the
    blood of your foes,
  while the tongues of your dogs
    have their share."

²⁴Your procession has come into view,
    O God,
  the procession of my God and
    King into the sanctuary.
²⁵In front are the singers, after them
    the musicians;
  with them are the maidens playing
    tambourines.
²⁶Praise God in the great congregation;
  praise the LORD in the assembly of
    Israel.
²⁷There is the little tribe of Benjamin,
    leading them,
  there the great throng of Judah's
    princes,
  and there the princes of Zebulun
    and of Naphtali.

²⁸Summon your power, O God[a];
  show us your strength, O God, as
    you have done before.
²⁹Because of your temple at Jerusalem
  kings will bring you gifts.
³⁰Rebuke the beast among the reeds,
  the herd of bulls among the calves
    of the nations.
  Humbled, may it bring bars of silver.
  Scatter the nations who delight in
    war.
³¹Envoys will come from Egypt;
  Cush[b] will submit herself to God.

³²Sing to God, O kingdoms of the
    earth,
  sing praise to the Lord,   *Selah*
³³to him who rides the ancient skies
    above,
  who thunders with mighty voice.
³⁴Proclaim the power of God,
  whose majesty is over Israel,
  whose power is in the skies.
³⁵You are awesome, O God, in your
    sanctuary;
  the God of Israel gives power and
    strength to his people.

  Praise be to God!

Psalm 69

For the director of music. To ⌊the tune
of⌋ "Lilies." Of David.

¹Save me, O God,
  for the waters have come up to my
    neck.
²I sink in the miry depths,
  where there is no foothold.
  I have come into the deep waters;
  the floods engulf me.
³I am worn out calling for help;
  my throat is parched.
  My eyes fail,
  looking for my God.
⁴Those who hate me without reason
  outnumber the hairs of my head;
  many are my enemies without cause,
  those who seek to destroy me.
  I am forced to restore
  what I did not steal.

⁵You know my folly, O God;
  my guilt is not hidden from you.

⁶May those who hope in you
  not be disgraced because of me,
  O Lord, the LORD Almighty;
  may those who seek you
  not be put to shame because of
    me,
  O God of Israel.
⁷For I endure scorn for your sake,
  and shame covers my face.
⁸I am a stranger to my brothers,
  an alien to my own mother's sons;
⁹for zeal for your house consumes
    me,
  and the insults of those who
  insult you fall on me.
¹⁰When I weep and fast,
  I must endure scorn;
¹¹when I put on sackcloth,
  people make sport of me.
¹²Those who sit at the gate mock me,
  and I am the song of the
    drunkards.

¹³But I pray to you, O LORD,
  in the time of your favor;
  in your great love, O God,
  answer me with your sure
    salvation.
¹⁴Rescue me from the mire,
  do not let me sink;
  deliver me from those who hate me,
  from the deep waters.

---

[a]28 Many Hebrew manuscripts, Septuagint and Syriac; most Hebrew manuscripts *Your God has
summoned power for you*   [b]31 That is, the upper Nile region

¹⁵Do not let the floodwaters engulf me
  or the depths swallow me up
  or the pit close its mouth over me.
¹⁶Answer me, O LORD, out of the
    goodness of your love;
  in your great mercy turn to me.
¹⁷Do not hide your face from your
    servant;
  answer me quickly, for I am in
    trouble.
¹⁸Come near and rescue me;
  redeem me because of my foes.

¹⁹You know how I am scorned,
    disgraced and shamed;
  all my enemies are before you.
²⁰Scorn has broken my heart
  and has left me helpless;
  I looked for sympathy, but there was
    none,
  for comforters, but I found none.
²¹They put gall in my food
  and gave me vinegar for my thirst.

²²May the table set before them
    become a snare;
  may it become retribution and[a] a
    trap.
²³May their eyes be darkened so they
    cannot see,
  and their backs be bent forever.
²⁴Pour out your wrath on them;
  let your fierce anger overtake them.
²⁵May their place be deserted;
  let there be no one to dwell in
    their tents.
²⁶For they persecute those you wound
  and talk about the pain of those
    you hurt.
²⁷Charge them with crime upon crime;
  do not let them share in your
    salvation.
²⁸May they be blotted out of the book
    of life
  and not be listed with the
    righteous.

²⁹I am in pain and distress;
  may your salvation, O God,
    protect me.

³⁰I will praise God's name in song
  and glorify him with thanksgiving.
³¹This will please the LORD more than
    an ox,
  more than a bull with its horns
    and hoofs.
³²The poor will see and be glad—

you who seek God, may your
    hearts live!
³³The LORD hears the needy
  and does not despise his captive
    people.

³⁴Let heaven and earth praise him,
  the seas and all that move in
    them,
³⁵for God will save Zion
  and rebuild the cities of Judah.
  Then people will settle there and
    possess it;
³⁶ the children of his servants will
    inherit it,
  and those who love his name will
    dwell there.

Psalm 70

For the director of music. Of David.
A petition.

¹Hasten, O God, to save me;
  O LORD, come quickly to help me.
²May those who seek my life
  be put to shame and confusion;
  may all who desire my ruin
  be turned back in disgrace.
³May those who say to me, "Aha!
    Aha!"
  turn back because of their shame.
⁴But may all who seek you
  rejoice and be glad in you;
  may those who love your salvation
    always say,
  "Let God be exalted!"

⁵Yet I am poor and needy;
  come quickly to me, O God.
  You are my help and my deliverer;
  O LORD, do not delay.

Psalm 71

¹In you, O LORD, I have taken refuge;
  let me never be put to shame.
²Rescue me and deliver me in your
    righteousness;
  turn your ear to me and save me.
³Be my rock of refuge,
  to which I can always go;
  give the command to save me,
  for you are my rock and my
    fortress.
⁴Deliver me, O my God, from the
    hand of the wicked,

---

a 22 Or snare / and their fellowship become

from the grasp of evil and cruel
men.

[5]For you have been my hope,
O Sovereign LORD,
my confidence since my youth.
[6]From birth I have relied on you;
you brought me forth from my
mother's womb.
I will ever praise you.
[7]I have become like a portent to
many,
but you are my strong refuge.
[8]My mouth is filled with your praise,
declaring your splendor all day
long.

[9]Do not cast me away when I am old;
do not forsake me when my
strength is gone.
[10]For my enemies speak against me;
those who wait to kill me conspire
together.
[11]They say, "God has forsaken him;
pursue him and seize him,
for no one will rescue him."
[12]Be not far from me, O God;
come quickly, O my God, to help
me.
[13]May my accusers perish in shame;
may those who want to harm me
be covered with scorn and
disgrace.

[14]But as for me, I will always have
hope;
I will praise you more and more.
[15]My mouth will tell of your
righteousness,
of your salvation all day long,
though I know not its measure.
[16]I will come and proclaim your
mighty acts, O Sovereign LORD;
I will proclaim your righteousness,
yours alone.
[17]Since my youth, O God, you have
taught me,
and to this day I declare your
marvelous deeds.
[18]Even when I am old and gray,
do not forsake me, O God,
till I declare your power to the next
generation,
your might to all who are to come.

[19]Your righteousness reaches to the
skies, O God,
you who have done great things.

Who, O God, is like you?
[20]Though you have made me see
troubles, many and bitter,
you will restore my life again;
from the depths of the earth
you will again bring me up.
[21]You will increase my honor
and comfort me once again.

[22]I will praise you with the harp
for your faithfulness, O my God;
I will sing praise to you with the
lyre,
O Holy One of Israel.
[23]My lips will shout for joy
when I sing praise to you—
I, whom you have redeemed.
[24]My tongue will tell of your righteous
acts
all day long,
for those who wanted to harm me
have been put to shame and
confusion.

Psalm 72

Of Solomon.

[1]Endow the king with your justice,
O God,
the royal son with your
righteousness.
[2]He will[a] judge your people in
righteousness,
your afflicted ones with justice.
[3]The mountains will bring prosperity
to the people,
the hills the fruit of righteousness.
[4]He will defend the afflicted among
the people
and save the children of the needy;
he will crush the oppressor.

[5]He will endure[b] as long as the sun,
as long as the moon, through all
generations.
[6]He will be like rain falling on a
mown field,
like showers watering the earth.
[7]In his days the righteous will
flourish;
prosperity will abound till the
moon is no more.

[8]He will rule from sea to sea
and from the River[c] to the ends
of the earth.[d]

---

[a]2 Or *May he;* similarly in verses 3–11 and 17   [b]5 Septuagint; Hebrew *You will be feared*
[c]8 That is, the Euphrates   [d]8 Or *the end of the land*

⁹The desert tribes will bow before
    him
  and his enemies will lick the dust.
¹⁰The kings of Tarshish and of distant
    shores
  will bring tribute to him;
 the kings of Sheba and Seba
  will present him gifts.
¹¹All kings will bow down to him
  and all nations will serve him.

¹²For he will deliver the needy who cry
    out,
  the afflicted who have no one to
    help.
¹³He will take pity on the weak and
    the needy
  and save the needy from death.
¹⁴He will rescue them from oppression
    and violence,
  for precious is their blood in his
    sight.

¹⁵Long may he live!
  May gold from Sheba be given
    him.
 May people ever pray for him
  and bless him all day long.
¹⁶Let grain abound throughout the
    land;
  on the tops of the hills may it
    sway.
 Let its fruit flourish like Lebanon;
  let it thrive like the grass of the
    field.
¹⁷May his name endure forever;
  may it continue as long as the
    sun.

All nations will be blessed through
    him,
  and they will call him blessed.

¹⁸Praise be to the LORD God, the God
    of Israel,
  who alone does marvelous deeds.
¹⁹Praise be to his glorious name
    forever;
  may the whole earth be filled with
    his glory.
      Amen and Amen.

²⁰This concludes the prayers of David
    son of Jesse.

BOOK III

Psalms 73–89

Psalm 73

A psalm of Asaph.

¹Surely God is good to Israel,
  to those who are pure in heart.

²But as for me, my feet had almost
    slipped;
  I had nearly lost my foothold.
³For I envied the arrogant
  when I saw the prosperity of the
    wicked.

⁴They have no struggles;
  their bodies are healthy and
    strong.ᵃ
⁵They are free from the burdens
    common to man;
  they are not plagued by human
    ills.
⁶Therefore pride is their necklace;
  they clothe themselves with
    violence.
⁷From their callous hearts comes
    iniquityᵇ;
  the evil conceits of their minds
    know no limits.
⁸They scoff, and speak with malice;
  in their arrogance they threaten
    oppression.
⁹Their mouths lay claim to heaven,
  and their tongues take possession
    of the earth.
¹⁰Therefore their people turn to them
  and drink up waters in
    abundance.ᶜ
¹¹They say, "How can God know?
  Does the Most High have
    knowledge?"

¹²This is what the wicked are like—
  always carefree, they increase in
    wealth.

¹³Surely in vain have I kept my heart
    pure;
  in vain have I washed my hands
    in innocence.
¹⁴All day long I have been plagued;
  I have been punished every
    morning.

¹⁵If I had said, "I will speak thus,"

ᵃ4 With a different word division of the Hebrew; Masoretic Text *struggles at their death; / their bodies are
healthy*   ᵇ7 Syriac (see also Septuagint); Hebrew *Their eyes bulge with fat*   ᶜ10 The meaning of the
Hebrew for this verse is uncertain.

I would have betrayed your
   children.
16When I tried to understand all this,
   it was oppressive to me
17till I entered the sanctuary of God;
   then I understood their final
     destiny.

18Surely you place them on slippery
   ground;
   you cast them down to ruin.
19How suddenly are they destroyed,
   completely swept away by terrors!
20As a dream when one awakes,
   so when you arise, O Lord,
   you will despise them as fantasies.

21When my heart was grieved
   and my spirit embittered,
22I was senseless and ignorant;
   I was a brute beast before you.

23Yet I am always with you;
   you hold me by my right hand.
24You guide me with your counsel,
   and afterward you will take me
     into glory.
25Whom have I in heaven but you?
   And earth has nothing I desire
     besides you.
26My flesh and my heart may fail,
   but God is the strength of my
     heart
   and my portion forever.

27Those who are far from you will
   perish;
   you destroy all who are unfaithful
     to you.
28But as for me, it is good to be near
   God.
   I have made the Sovereign Lord
     my refuge;
   I will tell of all your deeds.

Psalm 74

A maskil[a] of Asaph.

1Why have you rejected us forever,
   O God?
   Why does your anger smolder
     against the sheep of your
     pasture?
2Remember the people you purchased
   of old,
   the tribe of your inheritance,
     whom you redeemed—
   Mount Zion, where you dwelt.

3Turn your steps toward these
   everlasting ruins,
   all this destruction the enemy has
     brought on the sanctuary.

4Your foes roared in the place where
   you met with us;
   they set up their standards as
     signs.
5They behaved like men wielding axes
   to cut through a thicket of trees.
6They smashed all the carved paneling
   with their axes and hatchets.
7They burned your sanctuary to the
   ground;
   they defiled the dwelling place of
     your Name.
8They said in their hearts, "We will
   crush them completely!"
   They burned every place where
     God was worshiped in the
     land.
9We are given no miraculous signs;
   no prophets are left,
   and none of us knows how long
     this will be.

10How long will the enemy mock you,
   O God?
   Will the foe revile your name
     forever?
11Why do you hold back your hand,
   your right hand?
   Take it from the folds of your
     garment and destroy them!

12But you, O God, are my king from of
   old;
   you bring salvation upon the
     earth.
13It was you who split open the sea by
   your power;
   you broke the heads of the
     monster in the waters.
14It was you who crushed the heads of
   Leviathan
   and gave him as food to the
     creatures of the desert.
15It was you who opened up springs
   and streams;
   you dried up the ever flowing
     rivers.
16The day is yours, and yours also the
   night;
   you established the sun and
     moon.
17It was you who set all the
   boundaries of the earth;

---

*a*Title: Probably a literary or musical term

you made both summer and
winter.
18Remember how the enemy has
mocked you, O LORD,
how foolish people have reviled
your name.
19Do not hand over the life of your
dove to wild beasts;
do not forget the lives of your
afflicted people forever.
20Have regard for your covenant,
because haunts of violence fill the
dark places of the land.
21Do not let the oppressed retreat in
disgrace;
may the poor and needy praise
your name.

22Rise up, O God, and defend your
cause;
remember how fools mock you all
day long.
23Do not ignore the clamor of your
adversaries,
the uproar of your enemies, which
rises continually.

Psalm 75

For the director of music. To the tune
of "Do Not Destroy." A psalm of
Asaph. A song.

1We give thanks to you, O God,
we give thanks, for your Name is
near;
men tell of your wonderful deeds.

2You say, "I choose the appointed
time;
it is I who judge uprightly.
3When the earth and all its people
quake,
it is I who hold its pillars firm. Selah

4To the arrogant I say, 'Boast no
more,'
and to the wicked, 'Do not lift up
your horns.
5Do not lift your horns against
heaven;
do not speak with outstretched
neck.'"

6No one from the east or the west
or from the desert can exalt a man.
7But it is God who judges:

He brings one down, he exalts
another.
8In the hand of the LORD is a cup
full of foaming wine mixed with
spices;
he pours it out, and all the wicked of
the earth
drink it down to its very dregs.

9As for me, I will declare this forever;
I will sing praise to the God of
Jacob.
10I will cut off the horns of all the
wicked,
but the horns of the righteous will
be lifted up.

Psalm 76

For the director of music. With stringed
instruments. A psalm of Asaph.
A song.

1In Judah God is known;
his name is great in Israel.
2His tent is in Salem,
his dwelling place in Zion.
3There he broke the flashing arrows,
the shields and the swords, the
weapons of war. Selah

4You are resplendent with light,
more majestic than mountains rich
with game.
5Valiant men lie plundered,
they sleep their last sleep;
not one of the warriors
can lift his hands.
6At your rebuke, O God of Jacob,
both horse and chariot lie still.
7You alone are to be feared.
Who can stand before you when
you are angry?
8From heaven you pronounced
judgment,
and the land feared and was
quiet—
9when you, O God, rose up to judge,
to save all the afflicted of the land. Selah
10Surely your wrath against men brings
you praise,
and the survivors of your wrath
are restrained.[a]

11Make vows to the LORD your God
and fulfill them;
let all the neighboring lands
bring gifts to the One to be feared.

[a]10 Or Surely the wrath of men brings you praise, / and with the remainder of wrath you arm yourself

¹²He breaks the spirit of rulers;
  he is feared by the kings of the
    earth.

Psalm 77

For the director of music. For Jeduthun.
Of Asaph. A psalm.

¹I cried out to God for help;
  I cried out to God to hear me.
²When I was in distress, I sought the
    Lord;
  at night I stretched out untiring
    hands
  and my soul refused to be
    comforted.

³I remembered you, O God, and I
    groaned;
  I mused, and my spirit grew faint.
                                    Selah

⁴You kept my eyes from closing;
  I was too troubled to speak.
⁵I thought about the former days,
  the years of long ago;
⁶I remembered my songs in the night.
  My heart mused and my spirit
    inquired:

⁷"Will the Lord reject forever?
  Will he never show his favor
    again?
⁸Has his unfailing love vanished
    forever?
  Has his promise failed for all
    time?
⁹Has God forgotten to be merciful?
  Has he in anger withheld his
    compassion?"   *Selah*

¹⁰Then I thought, "To this I will
    appeal:
  the years of the right hand of the
    Most High."
¹¹I will remember the deeds of the
    LORD;
  yes, I will remember your miracles
    of long ago.
¹²I will meditate on all your works
  and consider all your mighty
    deeds.

¹³Your ways, O God, are holy.
  What god is so great as our God?
¹⁴You are the God who performs
    miracles;
  you display your power among the
    peoples.

¹⁵With your mighty arm you redeemed
    your people,
  the descendants of Jacob and
    Joseph.   *Selah*

¹⁶The waters saw you, O God,
  the waters saw you and writhed;
  the very depths were convulsed.
¹⁷The clouds poured down water,
  the skies resounded with thunder;
  your arrows flashed back and
    forth.
¹⁸Your thunder was heard in the
    whirlwind,
  your lightning lit up the world;
  the earth trembled and quaked.
¹⁹Your path led through the sea,
  your way through the mighty
    waters,
  though your footprints were not
    seen.

²⁰You led your people like a flock
  by the hand of Moses and Aaron.

Psalm 78

A *maskil*[a] of Asaph.

¹O my people, hear my teaching;
  listen to the words of my mouth.
²I will open my mouth in parables,
  I will utter hidden things, things
    from of old—
³what we have heard and known,
  what our fathers have told us.
⁴We will not hide them from their
    children;
  we will tell the next generation
the praiseworthy deeds of the
    LORD,
  his power, and the wonders he
    has done.
⁵He decreed statutes for Jacob
  and established the law in Israel,
which he commanded our
    forefathers
  to teach their children,
⁶so the next generation would know
    them,
  even the children yet to be born,
  and they in turn would tell their
    children.
⁷Then they would put their trust in
    God
  and would not forget his deeds
  but would keep his commands.

---

[a]Title: Probably a literary or musical term

8They would not be like their
forefathers—
a stubborn and rebellious
generation,
whose hearts were not loyal to God,
whose spirits were not faithful to
him.

9The men of Ephraim, though armed
with bows,
turned back on the day of battle;
10they did not keep God's covenant
and refused to live by his law.
11They forgot what he had done,
the wonders he had shown them.
12He did miracles in the sight of their
fathers
in the land of Egypt, in the region
of Zoan.
13He divided the sea and led them
through;
he made the water stand firm like
a wall.
14He guided them with the cloud by day
and with light from the fire all
night.
15He split the rocks in the desert
and gave them water as abundant
as the seas;
16he brought streams out of a rocky
crag
and made water flow down like
rivers.

TUESDAY

VERSE:	AUTHOR:	PASSAGE:
Psalm 78:5	Grace H. Ketterman	Psalm 78

Love Teaches

One of the most essential ingredients of education is the parents' attitude and example regarding basic curiosity and a desire to learn.

It is not so much the didactic or "book" learning that is important in parent-child relationships, however. It is, instead, educating children about life—and death; about themselves—and others; about their world—and how they fit into it. The love of learning and the curiosity that will *only* be satisfied through finding out about something—that is a parent's means of prompting a child to become wise and to respect and appreciate the teacher.

My parents encouraged my love for learning (and for them) by their examples. The dad who took time out during a busy day to show a little girl a baby chick being hatched, a brand-new baby colt on its first wobbly walk, or a litter of pink squealing piglets did not know the impact those simple sights would have on her life! He was teaching her about creation, the Creator and her own place in God's scheme of things.

Through my parents' reading, I learned to love books; through their philosophy, I learned to think; through their humor, I learned to laugh; through their discipline, I learned obedience, respect and self-control. It was through their faith that my own was born.

ADDITIONAL SCRIPTURE READINGS:
Deuteronomy 4:9; Ephesians 6:4

Go to page 459 for your next devotional reading.

¹⁷But they continued to sin against
        him,
    rebelling in the desert against the
        Most High.
¹⁸They willfully put God to the test
    by demanding the food they
        craved.
¹⁹They spoke against God, saying,
    "Can God spread a table in the
        desert?
²⁰When he struck the rock, water
        gushed out,
    and streams flowed abundantly.
    But can he also give us food?
    Can he supply meat for his
        people?"
²¹When the LORD heard them, he was
        very angry;
    his fire broke out against Jacob,
    and his wrath rose against Israel,
²²for they did not believe in God
    or trust in his deliverance.
²³Yet he gave a command to the skies
        above
    and opened the doors of the
        heavens;
²⁴he rained down manna for the
        people to eat,
    he gave them the grain of heaven.
²⁵Men ate the bread of angels;
    he sent them all the food they
        could eat.
²⁶He let loose the east wind from the
        heavens
    and led forth the south wind by
        his power.
²⁷He rained meat down on them like
        dust,
    flying birds like sand on the
        seashore.
²⁸He made them come down inside
        their camp,
    all around their tents.
²⁹They ate till they had more than
        enough,
    for he had given them what they
        craved.
³⁰But before they turned from the food
        they craved,
    even while it was still in their
        mouths,
³¹God's anger rose against them;
    he put to death the sturdiest
        among them,
    cutting down the young men of
        Israel.

³²In spite of all this, they kept on
        sinning;

in spite of his wonders, they did
        not believe.
³³So he ended their days in futility
    and their years in terror.
³⁴Whenever God slew them, they
        would seek him;
    they eagerly turned to him again.
³⁵They remembered that God was their
        Rock,
    that God Most High was their
        Redeemer.
³⁶But then they would flatter him with
        their mouths,
    lying to him with their tongues;
³⁷their hearts were not loyal to him,
    they were not faithful to his
        covenant.
³⁸Yet he was merciful;
    he forgave their iniquities
    and did not destroy them.
    Time after time he restrained his
        anger
    and did not stir up his full wrath.
³⁹He remembered that they were but
        flesh,
    a passing breeze that does not
        return.
⁴⁰How often they rebelled against him
        in the desert
    and grieved him in the wasteland!
⁴¹Again and again they put God to the
        test;
    they vexed the Holy One of Israel.
⁴²They did not remember his power—
    the day he redeemed them from
        the oppressor,
⁴³the day he displayed his miraculous
        signs in Egypt,
    his wonders in the region of Zoan.
⁴⁴He turned their rivers to blood;
    they could not drink from their
        streams.
⁴⁵He sent swarms of flies that
        devoured them,
    and frogs that devastated them.
⁴⁶He gave their crops to the
        grasshopper,
    their produce to the locust.
⁴⁷He destroyed their vines with hail
    and their sycamore-figs with sleet.
⁴⁸He gave over their cattle to the hail,
    their livestock to bolts of lightning.
⁴⁹He unleashed against them his hot
        anger,
    his wrath, indignation and
        hostility—
    a band of destroying angels.
⁵⁰He prepared a path for his anger;

he did not spare them from death
but gave them over to the plague.
⁵¹He struck down all the firstborn of
Egypt,
the firstfruits of manhood in the
tents of Ham.
⁵²But he brought his people out like a
flock;
he led them like sheep through the
desert.
⁵³He guided them safely, so they were
unafraid;
but the sea engulfed their enemies.
⁵⁴Thus he brought them to the border
of his holy land,
to the hill country his right hand
had taken.
⁵⁵He drove out nations before them
and allotted their lands to them as
an inheritance;
he settled the tribes of Israel in
their homes.

⁵⁶But they put God to the test
and rebelled against the Most
High;
they did not keep his statutes.
⁵⁷Like their fathers they were disloyal
and faithless,
as unreliable as a faulty bow.
⁵⁸They angered him with their high
places;
they aroused his jealousy with
their idols.
⁵⁹When God heard them, he was very
angry;
he rejected Israel completely.
⁶⁰He abandoned the tabernacle of
Shiloh,
the tent he had set up among
men.
⁶¹He sent ˻the ark of˼ his might into
captivity,
his splendor into the hands of the
enemy.
⁶²He gave his people over to the
sword;
he was very angry with his
inheritance.
⁶³Fire consumed their young men,
and their maidens had no wedding
songs;
⁶⁴their priests were put to the sword,
and their widows could not weep.

⁶⁵Then the Lord awoke as from sleep,
as a man wakes from the stupor
of wine.
⁶⁶He beat back his enemies;

he put them to everlasting shame.
⁶⁷Then he rejected the tents of Joseph,
he did not choose the tribe of
Ephraim;
⁶⁸but he chose the tribe of Judah,
Mount Zion, which he loved.
⁶⁹He built his sanctuary like the
heights,
like the earth that he established
forever.
⁷⁰He chose David his servant
and took him from the sheep
pens;
⁷¹from tending the sheep he brought
him
to be the shepherd of his people
Jacob,
of Israel his inheritance.
⁷²And David shepherded them with
integrity of heart;
with skillful hands he led them.

Psalm 79

A psalm of Asaph.

¹O God, the nations have invaded
your inheritance;
they have defiled your holy temple,
they have reduced Jerusalem to
rubble.
²They have given the dead bodies of
your servants
as food to the birds of the air,
the flesh of your saints to the
beasts of the earth.
³They have poured out blood like
water
all around Jerusalem,
and there is no one to bury the
dead.
⁴We are objects of reproach to our
neighbors,
of scorn and derision to those
around us.

⁵How long, O LORD? Will you be angry
forever?
How long will your jealousy burn
like fire?
⁶Pour out your wrath on the nations
that do not acknowledge you,
on the kingdoms
that do not call on your name;
⁷for they have devoured Jacob
and destroyed his homeland.
⁸Do not hold against us the sins of
the fathers;

may your mercy come quickly to
    meet us,
for we are in desperate need.

⁹Help us, O God our Savior,
    for the glory of your name;
deliver us and forgive our sins
    for your name's sake.
¹⁰Why should the nations say,
    "Where is their God?"
Before our eyes, make known among
        the nations
    that you avenge the outpoured
        blood of your servants.
¹¹May the groans of the prisoners
        come before you;
    by the strength of your arm
        preserve those condemned to die.

¹²Pay back into the laps of our
        neighbors seven times
    the reproach they have hurled at
        you, O Lord.
¹³Then we your people, the sheep of
        your pasture,
    will praise you forever;
from generation to generation
    we will recount your praise.

Psalm 80

For the director of music. To ⌊the tune
of⌋ "The Lilies of the Covenant."
Of Asaph. A psalm.

¹Hear us, O Shepherd of Israel,
    you who lead Joseph like a flock;
you who sit enthroned between the
        cherubim, shine forth
²   before Ephraim, Benjamin and
        Manasseh.
Awaken your might;
    come and save us.

³Restore us, O God;
    make your face shine upon us,
    that we may be saved.

⁴O LORD God Almighty,
    how long will your anger smolder
    against the prayers of your people?
⁵You have fed them with the bread of
        tears;
    you have made them drink tears
        by the bowlful.
⁶You have made us a source of
        contention to our neighbors,
    and our enemies mock us.

⁷Restore us, O God Almighty;
    make your face shine upon us,
    that we may be saved.

⁸You brought a vine out of Egypt;
    you drove out the nations and
        planted it.
⁹You cleared the ground for it,
    and it took root and filled the
        land.
¹⁰The mountains were covered with its
        shade,
    the mighty cedars with its
        branches.
¹¹It sent out its boughs to the Sea,ᵃ
    its shoots as far as the River.ᵇ

¹²Why have you broken down its walls
    so that all who pass by pick its
        grapes?
¹³Boars from the forest ravage it
    and the creatures of the field feed
        on it.
¹⁴Return to us, O God Almighty!
    Look down from heaven and see!
Watch over this vine,
¹⁵   the root your right hand has
        planted,
    the sonᶜ you have raised up for
        yourself.

¹⁶Your vine is cut down, it is burned
        with fire;
    at your rebuke your people perish.
¹⁷Let your hand rest on the man at
        your right hand,
    the son of man you have raised
        up for yourself.
¹⁸Then we will not turn away from
        you;
    revive us, and we will call on your
        name.

¹⁹Restore us, O LORD God Almighty;
    make your face shine upon us,
    that we may be saved.

Psalm 81

For the director of music. According to
gittith.ᵈ Of Asaph.

¹Sing for joy to God our strength;
    shout aloud to the God of Jacob!
²Begin the music, strike the
        tambourine,
    play the melodious harp and lyre.

ᵃ11 Probably the Mediterranean   ᵇ11 That is, the Euphrates   ᶜ15 Or branch   ᵈTitle:
Probably a musical term

³Sound the ram's horn at the New
 Moon,
  and when the moon is full, on the
  day of our Feast;
⁴this is a decree for Israel,
  an ordinance of the God of Jacob.
⁵He established it as a statute for
  Joseph
  when he went out against Egypt,
  where we heard a language we did
  not understand.ᵃ

⁶He says, "I removed the burden from
  their shoulders;
  their hands were set free from the
  basket.
⁷In your distress you called and I
  rescued you,
  I answered you out of a
  thundercloud;
  I tested you at the waters of
  Meribah.   *Selah*

⁸"Hear, O my people, and I will warn
  you—
  if you would but listen to me,
  O Israel!
⁹You shall have no foreign god
  among you;
  you shall not bow down to an
  alien god.
¹⁰I am the LORD your God,
  who brought you up out of Egypt.
  Open wide your mouth and I will
  fill it.

¹¹"But my people would not listen to
  me;
  Israel would not submit to me.
¹²So I gave them over to their
  stubborn hearts
  to follow their own devices.

¹³"If my people would but listen to
  me,
  if Israel would follow my ways,
¹⁴how quickly would I subdue their
  enemies
  and turn my hand against their
  foes!
¹⁵Those who hate the LORD would
  cringe before him,
  and their punishment would last
  forever.
¹⁶But you would be fed with the finest
  of wheat;
  with honey from the rock I would
  satisfy you."

Psalm 82

A psalm of Asaph.

¹God presides in the great assembly;
  he gives judgment among the
  "gods":

²"How long will youᵇ defend the
  unjust
  and show partiality to the wicked?
                                    Selah
³Defend the cause of the weak and
  fatherless;
  maintain the rights of the poor
  and oppressed.
⁴Rescue the weak and needy;
  deliver them from the hand of the
  wicked.

⁵"They know nothing, they
  understand nothing.
  They walk about in darkness;
  all the foundations of the earth are
  shaken.

⁶"I said, 'You are "gods";
  you are all sons of the Most High.'
⁷But you will die like mere men;
  you will fall like every other ruler."

⁸Rise up, O God, judge the earth,
  for all the nations are your
  inheritance.

Psalm 83

A song. A psalm of Asaph.

¹O God, do not keep silent;
  be not quiet, O God, be not still.
²See how your enemies are astir,
  how your foes rear their heads.
³With cunning they conspire against
  your people;
  they plot against those you
  cherish.
⁴"Come," they say, "let us destroy
  them as a nation,
  that the name of Israel be
  remembered no more."

⁵With one mind they plot together;
  they form an alliance against you—
⁶the tents of Edom and the
  Ishmaelites,
  of Moab and the Hagrites,
⁷Gebal,ᶜ Ammon and Amalek,
  Philistia, with the people of Tyre.
⁸Even Assyria has joined them

ᵃ5 Or / and we heard a voice we had not known   ᵇ2 The Hebrew is plural.   ᶜ7 That is, Byblos

to lend strength to the
  descendants of Lot.   *Selah*

⁹Do to them as you did to Midian,
  as you did to Sisera and Jabin at
    the river Kishon,
¹⁰who perished at Endor
  and became like refuse on the
    ground.
¹¹Make their nobles like Oreb and
    Zeeb,
  all their princes like Zebah and
    Zalmunna,
¹²who said, "Let us take possession
  of the pasturelands of God."

¹³Make them like tumbleweed, O my
    God,
  like chaff before the wind.
¹⁴As fire consumes the forest
  or a flame sets the mountains
    ablaze,
¹⁵so pursue them with your tempest
  and terrify them with your storm.
¹⁶Cover their faces with shame
  so that men will seek your name,
    O LORD.

¹⁷May they ever be ashamed and
    dismayed;
  may they perish in disgrace.
¹⁸Let them know that you, whose
    name is the LORD—
  that you alone are the Most High
    over all the earth.

Psalm 84

For the director of music. According to
gittith. ᵃ Of the Sons of Korah.
A psalm.

¹How lovely is your dwelling place,
  O LORD Almighty!
²My soul yearns, even faints,
  for the courts of the LORD;
  my heart and my flesh cry out
    for the living God.

³Even the sparrow has found a home,
  and the swallow a nest for herself,
  where she may have her young—
  a place near your altar,
    O LORD Almighty, my King and my
    God.
⁴Blessed are those who dwell in your
    house;
  they are ever praising you.   *Selah*

⁵Blessed are those whose strength is
    in you,
  who have set their hearts on
    pilgrimage.
⁶As they pass through the Valley of
    Baca,
  they make it a place of springs;
  the autumn rains also cover it with
    pools.ᵇ
⁷They go from strength to strength,
  till each appears before God in
    Zion.

⁸Hear my prayer, O LORD God
    Almighty;
  listen to me, O God of Jacob.   *Selah*
⁹Look upon our shield,ᶜ O God;
  look with favor on your anointed
    one.

¹⁰Better is one day in your courts
  than a thousand elsewhere;
  I would rather be a doorkeeper in
    the house of my God
  than dwell in the tents of the
    wicked.
¹¹For the LORD God is a sun and
    shield;
  the LORD bestows favor and honor;
  no good thing does he withhold
    from those whose walk is
    blameless.

¹²O LORD Almighty,
  blessed is the man who trusts in
    you.

Psalm 85

For the director of music. Of the Sons
of Korah. A psalm.

¹You showed favor to your land,
    O LORD;
  you restored the fortunes of Jacob.
²You forgave the iniquity of your
    people
  and covered all their sins.   *Selah*
³You set aside all your wrath
  and turned from your fierce anger.

⁴Restore us again, O God our Savior,
  and put away your displeasure
    toward us.
⁵Will you be angry with us forever?
  Will you prolong your anger
    through all generations?
⁶Will you not revive us again,

ᵃTitle: Probably a musical term   ᵇ6 Or *blessings*   ᶜ9 Or *sovereign*

that your people may rejoice in
you?
[7]Show us your unfailing love, O LORD,
and grant us your salvation.

[8]I will listen to what God the LORD
will say;
he promises peace to his people,
his saints —
but let them not return to folly.
[9]Surely his salvation is near those
who fear him,
that his glory may dwell in our
land.

[10]Love and faithfulness meet together;
righteousness and peace kiss each
other.
[11]Faithfulness springs forth from the
earth,
and righteousness looks down
from heaven.
[12]The LORD will indeed give what is
good,
and our land will yield its harvest.
[13]Righteousness goes before him
and prepares the way for his
steps.

Psalm 86

A prayer of David.

[1]Hear, O LORD, and answer me,
for I am poor and needy.
[2]Guard my life, for I am devoted to
you.
You are my God; save your servant
who trusts in you.
[3]Have mercy on me, O Lord,
for I call to you all day long.
[4]Bring joy to your servant,
for to you, O Lord,
I lift up my soul.

[5]You are forgiving and good, O Lord,
abounding in love to all who call
to you.
[6]Hear my prayer, O LORD;
listen to my cry for mercy.
[7]In the day of my trouble I will call to
you,
for you will answer me.

[8]Among the gods there is none like
you, O Lord;
no deeds can compare with yours.
[9]All the nations you have made

will come and worship before you,
O Lord;
they will bring glory to your name.
[10]For you are great and do marvelous
deeds;
you alone are God.

[11]Teach me your way, O LORD,
and I will walk in your truth;
give me an undivided heart,
that I may fear your name.
[12]I will praise you, O Lord my God,
with all my heart;
I will glorify your name forever.
[13]For great is your love toward me;
you have delivered me from the
depths of the grave.[a]

[14]The arrogant are attacking me,
O God;
a band of ruthless men seeks my
life—
men without regard for you.
[15]But you, O Lord, are a
compassionate and gracious
God,
slow to anger, abounding in love
and faithfulness.
[16]Turn to me and have mercy on me;
grant your strength to your servant
and save the son of your
maidservant.[b]
[17]Give me a sign of your goodness,
that my enemies may see it and be
put to shame,
for you, O LORD, have helped me
and comforted me.

Psalm 87

*Of the Sons of Korah. A psalm.
A song.*

[1]He has set his foundation on the
holy mountain;
[2]   the LORD loves the gates of Zion
more than all the dwellings of
Jacob.
[3]Glorious things are said of you,
O city of God: *Selah*
[4]"I will record Rahab[c] and Babylon
among those who acknowledge
me—
Philistia too, and Tyre, along with
Cush[d]—

---

[a]13 Hebrew *Sheol*   [b]16 Or *save your faithful son*   [c]4 A poetic name for Egypt   [d]4 That is, the
upper Nile region

and will say, 'This[a] one was born
in Zion.' "

5Indeed, of Zion it will be said,
"This one and that one were born
in her,
and the Most High himself will
establish her."
6The LORD will write in the register of
the peoples:
"This one was born in Zion." *Selah*
7As they make music they will sing,
"All my fountains are in you."

Psalm 88

A song. A psalm of the Sons of Korah.
For the director of music. According to
mahalath leannoth.[b] A *maskil*[c] of
Heman the Ezrahite.

1O LORD, the God who saves me,
day and night I cry out before you.
2May my prayer come before you;
turn your ear to my cry.

3For my soul is full of trouble
and my life draws near the grave.[d]
4I am counted among those who go
down to the pit;
I am like a man without strength.
5I am set apart with the dead,
like the slain who lie in the grave,
whom you remember no more,
who are cut off from your care.

6You have put me in the lowest pit,
in the darkest depths.
7Your wrath lies heavily upon me;
you have overwhelmed me with all
your waves. *Selah*
8You have taken from me my closest
friends
and have made me repulsive to
them.
I am confined and cannot escape;
9 my eyes are dim with grief.

I call to you, O LORD, every day;
I spread out my hands to you.
10Do you show your wonders to the
dead?
Do those who are dead rise up
and praise you? *Selah*
11Is your love declared in the grave,
your faithfulness in Destruction[e]?
12Are your wonders known in the
place of darkness,

or your righteous deeds in the
land of oblivion?

13But I cry to you for help, O LORD;
in the morning my prayer comes
before you.
14Why, O LORD, do you reject me
and hide your face from me?

15From my youth I have been afflicted
and close to death;
I have suffered your terrors and
am in despair.
16Your wrath has swept over me;
your terrors have destroyed me.
17All day long they surround me like a
flood;
they have completely engulfed me.
18You have taken my companions and
loved ones from me;
the darkness is my closest friend.

Psalm 89

A *maskil*[c] of Ethan the Ezrahite.

1I will sing of the LORD's great love
forever;
with my mouth I will make your
faithfulness known through
all generations.
2I will declare that your love stands
firm forever,
that you established your
faithfulness in heaven itself.

3You said, "I have made a covenant
with my chosen one,
I have sworn to David my servant,
4'I will establish your line forever
and make your throne firm
through all generations.' "
Selah

5The heavens praise your wonders,
O LORD,
your faithfulness too, in the
assembly of the holy ones.
6For who in the skies above can
compare with the LORD?
Who is like the LORD among the
heavenly beings?
7In the council of the holy ones God
is greatly feared;
he is more awesome than all who
surround him.

---

*a*4 Or "O Rahab and Babylon, / Philistia, Tyre and Cush, / I will record concerning those who acknowledge me:
/ 'This   *b*Title: Possibly a tune, "The Suffering of Affliction"   *c*Title: Probably a literary or
musical term   *d*3 Hebrew *Sheol*   *e*11 Hebrew *Abaddon*

8O LORD God Almighty, who is like
  you?
    You are mighty, O LORD, and your
      faithfulness surrounds you.

9You rule over the surging sea;
    when its waves mount up, you
      still them.
10You crushed Rahab like one of the
  slain;
    with your strong arm you scattered
      your enemies.
11The heavens are yours, and yours
  also the earth;
    you founded the world and all that
      is in it.
12You created the north and the south;
    Tabor and Hermon sing for joy at
      your name.
13Your arm is endued with power;
    your hand is strong, your right
      hand exalted.

14Righteousness and justice are the
    foundation of your throne;
    love and faithfulness go before
      you.
15Blessed are those who have learned
    to acclaim you,
    who walk in the light of your
      presence, O LORD.
16They rejoice in your name all day
  long;
    they exult in your righteousness.
17For you are their glory and strength,
    and by your favor you exalt our
      horn.a
18Indeed, our shieldb belongs to the
  LORD,
    our king to the Holy One of Israel.

19Once you spoke in a vision,
    to your faithful people you said:
  "I have bestowed strength on a
    warrior;
    I have exalted a young man from
      among the people.
20I have found David my servant;
    with my sacred oil I have anointed
      him.
21My hand will sustain him;
    surely my arm will strengthen him.
22No enemy will subject him to tribute;
    no wicked man will oppress him.
23I will crush his foes before him
    and strike down his adversaries.
24My faithful love will be with him,

and through my name his hornc
  will be exalted.
25I will set his hand over the sea,
    his right hand over the rivers.
26He will call out to me, 'You are my
  Father,
    my God, the Rock my Savior.'
27I will also appoint him my firstborn,
    the most exalted of the kings of
      the earth.
28I will maintain my love to him
  forever,
    and my covenant with him will
      never fail.
29I will establish his line forever,
    his throne as long as the heavens
      endure.

30"If his sons forsake my law
    and do not follow my statutes,
31if they violate my decrees
    and fail to keep my commands,
32I will punish their sin with the rod,
    their iniquity with flogging;
33but I will not take my love from him,
    nor will I ever betray my
      faithfulness.
34I will not violate my covenant
    or alter what my lips have uttered.
35Once for all, I have sworn by my
  holiness—
    and I will not lie to David—
36that his line will continue forever
    and his throne endure before me
      like the sun;
37it will be established forever like the
  moon,
    the faithful witness in the sky."
                                              Selah

38But you have rejected, you have
  spurned,
    you have been very angry with
      your anointed one.
39You have renounced the covenant
    with your servant
    and have defiled his crown in the
      dust.
40You have broken through all his
  walls
    and reduced his strongholds to
      ruins.
41All who pass by have plundered
  him;
    he has become the scorn of his
      neighbors.
42You have exalted the right hand of
    his foes;

a17 Horn here symbolizes strong one.   b18 Or sovereign   c24 Horn here symbolizes strength.

you have made all his enemies
rejoice.
⁴³You have turned back the edge of his
sword
and have not supported him in
battle.
⁴⁴You have put an end to his splendor
and cast his throne to the ground.
⁴⁵You have cut short the days of his
youth;
you have covered him with a
mantle of shame.   *Selah*

⁴⁶How long, O LORD? Will you hide
yourself forever?
How long will your wrath burn
like fire?
⁴⁷Remember how fleeting is my life.
For what futility you have created
all men!
⁴⁸What man can live and not see
death,
or save himself from the power of
the grave*ᵃ*?   *Selah*
⁴⁹O Lord, where is your former great
love,
which in your faithfulness you
swore to David?
⁵⁰Remember, Lord, how your servant
has*ᵇ* been mocked,
how I bear in my heart the taunts
of all the nations,
⁵¹the taunts with which your enemies
have mocked, O LORD,
with which they have mocked
every step of your anointed
one.

⁵²Praise be to the LORD forever!
Amen and Amen.

BOOK IV

Psalms 90–106

Psalm 90

A prayer of Moses the man of God.

¹Lord, you have been our dwelling
place
throughout all generations.
²Before the mountains were born
or you brought forth the earth and
the world,
from everlasting to everlasting you
are God.

³You turn men back to dust,
saying, "Return to dust, O sons of
men."
⁴For a thousand years in your sight
are like a day that has just gone
by,
or like a watch in the night.
⁵You sweep men away in the sleep of
death;
they are like the new grass of the
morning—
⁶though in the morning it springs up
new,
by evening it is dry and withered.

⁷We are consumed by your anger
and terrified by your indignation.
⁸You have set our iniquities before
you,
our secret sins in the light of your
presence.
⁹All our days pass away under your
wrath;
we finish our years with a moan.
¹⁰The length of our days is seventy
years—
or eighty, if we have the strength;
yet their span*ᶜ* is but trouble and
sorrow,
for they quickly pass, and we fly
away.

¹¹Who knows the power of your
anger?
For your wrath is as great as the
fear that is due you.
¹²Teach us to number our days aright,
that we may gain a heart of
wisdom.

¹³Relent, O LORD! How long will it
be?
Have compassion on your
servants.
¹⁴Satisfy us in the morning with your
unfailing love,
that we may sing for joy and be
glad all our days.
¹⁵Make us glad for as many days as
you have afflicted us,
for as many years as we have seen
trouble.
¹⁶May your deeds be shown to your
servants,
your splendor to their children.
¹⁷May the favor*ᵈ* of the Lord our God
rest upon us;

ᵃ48 Hebrew *Sheol*   *ᵇ50* Or *your servants have*   *ᶜ10* Or *yet the best of them*   *ᵈ17* Or *beauty*

establish the work of our hands
for us—
yes, establish the work of our
hands.

Psalm 91

¹He who dwells in the shelter of the
Most High
will rest in the shadow of the
Almighty.ᵃ
²I will sayᵇ of the LORD, "He is my
refuge and my fortress,
my God, in whom I trust."

ᵃ1 Hebrew *Shaddai*   ᵇ2 Or *He says*

³Surely he will save you from the
fowler's snare
and from the deadly pestilence.
⁴He will cover you with his feathers,
and under his wings you will find
refuge;
his faithfulness will be your shield
and rampart.
⁵You will not fear the terror of night,
nor the arrow that flies by day,
⁶nor the pestilence that stalks in the
darkness,
nor the plague that destroys at
midday.

WEDNESDAY

VERSE:	AUTHOR:	PASSAGE:
Psalm 90:17	Catherine Doherty	Psalm 90

Handicrafts and Creativity

Handicrafts serve as a means of communication among people who are afraid, shy or sick, or even people who speak different languages. There is something reassuring, homey, pleasant and relaxing to see someone embroidering or knitting in an airport or on a train. One feels a trust and confidence about such a person. If one has some similar work at hand, one becomes friends almost without words. Or one might ask what the other is doing; and a bond of friendship, gentle and warm, is established with this person who only a short time ago was a stranger. The handicraft is a bridge.

All creative effort is from God, and people who do handicrafts create. To create is to be at peace, for in creating one is joined with the Creator. Creativeness is one of the needs of our humanity and one of the gifts of God to us. Handicrafts also are one more way of restoring us to wholeness in the natural and psychological order so as to better restore us to Christ. The loneliness of modern people has almost reached a point of no return; but in a common effort of creativity, men and women may find someone else who is interested in similar crafts, and become friends through their craftsmanship. Friendship is still the most precious possession that a human being can share. So handicrafts open the door to both friendship and creativity. These aspects go together, for friendship both creates and demands creativity to grow.

ADDITIONAL SCRIPTURE READINGS:
Proverbs 31:13; Colossians 3:17

Go to page 460 for your next devotional reading.

⁷A thousand may fall at your side,
  ten thousand at your right hand,
  but it will not come near you.
⁸You will only observe with your
    eyes
  and see the punishment of the
    wicked.

⁹If you make the Most High your
    dwelling—
  even the LORD, who is my refuge—
¹⁰then no harm will befall you,
  no disaster will come near your
    tent.
¹¹For he will command his angels
    concerning you
  to guard you in all your ways;
¹²they will lift you up in their hands,
  so that you will not strike your
    foot against a stone.
¹³You will tread upon the lion and the
    cobra;

you will trample the great lion and
  the serpent.

¹⁴"Because he loves me," says the
    LORD, "I will rescue him;
  I will protect him, for he
    acknowledges my name.
¹⁵He will call upon me, and I will
    answer him;
  I will be with him in trouble,
  I will deliver him and honor him.
¹⁶With long life will I satisfy him
  and show him my salvation."

Psalm 92

A psalm. A song. For the Sabbath day.

¹It is good to praise the LORD
  and make music to your name,
    O Most High,
²to proclaim your love in the morning
  and your faithfulness at night,

THURSDAY

VERSE: AUTHOR: PASSAGE:
Psalm 91:4   Kay Arthur   Psalm 91

God's Promises!

She had stopped at a red light. Before she even realized the car
door had opened, a man had a gun stuck in her side. He
demanded, "Lady, just drive. Don't do anything dumb!"

She had just heard a message on Psalm 91. This psalm told
her that God was her refuge, that he was her fortress, that he
would deliver her from the snare of the fowler, that he covered
her with his feathers, that he was her shield and rampart. But in
this instant, with a gun in her side and her mind in a whirl, she
could not think of the exact words of the Scripture.

In desperation, all she could come up with and exclaim was,
"Feathers! Feathers! Feathers!"

The hijacker panicked. He shouted, "Lady, you are crazy!" And
as quickly as he had appeared, he disappeared!

Oh, how precious to know that when we can't think of a
promise word for word, or when we don't have time to quote a
promise for the situation in which we find ourselves, God knows
his promises and he knows our heart.

ADDITIONAL SCRIPTURE READINGS:
1 Samuel 16:7; Nahum 1:7

Go to page 467 for your next devotional reading.

³to the music of the ten-stringed lyre
  and the melody of the harp.

⁴For you make me glad by your
      deeds, O LORD;
  I sing for joy at the works of your
      hands.
⁵How great are your works, O LORD,
  how profound your thoughts!
⁶The senseless man does not know,
  fools do not understand,
⁷that though the wicked spring up like
      grass
  and all evildoers flourish,
  they will be forever destroyed.

⁸But you, O LORD, are exalted forever.

⁹For surely your enemies, O LORD,
  surely your enemies will perish;
  all evildoers will be scattered.
¹⁰You have exalted my horn*a* like that
      of a wild ox;
  fine oils have been poured upon
      me.
¹¹My eyes have seen the defeat of my
      adversaries;
  my ears have heard the rout of my
      wicked foes.

¹²The righteous will flourish like a
      palm tree,
  they will grow like a cedar of
      Lebanon;
¹³planted in the house of the LORD,
  they will flourish in the courts of
      our God.
¹⁴They will still bear fruit in old age,
  they will stay fresh and green,
¹⁵proclaiming, "The LORD is upright;
  he is my Rock, and there is no
      wickedness in him."

Psalm 93

¹The LORD reigns, he is robed in
      majesty;
  the LORD is robed in majesty
  and is armed with strength.
  The world is firmly established;
  it cannot be moved.
²Your throne was established long
      ago;
  you are from all eternity.

³The seas have lifted up, O LORD,
  the seas have lifted up their voice;
  the seas have lifted up their
      pounding waves.

⁴Mightier than the thunder of the
      great waters,
  mightier than the breakers of the
      sea—
  the LORD on high is mighty.

⁵Your statutes stand firm;
  holiness adorns your house
  for endless days, O LORD.

Psalm 94

¹O LORD, the God who avenges,
  O God who avenges, shine forth.
²Rise up, O Judge of the earth;
  pay back to the proud what they
      deserve.
³How long will the wicked, O LORD,
  how long will the wicked be
      jubilant?

⁴They pour out arrogant words;
  all the evildoers are full of
      boasting.
⁵They crush your people, O LORD;
  they oppress your inheritance.
⁶They slay the widow and the alien;
  they murder the fatherless.
⁷They say, "The LORD does not see;
  the God of Jacob pays no heed."

⁸Take heed, you senseless ones
      among the people;
  you fools, when will you become
      wise?
⁹Does he who implanted the ear not
      hear?
  Does he who formed the eye not
      see?
¹⁰Does he who disciplines nations not
      punish?
  Does he who teaches man lack
      knowledge?
¹¹The LORD knows the thoughts of
      man;
  he knows that they are futile.

¹²Blessed is the man you discipline,
      O LORD,
  the man you teach from your law;
¹³you grant him relief from days of
      trouble,
  till a pit is dug for the wicked.
¹⁴For the LORD will not reject his
      people;
  he will never forsake his
      inheritance.
¹⁵Judgment will again be founded on
      righteousness,

---

a 10 Horn here symbolizes strength.

and all the upright in heart will
    follow it.

16Who will rise up for me against the
        wicked?
    Who will take a stand for me
        against evildoers?
17Unless the LORD had given me help,
    I would soon have dwelt in the
        silence of death.
18When I said, "My foot is slipping,"
    your love, O LORD, supported me.
19When anxiety was great within me,
    your consolation brought joy to
        my soul.

20Can a corrupt throne be allied with
        you—
    one that brings on misery by its
        decrees?
21They band together against the
        righteous
    and condemn the innocent to
        death.
22But the LORD has become my
        fortress,
    and my God the rock in whom I
        take refuge.
23He will repay them for their sins
    and destroy them for their
        wickedness;
    the LORD our God will destroy
        them.

Psalm 95

1Come, let us sing for joy to the LORD;
    let us shout aloud to the Rock of
        our salvation.
2Let us come before him with
        thanksgiving
    and extol him with music and
        song.

3For the LORD is the great God,
    the great King above all gods.
4In his hand are the depths of the
        earth,
    and the mountain peaks belong to
        him.
5The sea is his, for he made it,
    and his hands formed the dry
        land.

6Come, let us bow down in worship,
    let us kneel before the LORD our
        Maker;
7for he is our God

and we are the people of his
        pasture,
    the flock under his care.

Today, if you hear his voice,
8   do not harden your hearts as you
        did at Meribah,a
    as you did that day at Massahb in
        the desert,
9where your fathers tested and tried
        me,
    though they had seen what I did.
10For forty years I was angry with that
        generation;
    I said, "They are a people whose
        hearts go astray,
    and they have not known my
        ways."
11So I declared on oath in my anger,
    "They shall never enter my rest."

Psalm 96

1Sing to the LORD a new song;
    sing to the LORD, all the earth.
2Sing to the LORD, praise his name;
    proclaim his salvation day after
        day.
3Declare his glory among the nations,
    his marvelous deeds among all
        peoples.

4For great is the LORD and most
        worthy of praise;
    he is to be feared above all gods.
5For all the gods of the nations are
        idols,
    but the LORD made the heavens.
6Splendor and majesty are before him;
    strength and glory are in his
        sanctuary.

7Ascribe to the LORD, O families of
        nations,
    ascribe to the LORD glory and
        strength.
8Ascribe to the LORD the glory due his
        name;
    bring an offering and come into
        his courts.
9Worship the LORD in the splendor of
        hisc holiness;
    tremble before him, all the earth.

10Say among the nations, "The LORD
        reigns."
    The world is firmly established, it
        cannot be moved;

---

a8 Meribah means quarreling.   b8 Massah means testing.   c9 Or LORD with the splendor of

he will judge the peoples with
  equity.
¹¹Let the heavens rejoice, let the earth
  be glad;
  let the sea resound, and all that is
  in it;
¹² let the fields be jubilant, and
  everything in them.
Then all the trees of the forest will
  sing for joy;
¹³ they will sing before the LORD, for
  he comes,
  he comes to judge the earth.
He will judge the world in
  righteousness
  and the peoples in his truth.

Psalm 97

¹The LORD reigns, let the earth be glad;
  let the distant shores rejoice.

²Clouds and thick darkness surround
  him;
  righteousness and justice are the
  foundation of his throne.
³Fire goes before him
  and consumes his foes on every
  side.
⁴His lightning lights up the world;
  the earth sees and trembles.
⁵The mountains melt like wax before
  the LORD,
  before the Lord of all the earth.
⁶The heavens proclaim his
  righteousness,
  and all the peoples see his glory.

⁷All who worship images are put to
  shame,
  those who boast in idols—
  worship him, all you gods!

⁸Zion hears and rejoices
  and the villages of Judah are glad
  because of your judgments,
  O LORD.
⁹For you, O LORD, are the Most High
  over all the earth;
  you are exalted far above all gods.

¹⁰Let those who love the LORD hate
  evil,
  for he guards the lives of his
  faithful ones
  and delivers them from the hand
  of the wicked.
¹¹Light is shed upon the righteous
  and joy on the upright in heart.

¹²Rejoice in the LORD, you who are
  righteous,
  and praise his holy name.

Psalm 98

A psalm.

¹Sing to the LORD a new song,
  for he has done marvelous things;
  his right hand and his holy arm
  have worked salvation for him.
²The LORD has made his salvation
  known
  and revealed his righteousness to
  the nations.
³He has remembered his love
  and his faithfulness to the house
  of Israel;
  all the ends of the earth have seen
  the salvation of our God.

⁴Shout for joy to the LORD, all the
  earth,
  burst into jubilant song with
  music;
⁵make music to the LORD with the
  harp,
  with the harp and the sound of
  singing,
⁶with trumpets and the blast of the
  ram's horn—
  shout for joy before the LORD, the
  King.

⁷Let the sea resound, and everything
  in it,
  the world, and all who live in it.
⁸Let the rivers clap their hands,
  let the mountains sing together for
  joy;
⁹let them sing before the LORD,
  for he comes to judge the earth.
He will judge the world in
  righteousness
  and the peoples with equity.

Psalm 99

¹The LORD reigns,
  let the nations tremble;
  he sits enthroned between the
  cherubim,
  let the earth shake.
²Great is the LORD in Zion;
  he is exalted over all the nations.
³Let them praise your great and
  awesome name—
  he is holy.

⁴The King is mighty, he loves justice—
    you have established equity;
  in Jacob you have done
    what is just and right.
⁵Exalt the LORD our God
    and worship at his footstool;
  he is holy.

⁶Moses and Aaron were among his
      priests,
    Samuel was among those who
      called on his name;
  they called on the LORD
    and he answered them.
⁷He spoke to them from the pillar of
      cloud;
    they kept his statutes and the
      decrees he gave them.

⁸O LORD our God,
    you answered them;
  you were to Israel[a] a forgiving God,
    though you punished their
      misdeeds.[b]
⁹Exalt the LORD our God
    and worship at his holy mountain,
  for the LORD our God is holy.

Psalm 100

A psalm. For giving thanks.

¹Shout for joy to the LORD, all the
    earth.
²   Worship the LORD with gladness;
    come before him with joyful
      songs.
³Know that the LORD is God.
    It is he who made us, and we are
      his[c];
  we are his people, the sheep of his
    pasture.

⁴Enter his gates with thanksgiving
    and his courts with praise;
  give thanks to him and praise his
    name.
⁵For the LORD is good and his love
      endures forever;
  his faithfulness continues through
    all generations.

Psalm 101

Of David. A psalm.

¹I will sing of your love and justice;
    to you, O LORD, I will sing praise.

²I will be careful to lead a blameless
      life—
    when will you come to me?

  I will walk in my house
    with blameless heart.
³I will set before my eyes
    no vile thing.

  The deeds of faithless men I hate;
    they will not cling to me.
⁴Men of perverse heart shall be far
      from me;
    I will have nothing to do with evil.

⁵Whoever slanders his neighbor in
      secret,
    him will I put to silence;
  whoever has haughty eyes and a
      proud heart,
    him will I not endure.

⁶My eyes will be on the faithful in the
      land,
    that they may dwell with me;
  he whose walk is blameless
    will minister to me.

⁷No one who practices deceit
    will dwell in my house;
  no one who speaks falsely
    will stand in my presence.

⁸Every morning I will put to silence
    all the wicked in the land;
  I will cut off every evildoer
    from the city of the LORD.

Psalm 102

*A prayer of an afflicted man. When he
is faint and pours out his lament
before the LORD.*

¹Hear my prayer, O LORD;
    let my cry for help come to you.
²Do not hide your face from me
    when I am in distress.
  Turn your ear to me;
    when I call, answer me quickly.

³For my days vanish like smoke;
    my bones burn like glowing
      embers.
⁴My heart is blighted and withered
      like grass;
    I forget to eat my food.
⁵Because of my loud groaning
    I am reduced to skin and bones.
⁶I am like a desert owl,
    like an owl among the ruins.

a 8 Hebrew *them*   *b 8* Or / *an avenger of the wrongs done to them*   *c 3* Or *and not we ourselves*

7I lie awake; I have become
   like a bird alone on a roof.
8All day long my enemies taunt me;
   those who rail against me use my
      name as a curse.
9For I eat ashes as my food
   and mingle my drink with tears
10because of your great wrath,
   for you have taken me up and
      thrown me aside.
11My days are like the evening shadow;
   I wither away like grass.

12But you, O LORD, sit enthroned
      forever;
   your renown endures through all
      generations.
13You will arise and have compassion
      on Zion,
   for it is time to show favor to her;
      the appointed time has come.
14For her stones are dear to your
      servants;
   her very dust moves them to pity.
15The nations will fear the name of the
      LORD,
   all the kings of the earth will
      revere your glory.
16For the LORD will rebuild Zion
   and appear in his glory.
17He will respond to the prayer of the
      destitute;
   he will not despise their plea.

18Let this be written for a future
      generation,
   that a people not yet created may
      praise the LORD:
19"The LORD looked down from his
      sanctuary on high,
   from heaven he viewed the earth,
20to hear the groans of the prisoners
   and release those condemned to
      death."
21So the name of the LORD will be
      declared in Zion
   and his praise in Jerusalem
22when the peoples and the kingdoms
   assemble to worship the LORD.

23In the course of my life[a] he broke
      my strength;
   he cut short my days.
24So I said:
   "Do not take me away, O my God,
      in the midst of my days;
   your years go on through all
      generations.

25In the beginning you laid the
      foundations of the earth,
   and the heavens are the work of
      your hands.
26They will perish, but you remain;
   they will all wear out like a
      garment.
   Like clothing you will change them
   and they will be discarded.
27But you remain the same,
   and your years will never end.
28The children of your servants will
      live in your presence;
   their descendants will be
      established before you."

Psalm 103

Of David.

1Praise the LORD, O my soul;
   all my inmost being, praise his
      holy name.
2Praise the LORD, O my soul,
   and forget not all his benefits—
3who forgives all your sins
   and heals all your diseases,
4who redeems your life from the pit
   and crowns you with love and
      compassion,
5who satisfies your desires with good
      things
   so that your youth is renewed like
      the eagle's.

6The LORD works righteousness
   and justice for all the oppressed.

7He made known his ways to Moses,
   his deeds to the people of Israel:
8The LORD is compassionate and
      gracious,
   slow to anger, abounding in love.
9He will not always accuse,
   nor will he harbor his anger
      forever;
10he does not treat us as our sins
      deserve
   or repay us according to our
      iniquities.
11For as high as the heavens are above
      the earth,
   so great is his love for those who
      fear him;
12as far as the east is from the west,
   so far has he removed our
      transgressions from us.

a 23 Or By his power

¹³As a father has compassion on his
    children,
    so the LORD has compassion on
      those who fear him;
¹⁴for he knows how we are formed,
    he remembers that we are dust.
¹⁵As for man, his days are like grass,
    he flourishes like a flower of the
      field;
¹⁶the wind blows over it and it is
      gone,
    and its place remembers it no
      more.
¹⁷But from everlasting to everlasting
    the LORD's love is with those who
      fear him,
    and his righteousness with their
      children's children—
¹⁸with those who keep his covenant
    and remember to obey his
      precepts.

¹⁹The LORD has established his throne
    in heaven,
    and his kingdom rules over all.

²⁰Praise the LORD, you his angels,
    you mighty ones who do his
      bidding,
    who obey his word.
²¹Praise the LORD, all his heavenly
      hosts,
    you his servants who do his will.
²²Praise the LORD, all his works
    everywhere in his dominion.

    Praise the LORD, O my soul.

Psalm 104

¹Praise the LORD, O my soul.

O LORD my God, you are very great;
    you are clothed with splendor and
      majesty.
²He wraps himself in light as with a
      garment;
    he stretches out the heavens like a
      tent
³   and lays the beams of his upper
      chambers on their waters.
    He makes the clouds his chariot
    and rides on the wings of the
      wind.
⁴He makes winds his messengers,ᵃ
    flames of fire his servants.

⁵He set the earth on its foundations;
    it can never be moved.

⁶You covered it with the deep as with
      a garment;
    the waters stood above the
      mountains.
⁷But at your rebuke the waters fled,
    at the sound of your thunder they
      took to flight;
⁸they flowed over the mountains,
    they went down into the valleys,
    to the place you assigned for
      them.
⁹You set a boundary they cannot
      cross;
    never again will they cover the
      earth.

¹⁰He makes springs pour water into
      the ravines;
    it flows between the mountains.
¹¹They give water to all the beasts of
      the field;
    the wild donkeys quench their
      thirst.
¹²The birds of the air nest by the
      waters;
    they sing among the branches.
¹³He waters the mountains from his
      upper chambers;
    the earth is satisfied by the fruit of
      his work.
¹⁴He makes grass grow for the cattle,
    and plants for man to cultivate—
    bringing forth food from the earth:
¹⁵wine that gladdens the heart of man,
    oil to make his face shine,
    and bread that sustains his heart.
¹⁶The trees of the LORD are well
      watered,
    the cedars of Lebanon that he
      planted.
¹⁷There the birds make their nests;
    the stork has its home in the pine
      trees.
¹⁸The high mountains belong to the
      wild goats;
    the crags are a refuge for the
      coneys.ᵇ

¹⁹The moon marks off the seasons,
    and the sun knows when to go
      down.
²⁰You bring darkness, it becomes
      night,
    and all the beasts of the forest
      prowl.
²¹The lions roar for their prey
    and seek their food from God.
²²The sun rises, and they steal away;

ᵃ4 Or *angels*   ᵇ18 That is, the hyrax or rock badger

VERSE:
Psalm 103:13

AUTHOR:
Joni Eareckson Tada

PASSAGE:
Psalm 103

God of the Little Things

Is God concerned about the details of your life? Does he care about the "little things"?

Piles of dishes need to be done. The washer leaks a big soapy puddle on the floor—and you've got people coming in an hour. Little things.

Nobody else seems to notice or pay that much mind . . . so why should God? After all, isn't he the God of the BIG things? Isn't he the one who spoke swirling galaxies into the vast frontiers of space, who measured the waters in the hollow of his hand and calculated the dust of the earth (Isaiah 40:12)?

Why should this great, awesome God notice the tears that came to my eyes this morning at breakfast—when no one else noticed? Why should the Creator of the universe care about the worries that kept me awake until two in the morning? Why should the mighty Sovereign of eternity be concerned about the fact that I'm late for an appointment and can't find a parking place?

Sure, the Bible says he has compassion for his people. But isn't that sort of a "general" compassion for humankind? Isn't that an arms-length kind of compassion? Just how intimately is God involved in our small, petty problems? David says he has the compassion of a father.

I remember my father having a kind of intimate, heartfelt compassion with me. Often when my dad would be busy at his easel, I'd sit on the floor at his side with my crayons and coloring book. Sometimes he'd set his brushes aside, reach down and lift me into his lap. Then he'd fix my hand on one of his brushes and enfold his larger, stronger hand around mine. Ever so gently, he would guide my hand and the brush, and I would watch in amazement as, together, we made something beautiful.

This is the kind of love our God has for us. Fatherlove. The kind, gentle compassion of a dad who deeply cares for his sons and daughters. Maybe you never had a dad like that . . . but you do have such a Father.

Let God's big hand close gently over yours. With his help, even the discouraging scribbles of your life can become a masterpiece. Nothing would delight a father's heart more.

ADDITIONAL SCRIPTURE READINGS:
Exodus 3:7; Matthew 6:9–13; Romans 8:8–15

Go to page 472 for your next devotional reading.

they return and lie down in their
    dens.
23Then man goes out to his work,
    to his labor until evening.

24How many are your works, O LORD!
    In wisdom you made them all;
    the earth is full of your creatures.
25There is the sea, vast and spacious,
    teeming with creatures beyond
      number—
    living things both large and small.
26There the ships go to and fro,
    and the leviathan, which you
      formed to frolic there.

27These all look to you
    to give them their food at the
      proper time.
28When you give it to them,
    they gather it up;
    when you open your hand,
    they are satisfied with good things.
29When you hide your face,
    they are terrified;
    when you take away their breath,
    they die and return to the dust.
30When you send your Spirit,
    they are created,
    and you renew the face of the
      earth.

31May the glory of the LORD endure
    forever;
    may the LORD rejoice in his
      works—
32he who looks at the earth, and it
    trembles,
    who touches the mountains, and
      they smoke.

33I will sing to the LORD all my life;
    I will sing praise to my God as
      long as I live.
34May my meditation be pleasing to
    him,
    as I rejoice in the LORD.
35But may sinners vanish from the
    earth
    and the wicked be no more.

Praise the LORD, O my soul.

Praise the LORD.a

Psalm 105

1Give thanks to the LORD, call on his
    name;

make known among the nations
    what he has done.
2Sing to him, sing praise to him;
    tell of all his wonderful acts.
3Glory in his holy name;
    let the hearts of those who seek
      the LORD rejoice.
4Look to the LORD and his strength;
    seek his face always.

5Remember the wonders he has done,
    his miracles, and the judgments he
      pronounced,
6O descendants of Abraham his
    servant,
    O sons of Jacob, his chosen ones.
7He is the LORD our God;
    his judgments are in all the earth.

8He remembers his covenant forever,
    the word he commanded, for a
      thousand generations,
9the covenant he made with Abraham,
    the oath he swore to Isaac.
10He confirmed it to Jacob as a decree,
    to Israel as an everlasting
      covenant:
11"To you I will give the land of
    Canaan
    as the portion you will inherit."

12When they were but few in number,
    few indeed, and strangers in it,
13they wandered from nation to nation,
    from one kingdom to another.
14He allowed no one to oppress them;
    for their sake he rebuked kings:
15"Do not touch my anointed ones;
    do my prophets no harm."

16He called down famine on the land
    and destroyed all their supplies of
      food;
17and he sent a man before them—
    Joseph, sold as a slave.
18They bruised his feet with shackles,
    his neck was put in irons,
19till what he foretold came to pass,
    till the word of the LORD proved
      him true.
20The king sent and released him,
    the ruler of peoples set him free.
21He made him master of his
    household,
    ruler over all he possessed,
22to instruct his princes as he pleased
    and teach his elders wisdom.

23Then Israel entered Egypt;

---

a35 Hebrew Hallelu Yah; in the Septuagint this line stands at the beginning of Psalm 105.

Jacob lived as an alien in the land
of Ham.
24The LORD made his people very
fruitful;
he made them too numerous for
their foes,
25whose hearts he turned to hate his
people,
to conspire against his servants.
26He sent Moses his servant,
and Aaron, whom he had chosen.
27They performed his miraculous signs
among them,
his wonders in the land of Ham.
28He sent darkness and made the land
dark—
for had they not rebelled against
his words?
29He turned their waters into blood,
causing their fish to die.
30Their land teemed with frogs,
which went up into the bedrooms
of their rulers.
31He spoke, and there came swarms of
flies,
and gnats throughout their
country.
32He turned their rain into hail,
with lightning throughout their
land;
33he struck down their vines and fig
trees
and shattered the trees of their
country.
34He spoke, and the locusts came,
grasshoppers without number;
35they ate up every green thing in their
land,
ate up the produce of their soil.
36Then he struck down all the firstborn
in their land,
the firstfruits of all their manhood.

37He brought out Israel, laden with
silver and gold,
and from among their tribes no
one faltered.
38Egypt was glad when they left,
because dread of Israel had fallen
on them.
39He spread out a cloud as a covering,
and a fire to give light at night.
40They asked, and he brought them
quail
and satisfied them with the bread
of heaven.

41He opened the rock, and water
gushed out;
like a river it flowed in the desert.

42For he remembered his holy promise
given to his servant Abraham.
43He brought out his people with
rejoicing,
his chosen ones with shouts of
joy;
44he gave them the lands of the
nations,
and they fell heir to what others
had toiled for—
45that they might keep his precepts
and observe his laws.

Praise the LORD.*a*

Psalm 106

1Praise the LORD.*b*

Give thanks to the LORD, for he is
good;
his love endures forever.
2Who can proclaim the mighty acts of
the LORD
or fully declare his praise?
3Blessed are they who maintain
justice,
who constantly do what is right.
4Remember me, O LORD, when you
show favor to your people,
come to my aid when you save
them,
5that I may enjoy the prosperity of
your chosen ones,
that I may share in the joy of your
nation
and join your inheritance in giving
praise.

6We have sinned, even as our fathers
did;
we have done wrong and acted
wickedly.
7When our fathers were in Egypt,
they gave no thought to your
miracles;
they did not remember your many
kindnesses,
and they rebelled by the sea, the
Red Sea.*c*
8Yet he saved them for his name's
sake,
to make his mighty power known.

*a*45 Hebrew *Hallelu Yah*   *b*1 Hebrew *Hallelu Yah*; also in verse 48   *c*7 Hebrew *Yam Suph*; that is,
Sea of Reeds; also in verses 9 and 22

⁹He rebuked the Red Sea, and it dried
    up;
  he led them through the depths as
    through a desert.
¹⁰He saved them from the hand of the
    foe;
  from the hand of the enemy he
    redeemed them.
¹¹The waters covered their adversaries;
  not one of them survived.
¹²Then they believed his promises
  and sang his praise.

¹³But they soon forgot what he had
    done
  and did not wait for his counsel.
¹⁴In the desert they gave in to their
    craving;
  in the wasteland they put God to
    the test.
¹⁵So he gave them what they asked for,
  but sent a wasting disease upon
    them.

¹⁶In the camp they grew envious of
    Moses
  and of Aaron, who was
    consecrated to the LORD.
¹⁷The earth opened up and swallowed
    Dathan;
  it buried the company of Abiram.
¹⁸Fire blazed among their followers;
  a flame consumed the wicked.

¹⁹At Horeb they made a calf
  and worshiped an idol cast from
    metal.
²⁰They exchanged their Glory
  for an image of a bull, which eats
    grass.
²¹They forgot the God who saved
    them,
  who had done great things in
    Egypt,
²²miracles in the land of Ham
  and awesome deeds by the Red
    Sea.
²³So he said he would destroy them—
  had not Moses, his chosen one,
  stood in the breach before him
    to keep his wrath from destroying
    them.

²⁴Then they despised the pleasant
    land;
  they did not believe his promise.
²⁵They grumbled in their tents
  and did not obey the LORD.

²⁶So he swore to them with uplifted
    hand
  that he would make them fall in
    the desert,
²⁷make their descendants fall among
    the nations
  and scatter them throughout the
    lands.

²⁸They yoked themselves to the Baal of
    Peor
  and ate sacrifices offered to lifeless
    gods;
²⁹they provoked the LORD to anger by
    their wicked deeds,
  and a plague broke out among
    them.
³⁰But Phinehas stood up and
    intervened,
  and the plague was checked.
³¹This was credited to him as
    righteousness
  for endless generations to come.

³²By the waters of Meribah they
    angered the LORD,
  and trouble came to Moses
    because of them;
³³for they rebelled against the Spirit of
    God,
  and rash words came from Moses'
    lips.ᵃ

³⁴They did not destroy the peoples
  as the LORD had commanded them,
³⁵but they mingled with the nations
  and adopted their customs.
³⁶They worshiped their idols,
  which became a snare to them.
³⁷They sacrificed their sons
  and their daughters to demons.
³⁸They shed innocent blood,
  the blood of their sons and
    daughters,
  whom they sacrificed to the idols of
    Canaan,
  and the land was desecrated by
    their blood.
³⁹They defiled themselves by what they
    did;
  by their deeds they prostituted
    themselves.

⁴⁰Therefore the LORD was angry with
    his people
  and abhorred his inheritance.
⁴¹He handed them over to the nations,
  and their foes ruled over them.
⁴²Their enemies oppressed them

ᵃ33 Or *against his spirit, / and rash words came from his lips*

and subjected them to their power.
⁴³Many times he delivered them,
  but they were bent on rebellion
  and they wasted away in their sin.

⁴⁴But he took note of their distress
  when he heard their cry;
⁴⁵for their sake he remembered his
   covenant
  and out of his great love he
   relented.
⁴⁶He caused them to be pitied
  by all who held them captive.

⁴⁷Save us, O LORD our God,
  and gather us from the nations,
that we may give thanks to your holy
   name
  and glory in your praise.

⁴⁸Praise be to the LORD, the God of
   Israel,
  from everlasting to everlasting.
Let all the people say, "Amen!"

Praise the LORD.

BOOK V

Psalms 107–150

Psalm 107

¹Give thanks to the LORD, for he is
  good;
  his love endures forever.
²Let the redeemed of the LORD say
  this—
  those he redeemed from the hand
   of the foe,
³those he gathered from the lands,
  from east and west, from north
   and south.ᵃ

⁴Some wandered in desert wastelands,
  finding no way to a city where
   they could settle.
⁵They were hungry and thirsty,
  and their lives ebbed away.
⁶Then they cried out to the LORD in
   their trouble,
  and he delivered them from their
   distress.
⁷He led them by a straight way
  to a city where they could settle.
⁸Let them give thanks to the LORD for
  his unfailing love
  and his wonderful deeds for men,
⁹for he satisfies the thirsty

and fills the hungry with good
  things.

¹⁰Some sat in darkness and the
   deepest gloom,
  prisoners suffering in iron chains,
¹¹for they had rebelled against the
   words of God
  and despised the counsel of the
   Most High.
¹²So he subjected them to bitter labor;
  they stumbled, and there was no
   one to help.
¹³Then they cried to the LORD in their
   trouble,
  and he saved them from their
   distress.
¹⁴He brought them out of darkness
   and the deepest gloom
  and broke away their chains.
¹⁵Let them give thanks to the LORD for
  his unfailing love
  and his wonderful deeds for men,
¹⁶for he breaks down gates of bronze
  and cuts through bars of iron.

¹⁷Some became fools through their
   rebellious ways
  and suffered affliction because of
   their iniquities.
¹⁸They loathed all food
  and drew near the gates of death.
¹⁹Then they cried to the LORD in their
   trouble,
  and he saved them from their
   distress.
²⁰He sent forth his word and healed
   them;
  he rescued them from the grave.
²¹Let them give thanks to the LORD for
  his unfailing love
  and his wonderful deeds for men.
²²Let them sacrifice thank offerings
  and tell of his works with songs
   of joy.

²³Others went out on the sea in ships;
  they were merchants on the
   mighty waters.
²⁴They saw the works of the LORD,
  his wonderful deeds in the deep.
²⁵For he spoke and stirred up a
   tempest
  that lifted high the waves.
²⁶They mounted up to the heavens and
   went down to the depths;
  in their peril their courage melted
   away.

ᵃ3 Hebrew *north and the sea*

WEEKENDING

RECHARGE

All of us face times when we wonder if we will ever laugh again . . . I have known these moments and wondered where laughter has gone, only to discover that laughter cloaks itself in disguise and springs out from its hiding place to surprise us when we are most garroted with the enormity of life; it shouts, *Olly, Olly, oxen free!* It invites us to rush to life's game again, to cast aside for a moment the weights of labor and responsibility, and to roll down the greening hillside, over and over, tumbling faster, bumping, plummeting, strangling for air between chortled shouts and gasps.

Laughter is God's good friend!

Karen Burton Mains

REVIVE

Saturday: Job 8:20–22
Sunday: Psalm 118

Go to page 478 for your next devotional reading.

²⁷They reeled and staggered like
  drunken men;
  they were at their wits' end.
²⁸Then they cried out to the LORD in
  their trouble,
  and he brought them out of their
  distress.
²⁹He stilled the storm to a whisper;
  the waves of the sea were hushed.
³⁰They were glad when it grew calm,
  and he guided them to their
  desired haven.
³¹Let them give thanks to the LORD for
  his unfailing love
  and his wonderful deeds for men.
³²Let them exalt him in the assembly
  of the people
  and praise him in the council of
  the elders.

³³He turned rivers into a desert,
  flowing springs into thirsty
  ground,
³⁴and fruitful land into a salt waste,
  because of the wickedness of
  those who lived there.
³⁵He turned the desert into pools of
  water
  and the parched ground into
  flowing springs;
³⁶there he brought the hungry to live,
  and they founded a city where they
  could settle.
³⁷They sowed fields and planted
  vineyards
  that yielded a fruitful harvest;
³⁸he blessed them, and their numbers
  greatly increased,
  and he did not let their herds
  diminish.

³⁹Then their numbers decreased, and
  they were humbled
  by oppression, calamity and
  sorrow;
⁴⁰he who pours contempt on nobles
  made them wander in a trackless
  waste.
⁴¹But he lifted the needy out of their
  affliction
  and increased their families like
  flocks.
⁴²The upright see and rejoice,
  but all the wicked shut their
  mouths.

⁴³Whoever is wise, let him heed these
  things
  and consider the great love of the
  LORD.

Psalm 108

A song. A psalm of David.

¹My heart is steadfast, O God;
  I will sing and make music with
  all my soul.
²Awake, harp and lyre!
  I will awaken the dawn.
³I will praise you, O LORD, among the
  nations;
  I will sing of you among the
  peoples.
⁴For great is your love, higher than
  the heavens;
  your faithfulness reaches to the
  skies.
⁵Be exalted, O God, above the
  heavens,
  and let your glory be over all the
  earth.

⁶Save us and help us with your right
  hand,
  that those you love may be
  delivered.
⁷God has spoken from his sanctuary:
  "In triumph I will parcel out
  Shechem
  and measure off the Valley of
  Succoth.
⁸Gilead is mine, Manasseh is mine;
  Ephraim is my helmet,
  Judah my scepter.
⁹Moab is my washbasin,
  upon Edom I toss my sandal;
  over Philistia I shout in triumph."

¹⁰Who will bring me to the fortified
  city?
  Who will lead me to Edom?
¹¹Is it not you, O God, you who have
  rejected us
  and no longer go out with our
  armies?
¹²Give us aid against the enemy,
  for the help of man is worthless.
¹³With God we will gain the victory,
  and he will trample down our
  enemies.

Psalm 109

For the director of music. Of David.
A psalm.

¹O God, whom I praise,
  do not remain silent,
²for wicked and deceitful men

have opened their mouths against
    me;
they have spoken against me with
    lying tongues.
³With words of hatred they surround
    me;
they attack me without cause.
⁴In return for my friendship they
    accuse me,
but I am a man of prayer.
⁵They repay me evil for good,
    and hatred for my friendship.

⁶Appoint*a* an evil man*b* to oppose
    him;
let an accuser*c* stand at his right
    hand.
⁷When he is tried, let him be found
    guilty,
and may his prayers condemn
    him.
⁸May his days be few;
    may another take his place of
    leadership.
⁹May his children be fatherless
    and his wife a widow.
¹⁰May his children be wandering
    beggars;
may they be driven*d* from their
    ruined homes.
¹¹May a creditor seize all he has;
    may strangers plunder the fruits of
    his labor.
¹²May no one extend kindness to him
    or take pity on his fatherless
    children.
¹³May his descendants be cut off,
    their names blotted out from the
    next generation.
¹⁴May the iniquity of his fathers be
    remembered before the LORD;
may the sin of his mother never
    be blotted out.
¹⁵May their sins always remain before
    the LORD,
that he may cut off the memory of
    them from the earth.

¹⁶For he never thought of doing a
    kindness,
but hounded to death the poor
    and the needy and the
    brokenhearted.
¹⁷He loved to pronounce a curse—
    may it*e* come on him;
he found no pleasure in blessing—

may it be*f* far from him.
¹⁸He wore cursing as his garment;
    it entered into his body like water,
    into his bones like oil.
¹⁹May it be like a cloak wrapped about
    him,
like a belt tied forever around him.
²⁰May this be the LORD's payment to
    my accusers,
to those who speak evil of me.

²¹But you, O Sovereign LORD,
    deal well with me for your name's
    sake;
out of the goodness of your love,
    deliver me.
²²For I am poor and needy,
    and my heart is wounded within
    me.
²³I fade away like an evening shadow;
    I am shaken off like a locust.
²⁴My knees give way from fasting;
    my body is thin and gaunt.
²⁵I am an object of scorn to my
    accusers;
when they see me, they shake their
    heads.

²⁶Help me, O LORD my God;
    save me in accordance with your
    love.
²⁷Let them know that it is your hand,
    that you, O LORD, have done it.
²⁸They may curse, but you will bless;
    when they attack they will be put
    to shame,
but your servant will rejoice.
²⁹My accusers will be clothed with
    disgrace
and wrapped in shame as in a
    cloak.

³⁰With my mouth I will greatly extol
    the LORD;
in the great throng I will praise
    him.
³¹For he stands at the right hand of
    the needy one,
to save his life from those who
    condemn him.

Psalm 110

Of David. A psalm.

¹The LORD says to my Lord:
    "Sit at my right hand

---

a6 Or ⌊*They say:*⌋ *"Appoint* (with quotation marks at the end of verse 19)   *b6* Or *the Evil One*
c6 Or *let Satan*   *d10* Septuagint; Hebrew *sought*   *e17* Or *curse, / and it has*   *f17* Or *blessing, /*
and it is

until I make your enemies
    a footstool for your feet."

²The LORD will extend your mighty
    scepter from Zion;
  you will rule in the midst of your
    enemies.
³Your troops will be willing
    on your day of battle.
  Arrayed in holy majesty,
    from the womb of the dawn
  you will receive the dew of your
    youth.ᵃ

⁴The LORD has sworn
    and will not change his mind:
  "You are a priest forever,
    in the order of Melchizedek."

⁵The Lord is at your right hand;
    he will crush kings on the day of
    his wrath.
⁶He will judge the nations, heaping
    up the dead
  and crushing the rulers of the
    whole earth.
⁷He will drink from a brook beside
    the wayᵇ;
  therefore he will lift up his head.

Psalm 111ᶜ

¹Praise the LORD.ᵈ

I will extol the LORD with all my heart
  in the council of the upright and
    in the assembly.

²Great are the works of the LORD;
  they are pondered by all who
    delight in them.
³Glorious and majestic are his deeds,
  and his righteousness endures
    forever.
⁴He has caused his wonders to be
    remembered;
  the LORD is gracious and
    compassionate.
⁵He provides food for those who fear
    him;
  he remembers his covenant
    forever.
⁶He has shown his people the power
    of his works,
  giving them the lands of other
    nations.

⁷The works of his hands are faithful
    and just;
  all his precepts are trustworthy.
⁸They are steadfast for ever and ever,
  done in faithfulness and
    uprightness.
⁹He provided redemption for his
    people;
  he ordained his covenant forever—
  holy and awesome is his name.

¹⁰The fear of the LORD is the beginning
    of wisdom;
  all who follow his precepts have
    good understanding.
  To him belongs eternal praise.

Psalm 112ᶜ

¹Praise the LORD.ᵈ

Blessed is the man who fears the
    LORD,
  who finds great delight in his
    commands.

²His children will be mighty in the
    land;
  the generation of the upright will
    be blessed.
³Wealth and riches are in his house,
  and his righteousness endures
    forever.
⁴Even in darkness light dawns for the
    upright,
  for the gracious and
    compassionate and righteous
    man.ᵉ
⁵Good will come to him who is
    generous and lends freely,
  who conducts his affairs with
    justice.
⁶Surely he will never be shaken;
  a righteous man will be
    remembered forever.
⁷He will have no fear of bad news;
  his heart is steadfast, trusting in
    the LORD.
⁸His heart is secure, he will have no
    fear;
  in the end he will look in triumph
    on his foes.
⁹He has scattered abroad his gifts to
    the poor,
  his righteousness endures forever;

ᵃ3 Or / your young men will come to you like the dew
in authority   ᶜThis psalm is an acrostic poem, the lines of which begin with the successive letters of
the Hebrew alphabet.   ᵈ1 Hebrew Hallelu Yah
and righteous

ᵇ7 Or / The One who grants succession will set him
ᵉ4 Or / for ⌊the LORD⌋ is gracious and compassionate

his horn[a] will be lifted high in
    honor.

¹⁰The wicked man will see and be
    vexed,
    he will gnash his teeth and waste
      away;
    the longings of the wicked will
      come to nothing.

Psalm 113

¹Praise the LORD.[b]

Praise, O servants of the LORD,
    praise the name of the LORD.
²Let the name of the LORD be praised,
    both now and forevermore.
³From the rising of the sun to the
    place where it sets,
    the name of the LORD is to be
      praised.
⁴The LORD is exalted over all the
    nations,
    his glory above the heavens.
⁵Who is like the LORD our God,
    the One who sits enthroned on
      high,
⁶who stoops down to look
    on the heavens and the earth?

⁷He raises the poor from the dust
    and lifts the needy from the ash
      heap;
⁸he seats them with princes,
    with the princes of their people.
⁹He settles the barren woman in her
    home
    as a happy mother of children.

Praise the LORD.

Psalm 114

¹When Israel came out of Egypt,
    the house of Jacob from a people
      of foreign tongue,
²Judah became God's sanctuary,
    Israel his dominion.

³The sea looked and fled,
    the Jordan turned back;
⁴the mountains skipped like rams,
    the hills like lambs.

⁵Why was it, O sea, that you fled,
    O Jordan, that you turned back,
⁶you mountains, that you skipped like
    rams,
    you hills, like lambs?

⁷Tremble, O earth, at the presence of
    the Lord,
    at the presence of the God of
      Jacob,
⁸who turned the rock into a pool,
    the hard rock into springs of
      water.

Psalm 115

¹Not to us, O LORD, not to us
    but to your name be the glory,
    because of your love and
      faithfulness.

²Why do the nations say,
    "Where is their God?"
³Our God is in heaven;
    he does whatever pleases him.
⁴But their idols are silver and gold,
    made by the hands of men.
⁵They have mouths, but cannot speak,
    eyes, but they cannot see;
⁶they have ears, but cannot hear,
    noses, but they cannot smell;
⁷they have hands, but cannot feel,
    feet, but they cannot walk;
    nor can they utter a sound with
      their throats.
⁸Those who make them will be like
    them,
    and so will all who trust in them.

⁹O house of Israel, trust in the LORD—
    he is their help and shield.
¹⁰O house of Aaron, trust in the
    LORD—
    he is their help and shield.
¹¹You who fear him, trust in the
    LORD—
    he is their help and shield.

¹²The LORD remembers us and will
    bless us:
    He will bless the house of Israel,
    he will bless the house of Aaron,
¹³he will bless those who fear the
    LORD—
    small and great alike.

¹⁴May the LORD make you increase,
    both you and your children.
¹⁵May you be blessed by the LORD,
    the Maker of heaven and earth.

¹⁶The highest heavens belong to the
    LORD,
    but the earth he has given to man.

---

[a]9 *Horn* here symbolizes dignity.   [b]1 Hebrew *Hallelu Yah*; also in verse 9

17It is not the dead who praise the
  LORD,
  those who go down to silence;
18it is we who extol the LORD,
  both now and forevermore.

Praise the LORD. [a]

Psalm 116

1I love the LORD, for he heard my
  voice;
  he heard my cry for mercy.
2Because he turned his ear to me,
  I will call on him as long as I live.

3The cords of death entangled me,
  the anguish of the grave [b] came
    upon me;
  I was overcome by trouble and
    sorrow.
4Then I called on the name of the
  LORD:
  "O LORD, save me!"

5The LORD is gracious and righteous;
  our God is full of compassion.
6The LORD protects the simplehearted;
  when I was in great need, he saved
    me.

7Be at rest once more, O my soul,
  for the LORD has been good to you.

8For you, O LORD, have delivered my
  soul from death,
  my eyes from tears,
  my feet from stumbling,
9that I may walk before the LORD
  in the land of the living.
10I believed; therefore [c] I said,
  "I am greatly afflicted."
11And in my dismay I said,
  "All men are liars."

12How can I repay the LORD
  for all his goodness to me?
13I will lift up the cup of salvation
  and call on the name of the LORD.
14I will fulfill my vows to the LORD
  in the presence of all his people.

15Precious in the sight of the LORD
  is the death of his saints.
16O LORD, truly I am your servant;
  I am your servant, the son of your
    maidservant [d];
  you have freed me from my
    chains.

17I will sacrifice a thank offering to
  you
  and call on the name of the LORD.
18I will fulfill my vows to the LORD
  in the presence of all his people,
19in the courts of the house of the
  LORD—
  in your midst, O Jerusalem.

Praise the LORD. [a]

Psalm 117

1Praise the LORD, all you nations;
  extol him, all you peoples.
2For great is his love toward us,
  and the faithfulness of the LORD
    endures forever.

Praise the LORD. [a]

Psalm 118

1Give thanks to the LORD, for he is
  good;
  his love endures forever.

2Let Israel say:
  "His love endures forever."
3Let the house of Aaron say:
  "His love endures forever."
4Let those who fear the LORD say:
  "His love endures forever."

5In my anguish I cried to the LORD,
  and he answered by setting me
    free.
6The LORD is with me; I will not be
  afraid.
  What can man do to me?
7The LORD is with me; he is my
  helper.
  I will look in triumph on my
    enemies.

8It is better to take refuge in the LORD
  than to trust in man.
9It is better to take refuge in the LORD
  than to trust in princes.

10All the nations surrounded me,
  but in the name of the LORD I cut
    them off.
11They surrounded me on every side,
  but in the name of the LORD I cut
    them off.
12They swarmed around me like bees,
  but they died out as quickly as
    burning thorns;

a18,19,2 Hebrew Hallelu Yah   b3 Hebrew Sheol   c10 Or believed even when   d16 Or servant,
your faithful son

in the name of the LORD I cut them off.

¹³I was pushed back and about to fall,
but the LORD helped me.
¹⁴The LORD is my strength and my song;
he has become my salvation.

¹⁵Shouts of joy and victory
resound in the tents of the righteous:

"The LORD's right hand has done mighty things!
¹⁶ The LORD's right hand is lifted high;
the LORD's right hand has done mighty things!"

¹⁷I will not die but live,
and will proclaim what the LORD has done.
¹⁸The LORD has chastened me severely,

MONDAY

VERSE:	AUTHOR:	PASSAGE:
Psalm 116:6	June Masters Bacher	Psalm 116:5-9

How to Eat an Elephant

There is only one way to eat an elephant: a bite at a time. Maybe you know that already. I didn't—until Beverly Johnson told the world after she, the first woman to do so alone, reached the top of thirty-six hundred feet high El Capitan in Yosemite National Park, California.

"That's what I kept saying, 'A bite at a time, a bite at a time . . . '," the smiling Beverly said of her ten-day struggle up the gigantic granite mass that rises unbroken from the Yosemite Valley.

She was weary and afraid up there all alone, strapped with a hundred pounds of gear . . . climbing . . . climbing. Day after day she rose higher and higher, clutching to rocks and ropes self-hammered into the rock—praying that they would hold. What sleep she had was in slings on the sheer granite wall. "I often thought if I could magically leave, I would—" but there was no way but up.

She kept climbing, saying to herself, "I'll climb here today." You can't do it, she told reporters, if you count the days. "Just a step at a time . . . a day at a time," she laughed victoriously, "and a bite at a time!"

We can all "eat elephants" by Beverly's formula, can't we? It makes little difference whether it's all the things we have to accomplish, a test we have to take, a physical condition we have to live with, a broken heart that needs healing. Her reasoning works.

Haven't you often wished, as she did, that you could magically leave your problems? Most of us feel that way, but the world doesn't stop for us to get off. We dig in with whatever equipment we have; we work our way up slowly; and, remember this: We have the solid Rock to lean upon! God is always there.

ADDITIONAL SCRIPTURE READINGS:
Philippians 3:13-14; Hebrews 12:1-3

Go to page 483 for your next devotional reading.

but he has not given me over to
death.

¹⁹Open for me the gates of
righteousness;
I will enter and give thanks to the
LORD.
²⁰This is the gate of the LORD
through which the righteous may
enter.
²¹I will give you thanks, for you
answered me;
you have become my salvation.

²²The stone the builders rejected
has become the capstone;
²³the LORD has done this,
and it is marvelous in our eyes.
²⁴This is the day the LORD has made;
let us rejoice and be glad in it.

²⁵O LORD, save us;
O LORD, grant us success.
²⁶Blessed is he who comes in the
name of the LORD.
From the house of the LORD we
bless you.ᵃ
²⁷The LORD is God,
and he has made his light shine
upon us.
With boughs in hand, join in the
festal procession
upᵇ to the horns of the altar.

²⁸You are my God, and I will give you
thanks;
you are my God, and I will exalt
you.

²⁹Give thanks to the LORD, for he is
good;
his love endures forever.

Psalm 119ᶜ

א   Aleph

¹Blessed are they whose ways are
blameless,
who walk according to the law of
the LORD.
²Blessed are they who keep his
statutes
and seek him with all their heart.
³They do nothing wrong;
they walk in his ways.
⁴You have laid down precepts
that are to be fully obeyed.
⁵Oh, that my ways were steadfast

in obeying your decrees!
⁶Then I would not be put to shame
when I consider all your
commands.
⁷I will praise you with an upright
heart
as I learn your righteous laws.
⁸I will obey your decrees;
do not utterly forsake me.

ב   Beth

⁹How can a young man keep his way
pure?
By living according to your word.
¹⁰I seek you with all my heart;
do not let me stray from your
commands.
¹¹I have hidden your word in my heart
that I might not sin against you.
¹²Praise be to you, O LORD;
teach me your decrees.
¹³With my lips I recount
all the laws that come from your
mouth.
¹⁴I rejoice in following your statutes
as one rejoices in great riches.
¹⁵I meditate on your precepts
and consider your ways.
¹⁶I delight in your decrees;
I will not neglect your word.

ג   Gimel

¹⁷Do good to your servant, and I will
live;
I will obey your word.
¹⁸Open my eyes that I may see
wonderful things in your law.
¹⁹I am a stranger on earth;
do not hide your commands from
me.
²⁰My soul is consumed with longing
for your laws at all times.
²¹You rebuke the arrogant, who are
cursed
and who stray from your
commands.
²²Remove from me scorn and
contempt,
for I keep your statutes.
²³Though rulers sit together and
slander me,
your servant will meditate on your
decrees.
²⁴Your statutes are my delight;
they are my counselors.

ᵃ26 The Hebrew is plural.   ᵇ27 Or *Bind the festal sacrifice with ropes / and take it*   ᶜThis psalm is
an acrostic poem; the verses of each stanza begin with the same letter of the Hebrew alphabet.

ד   Daleth

²⁵I am laid low in the dust;
preserve my life according to your
word.
²⁶I recounted my ways and you
answered me;
teach me your decrees.
²⁷Let me understand the teaching of
your precepts;
then I will meditate on your
wonders.
²⁸My soul is weary with sorrow;
strengthen me according to your
word.
²⁹Keep me from deceitful ways;
be gracious to me through your
law.
³⁰I have chosen the way of truth;
I have set my heart on your laws.
³¹I hold fast to your statutes, O LORD;
do not let me be put to shame.
³²I run in the path of your commands,
for you have set my heart free.

ה   He

³³Teach me, O LORD, to follow your
decrees;
then I will keep them to the
end.
³⁴Give me understanding, and I will
keep your law
and obey it with all my heart.
³⁵Direct me in the path of your
commands,
for there I find delight.
³⁶Turn my heart toward your statutes
and not toward selfish gain.
³⁷Turn my eyes away from worthless
things;
preserve my life according to your
word.ᵃ
³⁸Fulfill your promise to your servant,
so that you may be feared.
³⁹Take away the disgrace I dread,
for your laws are good.
⁴⁰How I long for your precepts!
Preserve my life in your
righteousness.

ו   Waw

⁴¹May your unfailing love come to me,
O LORD,
your salvation according to your
promise;

⁴²then I will answer the one who
taunts me,
for I trust in your word.
⁴³Do not snatch the word of truth
from my mouth,
for I have put my hope in your
laws.
⁴⁴I will always obey your law,
for ever and ever.
⁴⁵I will walk about in freedom,
for I have sought out your
precepts.
⁴⁶I will speak of your statutes before
kings
and will not be put to shame,
⁴⁷for I delight in your commands
because I love them.
⁴⁸I lift up my hands toᵇ your
commands, which I love,
and I meditate on your decrees.

ז   Zayin

⁴⁹Remember your word to your
servant,
for you have given me hope.
⁵⁰My comfort in my suffering is this:
Your promise preserves my life.
⁵¹The arrogant mock me without
restraint,
but I do not turn from your law.
⁵²I remember your ancient laws,
O LORD,
and I find comfort in them.
⁵³Indignation grips me because of the
wicked,
who have forsaken your law.
⁵⁴Your decrees are the theme of my
song
wherever I lodge.
⁵⁵In the night I remember your name,
O LORD,
and I will keep your law.
⁵⁶This has been my practice:
I obey your precepts.

ח   Heth

⁵⁷You are my portion, O LORD;
I have promised to obey your
words.
⁵⁸I have sought your face with all my
heart;
be gracious to me according to
your promise.
⁵⁹I have considered my ways
and have turned my steps to your
statutes.

ᵃ37 Two manuscripts of the Masoretic Text and Dead Sea Scrolls; most manuscripts of the Masoretic
Text *life in your way*   ᵇ48 Or *for*

⁶⁰I will hasten and not delay
    to obey your commands.
⁶¹Though the wicked bind me with
        ropes,
    I will not forget your law.
⁶²At midnight I rise to give you thanks
    for your righteous laws.
⁶³I am a friend to all who fear you,
    to all who follow your precepts.
⁶⁴The earth is filled with your love,
        O LORD;
    teach me your decrees.

ט   Teth

⁶⁵Do good to your servant
    according to your word, O LORD.
⁶⁶Teach me knowledge and good
        judgment,
    for I believe in your commands.
⁶⁷Before I was afflicted I went astray,
    but now I obey your word.
⁶⁸You are good, and what you do is
        good;
    teach me your decrees.
⁶⁹Though the arrogant have smeared
        me with lies,
    I keep your precepts with all my
        heart.
⁷⁰Their hearts are callous and
        unfeeling,
    but I delight in your law.
⁷¹It was good for me to be afflicted
    so that I might learn your decrees.
⁷²The law from your mouth is more
        precious to me
    than thousands of pieces of silver
        and gold.

י   Yodh

⁷³Your hands made me and formed
        me;
    give me understanding to learn
        your commands.
⁷⁴May those who fear you rejoice when
        they see me,
    for I have put my hope in your
        word.
⁷⁵I know, O LORD, that your laws are
        righteous,
    and in faithfulness you have
        afflicted me.
⁷⁶May your unfailing love be my
        comfort,
    according to your promise to your
        servant.
⁷⁷Let your compassion come to me
        that I may live,
    for your law is my delight.

⁷⁸May the arrogant be put to shame
        for wronging me without
        cause;
    but I will meditate on your
        precepts.
⁷⁹May those who fear you turn to
        me,
    those who understand your
        statutes.
⁸⁰May my heart be blameless toward
        your decrees,
    that I may not be put to shame.

כ   Kaph

⁸¹My soul faints with longing for your
        salvation,
    but I have put my hope in your
        word.
⁸²My eyes fail, looking for your
        promise;
    I say, "When will you comfort
        me?"
⁸³Though I am like a wineskin in the
        smoke,
    I do not forget your decrees.
⁸⁴How long must your servant wait?
    When will you punish my
        persecutors?
⁸⁵The arrogant dig pitfalls for me,
    contrary to your law.
⁸⁶All your commands are trustworthy;
    help me, for men persecute me
        without cause.
⁸⁷They almost wiped me from the
        earth,
    but I have not forsaken your
        precepts.
⁸⁸Preserve my life according to your
        love,
    and I will obey the statutes of
        your mouth.

ל   Lamedh

⁸⁹Your word, O LORD, is eternal;
    it stands firm in the heavens.
⁹⁰Your faithfulness continues through
        all generations;
    you established the earth, and it
        endures.
⁹¹Your laws endure to this day,
    for all things serve you.
⁹²If your law had not been my delight,
    I would have perished in my
        affliction.
⁹³I will never forget your precepts,
    for by them you have preserved
        my life.

94Save me, for I am yours;
 I have sought out your precepts.
95The wicked are waiting to destroy
   me,
 but I will ponder your statutes.
96To all perfection I see a limit;
 but your commands are
   boundless.

ם   Mem

97Oh, how I love your law!
 I meditate on it all day long.
98Your commands make me wiser
   than my enemies,
 for they are ever with me.
99I have more insight than all my
   teachers,
 for I meditate on your statutes.
100I have more understanding than the
   elders,
 for I obey your precepts.
101I have kept my feet from every evil
   path
 so that I might obey your word.
102I have not departed from your laws,
 for you yourself have taught me.
103How sweet are your words to my
   taste,
 sweeter than honey to my mouth!
104I gain understanding from your
   precepts;
 therefore I hate every wrong path.

נ   Nun

105Your word is a lamp to my feet
 and a light for my path.
106I have taken an oath and
   confirmed it,
 that I will follow your righteous
   laws.
107I have suffered much;
 preserve my life, O LORD, according
   to your word.
108Accept, O LORD, the willing praise of
   my mouth,
 and teach me your laws.
109Though I constantly take my life in
   my hands,
 I will not forget your law.
110The wicked have set a snare for me,
 but I have not strayed from your
   precepts.
111Your statutes are my heritage
   forever;
 they are the joy of my heart.
112My heart is set on keeping your
   decrees
 to the very end.

ס   Samekh

113I hate double-minded men,
 but I love your law.
114You are my refuge and my shield;
 I have put my hope in your word.
115Away from me, you evildoers,
 that I may keep the commands of
   my God!
116Sustain me according to your
   promise, and I will live;
 do not let my hopes be dashed.
117Uphold me, and I will be delivered;
 I will always have regard for your
   decrees.
118You reject all who stray from your
   decrees,
 for their deceitfulness is in vain.
119All the wicked of the earth you
   discard like dross;
 therefore I love your statutes.
120My flesh trembles in fear of you;
 I stand in awe of your laws.

ע   Ayin

121I have done what is righteous and
   just;
 do not leave me to my oppressors.
122Ensure your servant's well-being;
 let not the arrogant oppress me.
123My eyes fail, looking for your
   salvation,
 looking for your righteous
   promise.
124Deal with your servant according to
   your love
 and teach me your decrees.
125I am your servant; give me
   discernment
 that I may understand your
   statutes.
126It is time for you to act, O LORD;
 your law is being broken.
127Because I love your commands
   more than gold, more than pure
   gold,
128and because I consider all your
   precepts right,
 I hate every wrong path.

פ   Pe

129Your statutes are wonderful;
 therefore I obey them.
130The unfolding of your words gives
   light;
 it gives understanding to the
   simple.
131I open my mouth and pant,
 longing for your commands.

132Turn to me and have mercy on me,
   as you always do to those who
      love your name.
133Direct my footsteps according to
      your word;
   let no sin rule over me.
134Redeem me from the oppression of
      men,
   that I may obey your precepts.
135Make your face shine upon your
      servant
   and teach me your decrees.
136Streams of tears flow from my eyes,
   for your law is not obeyed.

צ Tsadhe

137Righteous are you, O LORD,
   and your laws are right.
138The statutes you have laid down are
      righteous;
   they are fully trustworthy.
139My zeal wears me out,
   for my enemies ignore your words.

140Your promises have been
      thoroughly tested,
   and your servant loves them.
141Though I am lowly and despised,
   I do not forget your precepts.
142Your righteousness is everlasting
   and your law is true.
143Trouble and distress have come
      upon me,
   but your commands are my
      delight.
144Your statutes are forever right;
   give me understanding that I may
      live.

ק Qoph

145I call with all my heart; answer me,
      O LORD,
   and I will obey your decrees.
146I call out to you; save me
   and I will keep your statutes.
147I rise before dawn and cry for help;
   I have put my hope in your word.

⟨ TUESDAY ⟩

VERSE:	AUTHOR:	PASSAGE:
Psalm 119:130	Joan C. Webb	Psalm 119:130–133

Step by Step

When our children were born, my husband and I lovingly
cared for them daily. We held them close, rocked them to sleep
and fed them. As they were able, we encouraged them to learn
to walk, dress themselves and communicate. We watched excitedly as they grew.

Likewise, our heavenly Father is actively involved in our growth;
he encourages us according to our capabilities and understanding
at the time. He does not push us; he waits until we are ready. If God
told us everything about ourselves and life all at once, we would be
confused and crushed. Instead he teaches us based on our spiritual
and emotional age level. God's gentle unfolding plan increases our
insight and encourages our consistent growth.

Lord, you are a compassionate and caring Father. Thank you for nur-
turing my development step by step and giving me understanding just as
I need it. Help me to be as patient as you are with my simple and imper-
fect attempts at gaining maturity.

ADDITIONAL SCRIPTURE READINGS:
Isaiah 40:11; Matthew 7:9–11; Luke 15:11–32

Go to page 486 for your next devotional reading.

148My eyes stay open through the
watches of the night,
that I may meditate on your
promises.
149Hear my voice in accordance with
your love;
preserve my life, O LORD, according
to your laws.
150Those who devise wicked schemes
are near,
but they are far from your law.
151Yet you are near, O LORD,
and all your commands are true.
152Long ago I learned from your
statutes
that you established them to last
forever.

ר Resh

153Look upon my suffering and
deliver me,
for I have not forgotten your law.
154Defend my cause and redeem me;
preserve my life according to your
promise.
155Salvation is far from the wicked,
for they do not seek out your
decrees.
156Your compassion is great, O LORD;
preserve my life according to your
laws.
157Many are the foes who
persecute me,
but I have not turned from your
statutes.
158I look on the faithless with loathing,
for they do not obey your word.
159See how I love your precepts;
preserve my life, O LORD, according
to your love.
160All your words are true;
all your righteous laws are eternal.

ש Sin and Shin

161Rulers persecute me without cause,
but my heart trembles at your
word.
162I rejoice in your promise
like one who finds great spoil.
163I hate and abhor falsehood
but I love your law.
164Seven times a day I praise you
for your righteous laws.
165Great peace have they who love your
law,
and nothing can make them
stumble.
166I wait for your salvation, O LORD,

and I follow your commands.
167I obey your statutes,
for I love them greatly.
168I obey your precepts and your
statutes,
for all my ways are known to you.

ת Taw

169May my cry come before you,
O LORD;
give me understanding according
to your word.
170May my supplication come before
you;
deliver me according to your
promise.
171May my lips overflow with praise,
for you teach me your decrees.
172May my tongue sing of your word,
for all your commands are
righteous.
173May your hand be ready to help me,
for I have chosen your precepts.
174I long for your salvation, O LORD,
and your law is my delight.
175Let me live that I may praise you,
and may your laws sustain me.
176I have strayed like a lost sheep.
Seek your servant,
for I have not forgotten your
commands.

Psalm 120

A song of ascents.

1I call on the LORD in my distress,
and he answers me.
2Save me, O LORD, from lying lips
and from deceitful tongues.

3What will he do to you,
and what more besides,
O deceitful tongue?
4He will punish you with a warrior's
sharp arrows,
with burning coals of the broom
tree.

5Woe to me that I dwell in Meshech,
that I live among the tents of
Kedar!
6Too long have I lived
among those who hate peace.
7I am a man of peace;
but when I speak, they are for war.

Psalm 121

A song of ascents.

¹I lift up my eyes to the hills—
  where does my help come from?
²My help comes from the LORD,
  the Maker of heaven and earth.

³He will not let your foot slip—
  he who watches over you will not
    slumber;
⁴indeed, he who watches over Israel
  will neither slumber nor sleep.

⁵The LORD watches over you—
  the LORD is your shade at your
    right hand;
⁶the sun will not harm you by day,
  nor the moon by night.

⁷The LORD will keep you from all
    harm—
  he will watch over your life;
⁸the LORD will watch over your coming
    and going
  both now and forevermore.

Psalm 122

A song of ascents. Of David.

¹I rejoiced with those who said to me,
  "Let us go to the house of the
    LORD."
²Our feet are standing
  in your gates, O Jerusalem.

³Jerusalem is built like a city
  that is closely compacted together.
⁴That is where the tribes go up,
  the tribes of the LORD,
to praise the name of the LORD
  according to the statute given to
    Israel.
⁵There the thrones for judgment
    stand,
  the thrones of the house of David.

⁶Pray for the peace of Jerusalem:
  "May those who love you be
    secure.
⁷May there be peace within your walls
  and security within your citadels."
⁸For the sake of my brothers and
    friends,
  I will say, "Peace be within you."
⁹For the sake of the house of the LORD
  our God,
  I will seek your prosperity.

Psalm 123

A song of ascents.

¹I lift up my eyes to you,
  to you whose throne is in heaven.
²As the eyes of slaves look to the
    hand of their master,
as the eyes of a maid look to the
    hand of her mistress,
so our eyes look to the LORD our
    God,
  till he shows us his mercy.

³Have mercy on us, O LORD, have
    mercy on us,
  for we have endured much
    contempt.
⁴We have endured much ridicule from
    the proud,
  much contempt from the arrogant.

Psalm 124

A song of ascents. Of David.

¹If the LORD had not been on our
    side—
  let Israel say—
²if the LORD had not been on our side
  when men attacked us,
³when their anger flared against us,
  they would have swallowed us
    alive;
⁴the flood would have engulfed us,
  the torrent would have swept over
    us,
⁵the raging waters
  would have swept us away.

⁶Praise be to the LORD,
  who has not let us be torn by
    their teeth.
⁷We have escaped like a bird
  out of the fowler's snare;
the snare has been broken,
  and we have escaped.
⁸Our help is in the name of the LORD,
  the Maker of heaven and earth.

Psalm 125

A song of ascents.

¹Those who trust in the LORD are like
  Mount Zion,
which cannot be shaken but
  endures forever.
²As the mountains surround
  Jerusalem,

so the LORD surrounds his people
both now and forevermore.

³The scepter of the wicked will not
remain
over the land allotted to the
righteous,

for then the righteous might use
their hands to do evil.

⁴Do good, O LORD, to those who are
good,
to those who are upright in heart.
⁵But those who turn to crooked ways

WEDNESDAY

VERSE:
Psalm 121:1

AUTHOR:
Debra Klingsporn

PASSAGE:
Psalm 121:1–8

Ballerina

When television coverage of the Winter Olympics brought
visions of twirling, whirling ice skaters into our home, we had
two diminutive skaters in our living room. Spin after spin cat-
apulted them into tangled heaps of arms and legs on the floor.
Finally, my five-year-old asked in exasperation, "Mommy, how
do they spin so fast?"

I tried to explain a technique learned many years ago when I was
the ballerina-to-be—the technique of spotting. Start by focusing
your sight on a fixed spot and with each rapid turn of the head,
return your gaze to the same place. No dramatic improvement
resulted from my little ballerina's initial efforts as she began trying
this technique. Spotting does not come naturally at any age. She
and her sister continued to look like they were playing a musical
game of Twister®, ending in the same heap on the floor. But
slowly, ever so slowly, spotting took effect. Her turns were more
controlled, she retained her balance and before long she was trying to explain spotting to her little sister.

Spotting takes practice, but it works. And it's no different for
grownups. On what do we set our sights? Are we spotting on career
moves, relationships, things? What occupies our minds as we wake
in the morning or creeps in unsolicited to our thoughts as we close
our eyes at the end of the day? Our uninvited thoughts and recur-
ring worries are probably a good indicator of what we're using to
spot.

The psalmist wrote, "I lift up my eyes . . ." (v. 1). He knew about
spotting, even if he didn't call it that. He knew where to set his
sights. Only one thing is worthy of our practiced focus, and only
one thing will enable us to maintain balance. When my head is
spinning and my world is turning too fast, I can spot on One
whose power is greater than mine, One who never loses his balance.

ADDITIONAL SCRIPTURE READINGS:
2 Samuel 6:14; 2 Peter 1:5–9

Go to page 490 for your next devotional reading.

the LORD will banish with the evildoers.

Peace be upon Israel.

Psalm 126

A song of ascents.

[1]When the LORD brought back the captives to[a] Zion,
we were like men who dreamed.[b]
[2]Our mouths were filled with laughter,
our tongues with songs of joy.
Then it was said among the nations,
"The LORD has done great things for them."
[3]The LORD has done great things for us,
and we are filled with joy.

[4]Restore our fortunes,[c] O LORD,
like streams in the Negev.
[5]Those who sow in tears
will reap with songs of joy.
[6]He who goes out weeping,
carrying seed to sow,
will return with songs of joy,
carrying sheaves with him.

Psalm 127

A song of ascents. Of Solomon.

[1]Unless the LORD builds the house,
its builders labor in vain.
Unless the LORD watches over the city,
the watchmen stand guard in vain.
[2]In vain you rise early
and stay up late,
toiling for food to eat—
for he grants sleep to[d] those he loves.

[3]Sons are a heritage from the LORD,
children a reward from him.
[4]Like arrows in the hands of a warrior
are sons born in one's youth.
[5]Blessed is the man
whose quiver is full of them.
They will not be put to shame
when they contend with their enemies in the gate.

Psalm 128

A song of ascents.

[1]Blessed are all who fear the LORD,
who walk in his ways.
[2]You will eat the fruit of your labor;
blessings and prosperity will be yours.
[3]Your wife will be like a fruitful vine
within your house;
your sons will be like olive shoots
around your table.
[4]Thus is the man blessed
who fears the LORD.

[5]May the LORD bless you from Zion
all the days of your life;
may you see the prosperity of Jerusalem,
[6]   and may you live to see your children's children.

Peace be upon Israel.

Psalm 129

A song of ascents.

[1]They have greatly oppressed me from my youth—
let Israel say—
[2]they have greatly oppressed me from my youth,
but they have not gained the victory over me.
[3]Plowmen have plowed my back
and made their furrows long.
[4]But the LORD is righteous;
he has cut me free from the cords of the wicked.

[5]May all who hate Zion
be turned back in shame.
[6]May they be like grass on the roof,
which withers before it can grow;
[7]with it the reaper cannot fill his hands,
nor the one who gathers fill his arms.
[8]May those who pass by not say,
"The blessing of the LORD be upon you;
we bless you in the name of the LORD."

---

[a]1 Or LORD restored the fortunes of   [b]1 Or men restored to health   [c]4 Or Bring back our captives
[d]2 Or eat— / for while they sleep he provides for

Psalm 130

A song of ascents.

¹Out of the depths I cry to you,
    O LORD;
² O Lord, hear my voice.
Let your ears be attentive
    to my cry for mercy.

³If you, O LORD, kept a record of
        sins,
    O Lord, who could stand?
⁴But with you there is forgiveness;
    therefore you are feared.

⁵I wait for the LORD, my soul waits,
    and in his word I put my hope.
⁶My soul waits for the Lord
    more than watchmen wait for the
        morning,
    more than watchmen wait for the
        morning.

⁷O Israel, put your hope in the LORD,
    for with the LORD is unfailing love
    and with him is full redemption.
⁸He himself will redeem Israel
    from all their sins.

Psalm 131

A song of ascents. Of David.

¹My heart is not proud, O LORD,
    my eyes are not haughty;
I do not concern myself with great
        matters
    or things too wonderful for me.
²But I have stilled and quieted my
        soul;
    like a weaned child with its
        mother,
    like a weaned child is my soul
        within me.

³O Israel, put your hope in the LORD
    both now and forevermore.

Psalm 132

A song of ascents.

¹O LORD, remember David
    and all the hardships he endured.

²He swore an oath to the LORD

and made a vow to the Mighty
        One of Jacob:
³"I will not enter my house
    or go to my bed—
⁴I will allow no sleep to my eyes,
    no slumber to my eyelids,
⁵till I find a place for the LORD,
    a dwelling for the Mighty One of
        Jacob."

⁶We heard it in Ephrathah,
    we came upon it in the fields of
        Jaar[a; b]
⁷"Let us go to his dwelling place;
    let us worship at his footstool—
⁸arise, O LORD, and come to your
        resting place,
    you and the ark of your might.
⁹May your priests be clothed with
        righteousness;
    may your saints sing for joy."

¹⁰For the sake of David your servant,
    do not reject your anointed one.

¹¹The LORD swore an oath to David,
    a sure oath that he will not
        revoke:
"One of your own descendants
    I will place on your throne—
¹²if your sons keep my covenant
    and the statutes I teach them,
then their sons will sit
    on your throne for ever and
        ever."

¹³For the LORD has chosen Zion,
    he has desired it for his dwelling:
¹⁴"This is my resting place for ever
        and ever;
    here I will sit enthroned, for I have
        desired it—
¹⁵I will bless her with abundant
        provisions;
    her poor will I satisfy with food.
¹⁶I will clothe her priests with
        salvation,
    and her saints will ever sing for
        joy.

¹⁷"Here I will make a horn[c] grow for
        David
    and set up a lamp for my anointed
        one.
¹⁸I will clothe his enemies with shame,
    but the crown on his head will be
        resplendent."

---

[a]6 That is, Kiriath Jearim   [b]6 Or heard of it in Ephrathah, / we found it in the fields of Jaar. (And no
quotes around verses 7-9)   [c]17 Horn here symbolizes strong one, that is, king.

Psalm 133

A song of ascents. Of David.

[1]How good and pleasant it is
  when brothers live together in
    unity!
[2]It is like precious oil poured on the
    head,
  running down on the beard,
running down on Aaron's beard,
  down upon the collar of his robes.
[3]It is as if the dew of Hermon
  were falling on Mount Zion.
For there the LORD bestows his
    blessing,
  even life forevermore.

Psalm 134

A song of ascents.

[1]Praise the LORD, all you servants of
    the LORD
  who minister by night in the
    house of the LORD.
[2]Lift up your hands in the sanctuary
  and praise the LORD.

[3]May the LORD, the Maker of heaven
    and earth,
  bless you from Zion.

Psalm 135

[1]Praise the LORD.[a]

 Praise the name of the LORD;
  praise him, you servants of the
    LORD,
[2]you who minister in the house of
    the LORD,
  in the courts of the house of our
    God.

[3]Praise the LORD, for the LORD is good;
  sing praise to his name, for that is
    pleasant.
[4]For the LORD has chosen Jacob to be
    his own,
  Israel to be his treasured
    possession.

[5]I know that the LORD is great,
  that our Lord is greater than all
    gods.
[6]The LORD does whatever pleases him,
  in the heavens and on the earth,
  in the seas and all their depths.

[7]He makes clouds rise from the ends
    of the earth;
  he sends lightning with the rain
  and brings out the wind from his
    storehouses.

[8]He struck down the firstborn of
    Egypt,
  the firstborn of men and animals.
[9]He sent his signs and wonders into
    your midst, O Egypt,
  against Pharaoh and all his
    servants.
[10]He struck down many nations
  and killed mighty kings—
[11]Sihon king of the Amorites,
  Og king of Bashan
  and all the kings of Canaan—
[12]and he gave their land as an
    inheritance,
  an inheritance to his people Israel.

[13]Your name, O LORD, endures forever,
  your renown, O LORD, through all
    generations.
[14]For the LORD will vindicate his people
  and have compassion on his
    servants.

[15]The idols of the nations are silver
    and gold,
  made by the hands of men.
[16]They have mouths, but cannot speak,
  eyes, but they cannot see;
[17]they have ears, but cannot hear,
  nor is there breath in their
    mouths.
[18]Those who make them will be like
    them,
  and so will all who trust in them.

[19]O house of Israel, praise the LORD;
  O house of Aaron, praise the LORD;
[20]O house of Levi, praise the LORD;
  you who fear him, praise the LORD.
[21]Praise be to the LORD from Zion,
  to him who dwells in Jerusalem.

 Praise the LORD.

Psalm 136

[1]Give thanks to the LORD, for he is
    good.
                    His love endures forever.
[2]Give thanks to the God of gods.
                    His love endures forever.
[3]Give thanks to the Lord of lords:
                    His love endures forever.

---

[a]1 Hebrew *Hallelu Yah;* also in verses 3 and 21

⁴to him who alone does great wonders,
His love endures forever.
⁵who by his understanding made the
heavens,
His love endures forever.

⁶who spread out the earth upon the
waters,
His love endures forever.
⁷who made the great lights—
His love endures forever.

THURSDAY

VERSE:
Psalm 136:1

AUTHOR:
Ruth Senter

PASSAGE:
Psalm 136:1–26

When the Moon Doesn't Shine

Usually the moon shines bright on clear May nights in eastern Pennsylvania. But tonight the moon is missing. All is dark. I notice brown circles under the lamp in the hall when mother welcomes our 2:00 A.M. arrival from Illinois. I also notice brown circles under her eyes. Tired skin under gentle folds.

But here she stands, my mother for forty years. I sense an accumulation of nights waiting up for home-coming children, as though the years have cast shadows from the lamp onto her face. I see the years in the black and blue veins that have just this week felt the heart specialist's probe. I hear the years—like the ocean ringing in a seashell—in the doctor's diagnosis: "Enlarged heart . . . slow the pace . . ." I stare into uncertainty. Tomorrow has been an assumed promise—a grand procession of weddings, births, celebrations. Time has been an event, not a sequence.

As I look at Mother, I sense that someone has wound the clock. Years have become increments. History has a beginning and an end. I shiver in the early morning chill. But then Mother's arms wrap me in warmth, and I am home. A forty-year-old child reassured by her mother's touch. There is no time in touch.

I hear the tea kettle whistling. Mother's chocolate chip cookies on Grandma Hollinger's ironstone plate pull me back into timelessness. Our laughter drowns out the clock. There is no time in laughter. Mother laughs the hardest of all. Dark circles. Tired circles of joy. Her children are home.

For a moment I forget bruised veins and ticking clocks. I am held together by things that do not change—a mother's early morning welcome, freshly baked chocolate chip cookies, an ironstone plate and laughter. I am held together by a God who does not change. I know the God of time who is yet above time. I see tonight in my mother's face the strange paradox of time and timelessness. A rare glimpse of the divine.

ADDITIONAL SCRIPTURE READINGS:
Deuteronomy 33:27; Revelation 21:1–7

Go to page 493 for your next devotional reading.

⁸the sun to govern the day,
His love endures forever.
⁹the moon and stars to govern the
night;
His love endures forever.

¹⁰to him who struck down the
firstborn of Egypt
His love endures forever.
¹¹and brought Israel out from among
them
His love endures forever.
¹²with a mighty hand and outstretched
arm;
His love endures forever.

¹³to him who divided the Red Sea*a*
asunder
His love endures forever.
¹⁴and brought Israel through the midst
of it,
His love endures forever.
¹⁵but swept Pharaoh and his army into
the Red Sea;
His love endures forever.

¹⁶to him who led his people through
the desert,
His love endures forever.
¹⁷who struck down great kings,
His love endures forever.
¹⁸and killed mighty kings—
His love endures forever.
¹⁹Sihon king of the Amorites
His love endures forever.
²⁰and Og king of Bashan—
His love endures forever.
²¹and gave their land as an inheritance,
His love endures forever.
²²an inheritance to his servant Israel;
His love endures forever.

²³to the One who remembered us in
our low estate
His love endures forever.
²⁴and freed us from our enemies,
His love endures forever.
²⁵and who gives food to every creature.
His love endures forever.

²⁶Give thanks to the God of heaven.
His love endures forever.

Psalm 137

¹By the rivers of Babylon we sat and
wept
when we remembered Zion.
²There on the poplars

we hung our harps,
³for there our captors asked us for
songs,
our tormentors demanded songs
of joy;
they said, "Sing us one of the
songs of Zion!"

⁴How can we sing the songs of the
LORD
while in a foreign land?
⁵If I forget you, O Jerusalem,
may my right hand forget ⌞its
skill⌟.
⁶May my tongue cling to the roof of
my mouth
if I do not remember you,
if I do not consider Jerusalem
my highest joy.

⁷Remember, O LORD, what the
Edomites did
on the day Jerusalem fell.
"Tear it down," they cried,
"tear it down to its foundations!"

⁸O Daughter of Babylon, doomed to
destruction,
happy is he who repays you
for what you have done to us—
⁹he who seizes your infants
and dashes them against the
rocks.

Psalm 138

Of David.

¹I will praise you, O LORD, with all my
heart;
before the "gods" I will sing your
praise.
²I will bow down toward your holy
temple
and will praise your name
for your love and your
faithfulness,
for you have exalted above all things
your name and your word.
³When I called, you answered me;
you made me bold and
stouthearted.

⁴May all the kings of the earth praise
you, O LORD,
when they hear the words of your
mouth.

---

a13 Hebrew *Yam Suph;* that is, Sea of Reeds; also in verse 15

5May they sing of the ways of the
　LORD,
　　for the glory of the LORD is great.

6Though the LORD is on high, he looks
　upon the lowly,
　　but the proud he knows from afar.
7Though I walk in the midst of
　trouble,
　you preserve my life;
　you stretch out your hand against
　　the anger of my foes,
　with your right hand you save me.
8The LORD will fulfill ⌞his purpose⌟ for
　me;
　　your love, O LORD, endures
　　　forever—
　　do not abandon the works of your
　　　hands.

Psalm 139

For the director of music. Of David.
A psalm.

1O LORD, you have searched me
　and you know me.
2You know when I sit and when I
　rise;
　　you perceive my thoughts from
　　　afar.
3You discern my going out and my
　lying down;
　　you are familiar with all my ways.
4Before a word is on my tongue
　you know it completely, O LORD.

5You hem me in—behind and before;
　you have laid your hand upon me.
6Such knowledge is too wonderful for
　me,
　　too lofty for me to attain.

7Where can I go from your Spirit?
　Where can I flee from your
　　presence?
8If I go up to the heavens, you are
　there;
　　if I make my bed in the depths,[a]
　　　you are there.
9If I rise on the wings of the dawn,
　if I settle on the far side of the
　　sea,
10even there your hand will guide me,
　your right hand will hold me fast.

11If I say, "Surely the darkness will
　hide me
　and the light become night around
　　me,"
12even the darkness will not be dark to
　you;
　the night will shine like the day,
　　for darkness is as light to you.

13For you created my inmost being;
　you knit me together in my
　　mother's womb.
14I praise you because I am fearfully
　and wonderfully made;
　your works are wonderful,
　　I know that full well.
15My frame was not hidden from you
　when I was made in the secret
　　place.
　When I was woven together in the
　　depths of the earth,
16　your eyes saw my unformed body.
　All the days ordained for me
　were written in your book
　　before one of them came to be.

17How precious to[b] me are your
　thoughts, O God!
　　How vast is the sum of them!
18Were I to count them,
　they would outnumber the grains
　　of sand.
　When I awake,
　　I am still with you.

19If only you would slay the wicked,
　O God!
　　Away from me, you bloodthirsty
　　　men!
20They speak of you with evil intent;
　your adversaries misuse your
　　name.
21Do I not hate those who hate you,
　O LORD,
　　and abhor those who rise up
　　　against you?
22I have nothing but hatred for them;
　I count them my enemies.

23Search me, O God, and know my
　heart;
　　test me and know my anxious
　　　thoughts.
24See if there is any offensive way in
　me,
　　and lead me in the way
　　　everlasting.

---

a8 Hebrew Sheol　　b17 Or concerning

VERSE:
Psalm 139:14

AUTHOR:
Joy Morgan Davis

PASSAGE:
Psalm 139:13–16

Art Appreciation

Lord,
Sometimes when I look
At my life
It seems like a homespun
Patch-work quilt . . .
Quaint, but not quite "together"!
There are bits and pieces of
Cloths and colors,
Scraps of material,
The days of my life . . .

When you began to put together
The days of my life
You must have known
Where each piece would go . . .
You've told me that I am
Fearfully and wonderfully
Made . . .
And I believe you, Lord,
I do!
I may not be a velvet tapestry,
But even crazy-quilts
Have purpose,
To give warmth and
Cozy comfort and
Color to a room!

Whatever I am, Lord,
You made me . . .
Lovingly,
Carefully,
Reverently,
And exactly right!

ADDITIONAL SCRIPTURE READINGS:
2 Timothy 1:9; 1 John 3:1–3

Go to page 495 for your next devotional reading.

Psalm 140

For the director of music. A psalm
of David.

¹Rescue me, O LORD, from evil men;
  protect me from men of violence,
²who devise evil plans in their hearts
  and stir up war every day.
³They make their tongues as sharp as
    a serpent's;
  the poison of vipers is on their
    lips.   *Selah*

⁴Keep me, O LORD, from the hands of
    the wicked;
  protect me from men of violence
    who plan to trip my feet.
⁵Proud men have hidden a snare for
    me;
  they have spread out the cords of
    their net
  and have set traps for me along
    my path.   *Selah*

⁶O LORD, I say to you, "You are my
    God."
  Hear, O LORD, my cry for mercy.
⁷O Sovereign LORD, my strong
    deliverer,
  who shields my head in the day of
    battle—
⁸do not grant the wicked their desires,
    O LORD;
  do not let their plans succeed,
    or they will become proud.   *Selah*

⁹Let the heads of those who surround
    me
  be covered with the trouble their
    lips have caused.
¹⁰Let burning coals fall upon them;
  may they be thrown into the fire,
    into miry pits, never to rise.
¹¹Let slanderers not be established in
    the land;
  may disaster hunt down men of
    violence.

¹²I know that the LORD secures justice
    for the poor
  and upholds the cause of the
    needy.
¹³Surely the righteous will praise your
    name
  and the upright will live before
    you.

Psalm 141

A psalm of David.

¹O LORD, I call to you; come quickly to
    me.
  Hear my voice when I call to you.
²May my prayer be set before you like
    incense;
  may the lifting up of my hands be
    like the evening sacrifice.

³Set a guard over my mouth, O LORD;
  keep watch over the door of my
    lips.
⁴Let not my heart be drawn to what is
    evil,
  to take part in wicked deeds
with men who are evildoers;
  let me not eat of their delicacies.

⁵Let a righteous man*ᵃ* strike me—it is
    a kindness;
  let him rebuke me—it is oil on my
    head.
  My head will not refuse it.

Yet my prayer is ever against the
    deeds of evildoers;
⁶ their rulers will be thrown down
    from the cliffs,
  and the wicked will learn that my
    words were well spoken.
⁷⌊They will say,⌋ "As one plows and
    breaks up the earth,
  so our bones have been scattered
    at the mouth of the grave.*ᵇ*"

⁸But my eyes are fixed on you,
    O Sovereign LORD;
  in you I take refuge—do not give
    me over to death.
⁹Keep me from the snares they have
    laid for me,
  from the traps set by evildoers.
¹⁰Let the wicked fall into their own
    nets,
  while I pass by in safety.

Psalm 142

A *maskil*ᶜ of David. When he was in
    the cave. A prayer.

¹I cry aloud to the LORD;
  I lift up my voice to the LORD for
    mercy.
²I pour out my complaint before him;
  before him I tell my trouble.

ᵃ5 Or Let the Righteous One   *ᵇ7 Hebrew Sheol*   *ᶜTitle: Probably a literary or musical term*

WEEKENDING

REALIZE

If I could, I'd write for you a rainbow
And splash it with all the colors of God
And hang it in the window of your being
So that each new God's morning
Your eyes would open first
                    to Hope and Promise.
If I could, I'd wipe away your tears
And hold you close forever in shalom.
But God never promised
I could write a rainbow,
Never promised I could suffer for you,
Only promised I could love you.
That I do.

Ann Weems

REFLECT

Saturday: Genesis 9:13–16
Sunday: Lamentations 3:22–23

*Go to page 497 for your
next devotional reading.*

³When my spirit grows faint within
    me,
  it is you who know my way.
In the path where I walk
  men have hidden a snare for me.
⁴Look to my right and see;
  no one is concerned for me.
I have no refuge;
  no one cares for my life.

⁵I cry to you, O LORD;
  I say, "You are my refuge,
  my portion in the land of the
    living."
⁶Listen to my cry,
  for I am in desperate need;
rescue me from those who pursue
    me,
  for they are too strong for me.
⁷Set me free from my prison,
  that I may praise your name.

Then the righteous will gather about
    me
  because of your goodness to me.

Psalm 143

A psalm of David.

¹O LORD, hear my prayer,
  listen to my cry for mercy;
in your faithfulness and
    righteousness
  come to my relief.
²Do not bring your servant into
    judgment,
  for no one living is righteous
    before you.

³The enemy pursues me,
  he crushes me to the ground;
he makes me dwell in darkness
  like those long dead.
⁴So my spirit grows faint within me;
  my heart within me is dismayed.

⁵I remember the days of long ago;
  I meditate on all your works
  and consider what your hands
    have done.
⁶I spread out my hands to you;
  my soul thirsts for you like a
    parched land.   Selah

⁷Answer me quickly, O LORD;
  my spirit fails.
Do not hide your face from me

or I will be like those who go
  down to the pit.
⁸Let the morning bring me word of
  your unfailing love,
  for I have put my trust in you.
Show me the way I should go,
  for to you I lift up my soul.
⁹Rescue me from my enemies,
  O LORD,
  for I hide myself in you.
¹⁰Teach me to do your will,
  for you are my God;
may your good Spirit
  lead me on level ground.

¹¹For your name's sake, O LORD,
  preserve my life;
in your righteousness, bring me
  out of trouble.
¹²In your unfailing love, silence my
    enemies;
  destroy all my foes,
  for I am your servant.

Psalm 144

Of David.

¹Praise be to the LORD my Rock,
  who trains my hands for war,
  my fingers for battle.
²He is my loving God and my
    fortress,
  my stronghold and my deliverer,
my shield, in whom I take refuge,
  who subdues peoplesᵃ under me.

³O LORD, what is man that you care
    for him,
  the son of man that you think of
    him?
⁴Man is like a breath;
  his days are like a fleeting shadow.

⁵Part your heavens, O LORD, and come
    down;
  touch the mountains, so that they
    smoke.
⁶Send forth lightning and scatter ⌊the
    enemies⌋;
  shoot your arrows and rout them.
⁷Reach down your hand from on
    high;
  deliver me and rescue me
from the mighty waters,
  from the hands of foreigners
⁸whose mouths are full of lies,
  whose right hands are deceitful.

ᵃ2 Many manuscripts of the Masoretic Text, Dead Sea Scrolls, Aquila, Jerome and Syriac; most
manuscripts of the Masoretic Text *subdues my people*

⁹I will sing a new song to you,
　　O God;
　on the ten-stringed lyre I will
　　make music to you,
¹⁰to the One who gives victory to
　　kings,
　who delivers his servant David
　　from the deadly sword.

¹¹Deliver me and rescue me
　　from the hands of foreigners
　whose mouths are full of lies,
　　whose right hands are deceitful.

¹²Then our sons in their youth
　　will be like well-nurtured plants,
　and our daughters will be like pillars

MONDAY

VERSE:	AUTHOR:	PASSAGE:
Psalm 143:5	Brenda M. Josee, Ed.	Psalm 143:5–6

Imagine That

What would you think if you saw your neighbor and her four children lying in the grass and pointing up to the sky? That's one of the things we'd do during the summer when I was growing up. Mom would have us find pictures in the clouds and then draw them. While we drew, Mom would teach us about clouds or whatever we were drawing.

Other times we would write and perform plays. We had a big hearth that made a great stage. Sometimes we wrote in parts for Mom and Dad and performed for our own pleasure.

My favorite was to pretend that our house was a giant boat on an imaginary journey. Our travels took us to the Coral Sea, across the Atlantic, up the Nile River and down the Mississippi River. And we never failed to sail right into a monsoon, which made the game much more exciting. We'd scream and bounce around like we were being tossed about on the waves. Not only did we have fun, but we learned more about geography and boats than we ever did in school.

Now as an adult, my imagination is the servant of my creativity and my faith. I love to research the facts about Bible times and places—I dig right into those history books. Then, as I read the Bible, I don't have any trouble imagining what things were really like. I can almost smell the pungent passengers on Noah's ark or feel the rough wood of a tiny boat rocking on the Galilean waves. My Bible study comes alive as I put myself in the times, the places and the personalities of the men and women whose faith is my example.

Your imagination can be used for good or for evil (Psalm 104:34; Genesis 8:21). To empathize with the feelings and thoughts of others . . . or to enhance your prayer life are [two] of the uses of your imagination that please and glorify God.

ADDITIONAL SCRIPTURE READINGS:
Psalm 139:1-2; Isaiah 66:18; 2 Corinthians 10:5

Go to page 500 for your next devotional reading.

carved to adorn a palace.
¹³Our barns will be filled
with every kind of provision.
Our sheep will increase by
thousands,
by tens of thousands in our fields;
¹⁴ our oxen will draw heavy loads.ᵃ
There will be no breaching of walls,
no going into captivity,
no cry of distress in our streets.

¹⁵Blessed are the people of whom this
is true;
blessed are the people whose God
is the LORD.

Psalm 145ᵇ

A psalm of praise. Of David.

¹I will exalt you, my God the King;
I will praise your name for ever
and ever.
²Every day I will praise you
and extol your name for ever and
ever.

³Great is the LORD and most worthy of
praise;
his greatness no one can fathom.
⁴One generation will commend your
works to another;
they will tell of your mighty acts.
⁵They will speak of the glorious
splendor of your majesty,
and I will meditate on your
wonderful works.ᶜ
⁶They will tell of the power of your
awesome works,
and I will proclaim your great
deeds.
⁷They will celebrate your abundant
goodness
and joyfully sing of your
righteousness.

⁸The LORD is gracious and
compassionate,
slow to anger and rich in love.
⁹The LORD is good to all;
he has compassion on all he has
made.
¹⁰All you have made will praise you,
O LORD;

your saints will extol you.
¹¹They will tell of the glory of your
kingdom
and speak of your might,
¹²so that all men may know of your
mighty acts
and the glorious splendor of your
kingdom.
¹³Your kingdom is an everlasting
kingdom,
and your dominion endures
through all generations.

The LORD is faithful to all his
promises
and loving toward all he has
made.ᵈ
¹⁴The LORD upholds all those who fall
and lifts up all who are bowed
down.
¹⁵The eyes of all look to you,
and you give them their food at
the proper time.
¹⁶You open your hand
and satisfy the desires of every
living thing.

¹⁷The LORD is righteous in all his ways
and loving toward all he has
made.
¹⁸The LORD is near to all who call on
him,
to all who call on him in truth.
¹⁹He fulfills the desires of those who
fear him;
he hears their cry and saves them.
²⁰The LORD watches over all who love
him,
but all the wicked he will destroy.

²¹My mouth will speak in praise of the
LORD.
Let every creature praise his holy
name
for ever and ever.

Psalm 146

¹Praise the LORD.ᵉ

Praise the LORD, O my soul.
² I will praise the LORD all my life;
I will sing praise to my God as
long as I live.

ᵃ14 Or our chieftains will be firmly established   ᵇThis psalm is an acrostic poem, the verses of which
(including verse 13b) begin with the successive letters of the Hebrew alphabet.   ᶜ5 Dead Sea
Scrolls and Syriac (see also Septuagint); Masoretic Text On the glorious splendor of your majesty / and on
your wonderful works I will meditate   ᵈ13 One manuscript of the Masoretic Text, Dead Sea Scrolls and
Syriac (see also Septuagint); most manuscripts of the Masoretic Text do not have the last two lines of
verse 13.   ᵉ1 Hebrew Hallelu Yah; also in verse 10

³Do not put your trust in princes,
in mortal men, who cannot save.
⁴When their spirit departs, they return
to the ground;
on that very day their plans come
to nothing.

⁵Blessed is he whose help is the God
of Jacob,
whose hope is in the LORD his
God,
⁶the Maker of heaven and earth,
the sea, and everything in them—
the LORD, who remains faithful
forever.
⁷He upholds the cause of the
oppressed
and gives food to the hungry.
The LORD sets prisoners free,
⁸ the LORD gives sight to the blind,
the LORD lifts up those who are
bowed down,
the LORD loves the righteous.
⁹The LORD watches over the alien
and sustains the fatherless and the
widow,
but he frustrates the ways of the
wicked.

¹⁰The LORD reigns forever,
your God, O Zion, for all
generations.

Praise the LORD.

Psalm 147

¹Praise the LORD.ᵃ

How good it is to sing praises to our
God,
how pleasant and fitting to praise
him!

²The LORD builds up Jerusalem;
he gathers the exiles of Israel.
³He heals the brokenhearted
and binds up their wounds.

⁴He determines the number of the
stars
and calls them each by name.
⁵Great is our Lord and mighty in
power;
his understanding has no limit.
⁶The LORD sustains the humble
but casts the wicked to the
ground.

⁷Sing to the LORD with thanksgiving;
make music to our God on the
harp.

⁸He covers the sky with clouds;
he supplies the earth with rain
and makes grass grow on the
hills.
⁹He provides food for the cattle
and for the young ravens when
they call.

¹⁰His pleasure is not in the strength of
the horse,
nor his delight in the legs of a
man;
¹¹the LORD delights in those who fear
him,
who put their hope in his
unfailing love.

¹²Extol the LORD, O Jerusalem;
praise your God, O Zion,
¹³for he strengthens the bars of your
gates
and blesses your people within
you.
¹⁴He grants peace to your borders
and satisfies you with the finest of
wheat.

¹⁵He sends his command to the earth;
his word runs swiftly.
¹⁶He spreads the snow like wool
and scatters the frost like ashes.
¹⁷He hurls down his hail like pebbles.
Who can withstand his icy blast?
¹⁸He sends his word and melts them;
he stirs up his breezes, and the
waters flow.

¹⁹He has revealed his word to Jacob,
his laws and decrees to Israel.
²⁰He has done this for no other
nation;
they do not know his laws.

Praise the LORD.

Psalm 148

¹Praise the LORD.ᵇ

Praise the LORD from the heavens,
praise him in the heights above.
²Praise him, all his angels,
praise him, all his heavenly hosts.
³Praise him, sun and moon,
praise him, all you shining stars.

ᵃ1 Hebrew *Hallelu Yah*; also in verse 20   ᵇ1 Hebrew *Hallelu Yah*; also in verse 14

⁴Praise him, you highest heavens
    and you waters above the skies.
⁵Let them praise the name of the
    LORD,
    for he commanded and they were
      created.
⁶He set them in place for ever and
    ever;
    he gave a decree that will never
      pass away.

⁷Praise the LORD from the earth,
    you great sea creatures and all
      ocean depths,
⁸lightning and hail, snow and clouds,
    stormy winds that do his bidding,

⁹you mountains and all hills,
    fruit trees and all cedars,
¹⁰wild animals and all cattle,
    small creatures and flying
      birds,
¹¹kings of the earth and all nations,
    you princes and all rulers on
      earth,
¹²young men and maidens,
    old men and children.

¹³Let them praise the name of the
    LORD,
    for his name alone is exalted;
    his splendor is above the earth
      and the heavens.

TUESDAY

VERSE:
Psalm 148:13

AUTHOR:
Bernie Sheahan

PASSAGE:
Psalm 148:1–14

Holy Awe

If you've never read the book, then maybe you've seen Cecil B. DeMille's epic movie *The Ten Commandments*. Do you remember the scene when Moses went to the top of the mountain to meet with God? Moses met the Almighty in the form of a burning bush, and he was informed by the voice of God that where he was standing was holy ground. His response was that of reverence, awe and holy fear; he took off his shoes.

The Japanese know about reverence and respect; they take off their shoes when they enter a house. It's not something we Americans do out of any particular courtesy. If we do it at all, it's to be comfortable or because our feet hurt. I love what Browning says in her poem. All around us is God's creation, "Earth's crammed with heaven." Do we really respect it, revere it and hold it in awe? Or do we simply take it for granted?

We live in a time of great awareness of the earth's frailty. Some say that if we don't do something radical, we won't be able to pass on all its beauty to our descendants. Most of us do more than ever to make adjustments to help the earth—recycling, buying eco-friendly products and generally "thinking green."

Some take concern for the environment to the extreme by worshiping nature. As a Christian, I can't buy that. But to revere the earth and its beauty as the wondrous work of God, to honor its loveliness with awe—that's something I can take my shoes off for.

ADDITIONAL SCRIPTURE READINGS:
Exodus 20; Ecclesiastes 11:1–5; Isaiah 44:23

Go to page 505 for your next devotional reading.

[14]He has raised up for his people a
        horn,[a]
    the praise of all his saints,
    of Israel, the people close to his
        heart.

Praise the LORD.

Psalm 149

[1]Praise the LORD.[b]

Sing to the LORD a new song,
    his praise in the assembly of the
        saints.
[2]Let Israel rejoice in their Maker;
    let the people of Zion be glad in
        their King.
[3]Let them praise his name with
        dancing
    and make music to him with
        tambourine and harp.
[4]For the LORD takes delight in his
        people;
    he crowns the humble with
        salvation.
[5]Let the saints rejoice in this honor
    and sing for joy on their beds.

[6]May the praise of God be in their
        mouths
    and a double-edged sword in their
        hands,
[7]to inflict vengeance on the nations

and punishment on the peoples,
[8]to bind their kings with fetters,
    their nobles with shackles of iron,
[9]to carry out the sentence written
        against them.
    This is the glory of all his saints.

Praise the LORD.

Psalm 150

[1]Praise the LORD.[c]

Praise God in his sanctuary;
    praise him in his mighty heavens.
[2]Praise him for his acts of power;
    praise him for his surpassing
        greatness.
[3]Praise him with the sounding of the
        trumpet,
    praise him with the harp and lyre,
[4]praise him with tambourine and
        dancing,
    praise him with the strings and
        flute,
[5]praise him with the clash of
        cymbals,
    praise him with resounding
        cymbals.

[6]Let everything that has breath praise
        the LORD.

Praise the LORD.

---

[a]14 *Horn* here symbolizes strong one, that is, king.
[c]1 Hebrew *Hallelu Yah;* also in verse 6
[b]1 Hebrew *Hallelu Yah;* also in verse 9

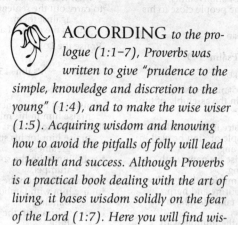

ACCORDING to the prologue (1:1–7), Proverbs was written to give "prudence to the simple, knowledge and discretion to the young" (1:4), and to make the wise wiser (1:5). Acquiring wisdom and knowing how to avoid the pitfalls of folly will lead to health and success. Although Proverbs is a practical book dealing with the art of living, it bases wisdom solidly on the fear of the Lord (1:7). Here you will find wisdom that works and insights that will not wear out.

PROVERBS

Prologue: Purpose and Theme

1 The proverbs of Solomon son of David, king of Israel:

²for attaining wisdom and discipline;
  for understanding words of insight;
³for acquiring a disciplined and
    prudent life,
  doing what is right and just and
    fair;
⁴for giving prudence to the simple,
  knowledge and discretion to the
    young—

⁵let the wise listen and add to their
    learning,
  and let the discerning get
    guidance—
⁶for understanding proverbs and
    parables,
  the sayings and riddles of the
    wise.

⁷The fear of the LORD is the beginning
    of knowledge,
  but fools*ᵃ* despise wisdom and
    discipline.

ᵃ 7 The Hebrew words rendered *fool* in Proverbs, and often elsewhere in the Old Testament, denote one who is morally deficient.

Exhortations to Embrace Wisdom

Warning Against Enticement

[8]Listen, my son, to your father's
    instruction
    and do not forsake your mother's
        teaching.
[9]They will be a garland to grace your
        head
    and a chain to adorn your neck.

[10]My son, if sinners entice you,
    do not give in to them.
[11]If they say, "Come along with us;
    let's lie in wait for someone's
        blood,
    let's waylay some harmless soul;
[12]let's swallow them alive, like the
        grave,[a]
    and whole, like those who go
        down to the pit;
[13]we will get all sorts of valuable
        things
    and fill our houses with plunder;
[14]throw in your lot with us,
    and we will share a common
        purse"—
[15]my son, do not go along with them,
    do not set foot on their paths;
[16]for their feet rush into sin,
    they are swift to shed blood.
[17]How useless to spread a net
    in full view of all the birds!
[18]These men lie in wait for their own
        blood;
    they waylay only themselves!
[19]Such is the end of all who go after
        ill-gotten gain;
    it takes away the lives of those
        who get it.

Warning Against Rejecting Wisdom

[20]Wisdom calls aloud in the street,
    she raises her voice in the public
        squares;
[21]at the head of the noisy streets[b] she
        cries out,
    in the gateways of the city she
        makes her speech:

[22]"How long will you simple ones[c]
        love your simple ways?
    How long will mockers delight in
        mockery
    and fools hate knowledge?
[23]If you had responded to my rebuke,

I would have poured out my heart
    to you
    and made my thoughts known to
        you.
[24]But since you rejected me when I
        called
    and no one gave heed when I
        stretched out my hand,
[25]since you ignored all my advice
    and would not accept my rebuke,
[26]I in turn will laugh at your disaster;
    I will mock when calamity
        overtakes you—
[27]when calamity overtakes you like a
        storm,
    when disaster sweeps over you
        like a whirlwind,
    when distress and trouble
        overwhelm you.

[28]"Then they will call to me but I will
        not answer;
    they will look for me but will not
        find me.
[29]Since they hated knowledge
    and did not choose to fear the
        LORD,
[30]since they would not accept my
        advice
    and spurned my rebuke,
[31]they will eat the fruit of their ways
    and be filled with the fruit of their
        schemes.
[32]For the waywardness of the simple
    will kill them,
    and the complacency of fools will
        destroy them;
[33]but whoever listens to me will live in
        safety
    and be at ease, without fear of
        harm."

Moral Benefits of Wisdom

2 My son, if you accept my words
    and store up my commands
        within you,
[2]turning your ear to wisdom
    and applying your heart to
        understanding,
[3]and if you call out for insight
    and cry aloud for understanding,
[4]and if you look for it as for silver
    and search for it as for hidden
        treasure,
[5]then you will understand the fear of
    the LORD

---

[a]12 Hebrew *Sheol*   [b]21 Hebrew; Septuagint / *on the tops of the walls*   [c]22 The Hebrew word
rendered *simple* in Proverbs generally denotes one without moral direction and inclined to evil.

and find the knowledge of God.
⁶For the LORD gives wisdom,
    and from his mouth come
        knowledge and understanding.
⁷He holds victory in store for the
        upright,
    he is a shield to those whose walk
        is blameless,
⁸for he guards the course of the just
    and protects the way of his faithful
        ones.

⁹Then you will understand what is
        right and just
    and fair—every good path.
¹⁰For wisdom will enter your heart,
    and knowledge will be pleasant to
        your soul.
¹¹Discretion will protect you,
    and understanding will guard you.

¹²Wisdom will save you from the ways
        of wicked men,
    from men whose words are
        perverse,
¹³who leave the straight paths
    to walk in dark ways,
¹⁴who delight in doing wrong
    and rejoice in the perverseness of
        evil,
¹⁵whose paths are crooked
    and who are devious in their ways.

¹⁶It will save you also from the
        adulteress,
    from the wayward wife with her
        seductive words,
¹⁷who has left the partner of her youth
    and ignored the covenant she
        made before God.[a]
¹⁸For her house leads down to death
    and her paths to the spirits of the
        dead.
¹⁹None who go to her return
    or attain the paths of life.

²⁰Thus you will walk in the ways of
        good men
    and keep to the paths of the
        righteous.
²¹For the upright will live in the land,
    and the blameless will remain in
        it;
²²but the wicked will be cut off from
        the land,
    and the unfaithful will be torn
        from it.

Further Benefits of Wisdom

3 My son, do not forget my
        teaching,
    but keep my commands in your
        heart,
²for they will prolong your life many
        years
    and bring you prosperity.

³Let love and faithfulness never leave
        you;
    bind them around your neck,
    write them on the tablet of your
        heart.
⁴Then you will win favor and a good
        name
    in the sight of God and man.

⁵Trust in the LORD with all your heart
    and lean not on your own
        understanding;
⁶in all your ways acknowledge him,
    and he will make your paths
        straight.[b]

⁷Do not be wise in your own eyes;
    fear the LORD and shun evil.
⁸This will bring health to your body
    and nourishment to your bones.

⁹Honor the LORD with your wealth,
    with the firstfruits of all your
        crops;
¹⁰then your barns will be filled to
        overflowing,
    and your vats will brim over with
        new wine.

¹¹My son, do not despise the LORD's
        discipline
    and do not resent his rebuke,
¹²because the LORD disciplines those
        he loves,
    as a father[c] the son he delights
        in.

¹³Blessed is the man who finds
        wisdom,
    the man who gains understanding,
¹⁴for she is more profitable than silver
    and yields better returns than gold.
¹⁵She is more precious than rubies;
    nothing you desire can compare
        with her.
¹⁶Long life is in her right hand;
    in her left hand are riches and
        honor.
¹⁷Her ways are pleasant ways,
    and all her paths are peace.

---

[a] 17 Or *covenant of her God*   [b] 6 Or *will direct your paths*   [c] 12 Hebrew; Septuagint / *and he punishes*

¹⁸She is a tree of life to those who
embrace her;
those who lay hold of her will be
blessed.

¹⁹By wisdom the LORD laid the earth's
foundations,
by understanding he set the
heavens in place;
²⁰by his knowledge the deeps were
divided,
and the clouds let drop the dew.

²¹My son, preserve sound judgment
and discernment,
do not let them out of your sight;
²²they will be life for you,
an ornament to grace your neck.
²³Then you will go on your way in
safety,
and your foot will not stumble;
²⁴when you lie down, you will not be
afraid;
when you lie down, your sleep will
be sweet.

WEDNESDAY

VERSE:	AUTHOR:	PASSAGE:
Proverbs 3:27	Bernie Sheahan	Proverbs 3:27–28

Give Yourself

"I just want you to know that your child was delightful in the nursery this morning." "You have a wonderful way with people, and I admire that." "Your house is so warm and welcoming." "You told that guy the truth on that deal, and I respect you for it."

Wouldn't it be great to hear things like that all the time? How many times do you think about saying something encouraging or uplifting to someone else, but you just don't feel comfortable? It's a risk; what if they think you're just trying to butter them up? You could come off sounding insincere. So you keep it to yourself, instead, and the encouraging word never gets said. Oh, maybe you think about it later and have every good intention of writing a note, but you never get it written. Time goes by and you've lost that moment forever.

It's not just words, of course. There are times when you might see a situation that could use something—time, money, skills—that you possess and could share. It might be as simple as offering to drive an elderly neighbor to the store or washing a friend's car when they're too busy to take care of it. Or it might be a case where you have extra money and know of someone who's struggling financially. What a joy to send an anonymous gift!

Think of the times that someone has given you something right when you needed it—an encouraging note or phone call, a helping hand with a project or a few bucks when you were strapped for cash. It meant a lot to you, didn't it? Don't miss the opportunity to give to someone else.

ADDITIONAL SCRIPTURE READINGS:
Isaiah 58:6–11; 2 Corinthians 9:6–15

Go to page 508 for your next devotional reading.

²⁵Have no fear of sudden disaster
   or of the ruin that overtakes the
      wicked,
²⁶for the LORD will be your confidence
   and will keep your foot from being
      snared.

²⁷Do not withhold good from those
      who deserve it,
   when it is in your power to act.
²⁸Do not say to your neighbor,
   "Come back later; I'll give it
      tomorrow"—
   when you now have it with you.

²⁹Do not plot harm against your
      neighbor,
   who lives trustfully near you.
³⁰Do not accuse a man for no
      reason—
   when he has done you no harm.

³¹Do not envy a violent man
   or choose any of his ways,
³²for the LORD detests a perverse man
   but takes the upright into his
      confidence.

³³The LORD's curse is on the house of
      the wicked,
   but he blesses the home of the
      righteous.
³⁴He mocks proud mockers
   but gives grace to the humble.
³⁵The wise inherit honor,
   but fools he holds up to shame.

Wisdom Is Supreme

4 Listen, my sons, to a father's
      instruction;
   pay attention and gain
      understanding.
²I give you sound learning,
   so do not forsake my teaching.
³When I was a boy in my father's
      house,
   still tender, and an only child of
      my mother,
⁴he taught me and said,
   "Lay hold of my words with all
      your heart;
   keep my commands and you will
      live.
⁵Get wisdom, get understanding;
   do not forget my words or swerve
      from them.
⁶Do not forsake wisdom, and she will
      protect you;

love her, and she will watch over
      you.
⁷Wisdom is supreme; therefore get
      wisdom.
   Though it cost all you have,ᵃ get
      understanding.
⁸Esteem her, and she will exalt you;
   embrace her, and she will honor
      you.
⁹She will set a garland of grace on
      your head
   and present you with a crown of
      splendor."

¹⁰Listen, my son, accept what I say,
   and the years of your life will be
      many.
¹¹I guide you in the way of wisdom
   and lead you along straight paths.
¹²When you walk, your steps will not
      be hampered;
   when you run, you will not
      stumble.
¹³Hold on to instruction, do not let it
      go;
   guard it well, for it is your life.
¹⁴Do not set foot on the path of the
      wicked
   or walk in the way of evil men.
¹⁵Avoid it, do not travel on it;
   turn from it and go on your way.
¹⁶For they cannot sleep till they do
      evil;
   they are robbed of slumber till
      they make someone fall.
¹⁷They eat the bread of wickedness
   and drink the wine of violence.

¹⁸The path of the righteous is like the
      first gleam of dawn,
   shining ever brighter till the full
      light of day.
¹⁹But the way of the wicked is like
      deep darkness;
   they do not know what makes
      them stumble.

²⁰My son, pay attention to what I say;
   listen closely to my words.
²¹Do not let them out of your sight,
   keep them within your heart;
²²for they are life to those who find
      them
   and health to a man's whole body.
²³Above all else, guard your heart,
   for it is the wellspring of life.
²⁴Put away perversity from your
      mouth;

ᵃ7 Or *Whatever else you get*

keep corrupt talk far from your
lips.
25Let your eyes look straight ahead,
fix your gaze directly before you.
26Make level*a* paths for your feet
and take only ways that are firm.
27Do not swerve to the right or the left;
keep your foot from evil.

Warning Against Adultery

5 My son, pay attention to my
wisdom,
listen well to my words of insight,
2that you may maintain discretion
and your lips may preserve
knowledge.
3For the lips of an adulteress drip
honey,
and her speech is smoother than
oil;
4but in the end she is bitter as gall,
sharp as a double-edged sword.
5Her feet go down to death;
her steps lead straight to the
grave.*b*
6She gives no thought to the way of
life;
her paths are crooked, but she
knows it not.

7Now then, my sons, listen to me;
do not turn aside from what I say.
8Keep to a path far from her,
do not go near the door of her
house,
9lest you give your best strength to
others
and your years to one who is
cruel,
10lest strangers feast on your wealth
and your toil enrich another man's
house.
11At the end of your life you will
groan,
when your flesh and body are
spent.
12You will say, "How I hated
discipline!
How my heart spurned correction!
13I would not obey my teachers
or listen to my instructors.
14I have come to the brink of utter ruin
in the midst of the whole
assembly."

15Drink water from your own cistern,
running water from your own well.

16Should your springs overflow in the
streets,
your streams of water in the
public squares?
17Let them be yours alone,
never to be shared with strangers.
18May your fountain be blessed,
and may you rejoice in the wife of
your youth.
19A loving doe, a graceful deer—
may her breasts satisfy you
always,
may you ever be captivated by her
love.
20Why be captivated, my son, by an
adulteress?
Why embrace the bosom of
another man's wife?
21For a man's ways are in full view of
the LORD,
and he examines all his paths.
22The evil deeds of a wicked man
ensnare him;
the cords of his sin hold him fast.
23He will die for lack of discipline,
led astray by his own great folly.

Warnings Against Folly

6 My son, if you have put up
security for your neighbor,
if you have struck hands in pledge
for another,
2if you have been trapped by what
you said,
ensnared by the words of your
mouth,
3then do this, my son, to free
yourself,
since you have fallen into your
neighbor's hands:
Go and humble yourself;
press your plea with your
neighbor!
4Allow no sleep to your eyes,
no slumber to your eyelids.
5Free yourself, like a gazelle from the
hand of the hunter,
like a bird from the snare of the
fowler.

6Go to the ant, you sluggard;
consider its ways and be wise!
7It has no commander,
no overseer or ruler,
8yet it stores its provisions in
summer
and gathers its food at harvest.

a26 Or *Consider the*   *b5* Hebrew *Sheol*

⁹How long will you lie there, you
   sluggard?
   When will you get up from your
      sleep?
¹⁰A little sleep, a little slumber,
   a little folding of the hands to
      rest—
¹¹and poverty will come on you like a
      bandit
   and scarcity like an armed man.ᵃ

¹²A scoundrel and villain,
   who goes about with a corrupt
      mouth,
¹³ who winks with his eye,
   signals with his feet
   and motions with his fingers,

ᵃ11 Or like a vagrant / and scarcity like a beggar

¹⁴ who plots evil with deceit in his
      heart—
   he always stirs up dissension.
¹⁵Therefore disaster will overtake him
      in an instant;
   he will suddenly be destroyed—
      without remedy.

¹⁶There are six things the LORD hates,
   seven that are detestable to him:
¹⁷   haughty eyes,
      a lying tongue,
      hands that shed innocent blood,
¹⁸   a heart that devises wicked
         schemes,
      feet that are quick to rush into
         evil,

═══ THURSDAY ═══

VERSE: AUTHOR: PASSAGE:
Proverbs 5:18   Marjorie Holmes   Proverbs 5:15-23

The Good Days of Marriage

Dear Lord, thank you for the good days of marriage. The days
when we wake up pleased with each other, our jobs, our children, our home and ourselves.

Thank you for our communication—the times when we can
really talk to each other; and the times when we understand
each other without so much as a gesture or a word.

Thank you for our companionship—the times when we can
work together at projects we both enjoy. Or work in our separate
fields and yet have that sense of sharing that can only come when
two persons' lives have merged in so many other ways for so long.
Thank you that we don't feel cut off from each other, no matter
how divergent the things we do.

Thank you for our times of privacy. Our times of freedom. Our
relaxed sense of personal trust. Thank you that we don't have to
clutch and stifle each other, that we have learned to respect ourselves enough to respect the other's individuality.

Thank you, Lord, that despite the many storms of marriage we
have reached these particular shores. Help us to remember them.
Help us to hold fast to them, Lord.

ADDITIONAL SCRIPTURE READINGS:
Ecclesiastes 9:9; Ephesians 5:25

Go to page 511 for your next devotional reading.

19   a false witness who pours out
             lies
       and a man who stirs up
             dissension among brothers.

Warning Against Adultery

20My son, keep your father's
       commands
       and do not forsake your mother's
             teaching.
21Bind them upon your heart forever;
       fasten them around your neck.
22When you walk, they will guide you;
       when you sleep, they will watch
             over you;
       when you awake, they will speak
             to you.
23For these commands are a lamp,
       this teaching is a light,
   and the corrections of discipline
       are the way to life,
24keeping you from the immoral
             woman,
       from the smooth tongue of the
             wayward wife.
25Do not lust in your heart after her
             beauty
       or let her captivate you with her
             eyes,
26for the prostitute reduces you to a
             loaf of bread,
       and the adulteress preys upon
             your very life.
27Can a man scoop fire into his lap
       without his clothes being burned?
28Can a man walk on hot coals
       without his feet being scorched?
29So is he who sleeps with another
             man's wife;
       no one who touches her will go
             unpunished.

30Men do not despise a thief if he
             steals
       to satisfy his hunger when he is
             starving.
31Yet if he is caught, he must pay
             sevenfold,
       though it costs him all the wealth
             of his house.
32But a man who commits adultery
             lacks judgment;
       whoever does so destroys himself.
33Blows and disgrace are his lot,
       and his shame will never be wiped
             away;

34for jealousy arouses a husband's
             fury,
       and he will show no mercy when
             he takes revenge.
35He will not accept any
             compensation;
       he will refuse the bribe, however
             great it is.

Warning Against the Adulteress

7 My son, keep my words
     and store up my commands
             within you.
2Keep my commands and you will
             live;
       guard my teachings as the apple of
             your eye.
3Bind them on your fingers;
       write them on the tablet of your
             heart.
4Say to wisdom, "You are my sister,"
       and call understanding your
             kinsman;
5they will keep you from the
             adulteress,
       from the wayward wife with her
             seductive words.

6At the window of my house
       I looked out through the lattice.
7I saw among the simple,
       I noticed among the young men,
       a youth who lacked judgment.
8He was going down the street near
             her corner,
       walking along in the direction of
             her house
9at twilight, as the day was fading,
       as the dark of night set in.

10Then out came a woman to meet
             him,
       dressed like a prostitute and with
             crafty intent.
11(She is loud and defiant,
       her feet never stay at home;
12now in the street, now in the
             squares,
       at every corner she lurks.)
13She took hold of him and kissed
             him
       and with a brazen face she said:

14"I have fellowship offerings*a* at
             home;
       today I fulfilled my vows.
15So I came out to meet you;

a14 Traditionally *peace offerings*

I looked for you and have found
you!
¹⁶I have covered my bed
with colored linens from Egypt.
¹⁷I have perfumed my bed
with myrrh, aloes and cinnamon.
¹⁸Come, let's drink deep of love till
morning;
let's enjoy ourselves with love!
¹⁹My husband is not at home;
he has gone on a long journey.
²⁰He took his purse filled with money
and will not be home till full
moon."

²¹With persuasive words she led him
astray;
she seduced him with her smooth
talk.
²²All at once he followed her
like an ox going to the slaughter,
like a deer[a] stepping into a noose[b]
²³ till an arrow pierces his liver,
like a bird darting into a snare,
little knowing it will cost him his
life.

²⁴Now then, my sons, listen to me;
pay attention to what I say.
²⁵Do not let your heart turn to her
ways
or stray into her paths.
²⁶Many are the victims she has
brought down;
her slain are a mighty throng.
²⁷Her house is a highway to the
grave,[c]
leading down to the chambers of
death.

Wisdom's Call

8 Does not wisdom call out?
Does not understanding raise her
voice?
²On the heights along the way,
where the paths meet, she takes
her stand;
³beside the gates leading into the city,
at the entrances, she cries aloud:
⁴"To you, O men, I call out;
I raise my voice to all mankind.
⁵You who are simple, gain prudence;
you who are foolish, gain
understanding.

⁶Listen, for I have worthy things to
say;
I open my lips to speak what is
right.
⁷My mouth speaks what is true,
for my lips detest wickedness.
⁸All the words of my mouth are just;
none of them is crooked or
perverse.
⁹To the discerning all of them are
right;
they are faultless to those who
have knowledge.
¹⁰Choose my instruction instead of
silver,
knowledge rather than choice gold,
¹¹for wisdom is more precious than
rubies,
and nothing you desire can
compare with her.

¹²"I, wisdom, dwell together with
prudence;
I possess knowledge and
discretion.
¹³To fear the LORD is to hate evil;
I hate pride and arrogance,
evil behavior and perverse speech.
¹⁴Counsel and sound judgment are
mine;
I have understanding and power.
¹⁵By me kings reign
and rulers make laws that are just;
¹⁶by me princes govern,
and all nobles who rule on
earth.[d]
¹⁷I love those who love me,
and those who seek me find me.
¹⁸With me are riches and honor,
enduring wealth and prosperity.
¹⁹My fruit is better than fine gold;
what I yield surpasses choice
silver.
²⁰I walk in the way of righteousness,
along the paths of justice,
²¹bestowing wealth on those who love
me
and making their treasuries full.

²²"The LORD brought me forth as the
first of his works,[e, f]
before his deeds of old;
²³I was appointed[g] from eternity,

---

[a]22 Syriac (see also Septuagint); Hebrew *fool*   [b]22 The meaning of the Hebrew for this line is
uncertain.   [c]27 Hebrew *Sheol*   [d]16 Many Hebrew manuscripts and Septuagint; most Hebrew
manuscripts *and nobles—all righteous rulers*   [e]22 Or *way*; or *dominion*   [f]22 Or *The LORD possessed
me at the beginning of his work*; or *The LORD brought me forth at the beginning of his work*   [g]23 Or
fashioned

from the beginning, before the world began.
²⁴When there were no oceans, I was given birth,
when there were no springs abounding with water;

²⁵before the mountains were settled in place,
before the hills, I was given birth,
²⁶before he made the earth or its fields
or any of the dust of the world.

FRIDAY

VERSE:
Proverbs 8:30

AUTHOR:
Carole Mayhall

PASSAGE:
Proverbs 8:22–31

Beyond Boredom

Boredom can rob a person of *joy*. Apathy may not sink my boat but it can becalm me and cause despair as the wind is taken out of the sails of my life. I thought about two verses in Proverbs. Wisdom . . . is speaking, "I was filled with delight day after day, rejoicing always in his presence, rejoicing in his whole world and delighting in mankind" (vv. 30–31).

Because Christ lives in us, these verses are ours! We can be filled with delight day after day. Let's emphasize that: *We can be filled with* delight *day after day*. And those things that can and will delight us have nothing to do with position or ministry or fascinating things to do. We can have delight in the dull, monotonous months, in the routine, mundane days, in the lean, hungry years.

Three things will bring rejoicing to our souls: (1) God's very presence, (2) his world around us and (3) people! God's promise to be present with us always can bring us comfort and delight. So can the complexity and variety of his creation: a flower, the misty rain, the billowing clouds. Sometimes we may have to look hard into some of the people we encounter, but as we ask, God will help us delight in them too. These are three pools of delight we can bathe in when we're young and strong, old and feeble or incapacitated or ill.

Anytime. Anyplace. Any condition.

I'll probably have to remind myself often when dullness of soul creeps over me, but the truth is that God provides . . . *no excuse for boredom*!

Father, when I feel disgruntled—dissatisfied with the "ordinary" life you've given me—please remind me that my circumstances aren't necessarily the problem. When I feel like a plug has been pulled from the bottom of my soul and all the meaning has disappeared down a dark drain, remind me to look for your delights—your purpose in my everyday life—until I find fresh joy in your presence, your world and your people.

ADDITIONAL SCRIPTURE READINGS:
Habakkuk 3:18; John 15:11

Go to page 514 for your next devotional reading.

27I was there when he set the heavens
in place,
when he marked out the horizon
on the face of the deep,
28when he established the clouds
above
and fixed securely the fountains of
the deep,
29when he gave the sea its boundary
so the waters would not overstep
his command,
and when he marked out the
foundations of the earth.
30 Then I was the craftsman at his
side.
I was filled with delight day after
day,
rejoicing always in his presence,
31rejoicing in his whole world
and delighting in mankind.
32"Now then, my sons, listen to me;
blessed are those who keep my
ways.
33Listen to my instruction and be wise;
do not ignore it.
34Blessed is the man who listens to
me,
watching daily at my doors,
waiting at my doorway.
35For whoever finds me finds life
and receives favor from the LORD.
36But whoever fails to find me harms
himself;
all who hate me love death."

Invitations of Wisdom and of Folly

9 Wisdom has built her house;
she has hewn out its seven
pillars.
2She has prepared her meat and
mixed her wine;
she has also set her table.
3She has sent out her maids, and she
calls
from the highest point of the city.
4"Let all who are simple come in
here!"
she says to those who lack
judgment.
5"Come, eat my food
and drink the wine I have mixed.
6Leave your simple ways and you will
live;
walk in the way of understanding.
7"Whoever corrects a mocker invites
insult;

whoever rebukes a wicked man
incurs abuse.
8Do not rebuke a mocker or he will
hate you;
rebuke a wise man and he will
love you.
9Instruct a wise man and he will be
wiser still;
teach a righteous man and he will
add to his learning.
10"The fear of the LORD is the
beginning of wisdom,
and knowledge of the Holy One is
understanding.
11For through me your days will be
many,
and years will be added to your
life.
12If you are wise, your wisdom will
reward you;
if you are a mocker, you alone will
suffer."
13The woman Folly is loud;
she is undisciplined and without
knowledge.
14She sits at the door of her house,
on a seat at the highest point of
the city,
15calling out to those who pass by,
who go straight on their way.
16"Let all who are simple come in
here!"
she says to those who lack
judgment.
17"Stolen water is sweet;
food eaten in secret is delicious!"
18But little do they know that the dead
are there,
that her guests are in the depths
of the grave.*a*

Proverbs of Solomon

10 The proverbs of Solomon:

A wise son brings joy to his father,
but a foolish son grief to his
mother.
2Ill-gotten treasures are of no value,
but righteousness delivers from
death.
3The LORD does not let the righteous
go hungry
but he thwarts the craving of the
wicked.

a18 Hebrew Sheol

[4]Lazy hands make a man poor,
  but diligent hands bring wealth.

[5]He who gathers crops in summer is
    a wise son,
  but he who sleeps during harvest
    is a disgraceful son.

[6]Blessings crown the head of the
    righteous,
  but violence overwhelms the
    mouth of the wicked.[a]

[7]The memory of the righteous will be
    a blessing,
  but the name of the wicked will
    rot.

[8]The wise in heart accept commands,
  but a chattering fool comes to
    ruin.

[9]The man of integrity walks securely,
  but he who takes crooked paths
    will be found out.

[10]He who winks maliciously causes
    grief,
  and a chattering fool comes to
    ruin.

[11]The mouth of the righteous is a
    fountain of life,
  but violence overwhelms the
    mouth of the wicked.

[12]Hatred stirs up dissension,
  but love covers over all wrongs.

[13]Wisdom is found on the lips of the
    discerning,
  but a rod is for the back of him
    who lacks judgment.

[14]Wise men store up knowledge,
  but the mouth of a fool invites
    ruin.

[15]The wealth of the rich is their
    fortified city,
  but poverty is the ruin of the poor.

[16]The wages of the righteous bring
    them life,
  but the income of the wicked
    brings them punishment.

[17]He who heeds discipline shows the
    way to life,
  but whoever ignores correction
    leads others astray.

[18]He who conceals his hatred has
    lying lips,

and whoever spreads slander is a
    fool.

[19]When words are many, sin is not
    absent,
  but he who holds his tongue is
    wise.

[20]The tongue of the righteous is choice
    silver,
  but the heart of the wicked is of
    little value.

[21]The lips of the righteous nourish
    many,
  but fools die for lack of judgment.

[22]The blessing of the LORD brings
    wealth,
  and he adds no trouble to it.

[23]A fool finds pleasure in evil conduct,
  but a man of understanding
    delights in wisdom.

[24]What the wicked dreads will overtake
    him;
  what the righteous desire will be
    granted.

[25]When the storm has swept by, the
    wicked are gone,
  but the righteous stand firm
    forever.

[26]As vinegar to the teeth and smoke to
    the eyes,
  so is a sluggard to those who
    send him.

[27]The fear of the LORD adds length to
    life,
  but the years of the wicked are cut
    short.

[28]The prospect of the righteous is joy,
  but the hopes of the wicked come
    to nothing.

[29]The way of the LORD is a refuge for
    the righteous,
  but it is the ruin of those who do
    evil.

[30]The righteous will never be uprooted,
  but the wicked will not remain in
    the land.

[31]The mouth of the righteous brings
    forth wisdom,
  but a perverse tongue will be cut
    out.

---

[a]6 Or *but the mouth of the wicked conceals violence*; also in verse 11

WEEKENDING

REFLECT

Home is where I hope to stay . . . I hope to be here when any of the children or grandchildren need me. From my vantage point, I can look back on circumstances involving our children, situations I once felt were hopeless, only to see in disbelief and amazement as God brought order out of chaos, light out of darkness.

I will follow their struggles with peace in my heart. Battles may be lost, but God will win out in the end. We gave them to him, each one uniquely loved, each as dear as the other: our most treasured possessions . . . As each little family builds its nest, I shall be watching with interest and love, concern at times, but concern undergirded with confidence, knowing God is in control.

Ruth Bell Graham

RESTORE

Saturday: Psalm 128
Sunday: Proverbs 17:6

*Go to page 516 for your
next devotional reading.*

³²The lips of the righteous know what
is fitting,
but the mouth of the wicked only
what is perverse.

11 The LORD abhors dishonest
scales,
but accurate weights are his
delight.

²When pride comes, then comes
disgrace,
but with humility comes wisdom.

³The integrity of the upright guides
them,
but the unfaithful are destroyed by
their duplicity.

⁴Wealth is worthless in the day of
wrath,
but righteousness delivers from
death.

⁵The righteousness of the blameless
makes a straight way for
them,
but the wicked are brought down
by their own wickedness.

⁶The righteousness of the upright
delivers them,
but the unfaithful are trapped by
evil desires.

⁷When a wicked man dies, his hope
perishes;
all he expected from his power
comes to nothing.

⁸The righteous man is rescued from
trouble,
and it comes on the wicked
instead.

⁹With his mouth the godless destroys
his neighbor,
but through knowledge the
righteous escape.

¹⁰When the righteous prosper, the city
rejoices;
when the wicked perish, there are
shouts of joy.

¹¹Through the blessing of the upright a
city is exalted,
but by the mouth of the wicked it
is destroyed.

¹²A man who lacks judgment derides
his neighbor,
but a man of understanding holds
his tongue.

¹³A gossip betrays a confidence,
but a trustworthy man keeps a
secret.

¹⁴For lack of guidance a nation falls,
but many advisers make victory
sure.

¹⁵He who puts up security for another
will surely suffer,
but whoever refuses to strike
hands in pledge is safe.

¹⁶A kindhearted woman gains respect,
but ruthless men gain only wealth.

¹⁷A kind man benefits himself,
but a cruel man brings trouble on
himself.

¹⁸The wicked man earns deceptive
wages,
but he who sows righteousness
reaps a sure reward.

¹⁹The truly righteous man attains life,
but he who pursues evil goes to
his death.

²⁰The LORD detests men of perverse
heart
but he delights in those whose
ways are blameless.

²¹Be sure of this: The wicked will not
go unpunished,
but those who are righteous will
go free.

²²Like a gold ring in a pig's snout
is a beautiful woman who shows
no discretion.

²³The desire of the righteous ends only
in good,
but the hope of the wicked only in
wrath.

²⁴One man gives freely, yet gains even
more;
another withholds unduly, but
comes to poverty.

²⁵A generous man will prosper;
he who refreshes others will
himself be refreshed.

²⁶People curse the man who hoards
grain,
but blessing crowns him who is
willing to sell.

²⁷He who seeks good finds goodwill,
but evil comes to him who
searches for it.

²⁸Whoever trusts in his riches will fall,
    but the righteous will thrive like a
    green leaf.

²⁹He who brings trouble on his family
    will inherit only wind,
    and the fool will be servant to the
    wise.

³⁰The fruit of the righteous is a tree of
    life,
    and he who wins souls is wise.

³¹If the righteous receive their due on
    earth,
    how much more the ungodly and
    the sinner!

12 Whoever loves discipline loves
    knowledge,
    but he who hates correction is
    stupid.

²A good man obtains favor from the
    LORD,
    but the LORD condemns a crafty
    man.

³A man cannot be established
    through wickedness,
    but the righteous cannot be
    uprooted.

⁴A wife of noble character is her
    husband's crown,
    but a disgraceful wife is like decay
    in his bones.

⁵The plans of the righteous are just,
    but the advice of the wicked is
    deceitful.

⁶The words of the wicked lie in wait
    for blood,

MONDAY

VERSE:	AUTHOR:	PASSAGE:
Proverbs 11:25	Barbara Johnson	Proverbs 11:24–28

Encouraging Thoughts

I often get "encouraging thoughts" from my good friend, Mary Lou, and one of her timeliest contributions came on a day when trying to help so many people who were down in the pit almost had me down there, too. I opened the envelope and here was a cartoon of a bewildered-looking woman tied hand and foot, lying on the railroad tracks. The cutline said: "I don't recall asking for any of this!" As I chuckled, I thought: *That's right! I didn't ASK for any of this, but it's what I've GOT, so I'll just take my own advice and stick a geranium in my hat and be happy!*

That little envelope from Mary Lou didn't contain anything expensive, profound or "deep," but nonetheless, it picked me up and refreshed me for the rest of the day. I think that's the secret to being a real friend—to always be looking for ways to encourage and refresh others.

As you refresh others, you relieve your own pain. You may be going through a painful time right now or trying to get over a tremendous loss. If so, try "refreshing" or "watering" another person's life; and as you encourage that person, you will find that your own pain is lessened.

ADDITIONAL SCRIPTURE READINGS:
Proverbs 16:24; Proverbs 25:11; Isaiah 50:4

Go to page 518 for your next devotional reading.

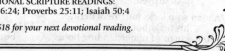

but the speech of the upright
rescues them.

⁷Wicked men are overthrown and are
no more,
but the house of the righteous
stands firm.

⁸A man is praised according to his
wisdom,
but men with warped minds are
despised.

⁹Better to be a nobody and yet have a
servant
than pretend to be somebody and
have no food.

¹⁰A righteous man cares for the needs
of his animal,
but the kindest acts of the wicked
are cruel.

¹¹He who works his land will have
abundant food,
but he who chases fantasies lacks
judgment.

¹²The wicked desire the plunder of evil
men,
but the root of the righteous
flourishes.

¹³An evil man is trapped by his sinful
talk,
but a righteous man escapes
trouble.

¹⁴From the fruit of his lips a man is
filled with good things
as surely as the work of his hands
rewards him.

¹⁵The way of a fool seems right to
him,
but a wise man listens to advice.

¹⁶A fool shows his annoyance at once,
but a prudent man overlooks an
insult.

¹⁷A truthful witness gives honest
testimony,
but a false witness tells lies.

¹⁸Reckless words pierce like a sword,
but the tongue of the wise brings
healing.

¹⁹Truthful lips endure forever,
but a lying tongue lasts only a
moment.

²⁰There is deceit in the hearts of those
who plot evil,
but joy for those who promote
peace.

²¹No harm befalls the righteous,
but the wicked have their fill of
trouble.

²²The LORD detests lying lips,
but he delights in men who are
truthful.

²³A prudent man keeps his knowledge
to himself,
but the heart of fools blurts out
folly.

²⁴Diligent hands will rule,
but laziness ends in slave labor.

²⁵An anxious heart weighs a man
down,
but a kind word cheers him up.

²⁶A righteous man is cautious in
friendship,ᵃ
but the way of the wicked leads
them astray.

²⁷The lazy man does not roastᵇ his
game,
but the diligent man prizes his
possessions.

²⁸In the way of righteousness there is
life;
along that path is immortality.

13 A wise son heeds his father's
instruction,
but a mocker does not listen to
rebuke.

²From the fruit of his lips a man
enjoys good things,
but the unfaithful have a craving
for violence.

³He who guards his lips guards his
life,
but he who speaks rashly will
come to ruin.

⁴The sluggard craves and gets
nothing,
but the desires of the diligent are
fully satisfied.

⁵The righteous hate what is false,
but the wicked bring shame and
disgrace.

ᵃ26 Or *man is a guide to his neighbor*   ᵇ27 The meaning of the Hebrew for this word is uncertain.

6Righteousness guards the man of
 integrity,
  but wickedness overthrows the
   sinner.

7One man pretends to be rich, yet has
 nothing;
  another pretends to be poor, yet
   has great wealth.

8A man's riches may ransom his life,
  but a poor man hears no threat.

9The light of the righteous shines
 brightly,
  but the lamp of the wicked is
   snuffed out.

10Pride only breeds quarrels,
  but wisdom is found in those who
   take advice.

11Dishonest money dwindles away,
  but he who gathers money little by
   little makes it grow.

TUESDAY

VERSE:	AUTHOR:	PASSAGE:
Proverbs 12:18	Nancy Corbett Cole	Proverbs 12:18–23

Men: They're Human, Too

Much is said today about how men treat women, but we rarely hear about how women treat men. We need to admit that as women we are not always in the right in relationship to men. There is a plethora of advice in women's magazines about how to appeal to a man sexually, and how to live with his "male ego." Let's remember that beyond a man's ego and sexuality lies a real human being, a regular "guy." Men know feelings of hurt, embarrassment, failure and tenderness, just as women do.

I overheard a woman recently talking about her husband in a deprecating way while he stood there mute, not knowing what to say. I cringed inside, wishing she would stop telling the personal details and embarrassing moments of his life. This was a human being she was talking about! He was obviously respected by others, but his wife took center stage by getting some laughs at his expense.

A woman's tendency to treat a man as if he has no feelings seems to begin in adolescence, when girls run roughshod over boys' feelings, turning them down for dates and telling everyone that they did, or spitefully making fun of the boy who doesn't return some flirting gesture. We know this is a mark of immaturity, but some women simply don't mature beyond that point.

It is easy to fall into a habit of deprecative humor. If you are constantly using someone in your family or group of friends to laugh about, think it over. "Oh, it doesn't bother him," is not really a valid statement. If he is alive and breathing, he is affected by the words of others as that is part of being human.

ADDITIONAL SCRIPTURE READINGS:
Ecclesiastes 10:12; James 1:26; James 3:2

Go to page 521 for your next devotional reading.

[12]Hope deferred makes the heart sick,
but a longing fulfilled is a tree of
life.

[13]He who scorns instruction will pay
for it,
but he who respects a command is
rewarded.

[14]The teaching of the wise is a
fountain of life,
turning a man from the snares of
death.

[15]Good understanding wins favor,
but the way of the unfaithful is
hard.[a]

[16]Every prudent man acts out of
knowledge,
but a fool exposes his folly.

[17]A wicked messenger falls into
trouble,
but a trustworthy envoy brings
healing.

[18]He who ignores discipline comes to
poverty and shame,
but whoever heeds correction is
honored.

[19]A longing fulfilled is sweet to the
soul,
but fools detest turning from evil.

[20]He who walks with the wise grows
wise,
but a companion of fools suffers
harm.

[21]Misfortune pursues the sinner,
but prosperity is the reward of the
righteous.

[22]A good man leaves an inheritance for
his children's children,
but a sinner's wealth is stored up
for the righteous.

[23]A poor man's field may produce
abundant food,
but injustice sweeps it away.

[24]He who spares the rod hates his
son,
but he who loves him is careful to
discipline him.

[25]The righteous eat to their hearts'
content,
but the stomach of the wicked
goes hungry.

14 The wise woman builds her
house,
but with her own hands the
foolish one tears hers down.

[2]He whose walk is upright fears the
LORD,
but he whose ways are devious
despises him.

[3]A fool's talk brings a rod to his back,
but the lips of the wise protect
them.

[4]Where there are no oxen, the manger
is empty,
but from the strength of an ox
comes an abundant harvest.

[5]A truthful witness does not deceive,
but a false witness pours out lies.

[6]The mocker seeks wisdom and finds
none,
but knowledge comes easily to the
discerning.

[7]Stay away from a foolish man,
for you will not find knowledge on
his lips.

[8]The wisdom of the prudent is to give
thought to their ways,
but the folly of fools is deception.

[9]Fools mock at making amends for
sin,
but goodwill is found among the
upright.

[10]Each heart knows its own bitterness,
and no one else can share its joy.

[11]The house of the wicked will be
destroyed,
but the tent of the upright will
flourish.

[12]There is a way that seems right to a
man,
but in the end it leads to death.

[13]Even in laughter the heart may ache,
and joy may end in grief.

[14]The faithless will be fully repaid for
their ways,
and the good man rewarded for
his.

[15]A simple man believes anything,
but a prudent man gives thought
to his steps.

[a]15 Or *unfaithful does not endure*

16A wise man fears the Lord and
shuns evil,
but a fool is hotheaded and
reckless.

17A quick-tempered man does foolish
things,
and a crafty man is hated.

18The simple inherit folly,
but the prudent are crowned with
knowledge.

19Evil men will bow down in the
presence of the good,
and the wicked at the gates of the
righteous.

20The poor are shunned even by their
neighbors,
but the rich have many friends.

21He who despises his neighbor sins,
but blessed is he who is kind to
the needy.

22Do not those who plot evil go
astray?
But those who plan what is good
find*a* love and faithfulness.

23All hard work brings a profit,
but mere talk leads only to
poverty.

24The wealth of the wise is their
crown,
but the folly of fools yields folly.

25A truthful witness saves lives,
but a false witness is deceitful.

26He who fears the Lord has a secure
fortress,
and for his children it will be a
refuge.

27The fear of the Lord is a fountain of
life,
turning a man from the snares of
death.

28A large population is a king's glory,
but without subjects a prince is
ruined.

29A patient man has great
understanding,
but a quick-tempered man
displays folly.

30A heart at peace gives life to the
body,
but envy rots the bones.

31He who oppresses the poor shows
contempt for their Maker,
but whoever is kind to the needy
honors God.

32When calamity comes, the wicked are
brought down,
but even in death the righteous
have a refuge.

33Wisdom reposes in the heart of the
discerning
and even among fools she lets
herself be known.*b*

34Righteousness exalts a nation,
but sin is a disgrace to any people.

35A king delights in a wise servant,
but a shameful servant incurs his
wrath.

15 A gentle answer turns away
wrath,
but a harsh word stirs up anger.

2The tongue of the wise commends
knowledge,
but the mouth of the fool gushes
folly.

3The eyes of the Lord are everywhere,
keeping watch on the wicked and
the good.

4The tongue that brings healing is a
tree of life,
but a deceitful tongue crushes the
spirit.

5A fool spurns his father's discipline,
but whoever heeds correction
shows prudence.

6The house of the righteous contains
great treasure,
but the income of the wicked
brings them trouble.

7The lips of the wise spread
knowledge;
not so the hearts of fools.

8The Lord detests the sacrifice of the
wicked,
but the prayer of the upright
pleases him.

9The Lord detests the way of the
wicked
but he loves those who pursue
righteousness.

*a*22 Or *show*   *b*33 Hebrew; Septuagint and Syriac / *but in the heart of fools she is not known*

¹⁰Stern discipline awaits him who
　　leaves the path;
　he who hates correction will die.

¹¹Death and Destruction*a* lie open
　　before the LORD—
　how much more the hearts of
　　men!

¹²A mocker resents correction;
　he will not consult the wise.

¹³A happy heart makes the face
　　cheerful,
　but heartache crushes the spirit.

¹⁴The discerning heart seeks
　　knowledge,
　but the mouth of a fool feeds on
　　folly.

a11 Hebrew Sheol and Abaddon

¹⁵All the days of the oppressed are
　　wretched,
　but the cheerful heart has a
　　continual feast.

¹⁶Better a little with the fear of the
　　LORD
　than great wealth with turmoil.

¹⁷Better a meal of vegetables where
　　there is love
　than a fattened calf with hatred.

¹⁸A hot-tempered man stirs up
　　dissension,
　but a patient man calms a quarrel.

¹⁹The way of the sluggard is blocked
　　with thorns,

WEDNESDAY

VERSE:	AUTHOR:	PASSAGE:
Proverbs 15:15	Emilie Barnes	Proverbs 15:13–15

Celebrating Laughter

Laughter is a gift of God that brightens our good times and lightens the rough ones. Laughter even has a healing quality to it. People have recovered from serious diseases by learning to laugh each day. Even more people have regained the courage to go on in painful circumstances when they were able to laugh.

Proverbs 17:22 says that a cheerful heart is good medicine. Laughter can draw others to you and lighten your load in life. When you begin to laugh at life and at yourself you gain new perspective on your struggles. You begin to see a speck of light at the end of the tunnel.

A life without laughter quickly becomes a breeding ground for depression, physical illness and a critical spirit. But a laughter-filled life unleashes the spirit of celebration.

So cultivate the spirit of celebration in your life by making room for laughter. Deliberately seek it out. Begin today as you smile at someone and find something worth laughing about. As the laughter permeates your life, the spirit of celebration will take root in your heart and you will discover the meaning of another proverb: "The cheerful heart has a continual feast" (v. 15).

ADDITIONAL SCRIPTURE READINGS:
Psalm 126:1–3; Proverbs 17:22; 1 Thessalonians 5:16–18; James 1:2–4

Go to page 524 for your next devotional reading.

but the path of the upright is a highway.

²⁰A wise son brings joy to his father,
but a foolish man despises his mother.

²¹Folly delights a man who lacks judgment,
but a man of understanding keeps a straight course.

²²Plans fail for lack of counsel,
but with many advisers they succeed.

²³A man finds joy in giving an apt reply—
and how good is a timely word!

²⁴The path of life leads upward for the wise
to keep him from going down to the grave.[a]

²⁵The LORD tears down the proud man's house
but he keeps the widow's boundaries intact.

²⁶The LORD detests the thoughts of the wicked,
but those of the pure are pleasing to him.

²⁷A greedy man brings trouble to his family,
but he who hates bribes will live.

²⁸The heart of the righteous weighs its answers,
but the mouth of the wicked gushes evil.

²⁹The LORD is far from the wicked
but he hears the prayer of the righteous.

³⁰A cheerful look brings joy to the heart,
and good news gives health to the bones.

³¹He who listens to a life-giving rebuke
will be at home among the wise.

³²He who ignores discipline despises himself,
but whoever heeds correction gains understanding.

³³The fear of the LORD teaches a man wisdom,[b]

and humility comes before honor.

16

To man belong the plans of the heart,
but from the LORD comes the reply of the tongue.

²All a man's ways seem innocent to him,
but motives are weighed by the LORD.

³Commit to the LORD whatever you do,
and your plans will succeed.

⁴The LORD works out everything for his own ends—
even the wicked for a day of disaster.

⁵The LORD detests all the proud of heart.
Be sure of this: They will not go unpunished.

⁶Through love and faithfulness sin is atoned for;
through the fear of the LORD a man avoids evil.

⁷When a man's ways are pleasing to the LORD,
he makes even his enemies live at peace with him.

⁸Better a little with righteousness
than much gain with injustice.

⁹In his heart a man plans his course,
but the LORD determines his steps.

¹⁰The lips of a king speak as an oracle,
and his mouth should not betray justice.

¹¹Honest scales and balances are from the LORD;
all the weights in the bag are of his making.

¹²Kings detest wrongdoing,
for a throne is established through righteousness.

¹³Kings take pleasure in honest lips;
they value a man who speaks the truth.

¹⁴A king's wrath is a messenger of death,
but a wise man will appease it.

---

[a]24 Hebrew *Sheol*   [b]33 Or *Wisdom teaches the fear of the LORD*

15When a king's face brightens, it
        means life;
    his favor is like a rain cloud in
        spring.

16How much better to get wisdom than
        gold,
    to choose understanding rather
        than silver!

17The highway of the upright avoids
        evil;
    he who guards his way guards his
        life.

18Pride goes before destruction,
    a haughty spirit before a fall.

19Better to be lowly in spirit and
        among the oppressed
    than to share plunder with the
        proud.

20Whoever gives heed to instruction
        prospers,
    and blessed is he who trusts in
        the LORD.

21The wise in heart are called
        discerning,
    and pleasant words promote
        instruction.[a]

22Understanding is a fountain of life to
        those who have it,
    but folly brings punishment to
        fools.

23A wise man's heart guides his
        mouth,
    and his lips promote instruction.[b]

24Pleasant words are a honeycomb,
    sweet to the soul and healing to
        the bones.

25There is a way that seems right to a
        man,
    but in the end it leads to death.

26The laborer's appetite works for him;
    his hunger drives him on.

27A scoundrel plots evil,
    and his speech is like a scorching
        fire.

28A perverse man stirs up dissension,
    and a gossip separates close
        friends.

29A violent man entices his neighbor

and leads him down a path that is
        not good.

30He who winks with his eye is
        plotting perversity;
    he who purses his lips is bent on
        evil.

31Gray hair is a crown of splendor;
    it is attained by a righteous life.

32Better a patient man than a warrior,
    a man who controls his temper
        than one who takes a city.

33The lot is cast into the lap,
    but its every decision is from the
        LORD.

17 Better a dry crust with peace
        and quiet
    than a house full of feasting,[c]
        with strife.

2A wise servant will rule over a
        disgraceful son,
    and will share the inheritance as
        one of the brothers.

3The crucible for silver and the
        furnace for gold,
    but the LORD tests the heart.

4A wicked man listens to evil lips;
    a liar pays attention to a malicious
        tongue.

5He who mocks the poor shows
        contempt for their Maker;
    whoever gloats over disaster will
        not go unpunished.

6Children's children are a crown to
        the aged,
    and parents are the pride of their
        children.

7Arrogant[d] lips are unsuited to a
        fool—
    how much worse lying lips to a
        ruler!

8A bribe is a charm to the one who
        gives it;
    wherever he turns, he succeeds.

9He who covers over an offense
        promotes love,
    but whoever repeats the matter
        separates close friends.

10A rebuke impresses a man of
        discernment

---

[a]21 Or words make a man persuasive   [b]23 Or mouth / and makes his lips persuasive   [c]1 Hebrew
sacrifices   [d]7 Or Eloquent

more than a hundred lashes a
    fool.

[11]An evil man is bent only on
    rebellion;
a merciless official will be sent
    against him.

[12]Better to meet a bear robbed of her
    cubs
than a fool in his folly.

[13]If a man pays back evil for good,
    evil will never leave his
    house.

THURSDAY

VERSE:
Proverbs 17:6

AUTHOR:
Nancy Corbett Cole

PASSAGE:
Proverbs 17:1–6

Grandma: A Glorious Crown

I will never forget the day my first grandchild, Lindsay, was born. What a happy time! After all the years of raising my own children with all the struggles, I could now see the fruits of my labors in my grandchildren. It was as though life's cycle was completed. First I was a child, then a married adult, then a mother, and then my children were reproducing tiny composites of genes with some of me in them.

When that first squeaky "Grandma" came from Lindsay's mouth, it was like sweet music. Then there were two more babies, then four and five. Now we have seven grandchildren! When I hear of people who have perhaps twenty grandchildren, or family reunions with as many as five hundred people, I think how fortunate they are, especially if the original mother and father instilled godly values into their children, who also did the same with their children.

Every individual in a family counts. The beauty of family does not have to be blighted when there has been divorce and remarriage. We can accept stepchildren and love them unconditionally, just as we do those who are born into the family. Everyone needs acceptance, and a child of divorce, death or abandonment needs more attention than those born into the family naturally. It is easy to favor one above another, particularly those who share our physical characteristics or disposition—characteristics that we secretly admire in ourselves. But we must love them all equally.

I admire greatly those grandparents who, because of circumstances, are raising their grandchildren. I read of a famous athlete who attributed all of his success to his grandmother who raised him. What a struggle, but how rewarding!

The Bible says that an old man's (and woman's) grandchildren are his crowning glory. What a privilege to wear that glorious crown!

ADDITIONAL SCRIPTURE READINGS:
Psalm 127:3; Acts 2:39; James 3:17

Go to page 527 for your next devotional reading.

¹⁴Starting a quarrel is like breaching a dam;
so drop the matter before a dispute breaks out.

¹⁵Acquitting the guilty and condemning the innocent—
the LORD detests them both.

¹⁶Of what use is money in the hand of a fool,
since he has no desire to get wisdom?

¹⁷A friend loves at all times,
and a brother is born for adversity.

¹⁸A man lacking in judgment strikes hands in pledge
and puts up security for his neighbor.

¹⁹He who loves a quarrel loves sin;
he who builds a high gate invites destruction.

²⁰A man of perverse heart does not prosper;
he whose tongue is deceitful falls into trouble.

²¹To have a fool for a son brings grief;
there is no joy for the father of a fool.

²²A cheerful heart is good medicine,
but a crushed spirit dries up the bones.

²³A wicked man accepts a bribe in secret
to pervert the course of justice.

²⁴A discerning man keeps wisdom in view,
but a fool's eyes wander to the ends of the earth.

²⁵A foolish son brings grief to his father
and bitterness to the one who bore him.

²⁶It is not good to punish an innocent man,
or to flog officials for their integrity.

²⁷A man of knowledge uses words with restraint,
and a man of understanding is even-tempered.

²⁸Even a fool is thought wise if he keeps silent,
and discerning if he holds his tongue.

18 An unfriendly man pursues selfish ends;
he defies all sound judgment.

²A fool finds no pleasure in understanding
but delights in airing his own opinions.

³When wickedness comes, so does contempt,
and with shame comes disgrace.

⁴The words of a man's mouth are deep waters,
but the fountain of wisdom is a bubbling brook.

⁵It is not good to be partial to the wicked
or to deprive the innocent of justice.

⁶A fool's lips bring him strife,
and his mouth invites a beating.

⁷A fool's mouth is his undoing,
and his lips are a snare to his soul.

⁸The words of a gossip are like choice morsels;
they go down to a man's inmost parts.

⁹One who is slack in his work
is brother to one who destroys.

¹⁰The name of the LORD is a strong tower;
the righteous run to it and are safe.

¹¹The wealth of the rich is their fortified city;
they imagine it an unscalable wall.

¹²Before his downfall a man's heart is proud,
but humility comes before honor.

¹³He who answers before listening—
that is his folly and his shame.

¹⁴A man's spirit sustains him in sickness,
but a crushed spirit who can bear?

¹⁵The heart of the discerning acquires knowledge;
the ears of the wise seek it out.

¹⁶A gift opens the way for the giver
and ushers him into the presence
of the great.

¹⁷The first to present his case seems
right,
till another comes forward and
questions him.

¹⁸Casting the lot settles disputes
and keeps strong opponents apart.

¹⁹An offended brother is more
unyielding than a fortified city,
and disputes are like the barred
gates of a citadel.

²⁰From the fruit of his mouth a man's
stomach is filled;
with the harvest from his lips he
is satisfied.

²¹The tongue has the power of life and
death,
and those who love it will eat its
fruit.

²²He who finds a wife finds what is
good
and receives favor from the LORD.

²³A poor man pleads for mercy,
but a rich man answers harshly.

²⁴A man of many companions may
come to ruin,
but there is a friend who sticks
closer than a brother.

19 Better a poor man whose walk
is blameless
than a fool whose lips are
perverse.

²It is not good to have zeal without
knowledge,
nor to be hasty and miss the way.

³A man's own folly ruins his life,
yet his heart rages against the
LORD.

⁴Wealth brings many friends,
but a poor man's friend deserts
him.

⁵A false witness will not go
unpunished,
and he who pours out lies will not
go free.

⁶Many curry favor with a ruler,
and everyone is the friend of a
man who gives gifts.

⁷A poor man is shunned by all his
relatives—
how much more do his friends
avoid him!
Though he pursues them with
pleading,
they are nowhere to be found.ᵃ

⁸He who gets wisdom loves his own
soul;
he who cherishes understanding
prospers.

⁹A false witness will not go
unpunished,
and he who pours out lies will
perish.

¹⁰It is not fitting for a fool to live in
luxury—
how much worse for a slave to
rule over princes!

¹¹A man's wisdom gives him patience;
it is to his glory to overlook an
offense.

¹²A king's rage is like the roar of a
lion,
but his favor is like dew on the
grass.

¹³A foolish son is his father's ruin,
and a quarrelsome wife is like a
constant dripping.

¹⁴Houses and wealth are inherited
from parents,
but a prudent wife is from the
LORD.

¹⁵Laziness brings on deep sleep,
and the shiftless man goes
hungry.

¹⁶He who obeys instructions guards
his life,
but he who is contemptuous of
his ways will die.

¹⁷He who is kind to the poor lends to
the LORD,
and he will reward him for what
he has done.

¹⁸Discipline your son, for in that there
is hope;
do not be a willing party to his
death.

¹⁹A hot-tempered man must pay the
penalty;

ᵃ7 The meaning of the Hebrew for this sentence is uncertain.

if you rescue him, you will have to
do it again.

²⁰Listen to advice and accept
instruction,
and in the end you will be wise.

²¹Many are the plans in a man's heart,
but it is the LORD's purpose that
prevails.

^a22 Or A man's greed is his shame

²²What a man desires is unfailing
love^a;
better to be poor than a liar.

²³The fear of the LORD leads to life:
Then one rests content, untouched
by trouble.

²⁴The sluggard buries his hand in the
dish;

FRIDAY

VERSE:	AUTHOR:	PASSAGE:
Proverbs 19:11	Jeanne Zornes	Proverbs 19:1–11

The Waiting Game

Impatient people are like cats petted backwards—apt to yowl
over the discomfort of things not done right or not done at all.
But Proverbs 19:11 spells out the divine imperative: "A man's
wisdom gives him patience; it is to his glory to overlook an
offense."

Unlike jigsaw puzzles, people don't always fit together perfectly. Everyone's personality has unique ins and outs. Some are
busy, get-it-done types, for whom people are a means to an end.
Others are more laid-back; they talk about getting something
done, but never quite get to it. To them, people and relationships
are the end.

When these two types get together, they can despair over the
other's failures, blind to their own. Or they can see those conflicts
as opportunities for their own growth.

Single until her mid-thirties, Dora had numerous roommates
who stretched her comfort zone.

"I like the dishes always done and the floor vacuumed," she
says. "But the Lord needed to expose my inflexibility. The roommates he sent were my opposites. They lived on the telephone and
were blind to dust. But they also drew me out of myself and taught
me how to care for people."

In [my] family, cartoons help us celebrate our differences and
be patient with one another. Any comic strip that hits home is
clipped and posted on the refrigerator for laughs. Then I paste it in
a notebook, kept with the family photo albums, for repeat laughs
and long-term reminders of how human we all really are.

ADDITIONAL SCRIPTURE READINGS:
Ecclesiastes 7:8; Luke 10:38–42; 1 Thessalonians 5:14

Go to page 530 for your next devotional reading.

he will not even bring it back to
   his mouth!

²⁵Flog a mocker, and the simple will
   learn prudence;
   rebuke a discerning man, and he
   will gain knowledge.

²⁶He who robs his father and drives
   out his mother
   is a son who brings shame and
   disgrace.

²⁷Stop listening to instruction, my son,
   and you will stray from the words
   of knowledge.

²⁸A corrupt witness mocks at justice,
   and the mouth of the wicked gulps
   down evil.

²⁹Penalties are prepared for mockers,
   and beatings for the backs of
   fools.

20 Wine is a mocker and beer a
   brawler;
   whoever is led astray by them is
   not wise.

²A king's wrath is like the roar of a
   lion;
   he who angers him forfeits his
   life.

³It is to a man's honor to avoid strife,
   but every fool is quick to quarrel.

⁴A sluggard does not plow in season;
   so at harvest time he looks but
   finds nothing.

⁵The purposes of a man's heart are
   deep waters,
   but a man of understanding draws
   them out.

⁶Many a man claims to have unfailing
   love,
   but a faithful man who can find?

⁷The righteous man leads a blameless
   life;
   blessed are his children after him.

⁸When a king sits on his throne to
   judge,
   he winnows out all evil with his
   eyes.

⁹Who can say, "I have kept my heart
   pure;
   I am clean and without sin"?

¹⁰Differing weights and differing
   measures—
   the LORD detests them both.

¹¹Even a child is known by his
   actions,
   by whether his conduct is pure
   and right.

¹²Ears that hear and eyes that see—
   the LORD has made them both.

¹³Do not love sleep or you will grow
   poor;
   stay awake and you will have food
   to spare.

¹⁴"It's no good, it's no good!" says the
   buyer;
   then off he goes and boasts about
   his purchase.

¹⁵Gold there is, and rubies in
   abundance,
   but lips that speak knowledge are
   a rare jewel.

¹⁶Take the garment of one who puts
   up security for a stranger;
   hold it in pledge if he does it for a
   wayward woman.

¹⁷Food gained by fraud tastes sweet to
   a man,
   but he ends up with a mouth full
   of gravel.

¹⁸Make plans by seeking advice;
   if you wage war, obtain guidance.

¹⁹A gossip betrays a confidence;
   so avoid a man who talks too
   much.

²⁰If a man curses his father or mother,
   his lamp will be snuffed out in
   pitch darkness.

²¹An inheritance quickly gained at the
   beginning
   will not be blessed at the end.

²²Do not say, "I'll pay you back for
   this wrong!"
   Wait for the LORD, and he will
   deliver you.

²³The LORD detests differing weights,
   and dishonest scales do not
   please him.

²⁴A man's steps are directed by the
   LORD.
   How then can anyone understand
   his own way?

²⁵It is a trap for a man to dedicate
something rashly
and only later to consider his
vows.

²⁶A wise king winnows out the wicked;
he drives the threshing wheel over
them.

²⁷The lamp of the LORD searches the
spirit of a man^a;
it searches out his inmost being.

²⁸Love and faithfulness keep a king
safe;
through love his throne is made
secure.

²⁹The glory of young men is their
strength,
gray hair the splendor of the old.

³⁰Blows and wounds cleanse away
evil,
and beatings purge the inmost
being.

21 The king's heart is in the hand
of the LORD;
he directs it like a watercourse
wherever he pleases.

²All a man's ways seem right to him,
but the LORD weighs the heart.

³To do what is right and just
is more acceptable to the LORD
than sacrifice.

⁴Haughty eyes and a proud heart,
the lamp of the wicked, are sin!

⁵The plans of the diligent lead to
profit
as surely as haste leads to poverty.

⁶A fortune made by a lying tongue
is a fleeting vapor and a deadly
snare.^b

⁷The violence of the wicked will drag
them away,
for they refuse to do what is right.

⁸The way of the guilty is devious,
but the conduct of the innocent is
upright.

⁹Better to live on a corner of the roof
than share a house with a
quarrelsome wife.

¹⁰The wicked man craves evil;
his neighbor gets no mercy from
him.

¹¹When a mocker is punished, the
simple gain wisdom;
when a wise man is instructed, he
gets knowledge.

¹²The Righteous One^c takes note of
the house of the wicked
and brings the wicked to ruin.

¹³If a man shuts his ears to the cry of
the poor,
he too will cry out and not be
answered.

¹⁴A gift given in secret soothes anger,
and a bribe concealed in the cloak
pacifies great wrath.

¹⁵When justice is done, it brings joy to
the righteous
but terror to evildoers.

¹⁶A man who strays from the path of
understanding
comes to rest in the company of
the dead.

¹⁷He who loves pleasure will become
poor;
whoever loves wine and oil will
never be rich.

¹⁸The wicked become a ransom for the
righteous,
and the unfaithful for the upright.

¹⁹Better to live in a desert
than with a quarrelsome and
ill-tempered wife.

²⁰In the house of the wise are stores
of choice food and oil,
but a foolish man devours all he
has.

²¹He who pursues righteousness and
love
finds life, prosperity^d and honor.

²²A wise man attacks the city of the
mighty
and pulls down the stronghold in
which they trust.

²³He who guards his mouth and his
tongue
keeps himself from calamity.

^a27 Or *The spirit of man is the LORD's lamp*   ^b6 Some Hebrew manuscripts, Septuagint and Vulgate;
most Hebrew manuscripts *vapor for those who seek death*   ^c12 Or *The righteous man*   ^d21 Or
righteousness

WEEKENDING

RECALL

Climbing a steep hill, I was pleased to meet a friend who stopped for a while to talk. Not only was the conversation good, but it also gave me a chance to rest before continuing the hard climb.

The road of life is sometimes steep too. It is a beautiful thing to have friends who encourage me by stopping to talk. It is also beautiful when I can provide a rest stop and brighten someone else's climb.

REFLECT

Direct me, O great encourager, in paths that cross with others', so we may refresh each other. Amen.

Sandra Drescher-Lehman

RECHARGE

Saturday: Ecclesiastes 4:9–10
Sunday: Romans 15:1–7

Go to page 533 for your next devotional reading.

²⁴The proud and arrogant man—
"Mocker" is his name;
he behaves with overweening
pride.

²⁵The sluggard's craving will be the
death of him,
because his hands refuse to work.

²⁶All day long he craves for more,
but the righteous give without
sparing.

²⁷The sacrifice of the wicked is
detestable—
how much more so when brought
with evil intent!

²⁸A false witness will perish,
and whoever listens to him will be
destroyed forever.ᵃ

²⁹A wicked man puts up a bold front,
but an upright man gives thought
to his ways.

³⁰There is no wisdom, no insight, no
plan
that can succeed against the LORD.

³¹The horse is made ready for the day
of battle,
but victory rests with the LORD.

22 A good name is more desirable
than great riches;
to be esteemed is better than silver
or gold.

²Rich and poor have this in common:
The LORD is the Maker of them all.

³A prudent man sees danger and
takes refuge,
but the simple keep going and
suffer for it.

⁴Humility and the fear of the LORD
bring wealth and honor and life.

⁵In the paths of the wicked lie thorns
and snares,
but he who guards his soul stays
far from them.

⁶Trainᵇ a child in the way he should
go,
and when he is old he will not
turn from it.

⁷The rich rule over the poor,
and the borrower is servant to the
lender.

⁸He who sows wickedness reaps
trouble,
and the rod of his fury will be
destroyed.

⁹A generous man will himself be
blessed,
for he shares his food with the
poor.

¹⁰Drive out the mocker, and out goes
strife;
quarrels and insults are ended.

¹¹He who loves a pure heart and
whose speech is gracious
will have the king for his friend.

¹²The eyes of the LORD keep watch over
knowledge,
but he frustrates the words of the
unfaithful.

¹³The sluggard says, "There is a lion
outside!"
or, "I will be murdered in the
streets!"

¹⁴The mouth of an adulteress is a deep
pit;
he who is under the LORD's wrath
will fall into it.

¹⁵Folly is bound up in the heart of a
child,
but the rod of discipline will drive
it far from him.

¹⁶He who oppresses the poor to
increase his wealth
and he who gives gifts to the
rich—both come to poverty.

Sayings of the Wise

¹⁷Pay attention and listen to the
sayings of the wise;
apply your heart to what I teach,

¹⁸for it is pleasing when you keep
them in your heart
and have all of them ready on
your lips.

¹⁹So that your trust may be in the
LORD,
I teach you today, even you.

²⁰Have I not written thirtyᶜ sayings
for you,
sayings of counsel and knowledge,

²¹teaching you true and reliable words,

ᵃ28 Or / but the words of an obedient man will live on
not written excellent   ᵇ6 Or Start   ᶜ20 Or not formerly written; or

so that you can give sound
    answers
  to him who sent you?

²²Do not exploit the poor because they
    are poor
  and do not crush the needy in
    court,
²³for the LORD will take up their case
  and will plunder those who
    plunder them.

²⁴Do not make friends with a
    hot-tempered man,
  do not associate with one easily
    angered,
²⁵or you may learn his ways
  and get yourself ensnared.

²⁶Do not be a man who strikes hands
    in pledge
  or puts up security for debts;
²⁷if you lack the means to pay,
  your very bed will be snatched
    from under you.

²⁸Do not move an ancient boundary
    stone
  set up by your forefathers.

²⁹Do you see a man skilled in his
    work?
  He will serve before kings;
  he will not serve before obscure
    men.

23 When you sit to dine with a
    ruler,
  note well what*a* is before you,
²and put a knife to your throat
  if you are given to gluttony.
³Do not crave his delicacies,
  for that food is deceptive.

⁴Do not wear yourself out to get rich;
  have the wisdom to show
    restraint.
⁵Cast but a glance at riches, and they
    are gone,
  for they will surely sprout wings
  and fly off to the sky like an eagle.

⁶Do not eat the food of a stingy man,
  do not crave his delicacies;
⁷for he is the kind of man
  who is always thinking about the
    cost.*b*
"Eat and drink," he says to you,
  but his heart is not with you.

⁸You will vomit up the little you have
    eaten
  and will have wasted your
    compliments.

⁹Do not speak to a fool,
  for he will scorn the wisdom of
    your words.

¹⁰Do not move an ancient boundary
    stone
  or encroach on the fields of the
    fatherless,
¹¹for their Defender is strong;
  he will take up their case against
    you.

¹²Apply your heart to instruction
  and your ears to words of
    knowledge.

¹³Do not withhold discipline from a
    child;
  if you punish him with the rod, he
    will not die.
¹⁴Punish him with the rod
  and save his soul from death.*c*

¹⁵My son, if your heart is wise,
  then my heart will be glad;
¹⁶my inmost being will rejoice
  when your lips speak what is
    right.

¹⁷Do not let your heart envy sinners,
  but always be zealous for the fear
    of the LORD.
¹⁸There is surely a future hope for you,
  and your hope will not be cut off.

¹⁹Listen, my son, and be wise,
  and keep your heart on the right
    path.
²⁰Do not join those who drink too
    much wine
  or gorge themselves on meat,
²¹for drunkards and gluttons become
    poor,
  and drowsiness clothes them in
    rags.

²²Listen to your father, who gave you
    life,
  and do not despise your mother
    when she is old.
²³Buy the truth and do not sell it;
  get wisdom, discipline and
    understanding.
²⁴The father of a righteous man has
    great joy;

a 1 Or *who*   *b 7* Or *for as he thinks within himself, / so he is;* or *for as he puts on a feast, / so he is*
c 14 Hebrew *Sheol*

he who has a wise son delights in
him.
25May your father and mother be glad;
may she who gave you birth
rejoice!

26My son, give me your heart
and let your eyes keep to my ways,
27for a prostitute is a deep pit

and a wayward wife is a narrow
well.
28Like a bandit she lies in wait,
and multiplies the unfaithful
among men.

29Who has woe? Who has sorrow?
Who has strife? Who has
complaints?

◁ MONDAY ▷

VERSE:	AUTHOR:	PASSAGE:
Proverbs 22:17	Marjorie Holmes	Proverbs 22:17-29

"Teach Me What I Need to Know"

Everybody should have a friend like Ralph.

He can fix a lamp or a lawn mower, refinish furniture, build bookshelves. All by himself he has transformed his garage into a workshop and completely remodeled his mother's house.

One day, marveling at these results over coffee, I asked, "Ralph, where did you learn to do all this? Who taught you—your father?"

Thoughtfully he sipped his coffee, his blue eyes twinkling. "I never knew my father," he said. "But I did meet a good carpenter a long time ago. And he still helps me. In fact, every time I have a problem, all I have to do is stop and ask him, 'Teach me what I need to know.' And he does. This morning, for instance, those boards just wouldn't work. But after I'd stopped and asked him, 'What am I doing wrong?' the answer came: I was cutting them too short."

Then Ralph gave me the words of his own special prayer:

> Jesus stand beside me.
> Guide and direct my life.
> Teach me what I need to know.
> Help me with my work.
> Let me serve You and others,
> That I may be worthy of God's grace.

Ralph's special prayer has become a part of my own life now. I say it every morning. And all day. Whenever I am anxious or confused about a situation, one phrase of the prayer comes to my rescue: "Teach me what I need to know." Of all the things Ralph has done to help me, his prayer has helped most of all.

ADDITIONAL SCRIPTURE READINGS:
Exodus 36:1; Proverbs 20:5; John 14:23-25

Go to page 536 for your next devotional reading.

Who has needless bruises? Who
has bloodshot eyes?
30Those who linger over wine,
who go to sample bowls of mixed
wine.
31Do not gaze at wine when it is red,
when it sparkles in the cup,
when it goes down smoothly!
32In the end it bites like a snake
and poisons like a viper.
33Your eyes will see strange sights
and your mind imagine confusing
things.
34You will be like one sleeping on the
high seas,
lying on top of the rigging.
35"They hit me," you will say, "but I'm
not hurt!
They beat me, but I don't feel it!
When will I wake up
so I can find another drink?"

24 Do not envy wicked men,
do not desire their company;
2for their hearts plot violence,
and their lips talk about making
trouble.

3By wisdom a house is built,
and through understanding it is
established;
4through knowledge its rooms are
filled
with rare and beautiful treasures.

5A wise man has great power,
and a man of knowledge increases
strength;
6for waging war you need guidance,
and for victory many advisers.

7Wisdom is too high for a fool;
in the assembly at the gate he has
nothing to say.

8He who plots evil
will be known as a schemer.
9The schemes of folly are sin,
and men detest a mocker.

10If you falter in times of trouble,
how small is your strength!

11Rescue those being led away to
death;
hold back those staggering toward
slaughter.
12If you say, "But we knew nothing
about this,"
does not he who weighs the heart
perceive it?

Does not he who guards your life
know it?
Will he not repay each person
according to what he has
done?

13Eat honey, my son, for it is good;
honey from the comb is sweet to
your taste.
14Know also that wisdom is sweet to
your soul;
if you find it, there is a future
hope for you,
and your hope will not be cut off.

15Do not lie in wait like an outlaw
against a righteous man's
house,
do not raid his dwelling place;
16for though a righteous man falls
seven times, he rises again,
but the wicked are brought down
by calamity.

17Do not gloat when your enemy falls;
when he stumbles, do not let your
heart rejoice,
18or the LORD will see and disapprove
and turn his wrath away from him.

19Do not fret because of evil men
or be envious of the wicked,
20for the evil man has no future hope,
and the lamp of the wicked will be
snuffed out.

21Fear the LORD and the king, my son,
and do not join with the
rebellious,
22for those two will send sudden
destruction upon them,
and who knows what calamities
they can bring?

Further Sayings of the Wise

23These also are sayings of the wise:

To show partiality in judging is not
good:
24Whoever says to the guilty, "You are
innocent"—
peoples will curse him and
nations denounce him.
25But it will go well with those who
convict the guilty,
and rich blessing will come upon
them.

26An honest answer
is like a kiss on the lips.

27Finish your outdoor work

and get your fields ready;
  after that, build your house.

²⁸Do not testify against your neighbor
    without cause,
  or use your lips to deceive.
²⁹Do not say, "I'll do to him as he has
    done to me;
  I'll pay that man back for what he
    did."

³⁰I went past the field of the sluggard,
    past the vineyard of the man who
    lacks judgment;
³¹thorns had come up everywhere,
    the ground was covered with
    weeds,
  and the stone wall was in ruins.
³²I applied my heart to what I
    observed
  and learned a lesson from what I
    saw:
³³A little sleep, a little slumber,
    a little folding of the hands to
    rest—
³⁴and poverty will come on you like a
    bandit
  and scarcity like an armed man.[a]

More Proverbs of Solomon

25 These are more proverbs of Solomon, copied by the men of
Hezekiah king of Judah:

²It is the glory of God to conceal a
    matter;
  to search out a matter is the glory
    of kings.

³As the heavens are high and the
    earth is deep,
  so the hearts of kings are
    unsearchable.

⁴Remove the dross from the silver,
    and out comes material for[b] the
    silversmith;
⁵remove the wicked from the king's
    presence,
  and his throne will be established
    through righteousness.

⁶Do not exalt yourself in the king's
    presence,
  and do not claim a place among
    great men;
⁷it is better for him to say to you,
    "Come up here,"

than for him to humiliate you
    before a nobleman.

What you have seen with your eyes
⁸   do not bring[c] hastily to court,
  for what will you do in the end
    if your neighbor puts you to
    shame?

⁹If you argue your case with a
    neighbor,
  do not betray another man's
    confidence,
¹⁰or he who hears it may shame you
  and you will never lose your bad
    reputation.

¹¹A word aptly spoken
  is like apples of gold in settings of
    silver

¹²Like an earring of gold or an
    ornament of fine gold
  is a wise man's rebuke to a
    listening ear.

¹³Like the coolness of snow at harvest
    time
  is a trustworthy messenger to
    those who send him;
  he refreshes the spirit of his
    masters.

¹⁴Like clouds and wind without rain
  is a man who boasts of gifts he
    does not give.

¹⁵Through patience a ruler can be
    persuaded,
  and a gentle tongue can break a
    bone.

¹⁶If you find honey, eat just enough—
  too much of it, and you will vomit.
¹⁷Seldom set foot in your neighbor's
    house—
  too much of you, and he will hate
    you.

¹⁸Like a club or a sword or a sharp
    arrow
  is the man who gives false
    testimony against his
    neighbor.

¹⁹Like a bad tooth or a lame foot
  is reliance on the unfaithful in
    times of trouble.

²⁰Like one who takes away a garment
    on a cold day,

[a]34 Or like a vagrant / and scarcity like a beggar
whom you had set your eyes. / [8]Do not go   [b]4 Or comes a vessel from   [c]7,8 Or nobleman / on

or like vinegar poured on soda,
is one who sings songs to a heavy
  heart.

²¹If your enemy is hungry, give him
  food to eat;
if he is thirsty, give him water to
  drink.

²²In doing this, you will heap burning
  coals on his head,
and the LORD will reward you.

²³As a north wind brings rain,
  so a sly tongue brings angry
    looks.

²⁴Better to live on a corner of the roof

TUESDAY

VERSE:	AUTHOR:	PASSAGE:
Proverbs 25:11	Jean Shaw	Proverbs 25:11-12

A Word Aptly Spoken

The question is not whether or not we should speak the truth, but how to do it. To speak the truth in such a way that it is accepted as something which adds beauty to life, is a great gift.

In Ecclesiastes 12:9–10, we read about a wise teacher who imparted knowledge to the people: "He pondered and searched out and set in order many proverbs. [He] searched to find just the right words, and what he wrote was upright and true." To speak the truth is hard work. First, we must be sure it is the truth. How many times have we been absolutely sure of something, only to discover we were mistaken? The source must be reliable, as must be the transmitter. The person who brings a message must be sure that she has heard it correctly, not forgotten any of it, nor colored it with her own feelings.

Imparting the truth is not easy. The sensitivity of the listener also has to be considered. There is a right moment to speak—not at the end of an exhausting day. Sometimes it would be better to listen. The speaker must ask herself if this truth will be an encouragement, a positive force for growth.

Ephesians 4:15 tells us to speak "the truth in love." Our attitudes toward our listeners affect how our words will be received. The tone of voice and the look in a person's eyes can convey concern. Yet the truth, even from Scripture, can hurt and can subsequently be rejected if spoken from an unloving heart. The simile of truth as a two-edged sword is intended for use on our enemies, not our friends.

The "apples of gold in settings of silver" (v. 11) are thought to be golden balls arranged in silver filigree baskets. These were set on the table as ornaments, much like we use centerpieces today. No doubt they were carefully hand-crafted, valuable and very beautiful. So should our words be.

ADDITIONAL SCRIPTURE READINGS:
Ephesians 4:29-32; 2 Timothy 2:16

Go to page 539 for your next devotional reading.

than share a house with a
quarrelsome wife.

²⁵Like cold water to a weary soul
is good news from a distant land.

²⁶Like a muddied spring or a polluted
well
is a righteous man who gives way
to the wicked.

²⁷It is not good to eat too much
honey,
nor is it honorable to seek one's
own honor.

²⁸Like a city whose walls are broken
down
is a man who lacks self-control.

26 Like snow in summer or rain
in harvest,
honor is not fitting for a fool.

²Like a fluttering sparrow or a darting
swallow,
an undeserved curse does not
come to rest.

³A whip for the horse, a halter for the
donkey,
and a rod for the backs of fools!

⁴Do not answer a fool according to
his folly,
or you will be like him yourself.

⁵Answer a fool according to his folly,
or he will be wise in his own eyes.

⁶Like cutting off one's feet or drinking
violence
is the sending of a message by the
hand of a fool.

⁷Like a lame man's legs that hang
limp
is a proverb in the mouth of a
fool.

⁸Like tying a stone in a sling
is the giving of honor to a fool.

⁹Like a thornbush in a drunkard's
hand
is a proverb in the mouth of a
fool.

¹⁰Like an archer who wounds at
random
is he who hires a fool or any
passer-by.

¹¹As a dog returns to its vomit,
so a fool repeats his folly.

¹²Do you see a man wise in his own
eyes?
There is more hope for a fool than
for him.

¹³The sluggard says, "There is a lion in
the road,
a fierce lion roaming the streets!"

¹⁴As a door turns on its hinges,
so a sluggard turns on his bed.

¹⁵The sluggard buries his hand in the
dish;
he is too lazy to bring it back to
his mouth.

¹⁶The sluggard is wiser in his own
eyes
than seven men who answer
discreetly.

¹⁷Like one who seizes a dog by the
ears
is a passer-by who meddles in a
quarrel not his own.

¹⁸Like a madman shooting
firebrands or deadly arrows
¹⁹is a man who deceives his neighbor
and says, "I was only joking!"

²⁰Without wood a fire goes out;
without gossip a quarrel dies
down.

²¹As charcoal to embers and as wood
to fire,
so is a quarrelsome man for
kindling strife.

²²The words of a gossip are like choice
morsels;
they go down to a man's inmost
parts.

²³Like a coating of glaze*a* over
earthenware
are fervent lips with an evil heart.

²⁴A malicious man disguises himself
with his lips,
but in his heart he harbors deceit.

²⁵Though his speech is charming, do
not believe him,
for seven abominations fill his
heart.

²⁶His malice may be concealed by
deception,

a23 With a different word division of the Hebrew; Masoretic Text *of silver dross*

but his wickedness will be
exposed in the assembly.

²⁷If a man digs a pit, he will fall into
it;
if a man rolls a stone, it will roll
back on him.

²⁸A lying tongue hates those it hurts,
and a flattering mouth works ruin.

27 Do not boast about tomorrow,
for you do not know what a
day may bring forth.

²Let another praise you, and not your
own mouth;
someone else, and not your own
lips.

³Stone is heavy and sand a burden,
but provocation by a fool is
heavier than both.

⁴Anger is cruel and fury
overwhelming,
but who can stand before
jealousy?

⁵Better is open rebuke
than hidden love.

⁶Wounds from a friend can be
trusted,
but an enemy multiplies kisses.

⁷He who is full loathes honey,
but to the hungry even what is
bitter tastes sweet.

⁸Like a bird that strays from its nest
is a man who strays from his
home.

⁹Perfume and incense bring joy to the
heart,
and the pleasantness of one's
friend springs from his
earnest counsel.

¹⁰Do not forsake your friend and the
friend of your father,
and do not go to your brother's
house when disaster strikes
you—
better a neighbor nearby than a
brother far away.

¹¹Be wise, my son, and bring joy to
my heart;
then I can answer anyone who
treats me with contempt.

¹²The prudent see danger and take
refuge,
but the simple keep going and
suffer for it.

¹³Take the garment of one who puts
up security for a stranger;
hold it in pledge if he does it for a
wayward woman.

¹⁴If a man loudly blesses his neighbor
early in the morning,
it will be taken as a curse.

¹⁵A quarrelsome wife is like
a constant dripping on a rainy day;
¹⁶restraining her is like restraining the
wind
or grasping oil with the hand.

¹⁷As iron sharpens iron,
so one man sharpens another.

¹⁸He who tends a fig tree will eat its
fruit,
and he who looks after his master
will be honored.

¹⁹As water reflects a face,
so a man's heart reflects the man.

²⁰Death and Destruction[a] are never
satisfied,
and neither are the eyes of man.

²¹The crucible for silver and the
furnace for gold,
but man is tested by the praise he
receives.

²²Though you grind a fool in a mortar,
grinding him like grain with a
pestle,
you will not remove his folly from
him.

²³Be sure you know the condition of
your flocks,
give careful attention to your
herds;
²⁴for riches do not endure forever,
and a crown is not secure for all
generations.
²⁵When the hay is removed and new
growth appears
and the grass from the hills is
gathered in,
²⁶the lambs will provide you with
clothing,
and the goats with the price of a
field.
²⁷You will have plenty of goats' milk

a20 Hebrew *Sheol* and *Abaddon*

to feed you and your family
and to nourish your servant girls.

28 The wicked man flees though
no one pursues,
but the righteous are as bold as a
lion.

²When a country is rebellious, it has
many rulers,
but a man of understanding and
knowledge maintains order.

³A ruler*a* who oppresses the poor

is like a driving rain that leaves no
crops.

⁴Those who forsake the law praise the
wicked,
but those who keep the law resist
them.

⁵Evil men do not understand justice,
but those who seek the LORD
understand it fully.

⁶Better a poor man whose walk is
blameless

a3 Or A poor man

═══ WEDNESDAY ═══

VERSE:	AUTHOR:	PASSAGE:
Proverbs 27:24	Jean Shaw	Proverbs 27:23-27

What Is the Question?

If money is the answer for everything, what is the question?

Money, we know, cannot ensure health, happiness or immortality. It cannot buy peace of conscience or loving relationships. Yet it is not to be despised. Money supplies a thousand advantages. It can support a Christian college, send a missionary to Africa, supply Bibles for China, buy cooling fans for poor people in the city.

It is not money that is "a root of all kinds of evil," but the *love* of money (1 Timothy 6:10). Jesus condemns money when it becomes an object of devotion equal to God (Matthew 6:24). In his parable of the ten minas (Luke 19:11-26), the third servant who laid his money away in a piece of cloth was punished because he didn't put his money to work. He didn't even invest it so it could earn a little interest.

God is the ultimate supplier of all wealth. He puts us in a position where we have money, either by giving us employment, an inheritance, wise investments or perhaps a jackpot because we matched picture cards from a fast-food restaurant. However we got what money we have, God enabled us to have it. Therefore, he has a right to say what we do with the money he gave us.

The question is, what is my most versatile possession? The answer is, money. God's guideline to those who possess it is amazingly simple: "Command them to do good" (1 Timothy 6:18).

ADDITIONAL SCRIPTURE READINGS:
Proverbs 22:9; 2 Corinthians 9:6-8

Go to page 540 for your next devotional reading.

than a rich man whose ways are perverse.

⁷He who keeps the law is a discerning son,
but a companion of gluttons disgraces his father.

⁸He who increases his wealth by exorbitant interest

amasses it for another, who will be kind to the poor.

⁹If anyone turns a deaf ear to the law, even his prayers are detestable.

¹⁰He who leads the upright along an evil path
will fall into his own trap,
but the blameless will receive a good inheritance.

THURSDAY

VERSE:
Proverbs 28:1

AUTHOR:
Judith Lechman

PASSAGE:
Proverbs 28:1–4

Bold Service

No matter what painful experiences we undergo, we must continue to pursue servanthood in a manner reflecting the boldness of Christ. To bear witness against injustice, inhumanity and other aspects of our brokenness in a darkened world, we need to develop this quality of Christlike boldness in our thoughts and actions.

Boldness has a refreshingly honest and direct simplicity to it. Neither aggressive nor obnoxious, bold servants simply, quietly and effectively work to alleviate suffering in the most forthright method available. There are no hidden meanings behind their words. There are no half-measures taken either. Boldness is an all-or-nothing phenomenon, for bold servants have grown in their relationship with God enough to take risks in spite of the fear of involvement they feel. Acknowledging the specific ways the Lord wants them to serve, bold disciples of Christ opt for decisive rather than hesitant thoughts, and for daring rather than timid actions.

Boldness erases the limits we allow fear to place on our ability to serve. With boldness, we not only see but act from the belief that everyone we meet is our brother and sister in the family of God, deserving of respect, of dignity, of compassion, of giving. With boldness, we place the welfare of others before our own. With boldness, the unwanted and unloved become wanted and loved by us. With boldness, we refuse to hesitate for fear that we may be opposed, we may suffer, we may be rejected, we may offend, we may be in danger.

Having surrendered ourselves to God, we dare to become Christ's "slave to all" by letting God use us boldly in Christian service.

ADDITIONAL SCRIPTURE READINGS:
Mark 10:42–45; Acts 4:31

Go to page 544 for your next devotional reading.

[11]A rich man may be wise in his own
       eyes,
    but a poor man who has
       discernment sees through
       him.

[12]When the righteous triumph, there is
       great elation;
    but when the wicked rise to power,
       men go into hiding.

[13]He who conceals his sins does not
       prosper,
    but whoever confesses and
       renounces them finds mercy.

[14]Blessed is the man who always fears
       the LORD,
    but he who hardens his heart falls
       into trouble.

[15]Like a roaring lion or a charging bear
    is a wicked man ruling over a
       helpless people.

[16]A tyrannical ruler lacks judgment,
    but he who hates ill-gotten gain
       will enjoy a long life.

[17]A man tormented by the guilt of
       murder
    will be a fugitive till death;
    let no one support him.

[18]He whose walk is blameless is kept
       safe,
    but he whose ways are perverse
       will suddenly fall.

[19]He who works his land will have
       abundant food,
    but the one who chases fantasies
       will have his fill of poverty.

[20]A faithful man will be richly blessed,
    but one eager to get rich will not
       go unpunished.

[21]To show partiality is not good—
    yet a man will do wrong for a
       piece of bread.

[22]A stingy man is eager to get rich
    and is unaware that poverty awaits
       him.

[23]He who rebukes a man will in the
       end gain more favor
    than he who has a flattering
       tongue.

[24]He who robs his father or mother
    and says, "It's not wrong"—
    he is partner to him who destroys.

[25]A greedy man stirs up dissension,
    but he who trusts in the LORD will
       prosper.

[26]He who trusts in himself is a fool,
    but he who walks in wisdom is
       kept safe.

[27]He who gives to the poor will lack
       nothing,
    but he who closes his eyes to
       them receives many curses.

[28]When the wicked rise to power,
       people go into hiding;
    but when the wicked perish, the
       righteous thrive.

29 A man who remains
    stiff-necked after many
    rebukes
    will suddenly be destroyed—
       without remedy.

[2]When the righteous thrive, the
       people rejoice;
    when the wicked rule, the people
       groan.

[3]A man who loves wisdom brings joy
       to his father,
    but a companion of prostitutes
       squanders his wealth.

[4]By justice a king gives a country
       stability,
    but one who is greedy for bribes
       tears it down.

[5]Whoever flatters his neighbor
    is spreading a net for his feet.

[6]An evil man is snared by his own
       sin,
    but a righteous one can sing and
       be glad.

[7]The righteous care about justice for
       the poor,
    but the wicked have no such
       concern.

[8]Mockers stir up a city,
    but wise men turn away anger.

[9]If a wise man goes to court with a
       fool,
    the fool rages and scoffs, and
       there is no peace.

[10]Bloodthirsty men hate a man of
       integrity
    and seek to kill the upright.

11A fool gives full vent to his anger,
　but a wise man keeps himself
　　under control.

12If a ruler listens to lies,
　all his officials become wicked.

13The poor man and the oppressor
　have this in common:
　The Lord gives sight to the eyes of
　　both.

14If a king judges the poor with
　fairness,
　his throne will always be secure.

15The rod of correction imparts
　wisdom,
　but a child left to himself
　　disgraces his mother.

16When the wicked thrive, so does sin,
　but the righteous will see their
　　downfall.

17Discipline your son, and he will give
　you peace;
　he will bring delight to your soul.

18Where there is no revelation, the
　people cast off restraint;
　but blessed is he who keeps the
　　law.

19A servant cannot be corrected by
　mere words;
　though he understands, he will
　　not respond.

20Do you see a man who speaks in
　haste?
　There is more hope for a fool than
　　for him.

21If a man pampers his servant from
　youth,
　he will bring grief[a] in the end.

22An angry man stirs up dissension,
　and a hot-tempered one commits
　　many sins.

23A man's pride brings him low,
　but a man of lowly spirit gains
　　honor.

24The accomplice of a thief is his own
　enemy;
　he is put under oath and dare not
　　testify.

25Fear of man will prove to be a snare,

but whoever trusts in the Lord is
　kept safe.

26Many seek an audience with a ruler,
　but it is from the Lord that man
　　gets justice.

27The righteous detest the dishonest;
　the wicked detest the upright.

Sayings of Agur

30 The sayings of Agur son of Jakeh—an oracle[b]:

This man declared to Ithiel,
　to Ithiel and to Ucal:[c]

2"I am the most ignorant of men;
　I do not have a man's
　　understanding.
3I have not learned wisdom,
　nor have I knowledge of the Holy
　　One.
4Who has gone up to heaven and
　come down?
　Who has gathered up the wind in
　　the hollow of his hands?
　Who has wrapped up the waters in
　　his cloak?
　Who has established all the ends
　　of the earth?
　What is his name, and the name of
　　his son?
　Tell me if you know!

5"Every word of God is flawless;
　he is a shield to those who take
　　refuge in him.
6Do not add to his words,
　or he will rebuke you and prove
　　you a liar.

7"Two things I ask of you, O Lord;
　do not refuse me before I die:
8Keep falsehood and lies far from me;
　give me neither poverty nor riches,
　but give me only my daily bread.
9Otherwise, I may have too much and
　disown you
　and say, 'Who is the Lord?'
　Or I may become poor and steal,
　and so dishonor the name of my
　　God.

10"Do not slander a servant to his
　master,
　or he will curse you, and you will
　　pay for it.

---

[a]21 The meaning of the Hebrew for this word is uncertain.　[b]1 Or *Jakeh of Massa*　[c]1 Masoretic Text;
with a different word division of the Hebrew *declared,* "I am weary, O God; / I am weary, O God, and faint.

11"There are those who curse their
    fathers
    and do not bless their mothers;
12those who are pure in their own eyes
    and yet are not cleansed of their
      filth;
13those whose eyes are ever so
      haughty,
    whose glances are so disdainful;
14those whose teeth are swords
    and whose jaws are set with
      knives
to devour the poor from the earth,
    the needy from among mankind.

15"The leech has two daughters.
    'Give! Give!' they cry.

"There are three things that are never
    satisfied,
    four that never say, 'Enough!':
16the grave,[a] the barren womb,
    land, which is never satisfied with
      water,
    and fire, which never says,
      'Enough!'

17"The eye that mocks a father,
    that scorns obedience to a mother,
will be pecked out by the ravens of
    the valley,
    will be eaten by the vultures.

18"There are three things that are too
    amazing for me,
    four that I do not understand:
19the way of an eagle in the sky,
    the way of a snake on a rock,
the way of a ship on the high seas,
    and the way of a man with a
      maiden.

20"This is the way of an adulteress:
    She eats and wipes her mouth
    and says, 'I've done nothing
      wrong.'

21"Under three things the earth
    trembles,
    under four it cannot bear up:
22a servant who becomes king,
    a fool who is full of food,
23an unloved woman who is married,
    and a maidservant who displaces
      her mistress.

24"Four things on earth are small,
    yet they are extremely wise:
25Ants are creatures of little strength,
    yet they store up their food in the
      summer;
26coneys[b] are creatures of little power,
    yet they make their home in the
      crags;
27locusts have no king,
    yet they advance together in ranks;
28a lizard can be caught with the hand,
    yet it is found in kings' palaces.

29"There are three things that are
    stately in their stride,
    four that move with stately
      bearing:
30a lion, mighty among beasts,
    who retreats before nothing;
31a strutting rooster, a he-goat,
    and a king with his army around
      him.[c]

32"If you have played the fool and
    exalted yourself,
    or if you have planned evil,
    clap your hand over your mouth!
33For as churning the milk produces
    butter,
    and as twisting the nose produces
      blood,
    so stirring up anger produces
      strife."

Sayings of King Lemuel

31 The sayings of King Lemuel—
an oracle[d] his mother taught
him:

2"O my son, O son of my womb,
    O son of my vows,[e]
3do not spend your strength on
      women,
    your vigor on those who ruin
      kings.

4"It is not for kings, O Lemuel—
    not for kings to drink wine,
    not for rulers to crave beer,
5lest they drink and forget what the
    law decrees,
    and deprive all the oppressed of
      their rights.
6Give beer to those who are
      perishing,
    wine to those who are in anguish;
7let them drink and forget their
      poverty

---

[a]16 Hebrew *Sheol*   [b]26 That is, the hyrax or rock badger   [c]31 Or *king secure against revolt*
[d]1 Or *of Lemuel king of Massa, which*   [e]2 Or / *the answer to my prayers*

and remember their misery no
more.

8 "Speak up for those who cannot
speak for themselves,
for the rights of all who are
destitute.
9 Speak up and judge fairly;
defend the rights of the poor and
needy."

Epilogue: The Wife of Noble Character

10 *a* A wife of noble character who can
find?

She is worth far more than rubies.
11 Her husband has full confidence in
her
and lacks nothing of value.
12 She brings him good, not harm,
all the days of her life.
13 She selects wool and flax
and works with eager hands.
14 She is like the merchant ships,
bringing her food from afar.
15 She gets up while it is still dark;
she provides food for her family
and portions for her servant girls.
16 She considers a field and buys it;
out of her earnings she plants a
vineyard.

a 10 Verses 10-31 are an acrostic, each verse beginning with a successive letter of the Hebrew alphabet

---

FRIDAY

VERSE:	AUTHOR:	PASSAGE:
Proverbs 31:28	Jean E. Syswerda	Proverbs 31:10–31

Just Call Me Ma!

Fortunate woman!
My children usually arise and call me, "Ma!"
"Ma! Where are you?"
"Ma! Where is my blue shirt?"
"Ma! What's for supper?"
"Ma! Can you give me a ride to the football game?"
"Ma!!"
I wonder, does anyone know that my real name is twice as long
as the one I'm usually called? "Ma!"
My husband enters and calls me "Dear" or "Babe" or "Hon."
Granted each name is longer than "Ma," but they don't reflect the
real me.
Or do they? "Ma" is the one who can be depended on to pro-
vide the ride, the money, the answer to the homework crisis and
the meatloaf for supper. "Dear" provides the companionship,
"Hon" provides the listening ear and "Babe" provides the backrub.
My children may never rise up and call me blessed. But I'll settle for "Ma!"
*Dear Lord, help me to remember that who I am in my family is proba-
bly the most important who I am.*

ADDITIONAL SCRIPTURE READINGS:
1 Samuel 1:26–28; Psalm 128:1–6

Go to page 9 for your next devotional reading.

¹⁷She sets about her work vigorously;
her arms are strong for her tasks.
¹⁸She sees that her trading is
profitable,
and her lamp does not go out at
night.
¹⁹In her hand she holds the distaff
and grasps the spindle with her
fingers.
²⁰She opens her arms to the poor
and extends her hands to the
needy.
²¹When it snows, she has no fear for
her household;
for all of them are clothed in
scarlet.
²²She makes coverings for her bed;
she is clothed in fine linen and
purple.
²³Her husband is respected at the city
gate,
where he takes his seat among the
elders of the land.
²⁴She makes linen garments and sells
them,

and supplies the merchants with
sashes.
²⁵She is clothed with strength and
dignity;
she can laugh at the days to come.
²⁶She speaks with wisdom,
and faithful instruction is on her
tongue.
²⁷She watches over the affairs of her
household
and does not eat the bread of
idleness.
²⁸Her children arise and call her
blessed;
her husband also, and he praises
her:
²⁹"Many women do noble things,
but you surpass them all."
³⁰Charm is deceptive, and beauty
is fleeting;
but a woman who fears the
LORD is to be praised.
³¹Give her the reward she has
earned,
and let her works bring her
praise at the city gate.

WEIGHTS & MEASURES

The figures of the table are calculated on the basis of a shekel equaling 11.5 grams, a cubit equaling 18 inches and an ephah equaling 22 liters. The quart referred to is either a dry quart (slightly larger than a liter) or a liquid quart (slightly smaller than a liter), whichever is applicable. The ton referred to in the footnotes is the American ton of 2,000 pounds.

This table is based upon the best available information, but it is not intended to be mathematically precise; like the measurement equivalents in the footnotes, it merely gives approximate amounts and distances. Weights and measures differed somewhat at various times and places in the ancient world. There is uncertainty particularly about the ephah and the bath; further discoveries may shed more light on these units of capacity.

	BIBLICAL UNIT		APPROXIMATE AMERICAN EQUIVALENT		APPROXIMATE METRIC EQUIVALENT	
WEIGHTS	talent	*(60 minas)*	75	pounds	34	kilograms
	mina	*(50 shekels)*	1 1/4	pounds	0.6	kilogram
	shekel	*(2 bekas)*	2/5	ounce	11.5	grams
	pim	*(2/3 shekel)*	1/3	ounce	7.6	grams
	beka	*(10 gerahs)*	1/5	ounce	5.5	grams
	gerah		1/50	ounce	0.6	gram
LENGTH	cubit		18	inches	0.5	meter
	span		9	inches	23	centimeters
	handbreadth		3	inches	8	centimeters
CAPACITY						
Dry Measure	cor [homer]	*(10 ephahs)*	6	bushels	220	liters
	lethek	*(5 ephahs)*	3	bushels	110	liters
	ephah	*(10 omers)*	3/5	bushel	22	liters
	seah	*(1/3 ephah)*	7	quarts	7.3	liters
	omer	*(1/10 ephah)*	2	quarts	2	liters
	cab	*(1/18 ephah)*	1	quart	1	liter
Liquid Measure	bath	*(1 ephah)*	6	gallons	22	liters
	hin	*(1/6 bath)*	4	quarts	4	liters
	log	*(1/72 bath)*	1/3	quart	0.3	liter

INDEXES & READING PLANS

ACKNOWLEDGMENTS INDEX

Page 9: Taken from PRAYER: CONVERSING WITH GOD by Rosalind Rinker. Copyright © 1970 by Zondervan Publishing House. Used by permission.

Page 12: Taken from "Babbie Mason: Person to Person," an interview by Jane Johnson Struck. Adapted from TODAY'S CHRISTIAN WOMAN magazine (July/August 1994). Used by permission.

Page 18: Taken from CELEBRATE HIS GLORY by Sarah Jepson Coleman. Copyright © 1965, 1981 by Sarah Jepson Coleman. Used by permission.

Page 22: Taken from SURROUNDED BY MYSTERY: LIVING WITH THE CONTRADICTIONS OF FAITH by Ruth Senter. Copyright © 1988 by Ruth Senter. Published by Zondervan Publishing House. Used by permission.

Page 25: Taken from OPEN HEART, OPEN HOME by Karen Burton Mains. Copyright © 1976 by Karen Burton Mains. Published by David C. Cook Publishing. Used by permission.

Page 28: Taken from HOME IS WHERE YOU HANG YOUR HEART: A MOTHER'S DEVOTIONAL by Cynthia Culp Allen. Copyright © 1992 by Cynthia Culp Allen and published by Meridian Publishing. Used by permission.

Page 31: Taken from IMAGINATION: EMBRACING A THEOLOGY OF WONDER by Cheryl Forbes. Copyright © 1986 by Cheryl Forbes. Published by Multnomah Press. Used by permission.

Page 36: Taken from TIME OUT FOR COFFEE by Jeanette Lockerbie. Copyright © 1978 by Moody Bible Institute of Chicago. Moody Press. Used by permission.

Page 40: Taken from GOD SPEAKS TO WOMEN TODAY by Eugenia Price. Copyright © 1964 by Zondervan Publishing House. Used by permission.

Page 47: By Alice C. Peter. Taken from STILL MOMENTS, compiled by Mary Beckwith. Copyright © 1989 by Mary Beckwith. Published by Regal Books, Ventura, California. Used by permission.

Page 49: Taken from THE HEALING MOMENT by Betsy Lee. Copyright © 1994 by Betsy Lee. Published by Thomas Nelson Publishers. Used by permission.

Page 51: By Ruth DeJager. Copyright © 1995 by The Zondervan Corporation.

Page 53: Taken from REACHING FOR RAINBOWS by Ann Weems. Copyright © 1980 by Ann Weems. Used by permission of Westminster John Knox Press. All rights reserved.

Page 54: Taken from HE IS REAL by Millie Stamm. Copyright © 1991 by Millie Stamm. Published by Zondervan Publishing House. Used by permission.

Page 60: By Catherine Doherty. Taken from GRACE IN EVERY SEASON: THROUGH THE YEAR WITH CATHERINE DOHERTY, edited by Mary Achterhoff. Copyright © 1992 by Madonna House Publications. Published by Servant Publications and Madonna House Publications. Used by permission.

Page 65: Taken from BE STILL AND KNOW. Copyright © 1978 by Millie Stamm. Published by Zondervan Publishing House. Used by permission.

Page 69: Taken from A LAMP FOR MY FEET: THE BIBLE'S LIGHT FOR DAILY LIVING by Elisabeth Elliot. Copyright © 1985 by Servant Publications. Used by permission.

Page 73: Taken from WRITING THE RIVER © 1994 by Luci Shaw. Used by permission of Pinon Press, Colorado Springs, Colorado. All rights reserved.

Page 75: Taken from HORIZONS: EXPLORING CREATION by Luci Shaw. Copyright © 1992 by Luci Shaw and Timothy R. Botts. Published by Zondervan Publishing House. Used by permission.

Page 76: Taken from THE MIRACLE OF LIFE by Mary C. and Robert G. Wells, M.D.; Judy and Ken Gire. Copyright © 1993 Robert G. Wells, M.D. and Ken Gire. Published by Zondervan Publishing House. Used by permission.

Page 78: Taken from GOD MEETS US WHERE WE ARE by Marcia Hollis. Copyright © 1989 by Marcia Hollis. Published by Zondervan Publishing House. Used by permission.

Page 82: Taken from MEDITATIONS FOR CHRISTIANS WHO TRY TO BE PERFECT by Joan C. Webb. Copyright © 1993 by Joan C. Webb. Published by HarperCollins Publishers. Used by permission.

Page 84: Taken from GOD MEETS US WHERE WE ARE by Marcia Hollis. Copyright © 1989 by Marcia Hollis. Published by Zondervan Publishing House. Used by permission.

Page 90: Taken from TIME OUT FOR COFFEE by Jeanette Lockerbie. Copyright © 1978 by Moody Bible Institute of Chicago. Moody Press. Used by permission.

Page 92: Taken from YOU ARE WHAT YOU SAY by Karen Burton Mains. Copyright © 1988 by Karen Burton Mains. Published by Zondervan Publishing House. Used by permission.

Page 95: Taken from WHEN THE HEART WAITS by Sue Monk Kidd. Copyright © 1990 by Sue Monk Kidd. Published by HarperCollins Publishers. Used by permission.

Page 101: Taken from THE PRAYERS OF SUSANNA WESLEY by Susanna Wesley. Copyright © 1984 by The Zondervan Corporation. Used by permission of Zondervan Publishing House.

Page 103: "The Celebration" taken from POLISHING THE PETOSKEY STONE by Luci Shaw, © 1990. Used by permission of Harold Shaw Publishers.

Page 108: Taken from TIME OUT FOR COFFEE by Jeanette Lockerbie. Copyright © 1978 by Moody Bible Institute of Chicago. Moody Press. Used by permission.

Page 113: "The Look" taken from TAPESTRY: A WOMAN'S GUIDE TO INTIMACY WITH GOD, June 1994; edited by Brenda Josee. Used by permission.

Page 115: Taken from THE HELPER: HE WILL MEET YOUR EVERY NEED by Catherine Marshall. Copyright © 1978 by Catherine Marshall. Published by Word, Inc., Dallas, Texas. Used by permission.

Page 117: Taken from SURROUNDED BY MYSTERY: LIVING WITH THE CONTRADICTIONS OF FAITH by Ruth Senter. Copyright © 1988 by Ruth Senter. Published by Zondervan Publishing House. Used by permission.

Page 122: Taken from BECOMING FIRE by Jeanie Miley. Copyright © 1993 by Fleming H. Revell, a division of Baker Book House, Grand Rapids, Michigan. Used by permission.

Page 124: Taken from WHEN THE HEART WAITS by Sue Monk Kidd. Copyright © 1990 by Sue Monk Kidd. Published by HarperCollins Publishers. Used by permission.

Page 126: Taken from SINCERELY . . . GIGI by Gigi Graham Tchividjian. Copyright © 1984 by The Zondervan Corporation. Used by permission of Zondervan Publishing House.

Page 130: By Nellie C. Savicki. Taken from STILL MOMENTS, compiled by Mary Beckwith. Copyright © 1989 by Mary Beckwith. Published by Regal Books, Ventura, California. Used by permission.

Page 132: Taken from HE IS REAL by Millie Stamm. Copyright © 1991 by Millie Stamm. Published by Zondervan Publishing House. Used by permission.

Page 135: Taken from THE HEALING MOMENT by Betsy Lee. Copyright © 1994 by Betsy Lee. Published by Thomas Nelson Publishers. Used by permission.

Page 137: Taken from DIAMONDS IN THE DUST by Joni Eareckson Tada. Copyright © 1993 by Joni Eareckson Tada. Published by Zondervan Publishing House. Used by permission.

Page 139: By Edith Bajema. Copyright © 1995 by The Zondervan Corporation.

Page 143: By Gloria Gaither. Taken from 365 DEVOTIONS FOR GRANDMOTHERS by Gloria Gaither, et al. Copyright © 1994 by Gloria Gaither. Published by Dimensions for Living. Used by permission.

Page 146: Taken from SEEKING CHRIST: A WOMAN'S GUIDE TO PERSONAL WHOLENESS AND SPIRITUAL MATURITY by Kay Marshall Strom. Copyright © 1994 by Kay Marshall Strom. Published by Thomas Nelson Publishers. Used by permission.

Page 148: Taken from MAKE LOVE YOUR AIM by Eugenia Price. Copyright © 1967 by Eugenia Price. Published by Zondervan Publishing House. Used by permission.

Page 149: Taken from WE DIDN'T KNOW THEY WERE ANGELS by Doris W. Greig. Copyright © 1987 by Doris W. Greig. Published by Regal Books, Ventura, California. Used by permission.

Page 152: By Edith Bajema. Copyright © 1995 by The Zondervan Corporation.

Page 157: Taken from WINTER: A TIME FOR PEACE by Debra Klingsporn. Copyright © 1994 by Thomas Nelson Publishers. Used by permission.

Page 163: Taken from BY HOOK OR BY CROOK: HOW GOD SHAPED A FISHERMAN INTO A SHEPHERD by Jill Briscoe. Copyright © 1987 by Word, Inc., Dallas, Texas. All rights reserved.

Page 170: Taken from THE LIFE AND RELIGIOUS EXPERIENCE OF JARENA LEE IN HER WORDS: WOMEN'S WRITINGS IN THE HISTORY OF CHRISTIAN THOUGHT, edited by Amy Oden. Copyright © 1994 by Abingdon Press. Used by permission.

Page 173: Taken from QUIET STRENGTH by Rosa Parks. Copyright © 1995 by Rosa Parks. Published by Zondervan Publishing House. Used by permission.

Page 175: Taken from BY HOOK OR BY CROOK: HOW GOD SHAPED A FISHERMAN INTO A SHEPHERD by Jill Briscoe. Copyright © 1987 by Word, Inc., Dallas, Texas. All rights reserved.

Page 176: By Jean E. Syswerda. Copyright © 1995 by The Zondervan Corporation.

Page 183: Taken from MY SACRIFICE, HIS FIRE by Anne Ortlund. Copyright © 1993 by Word, Inc., Dallas, Texas. Used by permission. All rights reserved.

Page 184: Taken from OUR WISE COUNSELOR: SEEKING GOD'S GUIDANCE by Phyllis Bennett. Copyright © 1994 by Phyllis Bennett. Published by Zondervan Publishing House. Excerpt retold from THE HIDING PLACE by Corrie ten Boom, copyright © Corrie ten Boom with John and Elizabeth Sherrill. Chosen Books, Inc., Chappaqua, New York. Used by permission.

Page 189: Taken from MY LIFE FOR THE POOR by Mother Teresa of Calcutta; edited by Jose Luis Gonzalez-Balado and Janet N. Playfoot. Copyright © 1985 by HarperCollins Publishers. Used by permission.

Page 194: Taken from IMAGINATION: EMBRACING A THEOLOGY OF WONDER by Cheryl Forbes. Copyright © 1986 by Cheryl Forbes. Published by Multnomah Press. Used by permission.

Page 201: Taken from GIFTS FREELY GIVEN: DEVOTIONS FOR YOUR QUIET TIME by Marjorie Holmes. Copyright © 1992 by Guideposts Associates, Inc. Published by Fleming H. Revell, a division of Baker Book House, Grand Rapids, Michigan. Used by permission.

Page 206: Taken from SECRET STRENGTH FOR THOSE WHO SEARCH by Joni Eareckson Tada. Copyright © 1994 by Joni, Inc. Published by Questar Publishers, Multnomah Books. Used by permission.

Page 209: Taken from MY SACRIFICE, HIS FIRE by Anne Ortlund. Copyright © 1993 by Word, Inc., Dallas, Texas. Used by permission. All rights reserved.

Page 211: Taken from SURRENDERING HUNGER: 365 DEVOTIONS FOR CHRISTIANS RECOVERING FROM EATING DISORDERS by Jan Johnson. Copyright © 1993 by HarperCollins Publishers. Used by permission.

Page 214: Taken from MY SACRIFICE, HIS FIRE by Anne Ortlund. Copyright © 1993 by Word, Inc., Dallas, Texas. Used by permission. All rights reserved.

Page 216: Taken from A PATH THROUGH SUFFERING: DISCOVERING THE RELATIONSHIP BETWEEN GOD'S MERCY AND OUR PAIN by Elisabeth Elliot. Copyright © 1990 by Servant Publications. Used by permission.

Page 218: Taken from MEMORIES: A PRESENT FROM THE PAST by Kathryn Hillen. Copyright © 1987 by Kathryn Hillen. Published by Zondervan Publishing House. Used by permission.

Page 220:   Taken from HOME IS WHERE YOU HANG YOUR HEART: A MOTHER'S DEVOTIONAL by Cynthia Culp Allen. Copyright © 1992 by Cynthia Culp Allen and published by Meridian Publishing. Used by permission.

Page 222:   Taken from "Babbie Mason: Person to Person," an interview by Jane Johnson Struck. Adapted from TODAY'S CHRISTIAN WOMAN magazine (July/August 1994). Used by permission.

Page 224:   Taken from 'TIS IS GIFT TO BE SIMPLE by Barbara DeGrote-Sorensen and David Allen Sorensen. Copyright © 1992 by Augsburg Fortress. Used by permission.

Page 226:   Taken from A PLACE CALLED SIMPLICITY by Claire Cloninger. Copyright © 1993 by Harvest House Publishers, Eugene, Oregon. Used by permission.

Page 228:   Taken from IT'S MY TURN by Ruth Bell Graham. Copyright © 1982 by Fleming H. Revell, a division of Baker Book House, Grand Rapids, Michigan. Used by permission.

Page 229:   Taken from LORD, LET ME LOVE by Marjorie Holmes. Copyright © 1978 by Marjorie Holmes. Used by permission of Doubleday, a division of Bantam Doubleday Dell Publishing Group, Inc.

Page 234:   By Ann Kiemel Anderson. Taken from A DEEPER WALK. Copyright © 1994 by Thomas Nelson Publishers. Used by permission.

Page 236:   Taken from DELIGHT IN THE DAY by Shirley Pope Waite © 1993. Used by permission of Tyndale House Publishers, Inc. All rights reserved.

Page 239:   By Catherine Doherty. Taken from GRACE IN EVERY SEASON: THROUGH THE YEAR WITH CATHERINE DOHERTY, edited by Mary Achterhoff. Copyright © 1992 by Madonna House Publications. Published by Servant Publications and Madonna House Publications. Used by permission.

Page 242:   Taken from MUSIC AS MEDICINE by Deforia Lane with Rob Wilkins. Copyright © 1994 by Deforia Lane. Published by Zondervan Publishing House. Used by permission.

Page 244:   Taken from WOMANSPIRIT: RECLAIMING THE DEEP FEMININE IN OUR HUMAN SPIRITUALITY by Susan Muto. Copyright © 1991 by Susan Muto. Used by permission of The Crossroad Publishing Company, New York.

Page 246:   Taken from SUNNY-SIDE UP by Alma Barkman. Copyright © 1977 by Moody Bible Institute of Chicago. Moody Press. Used by permission.

Page 249:   Taken from CROSSING THE BRIDGE BETWEEN YOU AND ME by Susan Lenzkes. Copyright © 1994 by Susan Lenzkes. Used by permission of Discovery House Publishers, Box 3566, Grand Rapids, Michigan 49501. All rights reserved.

Page 251:   Taken from MY LIFE FOR THE POOR by Mother Teresa of Calcutta; edited by Jose Luis Gonzalez-Balado and Janet N. Playfoot. Copyright © 1985 by HarperCollins Publishers. Used by permission.

Page 254:   By Paula Michelsen. Taken from STILL MOMENTS, compiled by Mary Beckwith. Copyright © 1989 by Mary Beckwith. Published by Regal Books, Ventura, California. Used by permission.

Page 257:   Taken from BECOMING A WOMAN OF EXCELLENCE © 1986 by Cynthia Heald. Used by permission of NavPress, Colorado Springs, Colorado. All rights reserved.

Page 258:   Taken from LORD, LET ME LOVE by Marjorie Holmes. Copyright © 1978 by Marjorie Holmes. Used by permission of Doubleday, a division of Bantam Doubleday Dell Publishing Group, Inc.

Page 260:   Taken from THE CLEAVERS DON'T LIVE HERE ANYMORE by Paula Rinehart. Copyright © 1991, 1993 by Paula Rinehart. Published by Moody Press. Used by permission.

Page 263:   Taken from BECOMING A WOMAN OF EXCELLENCE © 1986 by Cynthia Heald. Used by permission of NavPress, Colorado Springs, Colorado. All rights reserved.

Page 266:   Taken from SEEKING CHRIST: A WOMAN'S GUIDE TO PERSONAL WHOLENESS AND SPIRITUAL MATURITY by Kay Marshall Strom. Copyright © 1994 by Kay Marshall Strom. Published by Thomas Nelson Publishers. Used by permission.

Page 268:   Taken from WINTER: A TIME FOR PEACE by Debra Klingsporn. Copyright © 1994 by Thomas Nelson Publishers. Used by permission.

Page 269:   Taken from A PLACE CALLED SIMPLICITY by Claire Cloninger. Copyright © 1993 by Harvest House Publishers, Eugene, Oregon. Used by permission.

Page 271:   Public Domain. Reprinted from PSALTER HYMNAL. Published by CRC Publications.

Page 273:   Taken from INTIMATE MOMENTS: DAILY DEVOTIONS FOR COUPLES by David and Teresa Ferguson, Chris and Holly Thurman. Copyright © 1993 by David Ferguson, Teresa Ferguson, Chris Thurman, Holly Thurman. Published by Thomas Nelson Publishers. Used by permission.

Page 275:   Taken from SEEKING CHRIST: A WOMAN'S GUIDE TO PERSONAL WHOLENESS AND SPIRITUAL MATURITY by Kay Marshall Strom. Copyright © 1994 by Kay Marshall Strom. Published by Thomas Nelson Publishers. Used by permission.

Page 277:   Taken from WHAT EVERY MOM NEEDS by Elisa Morgan and Carol Kuykendall. Copyright © 1995 by M.O.P.S. International, Inc. Published by Zondervan Publishing House. Used by permission.

Page 279:   Taken from DELIGHT IN THE DAY by Shirley Pope Waite © 1993. Used by permission of Tyndale House Publishers, Inc. All rights reserved.

Page 281:   Taken from A PLACE CALLED SIMPLICITY by Claire Cloninger. Copyright © 1993 by Harvest House Publishers, Eugene, Oregon. Used by permission.

Page 282:   Taken from MY SACRIFICE, HIS FIRE by Anne Ortlund. Copyright © 1993 by Word, Inc., Dallas, Texas. Used by permission. All rights reserved.

Page 284:   Taken from THE SPIRIT OF LOVELINESS by Emilie Barnes. Copyright © 1992 by Harvest House Publishers, Eugene, Oregon. Used by permission.

Page 286:   Taken from SEEKING CHRIST: A WOMAN'S GUIDE TO PERSONAL WHOLENESS AND SPIRITUAL MATURITY by Kay Marshall Strom. Copyright © 1994 by Kay Marshall Strom. Published by Thomas Nelson Publishers. Used by permission.

Page 289: Taken from MEMORIES: A PRESENT FROM THE PAST by Kathryn Hillen. Copyright © 1987 by Kathryn Hillen. Published by Zondervan Publishing House. Used by permission.

Page 291: Taken from WEATHER OF THE HEART: GLIMPSES OF GOD IN SUNLIGHT AND STORM by Gigi Graham Tchividjian. Copyright © 1991 by Gigi Graham Tchividjian. Published by Questar Publishers, Multnomah Books. Used by permission.

Page 292: By Sharon Mahoe. Taken from A MOMENT A DAY, compiled by Mary Beckwith and Kathi Mills. Copyright © 1988 by Mary Beckwith and Kathi Mills. Published by Regal Books, Ventura, California. Used by permission.

Page 294: Taken from QUIET STRENGTH by Rosa Parks. Copyright © 1995 by Rosa Parks. Published by Zondervan Publishing House. Used by permission.

Page 296: Taken from THE PRAYERS OF SUSANNA WESLEY by Susanna Wesley. Copyright © 1984 by The Zondervan Corporation. Used by permission of Zondervan Publishing House.

Page 297: By Deneese L. Jones. Taken from WOMEN TO WOMEN, edited by Novella Carter and Matthew Parker. Copyright © 1996 by The Institute for Black Family Development. Used by permission of Zondervan Publishing House.

Page 300: Author Unknown. Reprinted in PACK UP YOUR GLOOMIES IN A GREAT BIG BOX, THEN SIT ON THE LID AND LAUGH by Barbara Johnson. Published by Word, Inc., Dallas, Texas.

Page 302: Taken from THE UNSELFISHNESS OF GOD: MY SPIRITUAL AUTOBIOGRAPHY by Hannah Whitall Smith. Copyright © 1987 by Littlebrook Publishing, Inc., Princeton, New Jersey 08540. Used by permission.

Page 304: Taken from A NEW JOY by Colleen Townsend Evans. Copyright © 1973 by Fleming H. Revell, a division of Baker Book House, Grand Rapids, Michigan. Used by permission.

Page 305: Taken from EARLY NEW ENGLAND MEDITATIVE POETRY: ANNE BRADSTREET AND EDWARD TAYLOR, edited by Charles E. Hambrick Stowe. Copyright © 1988 by Paulist Press. Used by permission.

Page 307: Taken from THE GRANDMOTHER BOOK by Jan Stoop and Betty Southard. Copyright © 1993 by Jan Stoop and Betty Southard. Published by Thomas Nelson Publishers. Used by permission.

Page 309: Taken from THE CLEAVERS DON'T LIVE HERE ANYMORE by Paula Rinehart. Copyright © 1991, 1993 by Paula Rinehart. Published by Moody Press. Used by permission.

Page 312: Taken from WHAT EVERY MOM NEEDS by Elisa Morgan and Carol Kuykendall. Copyright © 1995 by M.O.P.S. International, Inc. Published by Zondervan Publishing House. Used by permission.

Page 313: Taken from SINCERELY . . . GIGI by Gigi Graham Tchividjian. Copyright © 1984 by The Zondervan Corporation. Used by permission of Zondervan Publishing House.

Page 316: Taken from CROSSING THE BRIDGE BETWEEN YOU AND ME by Susan Lenzkes. Copyright © 1994 by Susan Lenzkes. Used by permission of Discovery House Publishers, Box 3566, Grand Rapids, Michigan 49501. All rights reserved.

Page 317: Taken from JANE EYRE by Charlotte Bronte. A Norton Critical Edition. Copyright © 1987, 1971 by W.W. Norton & Company, Inc., New York, New York. Used by permission.

Page 319: Taken from THE UNSEEN WORLD OF ANGELS AND DEMONS by M. Basilia Schlink. Copyright © 1985 by the Evangelical Sisterhood of Mary. Published by HarperCollins Publishers. Used by permission.

Page 322: Taken from WHAT TO DO WHEN YOU CAN'T DO IT ALL by Carol Van Klompenburg. Copyright © 1989 by Augsburg Fortress. Used by permission.

Page 325: Taken from MUSIC AS MEDICINE by Deforia Lane with Rob Wilkins. Copyright © 1994 by Deforia Lane. Published by Zondervan Publishing House. Used by permission.

Page 327: By Zoe B. Metzger. Taken from STILL MOMENTS, compiled by Mary Beckwith. Copyright © 1989 by Mary Beckwith. Published by Regal Books, Ventura, California. Used by permission.

Page 330: Taken from WHEN GOD WHISPERS © 1994 by Carole Mayhall. Used by permission of NavPress, Colorado Springs, Colorado. All rights reserved.

Page 332: Taken from TAMING THE DRAGONS: CHRISTIAN WOMEN RESOLVING CONFLICT by Brenda Wilbee. Copyright © 1992 by Brenda Wilbee. Published by HarperCollins Publishers. Used by permission.

Page 333: Taken from THE GLORIOUS NAMES OF GOD by Mary Foxwell Loeks. Copyright © 1986 by Baker Book House, Grand Rapids, Michigan. Used by permission.

Page 334: Taken from A STRING OF PEARLS by Mary C. Crowley. Copyright © 1985 by Word, Inc., Dallas, Texas. Used by permission. All rights reserved.

Page 337: Taken from CROSSING THE BRIDGE BETWEEN YOU AND ME by Susan Lenzkes. Copyright © 1994 by Susan Lenzkes. Used by permission of Discovery House Publishers, Box 3566, Grand Rapids, Michigan 49501. All rights reserved.

Page 338: Taken from DELIGHT IN THE DAY by Shirley Pope Waite © 1993. Used by permission of Tyndale House Publishers, Inc. All rights reserved.

Page 340: Taken from SEEING YOURSELF THROUGH GOD'S EYES by June Hunt. Copyright © 1989 by June Hunt. Published by Zondervan Publishing House. Used by permission.

Page 342: Taken from PLAIN AND SIMPLE: A WOMAN'S JOURNEY TO THE AMISH by Sue Bender. Copyright © 1989 by Sue Bender. Published by HarperCollins Publishers. Used by permission.

Page 343: Taken from RECOVERY FROM GUILT: STUDY GUIDE by Juanita and Dale Ryan. Copyright © 1993 by Juanita and Dale Ryan. Published by InterVarsity Press. Used by permission.

Page 345: Taken from A PATH THROUGH SUFFERING: DISCOVERING THE RELATIONSHIP BETWEEN GOD'S MERCY AND OUR PAIN by Elisabeth Elliot. Copyright © 1990 by Servant Publications. Used by permission.

Page 347: Taken from DANCING IN THE ARMS OF GOD by Connie Neal. Copyright © 1995 by Connie Neal. Published by Zondervan Publishing House. Used by permission.

Page 349: Taken from MUSIC AS MEDICINE by Deforia Lane with Rob Wilkins. Copyright © 1994 by Deforia Lane. Published by Zondervan Publishing House. Used by permission.

Page 352: Taken from OPEN HEART, OPEN HOME by Karen Burton Mains. Copyright © 1976 by Karen Burton Mains. Published by David C. Cook Publishing. Used by permission.

Page 354: Taken from ELIZABETH SETON: SELECTED WRITINGS, edited by Dr. Ellin M. Kelly and Dr. Annabelle M. Melville. Copyright © 1987 by Paulist Press. Used by permission.

Page 355: By Mary Lou Carney. Taken from A MOMENT A DAY, compiled by Mary Beckwith and Kathi Mills. Copyright © 1988 by Mary Beckwith and Kathi Mills. Published by Regal Books, Ventura, California. Used by permission.

Page 358: Taken from HOPE HAS ITS REASONS: FROM THE SEARCH FOR SELF TO THE SURPRISE OF FAITH by Rebecca Manley Pippert. Copyright © 1989 by Rebecca Manley Pippert. Published by HarperCollins Publishers. Used by permission.

Page 359: Taken from HOME IS WHERE YOU HANG YOUR HEART: A MOTHER'S DEVOTIONAL by Cynthia Culp Allen. Copyright © 1992 by Cynthia Culp Allen and published by Meridian Publishing. Used by permission.

Page 362: Taken from 431 QUOTES FROM THE NOTES OF HENRIETTA MEARS, compiled by Eleanor L. Doan. Copyright © 1970 by Gospel Light Publications, Ventura, California. Used by permission.

Page 365: By Jean E. Syswerda. Copyright © 1995 by The Zondervan Corporation.

Page 367: Taken from WILD THINGS HAPPEN WHEN I PRAY by Becky Tirabassi. Copyright © 1993 by Becky Tirabassi. Published by Zondervan Publishing House. Used by permission.

Page 370: By Catherine DeVries. Copyright © 1995 by The Zondervan Corporation.

Page 373: Taken from HOPE HAS ITS REASONS: FROM THE SEARCH FOR SELF TO THE SURPRISE OF FAITH by Rebecca Manley Pippert. Copyright © 1989 by Rebecca Manley Pippert. Published by HarperCollins Publishers. Used by permission.

Page 377: Taken from BESIDE STILL WATERS © 1985 by Gien Karssen. Used by permission of NavPress, Colorado Springs, Colorado. All rights reserved.

Page 382: Taken from AN ANGEL A DAY by Ann Spangler. Copyright © 1994 by Ann Spangler. Published by Zondervan Publishing House. Used by permission.

Page 390: By Georgalyn Wilkinson. Taken from STILL MOMENTS, compiled by Mary Beckwith. Copyright © 1989 by Mary Beckwith. Published by Regal Books, Ventura, California. Used by permission.

Page 391: Taken from THOSE WHO LOVE HIM by M. Basilia Schlink. Copyright © 1969 by the Evangelical Sisterhood of Mary. Published by Bethany House Publishers. Used by permission.

Page 396: Taken from YOUNG WIDOW: LEARNING TO LIVE AGAIN by Kate Convissor. Copyright © 1992 by Kate Convissor. Published by Zondervan Publishing House. Used by permission.

Page 399: Taken from EDGES OF HIS WAYS: SELECTIONS FOR DAILY READING by Amy Carmichael. Copyright © 1955 by Dohnavur Fellowship. Reprinted 1994 by Christian Literature Crusade. Used by permission.

Page 408: By Jean E. Syswerda. Copyright © 1995 by The Zondervan Corporation.

Page 410: Taken from QUIET STRENGTH by Rosa Parks. Copyright © 1995 by Rosa Parks. Published by Zondervan Publishing House. Used by permission.

Page 412: Taken from WINTER: A TIME FOR PEACE by Debra Klingsporn. Copyright © 1994 by Thomas Nelson Publishers. Used by permission.

Page 414: Taken from LORD, HAVE YOU FORGOTTEN ME? THIRTY DEVOTIONS TO ENCOURAGE YOU WHEN LIFE LETS YOU DOWN by Judith Couchman. Copyright © 1992 by Judith Couchman. Published by Word, Inc., Dallas, Texas. Used by permission.

Page 416: Taken from SEEING YOURSELF THROUGH GOD'S EYES by June Hunt. Copyright © 1989 by June Hunt. Published by Zondervan Publishing House. Used by permission.

Page 420: Taken from THE SPIRITUALITY OF GENTLENESS: GROWING TOWARD CHRISTIAN WHOLENESS by Judith Lechman. Copyright © 1987 by Judith Lechman. Published by HarperCollins Publishers. Used by permission.

Page 424: Taken from WHAT EVERY MOM NEEDS by Elisa Morgan and Carol Kuykendall. Copyright © 1995 by M.O.P.S. International, Inc. Published by Zondervan Publishing House. Used by permission.

Page 428: Taken from LET'S MAKE A MEMORY by Gloria Gaither and Shirley Dobson. Copyright © 1983. Published by Word, Inc., Dallas, Texas. Used by permission. All rights reserved.

Page 431: Taken from THE FACES OF GOD by Gladis and Gordon DePree. Copyright © 1974 by Gladis and Gordon DePree. Published by HarperCollins Publishers. Used by permission.

Page 433: Taken from WHAT TO DO WHEN YOU CAN'T DO IT ALL by Carol Van Klompenburg. Copyright © 1989 by Augsburg Fortress. Used by permission.

Page 435: Taken from MEDITATIONS FOR CHRISTIANS WHO TRY TO BE PERFECT by Joan C. Webb. Copyright © 1993 by Joan C. Webb. Published by HarperCollins Publishers. Used by permission.

Page 449: Taken from A CIRCLE OF LOVE by Grace H. Ketterman. Copyright © 1987 by Fleming H. Revell, a division of Baker Book House, Grand Rapids, Michigan. Used by permission.

Page 459: By Catherine Doherty. Taken from GRACE IN EVERY SEASON: THROUGH THE YEAR WITH CATHERINE DOHERTY, edited by Mary Achterhoff. Copyright © 1992 by Madonna House Publications. Published by Servant Publications and Madonna House Publications. Used by permission.

Page 460: Taken from BELOVED by Kay Arthur. Copyright © 1994 by Kay Arthur. Published by Harvest House Publishers. Used by permission.

Page 467: Taken from SECRET STRENGTH FOR THOSE WHO SEARCH by Joni Eareckson Tada. Copyright © 1994 by Joni, Inc. Published by Questar Publishers, Multnomah Books. Used by permission.

Page 472: Taken from YOU ARE WHAT YOU SAY by Karen Burton Mains. Copyright © 1988 by Karen Burton Mains. Published by Zondervan Publishing House. Used by permission.

Page 478: Taken from QUIET MOMENTS by June Masters Bacher. Copyright © 1979 by Harvest House Publishers, Eugene, Oregon. Used by permission.

Page 483: Taken from MEDITATIONS FOR CHRISTIANS WHO TRY TO BE PERFECT by Joan C. Webb. Copyright © 1993 by Joan C. Webb. Published by HarperCollins Publishers. Used by permission.

Page 486: Taken from WINTER: A TIME FOR PEACE by Debra Klingsporn. Copyright © 1994 by Thomas Nelson Publishers. Used by permission.

Page 490: Taken from SURROUNDED BY MYSTERY: LIVING WITH THE CONTRADICTIONS OF FAITH by Ruth Senter. Copyright © 1988 by Ruth Senter. Published by Zondervan Publishing House. Used by permission.

Page 493: Taken from COULD YOU HURRY UP THE DAWN, LORD? by Joy Morgan Davis. Copyright © 1994 by Fleming H. Revell, a division of Baker Book House, Grand Rapids, Michigan. Used by permission.

Page 495: Taken from REACHING FOR RAINBOWS by Ann Weems. Copyright © 1980 by Ann Weems. Used by permission of Westminster John Knox Press. All rights reserved.

Page 497: "Imagine That" taken from TAPESTRY: A WOMAN'S GUIDE TO INTIMACY WITH GOD, June 1994; edited by Brenda Josee. Used by permission.

Page 500: Taken from SUMMER: A TIME TO ENJOY by Bernie Sheahan. Copyright © 1994 by Thomas Nelson Publishers. Used by permission.

Page 505: Taken from SUMMER: A TIME TO ENJOY by Bernie Sheahan. Copyright © 1994 by Thomas Nelson Publishers. Used by permission.

Page 508: Taken from LORD, LET ME LOVE by Marjorie Holmes. Copyright © 1978 by Marjorie Holmes. Used by permission of Doubleday, a division of Bantam Doubleday Dell Publishing Group, Inc.

Page 511: Taken from WHEN GOD WHISPERS © 1994 by Carole Mayhall. Used by permission of NavPress, Colorado Springs, Colorado. All rights reserved.

Page 514: Taken from IT'S MY TURN by Ruth Bell Graham. Copyright © 1982 by Fleming H. Revell, a division of Baker Book House, Grand Rapids, Michigan. Used by permission.

Page 516: Taken from SO STICK A GERANIUM IN YOUR HAT AND BE HAPPY by Barbara Johnson. Copyright © 1992. Published by Word, Inc,. Dallas, Texas. Used by permission. All rights reserved..

Page 518: Taken from TAPESTRY OF LIFE: DEVOTIONS FOR THE UNIQUE WOMAN by Nancy Corbett Cole. (Tulsa: Honor Books, Copyright © 1994.) Used by permission.

Page 521: Taken from THE SPIRIT OF LOVELINESS by Emilie Barnes. Copyright © 1992 by Harvest House Publishers, Eugene, Oregon. Used by permission.

Page 524: Taken from TAPESTRY OF LIFE: DEVOTIONS FOR THE UNIQUE WOMAN by Nancy Corbett Cole. (Tulsa: Honor Books, Copyright © 1994.) Used by permission.

Page 527: Taken from "The Waiting Game" by Jeanne Zornes. Adapted from TODAY'S CHRISTIAN WOMAN magazine (September/October 1994). Used by permission.

Page 530: Taken from JUST BETWEEN GOD AND ME by Sandra Drescher-Lehman. Copyright © 1977 by The Zondervan Corporation. Used by permission of Zondervan Publishing House.

Page 533: Taken from GIFTS FREELY GIVEN: DEVOTIONS FOR YOUR QUIET TIME by Marjorie Holmes. Copyright © 1992 by Guideposts Associates, Inc. Published by Fleming H. Revell, a division of Baker Book House, Grand Rapids, Michigan. Used by permission.

Page 536: Taken from SECOND CUP OF COFFEE by Jean Shaw. Copyright © 1981 by The Zondervan Corporation. Used by permission of Zondervan Publishing House.

Page 539: Taken from THE BETTER HALF OF LIFE: MEDITATIONS FROM ECCLESIASTES by Jean Shaw. Copyright © 1983 by The Zondervan Corporation. Used by permission of Zondervan Publishing House.

Page 540: Taken from YIELDING TO COURAGE by Judith Lechman. Copyright © 1988 by Judith Lechman. Published by HarperCollins Publishers. Used by permission.

Page 544: By Jean E. Syswerda. Copyright © 1995 The Zondervan Corporation.

Every effort has been made to trace the ownership of copyright items in this collection and to obtain permission for their use. The publisher would appreciate notification of, and copyright details for, any instances where further acknowledgment is due, so that adjustments may be made in a future reprint.

READING PLAN

God's Word is full of promises, encouragement and guidance for you. This reading plan gives you a simple structure for reading through the New Testament, Psalms and Proverbs in one year.

JANUARY	A.M.	P.M.	FEBRUARY	A.M.	P.M.
1	Matt 1	Prov 1:1–7	1	Mark 1:1–20	Prov 10:1–5
2	Matt 2	Prov 1:8–19	2	Mark 1:21–45	Prov 10:6–11
3	Matt 3	Prov 1:20–33	3	Mark 2	Prov 10:12–16
4	Matt 4	Prov 2:1–11	4	Mark 3:1–19	Prov 10:17–23
5	Matt 5	Prov 2:12–22	5	Mark 3:20–35	Prov 10:24–27
6	Matt 6	Prov 3:1–4	6	Mark 4:1–34	Prov 10:28–32
7	Matt 7	Prov 3:5–10	7	Mark 4:35–5:20	Prov 11:1–4
8	Matt 8	Prov 3:11–18	8	Mark 5:21–43	Prov 11:5–9
9	Matt 9	Prov 3:19–26	9	Mark 6:1–13	Prov 11:10–14
10	Matt 10	Prov 3:27–35	10	Mark 6:14–29	Prov 11:15–19
11	Matt 11	Prov 4:1–9	11	Mark 6:30–56	Prov 11:20–26
12	Matt 12	Prov 4:10–19	12	Mark 7:1–23	Prov 11:27–31
13	Matt 13:1–52	Prov 4:20–27	13	Mark 7:24–37	Prov 12:1–6
14	Matt 13:53–14:36	Prov 5:1–6	14	Mark 8:1–21	Prov 12:7–10
15	Matt 15	Prov 5:7–14	15	Mark 8:22–9:13	Prov 12:11–14
16	Matt 16	Prov 5:15–23	16	Mark 9:14–50	Prov 12:15–22
17	Matt 17	Prov 6:1–5	17	Mark 10:1–31	Prov 12:23–28
18	Matt 18	Prov 6:6–11	18	Mark 10:32–52	Prov 13:1–6
19	Matt 19:1–20:16	Prov 6:12–15	19	Mark 11:1–19	Prov 13:7–12
20	Matt 20:17–21:17	Prov 6:16–19	20	Mark 11:20–12:12	Prov 13:13–18
21	Matt 21:18–46	Prov 6:20–29	21	Mark 12:13–44	Prov 13:19–25
22	Matt 22:1–40	Prov 6:30–35	22	Mark 13	Prov 14:1–4
23	Matt 22:41–23:38	Prov 7:1–5	23	Mark 14:1–26	Prov 14:5–9
24	Matt 24:1–44	Prov 7:6–23	24	Mark 14:27–52	Prov 14:10–18
25	Matt 24:45–25:30	Prov 7:24–27	25	Mark 14:53–72	Prov 14:19–24
26	Matt 25:31–26:16	Prov 8:1–11	26	Mark 15:1–20	Prov 14:25–30
27	Matt 26:17–56	Prov 8:12–21	27	Mark 15:21–47	Prov 14:31–35
28	Matt 26:57–75	Prov 8:22–36	28	Mark 16	Prov 15:1–4
29	Matt 27:1–31	Prov 9:1–6			
30	Matt 27:32–66	Prov 9:7–12			
31	Matt 28	Prov 9:13–18			

MARCH	A.M.	P.M.		MAY	A.M.	P.M.
1	Luke 1:1–38	Prov 15:5–10		1	Acts 1	Prov 28:1–5
2	Luke 1:39–56	Prov 15:11–19		2	Acts 2	Prov 28:6–10
3	Luke 1:57–80	Prov 15:20–24		3	Acts 3:1–4:4	Prov 28:11–14
4	Luke 2	Prov 15:25–29		4	Acts 4:5–37	Prov 28:15–22
5	Luke 3	Prov 15:30–33		5	Acts 5:1–11	Prov 28:23–28
6	Luke 4	Prov 16:1–5		6	Acts 5:12–6:7	Prov 29:1–6
7	Luke 5	Prov 16:6–9		7	Acts 6:8–8:1a	Prov 29:7–11
8	Luke 6:1–16	Prov 16:10–15		8	Acts 8:1b–40	Prov 29:12–16
9	Luke 6:17–49	Prov 16:16–19		9	Acts 9	Prov 29:17–21
10	Luke 7:1–35	Prov 16:20–24		10	Acts 10	Prov 29:22–27
11	Luke 7:36–50	Prov 16:25–28		11	Acts 11	Prov 30:1–4
12	Luke 8	Prov 16:29–33		12	Acts 12	Prov 30:5–9
13	Luke 9:1–36	Prov 17:1–5		13	Acts 13	Prov 30:10–14
14	Luke 9:37–62	Prov 17:6–10		14	Acts 14	Prov 30:15–17
15	Luke 10	Prov 17:11–15		15	Acts 15:1–21	Prov 30:18–23
16	Luke 11	Prov 17:16–21		16	Acts 15:22–41	Prov 30:24–28
17	Luke 12	Prov 17:22–28		17	Acts 16:1–15	Prov 30:29–33
18	Luke 13	Prov 18:1–7		18	Acts 16:16–40	Prov 31:1–9
19	Luke 14	Prov 18:8–15		19	Acts 17	Prov 31:10–31
20	Luke 15	Prov 18:16–19		20	Acts 18	Psa 1
21	Luke 16	Prov 18:20–24		21	Acts 19:1–22	Psa 2
22	Luke 17	Prov 19:1–6		22	Acts 19:23–41	Psa 3
23	Luke 18	Prov 19:7–12		23	Acts 20	Psa 4
24	Luke 19	Prov 19:13–19		24	Acts 21:1–36	Psa 5
25	Luke 20	Prov 19:20–29		25	Acts 21:37–22:29	Psa 6
26	Luke 21:1–36	Prov 20:1–5		26	Acts 22:30–23:35	Psa 7:1–9
27	Luke 21:37–22:23	Prov 20:6–12		27	Acts 24	Psa 7:10–17
28	Luke 22:24–53	Prov 20:13–19		28	Acts 25:1–22	Psa 8
29	Luke 22:54–23:25	Prov 20:20–25		29	Acts 25:23–26:32	Psa 9:1–10
30	Luke 23:26–56	Prov 20:26–30		30	Acts 27	Psa 9:11–20
31	Luke 24	Prov 21:1–8		31	Acts 28	Psa 10

APRIL	A.M.	P.M.		JUNE	A.M.	P.M.
1	John 1:1–28	Prov 21:9–16		1	Rom 1:1–17	Psa 11
2	John 1:29–51	Prov 21:17–24		2	Rom 1:18–32	Psa 12
3	John 2	Prov 21:25–31		3	Rom 2:1–16	Psa 13
4	John 3	Prov 22:1–5		4	Rom 2:17–29	Psa 14
5	John 4:1–42	Prov 22:6–9		5	Rom 3:1–20	Psa 15
6	John 4:43–54	Prov 22:10–16		6	Rom 3:21–31	Psa 16
7	John 5	Prov 22:17–21		7	Rom 4:1–12	Psa 17
8	John 6:1–21	Prov 22:22–29		8	Rom 4:13–25	Psa 18:1–19
9	John 6:22–65	Prov 23:1–8		9	Rom 5:1–11	Psa 18:20–29
10	John 6:66–7:13	Prov 23:9–14		10	Rom 5:12–21	Psa 18:30–36
11	John 7:14–44	Prov 23:15–21		11	Rom 6:1–14	Psa 18:37–50
12	John 7:45–8:11	Prov 23:22–28		12	Rom 6:15–23	Psa 19
13	John 8:12–30	Prov 23:29–35		13	Rom 7:1–6	Psa 20
14	John 8:31–59	Prov 24:1–7		14	Rom 7:7–25	Psa 21
15	John 9	Prov 24:8–12		15	Rom 8:1–17	Psa 22:1–11
16	John 10:1–21	Prov 24:13–22		16	Rom 8:18–39	Psa 22:12–24
17	John 10:22–42	Prov 24:23–29		17	Rom 9:1–29	Psa 22:25–31
18	John 11	Prov 24:30–34		18	Rom 9:30–10:21	Psa 23
19	John 12:1–36	Prov 25:1–5		19	Rom 11:1–10	Psa 24
20	John 12:37–50	Prov 25:6–12		20	Rom 11:11–24	Psa 25:1–7
21	John 13:1–30	Prov 25:13–20		21	Rom 11:25–36	Psa 25:8–15
22	John 13:31–14:31	Prov 25:21–28		22	Rom 12:1–8	Psa 25:16–22
23	John 15	Prov 26:1–10		23	Rom 12:9–21	Psa 26
24	John 16	Prov 26:11–16		24	Rom 13:1–7	Psa 27
25	John 17	Prov 26:17–22		25	Rom 13:8–14	Psa 28
26	John 18	Prov 26:23–28		26	Rom 14:1–12	Psa 29
27	John 19:1–27	Prov 27:1–7		27	Rom 14:13–23	Psa 30
28	John 19:28–42	Prov 27:8–11		28	Rom 15:1–13	Psa 31:1–8
29	John 20	Prov 27:12–18		29	Rom 15:14–33	Psa 31:9–18
30	John 21	Prov 27:19–27		30	Rom 16	Psa 31:19–24

JULY	A.M.	P.M.	SEPTEMBER	A.M.	P.M.
1	1 Cor 1:1–2:5	Psa 32	1	1 Thess 1	Psa 78:40-55
2	1 Cor 2:5–16	Psa 33:1–11	2	1 Thess 2:1–16	Psa 78:56-72
3	1 Cor 3	Psa 33:12–22	3	1 Thess 2:17–3:13	Psa 79
4	1 Cor 4	Psa 34:1–10	4	1 Thess 4:1–12	Psa 80
5	1 Cor 5	Psa 34:11–22	5	1 Thess 4:13–18	Psa 81
6	1 Cor 6	Psa 35:1–18	6	1 Thess 5:1–11	Psa 82
7	1 Cor 7	Psa 35:19–28	7	1 Thess 5:12–28	Psa 83
8	1 Cor 8	Psa 36	8	2 Thess 1	Psa 84
9	1 Cor 9	Psa 37:1–22	9	2 Thess 2:1–12	Psa 85
10	1 Cor 10:1–11:1	Psa 37:23–40	10	2 Thess 2:13–3:5	Psa 86
11	1 Cor 11:2–34	Psa 38	11	2 Thess 3:6–18	Psa 87
12	1 Cor 12:1–31a	Psa 39	12	1 Tim 1:1–11	Psa 88
13	1 Cor 12:31b–13:13	Psa 40:1–10	13	1 Tim 1:12–20	Psa 89:1–13
14	1 Cor 14:1–25	Psa 40:11–17	14	1 Tim 2	Psa 89:14–29
15	1 Cor 14:26–40	Psa 41	15	1 Tim 3	Psa 89:30–45
16	1 Cor 15:1–34	Psa 42	16	1 Tim 4:1–10	Psa 89:46–52
17	1 Cor 15:35–58	Psa 43	17	1 Tim 4:11–5:8	Psa 90
18	1 Cor 16	Psa 44:1–8	18	1 Tim 5:9–6:2	Psa 91
19	2 Cor 1:1–2:11	Psa 44:9–26	19	1 Tim 6:3–10	Psa 92
20	2 Cor 2:12–3:18	Psa 45	20	1 Tim 6:11–21	Psa 93
21	2 Cor 4	Psa 46	21	2 Tim 1:1–14	Psa 94:1–15
22	2 Cor 5:1–10	Psa 47	22	2 Tim 1:15–2:13	Psa 94:16–23
23	2 Cor 5:11–6:2	Psa 48	23	2 Tim 2:14–26	Psa 95
24	2 Cor 6:3–7:1	Psa 49:1–15	24	2 Tim 3:1–9	Psa 96
25	2 Cor 7:2–16	Psa 49:16–20	25	2 Tim 3:10–4:8	Psa 97
26	2 Cor 8:1–15	Psa 50	26	2 Tim 4:9–22	Psa 98
27	2 Cor 8:16–9:15	Psa 51	27	Titus 1	Psa 99
28	2 Cor 10	Psa 52	28	Titus 2	Psa 100
29	2 Cor 11:1–15	Psa 53	29	Titus 3	Psa 101
30	2 Cor 11:16–12:10	Psa 54	30	Philemon	Psa 102:1-17
31	2 Cor 12:11–13:14	Psa 55			

AUGUST	A.M.	P.M.	OCTOBER	A.M.	P.M.
1	Gal 1	Psa 56	1	Heb 1	Psa 102:18-28
2	Gal 2	Psa 57	2	Heb 2:1–4	Psa 103:1–18
3	Gal 3:1–14	Psa 58	3	Heb 2:5–18	Psa 103:19–22
4	Gal 3:15–25	Psa 59:1–9	4	Heb 3:1–6	Psa 104:1–23
5	Gal 3:26–4:20	Psa 59:10–17	5	Heb 3:7–19	Psa 104:24–35
6	Gal 4:21–5:15	Psa 60	6	Heb 4:1–13	Psa 105:1–22
7	Gal 5:16–26	Psa 61	7	Heb 4:14–5:10	Psa 105:23–45
8	Gal 6	Psa 62	8	Heb 5:11–6:12	Psa 106:1–5
9	Eph 1:1–14	Psa 63	9	Heb 6:13–20	Psa 106:6–31
10	Eph 1:15–23	Psa 64	10	Heb 7:1–10	Psa 106:32–48
11	Eph 2:1–10	Psa 65	11	Heb 7:11–28	Psa 107:1–3
12	Eph 2:11–22	Psa 66:1–7	12	Heb 8	Psa 107:4–9
13	Eph 3	Psa 66:8–20	13	Heb 9:1–10	Psa 107:10–16
14	Eph 4:1–16	Psa 67	14	Heb 9:11–28	Psa 107:17–22
15	Eph 4:17–5:2	Psa 68:1–18	15	Heb 10:1–18	Psa 107:23–32
16	Eph 5:3–20	Psa 68:19–35	16	Heb 10:19–39	Psa 107:33–43
17	Eph 5:21–33	Psa 69:1–18	17	Heb 11:1–16	Psa 108
18	Eph 6:1–9	Psa 69:19–36	18	Heb 11:17–40	Psa 109:1–20
19	Eph 6:10–24	Psa 70	19	Heb 12:1–13	Psa 109:21–31
20	Php 1	Psa 71:1–18	20	Heb 12:14–29	Psa 110
21	Php 2:1–11	Psa 71:19–24	21	Heb 13	Psa 111
22	Php 2:12–18	Psa 72	22	James 1:1–18	Psa 112
23	Php 2:19–30	Psa 73:1–20	23	James 1:19–27	Psa 113
24	Php 3:1–14	Psa 73:21–28	24	James 2:1–13	Psa 114
25	Php 3:15–4:9	Psa 74:1–11	25	James 2:14–26	Psa 115
26	Php 4:10–23	Psa 74:12–23	26	James 3:1–12	Psa 116:1–6
27	Col 1:1–14	Psa 75	27	James 3:13–4:3	Psa 116:7–14
28	Col 1:15–2:5	Psa 76	28	James 4:4–12	Psa 116:15–19
29	Col 2:6–23	Psa 77	29	James 4:13–5:6	Psa 117
30	Col 3:1–4:1	Psa 78:1–8	30	James 5:7–12	Psa 118:1–7
31	Col 4:2–18	Psa 78:9–39	31	James 5:13–20	Psa 118:8–14

NOVEMBER	A.M.	P.M.	DECEMBER	A.M.	P.M.
1	1 Pet 1:1–12	Psa 118:15–21	1	Rev 1:1–8	Psa 126
2	1 Pet 1:13–2:3	Psa 118:22–29	2	Rev 1:9–20	Psa 127
3	1 Pet 2:4–12	Psa 119:1–8	3	Rev 2:1–11	Psa 128
4	1 Pet 2:13–25	Psa 119:9–16	4	Rev 2:12–29	Psa 129
5	1 Pet 3:1–7	Psa 119:17–24	5	Rev 3:1–6	Psa 130
6	1 Pet 3:8–22	Psa 119:25–32	6	Rev 3:7–13	Psa 131
7	1 Pet 4:1–11	Psa 119:33–40	7	Rev 3:14–22	Psa 132
8	1 Pet 4:12–19	Psa 119:41–48	8	Rev 4	Psa 133
9	1 Pet 5	Psa 119:49–56	9	Rev 5	Psa 134
10	2 Pet 1:1–11	Psa 119:57–64	10	Rev 6	Psa 135:1–12
11	2 Pet 1:12–21	Psa 119:65–72	11	Rev 7	Psa 135:13–21
12	2 Pet 2:1–9	Psa 119:73–80	12	Rev 8	Psa 136
13	2 Pet 2:10–22	Psa 119:81–88	13	Rev 9	Psa 137
14	2 Pet 3:1–9	Psa 119:89–96	14	Rev 10	Psa 138
15	2 Pet 3:10–18	Psa 119:97–104	15	Rev 11:1–14	Psa 139:1–16
16	1 John 1:1–4	Psa 119:105–112	16	Rev 11:15–19	Psa 139:17–24
17	1 John 1:5–2:2	Psa 119:113–120	17	Rev 12:1–13:1a	Psa 140
18	1 John 2:3–11	Psa 119:121–128	18	Rev 13:1b–10	Psa 141
19	1 John 2:12–17	Psa 119:129–136	19	Rev 13:11–18	Psa 142
20	1 John 2:18–27	Psa 119:137–144	20	Rev 14	Psa 143
21	1 John 2.28–3.10	Psa 119:145–152	21	Rev 15	Psa 144
22	1 John 3:11–24	Psa 119:153–160	22	Rev 16	Psa 145:1–7
23	1 John 4:1–6	Psa 119:161–168	23	Rev 17	Psa 145:8–13a
24	1 John 4:7–21	Psa 119:169–176	24	Rev 18	Psa 145:13b–21
25	1 John 5:1–12	Psa 120	25	Rev 19:1–10	Psa 146
26	1 John 5:13–21	Psa 121	26	Rev 19:11–21	Psa 147:1–6
27	2 John	Psa 122	27	Rev 20:1–6	Psa 147:7–11
28	3 John	Psa 123	28	Rev 20:7–15	Psa 147:12–20
29	Jude 1–16	Psa 124	29	Rev 21:1–8	Psa 148
30	Jude 17–25	Psa 125	30	Rev 21:9–27	Psa 149
			31	Rev 22	Psa 150

AUTHOR BIOGRAPHIES

Many gifted women contributed their insights to this Women's Devotional 2 New Testament with Psalms and Proverbs. This index gives information about each author and tells you where her contributions can be found.

Cynthia Culp Allen was awarded the Amy Award in 1989 in recognition of the last meditation—"The Special Santa Story"—in her book *Home Is Where You Hang Your Heart*. *Devotions by this author can be found on pages 28, 220, 359.*

Ann Kiemel Anderson is a former schoolteacher, youth director, college dean of women and author of nine books including *A Deeper Walk*. Ann has also coauthored the book *Struggling for Wholeness*. *A devotion by this author can be found on page 234.*

Kay Arthur and her husband, Jack, are the founders of Precept Ministries. Kay is the author of more than twenty books including *How to Study Your Bible; Lord, Teach Me to Pray* and *My Savior, My Friend*. *A devotion by this author can be found on page 460.*

June Masters Bacher is a gifted author whose credits include *Love Is a Gentle Stranger, Journey to Love* and *Love's Soft Whisper*, along with non-fiction and children's books. *A devotion by this author can be found on page 478.*

Edith Bajema is a free-lance writer and editor who has written numerous Bible studies for the Coffee Break evangelistic outreach program, as well as a book and articles on family worship and children in worship. *Devotions by this author can be found on pages 139, 152.*

Alma Barkman is a graduate of Moody Bible Institute and has written a humorous newspaper column and several award-winning books including *Days Remembered, Times to Treasure* and *Light Reflections*. *A devotion by this author can be found on page 246.*

Emilie Barnes is a popular speaker. She and her husband are the founders of the "More Hours in My Day Time Management Seminars." Emilie is the author of fourteen books including *More Hours in My Day* and *The Spirit of Loveliness*. *Devotions by this author can be found on pages 284, 521.*

Sue Bender is an artist and family therapist who lives in California. Her time spent with the Amish provided the material for her book *Plain and Simple*. *A devotion by this author can be found on page 342.*

Phyllis Bennett is a free-lance author and a frequent conference speaker. She lives with her husband and two children in Lake Oswego, Oregon. *A devotion by this author can be found on page 184.*

Anne Bradstreet (1612–1672) was an American poet and pastor's wife who made her home in Massachusetts. *A devotion by this author can be found on page 305.*

Jill Briscoe is known world-wide as a winsome and humorous speaker, teacher and author. Married to a busy senior pastor and involved in several ministries herself, Jill is keenly aware of the busy schedules confronting women today. Jill has written more than twenty books including *It Had to Be a Monday*. *Devotions by this author can be found on pages 163, 175.*

Charlotte Bronte (1816–1855) was an English novelist and poet. Charlotte is best known for her book *Jane Eyre*. *A devotion by this author can be found on page 317.*

Amy Carmichael (1867–1951) was a missionary to India who wrote poetry and devotional books with deep insight. *A devotion by this author can be found on page 399.*

Mary Lou Carney is the editor of *Guideposts for Kids* and the creative consultant for a new video series *Guideposts Junction*. A former teacher, Mary Lou is also an award-winning poet who has written nine books and numerous articles. *A devotion by this author can be found on page 355.*

Claire Cloninger is a gifted lyricist, three-time Dove Award winner, and well-known speaker and author. Her books include *A Place Called Simplicity, Faithfully Fit,* and *Postcards From Heaven*. Claire and her family live in rural Alabama. *Devotions by this author can be found on pages 226, 269, 281.*

Nancy Corbett Cole is a mother, grandmother, speaker and author of *The Unique Woman*. Nancy serves as an officer on the board of Edwin Cole Ministries and actively helps the widowed and disadvantaged through various church and civic groups. *Devotions by this author can be found on pages 518, 524.*

Sarah Jepson Coleman is a researcher, speech writer and journalist. She has written *Celebrate His Glory*. *A devotion by this author can be found on page 18.*

Kate Convissor is a free-lance writer. She is remarried and lives in Grand Rapids, Michigan, with her husband and six children. *A devotion by this author can be found on page 396.*

AUTHOR BIOGRAPHIES														559

Judith Couchman is the director of communications for the Navigators. Judith has written numerous articles for Christian periodicals as well as the books *Getting a Grip on Guilt* and *If I'm So Good Why Don't I Act That Way? A devotion by this author can be found on page 414.*

Mary C. Crowley has served as the president and sales manager for Home Interiors and Gifts. She has been involved in many civic groups and has published several books including *Decorate Your Home With Love. A devotion by this author can be found on page 334.*

Joy Morgan Davis is a popular women's club speaker living in Dallas, Texas, and the author of *A Woman's Song* and *You Bring the Umbrellas, Lord. A devotion by this author can be found on page 493.*

Ruth DeJager is an associate Bible editor at Zondervan Publishing House. She and her husband live in Marne, Michigan. *A devotion by this author can be found on page 51.*

Gladis and Gordon DePree have coauthored several books of inspirational poems and prose including *A Blade of Grass, A Time to Grow* and *Faces of God. A devotion by these authors can be found on page 431.*

Catherine DeVries is an associate Bible editor at Zondervan Publishing House. She and her husband, Brad, make their home in Grandville, Michigan. *A devotion by this author can be found on page 370.*

Catherine Doherty was a spiritual giant of the twentieth century who counted among her friends Thomas Merton and Dorothy Day. Her best known work is *Grace in Every Season. Devotions by this author can be found on pages 60, 239, 459.*

Elisabeth Elliot has written many books including *Shadow of the Almighty, Through Gates of Splendor,* and *A Path Through Suffering.* Elisabeth, twice-widowed, addresses the special needs of the single and widowed woman in her new book *Let Me Be a Woman. Devotions by this author can be found on pages 69, 216, 345.*

Colleen Townsend Evans is the author of more than eight books. She is currently spending time in renewal ministries with her husband, Lewis Evans, throughout the United States and abroad. A *devotion by this author can be found on page 304.*

Teresa and David Ferguson have coauthored the books *The Pursuit of Intimacy* and *Intimate Encounters.* Teresa is co-editor of the *Marriage and Family Intimacy Newsletter.* David is the executive director of the Center for Marriage and Family Intimacy. *A devotion by this author can be found on page 273.*

Cheryl Forbes has taught English on the college level and has written a daily column for the UPI radio network. *Catching Sight of God, Religion and Power* and *Backdoor Blessings* are a few of Cheryl's published works. *Devotions by this author can be found on pages 31, 194.*

Gloria Gaither has won two Grammy Awards and numerous Dove Awards for her songwriting and singing with the Bill Gaither Trio. She has authored or coauthored more than ten books and is the editor of *What My Parents Did Right. Devotions by this author can be found on pages 143, 428.*

Judy and Ken Gire are writers who live in Monument, Colorado. Judy and Ken coauthored *Miracle of Life* with Mary and Robert Wells. Ken has authored the *Moments With the Savior* series and *When You Can't Come Back* with Dave and Jan Dravecky. *A devotion by this author can be found on page 76.*

Ruth Bell Graham has written several books including *The Prodigals and Those Who Love Them, Legacy of a Pack Rat,* and *It's My Turn.* She is the wife of Billy Graham. They have five children and numerous grandchildren and great-grandchildren. *Devotions by this author can be found on pages 228, 514.*

Doris W. Greig is the mother of four children and is the founder, author and leader of the Joy of Living Bible Studies. *A devotion by this author can be found on page 149.*

Cynthia Heald is the author of the best-selling Bible studies *Becoming a Woman of Freedom, Becoming a Woman of Excellence* and *Becoming a Woman of Purpose.* She is a Navigator staff member in Tucson, Arizona. *Devotions by this author can be found on pages 257, 263.*

Kathryn Hillen retired from a position as an executive secretary to pursue studies in Biblical literature. She has written *There Came Unto him . . . Women* and *Memories. Devotions by this author can be found on pages 218, 289.*

Marcia Hollis is the author of several devotional books, including *God Meets Us Where We Are* from which the selections in this Bible were taken. She often speaks at conferences and retreats for women, focusing on themes of prayer, women, family life and gardening as seen from a Christian perspective. Having spent most of her life in Canada, she and her husband now live in Florida. *Devotions by this author can be found on pages 78, 84.*

Marjorie Holmes is well known for her books *I've Got to Talk to Somebody, God; Two From Galilee* and *Three From Galilee.* She has taught writing courses, written columns and articles and has spoken at many conferences. *Devotions by this author can be found on pages 201, 229, 258, 508, 533.*

June Hunt is the host of a daily radio broadcast "Hope for the Heart." She is an acclaimed speaker and Bible teacher and has written *Seeing Yourself Through God's Eyes. Devotions by this author can be found on pages 340, 416.*

Barbara Johnson is the founder of Spatula Ministries, a non-profit organization designed to guide hurting people through their despair. Her books include *Stick a Geranium in Your Hat and Be Happy,* and *Splashes of Joy in the Cesspools of Life. A devotion by this author can be found on page 516.*

Jan Johnson is a writer and retreat speaker living in Simi, California. *A devotion by this author can be found on page 211.*

Dr. Deneese L. Jones is an assistant professor at the University of Kentucky. Deneese serves in many capacities in her church and resides in Lexington, Illinois, with her husband, Steve, and their two daughters. *A devotion by this author can be found on page 297.*

Brenda M. Josee is editor-in-chief of *Tapestry*, a magazine that seeks to be "a woman's guide to intimacy with God." *Tapestry* is a publication of Walk Thru the Bible Ministries, Inc. *Devotions edited by this author can be found on pages 113, 497.*

Gien Karssen is the author of *Her Name Is Woman* and *Her Name Is Woman Book 2.* Gien is a leader for the Navigators' Women's Ministries in Europe. *A devotion by this author can be found on page 377.*

Grace H. Ketterman, M.D., is the medical director of the Crittenton Center in Kansas City, Missouri. She has authored several books including *The Complete Guide to Mothering, Depression Hits Every Family* and *Verbal Abuse.* *A devotion by this author can be found on page 449.*

Sue Monk Kidd is the author of several books including *God's Joyful Surprise* and *When the Heart Waits.* Longtime editor at *Guideposts,* Sue is also a contributor to *Reader's Digest, Weavings* and other periodicals. *Devotions by this author can be found on pages 95, 124.*

Debra Klingsporn is a free-lance writer and publicist and the author of *Winter: A Time for Peace* in *The Seasons of Life* Series. *Devotions by this author can be found on pages 157, 268, 412, 486.*

Carol Kuykendall is vice-president of educational resources for Mothers of Preschoolers (MOPS). The author of *Give Them Wings* and *Learning to Let Go,* Carol is also a regular columnist for *Parents of Teenagers. Devotions by this author can be found on pages 277, 312, 424.*

Dr. Deforia Lane is resident director of music therapy at the Ireland Cancer Center and Rainbow Babies and Children's Hospital, part of the University Hospitals of Cleveland. She has served as a spokesperson for the American Cancer Society for many years. Deforia lives in Cleveland with her husband and two sons. *Devotions by this author can be found on pages 242, 325, 349.*

Judith Lechman has over one hundred published short stories to her credit. She has also authored several books including *Yielding to Courage* and *The Spirituality of Gentleness. Devotions by this author can be found on pages 420, 540.*

Betsy Lee has been involved in prayer ministry for fifteen years and has written several books and numerous articles. *Devotions by this author can be found on pages 49, 135.*

Jarena Lee (1783–c.1850) was one of the outstanding preachers in the African Methodist Episcopal Church. She was a servant in Philadelphia when her conversion took place. *A devotion by this author can be found on page 170.*

Sandra Drescher-Lehman served as a prison chaplain for ten years; she is now a social worker in the field of mental health. Sandra has written *Waters of Reflection. A devotion by this author can be found on page 530.*

Susan Lenzkes is a mother and free-lance writer who has numerous articles and books to her credit. Some of her works include *When the Handwriting on the Wall Is in Brown Crayon* and *Crossing the Bridge Between You and Me. Devotions by this author can be found on pages 249, 316, 337.*

Jeanette Lockerbie is a former editor of *Psychology for Living.* She has authored *Salt in My Kitchen, More Salt in My Kitchen, Neighbor,* and *Time Out for Coffee. Devotions by this author can be found on pages 36, 90, 108.*

Mary Foxwell Loeks taught on the elementary level for almost four years. She has written *Devotions for Young Mothers, Christmas Activity Book,* and *Object Lessons for Children's Worship. A devotion by this author can be found on page 333.*

Sharon Mahoe edits a newsletter and makes her home in San Diego, California. *A devotion by this author can be found on page 292.*

Karen Burton Mains ministers with her husband, David, in the Chicago area through Chapel Ministries. Karen's book credits include the best-selling book *Open Heart, Open Home, Making Sunday Special,* and *The Fragile Curtain. Devotions by this author can be found on pages 25, 92, 352, 472.*

Catherine Marshall is one of America's most beloved authors. She wrote with candor, simplicity and eloquence until her death in 1983. Some of her best-loved works include *Beyond Ourselves, Christy,* and *Something More. A devotion by this author can be found on page 115.*

Babbie Mason is a singer/songwriter and a five-time Dove Award nominee. She is known for her inspirational albums, "With All My Heart," "A World of Difference" and "Standing in the Gap." She lives in Marietta, Georgia with her husband, Charles. *Devotions by this author can be found on pages 12, 222.*

Carole Mayhall is a popular Christian communicator and writer. She is the author of eight books including *Help, Lord, My Whole Life Hurts.* Carole has served in the Navigators for more than thirty-five years. *Devotions by this author can be found on pages 330, 511.*

Henrietta Mears founded Gospel Light Publications and Forest Home Christian Conference Center. Untold thousands were touched by her love for God until her death in 1963. *A devotion by this author can be found on page 362.*

Zoe B. Metzger writes many magazine articles. She teaches Bible classes and writes for her church. Zoe and her husband, John, reside in Lynden, Washington. *A devotion by this author can be found on page 327.*

Paula Michelsen is a preschool director and has initiated "7-11" clubs for the children in her church. Having completed her first book, she enjoys speaking and writing. *A devotion by this author can be found on page 254.*

Jeanie Miley is executive director of Growth Options, an organization promoting Christian growth and is the author of *Shared Splendor. A devotion by this author can be found on page 122.*

Elisa Morgan is the president and CEO of MOPS (Mothers of Preschoolers) International Inc. Elisa hosts a daily two-minute radio program "Mom Sense." She is also a regular columnist for *Christian Parenting Today* and has written *What Every Mom Needs. Devotions by this author can be found on pages 277, 312, 424.*

Susan Muto is the executive director of Epiphany Association. She has served as adjunct professor of literature and spirituality at the Pittsburgh School of Arts and Sciences. Susan has published many articles and books including *Celebrating the Single Life. A devotion by this author can be found on page 244.*

Connie Neal is an inspirational speaker who has written several books. A former businesswoman and youth minister, she lives in Antelope, California. *A devotion by this author can be found on page 347.*

Anne Ortlund is a best-selling Christian author known for her books *Children Are Wet Cement, The Best Half of Life* and *Disciplines of the Home.* She partners with her husband in a ministry of speaking and writing. *Devotions by this author can be found on pages 183, 209, 214, 282.*

Rosa Parks is the cofounder of the Rosa and Raymond Parks Institute for Self-Development and is recognized as the "mother of the modern-day civil rights movement." She lives in Detroit, Michigan. *Devotions by this author can be found on pages 173, 294, 410.*

Alice C. Peter has had several magazine articles published. She is the mother of three grown sons and makes her home in Seattle. *A devotion by this author can be found on page 47.*

Rebecca Manley Pippert is an internationally acclaimed teacher and lecturer and is the author of the best-selling *Out of the Salt Shaker* and *Hope Has Its Reasons. Devotions by this author can be found on pages 358, 373.*

Eugenia Price is an internationally known award-winning author who has more than thirty-five titles in print including both inspirational fiction and non-fiction. She lives on St. Simon's Island, Georgia. *Devotions by this author can be found on pages 40, 148.*

Paula Rinehart is the author of *Perfect Every Time: When Doing It All Leaves You with Nothing* and (with her husband) the award-winning best-seller, *Choices. Devotions by this author can be found on pages 260, 309.*

Rosalind Rinker served as a missionary in China and then worked with InterVarsity Christian Fellowship as a staff counselor. She is best known for her book *Prayer: Conversing With God. A devotion by this author can be found on page 9.*

Juanita and Dale Ryan are coauthors of the eight *Life Recovery Guides* and the book *Rooted in God's Love.* Juanita is a counselor in private practice in Hacienda Heights, California. Dale is the executive director of the Recovery Partnership. *A devotion by these authors can be found on page 343.*

Nellie C. Savicki is a writer and poet and is currently editing the "Children's Corner" for her church paper. She resides in Auburn, Washington. *A devotion by this author can be found on page 130.*

Basilea Schlink was the founder of the Evangelical Sisterhood of Mary in West Germany. She also founded a world-wide radio ministry "God Lives and Works Today." A prolific writer, Mother Basilea's teachings have reached around the world. *Devotions by this author can be found on pages 319, 391.*

Ruth Senter is the senior editor of *Campus Life* and the author of eight books including *The Seasons of Friendship, When You Are On Your Own,* and *Can I Afford Time for Friendships? Devotions by this author can be found on pages 22, 117, 490.*

Elizabeth Seton (1774–1821) was the founder of the American Sisters of Charity. *A devotion by this author can be found on page 354.*

Jean Shaw is a free-lance writer and charter member of Claywood Garden Club. Her other books include *Second Cup of Coffee* and *Devotions for Gardeners. Devotions by this author can be found on pages 536, 539.*

Luci Shaw is past president of Harold Shaw Publishers and is currently the writer-in-residence at Regent College in Vancouver. Her first book of prose, *God in the Dark,* met with critical acclaim. *Devotions by this author can be found on pages 73, 75, 103.*

Bernie Sheahan is the author of *Summer: A Time to Enjoy. Devotions by this author can be found on pages 500, 505.*

Hannah Whitall Smith (1832–1911) was a popular Bible conference leader for many years. Personal tragedy led Mrs. Smith to write several books on suffering and obedience including *The Christian's Secret to a Happy Life* and *The God of All Comfort. A devotion by this author can be found on page 302.*

Barbara DeGrote-Sorensen and **David Allen Sorensen** coauthored *Six Weeks to a Simpler Lifestyle* and *'Tis a Gift to Be Simple.* Barbara is a free-lance writer who has taught elementary and junior high school students. David is a pastor and free-lance writer. *A devotion by this author can be found on page 224.*

Betty Southard is a grandmother with a masters degree in theology from Fuller Theological Seminary. She leads seminars on choices, changes and challenges. With Jan Stoop she has written *The Grandmother Book. A devotion by this author can be found on page 307.*

Ann Spangler is a senior acquisitions editor for Zondervan Publishing House. She has published articles in *The Christian Reader, New Covenant, Pastoral Renewal*, and other magazines. *A devotion by this author can be found on page 382.*

Millie Stamm is the national executive prayer secretary of Stonecroft Ministries. A popular speaker, Millie has written *Be Still and Know, Beside Still Waters* and *He Is Real*. Millie lives in Kansas City, Missouri. *Devotions by this author can be found on pages 54, 65, 132.*

Jan Stoop is a counselor with the Minirth-Meier Clinic West and leads seminars on marriage and family issues. She has written *Saying Good-bye to Disappointments*. With Betty Southard she has authored *The Grandmother Book*. *A devotion by this author can be found on page 307.*

Kay Marshall Strom is a free-lance writer whose articles have appeared in *Virtue* and *Family Life Today*. She has also written *Chosen Families, Perfect in His Eyes*, and *Helping Women in Crisis*. *Devotions by this author can be found on pages 146, 266, 275, 286.*

Jean E. Syswerda is a senior editor with Zondervan Bible Publishers. She and her husband enjoy country life in West Michigan. *Devotions by this author can be found on pages 176, 365, 408, 544.*

Joni Eareckson Tada is the founder and president of JAF Ministries (Joni and Friends), an organization that accelerates Christian outreach in the disability community. Joni and her husband, Ken, make their home in California. *Devotions by this author can be found on pages 137, 206, 467.*

Gigi Graham Tchividjian is a renowned author, lecturer and counselor. She has written five books including the award-winning *Weather of the Heart*. Gigi and her husband, Stephan, have seven children and four grandchildren. *Devotions by this author can be found on pages 126, 291, 313.*

Mother Teresa of Calcutta (1910-1997) was the founder of the Missionary Sisters of Charity in Calcutta, India. She is the author of many books including *A Gift for God, My Life for the Poor, The Life of Christ: Spiritual Counsel* and *Seeking the Heart of God*. *Devotions by this author can be found on pages 189, 251.*

Holly and Chris Thurman have coauthored *The Pursuit of Intimacy* and *Intimate Moments*. Holly is active in Bible Study Fellowship. Chris maintains an active counseling practice in Austin, Texas. He is the author of *If Christ Were Your Counselor* and *The Twelve Best Kept Secrets for Living an Emotionally Healthy Life*. *A devotion by this author can be found on page 273.*

Becky Tirabassi is the founder of My Partner Ministries and the author of numerous books including *My Partner Prayer Notebook* and *Being a Wild, Wonderful Woman for God*. She has produced a series of Christian aerobic workout videos including *Making Fitness Fun*. *A devotion by this author can be found on page 367.*

Carol Van Klompenburg has worked as an instructor of English for Dordt College. She has also written numerous articles and resources, including *When the Kids Are Home From School*. Carol is a homemaker and mother who lives in Iowa. *Devotions by this author can be found on pages 322, 433.*

Shirley Pope Waite is a free-lance writer, speaker and instructor. She teaches "Writing to Sell" and "Writing Your Memoirs" through area community colleges and conducts workshops at Christian writer's conferences. *Devotions by this author can be found on pages 236, 279, 338.*

Joan C. Webb is a successful businesswoman, speaker and teacher. She has written *Meditations for Christians Who Try to Be Perfect*. *Devotions by this author can be found on pages 82, 435, 483.*

Ann Weems is a free-lance writer who has authored the books *Reaching for Rainbows, Kneeling in Bethlehem* and *Kneeling in Jerusalem*. *Devotions by this author can be found on pages 53, 495.*

Mary C. and Robert G. Wells, M.D., founded and run a menopause center in Long Beach, California. They authored *Menopause and Midlife* and coauthored *Miracle of Life* with Judy and Ken Gire. *A devotion by this author can be found on page 76.*

Susanna Wesley was an English pastor's wife and mother to fifteen children. Her most famous sons, Charles and John, became known as religious reformers. *Devotions by this author can be found on pages 101, 296.*

Brenda Wilbee is the author of the best-selling *Sweetbriar Pioneer Romance* series. She has begun work on *Classic Women of Faith* and has also written a non-fiction work *Taming the Dragons*. Brenda lives and writes from her home near Seattle. *A devotion by this author can be found on page 332.*

Georgalyn Wilkinson is executive director for GLINT (Gospel Literature International). She served as a missionary to Japan and a correspondent for the Foreign Press Association. *A devotion by this author can be found on page 390.*

Kate B. Wilkinson is a twentieth century poet best known for her verse set to music and found in most Protestant hymnals. *A devotion by this author can be found on page 271.*

Jeanne Zornes has published many articles, short stories and devotionals in more than one hundred periodicals. She is also the author of *The Power of Encouragement* and *When I Prayed for Patience God Let Me Have It*. *A devotion by this author can be found on page 527.*

SUBJECT INDEX

The subjects covered in the devotions are many and varied. This subject index will help you locate material on just about any topic or issue of interest, or about any problem confronting you.